LITERACY IN LOMBARD ITALY, c. 568–774

Italy had long experienced literacy under Roman rule, but what happened to literacy in Italy under the rule of a barbarian people? This book examines the evidence for the use of literacy in Lombard Italy c. 568–774, a period usually considered as the darkest of the Dark Ages in Italy owing to the poor survival of written evidence and the reputation of the Lombards as the fiercest of barbarian hordes ever to invade Italy.

A careful examination of the evidence, however, reveals quite a different story. The Lombards developed the literate traditions of the Roman world to suit the requirements of an early medieval society in which the use of the written word remained an integral part of government and administration. This study considers the different types of evidence in turn – legislation, charters, inscriptions and manuscripts – and offers a re-examination of the nature of Lombard settlement in Italy and the question of their cultural identity. Far from constituting a Dark Age in the history of literacy, Lombard Italy possessed relatively sophisticated written culture prior to the so-called Carolingian Renaissance of the ninth century.

NICHOLAS EVERETT is Lecturer in History and Literature, Harvard University.

Cambridge Studies in Medieval Life and Thought
Fourth Series

General Editor:
D.E. LUSCOMBE
Research Professor of Medieval History, University of Sheffield

Advisory Editors:
CHRISTINE CARPENTER
Reader in Medieval English History, University of Cambridge, and Fellow of New Hall

ROSAMOND MCKITTERICK
Professor of Medieval History, University of Cambridge, and Fellow of Newnham College

The series Cambridge Studies in Medieval Life and Thought was inaugurated by G.G. Coulton in 1921; Professor D.E. Luscombe now acts as General Editor of the Fourth Series, with Dr Christine Carpenter and Professor Rosamond McKitterick as Advisory Editors. The series brings together outstanding work by medieval scholars over a wide range of human endeavour extending from political economy to the history of ideas.

For a list of titles in the series, see end of book.

LITERACY IN LOMBARD ITALY, c. 568–774

NICHOLAS EVERETT

PUBLISHED BY THE PRESS SYNDICATE OF THE UNIVERSITY OF CAMBRIDGE
The Pitt Building, Trumpington Street, Cambridge, United Kingdom

CAMBRIDGE UNIVERSITY PRESS
The Edinburgh Building, Cambridge, CB2 2RU, UK
40 West 20th Street, New York, NY 10011-4211, USA
477 Williamstown Road, Port Melbourne, VIC 3207, Australia
Ruiz de Alarcón 13, 28014 Madrid, Spain
Dock House, The Waterfront, Cape Town 8001, South Africa

http://www.cambridge.org

© Nicholas Everett 2003

This book is in copyright. Subject to statutory exception
and to the provisions of relevant collective licensing agreements,
no reproduction of any part may take place without
the written permission of Cambridge University Press.

First published 2003

Printed in the United Kingdom at the University Press, Cambridge

Typeface Bembo 11/12 pt   *System* LaTeX 2$_\varepsilon$ [TB]

A catalogue record for this book is available from the British Library

ISBN 0 521 81905 9 hardback
ISBN 0 521 79639 3 paperback

CONTENTS

List of illustrations	*page* viii
Acknowledgements	ix
List of abbreviations	xi
INTRODUCTION	1
1 ITALY AND LITERACY BEFORE THE LOMBARDS	14
2 THE EARLY LOMBARDS AND THEIR SETTLEMENT IN ITALY	54
3 LANGUAGE AND LITERACY	100
4 LAW AND GOVERNMENT	163
5 CHARTERS	197
6 INSCRIPTIONS	235
7 MANUSCRIPTS	277
CONCLUSION	317
Bibliography	328
Index of manuscripts	371
Index	374

ILLUSTRATIONS

PLATES

I	Elementary script. Milan, Archivio di Stato, Museo Diplomatico, no. 14	page 216
II	Elementary script. Verona, Archivio di Stato, Ospitale Civico, no. 3	217
III	Elementary script. Verona, Biblioteca Capitolare, III.3–3v	218
IVa	Gaudentius. Lucca, Archivio arcivescovile, Diplomatico no. 13	228
IVb	Tanipert. Lucca, Archivio arcivescovile, Diplomatico no. 57 [++M3]	228
IVc	Osprand. Lucca, Archivio arcivescovile, Diplomatico no. 71 [+M, 65]	228
V	Epitaph of Cummianus. Bobbio, Museo dell'Abbazia	252
VI	Epitaph of Cunincperga. Pavia, Museo Civico Malaspina B21	257
VII	Epitaph of Audoald. Pavia, Museo Civico Malaspina, B20	259
VIII	RESPECE ET AUDI. Monza, Museo del Duomo	265
IX	Epitaph of Aldo. Milan, Castello Sforzesco	266
X	Inscriptions of Grimoald, Romoald and Romoald II. Gargano, Grotta di San Michele	270

MAPS

1	Cities, *castra* and ecclesiastical centres in early medieval Italy: the Lombard period	xiii
2	Lombard Italy, *c.* 740	xiv

ACKNOWLEDGEMENTS

First and foremost thanks must go to Rosamond McKitterick who supervised the thesis which formed the foundation of this book and who has been a constant source of encouragement and inspiration ever since. With characteristic generosity and acumen she has read the entire manuscript and offered invaluable advice. My debt to her scholarship will be apparent throughout. As will that to the work of Chris Wickham, who examined the crude ancestor of this study and has read most of its successive recensions, always generously sharing his expertise on Italy and offering constructive criticism.

Different chapters have been read and commented upon by Michael Gorman, John Moorhead, Walter Pohl and Roger Wright, and I have benefited greatly from their advice. David Luscombe made some insightful suggestions to make this a better book. Various aspects of this topic have been discussed formally and informally with many friends and colleagues over the years, but I wish to thank especially Ross Balzaretti, Tom Brown, Marios Costambeys, Maria Teresa Gigliozzi, Paul Kershaw, Simon Loseby, John Mitchell, John Morgan, Barbara Polci, Antonio Sennis and Geoff West.

The Cambridge Commonwealth Trust and the University of Queensland graciously provided the financial means to undertake the doctoral research which led to this study, and Clare Hall generously assisted also. The manuscript was written while I held an Australia Research Council Postdoctoral Fellowship in the Department of History at the University of Queensland. I gratefully thank those persons responsible at these institutions, in particular John Moorhead and Martin Stuart-Fox, for supporting my research and their many kindnesses shown while there. I should like to thank the librarians and staff at Cambridge University Library, the University of Queensland, and the Widener Library at Harvard for their assistance. In Italy, the Biblioteca Apostolica in the Vatican and the British School at Rome (*le sirene*) have provided a scholastic haven for this and other projects, and I would like to record here my sincere thanks to their staff for the generous help given.

Acknowledgements

Earlier versions of chapters 4 and 5 appeared as articles in *Early Medieval Europe* and *Studi Medievali* (both 2000), and I thank the publishers, Blackwells and the Centro Italiano di studi sull'alto medioevo, for permission to reprint parts of that material here. I also thank Urs Graf Verlag GmbH for permission to reproduce images from their ChLA series. All attempts have been made to obtain permission for the other plates.

This study would not have been possible without the support of dear friends – they know who they are – and above all my family. All of them but especially Charlie and Abbie for their patience and insightful criticism. As only she and I can know, my debt to Dita is beyond words, written or not.

ABBREVIATIONS

AA.SS.	*Acta sanctorum*, 3rd edn (Paris, 1863–)
AB	*Analecta Bollandiana*
Atti # CISAM	*Atti del # congresso internazionale di studi sull'alto medioevo del Centro italiano di studi sull'alto medioevo* (Spoleto, 1954–)
BHL	*Biblioteca hagiographica latina, antiquae et mediae aetatis*, 2 vols. (Brussels, 1898–1901; reprint 1914), and *Novum supplementum*, ed. Henricus Fros (Brussels, 1986), Subsidia Hagiographica 70
CCCM	Corpus Christianorum, Continuatio mediaevalis (Turnhout, 1966–)
CCSL	Corpus Christianorum series latina (Turnhout, 1952–)
CDL	Codice diplomatico longobardo
ChLA	Chartae latinae antiquiores. Facsimile Edition of the Latin Charter prior to the Ninth Century I–, ed. A. Bruckner and R. Marichal (Olten and Laussane, 1954–)
CIL	Corpus Inscriptionum Latinarum
CJ	*Codex Justinianus*
CLA	Codices Latini Antiquiores, ed. E.A. Lowe (Oxford, 1935–71)
CTh	*Codex Theodosianus*
EHR	*English Historical Review*
EME	*Early Medieval Europe*
EMI	C.J. Wickham, *Early Medieval Italy: Central Power and Local Society* (London and Basingstoke, 1981)
Gray	N. Gray, 'The palaeography of Latin inscriptions in the eighth and ninth centuries in Italy', *Papers of the British School at Rome* 16 (1948), 38–170
HL	Paul the Deacon, *Historia langobardorum*
HLCGoth.	*Historia langobardorum codicis gothani*

List of abbreviations

HR	Paul the Deacon, *Historia romana*
LP	*Liber pontificalis*, ed. L. Duchesne and C. Vogel, 2nd edn (Paris, 1955)
Mansi	J.D. Mansi, *Sacrorum conciliorum nova et amplissima collectio* (Florence and Venice, 1757–98)
MGH	Monumenta Germaniae Historica
AA.	Auctores Antiquissimi
Cap.	Capitularia, Legum Sectio II, Capitularia regum francorum
Dip. Kar.	Diplomata Karolinorum
Ep.	Epistulae
Form.	Formulae
Leges	Leges in folio
Leges n.g.	Leges nationum germanicarum
Poetae	Poetae aevi Karolini
SRM	Scriptores rerum merovingicarum
SRL	Scriptores rerum langobardicarum et italicarum saec. VI–IX
SS.	Scriptores
NCMH	R. McKitterick (ed.), *New Cambridge Medieval History*, II, *c. 700–c. 900* (Cambridge, 1995)
Panazza	G. Panazza, *Lapidi e sculture paleocristiane e pre-romaniche di Pavia, Arte del Primo Millenio Atti del II convegno per lo studio dell'arte dell'alto medioevo, tenuto presso l'Università di Pavia nel Settembre 1950* (Turin, 1953)
PBSR	*Papers of the British School at Rome*
PL	*Patrologiae cursus completus series latina*, ed. J.P. Migne (Paris, 1844–)
PLRE 2	J.R. Martindale, *The Prosopography of the Later Roman Empire*, 2, *A.D. 395–527* (Cambridge, 1980)
PLRE 3	J.R. Martindale, *The Prosopography of the Later Roman Empire*, 3, *A.D. 527–641* (Cambridge, 1993)
RB	*Regula Benedicti*
Settimane	*Settimane di studio del Centro italiano di studi sull'alto medioevo* 1– (Spoleto, 1954–)
ThLL	*Thesaurus linguae latinae* (Berlin and Munich, 1900–)
Tjäder	*Die nichtliterarischen lateinischen Papyri italiens aus der Zeit 445–700*, 3 vols., ed. J.O Tjäder (Lund, 1954/55–1982)

Map 1 Cities, *castra* and ecclesiastical centres in early medieval Italy:
The Lombard period

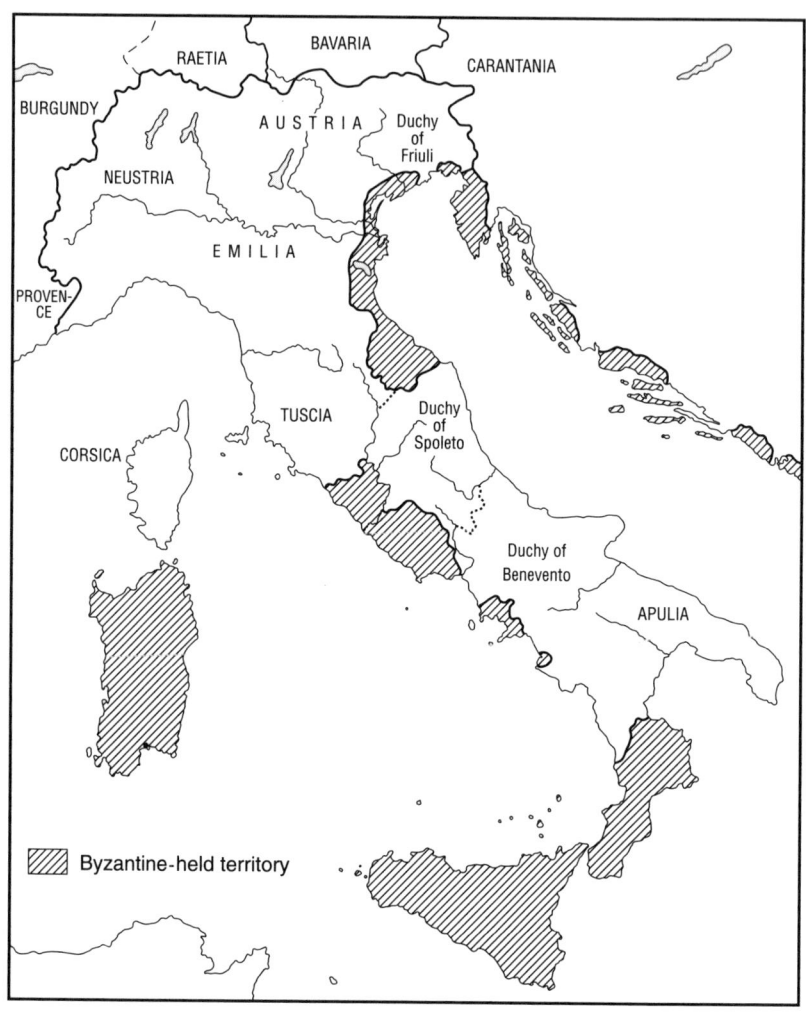

Map 2 Lombard Italy, c. 740

INTRODUCTION

The 'linguistic turn' in philosophy during the second half of the twentieth century caused much excitement about the acts of reading and writing amongst anthropologists, sociologists and historians.[1] For medieval historians, the refined notion of literacy as a mode of communication that works on numerous different levels has provided a better understanding of the paradox that medieval civilisation, despite a perceived dearth of literate skills when compared with later historical epochs in Europe, was a literate civilisation.[2] Literacy was an integral part of medieval culture. Religion was of the Holy Book. Laws, statutes, agreements and codes of required social behaviour were written down for everyone concerned to consult and (ideally) obey. Philosophical questioning and knowledge of the world and its wonders were passed on through writings. We can no longer agree with the picture that such activities were confined to a clerical and educated elite, while the rest of the population went on

---

[1] A great deal of debate was stimulated by the work of J. Goody, as found in Goody (ed.) *Literacy in Traditional Societies* (Cambridge, 1968), esp. Goody and I. Watt, 'The consequences of literacy', in *ibid*., pp. 69–83. See further J. Goody, *The Domestication of the Savage Mind* (Cambridge, 1977); *The Logic of Writing and the Organisation of Society* (Cambridge, 1986). Goody's general arguments have received a great deal of criticism, most convincingly in S. Scribner and S.M. Cole, *The Psychology of Literacy* (Cambridge, MA, 1981), cf. C. Lévi-Strauss, *Tristes-Tropiques*, trans. J. and D. Weightman (New York, 1974); J. Derrida, *Of Grammatology*, trans. G. C. Spivak (Baltimore, 1976), pp. 97–140. A different approach with similar conclusions similar to Goody's can be found in E. Havelock, *Origins of Western Literacy* (Toronto, 1976); Havelock, *The Literate Revolution in Ancient Greece and Its Cultural Consequences* (Princeton, 1982). See also W. J. Ong, *Interfaces of the Word* (Ithaca, 1977); Ong, *Orality and Literacy: The Technologising of the Word* (London and New York, 1982); B. Street, *Literacy in Theory and Practice* (Cambridge, 1984). H.J. Graff, *The Legacies of Literacy: Continuities and Contradictions in Western Culture and Society* (Bloomington, 1987). The 'industry' of studies in literacy now needs its own dictionary: S. Theodore, L. Harris and R. Hodges (eds.), *The Literacy Dictionary: The Vocabulary of Reading and Writing* (Newark, 1994).

[2] F. Bäuml, 'Varieties and consequences of medieval literacy and illiteracy', *Speculum* 55:2 (1980), 237–65, esp. p. 237; M. Camille, 'Seeing and reading: some visual implications of medieval literacy and illiteracy', *Art History* 8 (1995), 133–48. The term can be extended to cover many aspects of communication: see M. Mostert (ed.), *New Approaches to Medieval Communication* (Turnhout, 1999).

Literacy in Lombard Italy, c. 568–774

untouched by them and their interests, or, vice versa, that the elite were not affected by the world in which they lived and worked.[3]

New understandings of literacy sparked a number of important studies which drew back the chronological boundaries for a substantial dissemination of literate skills from the Renaissance, Reformation and early modern periods to the high middle ages.[4] Since then, the chronology has been pushed back even further. Rosamond McKitterick's *Carolingians and the Written Word* was in many ways a reaction against views that see a 'rebirth' of literacy in the higher middle ages. Instead, McKitterick called for continuity in our understanding of the history of literacy, seeing the post-millennium developments as 'an increase, extension and diversification of literate skills, the next stage in a continuous pattern from late antiquity to the early Germanic kingdoms'.[5] Having investigated the evidence of the Carolingian kingdoms, she concluded that 'The written word...was used by the Carolingians on an apparently larger scale than ever before in the barbarian kingdoms of Western Europe.'[6] It is difficult to doubt this conclusion when looking quantitatively at the surviving evidence: in manuscripts alone, some 7000 survive from the Carolingian period compared with around 1850 for the late antique and early medieval period prior to 800 AD.

Nevertheless we are entitled to ask the same questions concerning continuity for the period prior to the Carolingians. There has always been a sneaking suspicion amongst early medieval historians that Lombard Italy played a substantial role in providing foundations, or models, for the types of literate activity we see in the Carolingian period, in terms of both a 'high' literary culture of Latin letters and the everyday use of literacy at the administrative and governmental levels. The suspicion is not without foundation, but the paucity of surviving evidence for manuscript script production and literary composition allows little more than a nod to possibilities.[7]

---

[3] For 'classic overstatements of medieval illiteracy', Bäuml, 'Varieties and consequences', pp. 237–8. These views are still alive and well: M. Richter, *The Formation of the Medieval West: Studies in the Oral Culture of the Barbarians* (New York, 1994).

[4] Two works in particular merit special attention: B. Stock, *The Implications of Literacy: Written Language and Models of Interpretation in the Eleventh and Twelfth Centuries* (Princeton, 1983), and M. Clanchy, *From Memory to Written Record: England 1066–1307*, 2nd edn (Oxford, 1993).

[5] *The Carolingians and the Written Word* (Cambridge, 1989), p. 1. Also R. McKitterick (ed.), *The Uses of Literacy in Early Medieval Europe* (Cambridge, 1990).

[6] McKitterick, *Carolingians*, p. 273.

[7] See F. Brunhölzl, 'Der Bildungsauftrag der Hofschule', in B. Bischoff (ed.), *Karl der Grosse: Lebenswerk und Nachleben*, II, *Das Geistige Leben* (Düsseldorf, 1965), pp. 28–41; Brunhölzl, *Geschichte der lateinischen Literatur des Mittelalters* (Munich, 1975), II, pp. 243–85; G. Brown, 'The Carolingian Renaissance', in R. McKitterick (ed.), *Carolingian Culture: Emulation and Innovation* (Cambridge, 1994), pp. 1–51, esp. pp. 28–30; P. Riché, *Education and Culture in the Barbarian West: From the*

Introduction

With respect to the uses of literacy in administration and government, McKitterick was quick to point out the inherent biases towards Italy in arguing against Ganshof's views on the limited uses of writing in Carolingian administration.[8] She found two unpalatable assumptions in Ganshof's conclusions. The first was that the Franks primarily used ineffective oral methods of communication and, therefore, the evidence of literate practices in government were aberrations from the norm. The second assumption was:

that Italy, fount of civilisation, obviously preserved and was able to preserve and carry on literate methods of government. It is not my intention to dispute or refute the assumptions concerning Lombard Italy, albeit I retain grave doubts concerning their validity. It is time, indeed, that the question of literacy and levels of Latin learning in Lombard Italy were tackled head on.[9]

The present study is an attempt to take up the call of McKitterick's challenge. The description of Italy as the *fons civilitatis* neatly highlights the reason why the subject needs to be tackled head on. Western historiography has inherited a large number of assumptions concerning the connection between literacy and civilisation from Italian humanists and their successors, who believed ancient Roman urbanity and its texts were the height of human endeavour and the ideals to which the world should aspire.[10] Medieval historians are well aware that they work within the Petrarchian periodisation of a *medium aevum* based on such assumptions.[11] Early medieval historians are forced to contend with the real presence of ancient Roman culture in their field of investigation, a culture in which

---

Sixth through the Eighth Century, trans. J. Contreni (Columbia, SC, 1976), p. 497; D. Bullough, *The Age of Charlemagne*, 2nd edition (London, 1973), p. 100, 107; Bullough, 'Urban change in early medieval Italy: the example of Pavia', *Papers of the British School at Rome* 34 (1966), 82–131, esp. pp. 94–102; Bullough, 'Aula renovata: the Carolingian court before the Aachen palace', *Proceedings of the British Academy* 71 (1985), 267–301, esp. pp. 284–5. Similar arguments apply to illuminated manuscripts and art in general: A. Boeckler, 'Die Evangelistenbilder der Adagruppe', *Münchner Jahrbuch der Bildenden Kunst* 3:3–4 (1952–53), 121–44; Boeckler, 'Die Kanonbogen der Adagruppe und ihre Vorlagen', *Münchner Jahrbuch der Bildenden Kunst*, 5 (1954), 7–22; H. Fillitz. 'Die italienische Kunst des 8. Jahrhunderts als Voraussetzung der Kunst am Hofe Karls des Grossen', *Settimane* 20 (Spoleto, 1973), 783–802; H. Belting, 'Probleme der Kunstgeschichte Italiens im Frühmittelalter', *Frühmittelalterliche Studien* 1 (1967), 94–143; J. Mitchell, 'The display of script and the uses of painting in Longobard Italy', *Settimane* 41.2 (Spoleto, 1994), 887–951.
[8] McKitterick, *Carolingians*, p. 25. Similarly, J. Nelson, 'Literacy in Carolingian government', in McKitterick (ed.), *Uses*, pp. 258–96. F.L. Ganshof, 'Charlemagne et l'usage de l'écrit en matière administrative', *Le Moyen Age* 57 (1951), 1–25, Eng. trans. by J. Sondheimer in Ganshof, *The Carolingians and the Frankish Monarchy: Studies in Carolingian History* (Ithaca, NY, 1971), pp. 125–42.
[9] *Carolingians* p. 26. Similarly expressed in McKitterick (ed.), *Uses*, p. 10. Petrucci, *Scriptores* (note 13 below), p. 6, responded.
[10] See Clanchy, *Memory*, pp. 11–16.
[11] T. Mommsen, 'Petrarch's conception of the Dark Ages', *Speculum* 17 (1942), 226–42.

literacy was highly valued. The Roman heritage of Italy, of course, is of enormous importance in understanding the development of Italian society in the early medieval period (and, arguably, in any period of Italian history). The question to be 'tackled' is posed thus: in 568 the arrival of the Lombards heralded the end of the Roman empire in most parts of Italy, yet Italy had a long history of literacy under Roman rule. What happened to literacy in Italy under 'barbarian' rule?

The historiographical bias towards Italy as a repository of Roman literate culture, a *fons civilitatis*, is therefore spiced by another set of assumptions concerning the Lombards. Considered by Gibbon, and by many more recent commentators, as the quintessential barbarians, 'fierce and illiterate',[12] the Lombards were the third and final wave of Germanic invaders responsible for knocking Italy out of its late Roman orbit and pushing it into the early middle ages. The earlier Ostrogothic period, in contrast, is characterised as an 'Indian summer' of Roman continuity. The Ostrogothic regime essentially maintained a late Roman political framework, paid homage to senatorial values concerning the connections between literacy and *civilitas*, and nurtured *litterati* such as Boethius, Cassiodorus and Ennodius of Pavia. No such figures emerge from the Lombard kingdom until the time of its demise. The paucity of manuscript evidence and the dearth of narrative sources from the Lombard period are considered as further evidence of a Dark Age for literacy.

It has often been assumed that since the Lombards, as Germanic invaders, robbed the empire of Italy, they robbed Italy of literacy also. For example, Armando Petrucci, one of the foremost authorities on the palaeography of early medieval Italy, devoted an essay 'The Lombard problem' to the history of literacy in Italy. Petrucci explains the reason why the Lombards, in the earlier stages of their settlement and consolidation in Italy, had no 'need' for the use of written communication, or indeed any communication at all, owing to their German ethnicity:

If Roman society was a society of dialogue and communication, in which writing constituted the connective tissue of every practical and intellectual activity, Germanic society, and Lombard society in particular, were, to the contrary, societies devoid of a real need of communication or dialogue; or rather, societies in which the simplicity of administrative structures and the meagre sum of cultural traditions allowed the necessary web of social contacts to form and be governed through oral means.

[12] E. Gibbon, *The Decline and Fall of the Roman Empire*, ed. J.B. Bury, IV (London, 1909), p. 136.

Introduction

The Lombard invasion inaugurated a 'reversal of values and of prestige in the realm of culture', a culture in which the civility of literacy had no place.[13]

There are many assumptions here that are more than questionable in the light of recent research on the topics of barbarians, the later Roman empire and early medieval literacy. A loosely defined and often unhelpful Roman–German dichotomy, as an explanatory paradigm, has dogged much Italian historiography concerning the early medieval period, although it is easy to detect signs of its increasing obsolescence as we move further away from Italy's experiences of the twentieth century.[14] The notion of the 'simplicity' of oral culture is more than misleading, and we shall leave aside altogether the contention that Lombard society had no 'need to communicate'. The characterisation of Lombard administrative structures as 'simplistic', however, needs qualification. The Lombard settlement accelerated changes already taking place in relation to the uses of literacy: the integration of the civil and military in society; the decreasing power of the central imperial government in provincial Italian life; and the prevalence of land-owning as the predominant basis for wealth and social status in society. Chapter 1 seeks to explore these changes by examining the question of literacy in late antique and Ostrogothic Italy in order to place the establishment of Lombard rule in north-central Italy in its proper historical context. It is worth asking, however, just who the Lombards were and how they established their rule in Italy with respect to the adaptation of Roman literate traditions. This, then, is the goal of chapter 2, which proceeds to examine early court culture and the role of religion in helping to legitimate Lombard power and establish Lombard identity. Chapter 3 focuses upon the relationship between written and spoken language by examining the Latin of the sources and how this relates to the linguistic environment of Lombard Italy.

Chapters 4–7 focus upon a particular genre of evidence, namely law, charters, inscriptions and manuscripts. The arrangement is a result of the approach taken here to the subject of literacy in this period as much

---

[13] Petrucci's previous articles on early medieval Italy have been collected and re-edited with C. Romeo in *Scriptores in urbibus: alfabetismo e cultura scritta nell'Italia altomedievale* (Bologna, 1992), henceforth cited simply as Petrucci, *Scriptores*: 'Il problema', pp. 35–56, at pp. 38, 54. This essay, and others concerning Italy, have been published in English: *Writers and Readers in Medieval Italy: Studies in the History of Written Culture*, trans. C.M. Radding (New Haven and London, 1995), pp. 43–58, at pp. 45, 57.

[14] B. Luiselli, *Storia culturale dei rapporti tra mondo romano e mondo germanico* (Rome, 1992). But cf. G. Tabacco, 'Latinità e germanesimo nella tradizione medievalistica italiana', *Rivista Storica Italiana* 102 (1990), 691–716.

as a simple method of organising material. A preliminary few words, therefore, on the definition of literacy used in this study are in order.

Although the term 'literacy' encompasses the acts of both reading and writing, we need to remember that these are two separate skills, and that reading was far more widely practised than writing.[15] Definitions of literacy are notoriously vague and relative to different periods and places. In his *Ancient Literacy*, Harris cited the 1958 UNESCO definition of an illiterate person, as someone 'who cannot with understanding both read and write a short simple statement on his everyday life', and points out that even UNESCO dropped the definition twenty years later in a worldwide survey of literacy.[16] Richter has scoffed at scholars such as Clanchy and McKitterick for following an 'English empiricist tradition' and allegedly avoiding a real need for more theoretical approaches to the subject which might sharpen our understanding of how literacy operated in this period.[17] Yet it is also true that 'writing about literacy in the abstract is thus dangerous as it homogenizes culturally distinct and socially diverse practices'.[18] If cards are to be laid on the table, then I confess to an empiricist approach in the following study, not without reason. Literacy, as a set of skills pertaining to the separate acts of reading and writing, is essentially a highly individualistic and somewhat personal phenomenon. Our surviving sources are never particularly personal: no individual gives detailed descriptions of their own or someone else's attainment of literate skills and how this affected their lives. In the absence of direct references to the attainment of literate skills by individuals, we can do no more than focus upon the evidence for the uses of script and attempt to draw out the implications of its existence: who used it, how they used it and why they used it. Hence this study does not pretend to offer any precise definitions of literacy, but rather attempts to understand the different uses of literacy in Italo-Lombard society. Chapters 4–7 do this by focusing upon a particular genre of evidence and extrapolating from the individual circumstances surrounding the production and dissemination of a particular text, whether it be a hastily scribbled charter or a laboriously inscribed epitaph. Nevertheless, some points need to be made here concerning the relationship between reading and writing in this period as means of communication.

---

[15] See Riché, 'Apprendre à lire et à écrire dans le haut moyen-âge', *Bulletin de la Société Nationale des Antiquaires de France* (1978–79), 193–203.
[16] W. Harris, *Ancient Literacy* (Cambridge, MA and London, 1989), p. 3.
[17] Richter, *Formation*, p. 48 n. 9; cf. nn. 123, 125–7.
[18] M. Innes, 'Memory, orality and literacy in an early medieval society', *Past and Present* 158 (1998), 3–36, at p. 10.

Introduction

To begin with writing, let us take a statement by an anonymous scribe on the act of writing found in the colophon of a late eighth-century Italian legal manuscript: 'Whoever does not know how to write thinks it is no work at all. But oh how burdensome is script! It oppresses your eyes, bruises your kidneys, as well as making all your limbs sorrow at the same time. Three fingers write, but the whole body suffers.'[19] The fact that such statements are not found in the ancient world should not lead us to consider them as indicative of a 'profound cultural change' or a general devaluation of writing in the early middle ages.[20] It was a monastic topos to emphasise the labour involved in writing a manuscript and a plea for the reader to take care in using it 'ne subito litteras deleas'.[21] It might also suggest that demand for texts was overrunning supply. The colophon also draws attention to the physiological aspects of writing, an act which requires a degree of control and co-ordination of motor skills that were more threatened by ailments and disease than is common today. This is an important corrective to a definition of literacy as writing subscriptions on charters, because such physical ailments contributed significantly to the number of people who could write. In 765 the abbot Rignolf was called upon by his son, the young priest Rixolf, to provide legal consent for Rixolf's donation to a church in Lucca. Rignolf gave his consent, but because of his illness he required his son, who also wrote the charter, to subscribe for him.[22] Similarly, the Lucchese cleric Aniprand could not write 'propter neglegentia usui sui manibus suis propriis [*sic*]', that is, an inability to use his own hands.[23] In sixth-century Ravenna, the *vir devotus* Gregorius complained that he could not sign his own will owing to the gout in his feet.[24] Moreover, some witnesses in Lombard charters state that they could not write because of their poor eyesight.[25] As Umberto Eco reminded us in *The Name of the Rose*, the invention of spectacles in the late thirteenth century not only facilitated an increase in the percentage of the population who could read, but also greatly increased the longevity

---

[19] 'Qui nescit scribere, putat hoc esse nullum laborem. O quam gravis est scriptura: oculos gravat, renes frangit, simul et omnia membra contristat. Tria digita scribunt, totus corpus laborat', in W. Wattenbach, *Das Schriftwesen im Mittelalter*, 3rd edn (Leipzig, 1896), p. 283.
[20] Richter, *Formation*, p. 50.
[21] As is clear from rest of the colophon: 'beatissime lector, lava manus tuas et sic librum aprehende, leniter folia turna. longe a littera digito pone. Quia qui nescit scribere [etc.]. Wattenbach, *Schriftwesen*, pp. 282–3.
[22] CDL 194: 'hanc paginam fili mei me consentientem scribere, quia ego pre egredtudine mea non potuit scribere'.
[23] ChLA 948.   [24] Tjäder, P. 4–5.
[25] ChLA 966, 'propter caliginem oculorum menime potuit manu sua subscribere': ChLA 932. Also Tjäder, P. 34.

of a person's reading life.²⁶ If the questions we ask about the past are determined by the present, at the least we must try to avoid evaluating the position of literacy in past periods in comparison to the modern industrialised world in which we live, a world in which medical and optic sciences have permitted greater numbers of opportunities for reading, and as a corollary, writing.

The physiological element of reading and writing in the early middle ages forces us to acknowledge two interrelated aspects: first, the 'oral' nature of reading aloud in this period, and second, the communal or social component of reading. The oral nature of reading aloud in antiquity and in the early middle ages is well attested in the contemporary sources which do not have to be rehearsed here, although it is worth noting that reading aloud was not the only method of reading.²⁷ The importance of this factor for understanding the transmission of information in literate form cannot be underestimated: it was not necessary to be able to read in order to partake of the world of books, documents, inscriptions, and script in general.²⁸ To take an example from our period, Pope Gregory I's story of the quadruplegic Servulus serves as a poignant reminder of how even the most disadvantaged could take part in the world of reading:

> He did not know how to read or write; still he bought himself the sacred books of Scripture and had them read to him regularly by religious persons whom he used to invite to his home as guests. Thus, in his own way he acquired a knowledge of the whole of scripture, although, as I said, he was quite illiterate.²⁹

Reading, an act of recitation, was not only pronounced, but also performed. The performance aspect of communal reading in monastic circles can be heard in the stipulations of Benedict's *Rule*.³⁰ This type of communal reading was a reflection of that which was going on outside the monastery in the wider community. The oral nature of reading is further emphasised by the original form of early medieval Italian texts, for they are almost completely devoid of word-separation and use only minimal punctuation.³¹ A person reading from a text obtained its meaning by listening to sounds, rather than by seeing words or phrases and construing them according to their concordance with grammatical rules and

---

²⁶ See E. Rosen, 'Did Roger Bacon invent eyeglasses?', *Archives Internationales d'Histoire des Sciences* 33 (1954), 35–46, and Rosen, 'The invention of eyeglasses', *Journal of the History of Medicine* 11 (1956), 125–47; G.H. Oliver, *History of the Invention and Discovery of Spectacles* (London, 1913). Cf. K. Chiu, 'The introduction of spectacles into China', *Harvard Journal of Asiatic Studies* 1 (1936), 5–34; A. Crombie, *Augustine to Galileo*, 2 vols., 3rd edn in 1 vol. (London, 1979), pp. 233–7.
²⁷ J. Balogh, '*Voces paginarum*: Beiträge zur Geschichte des lauten Lesens und Schreibens', *Philologus* 82 (1927), 84–109, 202–40; Richter, *Formation*, pp. 52–55.
²⁸ See Stock, *Implications of Literacy*, p. 90. ²⁹ *Dialogues* IV.15.
³⁰ RB (see below, pp. 47–8) 38, 47, 12.4, 66, 4.10, 3.3.
³¹ See below, pp. 261, 307–8.

Introduction

regulations of the inflectional system of the Latin language. In such texts, the dual perception of the grapheme and the phoneme is inseparable in the signification of meaning.[32]

The evidence of administrative and governmental forms of literacy, such as laws and charters, points towards a society in which literacy played a fundamental role in the functioning of the Lombard state and in the everyday life of the kingdom. In particular, autographed subscriptions on charters are cited as evidence of literacy amongst a large proportion of the population.[33] The most thorough application of such evidence to the question of literacy has been Petrucci's examination of subscriptions (numbering 988 in all) in the witness lists of charters from the Lombard kingdom, which led him to four conclusions:

1 In eighth-century Lombard Italy there was a certain diffusion of the knowledge of writing among the middle and upper classes of society, which, however, completely excluded women.
2 The vast majority of ecclesiastics, in small centres or in cities, were literate.
3 Lay literacy seems to diminish in the countryside and less inhabited areas in comparison with the more populated centres.
4 Lay literacy does not appear to be connected with social functions or particular tradespeople. We find some royal functionaries, moneyers and goldsmiths who were unable to write, as well as others who could. The five identifiable craftsmen who appear as witnesses (a blacksmith, a *magister murorum*, a *magister commacinus*, a shoemaker and a tinker) are all illiterate.[34]

In sum, 32.7 per cent of subscribers were 'literate'. Petrucci's attempt to discern the 'graphic capacity' of the person subscribing redeems his quantitative method with more qualitative concerns.[35] The *vista paleografica*, however, can often neglect the social relations that constitute literate practices in favour of a specialised focus on textual concerns and the history of script, rather than the history of people. It is a problem of which palaeographers of Petrucci's calibre are well aware.[36]

---

[32] *Contra* Goody, *Domestication*, pp. 44–50, 78.
[33] For example T.S. Brown, 'The transformation of the Roman Mediterranean, 400–900', in G. Holmes (ed.), *The Oxford Illustrated History of Medieval Europe* (Oxford, 1988), p. 39; also, C. J. Wickham, *Early Medieval Italy: Central Power and Local Society 400–1000* (London and Basingstoke, 1981), p. 124 (hereafter *EMI*); Clanchy, *Memory*, p. 12.
[34] A. Petrucci 'Libro, scrittura e scuola', *Settimane* 19 (Spoleto,1972), 313–38; repr. 'Alle origini dell'alfabetismo altomedievale', *Scriptores*, pp. 13–34, at p. 23; trans. Radding, *Writers and Readers*, p. 68.
[35] See A. Petrucci, 'David Cressy: sull'alfabetismo in Inghilterra', *Quaderni Storici* 51/a. Dec. (1982), 1129–33. Cf. McKitterick, *Carolingians*, p. 3.
[36] See his 'Storia della scrittura e storia della società', *Anuario de Estudios Medievales* 21 (1991), 309–22.

The writing of a formulaic subscription involves a limited understanding of literacy. The problem is one not only of using autograph subscriptions as evidence for literacy, but also of using their absence or substitution with a cross *signum manus* as an indicator of illiteracy.[37] Chris Wickham remarked that Lombard autograph subscriptions were evidence of an awareness of what written law and proofs meant, even if such a 'functionally' literate person could not read particularly fluently, 'let alone read Virgil for pleasure'.[38] But the same could be said for witnesses who placed their *signum manus* upon a document. They may or may not have been able to read at all, but their participation in the act of conferring legitimacy upon a document demonstrates their acquaintance with the authority of the written word in legal affairs. In chapter 4, therefore, I explore the relationship of literacy to the socio-legal culture of Lombard Italy by examining the Lombard law code, both as a manifestation of legal literacy and as an instrument of Lombard government. In particular, I focus on the themes of women, manumission, and the uses of literacy in central and local government, in an attempt to provide a more satisfactory picture of how legal literacy affected Italo-Lombard society.

I then discuss who wrote charters, rather than just subscriptions, in chapter 5. The emphasis is on determining whether or not there existed any recognisable 'profession' for the redaction of documents, and if such skills were widespread or easily obtainable in this period. This raises the issues of the level of literacy required to write a charter and the type of education or training needed to do so. It further provides us with an insight into the type of documentary culture within which the scribe worked. Also considered are the social rituals surrounding the redaction of a charter, and the themes of 'public' and 'private' documentation with respect to both the redaction and the preservation of documents.

Chapter 6 focuses on the evidence of inscriptions in a further attempt to discern the 'script culture' of Lombard Italy and how the medium of epigraphy functioned as a form of literacy, a form which has not received its due attention in this context, at least not by medieval historians. In chapter 7 I turn to discuss the manuscript evidence of Lombard Italy, which too often has been erroneously considered negligible, in order to explore the role played by monasteries and churches as centres of written culture. This is followed by a brief discussion of the survival of classical works in Lombard Italy, and the implications of the diversity

---

[37] Bäuml, 'Varieties and consequences', pp. 240–1.
[38] *EMI*, p. 125. Cf. B. Rea, 'The context and meaning of popular literacy: some evidence from nineteenth-century rural England', *Past and Present* 131 (1991), 81–129.

Introduction

of script types for literacy, in particular the development of minuscule scripts.

I should now state what this study does not include, although the subjects are of direct or indirect relevance to the theme of literacy.

I have not included a discussion of the hagiographic evidence, owing to the technical difficulties involved in establishing secure date for many texts. These have been dealt with elsewhere in a manner which is complementary to the subject of this study,[39] and should be considered in the light of the other evidence presented here. Moreover, I have not directly addressed the theme of schools and education. Research on education in Lombard Italy revealed that the sources mention only monasteries and episcopal and clerical schools; there is no reference to urban schools except clerical ones.[40] The references, too, are just that; we do not know how these schools functioned, what they taught, who and how many people attended them.[41] There is no reason to presume that they did not operate along the same lines as monasteries and clerical schools elsewhere in Europe in this period.[42] A lay–ecclesiastical dichotomy in education has little validity. The *magister* and *discipuli* attested at the episcopal school at Lucca in this period wrote charters in an expert cursive script, in the best of late antique secular traditions.[43] The modern emphasis on schools as a means to obtaining literate skills is misleading. Literacy could be taught and learned in a number of different ways and places, particularly in the home.[44]

The problem of discerning different types of education and the different levels of literate culture in Lombard Italy is neatly encapsulated in the career of Paul the Deacon. Paul was a true scholar, historian, hagiographer and poet. He was born and raised in Friuli, and spent some time as a young man at the royal Lombard court in Pavia. His talents gained him employment at the Beneventan ducal court and the court of Charlemagne. He was also a monk of Monte Cassino. Precisely when

---

[39] Everett, 'The hagiography of Lombard Italy', *Hagiographica* 7 (2000), 49–126.
[40] G.H. Hörle, *Frümittelalterliche Mönchs- und Klerikerbildung in Italien: geistliche Bildungsideale und Bildungseinrichtungen vom 6. bis zum 9. Jahrhundert*, Freiburger Theologische Studien 13 (Freiburg, 1914), pp. 36–4; Riché, *Education*, pp. 406–9.
[41] D. Bullough, 'Le scuole cattedrali e la cultura dell'Italia settentrionale prima dei communi', *Italia Sacra* 5 (1964), 111–45; B. Pagnin, 'Scuola e cultura a Pavia nell'alto medioevo', *Atti* IV CISAM (Spoleto, 1969), 153–81; H. Schwarzmaier, *Lucca und das Reich bis zum Ende des 11. Jahrhunderts: Studien zur Sozialstruktur einer Herzogstadt in der Toscana* (Tübingen, 1972), pp. 266–70.
[42] P. Riché, *Ecoles et enseignement dans le haut moyen-âge* (Paris, 1979).
[43] Petrucci, 'Il codice e i documenti', *Scriptores*, pp. 77–108.
[44] See F. Niyi Akinnaso, 'Schooling, language and knowledge in literate and non-literate societies', *Comparative Studies in Society and History* 34 (1992), 68–109. McKitterick, *Carolingians*, pp. 212–27; Clanchy, *Memory*, pp. 12–20.

he became one is unknown.[45] Paul tells us nothing about his education, except briefly mentioning in some poems how he learned a Greek epigram 'in scholis' or, less informatively, how the muses had fled him in his monastic cell.[46] Paul's life (what we know of it) and works, and the levels of learning they demonstrate, have been adequately studied.[47] It is not my concern here to focus upon his literary culture, or upon evidence for high 'literary' culture in the Lombard kingdom at all.[48] Instead, the focus is on the more earthly evidence of laws, charters, inscriptions and manuscripts in order to understand further the background of literate culture from which figures such as Paul emerged.

A final word needs to be said concerning the social and economic environment of Lombard Italy. It has long been pointed out that the Lombard state was founded upon an infrastructural network of towns as organisational centres for political, administrative, cultural and economic activity.[49] A great deal of debate over the historical development of Italy in this period has been concerned with monitoring the levels of continuity and change of urban centres, for Italy constitutes a yardstick with which we can measure the transition from ancient to medieval civilisation.[50] Despite humanist assumptions concerning the connections

---

[45] Brunhölzl, *Geschichte*, pp. 256–66. A good account of Paul's life and career is W. Goffart, *The Narrators of Barbarian History A.D. 550–800: Jordanes, Gregory of Tours, Bede and Paul the Deacon* (Princeton, 1989), pp. 334–7; and see now the papers in P. Chiesa (ed.), *Paolo Diacono: uno scrittore fra tradizione e rinnovamento carolingio* (Udine, 2000).

[46] For Paul's poems, K. Neff, *Die Gedichte des Paulus Diaconus: Kritische und Erklärende Ausgabe*, Quellen und Untersuchungen zur lateinischen Philologie des Mittelalters 3.4 (Munich, 1908). Poems, VIII pp. 39–40, XIII, pp. 63–8.

[47] T. Mommsen, 'Die Quellen der Langobardengeschichte des Paulus Diaconus', in *Gesammelte Schriften* 6 (Berlin, 1910), pp. 485–539; M.L.W. Laistner, *Thought and Letters in Western Europe, A.D. 500–900* (London, 1957), pp. 266–72; E.F.J. Raby, *A History of Christian Latin Poetry* (Oxford, 1934), pp. 164–6; Raby, *A History of Secular Latin Poetry* (Oxford, 1936), pp. 192–3; D. Bianchi, 'Paolo Diacono e l'Ars Donatii', *Atti e Memorie della Deputazione Storica di Modena* s. VIII.10 (1958), pp. 158–202; V. Law, 'The sources of the Ars Donatii quam Paulus Diaconus exposuit', *Filologia Mediolatina* 1 (1994), 71–80; R. Cervani, *L'Epitome di Paolo del de verborum significatu di Pompeo Festo: struttura e metodo* (Rome, 1978). The individual essays in Chiesa (ed.), *Paolo Diacono*, help fill out the picture.

[48] An excellent survey is Riché, *Education*, pp. 336–45, 399–421.

[49] G. Tabacco, *Egemonie sociali e strutture del potere nel medioevo italiano* (Turin, 1979), trans. R. Brown Jensen, *The Struggle for Power in Medieval Italy: Structures of Political Rule* (Cambridge, 1989). C. Wickham, *EMI*; D. Harrison, *The Early State and the Towns: Forms of Integration in Lombard Italy AD, 568–774*, Lund Studies in International History 29 (Lund, 1993).

[50] Wickham, 'The other transition: from the ancient world to feudalism', *Past and Present* 113 (1984), 3–36, (repr. *Land and Power*, pp. 7–42); Wickham, 'Italy and the early middle ages', in K. Randsborg (ed.), *The Birth of Europe* (Rome, 1989), pp. 140–51 (repr. *Land and Power*, pp. 99–120). For the debate see R. Balzaretti, 'History, archaeology and early medieval urbanism: the north Italian debate', *The Journal of the Accordia Research Centre* 2 (1991), 87–104; B. Ward-Perkins, 'Continuitists, catastrophists and the towns of post-Roman northern Italy', *Papers of the British School at Rome* 65 (1997), 156–76. Also below, pp. 15–19.

Introduction

between ancient *urbanitas* and *litterae*, the history of literacy is full of examples that deny the validity of using urbanism as a guide to levels of literate activity.[51] The economic-determinist view of literacy, which holds that literate activity increases or decreases in accordance with the fortunes of large-scale socio-economic organisation, has been something of a hindrance to understanding the uses of literacy in the early medieval period.[52] Some archaeologists and historians have argued that the material culture of Italy became increasingly impoverished in the late antique and Lombard period, even to the point that 'Italy was reduced to aboriginal circumstances in the seventh and eighth centuries.'[53] It certainly was not, but we still need to establish how such changes affected literacy, if they did at all, rather than lapse into general assumptions of decline and devaluation. As I hope to demonstrate in the following pages, the surviving evidence of Lombard Italy suggests a development and diversification of the uses of literacy, the sophistication of which sheds a great deal of light on a period usually considered as Italy's Dark Age.

---

[51] See Gough, 'The implications', pp. 69–84; Clanchy, *Memory*, pp. 11–16. C. Radding, *The Origins of Medieval Jurisprudence: Pavia and Bologna 850–1150* (New Haven and London, 1988) p. 89, notes a similar historiographic fallacy for the history of law. An instructive counterpart is early medieval Ireland: see J. Stevenson, 'Literacy in Ireland: the evidence of the Patrick dossier in the Book of Armagh', in McKitterick (ed.), *Uses*, pp. 11–35, esp. pp. 11–12.

[52] Examples of the economic-determinist view are C. Cipolla, *Literacy and Development in the West* (Harmonds Worth, 1969); Harris, *Ancient Literacy*; H. Pirenne, 'L'instruction des marchands au moyen âge', *Annales d'Histoire Economique et Sociale* 1 (1929), 20–53; Pirenne, 'De l'état de l'instruction des laïques à l'époque mérovingienne', *Revue Bénédictine* 46 (1934), 165–76; Pirenne, *Mohammed and Charlemagne*, trans. B. Miall (New York and London, 1939). Cf. I. Wood, 'Administration, law and culture in Merovingian Gaul', in McKitterick (ed.), *Uses*, pp. 63–81.

[53] R. Hodges, 'In the shadow of Pirenne: San Vincenzo al Volturno and the revival of Mediterranean commerce', in R. Francovich and G. Noye (eds), *La storia dell'alto medioevo italiano (sec. VI–X) alla luce dell'archeologia* (Florence, 1994), pp. 109–27, at p. 124; Hodges, 'The riddle of St. Peter's Republic', in *La storia economica di Roma nell'alto medioevo alle luce dei recenti scavi archeologici*, Biblioteca di Archeologia Medievale (Florence, 1993), pp. 353–67.

1
ITALY AND LITERACY BEFORE THE LOMBARDS

In his Pragmatic Sanction of 554, the emperor Justinian decreed, among other things, that the state was to continue to provide, as it had under Theoderic the Ostrogoth, salaries for teachers of grammar, rhetoric, medicine and law, 'so that young men schooled in the liberal arts might flourish in the service of the state'.[1] That the state was to provide educated, literate recruits was an idea that was going to disappear in Italy. Justinian's decree highlights one of fundamental differences between the Italy of the first and second halves of the sixth century. Unlike their Ostrogothic predecessors, the Lombard rulers of Italy never sought imperial support or to construct a façade of imperial continuity for the parts of Italy they conquered. We hear no more of the 'liberal arts' as a key requisite for the art of government, nor as an ideal accomplishment for individuals to attain. This was not, however, a situation unique to the areas under Lombard control. At the same time, in the capitals of Byzantine-held Italy, Ravenna and Rome, the ranks of literate civil servants became increasingly irrelevant to the functioning of the state. By the middle of the seventh century, the administration of imperial Italy had come to rely on a network of predominantly military offices and personnel in a manner similar to its Lombard neighbours, employees 'schooled in the liberal arts' had little or no place in the service of the state, and such education is never heard of again.

In this chapter I explore possible reasons for this in order to provide the historical background for the developments that took place in Lombard Italy. It is simply too easy to cite the destruction caused by the Gothic wars as the instigator of irrevocable change. No doubt the wars were disastrous for Italian society, and for the imperial hold over the peninsula as a whole. But more important for the present study is to ask why that which was destroyed was not replaced; why a Roman education in the 'liberal arts' was no longer esteemed, or considered worthwhile, by a decisive proportion of the Italian population. Blaming Lombard ethnicity, or a

---

[1] *Const. prag.* 22; *CJ*, p. 802.

supposed primitivist antagonism towards Roman civilisation, does not square with their establishment as rulers, their relatively small numbers, or Italy's experience of barbarian government prior to their arrival. We need to look elsewhere for answers, and I propose to look in three places. First, the economic and social changes of Italy from the fourth to the sixth century will be sketched swiftly with a view towards understanding the long-term developments against which the Lombard conquest of Italy can be measured. Second, the emphasis on rhetoric in late Roman education needs to be understood as promoting a certain type of literacy, inextricably linked to Roman aristocratic identity, that became increasingly irrelevant to the needs, and ultimately the ideology, of government towards the end of the Ostrogothic regime. Finally, we shall consider how this type of literacy was under fire from another direction, that of the Christian polemic against rhetoric. While some fourth- and fifth-century Christian authors confessed to a degree of guilt over their love of Latin literature, nurtured through years of training, authors of the sixth century demonstrate a heightened awareness of a fundamental conflict of values. The tension between the emphasis on rhetoric in the secular schools and the Christian ideal of *sermo humilis* as the language of divine truth eventually eroded the uneasy alliance of traditional aristocratic tastes with episcopal office. As the edifice of empire diminished, and as more monastic sensibilities towards the wiles of the secular world gained momentum, Latin rhetoric appeared less to offer any benefits and more to be part of the problem. The seventh and eighth centuries inherited a clerical culture in which literate skills were prized for reasons other than the composition of new works, and this contributed to the silences in our historical record for that era.

ITALY BEFORE THE LOMBARDS: ECONOMY AND SOCIETY

There has been much debate concerning the economic and social conditions of late antique Italy and the degree of economic and population decline in both cities and the countryside. There is sufficient evidence, both literary and archaeological, to suggest that well before the arrival of the Lombards, Italy, at least in terms of material culture, urban density and the extent of its trade networks, was greatly impoverished compared to its imperial past.[2] The evidence of African Red Slip ware, which on the whole suggests economic retraction in Italy from the third century

---

[2] A good starting point is A. Giardina, 'Le due Italie nella forma tarda dell'impero', A. Giardina (ed.), *Società romana e impero tardoantico*, ed. (Rome and Bari, 1986), pp. 1–36; B. Ward Perkins, *From Classical Antiquity to the Middle Ages: Urban Public Building in Northern and Central Italy A.D. 300–850* (Oxford, 1984); Ward Perkins, 'Continuitists, catastrophists'; C. La Rocca, 'Trasformazioni

onwards, must be considered with respect to a great deal of regional and chronological variation. It seems that the imperial presence in Rome and in coastal regions to the south contributed to the maintenance of patterns of import and consumption of African wares in some cases into the seventh century, while central and northern Italy, and particularly the interior, were cut off from these networks of exchange long before the arrival of the Lombards. What effect this had on the economy in those regions is unclear.[3] When we look to the sixth century, an evil trinity of plague, famine and warfare seems to descend upon Italy to make it a shadow of its former imperial glory. An outbreak of bubonic plague in the east seems to have reached Italy in 543. At the same time it ravaged the population of Constantinople, where according to some sources it killed over a third of the population. We have no such information for Italy, and it is difficult to gauge the effect of the plague over the long term, though it surely delivered a debilitating blow to economic activity and population levels when it hit.[4] Italy was hit again by plague in 570–1, and the destruction wrought in Liguria was graphically characterised by Paul the Deacon: homes were deserted, fields abandoned, and 'the world

---

della città altomedievale in "Langobardia"', *Studi Storici* 4 (1989), 993–1011. Cf. G. Cantino Wataghin, 'Quadri urbani dell'Italia settentrionale: tarda antichità e alto medioevo', in C. Lepelley (ed.), *La Fin de la cité antique et le début de la cité médiévale* (Bari, 1996), pp. 239–71; G. Ciampoltrini, 'Città frammentate e città fortezza. Storie urbane della Toscana centrosettentrionale fra Teodosio e Carlo Magno', in R. Francovich and G. Noyé (eds.), *La storia dell'altomedioevo italiano alla luce dell'archeologia* (Florence, 1994), pp. 615–33; G.P. Brogiolo, 'Edilizia residenziale in Lombardia', in *Atti del 4 seminario sul tardoantico e l'altomedievo in Italia centrosettentrionale* (Mantua, 1994), pp. 103–14. On the countryside see N. Christie, 'Barren fields? Landscapes and settlements in Roman and post-Roman Italy', in G. Shipley and J. Salmon (eds.), *Human Landscapes in Classical Antiquity: Environment and Culture* (London, 1996), pp. 254–83.

[3] C. Wickham, 'Marx, Sherlock Holmes, and late Roman commerce', *Journal of Roman Studies* 78 (1988), 183–93; G.P. Brogiolo and S. Gelichi, 'La ceramica grezza medievale nella pianura padana', in D. Manacorda et al., *La ceramica medievale nel Mediterraneo occidentale* (Florence, 1986), pp. 293–316; R. Reynolds, *Trade in the Western Mediterranean A.D. 400–700: The Ceramic Evidence*, BAR International Series 604 (Oxford, 1995), pp. 22–7, 117–19. The papers collected in L. Paroli (ed.), *La ceramica invetriata tardoantica e altomedievale in Italia* (Florence, 1992), and L. Saguì (ed.), *La ceramica in Italia: VI–VII secolo: Atti del Colloquio in onore di John W. Hayes, Roma 11–13 Maggio 1995* (Florence, 1998) demonstrate the difficulty of establishing a synthesis, but see E. Zanini, 'Ricontando la terra sigillata africana', *Archeologia Medievale* 23 (1996), 677–88; Zanini, *Le Italie bizantine: territorio, insediamenti ed economia nella provincia bizantina d'Italia, (VI–VIII secolo)* (Bari, 1998).

[4] There is little agreement over its importance. A more catastrophic view is R. Hodges and D. Whitehouse, *Mohammed, Charlemagne and the Origins of Europe: Archaeology and the Pirenne Thesis* (Ithaca, NY, 1983), pp. 38–53; cf. J. Biraben and J. Le Goff, 'La peste dans haut moyen âge', *Annales* 24 (1969), 1484–1510, esp., pp. 1495–7; P. Allen, 'The "Justinianic" plague', *Byzantion* 49 (1979), 5–20; K. Leven, 'Die "Justinianische" peste', *Jahrbuch des Instituts für Geschichte der Medizin der Robert Bosch Stiftung* 6 (1987), 137–61; J. Moorhead, *Justinian* (London, 1994), pp. 99–101. Limiting its significance for the long term: J. Durliat, 'La peste du VIe siècle. Pour un nouvel examen des sources Byzantines', in G. Dagron (ed.), *Hommes et richesses dans l'Empire byzantin* (Paris, 1989), I.107–25; Wickham, 'Italy', in *Land and Power*, pp. 110–11.

was reduced to its primaeval silence'.[5] This is one of Paul's better literary flourishes, and the vivid description invites scepticism, not least that the plague spread 'right up to the borders of the Alemans and Bavarians, but only affected the Romans', though there is some confirmation of the damage it wrought in other sources.[6] Plague returned again in 590, when it killed Pope Pelagius II and ripped through the population of Rome. This last outbreak was directly linked by contemporaries to the floods 'believed not to have been seen since Noah' of the year before which devastated Veneto, Liguria and the city of Rome, where a huge dragon surrounded by water snakes floated down the flooded Tiber.[7]

Whether the importance of the plague has been under- or overstated, the search for the cause of the plague has led to some important findings concerning possible climate changes in this period. Literary sources, including confirmatory notices in Chinese chronicles, record a darkening of the sun and a winter that endured some twelve to eighteen months for the year 536–7, and dendrochronology further illustrates a dramatic decline in tree-growth for the years 536 and 540.[8] Various theories have been offered as to the cause, but the effect appears to have been a world-wide failure in crops and cycles of growth for most if not all plants, which must have been detrimental to pastoralism also.[9] Yet the early sixth century had seen other irregularities in weather patterns, and it has been argued that early medieval Europe experienced climatic warming from the fourth century onwards, interrupted in the sixth and seventh centuries by a cooling period which resulted in high levels of rainfall.[10] The data used to compile this picture are highly questionable, and archaeological investigation of some areas suggests heavy rainfall seriously affected settlement patterns well before the sixth century.[11] It is difficult to get any clear-cut picture here of climatic change, but clearly the sixth century witnessed more than its fair share of irregular weather and resulting natural disaster. Just how much this exacerbated political or economic difficulties

---

[5] *HL* II.4. [6] Marius, a. 569/570
[7] *HL* III.23, 24. Gregory, *Dialogues* III.19; Gregory, *Historiae* X.1.
[8] Michael the Syrian, *Chron.*, 26. Cf. Procopius, *Wars* IV.14.5; Cassiodorus, *Var.* XII.25; D. Keys, *Catastrophe: An Investigation into the Origins of the Modern World* (London, 1999).
[9] M.G.L. Baillie, *A Slice through Time: Dendrochronology and Precision Dating* (London, 1995), pp. 91–107. The theories are discussed by P. Farquharson, 'Byzantium, planet earth and the solar system', in E. Jeffreys and P. Allen, *The Sixth Century: End or Beginning?* (Brisbane, 1996), pp. 263–9; and J. Koder, 'Climactic change in the fifth and sixth centuries?', in *ibid.*, pp. 270–85.
[10] P. Brimblecome, 'Climatic traditions and population development in the Middle Ages', *Saeculum* 39 (1988), 141–8; cf. P. Squatriti, *Water and Culture in Early Medieval Italy* (Cambridge, 1998), pp. 65–75.
[11] See R. Hodges, *San Vincenzo al Volturno: The 1980–86 Excavations* (London, 1993), p. 133; and A. Marcello and A. Cornell, 'L'alluvione che seppellì Iulia Concordia', *Memorie di Biogeografia Adriatica dell'Istituto di Studi Adriatici* 5 (1957–63), 136–64.

is an open question, but significant changes in weather patterns have far more important and immediate consequences in a pre-industrial society than in the modern world. Disturbances in the rhythms of agricultural production cannot have helped Italians to recover from the effects of war and fundamental changes in political and social organisation.

Whatever economic gains were achieved under the Ostrogoths were soon eradicated by Justinian's attempt to reconquer the peninsula over more than twenty years of warfare.[12] Procopius tells us how, in the early stages of the war, the Gothic King Theodahad sought the advice of a Jewish soothsayer, who commanded the king to place three groups of ten pigs in three separate huts, naming each group after the Goths, the Romans and the soldiers of the emperor, and to wait for a number of days. On the appointed day they went to the huts to see the result: eight of the ten pigs called Goths were dead, nearly all the pigs representing the soldiers were alive except a few, and of the Roman pigs, all had lost their hair and half of them were dead.[13] Writing in the 550s at Constantinople, and surrounded by impoverished Italian aristocrats, Procopius could use the tale to reflect upon the state of Italy after the final defeat of the main contingents of the Gothic army.[14] For Procopius the destruction of Italy lay not in military intervention *per se*: his complaint was with the manner in which it was done.[15] Poor and cowardly generalship, and insufficient financial support from the emperor, were the primary reasons for what Procopius saw as a débâcle which ruined Italy once and for all. Behind the caustic criticism, and sensationalist stories of Romans eating rats owing to starvation, we can discern some undeniably catastrophic effects of the wars on the social fabric of Italy.[16] But north of the Po more damage may have been caused by the presence of Frankish troops. Procopius reports that 100,000 Franks, the 'most treacherous people in the world', and 'natural enemies' of the Lombards, took the opportunity to march into Liguria under the guise of being allies of the Goths.[17] The Franks found the land 'devoid all habitation' and complained about the lack of income it provided. One third of their troops died from diarrhoea and dysentery which they contracted from drinking water from the Po.[18]

---

[12] *Anon. Vales.* 60; Procopius, *Wars* VII.1.3. Cf. V.2.26 (Amalasuintha), and VIII.21.12. Cf. Ward Perkins, *Classical Antiquity*, pp. 158–66; M. Johnson, 'Toward a history of Theoderic's building program', *Dumbarton Oaks Papers* 42 (1988), 73–96; Lusuardi Siena, 'Sulle tracce della presenza gota in Italia: il contributo delle fonti archeologiche', in *Magistra Barbaritas* (Milan, 1984), pp. 513–48; J. Moorhead, *Theoderic in Italy* (Oxford, 1992), pp. 34, 136–7; cf. Zanini, *Le Italie bizantine*, who demonstrates a resumption of mercantile activity for the period *c.* 525–550, which he argues must be associated with the presence of Byzantine forces.
[13] *Wars* V.9.4–10.   [14] *Wars* VIII.21.16–17.
[15] A. Cameron, *Procopius and the Sixth Century* (London, 1985), pp. 242–60.
[16] *Wars* VII.17.12–19. Cf. VI.20.21; Cassiodorus, *Var.* XII.26.
[17] *Wars* VI.25 ff.   [18] Italy deserted, *Wars* VIII.24.4–11; VIII.24.25–9.

Italy and literacy before the Lombards

The important point here is the extent to which the north was now divorced, politically and culturally, from the imperial presence in the south, thus paving the way for independent rule by a barbarian people. When ordered out of Italy by Narses, a detachment of 1000 Goths broke away from the negotiations and 'proceeded to the city of Ticinum and the country beyond the Po',[19] the territory where proud Goths felt most at home, and far removed from imperial grasp.[20] It was this same city and the surrounding 'country beyond the Po' that the Lombards also found so congenial to their settlement.

Some sources sing Narses' praises and claim that during his time Italy was restored to prosperity and its former glory.[21] But such praises were hollow. The *Liber pontificalis* reports how the Romans complained to the emperor Justin II, stating that they preferred to live under the regime of the Goths rather than Romans while Narses continued to subject them to slavery.[22] Pope Pelagius I (556–61) complained about the loss of income to the church owing to the abandonment of fields in Italy which were now so desolate they could not be restored.[23] When the Lombards arrived in 568, they filled a political vacuum in an economically debilitated peninsula. As they went about the business of consolidating their conquests, to many Italians it must have seemed an opportunity to gain the political stability needed to facilitate any economic recovery.

LATIN *LITTERAE* AND THE CONSERVATION OF A CULTURE

The connection between literacy and the needs of the Roman state has a long history with an emphasis on training in the liberal arts. We should be careful, however, not to equate the ancient concept of being trained in the 'liberal arts' with anything as functional as the literate skills necessary for the reading and writing of documents. What Justinian had in mind when he legislated to ensure the continued supply of young men educated in the 'liberal arts' was that which was expressed by the emperor Constantius II and his Caesar Julian in 360:

---

[19] *Wars* VIII.35.37–8.
[20] Cf. Agathias I.1.1, who reports that Belisarius allowed the Goths to return to their estates. Procopius' understanding here may be influenced by the events of 540, when the Goths offered to submit to Justinian and cede to him large tracts of Italian territory, maintaining for themselves the lands north of the Po. *Wars* VI.29.1–3.
[21] *LP* 63.2, ed. Duchesne, I, p. 305: *Con. Prosp.*, c. 21, p. 339. Despite Justinian's attempts to alleviate the fiscal demands on Italy with the Pragmatic sanction (554) and the difficult to interpret 'Lex quae data est pro debitoribus' (c. 557), there seems to have been no respite in the levels of taxation exacted thereafter.
[22] *LP* 63.3, ed. Duchesne, I, p. 305: *Con. Prosp.*, c. 21, p. 339.
[23] MGH Ep. IV, pp. 72–3.

Among the various offices of the town councils... no person shall obtain a post of the first rank unless it shall be proved that he excels in long practice of liberal studies, and that he is so polished in literary matters that words flow from his pen faultlessly... and him who seems worthy in speech and study to obtain the position shall be raised by our sublimity to *honestior* status, lest the rewards of literature, which is the greatest of all virtues, be denied.[24]

A faultless flow of words was the ideal result of training in the 'liberal arts', rather than the acquisition of scientific or technical expertise, and even less so the intellectual skills necessary for any philosophical enquiry. Our sources do not provide any precise guide to the relationship between the attainment of literary skills and the levels of governmental office, probably because there was no direct correlation. Positions were filled on considerations other than meritocratic principles.[25] Birth certainly mattered, and money probably helped more than literary talent.[26] The command of rhetoric proved one worthy of commanding others, and late antiquity inherited a culture that placed high premium on the acquisition and demonstration of such skills.[27] Already in Quintilian's day (*fl.* 68–88), mastery of rhetoric provided 'power, honours, friendships, and glory in the present life and in that to come', and people were trying to fast-track their education to gain a veneer of rhetorical finesse.[28]

But in the late antique period other sciences imparted by the programme of the *quadrivium* – geometry, arithmetic, music and astronomy – were already relegated to the background, even at the highest levels of education, and the emphasis was squarely upon those skills of the *trivium*: grammar, dialectic and rhetoric. In the west, the gradual abandonment of instruction in Greek contributed to removing the more scientific studies of the *quadrivium* from the curriculum, and with them the philosophical training they were intended to complement disappeared.[29] Ferdinand Lot contemptuously noted that late antique literature is 'pathetically

---

[24] *CTh* 14.1.1. On *honestiores*, A.H.M. Jones, *Later Roman Empire: A Social, Economic and Administrative Survey*, 2 vols. (Oxford, 1973) (hereafter *LRE*), pp. 17–18, 749–51.

[25] F.S. Pederson, 'On professional qualifications for public posts in late antiquity', *Classica et Medievalia* 31 (1975), 161–213.

[26] See John Lydus, *De magistratibus* III.54.1–3, trans. T.F. Carney, in *Bureaucracy in Traditional Society: Romano-Byzantine Bureaucracies Viewed from Within*, III (Kansas, 1971), and below, pp. 33–5.

[27] See P.R.L. Brown, *Power and Persuasion in Late Antiquity: Towards a Christian Empire* (Madison, 1992), esp. pp. 35, 39.

[28] Quintilian, *Inst.* XII.11.29; I.9.6; II.1.1–13. See further M. Roberts, *Biblical Epic and Rhetorical Paraphrase in Late Antiquity*, ARCA Classical and Medieval Texts, Papers and Monographs 16 (Liverpool, 1985), pp. 5–28, 64–7.

[29] H. Marrou, *Histoire de l'éducation dans l'antiquité* (Paris, 1948), pp. 271–89, trans. G. Lamb, *A History of Education in Antiquity* (Madison, 1982), pp. 259–62; Marrou, 'L'école dans l'antiquité tardive', *Settimane* 19 (Spoleto, 1972), 127–43; W. Berschin, *Greek Letters and the Latin Middle Ages: From Jerome to Nicholas of Cusa*, trans. J.C. Frakes (Washington, 1988), pp. 41–55; Riché, *Education*, pp. 43–8.

Italy and literacy before the Lombards

academic', in that all of our surviving texts were written by teachers and students, rendering the entire corpus 'excessively dull and lifeless'.[30] But what was once dismissed as a sign of cultural decadence is now more sympathetically explained as a shift in aesthetics towards the ornamental and symbolic representation, in both the visual arts and language. Literature previously interpreted as a symptom of decline is now seen as manifestations of the vitality and vigour of late antique civilisation.[31]

Whatever the shifts in our own perception and evaluation of the predominance of rhetoric in this period, the result was the promotion of a certain type of literacy that was on the one hand a highly sophisticated mode of communication, yet on the other hand extremely limited in its application and dissemination. The type of education encouraged by elites generated uniformity among individuals from varied geographic and socio-economic backgrounds, producing a remarkable degree of cultural homogeneity.[32] Moreover, education separated them from the common rung of mankind. 'We are recognised to be as superior to the uneducated... as they themselves are to beasts', wrote a Latin grammarian in the late fourth century, an age in which the grammatical handbook, the *Ars grammatica*, flourished and in which grammarians were increasingly considered indispensable for the formation of the governing classes.[33]

Although practice varied greatly, the different stages of education, from learning under the supervision of the *primus* or *ludi magister* through to the *grammaticus* and finally the *rhetor*, and the methods of instruction each used, from the line-by-line explication of a canon of texts (*enarratio*) to the compositional exercises (*declamationes, controversiae, suasoriae*), are fairly clear to us.[34] That these exercises remained unchanged throughout the

---

[30] F. Lot, *The End of the Ancient World and the Beginnings of the Middle Ages*, trans. P. and M. Leon (London, 1931), p. 165.

[31] Besides the classic statements of Gibbon, for example *Decline and Fall* (ed. Bury), III, p. 134, cf. Lot, *The End*, pp. 151–65. The interpretative shift is witnessed in the *retractatio* of H. Marrou concerning his earlier views in *Saint Augustine et la fin de la culture antique*, 4th edn (Paris, 1958), p. 690, and his *Décadence romaine ou antiquité tardive? IIIe–VIe siècle* (Paris, 1977). Cf. M. Roberts, *The Jeweled Style: Poetry and Poetics in Late Antiquity* (Ithaca, NY and London, 1989), pp. 1–8, and *passim*.

[32] See R. Kaster, 'Notes on primary and secondary schools in late antiquity', *Transactions of the American Philological Association* 113 (1983), 323–46; Kaster, *Guardians of the Language: The Grammarians and Society in Late Antiquity* (Berkeley, 1988).

[33] Diomedes, *Ars Gram.*, *Grammatici Latini* (ed. H. Keil), I, p. 299. See L. Holtz, *Donat et la tradition de l'enseignement grammatical: étude sur l'Ars Donati et sa diffusion (IVe–IXe siècle) et édition critique* (Paris, 1981), pp. 15–48, 58–96; V. Law, 'Late Latin grammars in the early Middle Ages: a typological history', *Historiographia Linguistica* 13 (1986), 365–380, repr. in Law, *Grammar and Grammarians in the Early Middle Ages* (London and New York, 1997), pp. 54–69.

[34] For the process of *enarratio*, see M. Irvine, *The Making of a Textual Culture: 'Grammatica' and Literary Theory 350–1100* (Cambridge, 1994), pp. 49–87; *grammaticus* and *rhetor*, Kaster (above note 32). For the ancient terminology, H. Lausberg, *Handbook of Literary Rhetoric: A Foundation for Literary Study*, trans. M. Bliss, A. Jansen and D. Orton (Leiden, Cologne and Boston, 1998).

late antique period is a startling reminder of the cultural conservatism that buttressed Roman imperial power. Compositions on a particular theme drawn from mythology or history were typically set in a remote, seamless and usually pre-republican past of Trojan heroes, Vestal Virgins and pirates. Despite their abstract moralising and remoteness from the political realities of the empire, the speeches were viewed as necessary practice for the public life to come. Jerome and Augustine describe for us the process of learning to compose and perform their mock speeches, 'with slicked back hair and in little togas'.[35]

The increasing tendency towards abstracted and convoluted expression can be traced in late antique imperial law as much as literary works that are 'mannered to the point of absurdity'.[36] But convoluted expression in itself served a conservative function. By exclusively using a formalised speech, 'steeped in the vocabulary and examples of a distant age',[37] there was no room for surprises: late antique rhetoric is striking for its predictability. Such formalised mannerism finds little sympathy in our times, but for the aristocratic families of late antiquity, the cultivation of rhetoric was a sign that their position of dominance remained unchanged, and that Roman civilisation, as they defined it, still stood. As an exclusively aristocratic pastime, literary culture was restricted to ever narrowing circles. In the late fourth century the attainment of such skills permitted a newcomer such as Ausonius to rise through the ranks of the aristocracy. By the fifth century, literary education in Gaul was limited to those already born into the upper classes,[38] and it is difficult to believe that the situation in Italy was different. Sidonius Apollinaris (c. 431–89) acknowledged that literature was all that the aristocracy had left: 'because the imperial ranks and offices have now been swept away, through which it was possible to distinguish each best man from the worst, from now on to know literature will be the only indication of nobility'.[39]

---

[35] Jerome, *Contra Rufinum* I.30; Augustine, *Conf.* I.17. See further, S.F. Bonner, *Roman Declamation in the Late Republic and Early Empire* (Liverpool, 1949); M.L. Clarke, *Rhetoric at Rome: A Historical Survey*, 3rd edn (London, 1996), pp. 85–98.

[36] E. Auerbach, *Literary Language and Its Public in Late Antiquity and in the Middle Ages*, trans. Ralph Manheim (New York, 1965), p. 87.

[37] Brown, *Power and Persuasion*, p. 42, taking his cue from M. Bloch, 'Why oratory?', in *Political Language and Oratory in Traditional Society* (London, 1975), pp. 13–17.

[38] A. Loyen, *Sidoine Apollinaire et l'esprit précieux en Gaule aux derniers jours de l'Empire* (Paris, 1943), pp. 64–5, offers a pessimistic view of Gaul. Cf. R. Mathisen, 'The theme of literary decline in Late Roman Gaul', *Classical Philology* 83 (1988), 45–53; Harries, *Sidonius*, pp. 246–9.

[39] 'nam iam remotis gradibus dignitatum per quas solebant ultimo a quoque summus quisque discerni, solum erit posthac nobilitatis indicium litteras nosse'. Ep. VIII.2.2. cf. V.5.5. Cf. Ruricius of Limoges, Ep. I.3.56, MGH AA. VIII, pp. 299–300; Harries, *Sidonius*, pp. 11–16.

Italy and literacy before the Lombards

Litterae in Ostrogothic Italy

The same connection between rhetoric and aristocratic identity can be found in Ostrogothic Italy, where imperial ranks and offices were continued under the auspices of a 'barbarian' regime which promoted itself as the continuation of Rome's glorious past.[40] When Ennodius of Pavia (474–521) wrote to commemorate the commencement of his nephew's education at the hands of a *magister* in Milan, Deuterius, he reminds his nephew Lupercinus that by rhetorical traning 'you alone can restore and revive the nobility of our ancestors'.[41] Elsewhere Ennodius hails the vocation of the *venerabilis magister* as the 'sign of freedom, the testimony to good blood',[42] while Deuterius himself was the 'glory of Italy' and the 'custodian of empire'.[43]

Ennodius' love of rhetoric and its association with access to political power is a constant theme throughout the corpus of his surviving works and can best be seen in the educational treatise, the *Paraenesis didascalica*, which he wrote for two young men, Ambrosius and Beatus, to whom he appears to have been related. It is difficult to see how this work could be of pedagogical value, although its turgid verbosity could have been helpful as an exercise in vocabulary expansion. Although the first half of the work is taken up with rhetorical celebrations of the virtues of faith, modesty and chastity, Ennodius quickly moves on to his favourite subjects of grammar and rhetoric.[44] Ennodius has Rhetoric herself proclaim her supremacy in one of his typically tortured metaphors: 'poetry, legal science, dialectic and arithmetic use me as their mother, and when they are held for ransom it is I who redeem them'. Ambrosius took the advice to heart, and certainly used the contacts in Rome. He went on to become *quaestor* under King Athalaric (526–34) and later deputy to the praetorian prefect, continuing to serve the Goths after Belisarius had taken Rome. Beatus, however, chose a clerical career: a choice which, as we shall see, was in step with the times.[45]

---

[40] See C. La Rocca, 'Una prudente maschera "antiqua". La politica edilizia di Teoderico', *Atti XIII CISAM* (Spoleto, 1993), 451–516; Moorhead, *Theoderic*, pp. 252–8.

[41] *Op.* 69, p. 78: 'tibi uni concessum est claritatem dare aut reparare maiorum'. For Ennodius' works I cite the edition of F. Vogel, MGH AA. VII (Berlin, 1885).

[42] *Op.* 85, pp. 112–15, at p. 113: 'libertatis index, boni testimonium sanguinis'.

[43] *Op.* 213, pp. 168, 170: 'decus Italiae', 'custos imperii'. On Deuterius, see Kaster, *Guardians*, pp. 267–9.

[44] *Paraenesis didascalica* 10, pp. 314–15.

[45] Ambrosius, *PLRE* 2, p. 69. C. Schäfer, *Der weströmische Senatals Träger antiker Kontinuität unter den Ostrogoten Königen (490–540)* (St Katharinen, 1991), p. 20. Beatus, *PLRE* 2, pp. 209–11. On Arator, see below.

Literacy in Lombard Italy, c. 568–774

The works of Ennodius and his contemporary Cassiodorus demonstrate the type of education esteemed in Italy at the beginning of the sixth century and the literary activity it engendered. The collection of official correspondence or *Variae* which Cassiodorus published at the end of a long career of public service under Ostrogothic kings lets us see how rhetoric was used to upholster the machinery of government.[46] The letters were written for a wide range of purposes and occasions. Those announcing appointments often include miniature panegyrics on the individual and the particular office, and letters addressed to persons of high status or reputed for their learning frequently contain long digressions that give free rein to Cassiodorus' delight in piling up words. But we need to be careful in evaluating this evidence: Cassiodorus touched up the letters prior to publication, including the removal of names and dates. Hence the *Variae* often fail to constitute the historical source we would like them to be, and even their authenticity has been questioned.[47] The important point here, however, is that the Cassiodorus who returned to Italy c. 560, after a necessary sojourn in Constantinople during the height of the Gothic wars, no longer looked to rhetoric or Roman government for a sense of self-worth or solace. Instead he founded a monastic community on his family estates at Squillace, in Calabria, and wrote religious works and guidelines for his monks (*Institutiones*) for scriptural study and the copying of ancient texts to that end.[48] For the seasoned Cassiodorus, grammar was simply 'the source and foundation of liberal studies', rather than 'the mistress of the world, and the embellisher of the human race' she had been in the days of the *Variae*.[49] Accordingly, his language in the works after he adopted a religious life is markedly different. Rhetorical flourishes are restrained in the interests of clarity, and gone are pretentious digressions. The *Variae* sank without a trace in the west until the eleventh and twelfth centuries: the later works, particularly a commentary on the Psalms, proved much more popular.[50] His life

---

[46] See G. Vidéu, *The Roman Chancery Tradition: Studies in the Language of the Codex Theodosianus and Cassiodorus' Variae*, Studia Graeca et Latina Gothoburgensia 46 (Gothenburg, 1984); A. J. Fridh, *Terminologie et formules dans le Variae de Cassiodore: étude sur le développement du style administratif aux derniers siècles de l'antiquité*, Studia Graeca et Latina Gothoburgensia 2 (Stockholm, 1956).

[47] R. Macpherson, *Rome in Involution: Cassiodorus' Variae and Their Literary and Historical Setting* (Poznán, 1989); S. Krautschik, *Cassiodor und die Politik seiner Zeit* (Bonn, 1983). Authenticity challenged: P.S. Barnwell, *Emperors, Prefects and Kings: The Roman West 395–565* (London, 1992), pp. 168–9. On their publication, see A. Gillett, 'The purpose of Cassiodorus' *Variae*', in A. Callander Murray (ed.), *After Rome's Fall: Narrators and Sources of Early Medieval History. Essays presented to Walter Goffart* (Toronto, 1998), pp. 37–50.

[48] Cf. S. Barnish, 'The work of Cassiodorus after his conversion', *Latomus* 48 (1989), 157–98.

[49] *Inst.* II, pref.; cf. *Var.* IX.21.

[50] See Paul the Deacon, *HL* I.25. On MSS, see Mommsen, MGH, AA. XII, pp. lxviii–cx; O'Donnell, *Cassiodorus*, p. 242.

spanning the course of the sixth century, the vicissitudes of Cassiodorus' career have come to symbolise for us the momentous changes of the era in which he lived and worked, even if his achievements went relatively unnoticed by contemporaries, and have been further deflated by modern scholarship.[51]

Ennodius' corpus of writings, written when he was deacon in the church of Milan (503–11), stand as a baffling monument in the history of Latin literature. His highly convoluted style, and his propensity to move away from concrete description towards high-minded abstractions – never a strategy for clarity with a highly economical language such as Latin – often render his language impenetrable. Ennodius seems to go out of his way to use words in a deliberately different manner from their usual meaning.[52] The self-conscious and highly pretentious style makes 'almost every sentence as hard as a nut but too frequently deficient in any real kernel of meaning'.[53] The problem of citing Ennodius as evidence is that we can never be too sure what he is actually saying. This is particularly true when scholars have attempted to mine Ennodius' works for historical information, especially the *Panegyric* he wrote for King Theoderic, or his *Life of Epiphanius*.[54] Aside from these more famous works, there are nine books of letters, two books of poems, ten *opuscula miscella* and twenty-eight *dictiones* or rhetorical pieces, for the most part addressed to friends and relatives as examples of correct style.[55] Many of these last are the type

---

[51] He is not mentioned in the works of Procopius, Boethius or Ennodius. The failure of the latter and Cassiodorus to mention one another may be the result of being on opposing sides in the Laurentian schism: R. Bartlett, 'Ennodius of Pavia. A sixth-century churchman and his times', unpublished PhD thesis, University of Queensland, 1999, pp. 203–5; Moorhead, *Theodoric*, pp. 114–39. Cf. O'Donnell, *Cassiodorus*, pp. 13, 35; A. Momigliano, 'Cassiodorus and the Italian culture of his time', *Proceedings of the British Academy* 41 (1955), 207–45.

[52] C. Rohr, 'La tradizione culturale tardo-romana nel regno degli ostrogoti – il panegirico di Teoderico a Ennodio', *Romanobarbarica* 16 (1999), 261–84, at p. 261.

[53] H. Chadwick, *Boethius: The Consolation of Music, Logic, Theology and Philosophy* (Oxford, 1981), p. 15. A recent assessment of Ennodius, S. Kennell, *Magnus Felix Ennodius: A Gentleman of the Church* (Ann Arbor, 2000), puts forward an opposite view: the difficulty of understanding Ennodius comes not from his propensity to intellectual abstractions, but rather from the fact that his works 'convey highly topical material with exquisite elegance' (p. 3).

[54] *Op.* 80, pp. 84–109. Ed. with Italian trans. and excellent introduction is M. Cesa, *Ennodio: vita del beatissimo Epifanio vescovo della chiesa pavese* (Como, 1988), pp. 7–36. Eng. trans. by G. M. Cook, *The Life of Saint Epiphanius by Ennodius* (Washington, DC, 1942). See E. Pietrella, 'La figura del santo-vescovo nella *Vita Epiphani* di Ennodio di Pavia', *Augustinianum* 24 (1984), 213–26; M. Dumoulin, 'Le gouvernement de Théoderic et la domination des Ostrogoths en Italie d'après les œuvres d'Ennodius', *Revue Historique* 78 (1902), 1–7, 241–65; 79 (1902), 1–22. Bartlett, 'Ennodius', pp. 353–7, has argued cogently, if not entirely convincingly, that the *Vita Epiphani* was written upon Ennodius' accession to the bishopric of Pavia, c. 513. Certainly the dating to 501–4 is not secure.

[55] See L. Navarra, 'Le componenti letterarie e concettuali delle *dictiones* di Ennodio', *Augustinianum* 12 (1972), 465–78.

of school exercises (*suasoriae, controversiae*) which date back to Quintilian's day.[56]

Ennodius' aristocratic background, circle of contacts and attitude towards literature and education afford us a glimpse of how Roman literary traditions still survived under the aegis of the church at the beginning of the sixth century. Aside from his use of classical themes and mythology,[57] good examples of Ennodius' attachment to the literary life are his satiric epigrams. In one, entitled 'On a certain fool who was called Vergil', Ennodius attacks the man for claiming to stem from the same family as the 'holy' poet himself, and advises him that 'You can't be a Maro, but could be a moron.'[58] The atmosphere of schoolboy humour extends to light vulgarity, such as his attack on the philosopher Boethius' virility,[59] or that on 'the drunkard praetorian prefect who tends his vines' and who complained about receiving milk from his mother's breast instead of wine.[60] We might expect this from a cleric interested in horses, hunting dogs and falconry. Pride in his own prowess at this last extended to sending the dead ducks to friends.[61]

A higher order of aristocracy, intellect and literary talent is found in Boethius and his stepfather Symmachus.[62] Indeed the efforts of Boethius to translate Greek philosophical works into Latin, and his contributions to theological debates, attest real intellectual enquiry amid so much rhetorical froth in his contemporaries. Yet it is difficult to determine the extent to which Boethius and Symmachus, who among other things wrote a lost Roman history,[63] were exceptional in their pursuits. Their execution for treason by Theoderic has traditionally been viewed as the result of an inevitable clash between high-minded Roman values and the harsh realities of life for Romans under a barbarian government. But it has been pointed out that the accusers and witnesses called against them were fellow

---

[56] But cf. Kennell, *Ennodius*, pp. 72–79.

[57] F. Kennell, 'Ennodius and the pagan gods', *Athenaeum* 80 (1992), 236–42.

[58] *Op.* 326 a–d, p. 242.

[59] *Op.* 339, p. 249. See D. Schantzer, 'Ennodius, Boethius, and the date of Maximianus' *Elegia* III', *Rivista di Filologia e Istruzione Classica* 111 (1983), 183–95.

[60] *Op.* 364 b, p. 65.

[61] Horses: *Op.* 212 p. 169, 266 p. 215, 330 p. 243, 355 pp. 256–7, 359 p. 258, 397 p. 286; dogs: 231 p. 18; ducks: 351 p. 256, 337 p. 248 (to Maximus).

[62] *PLRE* 2, pp. 233–7. The volume of literature is enormous: but see M. Gibson (ed.), *Boethius: His Life, Thought and Influence* (Oxford, 1981), esp. J. Matthews, 'Anicius Manlius Severinus Boethius', in *ibid.*, pp. 15–43; and Chadwick, *Boethius*.

[63] On Symmachus, *PLRE* 2, pp. 1044–6. For speculation on the contents of his lost Roman history, see B. Croke, 'A.D. 474: the manufacture of a turning point', *Chiron* 13 (1983), 81–119; G. Zecchini, 'Il 476 nella storiografia tardoantica', *Aevum* 59 (1985), 3–23. On his subscription to a text of Macrobius, see S. Panciera, 'Iscrizioni senatorie di Roma e dintorni', *Tituli* 4 (1982), 591–678, at pp. 658–60.

senators, and that their trial followed strictly Roman procedures.⁶⁴ Whatever the precise nature of the machinations behind Boethius' downfall, one cannot help but gain the impression that the philosopher was not well liked among contemporaries. His brief and ill-fated period in office in Ravenna left him without any support there, and his earlier works include haughty comments on the inferior intellects of his 'stupid' contemporaries, monsters of men who were unworthy to read his works, let alone those 'frivolous persons who will not tolerate an argument unless it is made amusing'.⁶⁵ In short, both Symmachus and Boethius represent another order of aristocrat under the Ostrogothic regime, the 'Romans of Rome', the top shelf of nobility who by the second decade of the sixth century were generally excluded from the consulship and the urban prefecture.

Literary pursuits can be found at less lofty levels. Ennodius' brother-in-law, *Faustus niger*, who served under Odovacer and Theoderic, had cupboards full of books and wrote verses on Lake Como and on his favourite poets.⁶⁶ But it needs to be remembered that such figures represent only a small percentage of those who worked for the Ostrogothic government, and a much smaller percentage of the population as a whole. Some aristocratic families proved extremely fertile and had strong traditions of office holding, but many more seem to have faded away or are simply invisible in this period, while increasingly *novi homines* from less privileged backgrounds filled the ranks,⁶⁷ and we can only guess at their

---

⁶⁴ J. Moorhead, 'Boethius and Romans in Ostrogothic service', *Historia* 27 (1978), 604–12; S. Barnish, 'The anonymous Valesianus II as a source for the last years of Theoderic', *Latomus* 42 (1983), 572–96. Boethius' claim, *De cons*. I.4.130, 'nunc quingentis fere passuum milibus procul muti atque indefensi ob studium propensius in senatum morti proscriptionique damnamur', suggests the trial was not thoroughly Roman protocol: cf. Ensslin, *Theoderic*, p. 318; Matthews, 'Boethius', p. 23 n. 23; Moorhead, *Theoderic*, p. 223.

⁶⁵ *Quomodo sub.*, prol. Cf. *hominum monst[res]* (*De trin* prol), and *indoctorum gre[x]*. (*Contra Euty.*, prol.), and *De cons*. I.3: *stultitiae temeritate, errore lymphante, furiosi tumultus, grassanti stultitiae*, etc. See M.A. Wes, *Das Ende des Kaisertums in Western des römischen Reiches* (The Hague, 1967), pp. 94–6. Cf. Ennodius' satirical poem on a certain 'Boethius', *Carm*. II.132; and that of Maximian, *Elegy* III, S.J.B. Barnish, 'Maximian, Cassiodorus, Boethius, Theodahad: literature, philosophy and politics in Ostrogothic Italy', *Nottingham Medieval Studies* 34 (1990), 16–32, at pp. 21–8; D. Shanzer, 'Ennodius, Boethius and the date and interpretation of Maximianus' Elegia III', *Rivista di Filologia e di Istruzione Classica* 3 (1983), 183–95.

⁶⁶ *PLRE* 2, pp. 454–5. Possibly *magister officiorum*, under Odovacer, certainly *quaestor* (503–506) and praetorian prefect (507–512). Como, *Op.* 20, pp. 15–16. Books and poetry, *Op.* 20, p. 80. Faustus also appears to have theological works of Greek origin in his possession, as well as books on ethics, physics, history and comedies, although Ennodius' cramped lines reek of panegyric hyperbole: 'Attica per Graios ditentur dogmata sensus / et nostrum stupeat Graecia docta decus / Moralis strictis narrentur, fysica certis / Historiam monstrans indicet historia / Comica per limam numerentur, fortia plausu / Conueniunt operi lucida dicta tua'.

⁶⁷ S. Barnish, 'Transformation and survival of the western senatorial aristocracy, *c*. AD. 400–700', *PBSR* 43 (1988), 120–55, at pp. 128–9.

attitude to literature and degree of education. Even if some achieved the literary aplomb hailed by the likes of Cassiodorus and Ennodius, one gets the sense that they were becoming fewer. 'In our age it is not the talent [for literature] that is lacking but the study [of it]', wrote the late fifth-century rhetorician-cum-monk Claudius Mamertus, while Sidonius Apollinaris was forced to admit that 'the parade of learning is more valuable by however much it is more rare'.[68] The famous subscriptions to the manuscripts of classical works which can be dated to late fifth- and early sixth-century Italy testify to patterns of patronage and aristocratic involvement in scholarly projects of a considerable calibre. Yet in the half a dozen or so which do survive from this period, the same names keep appearing.[69] In any case, Justinian's conquest soon put an end to these vestiges of secular literary life. The few manuscript subscriptions which date from after the conquest reflect different kinds of activity and interests, now exclusively religious. In one of these, a copy of Eugippius' *excerpta* from the works of Augustine made in 581, the scribe, also the notary of the church of Naples, mentions that the Lombards are besieging the town.[70]

The shrinking base of aristocracy was one cause for the increasing demise of such activity. But there is evidence that many of the few had turned their back on the literary accomplishments that defined their

---

[68] Claudius, *Ep. ad Sapaudum*, PL 53, 784A: Sidonius, Ep. II.10.6. Cf. Ep. VIII.6.3, and Mathisen, 'The theme of literary decline', pp. 49, 52.

[69] Hence the *vir spectabilis* Securus Memor Felix, 'count of the consistory, rhetor of the city of Rome', appears as the *emendator* of one manuscript (Martianus Capella), and as the *magister* (and here *orator urbis Romae*) who supervised the emendation of a MS of Horace's *Epodes* by his student Vettius Agorius Basilius Mavortius, who was consul in 527, PLRE 3A, p. 481. Also consul (494), among other public honours such as holding the office of prefect of Rome and the title of *patricius*, was the *vir clarissimus et inlustris* Turcius Rufius Apronianus Asterius, who corrected a manuscript of Virgil's *Eclogues*, and also appears in a subscription to another manuscript of Sedulius' *Carmen paschale*, PLRE 2, pp. 173–4. For the subscription of Symmachus, above n 63. Finally, another fellow aristocrat of Ravenna, Rusticius Helpidius Domnulus, *vir clarissimus* and count of the consistory, and possibly one of Ennodius' correspondents, emended a codex of Pomponius Mela and an epitome of historical exempla based on a fourth-century collection by Valerius Maximus. PLRE 2, pp. 374–5. On the subscriptions, see O. Jahn, 'Über die Subscriptionen in den Handschriften römischer Classiker', *Berichte Sächsichen Gesellschaft der Wissenschaften zum Leipzig* 3 (1851), 327–73: and Kirkby, 'The scholar and his public', in Gibson (ed.), *Boethius*, pp. 51–3. See further C. Questa and R. Raffaelli, 'La tradizione dei testi latini fra IV e V secolo attraverso i libri sottoscritti', in A. Giardina (ed.), *Tradizione dei classici, trasformazioni della cultura*. Società Romana e Impero Tardoantico 4 (Rome and Bari, 1986), pp. 19–81, 210–46.

[70] The priest Donatus 'in aedibus beati Petri in castello Luccullano' emended a codex (Monte Cassino 150, CLA III.373) in 569 of the Latin translation of Origen's commentary on the Pauline epistles. Likewise, in 559, an anonymous scribe emended a copy of Augustine's *De trinitate* (Dijon, Bib. Mun. 141, saec. XI), 'in provincia Campania in territorio Cumano in possessione nostra Acheruscio'. Eugippius' *Excerpta* (Paris, lat. 11642, CLA V), 'indicitione quinta decima, obsidentibus Langobardis neapolitanam civitatem'. For the full text see Knöll, CSEL IX.1, pp. xxv–xxvi. See G. Cavallo, 'La circolazione libraria nell'età di Giustiniano', in *L'imperatore Giustiniano: storia e mito* (Milan, 1978), pp. 201–36.

class. Theoderic ordered Symmachus to detain the children of *spectabilis* Valerianus, a resident of Syracuse, who had brought them to Rome for their education. Theoderic's personal determination that they stay is striking. In referring to the mutual benefit of education to the state and its servants, the king does not mask his dependence on the system to provide loyal subjects:

For thus they will gain advancement in learning, while respect for my command is preserved. A man should not feel as a burden a gift for which he should pray. Rome, that fertile mother of eloquence, that vast temple of all virtue, cannot be called alien and should not be spurned by anyone. Let what is clear be plainly appreciated: he on whom such as residence is conferred is assuredly favoured.[71]

Around the same time, Ennodius chastised his aristocratic friend Asturius, *senator et doctor*, who had begun to remain in his Alpine villa and had shunned the literary life, wasting his own considerable talents 'and preferring to hear the burping of bloated sheep and mountain slang'.[72] *Otium* in a rustic setting was an aristocratic ideal, and similar complaints of elites avoiding their responsibilities to take public office can be found in the letters of Sidonius Apollinaris.[73] But in Ostrogothic Italy the rot had set in right down to the provincial level. In a letter (c. 526–7) to Severus, governor of Lucania and Bruttium, Athalaric railed against those land-owners and town-councillors (*possessores et curiales*) of Bruttium who had abandoned the cities of their official residence in favour of a retired life in the countryside at their villas. The educated are failing to live up to their responsibilities:

What does it profit so many men refined by education to hide themselves away? Young boys seek to enrol in liberal schools and as soon as they are ready to go out into the forum they immediately disappear into their rustic dwellings. They progress only to unlearn; they learn only to forget and although they love the countryside they do not know how to love themselves. The educated man should seek where he might live in fame. The wise man does not spurn the company of men who he knows will accord him praise.[74]

Coercion was needed to bring them back to the folds of civility: local notables must provide guarantors to ensure they spend the greater part

---

[71] *Var.* IV.6. Cf. Barnish trans., p. 76.
[72] *Op.* 31, Ep. 1.24, p. 33, 'in ructu turgidi pectoris et Alpini sermonis'. Asturius may be the same Turcius Rufius Apronianus Asterius who prepared an edition of Sedulius' *Carmen paschale* in 495 (n. 69 above), though there are other possible identifications: PRLE 2, pp. 170–4.
[73] Ep. I.6; VII.15; VIII.8; cf. Paulinus of Pella, *Euch.* 187–219.
[74] *Var.* VIII.31. The abandonment of urban life for the countryside was not limited to Italy: see L. Cracco Ruggini, 'Vicende rurali dell'Italia antica dall'età tetrarchia ai Longobardi', *Rivista Storica Italiana* 76 (1964), 261–86, at pp. 276–8.

of the year at their urban residence, 'redeant igitur civitates in pristinum decus'. The picture of the pleasures of city life which follows (conversations with peers, the forum, 'looking' at honest crafts, expounding your own version of the law, playing draughts, the baths and dinner parties), intended as enticement, probably seemed to the gentlemen of Bruttium as shallow as it would to Cassiodorus later in life.[75]

It is difficult to escape the impression that the tide continued to turn against education among the very people who stood to gain most from it. In the name of King Athalaric, Cassiodorus wrote to the senate (c. 533) to berate them for their lack of concern that the teachers of rhetoric at Rome were being deprived of their full salaries by corrupt officials: 'it is unbelievable that you should lack concern for something which brings honours to your offspring and gives your assembly the counsel that comes from assiduous reading'. Full salaries must be restored without delay so that 'the talent of eloquence is nurtured to serve my palace'. Senators were failing in their time-honoured duty to uphold Roman values. The barbarian king needed to remind them of the importance of eloquence to Roman identity and supremacy.[76]

As for the literacy of Ostrogothic rulers themselves, the tale of one chronicler that Theoderic was 'inliteratus' and used a stencil with the letters 'legi' ('I have read it') cut out in order to trace his signature upon the documents he authorised is untrustworthy, particularly since the same was said of the emperor Justin around the same time.[77] At the court of Constantinople from around the age of eight to eighteen, Theoderic probably experienced some education in the Greek language, and presumably Latin, the language of the army: we simply do not know how far this extended into reading and writing, if at all.[78] Theoderic's daughter, Amalasuintha, was praised in a letter addressed to the senate (533), which listed among her intellectual achievements complete fluency in Greek, Latin and 'her native tongue', as well as the 'priceless knowledge of literature',[79] talents which Procopius ascribed to her masculine

---

[75] See C. Lepelly, 'Un éloge nostalgique de la cité classique dans le *Variae* de Cassiodore', in *Haut Moyen-Age, culture, éducation et société: études offerts à Pierre Riché* (La Garenne-Colombe, 1990), pp. 334–348. Cf. S.J.B. Barnish, 'Pigs, plebeians and potentes: Rome's economic hinterland *c.* 530–600 A.D.', *Papers of the British School at Rome* 42 (1987), 157–85, at p. 179.

[76] *Var.* IX.21, and the famous lines: 'Grammatica magistra verborum, ornatrix humani generis... hac non utuntur barbari reges... arma enim et reliqua gentes habent: sola reperitur eloquentia, quae Romanorum dominis obscendat'.

[77] *Anon. Val.* 79, and 61; Procopius, *Anec.* 6.14–16.

[78] Moorhead, *Theoderic*, pp. 13–14 and 104–6, gives carefully considered judgements, but p. 87, 'better Greek than almost all his Roman subjects', is a little too optimistic.

[79] *Var.* XI.1, 'sermo nativus', 'inpretiabilis notitia litterarum'. References to Gothic language and interpreters at court are ignored by P. Amory, *People and Identity in Ostrogothic Italy, 489–544 A.D.* (Cambridge, 1997), pp. 102–8.

temper.⁸⁰ Moreover he reports her plans to provide her son Athalaric with a classical education, against the wishes of Gothic loyalists at court. Procopius' strong ethnographic prejudices aside, it is more likely that Amalasuintha's gender and her son's immaturity (he was eight years old on accession), rather than his classical education, were the major cause for political unrest, and the subsequent appointment of Theodahad as joint ruler tends to negate the picture of factions at court painted by Procopius. For Theodahad, by Procopius' and Amalasuintha's accounts, was a man of literature. Something of an entrepreneur in real estate, Theodahad was said to have been 'versed in Latin literature and the teachings of Plato', which rendered him completely useless for war.⁸¹ In her letter to the senate announcing Theodahad's accession (534), Amalasuintha listed among his qualities an 'enviable knowledge of letters', an attribute that can only make the wise man in him wiser, the warrior braver, and the ruler more just. Although she, the queen, is only acquainted with reading which sharpens the intellect ('quae lectio acuat ingenium'), Theodahad is 'eruditus ecclesiasticis litteris', which can only improve his qualities as a ruler, forever mindful of the coming judgement.⁸²

This, however, was the end of the line for highly literate Gothic rulers. Theodahad's successor, Witigis (536–40), had no truck with literacy or the niceties of *eloquentia* as extolled by Cassiodorus in the names of previous rulers. Procopius portrays the promotion of Witigis as a Gothic-nationalist reaction to the 'Romanised' character of Athalaric, Amalasuintha and Theodahad, Gothic leaders with bookish interests. While this simplification owes much to Procopius' ethnographic bias, the tone of arrogance found in Witigis' letters betrays a real change in the ideology now pervading the Gothic court.⁸³ Witigis reminded his Goths that he 'was not chosen in privy chambers' nor sought 'among the subtle debates of sycophants', but was raised up on a shield in the midst of battle by the Gothic troops 'in the ancestral way' (*more maiorum*).⁸⁴

We might expect this, given the diplomatic tension between the Ostrogoths and the Byzantine empire, but we may also detect change in

---

⁸⁰ *Wars*, V.2.2.
⁸¹ Procopius, *Wars* V.3.1–4 and 4.1. Cf. Marcellinus, *Chron.* a. 536. Gregory of Tours called him 'rex Tusciae', *Hist.* III:31. Cf. Moorhead, *Theoderic*, p. 103, but it is doubtful that Amalasuintha would have boasted to the senate that Theodahad was well versed in Arian literature. See also *Wars* I.3.1; I.6.10, 16. And *Var.* X.3, X.26, X.31.
⁸² *Var.* X.3. 'desiderabilis eruditio litterarum', 'gloriosa notitia litterarum'.
⁸³ *Var.* X.31, X.32. See H. Wolfram, *History of the Goths*, trans. T.J. Dunlap (Berkeley, 1988), pp. 342–3. On Procopius' literary strategy, Amory, *People and Identity*, pp. 155–7.
⁸⁴ In his panegyric on Witigis, Cassiodorus appealed solely to skills in arms and warlike ancestry: there are no allusions to the cultivation of 'knowledge' or 'wisdom' necessary for a just rule, and Witigis was implicitly contrasted with Athalaric. The text is, however, fragmentary: MGH AA. XII, pp. 473–84. Cf. Amory, *People and Identity*, p. 77.

the type of person who worked for the Ostrogothic kings. Cyprian, count of the sacred largesses under Theoderic, was described by Cassiodorus as 'trained in action rather than reading'.[85] The epithet seems doubly significant when we recall that it was Cyprian who brought the charges of treason against Albinus, and became an enemy of Boethius, and that it was Cyprian's brother, Opilio, who accused Boethius himself. For Cyprian represented a different order of *romanitas* from that of the senatorial aristocracy.[86] Cyprian was one of the few Romans we know of who served in the Gothic army. In reward he was made *referendarius*, the duties of which he performed on horseback while out riding with Theoderic. Cyprian himself was fluent in Gothic, as well as Latin and Greek, and had his sons brought up at the royal palace where they too learned Gothic and practised arms.[87] Like Cassiodorus, Cyprian was not 'socially out of the top drawer',[88] but belonged to the group of parvenu aristocracy who gravitated around Ravenna and advanced through the social ranks by holding posts in the public service, eventually to gain membership in the senate. But unlike Cassiodorus, Cyprian appears to have had no pretensions of literary culture and senatorial *otium*: Boethius placed him among the 'palatinae canes', and it seems significant that Cyprian was Cassiodorus' successor as *magister officiorum*, just as Cassiodorus succeeded Bocthius in the same position. Cyprian's brother Opilio was the only man to return from Theodahad's embassy to Constantinople to establish a treaty and avoid war, and the only man to defend the interests of the Ostrogothic king: the illustrious Liberius the patrician, veteran of Ostrogothic service, was also in the embassy, but stayed in Constantinople.[89]

The careers of Liberius, Cyprian and, to a lesser extent, his brother Opilio provide us with a glimpse of another type of aristocratic bureaucrat, highly literate yet seemingly unconcerned with literature, at least as a badge of identity. Liberius has left us no literary remains, nor even one document of which he was author, despite having served as praetorian prefect in three different places, spanning a record-breaking period of

---

[85] *Var.* V.40: 'agendo potius instructus es quam legendo'.
[86] As Barnish points out, trans. p. 90 n. 6, *Var.* V.41 seems to imply that Cyprian surpassed the rank achieved by his father.
[87] *Var.* VIII.21: 'infantia eorum est nota palatio ... nec cessant imbui fortibus institutis. Pueri stirpis Romanae nostra lingua loquuntur, eximie indicantes exhibere se nobis futuram fidem, quorum iam videntur affectasse sermonem'. Note that Cassiodorus (speaking for Athalaric here) implies that knowledge of the Gothic tongue is a guarantee of future loyalty to the regime. Army service as unusual: 'peculiare tibi fuit'.
[88] Moorhead, *Theodoric*, p. 227
[89] *Wars* V.4.22–31. Barnish, 'Maximinian', pp. 31–2, does not believe the Opilio of the embassy to be Cyprian's brother.

some thirty years for service in this office.⁹⁰ Liberius himself had one foot firmly in the military camp. He probably served Odovacer in some type of military command, and we later find him in war-torn Gaul. When Liberius switched sides Justinian used him to head a large body of infantry mustered to stave off the Goths in Sicily, and Liberius led an expedition to Spain immediately after.⁹¹ His son Venantius, basking in his father's glory and enjoying the consulship of 507,⁹² was advised by Cassiodorus 'to pursue the study of literature, the worth of which adorns all honours... thus in sweet measure adding to nobility the skill of eloquence'.⁹³ We hear nothing more of Venantius or his studies.

East and west

Not only in Italy but also in the east, the extant evidence conveys the impression that the rhetorical education traditionally associated with Roman aristocratic lifestyle and state service lost its *raison d'être* as government became more centralised and militarised throughout the course of the sixth century. A snapshot of the increasing irrelevance of literary studies to a career in the state bureaucracy during the time of Justinian is provided by John Lydus. John went to find his fortune in the city of Constantinople at the age of twenty-one when a relative from his home town who was serving a year as praetorian prefect managed to secure for him a position as a minor official on the prefecture, the minimum qualification for which, John assures us, was 'nine years of study in the liberal arts'.⁹⁴ John was promoted rapidly through the various ranks of different offices, and appears to have juggled several positions at once.⁹⁵ But John chose his career path badly: the prefecture was in rapid decline, and could not afford to offer

---

⁹⁰ See J. O'Donnell, 'Liberius the patrician', *Traditio* 37 (1981), 31–72.
⁹¹ Odovacer: *Var.* II.16.2. Although elliptic, it supports the notion that Liberius administered more than civilian personnel. The military office in Gaul is suggested by the letters of Avitus, *Ep.* 3, and Ennodius, *Ep.* IX.29. Procopius' comment, *Wars* III.39.7, that Liberius was 'inexperienced at war', is rightly dismissed by O'Donnell, 'Liberius', p. 66, as a 'canard'. Spain: Jordanes, *Getica*, 303. Ruled out by O'Donnell, 'Liberius', pp. 67–8.
⁹² *PLRE* 2, p. 1153. Venantius' consulship demonstrates that by 507 it was a completely empty dignity, no longer conferring senatorial status: O'Donnell, 'Liberius', p. 42.
⁹³ *Var.* II.15: 'litterarum siquidem studia, quae cunctis honoribus digna suffragio, sedulus perscrutator assequeris, addens claritate ingenium suaviter eloquentis. Incumbe ergo talibus studiis, ama quae remunerata cognoscis, ut nostra quoque iudicia cum tuis provectibus'. The letters of Ennodius to Venantius, *Op.* 250, p. 196; 429, p. 269 (Ep. IV.9, V.22), reveal nothing of Venantius' success at such studies, or his father's lack of them.
⁹⁴ *De mag.* II.18.2. The 'nine years' is probably culled from Horace, *Ars poetica*, 388; cf. Cassiodorus, *Var.*, pref. 1.
⁹⁵ On John's career, see M. Maas, *John Lydus and the Roman Past: Antiquarianism and Politics in the Age of Justinian* (London and New York, 1992), pp. 28–37; T.F. Carney, *Bureaucracy in Traditional Society: Romano-Byzantine Bureaucracies Viewed from Within* (Kansas, 1971), II, pp. 3–20.

to its staff the remunerations that once made it a profitable and illustrious choice for an ambitious, conscientious young man. At sixty years of age, looking back upon forty years of work, John's dissatisfaction with his lot caused him to interrupt his account of the history of Roman magistracies: 'For what purpose have I spent such a long time as a clerk of the court of law, since I got nothing from it by way of recompense? Was it right that this has happened to me after I had embarked upon public service of this type?'[96] The funding cut-backs, the redundancies, and the increasing centralisation and simplification of the state under Justin I and Justinian led John to hate his job in the civil service. His despondency was noticed and, owing to his proficiency in Latin, the emperor appointed him to a teaching position of some sort in the court of the capital: 'I was led on to entertain great notions.' The appointment, however, meant that John missed out on the important final stage of service in the prefecture which allowed bureaucrats to skim off some of the legal fees charged by the courts, and which furnished the long-standing employee with a decent sum of money for his retirement. By the time of John's retirement, the system, which once provided an income of 1000 gold pieces, now granted him only a small pittance of copper coins. At the ceremony held to signify the retirement of a court official, John received a banquet of words about his ability with words, instead of money.[97]

Two important points emerge from John's account of his career. First, John's increasing irrelevance as a Latin teacher provides further testimony to the increasing divorce between east and west in this period, most evident in Justinian legislating in Greek for his Novels. Latin was no longer the language of empire. John noted the decree of the ancient oracle that fortune will desert the Romans when they abandon their ancestral tongue.[98] John had not read the Latin classics he cites, but knew them through compilations or *florilegia*. As with his western counterparts Cassiodorus and Ennodius, there is much talk of erudition, but little sign of it.[99] Second, John's frustration documents the continual contraction of the state machinery which provided avenues for men such as himself hoping to gain reward and status for service and literary ability. The courts used to employ at least 1000 shorthand writers a year, but now only a fraction of that.[100] John's depiction of a Golden Age for literate bureaucrats during the reign of the emperor Anastasius (491–518) is probably

---

[96] *De mag.* III.25.6.   [97] *De mag.* III.29.1–3; III.30.10.   [98] *De mag.* III.42.1–3.
[99] On John's sources, see Carney, *Bureaucracy*, II, pp. 47–66. References to the exclusively literary nature of education in John's day are frequent: cf. II.13.4; III.20.6–10; III.67.1–6. Note his comments on philosophy, III.26.2–4.
[100] *De mag.* III.9.1–10

exaggeration, but clearly in John's own time Justin I and Justinian were seen as constituting a radical break with past traditions in their scaling down of the bureaucratic mandarinate of Constantinople.[101]

The new Roman elites which emerged throughout the course of the Gothic wars and which gained complete ascendancy in the second half of the sixth century paid no lip-service to the ideal of the highly literate Roman. Some vestiges of secular literary life remained in the east, but by the beginning of the seventh century Constantinople and the eastern provinces saw the 'rapid collapse of secular literary culture, a phenomenon which accompanied the disappearance of the old educated social elite and the conditions which maintained it'.[102] The bureaucracy was now recruited more directly through imperial service, and the rewards were distributed through a more centralised and more autocratic system of hierarchy. The officers and gentlemen who administered Byzantine Italy represented a different type of order and one in which traditional Roman rhetoric had no place. Education was no longer a channel to advancement, for power now rested in the hands of the military elite who owed their positions to their abilities on the field and in maintaining the best possible conditions for their soldiers. We know almost nothing about the bureaucracy who served them, as in Lombard Italy.[103] The reasons for these immense changes in the social and political order are complex and certainly not limited to Italy. We may well expose the complexity by asking a hypothetical 'what if' the Lombards turned around at the Piave river and left Italy in 568? It is difficult to believe that Roman control over the complete peninsula would have made any difference to the demise of Roman literary education.[104] Other forces were at work to undermine whatever vestiges of prestige the cultivation of *litterae liberales* or *scientia saeculare* remained in post-Justinianic *Ausonia*. We turn now to face them.

---

[101] *De mag.* III.47.1–4. On literature and emperors, cf. III.33.1–4. One suspects that the final note of optimism in III.76.6, which implies that orators were again in the public limelight, and 'publishing books and keen rivalry about them began recurring as part of the whole lifestyle of the state', is owed to John fishing for a commission from Justinian, as was suggested to him at his retirement ceremony: III:30.4–9. Cf. III.28.4–6. Justinian's reforms to the prefecture, Maas, *John Lydus*, pp. 25–7.

[102] J.F. Haldon, *Byzantium in the Seventh Century: The Transformation of a Culture* (Cambridge, 1990), p. 433. See also A. Cameron, 'The last days of the academy of Athens', *Proceedings of the Philosophical Society* 15 (1969), 7–29; H.J. Blumenthal, '529 and its sequel: what happened to the academy', *Byzantion* 48 (1978), 369–85; W. Treadgold, 'The break in Byzantium and the gap in Byzantine studies', *Byzantinische Forschungen* 14 (1990), 289–316.

[103] T.S. Brown, *Gentlemen and Officers* (Rome, 1984), pp. 79–80.

[104] *Contra* Marrou, *History of Education*, p. 349: 'The barbarism of the Lombards was appalling, but it never entirely put a stop to the literary tradition, primarily because it never covered the whole of the peninsula.'

CHRISTIANITY AND LETTERS

The Christian ideal of *sermo humilis*, of simple speech, the language of Christ and the scriptures, was inimical to the cultivation of Roman rhetoric, and Christian values cut through the core of the education system that had become one of the defining characteristics of the late Roman ruling classes. Aesthetic preferences for or against an ornate rhetorical style did not necessarily follow religious affiliation: pagans and Christians alike in the fourth century appear to have drawn upon the same techniques and formal styles of writing.[105] But by the fifth century many committed Christians were having trouble reconciling the form of their secular studies with the content of the scriptures. Although the fifth century saw a happy compromise in the merger between Roman aristocratic and Christian ideals in clerical office, by the end of that century and throughout the following one there are signs of tension, as the polemic against rhetoric gained ground at the expense, it seems, of any sort of literary composition, ushering in a period of silence. By the end of the sixth century in Italy, a beneficiary of secular education such as Pope Gregory had nothing positive to say about it, and even relegated basic literacy to the bottom of the list of qualities necessary for clerical office.

'It is no small thing for a noble man, a man fluent in speech... to mingle with the crowds, to cleave to the poor, to associate with peasants',[106] wrote Jerome in praise of Pammachius, the senator who sold his possessions and took up the monastic habit after the death of his wife. The role played by education in demarcating and possibly maintaining the social divisions of the empire was a source of guilt to many Christians who had benefited from a classical education. Jerome's guilt over his love of Latin literature, manifested in a famous dream in which the heavenly Judge accused him of being a Ciceronian rather than a Christian, reflected the wider problem of how to assimilate aristocratic literary tastes with the unadorned language of the scriptures, and with the growing Christian invective against rhetoric as vainglorious, worldly, and ultimately destructive to the soul. But Jerome's scholarly pride and love of intellectual skirmish meant this was not a subject he would address until old age,

---

[105] Marrou, *Saint Augustin*, pp. 692–3; and J. Fontaine, 'Unité et diversité du mélange des genres et des tons chez quelques écrivains latins de la fin du IVe siècle: Ausone, Ambroise, Ammien', in *Christianisme et formes littéraires de l'antiquité tardive en occident*, Fondation Hardt, Entretiens 23 (Vandouvres, 1977), 425–82 (= *Etudes sur la poésie latine tardive d'Ausone à Prudence* (Paris, 1980), 25–82).

[106] *Ep.* 66.6. On Jerome and Augustine see Kaster, *Guardians*, pp. 80–90, and B. Stock, *Augustine the Reader: Meditation, Self-Knowledge and the Ethics of Interpretation* (Cambridge, MA, 1996), *passim*.

when he claimed to have nightmares about his vainglorious behaviour at school trying to impress his teachers and classmates.[107]

Where Jerome was caught between two worlds, Augustine saw that the only way out was a radical break with an oppressive tradition. Augustine gave a damning portrait of his own miserable experiences with education in the *Confessions*, being beaten by first his elementary teacher, then the grammarian, while his parents merely looked on with approval and laughed, having suffered the same themselves.[108] Augustine recognised that the entire elementary educational system depended on fear.[109] The immorality behind this was one thing: but it was also fundamentally flawed pedagogy. Fear of beating prevented him from learning Greek, while his incipient Latin skills were owed to kind words, smiles and jokes among family members and friends as an infant. 'It seems clear from this that learning is better done with free curiosity, and not with threatening obligation.'[110] As an adult he recognised the absurdity that the canon of Latin literature taught by the grammarian was considered richer and more noble than that at the elementary level which taught him the skills of reading and writing.[111] The school of the rhetor, with its exercises in 'nonsense' (*deliramenta*), was an even greater waste of time.[112] Augustine had to admit that he learned 'many useful words', but the costs far outweighed the benefits: 'surely I could have learned these better in some sort of serious study: and this is the steady road boys should now take'.[113]

Augustine attempted to fill out his ideas on education in his *De doctrina christiana*, completed towards the end of his episcopate. But the importance of Augustine's message in the *De doctrina christiana* lay not purely in justifying the means of secular education by highlighting the profitable ends of understanding the mechanics of language. The treatise contains a scathing attack on the principles upon which the education system was founded. By divorcing the act of communication from correct Latinity, Augustine recognised that language differentiation over time and place was part of normal linguistic development, and that the training provided by the grammarian and rhetor in 'correct speech', an attempt to arrest linguistic development, was nothing short of perverse. The solemn rules of the grammarian concerning morphology, phonology and orthography, and their condemnation of barbarisms and solecisms, have no absolute validity, residing as they do only in the minds of men, and not in any perceived *integritas* of the Latin language as a system of communication. Adherence to the conventions of the past reflected a fundamental weakness

---

[107] *Ep.* 52.1. *Apology* I.30.   [108] *Conf.* I.9.
[109] *De doctrina christiana* II.7, the first of seven steps to wisdom.
[110] *Ibid.* I.14.   [111] *Ibid.* I.13.   [112] *Ibid.* I.17.   [113] *Ibid.* I.15.

in character: the more desirous of seeming learned in ancient grammatical standards, the weaker the person who needs such worldly assurances.[114] Schooling in the correctness of speech created a pernicious pride and self-consciousness that moved one further away from God.[115] But even more urgent was the need to demolish the haughty reputation of higher studies as the path to literate wisdom. Neither the grammarian nor the rhetor was necessary to learn the art of oratory: this could be learned by listening to eloquent people, just as infants learn to talk by listening to adults. Or the student could read ecclesiastical writings, in which there is an abundance of eloquence, and simply couple the reading with the practice of 'writing what he thinks'.[116]

The pomp of episcopal office

As a former professor of rhetoric, Augustine's attack on the intellectual and moral credibility of the secular education of his day was a radical departure from the uncritical eulogies in his day to the virtues of 'letters which only slaves of diverse passions call "liberal"'.[117] Such harsh criticisms could only be taken in bites by those who were proud of their hard-won skills. When Cassiodorus cribbed from Augustine's text for his own *Institutiones* in setting out a programme of Christian studies, he completely ignored Augustine's anti-grammar sentiment, which must have been anathema to the aged author of the *De orthographia*.[118] But Augustine's advocacy of simplicity in language and his heightened sensitivity to the plight of the young was shared by other churchmen in Italy. In the first half of the fifth century the archbishop of Ravenna, Peter Chrysologus, advised his congregation:

> The populace must be spoken to in the popular fashion, the community must be addressed in common speech. For the things necessary to all men should be said in the manner of all: natural language is clear to the simple, and sweet to the learned. He that teaches should speak in a way that profits everyone. Therefore today let the learned give pardon for the unlearned word.[119]

Peter 'the golden-worded' began his episcopate with an oration before the empress Galla Placidia, and his sermons demonstrate all the rhetorical

---

[114] *Ibid.* II.13.19–20.
[115] *Conf.* I.18; *De doc. christ.* II.14.21; II.41.62; IV.7.14. *De genesi ad litteram*, 10.39.
[116] *De doc. christ.* IV.4–5. The reference is to Cicero, *De oratore* II.23.96.
[117] *Ep.* 101.1.
[118] See below, chapter 3. The note of *Inst.* II.1, concerning the 'short treatise' written by Augustine on grammar 'for the simple brothers', must be an interpolation. *Institutiones*, ed. Mynors, p. 94, lines 13–17.
[119] *Sermo* 43. CCSL 24, a–b, ed. A. Olivar (Turnhout, 1975–82).

trappings of one well trained in the late antique schools.[120] But like Augustine, Peter was to look back on the experience as troubling for the child, and many of his dignified congregation would have nodded gravely as their archbishop drew the analogy of schooling and the acquisition of divine wisdom:

> In order to know the forms of letters and the rudiments of education, were you not assigned to a master and enrolled in a school? Then, completely ready to endure toil or pain, did you not forgo visits to your home and family? But how useful to you was that for which the teacher was assigned to you, to attend school? By his toil and the punishments he afflicts on you, the teacher implores you to conceive a desire to know those rudiments, and to be worthy of listening to such important things.[121]

Peter's rhetorical flourishes provide testimony to the enduring prestige of literary traditions among Italian churchmen at the highest levels, as well as a degree of ambiguity about the benefits of such traditions in clerical office. We know very little about Italian clergy in this period, but the majority of them appear to have been from aristocratic backgrounds.[122] Many would have received training in secular schools, but the lack of extant evidence prevents us from assessing how they may have reacted to Peter's precepts to speak 'in simple language', or whether they had turned their literate skills to interpreting the Gospels, in which 'not one letter-stroke, one letter, one syllable, one word, one name nor one person... is without divine allegory'.[123]

In order to gauge the degree of cultural change in attitudes of clerics towards literature, we can look to neighbouring Gaul. By the latter half of the fifth century, churchmen of aristocratic background such as Sidonius Apollinaris can be seen as struggling to reconcile their passion for a high Latin style with their new-found pastoral duties. By 470, at the time of his consecration as bishop of Clermont, Sidonius began to avoid

---

[120] Note *Sermo* 112: 'let us set aside the pursuit of declamation'. See further J.H. Baxter, 'The homilies of Peter Chrysologus', *Journal of Theological Studies* 22 (1920–1), 250–8; A. Olivar, *Los sermones de S. Pedro Crisologo* (Montserrat, 1962), pp. 47–51.

[121] *Sermo* 101.

[122] See C. Piétri, 'Une aristocracie provinciale et la mission chrétienne: l'example de la Venetia', in *Aquileia nel IV secolo* (Udine, 1981), pp. 89–137; Piétri, 'Aristocracie et société cléricale dans l'Italie chrétienne au temps d'Odovacre et de Théoderic', *Mélanges de l'Ecole Française du Rome, Antiquités* 93 (1981), 414–67; Piétri, 'Note sur la christianisation de la Ligure', *Atti del Convegno di Studi Lunensi e Prospettive sull'Occidente romano* (Luni, 1985–87), II, 351–80; C. Sontel, 'Le recrutement des évêques en Italie aux IVe et Ve siècles. Essai d'enquête prosopographique', in *Vescovi e pastori in epoca teodosiana. XXV Incontro di studiosi dell'antichità cristiana* (Rome, 1997), I, pp. 193–204; G.A. Cecconi, 'Vescovi e maggiorenti cristiani nell'Italia centrale fra il IV e il V secolo', in *ibid.*, pp. 205–24; R. Lizzi, 'Ambrose's contemporaries and the Christianisation of northern Italy', *Journal of Roman Studies* 80 (1990), 156–63.

[123] Peter, *Sermo* 46.

the theological controversies in which his contemporaries indulged. He refused their requests to write theological works, which he described as showing off (*iactantia*).[124] Sidonius also gave up other literary pursuits germane to his caste, such as the narrative history of the Huns which he had begun earlier in his career, or the history requested of him by King Euric's minister Leo of Narbonne. His preoccupation with the proper style is testimony both to his training and to the difficult position of the aristocratic Christian bishop: 'If we write simply we are called mad, if carefully, we are called presumptuous.'[125] Elsewhere, Sidonius recognised the incongruity of the literary and clerical life: 'I especially renounced this exercise of verse-writing from the very beginning of my religious profession because undoubtedly it might be a concession to weakness if I occupied myself with the levity of verse-writing when seriousness of action had become my duty.'[126] Yet for all his new-found religious scruples, Sidonius' aristocratic background, and his experience in the civil service at Rome, marked him as a creature anchored in the traditions of the past. He saw clerical office as another social dignity (*honoratus*), although it ranked above the loftiest of the secular offices.[127] And although undoubtedly sincere in his profession of the Christian faith,[128] in his works Sidonius never quoted the scriptures directly, reflecting the same distaste for the uncouth Latin of the Vulgate which so preoccupied Jerome, and instead preferred to paraphrase entire passages in his own arabesque style.[129]

By the end of the fifth century, in Gaul we hear adversarial attitudes towards Latin literary tradition which are echoed in sixth-century Italy. Pomerius Julianus, a rhetorician who had fled Africa in the wake of the Vandal persecution and settled in Arles where he was ordained a priest, anticipated the sensibilities of Pope Gregory a century later concerning the difficulties of reconciling an ascetic, contemplative lifestyle with the burdens of pastoral care.[130] Among the faults which cause a bishop to

---

[124] *Ep.* IV.2 and 3: 'iactantia', *Ep.* IV.17.
[125] *Ep.* VIII.15.1. *Ep.* IV.22.5: 'si quid simpliciter edamus insani, si quid exacte, praesumptiosi vocamur'.
[126] *Ep.* IX.12.1.   [127] *Ep.* IV.14.3.
[128] W. Daly, '*Christianitas* eclipses *Romanitas* in the life of Sidonius Apollinaris', in T. Noble and J. Contreni (eds.), *Religion, Society and Culture in the Early Middle Ages: Studies in Honour of R. Sullivan* (Kalamazoo, 1987), pp. 7–26.
[129] See *Carm.* 16.56–7. Harries, *Sidonius*, pp. 108–11. Cf. W. Daly, 'An adverse consensus question: does Sidonius' Eucharisticon (*Carmen* xvi) show that he was scripturally naïve?', *Traditio* 55 (2000), 19–72.
[130] Text, *PL* 59, 411–520. See M.J. Suelzer (trans.), *Julianus Pomerius: The Contemplative Life* (Westminster, MD, 1947); R.A. Markus, *The End of Ancient Christianity* (Cambridge, 1990), pp. 189–91. Another possible example is Domnulus. Two of his works survive; *PL* 62, 543–8, but the identification is not secure: *PLRE* 2, pp. 374–5, 537; cf. Harries, *Sidonius*, p. 123.

stray from the path of his calling, Pomerius singled out the cultivation of rhetoric, which caused the bishop 'to prefer leisured study to the fruitful service of the common good in ruling the many'.[131] Taking his cue from St Paul (II Cor. 6.6, 'etsi imperitus sermone, sed non scientia'), Pomerius launched into an attack on the high speech of bishops: 'a doctor of the church ought not to pride himself by a display of contrived speech, lest he appear not to want to build the church of God, but rather to show off the level of his own erudition'. The language of the bishop should be 'simple and accessible, even if less Latinate, yet still disciplined and dignified... so that it be comprehended by his own [congregation], and not exclude the unlearned'.[132]

It is difficult to imagine the same sentiments coming from Sidonius or Ennodius, and it is easy to imagine Pomerius' comments aimed at their like. Pomerius' own student, Caesarius of Arles (469/70–542), took the advice to heart. Like his contemporary the young Benedict of Nursia, Caesarius was a troubled youth who sought refuge in the monastic life. But under the tutorship of Pomerius, Caesarius' monastic simplicity was challenged by the 'teachings of worldly knowledge'. After experiencing a terrifying nightmare, in which he dreamt that the shoulder and arm which rested on the book he fell asleep upon were being gnawed by a serpent winding itself around him, he awoke petrified and vowed never to take up such studies again.[133] The account presented by Caesarius' hagiographers has obvious parallels with the famous dream of Jerome concerning his love of Cicero, and was intended to be read with a comparison in mind.[134] By the end of the sixth century in Gaul, the ghost of rhetoric no longer haunted bishops. Gregory of Tours dreamt that God reprimanded him for taking too long to learn shorthand, a far more pressing concern for busy bishops now responsible for administrative duties once handled by municipal councils of their cities.[135]

Ennodius, Arator and the generation gap

The combination of monastic humility and aristocratic status in the person of the bishop, as exemplified by Caesarius, could not take root in Italy until after the social divisions of late Roman society had been swept away with the demise of the Ostrogothic regime. Immersed in an aristocratic ethos of leadership, Italian bishops were too strongly tied to the traditions

---

[131] *Vita contemplativa* III.28.   [132] *Ibid.* I.24. PL 69, 458–9.
[133] *Vita Caesarii* I.9, in *Caesarius of Arles: Life, Testament, Letters*, trans. W. Klingshirn (Liverpool, 1994), pp. 13–14.
[134] See N. Adkin, 'Some notes on the dream of Jerome', *Philologus* 128 (1984), 119–26.
[135] P.R.L. Brown, *The World of Late Antiquity, A.D. 150–750* (London, 1971), p. 176.

of rhetorical education that furnished them with an indisputable sign of their right to lead and represent the interests of the cities under their sway. But there were signs of trouble. Writing to Pomerius, Ennodius, then still a deacon, confessed his weakness:

> I should not indulge dangerously in the pomp of eloquence, nor presume to make use of it in any way, when my profession requires me to study only simple doctrine. But if someone should strike me with the tooth of some novelty of the liberal arts, with all excuse I would prepare something becoming or something that would not be shameful to be put forward.[136]

It is perhaps testimony to the influence of the ideas of Pomerius and Caesarius that Ennodius' surviving corpus dates from his time as deacon of Milan (501–13), and that nothing survives from the period in which he was bishop of Pavia. Renunciation of literature appears to be the best explanation.[137] Theological or religious works play a small part in the surviving corpus of writings, and his addressees, for the most part, were members of aristocratic families.[138] He may have moved in too high circles for his fellow clerics. At the death of bishop Laurentius in 512, the Milanese clergy elected a certain Eustorgius. It was not the first time something had been snatched from Ennodius which he believed he deserved.[139]

A year earlier, Ennodius had been struck down with a grave illness, the effects of which caused him to turn a 'cloudy yellow colour', so that he was sure he had come to his end. He describes the sickness and his recovery in a short confessional work, titled by modern editors as *Eucharisticon de vita sua*, partly modelled on the *Confessions* of Augustine, and the only source in which Ennodius records his life prior to taking orders.[140] Recounting the steps which led to the sickness of his soul,

---

[136] *Op.* 39, p. 38.
[137] Vogel (pp. xxix–xxx) suggested two alternative reasons: another volume of works written during his episcopate has been lost; the surviving collection was put together by a previous amanuensis of Ennodius in Milan from the material preserved there. I find the first of these unconvincing. *Contra* Kennell, *Ennodius*, pp. 214–19. That Ennodius continued to be active in church affairs until his death in 521, including acting as the senior legate of the Roman church in two missions to Constantinople, and drawing up the *Collectio avellana*, suggests that he followed canonical strictures against bishops indulging in literary pursuits and turned his attention to church administration and settling doctrinal disputes under the auspices of the papacy.
[138] The *Libellus pro synodo* was more concerned to justify Theoderic's intervention into the Laurentian schism than to argue Laurence's case on the grounds of dogma and canon law: L. Duchesne, 'Observations sur quelques passages du *Libellus pro synodo* d'Ennode de Pavie', *Revue de Philologie, de Littérature et d'Histoire Anciennes* 7 (1883), 78–81: L. Navarra, 'Contributo storico di Ennodio', *Augustinianum* 14 (1974), 315–42, at pp. 320–4; but cf. Kennell, *Ennodius*, pp. 186–201.
[139] Cf. Ep. VII.9, p. 235, l.4–6.
[140] On his engagement, and possibly marriage, before orders: see L. Ferrai, 'Il matrimonio di Ennodio', *Archivio Storico Lombardo*, ser. 2, 20 (1893), 948–57, who identifies the lucky lass as

Italy and literacy before the Lombards

Ennodius highlights literature as the 'wages of sin' from which he first caught the virus that is a love of letters:

> For while the attraction of resounding superfluity was exercising me in the fields of rhetoric and poetry, I cut myself off from the true wisdom, instead following a false one, desiring nothing more to reach my ears than vain praise and to trade in my aversion to prayer, which I was wont to finish quickly.

After two months of suffering useless cures prescribed by the 'worn-out philosophy of secular pomp of Hippocrates and Galen', Ennodius was cured by continual prayer before the relics of St Victor. Luckily, the cure did not require a full renunciation of letters or his love of Latin rhetoric, merely a modification:

> I promised, that if He grant me through His grace a continued love of noble studies, I would write this present confession of mine, as a plump offering from the rewards of the little ability which He gave me, and that never again would my effort be fatigued by being executed in the conceited style of the secular world, and that I would refute the residual foulness from which I had been continually beaten, if He himself, who inspired me to speak at all, should wish me to do so.[141]

The *Eucharisticon* expresses clearly the tension in Ennodius' life between love of Latin literary traditions and his religious vocation, the combination of which he found embarrassing in others.[142]

Clerical opposition to Ennodius' love of literature can be found in his own favourite protégé, Arator, to whom Ennodius dedicated five of his *dictiones* and other works.[143] From these we can gleam a burgeoning difference of opinion between the two men about the place of literature in religious life. In an earlier *dictio* entitled 'the praise of letters' (*laus litterarum*), Ennodius admonished the promising young lawyer to 'pour libations to the divinity of literature which flows from its very altars'.[144] Such language and imagery, steeped in the pagan past, came naturally to Ennodius, but not to his student. When Arator failed to deliver an epithalamium on the occasion of their friend Maximus' marriage (*c*. 510), Ennodius chastised the young ascetic for allowing his religious sensibilities to get in the way of literature and its place in the maintenance of

---

Ennodius' correspondent Speciosa: cf. the refutation of A. Lumpe, 'Ennodiana', *Byzantinische Forschung* 1 (1966), 200–10, at p. 202. On the date of the *Eucharisticon*, J. Sundwall, *Abhandlungen zur Geschichte des ausgehenden Römertums* (Helsinki, 1919), p. 82.

[141] *Op.* 438, pp. 301–2. Further description of his illness: *Op.* 391, p. 280.
[142] See esp. *Op.* 43, p. 297.
[143] *Dictiones*: *Op.* 85, pp. 112–14, 'quando Arator auditorium ingressus est'; 239, pp. 184–5, 'in eum qui seni patri cibos subtraxit'; 243, pp. 191–192, 'In tyrannum qui praemi nomine parracidae statuam inter viros fortes dedit'; 320, pp. 238–9, 'laus litterarum'; 380, pp. 271–3, 'thema: lex'. Poems on Arator: *Op.* 237, p. 184, 'in natale infanti'; *Op.* 267, pp. 215–16, 'de flagello infantis'. Letters: *Op.* 378, p. 271; 387, p. 276; 422, p. 292.
[144] *Op.* 320, p. 238.

friendships.¹⁴⁵ Even if Arator himself had chosen the celibate life and found the subject of marriage too distasteful, he ought to put aside his own scruples and 'praise [it] for the sake of demonstrating your talent'.¹⁴⁶ Rather insensitively Ennodius even urged Arator to 'turn yourself to the problem of sowing your seed', and in his own epithalamium for Maximus, Ennodius had Cupid complain to Venus about Christian chastity and the monastic ideal of virginity.¹⁴⁷ Ennodius had already complained to Arator about his silence towards him and failure to write.¹⁴⁸

Sometime between 526 and 544, Arator abandoned his secular career altogether and became subdeacon in Rome: 'I entered the church as a shipwrecked man; I leave the faithless sails of the worldly sea.'¹⁴⁹ In the preface to his verse rendition of the Acts of the Apostles, Arator recalled his earlier education at Ravenna, and described this period of his life in terms of regret, and how through his love of poetry he had been 'carried off in the power of shallowness through an empty channel'.¹⁵⁰ Arator's verse paraphrase of Acts has been described by a modern critic as 'the worst of poems on an excellent subject', but it was obviously appreciated more in Arator's own day (544), for continual encores meant it took four days to read the entire text.¹⁵¹ Paul the Deacon cited it approvingly in the *HL* as a landmark of Roman literary achievements prior to the Lombard arrival.¹⁵² Arator was not alone in turning his back on secular literature and the legal profession it was intended to serve.

---

¹⁴⁵ *Op.* 387, p. 276.

¹⁴⁶ *Ibid.*: 'haec etsi non diligis, debes tamen pro ingenii tui ostentatione laudare'.

¹⁴⁷ *Op.* 422, p. 292: 'ergo post Musarum castra et inanes aetate nostra cantilenas ad curam te serendae subolis muta'. *Epithalamium: Op.* 387, p. 276.

¹⁴⁸ *Op.* 378, p. 271. Cf. *Op.* 422, p. 292: 'nam si quae mihi sit sententia flagites, ego ipsa studiorum liberalium nomina iam detestor'.

¹⁴⁹ There is some doubt as to whether this Arator is the same as Ennodius' student, since Cassiodorus speaks of Arator's father instructing his son in rhetoric (*Var.* VIII.12) whereas Ennodius tells us that he was orphaned at an early age and brought up under the tutelage of Bishop Laurentius of Milan, *Op.* 85, pp. 112–14. See R. Hillier, *Arator on the Acts of the Apostles: A Baptismal Commentary* (Oxford, 1993), pp. 5–12; cf. Sundwall, *Abhandlungen*, pp. 92–3.

¹⁵⁰ *PLRE* 2, pp. 126–7. Cf. *Var.* VIII.12: Ennodius, *Dictio* 9.22: Ep. VIII.4; 11; IX.1. See *Arator's Acts of the Apostles* (*De actibus apostolorum*), ed. and trans. R.J. Schrader (Atlanta, 1987). Ep. ad Parthenium, *ibid.*, p. 102. There is some dispute as to whether this Parthenius (*PLRE* 2, pp. 832–4) is to be identified as Ennodius' nephew: against the identification, Riché, *Education*, p. 26 n. 57; but cf. R. Mathisen, 'Epistolography, literary circles and family ties in late Roman Gaul', *Transactions of the American Philological Society* 111 (1981), 95–109, at pp. 102–4, and C. Leonardi, 'Aratore', in *Dizionario Biografico degli Italiani*, III (1961), pp. 725–9.

¹⁵¹ Schrader, *ibid.*, p. 5, citing E. Shipley Duckett, *Gateway to the Middle Ages* (New York, 1938), p. 70. On the political significance of the text's reading, Moorhead, '*Libertas* and *nomen romanum* in Ostrogothic Italy', *Latomus* 46 (1987), 164–5.

¹⁵² *HL* I.25, along with Cassiodorus' commentary on the Psalms, Dionysius Exiguus' calculations of the Easter cycle, and Priscian's works on grammar. A sign of reconciliation between religious sensibilities and literary ambition, Paul could not help but insert in the following chapter his own verse rendition of Book II of Gregory's *Dialogues* concerning the life of Benedict.

Italy and literacy before the Lombards

Venantius Fortunatus, a native of the area near Treviso, also trained in Ravenna to be a lawyer, and turned his considerable literary talents to the task of celebrating the celestial. But it seems all the more significant that Fortunatus should find conditions more favourable for his talents as a Christian rhetorican in ecclesiastical office outside of Italy. By 566, the first secure date we have of his career, Fortunatus was at the Merovingian court of King Sigibert and Queen Brunhild and was commissioned to write an epithalamium for the royal couple. Attempts to link his departure from Italy with political events,[153] particularly that of a perceived approach of the Lombards, or with the divisions caused by the Three Chapters schism,[154] are unfounded, and personal religious devotion to the cult of St Martin at Tours, as well as a sense of adventure befitting a talented young man on the make, appear to have been the primary motives for his initial journey northwards.[155] Fortunatus went on to take orders, and eventually achieved episcopal office, but he appears to have kept up little or no contact with his native Italy, so that Paul the Deacon needed to reclaim him as a fellow Ausonian when he wrote an epitaph for the poet's tomb.[156] But Paul never acknowledged Ennodius, despite his obvious knowledge of Pavese ecclesiastical history and possible use of the latter's *Vita Epiphanii* for the *Historia Romana*.[157] In this sense Ennodius was the last of the line in clerical rhetoricians who maintained the worth of the secular schooling tradition. The monastic sensibilities towards language and literacy we see in the generation after Ennodius could find no room for compromise.

Monasticism and written regulae

Fifteen years prior to the silence of bishop Ennodius, the young Benedict of Nursia (*c.* 480–547) had been horrified by the literary culture of the schools of Rome, seeing in its vacuity the very peril of his soul. According to Gregory, Benedict stood back appalled as he watched others fall into the vices of vanity and wordly pomp which these studies engendered.[158]

---

[153] J Sasel, 'Il viaggio di Venanzio Fortunato e la sua attività in ordine alla politica bizantina', *Antichità Altoadriatiche* 19 (1981), 359–75.

[154] G. Cuscito, 'Venanzio Fortunato e le chiese Istriane', *Atti e memorie della Società Istriana di Archeologia e storia patria* 78 (Trieste, 1978), 9–25; J. Herrin, *The Formation of Christendom* (Princeton, 1987), pp. 119–25.

[155] Following the arguments of J. George, *Venantius Fortunatus: A Latin Poet in Merovingian Gaul* (Oxford, 1992), pp. 18–28, who highlights the role of Nicetius of Trier as a link between Italy and the Frankish court.

[156] *HL* II.13, and see below, chapter 6, conclusion.

[157] Paul, *Historia romana*, Book 15 *passim*. The reference to Ennodius' mission to the east is taken directly from the *LP* 54.2–3.

[158] Gregory, *Dial.* II, prol., 'in eis [studiis] multos ire per abrupta vitiorum'.

Confirmation of Benedict's rejection of such training can be found in the language of his *Rule*, despite the problems raised by the relatively late manuscript tradition.[159] Orthography is one such problem: was Benedict's spelling as bad as we find in many of the earliest manuscripts? There can be no certain answers here, but given the deviancies from classical norms of grammar, syntax and vocabulary in language of the *Rule*, it is likely that Benedict shrugged off classical strictures on orthography also — as had, it seems, the 'Master' whose *Rule* Benedict used to compile his own.[160] In both texts we find traits common to other vulgar Latin texts of the period, including incorrect use of cases, an increased reliance on prepositions to express the noun's function (often with incorrect case, such as *post* with ablative (*post quibus*), or *de* with accusative (*de sedilia sua*), etc.), relative pronouns in disagreement with antecedents, the use of nominative absolutes, periphrases, and the auxiliary verb *habeo* to express past tense, and so on.[161] To some extent this type of language is a consequence of the genre — Cassian, Jerome and Sulpicius Severus were accomplished stylists who toned down their language when it came to compiling monastic rules.[162] Yet Benedict's rhetorical training shines through, so that the tricks of alliteration, assonance, anaphora, asyndeton, chiasmus and even the rhythmic *cursus* are used to create memorable and often striking phrases.[163] Nevertheless the Latin remains remarkably simple in style and

---

[159] Paul, *HL* IV.17, and cf. Ep. 13, MGH Ep. IV, pp. 509–14. I have used the text in *The Rule of St Benedict 1980*, ed. and trans. T. Frye *et al.* (Collegeville, MN, 1981), which is that of J. Neufville and A. De Vogüe, *La Règle de Saint Benoît*, 6 vols., Sources Chrétiennes 181–6 (Paris, 1971–72). Besides De Vogüe, *ibid.*, pp. 14–36, on the manuscript tradition see K. Zelzer, 'Zur Stellung der Textus receptus und des interpolierten Textes in der Textgeschichte der *Regula S. Benedicti*' *RB* 88 (1978), 205–46; Zelzer, 'Von Benedikt zu Hildemar: zur Textgestalt und Textgeschichte der Regula Benedicti auf ihrem Weg zur Alleingeltung', *Frühmittelalterliche Studien* 23 (1989), 112–30. Note Gregory's description of the *regula* as 'discretione praecipuam . . . sermone luculentam': on which, see A. De Vogüe, ' "Discretione praecipuam": a quoi Grégoire pensait-il?', *Benedictina* 22 (1975), 325–7.

[160] A. De Vogüe (ed.), *La Règle du Maître*, Sources Chrétiennes 105–7 (Paris, 1964–67). The relationship between the two texts has been the subject of much debate, see the revisionist views of M. Dunn, 'Mastering Benedict: monastic rules and their authors in the early medieval West', *EHR* 105 (1990), 567–94; De Vogüe's refutation of Dunn, *EHR* 107 (1992), 95–103, Dunn's response, pp. 104–11.

[161] The best study is still C. Mohrmann, 'La latinité de saint Benoît. Étude linguistique sur la tradition manuscrite de la règle', *Revue Bénédictine* 62 (1952), 108–39; repr. in Mohrmann *Etudes sur le Latin des Chrétiens*, Storia e Letteratura 65 (Rome, 1958), I, 403–35; Mohrmann, 'La langue de saint Benoît', in P. Schmitz, *Sancti Benedicti Regula Monachorum* (Maredsous, 1955), pp. 9–39. Cf. B. Lindebaurer, *S.B. Regula Monachorum, herausgegeben und philologisch Erklärt* (Metten, 1922).

[162] Mohrmann, 'La langue', pp. 10–11.

[163] See A. Lentini, *Il ritmo prosaico nella Regola di San Benedetto* (Montecassino, 1942); G. Widham, *Die rhetorische Elemente in der Regula Benedicti*, Regulae Benedicti Studia Supplementa 2 (Hildesheim, 1974).

structure, the *sermo humilis* of the Vulgate Bible serving as the principal model and source of inspiration.[164]

It is worth our while here to consider what type of literacy Benedict's *Rule* may have promoted or prevented.[165] Studies were not excluded from the rhythm of monastic life. At least two hours of private reading a day (three in the winter) was stipulated under the rubric of 'daily manual labour' (*opera manuum quotidiana*), although more was permitted. Sunday was devoted to reading: those unwilling or unable were to be found other tasks.[166] At the beginning of Lent each monk was 'to receive a single book from the library and read the whole of it straight through'.[167] Despite these strictures, Benedict never specified precisely what was to be read, the phrases *lectio divina, plena lectio* and *lectiones suae* being frustratingly vague.[168] In fact the *Rule of the Master* (*Regula magistri*), which Benedict knew and used for his own *Rule*, has more to say about education and literacy than Benedict, but this is still little to go on. Owing to the winter cold, the monks were spared manual labour in the morning, and for the first three hours of the day the monks were to be divided into groups of ten (*deceda*), with one monk reading to the others, while children were to practise their letters with one who was literate. Illiterates still under fifty years of age were to learn their letters also, and those ignorant of the Psalms were to learn them at this time.[169] The three hours between Terce and Sext were then devoted to manual labour, but after Sext one monk was to read 'from any codex' to the brothers while they worked; they were to move closer if they could not hear, or hear it another day.[170] In summer the reading activity of the *deceda* shifted to the evening.[171]

---

[164] It is interesting that by far the greater part of Benedict's citations is from Jerome's Vulgate, rather than from any variety of the *Vetus Latina* versions (only 19 of 132 citations from the Old Testament, and 18 of 189 from the New Testament), generally more common in Italy until the ninth century: see S. Pawlowsky, *Die biblischen Grundlagen der Regula Benedicti* (Vienna, 1965), pp. 30–5; De Vogüe, *La Règle*, II, pp. 882–6.

[165] See also below, pp. 292–300.   [166] RB 48.4, 10, 13, 22–3.

[167] RB 48.15: 'accipiant omnes singulos codices de bibliotheca, quos per ordinem ex integro legant'.

[168] J. Leclercq, *Love of Learning and Desire for God: A Study of Monastic Culture*, trans. C. Misrahi (New York, 1960), pp. 16–30, 87–95; D. Gorce, *La lectio divina des origines du cénobitisme à St. Benoît et Cassiodorus* (Wépion-sur-Meuse, 1925). The books taken 'ex bibliotheca' are something other than parts of the Bible, *contra* A. Mundó, 'Biblioteca, Bible et lecture de carême d'après S. Benoît', *Revue Bénédictine* 60 (1950), 65–92; Mundó, 'Las reglas de siglo VI y la lectio divina', *Studi Medievali* 9 (1967), 247–9. Cf. De Vogüe, *La Règle*, II, pp. 602–3 n. 15. In other contexts Benedict mentions the *Collationes*, RB 42.5, 73.5, which must be Cassian's *Collationes patrum et instituta*: De Vogüe, 'Les mentions des œuvres de Cassien chez Benoît et ses contemporains', *Studi Medievali* 20 (1978), 275–85.

[169] RM 58.10–17.   [170] RM 58.28–29.

[171] After Nones, 'alii legant, alii audiant, alii ad litteras discant et doceant, alii psalmos, quos habent superpositos, meditentur'. *Ibid.* 'superpositos' here presumably means 'inscribed on [wax] tablets'. De Vogüe, *La Règle*, II, p. 235 n. 64.

Those 'hard of heart' or simple brothers (*duricordes et simplices*) who refused or who were unable to learn their letters were to be found other tasks.

It has been suggested that the *Rule* of Benedict 'presupposes and promotes grammatical culture even though it does not explicitly prescribe an educational program'.[172] If this is true, 'grammatical culture' here must be interpreted in its broadest sense of a common use of written texts, and not the educational 'culture of grammar' that was part of the Roman liberal arts instruction, learned through the laborious *enarratio* of canonical texts. We might look to other literate traditions, namely those of late Roman legal culture, behind both the nature and the language of both *Rules*, which inform the text and perhaps help explain their success in Italy.[173] The very rite of admission into monastic life centres upon the use of texts. Already the procedure of the *Regula magistri* involved the postulant presenting a document listing the possessions he confers upon the monastery and placing it upon the altar. The transfer of property was integral to the ritual of the postulant's acceptance by the monastic community, and the following brief exchange between abbot and postulant echoes Roman *stipulatio* ritual in stating binding obligations in the presence of witnesses to create a unilateral contract.[174] Benedict's *Rule* takes the legal trappings a step further in a more personal direction. The document presented by the novice, written in his own hand if possible, or if not at least signed by him, does not concern property at all, which is a separate issue.[175] Instead, in this document (*petitio*) drawn up 'in the name of the saints whose relics are there, and of the abbot', the novice promises 'stability, fidelity to monastic life, and obedience'. In short, the document

---

[172] Irvine, *Textual Culture*, p. 191.
[173] Though it is difficult to know how successful: there were plenty of alternatives, and certainly no rules about Rules: see G. Jenal, *Italia ascetica atque monastica: des Apsketen- und Monchtum in Italien von den Anfangen bis zur Zeit der Langobarden (ca. 150/250–604)*, 2 vols., Monographien zur Geschichte des Mittelalters 39 (Stuttgart, 1995), II, pp. 215–62: G. Penco, 'La prima diffusione della Regola di Saint Benedetto', *Commentationes in Regulam S. Benedicti*, Studia Anselmiana 42 (Rome, 1957), pp. 321–54. Cf. G. Moyse, 'Monachisme et réglementation monastique en Gaule avant Benoît d'Aniane', in *Sous la règle de St Benoît: structures monastiques et sociétés en France du moyen âge à l'époque moderne* (Geneva and Paris, 1982), pp. 3–19; C. Leyser, 'St Benedict and Gregory the Great: another dialogue', in S. Pricoco, F. Rizzo Nervo and T. Sardello (eds.), *Sicilia e Italia suburbicaria tra IV e VIII secolo* (Catania, 1991), pp. 21–43; M. Costambeys, 'The transmission of tradition: Gregorian influence and innovation in eighth-century Italian monasticism', in Y. Hen and M. Innes (eds.), *The Uses of the Past in the Early Middle Ages* (Cambridge, 2000), pp. 78–101, at pp. 99–100.
[174] *RM* 89.11.
[175] RB 48.24–5: 'Res, si quas habet, aut eroget prius pauperibus aut facta sollemniter donatione conferat monasterio, nihil reservans ex omnibus, quippe qui ex illo die nec proprii corporis potestatem se habiturum scit.' Coming after the *promissio* of RB 48.17–23, the donation is envisaged as a separate act. *Contra*, De Vogüe, *La Règle*, VI, p. 956.

records the donation of the monk himself to the abbot's authority: a transaction further symbolised by the monastery's retention of the document for safe-keeping.[176] The written word was paramount to the procedure: already the postulant has had Benedict's *Rule* read to him three separate times over the course of the year, with the pronouncement: 'This is the law under which you are choosing to serve.'[177] The ritual for child oblation likewise centred on a solemn ceremony in which the child's hand and the *petitio*, written by his parents, were wrapped together in the altar cloth.[178]

The influence of Roman legal culture behind these rituals should not be overlooked: written documents bound individuals to follow the intentions expressed. The monastic vow, already imbued with a sense of the divinity, received greater solemnity for being couched in the legal culture of Roman property law. It is the very strength of that culture in Italy that spurred Peter Chrysologus, preaching in the first half of the fifth century, to draw a necessary distinction between the solemnity of legal writings and that of the Christian faith:

This faith, this sacrament is not to be committed to a charter, nor written in letters, because charters and letters declare law, not grace... Therefore in taking up this contract, that is, this treaty of life, this court case of salvation between you and God, prepare your hearts with the insoluble chain of faith, not with a charter: sharpen your sensibilities, not your reed-pen, and describe the things heard with the aid of the spirit rather than ink, because the eternal and celestial secret cannot be committed to corruptible and heirless documents, but instead should be filed in that cabinet of the soul, in that library of the interior spirit.[179]

Peter's comments reflect the importance of written law and legal documentation in daily life that Lombard Italy inherited, as we shall see in chapters 4 and 5. Benedict and the Master may have rejected Roman education, but not the legal culture which it was intended to serve. Their long lists of rules and regulations, with numerous subclauses, were intended to cover all aspects of the monk's life, and to provide the abbot with sure guidelines when the necessities of any individual establishment required changes.

---

[176] *RB* 58.29. Cf. *RM* 89.27, 89.31–35.
[177] *RB* 58.10: 'Ecce lex sub qua militare vis.' Cf. II Tim. 4.2 and *RM* 87.3.
[178] *RB* 59.1–2, 7–8. See at length, M. de Jonge, 'In Samuel's image: child oblation and the Rule of St Benedict in the early Middle Ages *c*. 600–900', *Regulae Benedicti Studia* 16 (1989), 69–79; De Vogüé, *La Règle*, VI, 951–61, 962–70.
[179] *Sermo* 57, *PL* 52, 360D–361B. Cf. *Sermo* 62, *PL* 52, 372B: 'inter Deum vero et homines symbolum fidei sola fide firmatur: non litterae, sed spiritui creditur: et mandatur cordi, non chartae', etc.

Literacy in Lombard Italy, c. 568–774

Pope Gregory and the Bible

Arator and Fortunatus were the last beneficiaries of ancient education in Italy who have left us literary works that attempt the compromise between traditions of rhetoric and clerical vocation. The move towards a strictly 'biblical literacy' can be seen in Pope Gregory the Great. Gregory's attitude towards secular studies and pagan learning, as expressed in his famous letters to Desiderius of Vienne and to Leander of Seville, has received a great deal of attention, for it has been read as constituting something of a landmark in the history of literature, though Gregory was merely following canonical prohibitions on bishops reading or teaching profane texts.[180] His invective was directed not towards pagan literature *per se*, but towards the danger of the neglect of pastoral duties in favour of pursuits that lead to worldly pomp and pride: the primary concern of the sacerdotal office was the *regimen animarum*, itself the *ars artium* which required all of one's energy.[181]

Gregory's writings furnish us with further evidence of the ideals of clerical education circulating in the Italy of his pontificate. We should not be too territorial here: Gregory did his best to exert influence in Lombard Italy and shape ecclesiastical policies. As he himself once complained, he had been made bishop of the Lombards for his sins.[182] Despite his own education and literary talents, Gregory went no further in setting standards of literacy and education for priests than the minimum set by canon law of knowing the Psalms. Throughout his corpus of surviving works we find contradictory messages regarding the need for priests to be literate. In his immensely successful *Pastoral Care*, Gregory admonishes the pastor to set aside time for daily reading of the holy scriptures and meditating over the application of divine *praecepta*.[183] This was important for two separate but related reasons: it helped the pastor achieve the necessary measure of *consideratio*, a state of introspection and reflection needed to counter active involvement in the affairs of the world for the task of *cura animarum*; and it provided infallible guidelines for the pastoral duty of preaching, for a misunderstanding of scripture may turn the most

---

[180] Ep. III.33; Ep. V.53. See Riché, *Education*, pp. 152–7, for a sensible discussion. The tract *In librum primum regum expositionum libri vi* is insecure: see A. De Vogüe, 'L'auteur du commentaire des rois attribué à Saint Grégoire: un moine de Cava?', *Revue Bénédictine* 106 (1996), 319–31; noted by Markus, *Gregory*, p. xiv.

[181] *Grégoire le Grand: Règle pastorale*, ed. F. Rommel, C. Morin and B. Jucic, Sources Chrétiennes 38, 2 vols. (Paris, 1992) (hereafter *Reg. Past*), prol.

[182] Ep. I.30: 'quia sicut peccata mea merebantur, non Romanorum, sed Langobardorum episcopus factus sum'.

[183] *Reg. past.* II.11: 'studiose cotidie sacri eloquii praecepta meditetur'.

wholesome draught of wine into a cup of poison.[184] While Gregory did not go so far as stating that only scripture was permitted in sermons,[185] he castigated those too eager to preach because of pride and worldly vanity. To look to the advice of others was antithetical to the fundamental humility that comes from speaking 'from God, before God' (II Cor. 2.17), a feat which is only achieved through a pure knowledge of scripture.

Knowledge and reading of scripture, then, were necessary for holy orders, but this was only one of the many other qualities necessary for office, and by no means the most important. The bishop elect of Ancona possessed *scripturae sacrae scientia*, but his old age was a worry, and rumour had it that his deacon was completely ignorant of the Psalms.[186] The second canon of the council of Nicaea had set knowledge of the Psalter as the minimum standard for those aspiring to episcopal office, and Gregory upheld the standard.[187] Only once in his correspondence, however, did Gregory refer to 'knowledge of letters' as a requirement for entry into holy orders, though again it was only one condition among many, such as not having married a nun, or being in a state of servitude, attached to the *curia*, a bigamist, a penitent or an African, whom Gregory saw as trouble.[188] The story of the Umbrian priest Sanctulus which Gregory recounted in the *Dialogues* suggests that even ability to read the scriptures could be waived. Sanctulus did not know his letters very well, nor did he know the precepts of divine law. He may never have read the precept of 1 John 3.16 concerning our Redeemer's self-sacrifice, but his practical application of it surpassed those who had. Like Benedict, Sanctulus was all the wiser for his ignorance:

Let us compare, if you will, his wise ignorance (*docta ignorantia*) with our unwise learning (*indocta scientia*); our learning lies low, whereas his wisdom rises high. We speak of virtue while we are devoid of it ourselves; we take our stand in the midst of the fruit-bearing trees to enjoy their pleasant fragrance, but we do not eat of their fruit. He, on the contrary, knew how to gather the fruits of virtue, though he may not have sensed the sweetness they exhaled through written word.[189]

---

[184] *Reg. past.* II.7. Scripture as wine, III.24. On Gregory's notion of *consideratio*, see G. Evans, *The Thought of Gregory the Great* (Cambridge, 1986) pp. 17–27, and preaching pp. 75–9. Cf. S. Boesch Gajano, 'Teoria e pratica pastorale nelle opere di Gregorio Magno', in J. Fontaine, R. Gillet and S. Pellistrandi (eds.), *Grégoire le Grand* (Paris, 1986), pp. 181–8; Markus, *Gregory*, pp. 1–33.
[185] Cf. *Breviatio Fulgentii canonum*, PL 88, 168, 228.
[186] Ep. XIV.11.
[187] For example, Ep. X.13. But cf. Ep. V.51, where Gregory refused a certain priest's candidacy for the bishopric of Ravenna, not so much on the grounds that the priest did not know the Psalms, but rather that he had made no effort to learn them.
[188] Ep. II.37.
[189] *Dialogues* III.37: 'elementa litterarum bene non noverat, legis praecepta nesciebat'. Benedict II.1: 'scienter nescius et sapienter indoctus'. Sanctulus was also from Norcia.

The road to sanctity, much less the path of priesthood, was not through the thorny fields of literacy. For Gregory, literacy still smacked of the rhetorical pomp and vanity of secular education still in operation in the Rome of his day: the very education Gregory received at the hands of the grammarian and rhetor and about which he was disturbingly silent, despite the evidence of such training in his own works.[190] If the *Pastoral Care* is the key to Gregory's overall message,[191] we find little there to promote the intellectual development of priests, or indeed bishops, beyond the daily reading of scripture.

CONCLUSION

The move towards a strictly biblical literacy as the ideal for clerical office has been characterised by Robert Markus as part of the process of 'de-secularisation' of society in Christian thought from the fourth to the end of the sixth century, as boundaries between secular and religious life became increasingly blurred.[192] As ascetic ideals rose to prominence among the clergy, and as traditions of civilian authority and secular administration were greatly weakened, the result was an 'epistemological excision' of secular knowledge and learning and subsequent constriction of discourse to an exclusively scriptural framework. Secular literary traditions did not disappear altogether: the study of grammar and concern for correct orthography were just part of the ancient heritage Christian culture adopted for its own ends. But gone was the model of the highly literate Christian who could grapple with the prestige and power of ancient literary culture on its own terms. In its place the 'holy rustic', who knew and lived out the precepts of the Bible whether or not he could read it, became the new hero. His humility, and as a corollary his simplicity of speech, directly linked him with the awesome power of the Divinity. Whatever prestige and power secular literary culture enjoyed in this world simply paled in comparison. As the political system of government and the social order it regulated were swept away over the course of the sixth century, secular literary culture increasingly had no point or purpose. This was the situation the Lombards found when they entered Italy, and this

---

[190] Particularly evident in Gregory's concern to rewrite and polish up his own works: cf. the prefatory letter to Leander of Seville for the *Moralia in Iob*: Ep. V.53a, and *Hom. in evang.* II.23.1, *PL* 86, 1282; also Ep. XII.6. On secular schools in Rome, Kirkby, 'The scholar and his public', p. 48; Riché, *Education*, pp. 79–152. On Gregory's language, M. Banniard, *Viva voce: Communication écrite et communication orale du IVe au IXe siècle en Occident latin* (Paris, 1992), pp. 105–79; E. Massa, 'Gregorio Magno e l'arte del linguaggio. Alcune osservazioni', in *Gregorio Magno e il suo tempo* (Rome, 1991), II, pp. 59–104; and U. Pizzani, 'S. Gregorio Magno, Cassiodorio, e le arti liberali', in *ibid.*, pp. 121–36.
[191] Markus, *Gregory*, p. 204.   [192] Markus, *End*, pp. 16–18, 224–7.

was the culture they and the clerics of the churches within their kingdom inherited. We may well ask what the constriction of literate discourse to an exclusively scriptural framework signifies for the history of literacy. The constriction of discourse to the scriptures need not necessarily mean an impoverishment of literary and intellectual culture, 'though the two things may go together'.[193] A society that has reduced its literate activity to reading, and occasionally writing about, just one book, irrespective of its complexity and comprehensiveness, might well be characterised as much less literate than, say, one in which people exchanged poetry and letters that echoed a canon of various texts learned since childhood. But at the more personal, individual level, the centrality of that book to the lives of those who read it, in determining their values, lifestyles, how they see others, and everyday decisions, perhaps points to a deeper type of literacy, a more intimate acquaintance with the written word, with extracting crucial meaning from a text. In becoming radically biblical, Christian culture of the early middle ages elevated writing and the book to the higher level of the sacred.

Whatever the merits and deficiencies of the concept of 'de-secularisation' – and it is difficult to escape the attraction of its comprehensiveness – it should not blind us from seeing the continuity of secular literate traditions in the spheres of law and administration. As I suggested above, the monasticism of Benedict and others owed much to the traditions of written law in Italy. But more importantly, as we shall see throughout the following chapters, the Lombards were to pick up and develop those written legal traditions to suit the needs of the society they governed, a society in which written law and documents were an integral component of self-regulation. It is time now to ask who the Lombards were and how they established their kingdom.

---

[193] *Ibid.*, p. 225.

2

THE EARLY LOMBARDS AND THEIR SETTLEMENT IN ITALY

The establishment of Lombard rule is thought to have so radically altered the social and cultural landscape of Italy that it removed the necessity of literate practices for the functioning of the new system of government, and rendered literacy irrelevant to the daily lives of Italy's inhabitants. In this chapter we shall explore the extent to which these claims are true by focusing on the nature of the Lombard settlement in Italy, the system of government which resulted, and the adoption of literate traditions by the early Lombard court. In this context it is also worth considering the religious disposition of the Lombards and their early relations with the church, for both subjects provide insight into the general cultural milieu of Italy in this period, and allow us to reassess some common myths concerning Lombard antipathy and aversion to Catholic Christianity and the religious life of late Roman Italy. Finally, the text of the *Origo gentis langobardorum* will be examined as representative of an alternative Lombard ethnic identity which pre-dates their settlement in Italy and which is read as evidence for a degree of cultural separatism among Lombard elites and the peninsula they governed.

THE EARLIEST LOMBARDS

Langobardi are first attested by classical writers as inhabiting the regions of the lower Elbe in the first and second centuries AD. 'Famous for being small in number, and set in the midst of innumerable and most powerful tribes, the Lombards are preserved not by submissiveness, but by peril and pitched battle', reported Tacitus, confirming Vellius Paterculus' allusion to the Lombards as 'a Germanic people more ferocious than ferocity itself'.[1] Cassius Dio reports that in 166, 6000 Langobardi and Ubii moved south and raided Pannonia, an event which appears to have opened

---

[1] Vellius Paterculus, *Res gestae divi Augusti*, ed. and trans. F.W. Shipley, Loeb edn (London and Cambridge, MA, 1967), II.cvi: 'gens etiam Germana feritate ferocior'. Tacitus, *Germania*, ed. and Italian trans. B. Ceva, BUR (Milan, 1995), 40.1: 'Contra Langobardos paucitas nobilitat: plurimis ac valentissimis nationibus cincti non per obsequium sed proeliis et periclitando tuti sunt.'

The early Lombards and their settlement in Italy

the proceedings of the Marcomannic war.[2] Strabo noted their nomadic character, and claimed they belonged to a larger Suevic realm.[3] Classical ethnography can tell us more about Roman attitudes to Germanic peoples than the peoples themselves, and these 'observations' of individual authors, often relying on hearsay or other literary sources, were tailored to fit with classical, 'ethnogeographic' theories of the effect of climate upon behaviour and character.[4] The Lombards, deep in the chilly north, were an exemplary barbarian horde, hardy and savage.

From these brief notices in classical authors there is a lacuna in our literary sources of over 400 years. We next hear of the Lombards when Procopius reports that the *Langobardi* occupied Rugiland in 488/9, and thereafter crossed the Danube to occupy part of the province of Pannonia in 526/7. Around 546/7, Justinian ceded portions of Noricum and Pannonia to the Lombards as *foederati* and employed Lombards as auxiliary troops under Narses to fight against the Ostrogoths, but the Lombards were too violent and undisciplined, and Narses had to send them home.[5] Attempts to fill in the gap in our literary sources have, rather unsuccessfully, relied upon archaeology in order to trace a line of 'Lombard' artefacts along a proposed 'migratory route' of a Lombard *Völkerwanderung* across a period of six or more centuries to Italy from Scandinavia, the place which, as we shall see, seventh- and eighth-century texts claim to be the Lombards' homeland.[6] The last few decades have witnessed a great deal of debate over early medieval ethnic identity amongst barbarian

---

[2] Dio, *Roman History*, 72.11.6; 72.12.1–3.
[3] Strabo, *Geographica*, trans. H.L. Jones, Loeb edn (London and New York, 1944), VII 1.3.291. Likewise Claudius Ptolemy, *Geographica*, ed. C. Nobbe (Leipzig, 1966), II.11.9, 17.
[4] J.P. Balsdon, *Romans and Aliens* (London, 1979); J. S. Romm, *The Edges of the Earth in Ancient Thought* (Princeton, 1992), pp. 44–9; Y.A. Dauge, *Le Barbare: recherches sur la conception romaine de la barbarie et de la civilisation*, Collection Latomus 176 (Brussels, 1981); K.E. Müller, *Geschichte der antiken Ethnographie und ethnologischen Theoriebildung* 2 vols. (Wiesbaden, 1982); Amory, *People and Identity*.
[5] Procopius, *Wars* II.22; III.25, 33.
[6] Some examples: V. Bierbrauer, 'Aspetti archeologici di Goti, Alamanni e Longobardi', in P. Caratelli (ed.), *Magistra Barbaritas* (Milan, 1984), pp. 445–508; O. von Hessen, 'Cultura materiale presso i Longobardi', in *I Longobardi e la Lombardia. Saggi* (Milan, 1978), pp. 261–7; and the catalogue to the exhibition of 'Lombard' artefacts, G.C. Menis (ed.) *I Longobardi* (Milan, 1990). Some modern general histories of the Lombards have used this material a little too incautiously: W. Menghin, *Die Langobarden: Archäologie und Geschichte* (Stuttgart, 1985); J. Jarnut, *Geschichte der Langobarden* (Stuttgart, 1982); N. Christie, *The Lombards* (Oxford, 1995), esp. pp. 1–30. On the fallacies of attributing ethnicity to artefacts: U. Veit, 'Ethnic concepts in German pre-history: a case study on the relationship between cultural identity and archaeological objectivity', in S. Shennan (ed.), *Archaeological Approaches to Cultural Identity* (London, 1989), pp. 35–56; R. Hachmann, 'Der Scandza-topos der frühmittelalterlichen Historiographie', and 'Kossina und der Skandinavientopos des 19. und 20. Jahrhunderts', in his *Die Goten und Skandinavien*, Quellen und Forschungen zu Sprach- und Kulturgeschichte der germanischen Völker 34 (Berlin, 1970), pp. 13–15, 138–45 respectively.

groups. In particular, the 'ethnogenesis' school of thought has attempted to fill the frustrating gaps in our sources with anthropological theories concerning the construction of ethnic identity amongst Germanic tribes for political and ideological purposes as they came within the Roman orbit.[7] Ethnogenesis theories have not been without criticism, although the debates for and against can often tell us more about twentieth-century history than the period supposedly under discussion.[8] The net result of this research, however, has been to stress the extreme fluidity of ethnic identity in this period, the essentially military character of these groups as a people-under-arms under the leadership of a mercenary-warrior elite, and the small numbers of people they comprised. As we shall see, it is not difficult to apply such findings to the case of the Lombards.[9] For the present study, it is relatively unimportant to ask where the Lombards came from six or more centuries before their arrival in the Roman province of Pannonia, a melting-pot of barbarian ethnicity. It is important that the Lombards remained in Pannonia for over two generations prior to their arrival in Italy and that they themselves promoted the idea of ancient Scandinavian origins with the use of texts well after their settlement.

ON THE HORIZONS OF LITERACY AND ITALY

By the time of their arrival in Pannonia, the Lombards, like other barbarian tribes of northern Europe, had been in constant contact with the Roman world for over five centuries in cultural, economic, military and political spheres of life. This contact with the empire facilitated familiarity with the Latin language and an awareness of the importance

---

[7] The 'ethnogenesis school' begins with the work of R. Wenskus, *Stammesbildung und Verfassung: das Werden der frühmittelalterlichen Gentes* (Cologne and Graz, 1961), and H. Wolfram's application of Wenskus' theories in reassessing the formation of the Goths, *Die Geschichte der Goten: von den Anfängen bis zur Mittel des sechsten Jahrhunderts. Entwurf einer historischen Ethnographie* (Munich, 1979), trans. T. Dunlap, *History of the Goths* (Berkeley, 1988). See further: P. Geary, 'Ethnic identity as a situational construct in the early middle ages', *Mitteilungen der Anthropologischen Gesellschaft in Wien* 113 (Vienna, 1983), 15–26; W. Pohl, 'Tradition, Ethnogenese und literarische Gestaltung: eine Zwischenbilanz', in K. Brunner and B. Merta (eds.), *Ethnogenese und Überlieferung: Angewandte Methoden der Frühmittelalterforschung* (Vienna, 1994), pp. 9–26; P. Amory, 'The meaning and purpose of ethnic terminology in the Burgundian laws', *EME* 2:1 (1993), 1–28, esp. p. 2 n. 6; Amory *People and Identity*, pp. 13–42.
[8] Criticism of Wenskus: F. Graus, *Historica* 7 (1963), 185–91; cf. H. Wolfram, 'Methodischen Fragen zur Kritik am "sakralen" Königtum germanischer Stämme', in H. Birkhan and O. Gschwantler (eds.), *Festschrift für Otto Höfler* (Vienna, 1968), pp. 473–90; P. Heather, 'Theoderic, king of the Goths', *EME*, 4:2 (1995), 145–74; H. Wolfram, '*Origo et religio*: ethnic traditions and literature in early medieval texts', *EME* 3:1 (1994), 19–38, esp. p. 25; W. Goffart, 'Two notes on Germanic antiquity today', *Traditio* 50 (1995), 9–30.
[9] Cf. D. Harrison, 'Dark Age migrations and subjective ethnicity: the example of the Lombards', *Scandia* 57:1 (1991), 19–36.

of literate communication, at least as part of Roman diplomatic procedures. Attila employed literate Romans as secretaries who drew up letters for diplomatic correspondence with the emperor, and both Gothic and Alemannic kings used letters to correspond with the emperor in the establishment of treaties and alliances.[10] Moreover, Christian missionaries conveyed literacy to barbarian groups in Pannonia and Noricum as early as the third century by the use of texts in no less than three literate languages: Gothic, Greek and Latin.[11] It might be argued that the success of the spread of early Christianity was more dependent upon intermediary personal contact with bishops or Christian missionaries who could translate the message of scripture into vernacular terms (that is, in both expression and language), and that therefore dissemination of the faith was primarily one of oral transmission.[12] The dichotomy of oral-literate communication is, however, misleading in relation to Christian missionary activity. Bishops and missionaries worked from texts, their ultimate source of authority for explaining the Christian message. A barbarian who accepted Christianity need not be able to read for him-/herself to practise the faith. Public ritual, such as attendance at a church, or private rituals, such as prayer or the use of decorative Christian symbols on clothing or household goods, were ways of professing the acceptance of Jesus Christ as personal saviour and the authority of his church as his representative on earth. All of these acts, however, denote an awareness of, if not direct acquaintance with, the power of the written word to convey Christ's teachings and his divinity. Christian missionaries and clergy went one step further than this: they emphasised the power of their sacred texts in this world, as weapons against demons and invaders.[13]

By the time of the Lombard settlement in Noricum the province had been nominally Catholic Christian (as opposed to any Arian varieties) for nearly a century.[14] Their next fixed address, Pannonia, had experienced more than two centuries of Christian influence, activity and ecclesiastical organisation prior to their arrival. Both provinces have yielded archaeological finds of fortress towns endowed with Christian basilicas and

---

[10] P. Heather, 'Literacy and power in the migration period', in A.K. Bowman and G. Woolf (eds.), *Literacy and Power in the Ancient World* (Cambridge, 1994), pp. 177–97, at 180; A.D. Lee, *Information and Frontiers: Roman Foreign Relations in Late Antiquity* (Cambridge, 1993), pp. 30–1.

[11] W.H.C. Friend, 'The missions of the early church 180–700 A.D.', *Miscellanea Historiae Christianae* 3 (1970), 3–23; J. Zeiller, *Les Origines chrétiennes dans les provinces danubiennes de l'empire romain* (Paris, 1918), pp. 572–4.

[12] See G. Cavallo, 'Alfabetismo e circolazione del libro', in M. Vegetti (ed.), *Oralità, scrittura, spettacolo* (Turin, 1983), pp. 166–86, esp. p. 181; also Richter, *Formation*, pp. 27–44.

[13] R. Lane Fox, 'Literacy and Power in early Christianity', in Bowman and Woolf (eds.), *Literacy and Power*, pp. 126–48.

[14] G. Alföldy, *Noricum*, trans. A. Birley (London and Boston, 1974), pp. 222–8, esp. p. 226.

cemeteries.[15] We know little about the Pannonian churches in this period, although a certain Bishop Vigilius is attested at *Scarbantia* (Sopron) until 568, and we know of an Arian bishop in Sirminium under Gepid rule.[16] Pannonian orthodoxy had enough vigour in the sixth century to produce St Martin of Braga, who was later active in the struggle against paganism and Arianism in Spain.[17]

The religious disposition of the Lombards in this pre-Italian period is recorded in two sources. First, Procopius assures us that the Lombards were 'a Christian people' who constantly sought peace 'calling on God as their witness' at the time they were subdued by the Heruli, that is before 491, although the Lombards had done nothing to provoke the wrath of their neighbours.[18] Moreover, they appear to have been Catholic, rather than Arian, Christians for some time, according to the speech of a Lombard legate made before Justinian at the court of Constantinople.[19] Such speeches are the least trustworthy parts of Procopius' narrative, and in this case the speech is rendered more dubious by Procopius' tendency to equate Arianism as a marker of anti-imperial sentiment, in line with Justinian's propaganda against the Vandal regime.[20]

Second, we have a letter (written 551–8) from the bishop of Trier, Nicetius, to Alboin's wife Queen Chlodosinda, daughter of the Frankish king Chlotar I, at the Lombard court in Pannonia.[21] Nicetius wrote to encourage the queen to be more active on behalf of her Catholic faith in following the example of Clothild and Clovis, and cited I Cor. 7.14, ever useful for motivating a barbarian queen to persuade her husband.[22] Moreover, Nicetius expressed surprise that King Alboin had allowed Arians to preach at his court, and that Alboin had sent some of his

---

[15] An instructive example is the excavated fortress town of *Valcum* and the surrounding region: see R. Müller, 'Die Spätromische Festung Valcum am Plattensee', in W. Menghin, T. Springer and E. Warmer (eds.), *Germanen Hunnen und Awaren: Schätze der Völkerwanderungszeit. Die Archäologie des 5. und 6. Jahrhunderts an der mittleren Donau und der östlich-merowingische Reihengräberkreis* (Nuremberg, 1987), pp. 270–4; N. Christie, 'The survival of Roman settlement along the Middle Danube: Pannonia from the fourth to the tenth century A.D.', *Oxford Journal of Archaeology* 11:3 (1992), 317–39; J. Haberl and C. Hawkes, 'The last of Roman Noricum: St. Severin on the Danube', in C. and S. Hawkes (eds.), *Greeks, Celts and Romans* (London, 1973), pp. 96–156.

[16] John of Biclar, *Chronica*, 212.26–7, 213.1–2, ed. T. Mommsen, MGH AA. XI, p. 265. See A. Mócsy, *Pannonia and Upper Moesia* (London and Boston, 1974), pp. 325–36, 351–3; also E. Thomas, 'Die Romanität Pannoniens im 5. und 6. Jahrhundert', in W. Menghin (eds.) *Germanen, Hunnen und Awaren*, pp. 284–94.

[17] Gregory of Tours, *Historiae* V.37.   [18] *Wars* VI.14.9–12ff.   [19] *Wars* VII.34.

[20] Cf. *Wars* I.21.17ff; II.14.21ff. See Cameron, *Procopius*, pp. 16–20, 126, 148–50, 171–87. Cf. M. Cesa, 'Etnografia e geografia nella visione storica di Procopius di Cesarea', *Studi Classici et Orientali* 32 (1982), 189–215.

[21] MGH Ep. III, 119–22. On the dating, see C. Blasel, 'Die Übertritt der Langobarden zum Christentum', *Archiv für Katholisches Kirchenrecht* 83 (1903), 585–634, at pp. 599–601.

[22] *Ibid*., p. 122. I Cor. 7.14: 'Salvabitur vir infidelis per mulierem fidelem'.

men to Italy to observe these Arian 'dogs' at work. We should not take too literally Nicetius' exhortation to Chlodosinda 'both to read this letter well and well to him [Alboin]'.[23] Functionaries, or the *legati* mentioned in the letter may have recited its contents, or perhaps Alboin could have read it for himself. But the letter does testify to the reception, if not the issuance, of written communications at the Lombard royal court at Pannonia, and to the presence of Christianity. Nicetius ended his letter with a plea guaranteed to stir a barbarian king's interest in the faith.[24]

LOMBARD ARIANISM

Nicetius' letter, and the presence of Arian bishops and followers in Pannonia, calls attention to the subject of Lombard Arianism, a subject of importance for understanding the politico-religious climate of Italian churches on the eve of the Lombards' arrival. Past historiography tended to associate Arianism with Germanic barbarism, and Catholicism with the empire and a degree of sophistication and civility not yet obtained by scruffy warriors.[25] This interpretative paradigm is frequently employed to explain the rebirth of 'culture', hence literate culture also, in the late seventh century under the 'Catholic' reign of Perctarit and continuing under Liutprand in the eighth century.[26] A close examination of the contemporary sources discredits much of this picture.[27] Both Gregory the Great and Gregory of Tours refer to Lombards as pagans, though clearly some Lombard kings such as Authari and Rothari were actively Arian. According to Pope Gregory, Authari promulgated a decree prohibiting the Catholic baptism of Lombard infants, which explains the king's subsequent death, and Paul tells us that in Rothari's time (636–52) all cities of the kingdom had two bishops, one Arian and one Catholic, but this is certainly an

---

[23] 'Quid est, quod nihil ibidem praesumere audent [scil. Ariani], nisi furtive, ut canes a foris, animas decipent, cum illos suos fideles rex Alboenus ibidem mittat et ad domni Petri, Pauli, Iohannis, vel reliquorum sanctorum limina perducat?', *ibid.*, p. 121; 'ut hanc epistulam et bene legas et bene illi', *ibid.*, p. 120.

[24] 'rogo, ut sic agas, ut et gentem Langobardorum fortem super inimicos facias', *ibid.*, p. 122.

[25] T. Hodgkin, *Italy and Her Invaders*, 8 vols. (London, 1892–99) V, p. 157; J.M. Wallace-Hadrill, *The Barbarian West 400–1000* (London, 1979), p. 54: 'The Lombards were not yet civilised', cf. pp. 44, 46; E.A. Thompson, *The Visigoths in the Time of Ulfila* (Oxford, 1966), p. 128 and *passim*.

[26] E.g. Riché, *Education*, pp. 341, 409–13; G.P. Bognetti, 'S. Maria foris portas di Castelseprio e la storia religiosa dei Langobardi', *L'età*, I, pp. 381–415, *passim*. Also Hodgkin, *Italy*, VI, p. 150; L.M. Hartmann, *Geschichte Italiens im Mittelalters*, 4 vols. (Gotha, 1900), II, p. 207. Cf. Wickham, *EMI*, pp. 34–6.

[27] S.C. Fanning, 'Lombard Arianism reconsidered', *Speculum* 56:2 (1981), 241–58, *contra* Bognetti, 'S. Maria'.

exaggeration.²⁸ Apart from Authari's decree, which may be ascribed to hearsay or hysteria on Gregory's part, the Lombards did not promote Arianism or persecute Catholics. Authari had Catholic followers: when one Lombard soldier tried to melt down St Peter's keys to make a knife, the wretch picked them up only to stab himself in the throat. But his comrade in arms, the pious Mimiulf, had no such trouble: he gave them to King Authari, who then sent the keys to Pope Pelagius II, with an account of the miracle.²⁹ There appears to have been no irreconcilable division between Arian and Catholic to contemporaries, witnessed by the support of Transpadane Catholic bishops for the usurpation of the throne by the Arian King Arioald (624–36), to the of horror of Pope Honorius I.³⁰ It may well be the case that elements of Arianism among the Lombards ultimately derived not from their pre-Italian period but from their settlement in Italy, where Arianism had very deep roots indeed. The Arian chuches in Aquileia and Milan date back to the fourth century, and those on the Via Merulana soon after. The *magistri militum* Ricimer, Gundobad and Odovacer were Arians, so we should not be surprised to find six or seven Arian churches in Ravenna which pre-date Theoderic and his munificence, which extended to setting aside tax revenues as salary for Arian clergy, commissioning magnificent manuscripts of the Gothic Bible, and founding and endowing churches as splendid as San Apollinare Nuovo.³¹ Gregory mentions a Lombard Arian bishop humbly asking for a place to perform his liturgical service in Spoleto, since the Arian church there had

---

²⁸ Gregory, Ep. I.17; Paul, *HL* IV.42. See J. Zeiller, 'Etude sur l'arianisme en Italie à l'époque ostrogothique et à l'époque lombarde', *Mélanges d'Archéologie et d'Histoire* 25 (1905), 121–53, at pp. 136, 145; Hartmann, *Geschichte Italiens*, II, p. 278; Bognetti, 'S. Maria', pp. 85, 107, 209; C. Cecchelli, 'L'arianesimo e le chiese ariene d'Italie', *Settimane* 7 (Spoleto, 1960), 743–74.
²⁹ Gregory, Ep. VII.23. Mimiulf, 'sciebatur in oratione et elemosinis deditus', may be the same as the Lombard duke of the Insula S. Giulio d'Orta, who was executed early in Agilulf's reign for collaborating with the Franks: Paul, *HL* IV.3; *PLRE* 3B, p. 890.
³⁰ MGH Ep. III, p. 694. Arioald is called *tyrannus* but Honorius does not mention his Arianism, of which we learn from Jonas, *Vita Columbani* II.24.
³¹ See M. Meslin, *Les Ariens d'Occident 335–430*, Patristica Sorbonensia 8 (Paris, 1967). Fourth-century Arian churches in Aquileia and Milan: Cecchello, 'L'arianesimo', pp. 757–9, 761–84 respectively. Six or seven Arian Italian churches pre-date Theoderic: Zeiller, 'Etude', pp. 128–30; Zeiller, 'Les églises ariennes de Rome à l'époque de la domination gotique', *Mélanges d'Archéologie et d'Histoire de l'Ecole Française de Rome* 24 (1904), 17–33. On Theoderic's religious policies, see F. Deichmann, *Ravenna: Haupstadt des spätantiken Abendlandes*, 3 vols. (Wiesbaden, 1969–76), I, pp. 43–7; Wolfram, *Goths*, pp. 325–6. Cf. Moorhead, *Theoderic*, pp. 89–97; T. Brown, 'Everyday life in Ravenna under Theoderic: an example of his "tolerance" and "prosperity"', *Atti XIII CISAM* (Spoleto, 1993), 77–100. On the Gothic Bible, see G.W. Friedrichsen, *The Gothic Version of the Gospels: A Study of Its Style and Textual History* (Oxford, 1926), and Friedrichsen, *The Gothic Version of the Epistles* (Oxford, 1936); W. Holmes Bennett (ed. and trans.), *The Gothic Commentary on the Gospel of St John*, MLA Monograph 21 (New York, 1960); M. J. Hunter, 'The Gothic Bible', in G. Lampe (ed.), *The Cambridge History of the Bible*, II (Cambridge, 1969), pp. 352–3; P. Heather and J.F. Matthews, *The Goths in the Fourth Century* (Liverpool, 1991), pp. 169–73.

been shut for years. Yet at the rude rebuttal from the Catholic bishop, the Arian prelate had no choice but to force entry, with a 'mob' of supporters behind him.[32] Proactive Arianism among certain kings should probably be seen as attempts to gain political support from certain sectors of Italian society. Arian sympathies may also have arisen owing to the Lombard's absorption of the Gepids after their defeat by the former in 567.[33] In any case, there is no reason to suppose that Arian Christianity in the sixth or seventh century had less affinity with the use of religious texts than had orthodox Catholicism. If anything, the presence of Arianism may have spurred on literary activity in this period, as it had done under the Ostrogoths.[34] Continuity of Arian–Orthodox debates into the Lombard period can be seen in the activity of the scriptorium at Bobbio, where the monks busily palimpsested Arian tracts to make room for patristic texts,[35] and we know that Columbanus wrote an anti-Arian tract during his stay in Milan which has unfortunately been lost.[36]

LOMBARD PAGANISM

Despite the evidence for both Catholicism and Arianism among the early Lombards, we also have references to them as pagans. Paul the Deacon was noticeably reticent about Lombard religious disposition, mentioning only in passing that the early Lombards were pagan when they arrived in Italy, and Gregory of Tours appears to have had the same impression.[37] Writing to the bishop of Autun in 580, Pope Pelagius II vaguely refers to a 'gentile disturbance' (*gentilis motus*) and the Catholic faith being 'insulted by idolators', but it is not clear that he is referring to the Lombards specifically.[38] Similarly, Pope Gregory referred to the Lombards only once as 'idolators' (*idolatres*) in his correspondence, a term which he also applied

---

[32] *Dialogues* III.30.
[33] As suggested by Fanning, 'Lombard Arianism', pp. 256–7. *HL* I.27; Procopius, *Wars* VII.34. Cf. Blasel, 'Übertritt der Langobarden', pp. 588–91.
[34] Such as the collection of Latin Arian sermons written in Verona *c*. 500, contained in MS Verona, LI (49) (CLA IV.504); see R. Gryson, *Le Recueil arien de Vérone*, Instrumenta Patristica (The Hague, 1992), pp. 21–8.
[35] CLA I.20; III.351, 364, 365. See M. Van der Hout, 'Gothic palimpsests of Bobbio', *Scriptorium* 6 (1952), 87–98. The copying of the *acta* of the councils of Ephesus and Chalcedon, CLA I.26, III.321, 334, 361, IV.451, is surely related to this activity, as is the revision of Hilary's *De trinitate*, CLA XI.1507, though this may date from *c*. 550: see H. Klos, 'Neue Fragmente des Hilarius-Papyruskodex', *Mitteilungen des Instituts für Österreichische Geschichtsforschung* 63 (1955), 47–52.
[36] Ep. V (ed. Walker), pp. 37ff.
[37] *HL* IV.6, 26. Until Theodelinda persuaded Agilulf to convert to Catholicism, the Lombards 'adhuc gentilitatis errore tenerentur'. Gregory of Tours, *Historiae* VI.6; IX.25; VIII.15.
[38] MGH Ep. III, p. 446ff. The 'gentilis motus' appears to be in Frankish territory: 'dum paene in conspectu vestro tanto sanguis innocentium sit effusus, ita sacra violentur altaria, ita catholicae fidei ab idolatris insultetur'.

to Romano-Italians living in parts of Byzantine-controlled Italy such as Sicily, Corsica and Sardinia, where even judges had become involved in pagan cults.[39] In his correspondence Gregory did not employ the terms 'idolater', 'gentilis', 'infidelis' and 'paganus' in any systematic way,[40] so that it is often impossible to know exactly to what types of pagan practices he is referring, aside from the somewhat generic description of people worshipping trees, or wood, and rocks. Jonas mentions that some Lombards worshipped at a woodland shrine, but this was among rural populations a fairly common practice against which churchmen across western Christendom often railed in a curiously uniform manner.[41]

Two passages in Gregory's *Dialogues*, however, refer to Lombard pagan practices specifically. In the first passage, Gregory seeks to answer the question put to him by his deacon Peter of what constitutes a martyr as opposed to a confessor. He refers to the recent example, which he had heard from others, of how forty peasants (*rustici*) had been captured by the Lombards and forced to eat food consecrated by pagan rites on pain of death. The peasants preferred to die rather than to eat the 'cibum sacrilegum', which for Gregory qualified the peasants for the crown of martyrdom.[42] The second passage, which follows immediately from the first, recounts how 400 prisoners were forced to participate in a ceremony in which Lombards 'sacrificed to the devil the head of a goat, running around it in circles and singing an abominable song, as is their custom'.[43]

These passages are favourites amongst scholars looking for early Lombard savagery and pagan religion prior to their conversion to Christianity.[44] The eating of consecrated food is a fairly standard target among ecclesiastical authors throughout the entire middle ages, and is therefore not a specifically Lombard custom. As for the second passage, Gregory's rhetoric ('[multitudo] cervicem quam semper creatori

---

[39] Sicily, Ep. V.32: Sardinia, Ep. IX.204; IV.23, 26; IX.29; XI.12; judges, V.38; bishop Ianuarius, XIX.38; cf. S. Boesch Gajano, 'Teoria e pratica pastorale nelle opere di Gregorio Magno', in J. Fontaine, R. Gillet and S. Pellistrandi (eds.), *Grégoire le Grand*, Colloques internationaux du CNRS (Paris, 1986), pp. 181–8, at pp. 185–7. Corsica, Ep. VIII.1.
[40] Markus, *Gregory*, p. 81 and n. 88.
[41] *Vita Columbani* II.25. Cf. J. Hillgarth, 'Popular religion in Visigothic Spain', in E. James (ed.), *Visigothic Spain: New Approaches* (Oxford, 1980), pp. 3–60; S. McKenna, *Paganism and Pagan Survivals in Spain up to the Fall of the Visgothic Kingdom* (Washington, DC, 1938), pp. 75–107. The similarity of descriptions has resulted in their being called into question as little more than literary topoi: see D. Harmening, *Superstitio: Überlieferungs und theoriegeschichtliche Untersuchungen zur kirchlich-theologischen Aberglaubsliteratur des Mittelalters* (Berlin, 1979), and cf. J.C. Schmidt, 'Les superstitions', in J. Le Goff (ed.), *Histoire de la France religieuse*, I (Paris, 1988), 423–53.
[42] *Dial.* III.27.   [43] *Dial.* III.28.
[44] E.g. R. Manselli, 'Gregorio Magno e due riti pagani dei Longobardi', in *Studi storici in onore di O. Bertolini*, 2 vols. (Pisa, 1972), I, pp. 435–41; and S. Gasparri, *La cultura tradizionale dei Longobardi: struttura tribale e resistenze pagane* (Spoleto, 1983), pp. 32–45.

flexerat creaturae inclinare contempsit'), a deliberate echo of Romans 1.25, alludes to the pagan barbarism of the ancient Romans and hence was intended to justify further his characterisation of murder by Lombards as a form of martyrdom. Despite scholarly attempts to find deep mythological resonances of sacrificing goats in Germanic religious cosmology, one suspects Gregory has employed a topos to describe German barbarism. The Franks, too, had been sacrificing to the heads of animals.[45] On the other hand, if the story of Lombards and their goat heads were a mere literary fabrication on Gregory's part, it would not have been received well by Queen Theudelinda, to whom Gregory sent a copy of the *Dialogues* and whose influence at court Gregory carefully cultivated as a means of furthering papal interests in northern Italy.

We hear no more of such practices in our sources. The ninth-century *Vita Barbati* records how the Lombards in mid-seventh-century Benevento, although Christian, still clung to a 'former rite of paganism' (*priscus gentilitatis ritus*) in which they bowed to a gold statue of a viper, promptly melted down by Bishop Barbatus to form a Eucharistic chalice. The late date of the text and the literary artifice of the tale, including the *dénouement* of Duke Romoald unwittingly drinking from the golden snake-cum-chalice, render the tale less than trustworthy as a reflection of pagan practices among the Lombards.[46] But another practice documented in the *Vita* is less suspect. On a certain day the Lombard men would gather about a 'sacred tree' upon which they hung an animal's hide and proceeded to charge at it on their horses with their lances, 'superstitiously' eating the part which remained on the lance.[47] At the bishop's remonstrations, some Beneventans were converted, but others 'remained blinded by their beastly dementia', and complained to the bishop that their practices were 'nothing other than that which they thought useful for the art of war, an excellent custom of their ancestors, who were, they boasted, the most martial of men, and so they spurned entirely the advice of the man of God'.[48] Unlike the theatricality of the golden viper, the custom, and perhaps also the Lombard response to the bishop, has a ring of truth to it, in that the martial culture of the Lombard warrior elites probably involved such practices of military skills which carried with them superstitions linked with ancestral cults or worship. Martial culture also appears to be behind other practices. Paul reports that it was a Lombard custom to commemorate those who died at war or in foreign

---

[45] E.g. Gregory, Ep. VIII.4, to Queen Brunhild: 'ut idolis non immolant [*scil.* Franci], cultores arborum non existant, de animalium capitibus sacrificia sacrilega non exhibeant'.
[46] In agreement with J.M. Martin, 'A propos de la "vita" de Barbatus évêque de Bénévent', *Mélanges de l'Ecole Française de Rome* 86 (1974), 137–64.
[47] *Vita Barbati*, 1, MGH SRL, p. 557.   [48] *Ibid.*, 2.

territory by placing stakes (*perticae*), with wooden images of doves on top, in between the graves of their ancestors, with the dove pointing in the direction of where the deceased perished.[49] Though this was not irreconcilable with Christian burial practices, Queen Rodelinda removed any ambiguities by founding a monastery (*c.* 675) on the site outside the walls of Pavia.[50] The practice does not appear to have been restricted to those who fell in battle, though these would probably have been the majority of those commemorated *ad perticas*.

Pagan practices and superstitions were not restricted to Lombards only but extended to the entire Italian population, as Pope Gregory's register of letters makes clear. In 599 Pope Gregory urged the bishop of Luni to encourage his clergy in their struggle against the pagan cults in the region, a region which remained under Byzantine control until the late 640s.[51] As late as the mid-eighth century, a Christian evangelist was commemorated for converting the populace of Luni and having 'smashed their various idols' which they worshipped.[52] The idols are more likely to have been of the Greco-Roman pantheon rather than, say, a Lombard golden viper. We should interpret the references to witches, charms and soothsayers in Lombard legislation in a similar light as addressed to the Italian population at large, particularly warning city-dwellers not to indulge in the follies of the *rustici*.[53]

No doubt some Lombards engaged in some pagan rituals, but recent studies have questioned the extent to which 'pagan' practices or superstitions can be equated with an alternative religious cosmology that was inimical or antithetical to Christianity. Sacred trees, fountains, woodland shrines and even howling at the full moon might be considered as merely parts of the pattern of traditional behaviour of rural communities whose lives, and livelihoods, were so intrinsically bound with the cycles

---

[49] *HL* V.34.
[50] Cf. Gasparri, *La cultura*, pp. 62–5. A. Zironi, 'Historia langobardorum V:34: "La colomba dei morti", fra bibbia gotica e sepulture franche', in Chiesa (ed.), *Paolo Diacono*, pp. 601–25, unsuccessfully searches for precedents among 'genti germaniche pagane' and 'populazioni delle steppe'.
[51] Ep. IX.102: 'illic populum ab infidelitate revocare, ac contendant a gentilium cultu suspendere'.
[52] 'gentilium varia hic idola fregit'. See U. Mazzini, 'Un epigrafe Lunigianese del secolo ottavo', *Giornale Storico della Lunigiana* 2 (1910), 153–60. Mazzini provided better and more complete readings of the damaged parts of the epitaph in 'L'epitaffio di Leodegar, vescovo di Luni del secolo VIII', *ibid.* 10 (1919), 81–111. His identification of the commemorated deceased as the bishop of Luni is strained, as are the arguments for the 'idols' being 'Lombard' (pp. 97–8).
[53] Note Liutprand 84, 'ad arborem quam rustici sanctivam vocant', and 85, concerning [h]arioli/ariolae, and the reference to the responsibilities of the *decanus* and *saltarius*, further suggesting a more rural environment for such practices. Liutprand uses language similar to the Roman council of 721, canon 12: Bognetti, 'S. Maria', p. 309. Cf. Gasparri *La cultura*, pp. 124–5. Other laws: Rothari 197, 198, 376 (witches), 368 (herbs). See V. Flint, *The Rise of Magic in Early Medieval Europe* (Oxford, 1991), pp. 6–8, 81, 204–5, 310–12.

The early Lombards and their settlement in Italy

and rhythms of the natural world.[54] Moreover, Italy's experience with the Greco-Roman pantheon and the forms of worship associated with it stretched far back before the time of Christ. Pagan customs and traditions were deeply rooted in the most Christianised parts of Italy. Pope Gregory could do little more than fulminate against Romans worshipping trees in nearby Terracina, nor could he prevent the practices of witchcraft, soothsaying or idol worship on the papal estates in Sicily, to mention nothing of the presence of insidious heresies such as Manicheism, Angellianism and, of course, Judaism.[55] Vestiges of paganism among some Lombards in the form of ritualistic practices constituted no real cultural barriers, for Italian religious culture was by no means uniform, and, as we shall see, the Lombard leadership was quick to appropriate late Roman symbols and trappings of power which had merged with Christian ceremonial centuries earlier.

THE LOMBARDS IN ITALY

Whatever doubts we might have about the religious affiliation of the majority of the Lombards who arrived in Italy in 568, the important point is that the first firmly established Lombard court, under the tutelage of the unquestionably Catholic Queen Theudelinda, became immediately involved in ecclesiastical politics and became the patron of some northern Italian churches. This seems at first difficult to square with the reports of hostile sources concerning the destruction caused by the Lombards' arrival, but is necessary to distinguish between the different phases of Lombard settlement in Italy: their initial entry and establishment under King Alboin (568–72) and his successor Cleph (572–4), the ten-year interregnum and Byzantine counter-attacks (574–84), the re-establishment of kingship under King Authari (584–90), and the court of King Agilulf and Queen Theudelinda (590–616) in Pavia.

After fifteen years of governing Italy as commander-in-chief, the now nonagenarian Narses had incurred the wrath of both the Italians and the imperial court at Constantinople for the excessive amount of wealth he had amassed. The story recorded by Paul, in which Narses sent baskets of Italian fruit and produce along with his invitation to the Lombards

---

54 Markus, *The End*, p. 206; and Markus, 'From Caesarius of Arles to Boniface: Christianity and paganism in Gaul', in J. Fontaine and J.N. Hillgarth (eds.), *The Seventh Century: Changes and Continuity* (London, 1992), pp. 154–72; Y. Hen, *Culture and Religion in Merovingian Gaul A.D. 481–751* (Leiden, 1995).
55 Terracina, Ep. VIII.19; Sicily, V.32 ('canterma'); XIV.1 and XI.33 (witches); III.59 (idols, Angelliores); V.13 (Manichees, Jews). Cf. Ep. I.17 (Narni).

in Pannonia, sounds suspiciously like a Greco-Roman historiographic topos, but earlier sixth-, seventh- and eighth-century sources also report Narses' invitation, some, like Paul, attributing the motive to the empress Sophia's threats and insults.[56] The more contemporary *Liber pontificalis* is perhaps our most trustworthy guide here, and the more suggestive for this study, for it also records *how* Narses invited the Lombards: he wrote them a letter.[57] The silence of the contemporary chroniclers, especially that of Gregory of Tours, suggests we are hearing the repeated echoes of a popular myth,[58] perhaps perpetuated by the Romans themselves, who could only conceive of losing a province in such terms. But it is possible that the imperial court at Constantinople sanctioned the initial settlement in northern Italy of Lombards as federate allies to repopulate and strengthen the Alpine passes of northern Italy, particularly against the Franks, whom Narses routed as late as 563 and who maintained a threatening presence on the northern borders. The rebellion and subsequent defeat in 566 of Sinduald and his Herulian army, whom Narses had employed to guard the Brenner Pass and Tirol valley since 553, meant a shortage of manpower to secure the region and the need to find a new source of military muscle.[59] The Lombards were an obvious choice: trusted allies of the empire for at least twenty years, they had proved themselves loyal and able in Narses' command against the Ostrogoths, their king Alboin had recently married the Frankish princess Clothsuinda, and they themselves were under pressure from the Avars. This is speculative, but it would explain the failure of contemporaries to describe the Lombard arrival as an invasion or to report the flight of refugee Italians, and the relative ease with which Alboin crossed the Alps and occupied the cities of Venetia in rapid succession and without bloodshed.[60] At this point Paul records the curious story that when Alboin came to Treviso on the march to Italy, the king was greeted by the bishop Felix, and subsequently re-confirmed

---

[56] Sophia's threats as a motive are recorded in Isidore, *Chron. maiora*, c. 402 (AA. XI, p. 476), and *Hav. Con. Chron.*, (AA. IX, p. 337). Fredegar, *Chron.* III.65. Otherwise the invitation is mentioned by Bede, *Chron. maiora*, c. 523 (using the *LP*); *Origo gentis*, c. 5, and Spanish continuator of Hydatius (AA. XI, p. 36). The chronicles of John of Biclar and Marius of Avenches fail to mention Narses' involvement.

[57] *LP* 63.3, ed. Duchesne, I, p. 305: 'scripsit genti Langobardorum ut venirent et possiderent Italiam'.

[58] Hodgkin, *Italy*, V, pp. 63–4, one of the first historians to consider the invitation story seriously: cf. L. Fauber, *Narses: Hammer of the Goths* (New York, 1990), pp. 177–83.

[59] *LP* 63.3, ed. Duchesne, I, p. 305; Agathias, *Historiae* I.20; II.7–9; Marius, *Chron.*, anno 566; *Excerpta Sangallensia* 710, anno 567 (MGH AA. IX.1, p. 335); *HL* II.3.

[60] See N. Christie, 'Invasion or invitation? The Longobard occupation of northern Italy, A.D. 568–569', *Romanobarbarica* 11 (1991), 79–108; and W. Pohl, 'L'armée romaine et les Lombards: stratégies militaires et politiques', in F. Vallet and M. Kazanski (eds.), *L'Armée romaine et les barbares du IIIe au VIIe siècle* (Rouen, 1993), pp. 291–6.

The early Lombards and their settlement in Italy

the church's property rights guaranteed by means of *suum pracmaticum*, that is, some type of royal charter or written instrument.[61] Such evidence, though scant, demonstrates Alboin's ability to communicate with a literate world on its own terms. It also lends weight to the notion that the Lombard entry into the Veneto region at least was a move sanctioned by imperial authorities. The flight of the patriarch of Aquileia to the island of Grado would suggest otherwise, though in this period relations between the patriarch and imperial authorities were poor, owing to the Three Chapters dispute. If Alboin was invited to occupy Veneto, relations must have broken down fast, for within the year he struck westwards into Liguria and met fierce resistance in Pavia, which endured a three-year siege, and was finally taken in 572, the same year in which Alboin, having taken most of Liguria, was killed by his wife Rosamund at the royal palace in Verona.[62]

It is worth asking just how many Lombards came with Alboin to Italy. A contemporary chronicler reports that Alboin came 'with his whole army, abandoning and scorching with fire his homeland Pannonia, and with women and all of his people he occupied Italy *in fara*'. The problematic reference to *fara* aside (here probably meaning some sort of kingroup), the notice suggests more of a migration of people than simply a band of warriors.[63] But exactly how many Lombards arrived with Alboin is an open question. Paul records that Alboin asked his old friends the Saxons to accompany him in occupying 'spacious Italy', to which the Saxons obliged by sending him 20,000 warriors 'together with their wives and children'.[64] Moreover, the Saxons were not the only people invited: Alboin arrived at the Italian border 'with all of his army and a multitude of mixed peoples',[65] including Gepids, Bulgars, Sarmartians, Pannonians,

---

[61] *HL* II.12, and note Waitz, MGH SRL, p. 79 n. 6. We may dismiss as fanciful the story recorded in the early ninth-century *Historia langobardorum codicis gothani* 5 (see below) that Alboin arranged a pact with the Avars concerning the possible return of the Lombards to Pannonia, up to 200 years later, with a *carta conscriptionis*. That a pact is also recorded by Paul, *HL* II.7, though not mentioning the 200-year period or charter, might further suggest an imperially sanctioned settlement in that Alboin was not confident of permanent settlement. Cf. W. Pohl, *Die Awaren: ein Steppenvolk in Mitteleuropa 567–822* (Munich, 1988), pp. 51–9.

[62] See A. Bracciotti, 'Il ruolo del Peredeo nell'assassinio di Alboino', *Romanobarbarica* 13 (1994–95), 99–123.

[63] Marius, *Chron.*, anno 569. On 'fara', below, pp. 106–7.

[64] *HL* II.6. But cf. III.7: 20,000 Saxon fighters perish against the Suevi, but another 6000 survive, swearing oaths of revenge. The Lombard contingent in the imperial armies numbered 2500 'good fighting men', with another 3000 fighting servants; Procopius, *Wars* VIII.26.12. Allied *foederati* were expected to have slaves , *CTh* 7.13.16. Cf. Heather, *Goths*, p. 325.

[65] *HL* II.8: '[Alboin] cum omni suo exercitu vulgique promiscui multitudine'. *Promiscuum vulgus* could refer both to mixed ethnic groups (as in the following passage of *HL* II.26) and to a mixed composition of people – in terms of different sexes, ages, etc. – within the same group.

Swabians, Noricans and other peoples whose places of settlement in Italy, according to Paul, were still named after them in his day.[66] From this evidence estimates have ranged from 80,000 to 200,000 adult males, hence up to 400,000 people *in toto*. But Paul's figure of the number of Saxons is itself unreliable, recorded more than two centuries after the event. The most optimistic assessments of the Ostrogothic army of the 530s and 540s give a figure of 25,000–30,000 fighting men, and therefore a round figure of 100,000 for the entire Ostrogothic population in Italy, the difficulties of ethnic labels notwithstanding.[67] Given their failure to conquer the entire peninsula, we might expect the number of people that came with Alboin to be less than this, say something of the order of 80,000, the figure which Victor of Vita recorded for the *total* number of Vandals, who crossed from Spain to Africa a century and half earlier, as opposed to Procopius' attribution of the same figure for the number for Vandal warriors.[68] Rumination on numbers is further frustrated by not knowing the population of Italy in this period. It has been suggested that the newcomers could not have exceeded more than 5 to 8 per cent of the population of the areas they occupied.[69] Whatever the demographic figures may have been, in their conquest and settlement of Italy the Lombards appear to have lived up to their Tacitian epithet: small in number, but undoubtedly effective.

By 571, the Lombards had pushed far enough south to establish the duchies of Spoleto and Benevento, and had made inroads into Tuscany. The death of Alboin in 572 appears to have unleashed hostilities that may have been kept in check under his obviously effective leadership. Under his successor, King Cleph, 'many powerful Roman men were killled by the sword, while others were exiled from Italy'.[70] With the murder of Cleph a year and a half later, the Lombard monarchy fell to pieces, and for the next ten years the Lombards were ruled by autonomous dukes. Our information at this point is even more fragmentary. What is clear is that many Lombard dukes and leaders sided with the

---

[66] *HL* II.26.
[67] K. Hannestad, 'Les forces militaires d'après la guerre gothique de Procope', *Classica et Medievalia* 21 (1960), 136–83; endorsed by Heather, *Goths*, pp. 164–5, 322–6, but cf. Brown, 'Everyday life', p. 82, putting the Gothic population at 10,000 (following S. Lazard). Amory, *People and Identity*, avoids figures altogether.
[68] Victor of Vita, *Historia persecutionis vandalicae* I.2.; Procopius, *Wars* I.5.8; cf. C. Courtois, *Les Vandales et L'Afrique* (Paris, 1955), pp. 215–17; Goffart, *Barbarians*, pp. 231–4. From this purely speculative figure we may subtract the 20,000-plus Saxons who were forced to leave Italy; *HL* III.16.
[69] Wickham, *EMI*, p. 65. Cf. Christie, *Lombards*, p. 53.
[70] *HL* II.31; Marius, anno 572: 'plures seniores et mediocres ab ipso interfecti sunt'.

Byzantines, many of them ended up fighting for the empire in the east.[71] Duke Grasulf of Friuli and later his son Grisulf both appear to have switched sides several times, and we learn of several other Lombard leaders who fought for the republic. It has even been suggested that the duchies of Spoleto and Benevento were originally founded by Lombard leaders in Byzantine pay as a foil to the Lombard monarchy in the north.[72] This was certainly possible, given the demonstrated ability of Lombard dukes and war-leaders to negotiate their own terms with imperial authorities.

DEAR GRASULF

The *voltafaccie* of some Lombard dukes and leaders demonstrates their ability to deal with the diplomatic procedures of the empire, and this involved an acquaintance with the role of literate communications in complex and delicate political arrangements. An example of such communications is a letter written some time between 571 and 581, by Gogo, the royal advisor to the Frankish king Childebert II, who writes on behalf of the king to the Lombard duke Grasulf of Friuli, urging Grasulf to confirm his alliance with the Franks and the emperor to oust the Lombards ('infestantes') from Italy.[73] The rhetoric of the letter can be obscure, but it is full of technical terms of imperial diplomacy: *ligationes* had moved between the two barbarian courts, and Roman ambassadors were waiting in Austrasia for Grasulf's reply lest the duke delay in replying directly to the emperor; *placita* had to be drawn up, and their provisions (*capitula*) scrutinised and agreed upon; correct procedure was important ('sicut ordo rationalibus exegit'), in order that the aim of a 'perpetuae pacis securitas' could be achieved, 'utriusque partibus opportunis intercurrentibus'. Although the letter was written at the Frankish court, its language and intent 'highlights the fact that within a decade of their invasion, Lombard dukes were supposed to be perfectly capable of dealing

---

[71] John of Ephesus records that a force of 60,000 Lombards fought in Syria in 575: *Historiae ecclesiasticae* VI.13. The figure is surely an exaggeration, but the presence in Syria seems feasible, given Lombards in active service in Persia and Thrace.

[72] As argued by Bognetti, 'Tradizione longobarda e politica bizantina nelle origini del ducato di Spoleto', *L'età*, III, pp. 439–76. Cf. S. Gasparri, *I duchi longobardi* (Rome, 1978), pp. 86–7.

[73] MGH Ep. III, p. 152. *PLRE* 3A, p. 545. The date of the letter is uncertain. Gogo died in 581, *PLRE* 3A, p. 541. W. Goffart, 'Byzantine policy in the west under Tiberius II and Maurice: the pretenders Hermenegild and Gundovald (579–585)', *Traditio* 13 (1957), 73–118, at pp. 74–82, dates it to 571, but this seems too early: cf. B. Bachrach, *Anatomy of a Little War: A Diplomatic and Military History of the Gundovald Affair (568–586)* (Boulder, 1994), pp. 155–9, who dates it to the reign of the Emperor Tiberius (577–582).

with sophisticated diplomatic procedures and the technical terms of Latin letters of state'.[74] While it would be hazardous to speak of a Friulian court culture, Friulian Lombards were proud of their traditions, and their ability to exact tribute (*pensio*) from settlements of the Slavs from the time of Gisulf (d. 614) to the accession of Duke Ratchis to the royal throne (744), suggesting a degree of administrative stability.[75]

We can only guess as to other ducal seats and the contours of their administrative mechanisms in this early period. Duke Ariulf of Spoleto (*c*. 591–601) wrote a menacing letter to Pope Gregory, taunting that the Tuscan city of Soana had now come over to his side. Gregory promptly forwarded Ariulf's letter to the Byzantine officers in charge of the region, and informed them of Ariulf's present whereabouts.[76] Gregory himself had been informed of Ariulf's movements by a letter from a certain Aldio, *vir magnificus*, probably a Lombard who later became *magister militum* of Fiesole or Perugia, and further wrote to the pope concerning the lack of clergy in the area.[77] Sharing similar pastoral concern was the Lombard Ansfrid, who wrote to Gregory from Bagnoreggio to request the ordination of a deacon whom Ansfrid thought worthy of episcopal office, though Gregory remained suspicious.[78] Another Lombard turncoat, Gulfaris, *magister militum*, received praise from Gregory for his efforts to win back Three Chapters schismatics in Istria,[79] and we know of other Lombard military men who received letters from the pope.[80] One thinks also of Nordulf, the Lombard-cum-Roman 'patricius' who was employed by the Byzantines to fight on behalf of the empire. Owing to a lack of pay, Nordulf's troops switched sides in 592 and joined forces with those of Duke Ariulf to menace the pope, but Nordulf himself appears to have returned to Constantinople where he became a chief adviser to the emperor on Italian affairs, his word counting for more than that of Gregory.[81] We know more about these Lombard *condottieri* than we do

---

[74] W. Pohl, 'The Empire and the Lombards: treaties and negotiations in the sixth century', in Pohl (ed.), *Kingdoms of the Empire: The Integration of Barbarians in Late Antiquity* (Leiden, New York and Cologne, 1997), pp. 75–133, at p. 101.

[75] Paul, *HL* IV.38, 50, 52, and Fredegar, *Chron.* IV:49. Grasulf I and II, *PLRE* 3A, p. 545.

[76] Ep. II.33 (July 592). That Ariulf was pagan, see Paul, *HL* IV.15, 16; Fredegar, *Chron.* IV.20. Ariulf may be the same mentioned by Theophylact Simocatta I.9.7–8 as fighting for the Roman army in Persia in 582. *PLRE* 3A, pp. 119–20.

[77] Ep. II.32; IX.102; Aldio, *PLRE* 3A, pp. 40–1; Brown, *Gentlemen*, p. 73.

[78] Ep. X.13 (*c*. 600): 'Gloriosus filius noster Ansfrid ad nos scripta transmisit indicans.' Gregory's reply ('sicut et suprascrito Ansfrid . . . scripsimus') is lost. Ansfrid, *PLRE* 3A, p. 84.

[79] Ep. IX.160. *PLRE* 3A, p. 563. He was probably the same Duke Ulfari who rebelled against Agilulf: Paul, *HL* IV.3; *PLRE* 3B, p. 1387.

[80] Gudiscalcus, duke of Campania, *PLRE* 3A, p. 561; Gregory, Ep. X.5; Guduin, *PRLE* 3A, pp. 561–2; Gregory, Ep. XIX.10, possibly the same mentioned by Theophylact, see note 82.

[81] Ep. II.45; V.36, 'novi, quoniam Nordulfus plus est creditum quam mihi'. *PLRE* 3B, pp. 949–50.

The early Lombards and their settlement in Italy

of the Lombards who continued to bat for the *gens*,[82] but this is still very little.

None of this is meant to suggest that these Lombard mercenaries were in any way 'men of letters', or that they were even literate, in the sense that they could either read or write with any fluency. Their own experience of literacy may have been limited to telling secretaries what to say and to say it in the appropriate manner. But secretarial skills were needed of a calibre that enabled compositions which balanced florid phraseology and technical vocabulary for diplomatic communications. They were probably needed at the more routine, quotidian level also. Any service in imperial forces exposed professional soldiers to the necessities of compiling lists and keeping records to ensure the equal distribution of pay, provisions and duties.[83] Of course, mercenary groups functioned on a much smaller scale. We have no idea how many men leaders like Ariulf or Nordulf had under their command at one time, but there seems little reason to rule out some use of basic, pragmatic literacy for methods of account keeping. But more importantly, these rulers moved in a world which valued literate communication beyond merely functional usage. Drotculf, a Suebian who had been captured by the Lombards when young and was later made duke of Brescello, was another who, perhaps not surprisingly, switched sides to fight for the Romans. Despite being defeated by Authari's troops at Brescello, Drotculf was an effective and dedicated soldier. He regained Classe from Duke Faroald of Spoleto, and when the three-year peace between Lombards and the exarch was signed in 584/5, he served as a subordinate commander (ὑποστρατεγός) in Thrace against the Avars. By 598, he was asking Pope Gregory for recommendations to help him gain a similar commission in Africa. The imperial authorities were grateful enough to record his brave deeds and

---

[82] Guduin: Theophylact, *Historiae* VII.2.12; VIII.5.6; Adobin, Aloin and Iugildus Grusingus: Gregory, Ep. II.7; *PLRE* 3A, p. 16; Authari: Fredegar, *Chron.* IV.45; *PLRE* 3A, p. 158, possibly the same 'Auctarit' whose troops served under Duke Ariulf: Gregory, Ep. II.45; Maurisio: Paul, *HL* IV.8; *PLRE* 3B, p. 863. A good synopsis of their activities is Brown, *Gentlemen*, pp. 70–5. Other ducal rebellions mentioned by Paul, such as Zangrulf of Verona (*HL* IV.13), Ulfari of Treviso (*HL* IV.3), and the 'catholic' Gaidoald of Trent, *HL* IV.27, may have been related to intrigue with the Romans.

[83] Vegetius, *De re militari* II.19. See G.R. Watson, 'Documentation in the Roman army', in H. Temporini *et al.*, *Aufstieg und Niedergang des römischer Welt* II.1 (Berlin, 1974), pp. 493–507; R.O. Fink, *Roman Military Records on Papyrus* (Cleveland, 1971); A.K. Bowman and J.D. Thomas, *The Vindolanda Writing Tablets*, Tabulae Vindolandenses 2 (London, 1994); R. Marichal, *Les Ostraca de Bu Njem*, Libya Antiqua, Suppl. 9 (Tripoli, 1992). C.B. Welles *et al.*, *The Excavations at Dura-Europas. Final Report V, part 1: The Parchments and the Papyri* (New Haven, 1959). Cf. M. Mersiowsky, 'Regierungspraxis und Schriftlichkeit im Karolingerreich: Das Fallbeispiel der Mandate und Briefe', in R. Schieffer, *Schriftkultur und Reichsverwantung unter den Karolingern*, Nordrhein-Westfälische Akademie der Wissenschaften Abhandlungen 97 (Opladen, 1996), pp. 110–66.

noble character, as well as his long beard, in an epitaph of thirteen elegiac couplets, situated in the church of San Vitale in Ravenna, Drotculf's chosen place of rest, where Paul the Deacon read it 200 years later.[84] Epitaphs for soldiers which proudly record their military prowess were not new in Italy: in the 560s the *magister militum* Asbad was commemorated in the church of Pavia because he 'expelled the tribes and gave the Gothic Alps back to the rule of Latium', and later the Lombards appear to have taken up the tradition, witnessed in the eighth-century epitaph of Duke Audoald of Liguria.[85] Drotculf's career and epitaph, as well as the careers of the Lombard mercenaries and dukes on the look-out for their own interests, demonstrate the relative ease with which individual Lombard leaders could negotiate, and even appropriate, literate traditions of late Roman culture, regardless of their ethnicity.

THE BEGINNINGS OF THE LOMBARD STATE

Pressure from the Byzantine and Frankish forces appears to have been the motive for a return to kingship under Authari (584–90), who spent much of his reign consolidating Lombard power as a necessary measure of defence against a series of attacks by the Byzantine–Frankish alliance in 584, 588 and 590. The failure of the last of these represents the withdrawal of Frankish troops from Italy in exchange for an annual tribute and recognition of their overlordship, while official Byzantine recognition of the Lombard state was not achieved until 680. In order to re-establish the kingship, Lombard dukes surrendered half of their property to the king, and hence provided a solid basis of landed wealth to ensure the monarchy's stability against wealthy, powerful and recalcitrant dukes in the future. Fiscal property in the form of *curtes* appears to have been organised according to the late Roman city circumscriptions and their surrounding territories.[86] Perhaps originally denoting a particular estate or block of holdings, the term *curtis regia* in our legal sources appears also to denote an administrative centre with a gastald as its chief officer, responsible for the collection of rents and dues owed by the lesser officials (*actores*, *scariones*) stationed in various estates or regions. They also functioned as judicial centres in terms of a local 'court', responsible for

---

[84] Drotculf (Drocton), Paul, *HL* III.18, 19; Theophylact Simocatta, *Historiae* II.17.9; Gregory, Ep. IX.9; *PLRE* 3A, pp. 425–7. Cf. Gasparri, *I duchi*, p. 54. Drotculf's house in Ravenna later became the episcopal palace; Agnellus, c. 86. Paul's phrase, 'ulciscendae suae captivitatis', is ambiguous: cf. Hodgkin, *Italy*, V, pp. 242–3, and Gasparri, *I duchi*, p. 54.
[85] Panazza, no. 80, see below, p. 258.
[86] See S. Gasparri, 'Il regno longobardo in Italia. Struttura e funzionamento di uno stato altomedievale', in P. Cammarosano and S. Gasparri (eds.), *Langobardia* (Udine, 1990), pp. 237–305, at pp. 241–62.

hearing cases, and exacting and receiving fines to be tallied up and consigned to the royal fisc.[87] There were *curtes ducales* too, in terms of both chunks of property and administrative centres, but we rarely hear of them in our sources beyond the references to such in the quasi-independent duchies of Spoleto and Benevento.[88]

Paul tells us that, after the death of Cleph, and therefore at the beginning of the ten-year interregnum, 'many Roman nobles were killed through greed. The rest (*reliqui*) were divided amongst their guests (*per hospites*) and were made tributary (*tributarii*), so that they paid a third part of their produce to the Lombards.'[89] This sounds much more organised than it probably was, but clearly the Lombard settlement employed the tried and trusted 'technique of accommodation' known as *hospitalitas*, in which barbarian troops received one to two thirds of land or tax assessments in return for their military service.[90] In the Lombard case, Paul provides the particulars that the Lombards received payment in kind for their sustenance, and he is probably drawing upon the relatively contemporary, but now lost, chronicle of Secundus of Trent for his information: that is, if he did not pilfer his terms from Gregory of Tours.[91] Scholars in the past have tended to misread 'the rest' (*reliqui*) as referring to the entire Roman population of Italy, thus envisaging a wholesale subjugation of ethnic Romans to their barbarian overlords. But future developments, not to mention the rules of Latin grammar, would suggest otherwise.

Paul did not conceive of the settlement of the Lombards in terms of the division of land, as he noted for the Suevi.[92] The reallocation of resources to Lombard leaders, rather than the confiscation or appropriation of land, suggests a greater degree of co-operation between the

---

[87] In some laws *curtis regia* (or *regis*) appears to mean Pavia, e.g. Rothari 221, and others local courts, Rothari 264. Cf. Rothari 15, 153, 158–60, 163 , 171, 182, 183, 185, 186, 195–7. Note Rothari 32, 33, and 269, 375, where *curtis* is used to refer to private estates. See Gasparri, 'Il regno longobardo', pp. 252–4; Harrison, *Early State*, pp. 62–6, 105–7.

[88] For *curtes ducales* in the north: Cremona, CDL III.14 (739); Brescia, CDL III.44 (772). This last speaks of property 'que pertenuerant ex iura curtis nostrae regie que ex iura curtis docalis' in Austria, Neustria, Spoleto, Fermo, Osimo and Benevento. See Gasparri, 'Il regno longobardo', p. 261 n. 54. Other mentions of *curtes ducales* date to the Carolingian period: C.R. Bruhl, *Fodrum, Gistum, Servitium Regis* (Cologne, 1968), pp. 363–6. For Spoleto, see S. Gasparri, 'Il ducato di Spoleto. Istituzioni, poteri, gruppi dominanti', *Atti IX CISAM* (Spoleto, 1983), pp. 77–122, at pp. 89–93.

[89] *HL* II.31–2.

[90] W. Goffart, *Barbarians and Romans: The Techniques of Accommodation* (Princeton, 1980), esp. pp. 188–216.

[91] K. Gardiner, 'Paul the Deacon and Secundus of Trent', in B. Croke and A. Emmet (eds.), *History and Historians in Late Antiquity* (Sydney, 1983), pp. 147–53. Cf. Gregory, *Historiae* IX.30, and Pohl, 'The Empire', pp. 120–1.

[92] *HL* III.8, a point made by Pohl, 'The Empire', pp. 112–31, the best discussion of Paul's famously cryptic passages, and whom I follow here.

Lombards and the late Roman aristocracy than our hostile papal and Byzantine sources would have us believe. Under such practical arrangements the establishment of Lombard rule caused no major upheaval in the social fabric of Italy. Interestingly, however, Paul's comments suggest that these arrangements were made by individual dukes acting on behalf of their own interests, though Paul's narrative is rarely chronologically precise, and it is more likely that the accommodation was negotiated and achieved under Alboin or Cleph. Fredegar records that after the death of Cleph the Lombards paid annual tribute to the Franks up until the accession of Agilulf's son Adaloald (616–26), and it is difficult to imagine Lombard dukes during the interregnum *instituting* a process in which they pooled together ever year to buy off their northern neighbours, rather than continuing a process established earlier by the centralised authority of a king.[93] The whole scenario is further complicated for us by Paul's comments concerning the re-establishment of kingship under Authari:

But the Lombards, having been under the rule of the dukes for ten years, unanimously elected as their king Authari, son of the above mentioned Cleph… In these times, for the restoration of the kingship, the dukes then gave one half of their property to the use of the king, in order to support the king himself, his retainers and those who were required to accompany him in virtue of the various offices which had been assigned to them. But the oppressed people (*populi adgravati*) were divided amongst the Lombard guests (*per hospites partiuntur*).[94]

What precisely is meant by 'the oppressed people'? One tendency has been to interpret the phrase as a comment on the 'fate of the Romans' in Italy. Taking a pessimistic view of the impact of the Lombards on Italy, it is thought that all Italo-Romans of free status were reduced to some sort of formal state of servitude, suffering a considerable loss of economic and personal freedom, and rendering such privileges as exclusive to the Lombard warrior elites.[95] This image of Italians as 'a dispersed people who have no name' certainly appealed to Risorgimento aspirations, and made for bad theatre.[96] But it is difficult to imagine how or why the entire population was divided up and distributed among the relatively few Lombard leaders for economic benefit, and difficult to reconcile this

---

[93] Fredegar, *Chron.* IV.43, but cf. IV.68, which suggests the overlordship continued for some time later. Paul, *HL* III.17; IV.13, 30 barely hints at the tribute.

[94] *HL* III.16.

[95] For example, Hartmann, *Geschichte Italiens*, II.1, pp. 41–58; Hodgkin, *Italy*, V, pp. 188–96; Bognetti, 'S. Maria', pp. 110–12; P. Delogu, 'Il regno longobardo', in G. Galasso (ed.), *Storia d'Italia*, I (Tuin, 1980) pp. 29–32, but cf. Delogu, 'Longobardi e Romani: altre congetture', in P. Cammarosano and P. Gasparri (eds.), *Langobardia* (Udine, 1990), pp. 111–64, at pp. 113–20.

[96] A. Manzoni, *Adelchi* (Milan, 1991), III. coro, 66; see N. Everett, 'Barbarian ethnicity and Italian history in Alessandro Manzoni's *Adelchi*', *Convivio: Journal of Ideas in Italian Studies* 6:2 (2000), 112–27.

with later evidence which tends to rule out such tightly drawn ethnic distinctions.

Another interpretation is that the term *populi adgravati* refers to the serfs and late Roman *coloni* who were by law and custom tied to the land which was, reading Paul's narrative closely, then handed over by Lombard dukes to the newly established royal fisc. In this scenario, the tenants were relocated and their rents were allocated to a particular Lombard leader or duke.[97] This would have involved a massive social upheaval of the underclasses, and there is no reason why land given to the royal fisc should be cleared of servile dependants. Ignoring the link implied in Paul's narrative between the property handed over to the king and the division of people among 'guests', and still reading *populi adgravati* as unfree tenants, a more likely explanation is that the same Roman landlords of the settlement of 573 were forced to relinquish their settled bondsmen to be divided amongst new Lombard *hospites*, a younger generation of Lombard leaders on the make.[98] But our text does not explicitly say that either. Moreover, if the *populi adgravati* were the bound cultivators who were previously subject to Roman landowners and now Lombard overlords, then the notion of continuity of tax obligations is a problematic one, for it needs to explain how the *reliqui nobiles* were still liable to pay tax to kings and dukes, having now lost a substantial amount of income.

Another reading of *populi adgravati* as the 'people burdened [by tax]' suggests a more coherent alternative.[99] The *populi adgravati* of the post-interregnum settlement need not refer to anything other than the *tributarii* mentioned in the first passage: that is to say, the tax payers in the first instance were simply reassigned to different *hospites* in the re-establishment of kingship under Authari. This redistribution of resources would have been necessary after ten years of unchecked ducal ambitions in order to strike a balance of power between the dukes and the king. If we take *populi adgravati* to include also the citizen population of Italy, which the term *populi* seems to imply, then it need not follow that free cultivators were subject to any loss of liberty. The people 'burdened' by

---

[97] See P.S. Leicht, *Studi sulla proprietà fondaria nel medioevo* (Padua, 1907), pp. 14–20; F. Schneider, *Die Reichsverwaltung in Toskana von der Gründung des Langobardenreiches bis zum Ausgang der Staufer* (Rome, 1914), pp. 193–200.
[98] Goffart, *Barbarians*, p. 187, would equate *populi adgravati* with the *agri cum mancipiis* of *Lex Burgundionum* 54, the potential 'fugitives' of *Codex Eurici* 277.2, and the *servi* (or *condumae cum cespitis suis*) in eighth-century Lombard charters, but clearly such references, distant from one another in time and place, denote completely different social relations and categories, and there is no use of anything akin to *populi adgravati* in Lombard charters. Cf. Goffart, 'From Roman taxation to medieval seigneurie: three notes', *Speculum* 47 (1972), 165–87, 373–94, at pp. 178–9 nn. 68, 70.
[99] As suggested by F. Thibault, 'L'impôt direct et la propriété foncière dans la royaume des Lombards', *Nouvelle Revue Historique de Droit Français et Etranger* 28 (1904), 53–79; see further Delogu, 'Longobardi e Romani', pp. 113–20; Pohl, 'The Empire', pp. 113–19.

taxes now simply transferred their tax obligations to Lombard overlords. This involved neither any loss of personal freedom nor economic disadvantage. The re-establishment of the Lombard state, after ten years of the interregnum, required more resources than the grand proprietors or *nobiles* made *tributarii* in the first instance under Cleph could provide. The *tertiae* from these estates had probably from the first been found to be insufficient; many of the estates would have been abandoned or suffering neglect after the Gothic wars, or were subsequently destroyed, damaged, or appropriated in full or in part, by ambitious Lombardced. The new distribution of resources, which required the dukes to render half of the produce to the royal fisc, required also a reorganisation of forms of income which reached further down the social scale beyond the grand proprietors and into smaller-scale freeholders.[100]

To accept this hypothesis, we have also to accept a considerable degree of stability and continuity of land-ownership among the Roman population. This means that four or five years after the invasion, Cleph could target grand proprietors, as opposed to smaller freeholders, and that these latter were still around in sufficient numbers and still relatively secure thirteen years after the invasion, their properties having remained intact throughout the ten years of the interregnum. While the destruction caused by the interregnum would seem to challenge the idea of a more extensive and systematic 'accommodation' between conquerors and conquered, we need also to consider the extent to which the re-establishment of kingship was a *desideratum* of all sectors of the population. The reallocation of tax revenues was a solution to social instability that satisfied the aspirations both of the Lombard warriors, who desired ready income to maintain their followers and equipment, and of the free Italian population, who retained their property rights and required a degree of social stability for the necessary exploitation of agricultural resources. As Pope Gregory remarked to King Agilulf in 598, the newly ratified peace treaty between

---

[100] J. Durliat, 'Le salaire de la paix sociale dans les royaumes barbares', in H. Wolfram and A. Schwarcz (eds.), *Anerkennung und Integration* (Vienna, 1988), pp. 21–72, at p. 49, and, at length, Durliat, *Les Finances publiques de Dioclétien aux Carolingiens (284–889)* (Sigmaringen, 1990), would go one step further here in reading all references in the two passages of Paul as references to taxation only: hence the *reliqui* were not Roman landowners burdened with the imposition of new taxes, but were those responsible for the collection and distribution of taxes, the *possessores* or 'rentiers de l'impôt', who were entitled to a small percentage of the taxes they collected for the state. But there are major problems with this interpretation of the late Roman tax system: see W. Liebeschütz, 'Cites, taxes and the accommodation of the barbarians', in Pohl (ed.), *Kingdoms of the Empire*, pp. 135–52, and more thoroughly, C. Wickham, 'La chute de Rome n'aura pas lieu', *Le Moyen Age* 99:1 (1993), 107–26. The language of Paul's text, 'reliqui [*nobiles* or, less convincingly, *populi*] per hospites divisi', suggests a direct relationship between Romans and 'guests', with no mention of a third party of *curiales* responsible for tax collection and distribution, and Paul specifically refers to tributaries, not tribute: cf. Goffart, *Barbarians*, pp. 184–5.

the Lombards and the Byzantines was necessary for both parties, for there was no gain from shedding 'the blood of the poor peasants (*rustici*), from whose labour we both profit'.[101]

The use of some form of taxation in the Lombard kingdom constitutes no anomaly in the history of Germanic successor kingdoms in the west. In the Visigothic kingdoms of both Gaul then Spain, 'Romani' continued to pay the land tax to the king which was previously owed to the state, perhaps up until the end of the seventh century, and the land tax was alive and well in Francia south of the Loire in the late sixth century, as Gregory of Tours attests.[102] Rothari's Edict, promulgated in 643, mentions nothing about taxes, and we can presume that any remnants of the land tax system were by then negligible, as they were to become in eighth-century Byzantine Italy, where the army became reliant on holding land for its sustenance.[103] But we are still left with the impression that, in the initial stages of settlement, the Lombards were beneficiaries of a financial arrangement based on the fiscal structures of late Roman Italy. When the Lombards wished to remember their entry into Italy in the solemn manner of a tribal history, they did so by reference to the indiction: 'Alboin, king of the Lombards, moved from Pannonia in the month of April, at Easter, in the first indiction. By the second indiction they began to plunder Italy. On the third indiction Alboin was made lord of Italy.'[104]

The survival of some type of redistribution of resources based on the late Roman tax system, at least in the initial stage of the Lombard settlement, has two important implications. First, it suggests a greater degree of co-operation between Italians and their new overlords than a literal reading of Paul's passages would otherwise have us believe. Second, it suggests a greater degree of administrative activity, both at the centre of power and among the local elites from whom the taxes, or rents, were collected. We should not expect this to have involved any high degree of literacy on behalf of those who collected the goods. Lists of names and the amounts owed, of the type we find in early seventh-century Spain written on slate, would have been sufficient.[105] Taxation usually involves more

---

[101] Ep. IX.66; included by Paul, *HL* IV.9.
[102] Receswinth (653–672), *Lex Visig.* V.4.19, and cf. P. D. King, *Law and Society in the Visigothic Kingdom* (Cambridge, 1972), pp. 62–77; Gregory, *Historiae* III.36; IV.2; V.28; 34; VII.15, 23; IX.30; X.71, and cf. W. Goffart 'Old and new in Merovingian taxation', *Past and Present* 96 (1982), 3–21.
[103] Wickham, *EMI*, p. 40; Brown, *Gentlemen*, pp. 86–8, 113–15.
[104] *Origo gentis*, 5. Indictions are not used elsewhere in the text, and this is the only instance of 'real' historical time, otherwise restricted to calculating the years of a king's reign.
[105] In I. Velázquez Soriano (ed.), *El Latín de las pizarras visigóticas*, 2vols. (Madrid, 1989). E.g. no. 45: the sides of the slate list some 24 and 35 names and holdings respectively, in a simple formula:

records than are strictly necessary, and both landlords and the Lombard government had incentives to keep well-documented accounts of the amounts owed and paid.

The evidence for the exaction of taxes in the Lombard kingdom is fairly thin and much later, all pertaining to the eighth century. We learn from a royal charter of 744 that the city of Piacenza was accustomed to paying an annual tribute of 30 pounds of soap to the royal government in Pavia. We do not know if such tribute was unique to Piacenza, or whether every city of the realm, as the focal point for the *curtis regia* in that region, was subject to render a certain amount of tribute to Pavia every year.[106] A document ascribed to Liutprand sets out carefully the tolls and mooring-dues to be collected from the inhabitants of Comacchio (near Ravenna) at various ports along the Po river.[107] A royal charter of 772 refers to taxes on the exploitation of uncultivated fiscal lands, as well as public corvée work, transport duties, tolls and customs fees, and some form of tribute paid by the *vici* to the *curtis regia* of the region.[108] Yet another, later charter of Charlemagne suggests that *vici* such as Sacco in Friuli customarily paid the central government in Pavia directly, without the intermediary of the *curtis regia*.[109] A later diploma of Louis the Pious refers to annual *pensiones* and *donationes* that were 'received at the royal court of the Lombard king, be it that of Lombard Tuscany or the duchy of Spoleto',[110] but we do

---

'Murildi sestarium I, Domnus magior sestarium I', etc., with some variation, 'unum Aiutor, Feruodus in alio cusso', etc. That the list refers to rents owed by dependants seems confirmed by the occasional obscure reference to a 'dominus'. Likewise, no. 46 lists some 38 or so names alongside phrases such as 'Vadentinus s[e]s[tarium] I ad modio et quartare', 'Ranila ad modio et quartare min[us] uncia'. There are also lists of the distribution of produce: 'notitia de ceuaria' (nos. 52, 96, the last of which uses '*solidi*' as a money of account), and 'notitia de casios' (no. 11, which appears to refer to the payment of cheese, cf. nos. 77 and 93). Other lists may have served similar purposes: 'notitiae pecoris' or of animals in general, which list their sex and age, and refer to them as payment of some kind: nos. 53, 54, 97 (these last two definitely refer to payments, revealed by the use of verbs such as *dedi*, *ispendit*, *consignemus*, etc.). Lists of furniture, nos. 49, 50, 51, 102. See further Velázquez Soriano, pp. 607 no. 641, 608 no. 644.

[106] CDL III.18. Brühl, *Fodrum*, p. 387, a Piacentine soap 'Handwerksgenossenschaft'.
[107] The *Pactus Commacinus*, ed. in Hartmann, *Wirtschaftgeschichte*, pp. 123–4; trans. Balzaretti, 'Cities, emporia', pp. 219–20.
[108] CDL III.44: 'Verum tamen concedimus per ipsa monasteria omnes scufias publicas et angarias atque operas et dationes vel collectas seu toleneo et seliquatico de singulas mercatoras et portoras.' *Scufias* = *excubias*, corvée services, cf. CDL 94, 223; Gasparri, 'Il regno longobardo', p. 268; *angariae* = public service, involving transport? Cf. Niermeyer, *Lexicon*, pp. 43–4. The charter also mentions that the sons and daughters of the *arimannae mulieres* who have joined with slaves of the monastery, and whose *mundii* are now property of the state 'secundum edicti tinore' (cf. Rothari 221, Liutprand 24), to be handed over to the monastery, their *mundium* now valued at six *solidi per caput*.
[109] MGH Dip. Kar. I, n. 134 (781). Cf. Gasparri, 'Il regno longobardo', p. 268, and Brühl, *Fodrum*, pp. 385–6.
[110] MGH Cap. II. 172 (817): 'censum et pensionem seu ceteras donationes quae annuatim in palatium regis Langobardorum sive de Tuscia Langobardorum sive de ducato Spoletino'.

not know of what these payments consisted, or how regular they were. Likewise, it is difficult to discern whether the reference to a tithe owed by the church of Aquileia to the central government in a diploma of Charlemagne refers to a practice instituted by the Carolingians upon conquest of Italy, or to a norm already established by Lombard leaders.[111] That the central government was aware of the exigencies of a poll tax is confirmed by the actions of Aistulf against the duchy of Rome, when he broke the forty-year truce he had made with the papacy after only four months, and imposed an 'honerosum tributum' on the inhabitants of Rome, consisting of one gold solidus *per caput*.[112] No such poll tax had existed in the Roman empire since the early fourth century: clearly the exigencies of a poll tax were not forgotten in Italy.[113] A little later (*c.* 768–72), the patriarch of Grado complained to the pope that the Lombards, by order of their king, were collecting taxes in kind (wheat and animals) from the church's properties, so that clergy and dependants on those lands were forced to serve two masters.[114]

In sum, our eighth-century sources provide testimony to several instances in which the wealth was directed from local society towards the central administration of the kingdom, whether it be from a city and its *curtis regia* (Piacenza) to the capital, from the duchies (Spoleto) or churches and church lands (Grado) to the *palatium regis*, from localities (*vici*) to the ducal or royal fisc (Sacco), the collection of fees and licences for the exploitation of public resources (San Salvatore, *Pactus Commacinus*), or a poll tax levied directly on conquered cities (Rome). These examples might be little more than temporary measures to meet needs created by particular circumstances: Aistulf's Roman poll tax, or the exaction of taxes from properties within the Aquileiese diocese of Grado, may be seen in punitive terms of military conquest and tribute. But it would also be unwise to deny the possibility that these practices stem from late Roman fiscal arrangements which the Lombards developed and adapted to meet the need of regular income to pay personnel and functionaries of state administration, as well as supplementary expenditure for military campaigns.

---

[111] MGH Dip. Kar. I, n. 174 (792).

[112] *LP* I, 94, p. 441: 'per unumquemque scilicet caput singulare auri solidos annue auferre iniabat [Aistulf] et iurisdictione civitatem hanc Romanam vel subiacentes ei castra subdere indignanter asserebat'.

[113] See the editors' introductory comments to *P. Oxy.* LV.3789. C.R. Brühl, 'Zentral- und Finanzverwaltung im Franken- und im Langobardenreich', *Settimane* 20 (Spoleto, 1973), 61–94, at pp. 91–3, suggests that Aistulf was here following a Roman model; but cf. Gasparri, 'Il regno longobardo', p. 267.

[114] MGH Ep. III, pp. 711–13. Ep. 19.

THE THREE CHAPTERS DISPUTE AND LOMBARD–CHURCH RELATIONS

In 551 Justinian convened an ecumenical council in Constantinople which condemned the work of three theologians who had previously been considered shining examples of Chalcedonian orthodoxy. Throughout the west, the news was received badly. In Italy, the duty of protest fell naturally to the papacy, but after some serious brow-beating by the emperor, Pope Vigilius caved in to the imperial will, and supported the decisions of the council. The north Italian churches of Italia *annonaria*, under the jurisdiction of the two metropolitan sees of Aquileia and Milan, broke from communion with the papacy for its acquiescence.

The Three Chapters dispute may have been 'an abstruse debate over the orthodoxy of three theological tracts',[115] yet arguably it also 'threatened the entire organisation of Christendom'.[116] By the eighth century, no one seemed to know what the dispute was about: Paul the Deacon clearly had little idea.[117] Its effect in Italy, however, was profound. In demonstrating the papacy's subordination to an emperor looking increasingly eastward, the schism undoubtedly contributed to the lack of resistance to Lombard rule, and the success with which the Lombards established themselves in north Italy.[118] The threats and strong-arm tactics employed by the papacy, with the help of the exarch of Ravenna, against the Aquileiese church only made its Istrian suffragans dig in their heels. In 591 the emperor Maurice wrote to Pope Gregory and ordered the pope to cease harassing the Aquileiese schismatics, reminding him that his actions are only serving to exacerbate the 'praesens rerum Italiacarum confusio'.[119] The conflict resulted in the creation of a pro-Roman 'new Aquileia' in Grado, whilst 'old Aquileia', defending its loyalty to decisions of the council of Chalcedon, sought the support of the Lombard king.[120] The situation got worse. 'Under the most severe threats by the Greeks', wrote the Archbishop John of old Aquileia to King Agilulf (c. 607), who with Duke Gisulf of Friuli had supported John's election, 'the Istrian bishops were dragged by force to Ravenna where they were denied the

---

[115] Wickham, *EMI*, p. 35.
[116] J. Herrin, *The Formation of Christendom* (Princeton, 1987), pp. 119–27, at p. 119.
[117] Cf. *HL* III.20, Helias, 'refused to accept the Three Chapters of the Chalcedonian synod', which is wrong; VI.14, confused with the monothelitist controversy.
[118] Cf. Bognetti, 'S. Maria', pp. 127–32; J. Richards, *The Popes and the Papacy in the Early Middle Ages 476–752* (London and Boston, 1979), pp. 164–7; Brown, *Gentlemen*, pp. 3, 151–3.
[119] Ep. I.16b.
[120] MGH SRL Ep. III, p. 393. See G. Cuscito, *Cristianesimo antico ad Aquilieia e in Istria*, Fonti per la Storia della Venezia Giulia 2.3 (Trieste, 1977), pp. 289–326; Markus, *Gregory*, pp. 127–33. Paul, *HL* IV.33.

right to speak'. Could the Lombard king please interfere in the election of the next bishop of Grado, 'so that the Catholic faith might flourish in your times'?[121]

The Milanese church similarly split in two: the clerics in exile with the archbishop in Genova kept their reservations quiet, while those in Milan, now the seat of the Lombard court, found favour with the Catholic queen Theudelinda, who, according to Gregory, 'little by little has been seduced by the words of depraved men'.[122] Meanwhile Agilulf himself was attempting to put forward his own candidate for the see of Ambrose.[123] Gregory had managed to get his own man elected in Genova, but within a year three suffragan bishops transferred their allegiance to old Aquileia, as did the church of Como.[124] Chalcedon hard-liners like Secundus of Trent (also godfather to the queen's son), and later the Irish holy man Columbanus, found favour at court and wrote to the pope, urging him to change his mind.[125]

Thus the two great, ancient metropolitan sees of *Italia annonaria* were split along geo-political lines, the schism helping to establish a territorial church within the Lombard sphere. To what extent did the creation of a separate Tricapitoline clergy with loyalties to the Lombard court contribute to the internal cohesion and sense of unity amongst the northern Italian churches? Bognetti saw, in the Three Chapters dispute, Agilulf's orientation towards a new 'theocratic conception of power' to govern his kingdom by means of establishing a 'national Catholic church', in emulation of the 'national' Visigothic and Frankish churches.[126] Although the schismatic churches found a sympathetic reception at court, nothing suggests an attempt at creating a Lombard 'national church', and one would hesitate to use such a term in reference to churches situated in the Frankish and Visigothic kingdoms. A letter of Columbanus to Pope Boniface IV, written in 613, suggests that, though the Three Chapters schism was still an issue, the Lombard monarchy wished to end it as a chance to reconcile themselves politically with the papacy: it was precisely Agilulf's prompting that caused Columbanus to write.[127]

---

[121] MGH Ep. III, p. 693.

[122] Ep. IV.2: 'pravorum hominum verbis ad paululum seducta est'. The queen had strong views: note Constantius' request that Gregory leave out mention of the fifth council in his admonitions, IV.37. In a later letter (603), Gregory appears to have accepted her schismatic resolve, Ep. XIV.12.

[123] Ep. XI.6.

[124] Ep. IV.2. One of these was the bishop of Brescia; Ep. IV.37. Como: Ep. IX.187.

[125] Gregrory, Ep. IX.148; *HL* IV.40. See P.T. Gray and M. Herren, 'Columbanus and the Three Chapters controversy – a new approach', *Journal of Theological Studies* 45 (1994), 160–70.

[126] Bognetti, 'S. Maria', pp. 214–15.

[127] Ep.V.8, ed. Walker, pp. 44–5: 'tum a rege rogor, ut singillatim suggeram tuis piis auribus sui negotium doloris; dolor namque suus et schisma populi pro regina, pro filio, forte et pro se ipso';

Agilulf was obviously concerned to take a leading part in the settlement of the dispute, for in doing so he demonstrated the court's concern for the welfare of the churches under his territorial jurisdiction.[128] But this did not extend to channelling the dissent of the northern churches into outright support for the Lombard monarchy against the papacy. The epitaph of one schismatic, the bishop of Como, Agrippinus (d. mid-seventh century), records how Agrippinus 'fought undefeated great battles for God' against the papacy and its erroneous declarations of orthodoxy, and how the Comascan clergy maintained their allegiance to Chalcedon and the patriarch of 'old' Aquileia, John.[129] The Lombards do not get a mention.

It is often presumed that a necessary distance between church and state was maintained in Lombard Italy owing to the religious indifference of the Lombard rulers, and to the fact they inherited a resolutely secular political system wherein the public ideology of the state was strong enough not to need the church as a buttress to secular power.[130] To some extent this seems true: while the Visigothic, Merovingian and Anglo-Saxon kings were expounding the idea of Christian reform in society through an educated priesthood, Lombard kings legislated 'for the salvation' of their Christian subjects, but without recourse to the church or its ministers. Aside from the Synod of Pavia in 698, the Lombard kings never summoned ecclesiastical councils to discuss doctrine, nor attempted to instigate administrative reforms for the church. The reasons for this, however, stem from the awkward geo-political situation of the divided peninsula. The proximity of the papacy made communications, even when strained, possible with north and central Italian churches, and the prestige the pope garnered as the indisputable head of churches in western Europe made it impossible to disregard his presence and make decisions concerning the church without his approval: not even Theoderic could have afforded to act in conjunction with northern Catholic churches in any independent manner.[131] Combined with the papacy's continued hostility to the Lombard regime, relations between church and state required a necessary measure of distance, and churches in Lombard territory found themselves in the difficult position of being located within the boundaries

---

ibid. V.17, p. 55: 'Post hanc autem scribendi occasionem insuper regis insistit iussio Agilulfi, cuius postulatio me in stuporem ac in sollicitudinem posuit multiplicem.'
[128] Bognetti,'S. Maria', p. 283.
[129] Text and plate in Menis (ed.), *Longobardi*, pp. 162–3. The reference to 'Hic patriam linquens propriam karosque parentes/ pro sancta studuit pereger esse fide' is unclear.
[130] Wickham, *EMI*, pp. 28–47. But cf. T. Brown, 'Gibbon, Hodgkin and the invaders of Italy', in R. McKitterick (ed.), *Edward Gibbon and Empire* (Cambridge, 1997), pp. 137–61, at p. 160 and n. 121.
[131] T. Noble, 'Theoderic and the papacy', *Atti XIII CISAM* (Spoleto, 1993), 395–425; Moorhead, *Theoderic*, pp. 54–60, 114–29.

The early Lombards and their settlement in Italy

of a kingdom opposed by their supreme executive head, to whom they owed the ultimate act of allegiance. The predicament is well illustrated by the formula preserved in the *Liber diurnus* for the appointment of a bishop in Lombard territory. The episcopal candidate is asked to provide a written promise that he 'always preserve the peace which God loves between the republic and us, that is the Lombard people, and I promise that I or anyone else in no manner shall do anything otherwise against this'. The bishop then signs the document placed on the grave of St Peter.[132] The formula was perhaps only used for bishoprics within the jurisdiction of Rome, which included all of south and central Italy, as well as Tuscany. Many of these bishoprics were located in frontier zones which witnessed first hand the struggles between the two powers for control over the peninsula, including hotspots like Bieda (Blera), Perugia, Terni and Narni. Churches in northern and other parts of central Italy (Emilia-Romagna) were under the metropolitan jurisdictions of the three northern archdioceses, Ravenna, Aquileia and Milan, and these maintained a degree of cultural separation from Rome by their varied liturgical traditions, employing combinations of Gallican and Ambrosian rites.[133]

The geo-political difficulties presented by a Lombard-loathing papacy notwithstanding, the Three Chapter dispute demonstrated how even in its earliest stages the Lombard monarchy sought to co-operate with ecclesiastical authorities situated within the boundaries of the kingdom. This necessarily involved acquaintance with, and concession to, the literary culture of Christianity. Manuscripts which preserve the dissenting tradition appear to have been produced and circulated around the schismatic areas, but next to nothing has survived.[134] From the Lombard court Secundus of Trent sent to Pope Gregory a *libellus exhortatorius*, setting out reasons for refusing the terms of the troublesome Fifth Oecumenical council. Gregory responded at length, praised Secundus for his simple and pure literary style, and sent to Secundus in return two codices of his *Homilies*, some incense, herbs, and a pullover for that chilly northern climate.[135] In his last letter addressed to the Lombard court (603),

---

[132] *Liber diurnus romanorum pontificum*, ed. H. Foerster (Berne, 1958), at V.76, A.65m, p. 377.

[133] The best discussion is O. Bertolini, 'I vescovi del *"regnum langobardorum"* al tempo dei Carolingi', *Italia Sacra* 5 (1964), pp. 1–26, repr. in *Scritti scelti di storia medioevale* (ed. O. Banti) (Livorno, 1968), pp. 71–92, esp. pp. 79–81, 90–2. The liturgical sources are conveniently listed in C. Vogel, *Medieval Liturgy: An Introduction to the Sources*, trans. and rev. W. Storey and N. Rasmussen (Washington, DC, 1986), pp. 72–3, 109–10, 282–4, 326–9.

[134] See R. Schieffer, 'Zur Beurteilung des norditalienischen Dreikapital Schismas', *Zeitschrift für Katholische Theologie* 87 (1976), 167–201.

[135] Ep. IX.147. Hartmann (ed.), p. 148 n. 7, notes that the 'duos omeliarum codices' probably refers to either the *Homiliae in evangelia* or *Homiliae in Hiezechielem*, rather than both, since both were divided into two books each.

Gregory congratulated Queen Theudelinda for the baptism of her son and heir to the throne Adaloald, and asked her to inform Secundus of Trent, 'dilectissimus filius', that bad health had prevented him from responding to all of Secundus'queries. But just as Secundus had requested, he was sending him a copy of the acts of the Fifth Oecumenical Council, convinced that upon reading these Secundus would no longer hurl accusations of doctrinal error against the papacy.[136] We can only wonder at the literary activity that took place at court, as Secundus and his fellow dissenters mustered arguments from scripture and the stock of patristic works and doctrinal treatises that supported Chalcedonian definitions of the faith.[137] It was perhaps also the ethos of *romanitas* surrounding the court of Agilulf and Theudelinda that gave one literate class of society, the clergy, the confidence to seek protection and patronage from the rulers of the new *regnum*.

LITERACY AND COURT CULTURE

Most scholars agree on the Romanising tendencies of the court under Queen Theudelinda and her two royal husbands, Authari and Agilulf. It was only under Agilulf that the court became centred on the city of Pavia, whereas previously the cities of Verona, under Alboin, and Milan, under Authari, had been the preferred cities of royal residence.[138] Authari assumed the title of *Flavius* in imitation of Constantine the Great, and of King Theoderic who had done likewise, and so did all subsequent Lombard kings.[139] On the famous Val di Nievole plaque, Agilulf was portrayed on a throne surrounded by warriors and flanked by winged victories of Roman-Byzantine type carrying banners reading 'D[omi]N[us] AGILULFUS' and the word 'VICTURIA'.[140] Agilulf's son Adaloald was elevated to the throne as co-regent in typically late Roman ceremonial style in the circus maximus in Milan before his proud father and a host of Frankish legates.[141] Theudelinda commissioned frescoes of Lombard

---

[136] Ep. XIV.12.
[137] Perhaps an exemplar for the eight-century Bobbiese fragment of Theodore of Mopsuestia's *De psalmis*, Milan, Ambr. C. 301 inf. (CLA III.326), and its copy, Turin, F.IV.1. Fasc. 5 + 6 (CLA IV.452). Theodore's works were rare.
[138] See S. Gasparri, 'Pavia longobarda', in *Storia di Pavia*, II, *L'alto medioevo* (Milan, 1987), pp. 19–68, at pp. 37–42.
[139] Paul, *HL* III.16. On *Flavius*, see Wolfram, 'Origo et religio', pp. 33–4.
[140] Interpretations of the plaque's symbolism vary: W. Kurze, 'La lamina di Agilulfo: usurpazione o diritto?', *Atti VI CISAM* (Spoleto, 1980), 224–61; M. McCormick, *Triumphal Rulership in Late Antiquity, Byzantium and the Early Middle Ages* (Cambridge, 1986), pp. 289–93. A cross from Bienasco contains the inscription 'AGLV. F. REX' and a bearded figure: S. Fuchs, *Die langobardischen Goldblattkreuze aus der Zone Sudwärts der Alpen* (Berlin, 1938), p. 45.
[141] *HL* IV.30. Also recorded by Fredegar, *Chron.* IV.31.

The early Lombards and their settlement in Italy

deeds (*gesta*) painted on the wall of the palace she built at Monza, from which Paul had to learn about Lombard dress and hair-styles.[142] The palace was built in conjuction with the church of San Giovanni, to which Paul gave a starring role as symbolising the fortunes of the kingdom.[143]

Literacy was part of this *romanitas*. Agilulf issued diplomas confirming the foundation of Bobbio by Columbanus.[144] The tile of San Simpliciano in Milan uses a typically Roman stamp to print Agilulf's and his son Adoald's names,[145] and a votive crown denoted by the king to the church of Monza bears the inscription, 'GRATIA DEI, VIR GLORIOSISSIMUS REX TOTIUS ITALIAE'.[146] Agilulf sent 'his' notary, Stabilicianus, to the emperor Phocas to obtain a treaty and sum of tribute owed.[147] Pope Gregory sent to Theudelinda the famous gold evangelary, and a book of his *Dialogues*.[148] Her reputation had even reached Spain, whence King Sisebut wrote to Adaloald (*c.* 616–20) exalting the studious orthodoxy of his co-regent mother.[149] When writing to Agilulf, Gregory urged the king to continue to send letters to his dukes on the borders around Rome to remind them of the treaty recently concluded.[150] We have already seen how some dukes and Lombard leaders had corresponded with the papacy, and as we shall see, Lombard legislation suggests letters between officials were common in the eighth century.[151]

An insight into the place of literacy in early Lombard court culture is afforded by Secundus of Trent's commission to write, as Paul called it, a 'succinct little history (*succincta historiola*) of Lombard deeds up to his own time'.[152] Secundus was a close confidant of Theudelinda's and something of a court adviser on religious affairs. Far from innocently

---

[142] *HL* IV.22. Cf. the trans. of Christie, *Lombards*, p. 43. W. Pohl, 'Telling the difference. Signs of ethnic identity', in W. Pohl and H. Reimitz (eds.), *Strategies of Distinction: The Construction of Ethnic Communities, 300–800* (Leiden Boston and Cologne, 1998), pp. 43–5, and n. 119, discusses the terms of dress used by Paul.

[143] IV.21, 22, cf. *HL* IV.27, 47, 51, and especially V.6. Monza was the link between his hero Pope Gregory and Theudelinda. Cf. Goffart, *Narrators*, p. 400.

[144] Brühl, CDL III.1, 2; Bruhl, *Studien zu den Langobardishen Königsurkunden* (Tübingen, 1970), pp. 19–27, 205–6; Bognetti, 'S. Maria', pp. 78, 210, 281, 290.

[145] Mitchell, 'Display of Script', p. 7. There is also the tile at San Giovanni Battista at Monza, Theudelinda's foundation, with 'SCI IOHA(nnis)', *ibid.*, p. 6.

[146] Cf. Delogu, 'Il regno', pp. 43–4.

[147] *HL* IV.35.

[148] Ep. XIV.12. It is not certain that the gold cover preserved at Monza belonged to Gregory's evangelary: R. Conti, *Il tesoro: guida alla conoscenza del Tesoro del Duomo di Monza* (Monza, 1993), pp. 38–9.

[149] MGH Ep. III, pp. 671–5, at p. 673: 'mater veneratione colenda, doctrix fidei firmissima. . oratione compuncta . . . suavis eloquio, acer ingenio', etc.

[150] Ep. IX.66. Included by Paul in the *HL* IV.9.

[151] See below, pp. 186–94. Cf. Gregory's letter to Duke Arichis of Benevento, Ep. IX.126, included by Paul, *HL* IV.19.

[152] *HL* IV.40. See K. Gardiner, 'Paul the Deacon', pp. 147–53.

preserving memory, history-writing also constructed a common identity and purpose in order to unite the audience in the achievement of particular goals.[153] We are given some idea of the contents of Secundus' *historiola* when Paul pauses to marvel that Secundus omitted to narrate the details of a particularly glorious Lombard victory over the Franks:

> In that fight the Lombards were victorious; the Franks were truly slaughtered, many of them were captured, even more took flight and attempted to head back to their own country. It was the greatest massacre of the Frankish army ever remembered. It is truly a mystery, therefore, why Secundus, who wrote something about the history of the Lombards, did not mention this victory, when indeed we have found the very same words written above concerning the massacre of the Franks in their own history.[154]

The implication of Paul's perplexity is that the *historiola* included similar episodes which celebrated other victories of the Lombards as a united force against foes who threatened the unity of the kingdom, as the Franks certainly were in this period. We can only wonder what else Secundus may have included in his *historiola*, though it possibly focused on the Lombards in Italy only: Paul had to learn of traditional Lombard costume and hair-styles from the frescoes of the palace at Monza, and he never mentions Secundus' work as a source or confirmation for the fantastical, pre-Pannonian Lombard past he portrays in the first book of his own *Historia Langobardorum*. Given Secundus' monastic vocation, and Theudelinda's undoubted piety, he probably included material on ecclesiastical affairs, perhaps setting the Lombard invasion in a Eusebian framework of history by divine purpose.[155] We have no idea how widely the text was disseminated, but it was obviously still known in Paul the Deacon's day. Whether he first encountered the text at the court of Ratchis, where he was brought up, or at a later stage in his literary career, is purely speculative.

We may well ask the same questions of the *Prosperi Continuatio haveniensis*, a continuation of Prosper's Chronicle which was written by a cleric in Pavia around 625.[156] The anonymous continuator was no simple compiler of straightforward annalistic information, but used the materials at

---

[153] See R. McKitterick, 'The audience for Carolingian historiography ', in G. Scheibelreiter and A. Scharer (eds.), *Historiographie im Frühmittelalter* (Vienna, 1994), pp. 96–114; McKitterick, 'Constructing the past in the early Middle Ages: the case of the Royal Frankish Annals', *Transactions of the Royal Historical Society*, sixth series, 7 (1997), 101–29.

[154] *HL* III.29. Paul's Frankish source ('their own history') is Gregory of Tours, *Historiae* IX.25.

[155] Paul's description of Secundus as 'servus Christi de Tridento', twice, *HL* IV.27, 40, suggests a monastic vocation.

[156] The *Continuatio*, MGH AA. IX, pp. 266–339, ed. Mommsen. See D. Wattenbach-Levison, *Deutschlands Geschichtsquellen*, I, p. 205. Further, R. Cessi, 'Studi sulle fonti dell'età gotica e longobarda, II: *Prosperi Continuatio Haveniensis*', *Bollettino Storico Italiano per il Medioevo* 22 (1922),

The early Lombards and their settlement in Italy

hand to shape and interpret history in a particular fashion. His main concern, as becomes clear in the part of his narrative where his sources appear to have run dry, was to record events in Italy, particularly the arrival of the Lombards and their establishment, since they were now indisputably the new masters of the peninsula.[157] The continuator even informs us of a meeting between Pope Gregory and King Agilulf on the stairs of the basilica of St Peter, no doubt modelled on that of the meeting between Pope Leo and Attila which he found in Prosper's chronicle. Indeed, the chronicler's ignorance of events nearly 100 years earlier is alarming. Yet behind the curt and confused entries lies a sensitivity, if somewhat simplified, to the notion of historical change, as the continuator attempts to explain the success of the Lombards in terms of their unity and military prowess, as opposed to the disunity of the Romans and their subsequent failure in the field. Owing to divisions in the Roman hierarchy, Italy lay open to the Lombards, who settled 'quietly' (*quiete*) along with their wives and children. The death of Alboin and the interregnum were a blow to Lombard rule: this allowed ambitious dukes such as Zafan of Pavia to waste the strength of the Lombards in unrealistic pursuits, while the peninsula was tormented by the destructive presence of yet another people, the Franks, who were 'wreaking devastation widely in Italy'. The anonymous chronicler drew an 'intentional contrast between the warlike and effective Lombards and the disunited and demoralised Romans'.[158] Similar sentiments can be found in the works of other seventh-century clergymen, such as Isidore of Seville, which represent a shift in clerical culture towards a positive attitude to military virtue as necessary for a stable and just society.[159] Moreover, the chronicler had no illusions about the eternal victory of the Romans. In a country divided between two powers, the chronicler was in favour of a united Italy, and looked to the Lombards with hope. We can only wonder if Secundus' lost *historiola* shared similar sentiments, as a reflection of the court culture of Agilulf, 'gloriosissimus rex totius Italiae'.

THE *ORIGO GENTIS LANGOBARDORUM*

Another historiographical text which is thought to have emanated from the Lombard court of Rothari is the potted history of the Lombards

---

587–641; S. Muhlberger, 'Heroic kings and unruly generals: the Copenhagen continuation of Prosper reconsidered', *Florilegium* 6 (1984), 50–70, and trans. *ibid.*, pp. 71–95. The argument that he wrote in Pavia (Cessi, 'Studi', p. 625) is not water-tight.

[157] 'partem Italiae, quam nondum Langobardi occupaverant', p. 339.
[158] Mulhberger, 'Heroic kings', p. 60.
[159] See Muhlberger, 'War, warlords, and Christian historians from the fifth to the seventh century', in A. Murray (ed.), *After Rome's Fall* (Toronto, Buffalo and London, 1988), pp. 83–98.

known as the *Origo gentis langobardorum* (hereafter simply *Origo*).[160] An anonymously written and obscure text of only two or three manuscript folios in length, it constitutes the only statement we have by Lombards themselves on their own ethnic identity, in terms of proposing a Scandinavian origin for the *gens*, and recounting how the name of *Langobardi* was bestowed upon the Winili by the Germanic gods Woden and Frea. The legends of the text, repeated by Paul the Deacon in his *Historia Langobardorum*, are often considered examples of orally transmitted Germanic *Heldensage* redacted in Latin prose.[161] It has even been argued that behind the barbaric Latin one can hear the rhythm and cadences of heroic verse in Old High German.[162] According to such views, the text of the *Origo*, therefore, would seem to stand at the crossroads of orality and literacy, and additionally at the intersection of barbarian and Roman-Christian culture.

The *Origo* begins in a matter-of-fact fashion: 'There is an island called Scadanan, which means "destruction(s)", in the northern regions, where many peoples live. Amongst whom was a small people called the Winili.'[163] The text then narrates, in an extremely terse manner, how the Winili, under the rule of the woman Gambara and her two sons Ibor and Agio, changed their name to *Langobardi* through divine intervention from the Germanic god Woden, their subsequent victory over the threatening Vandals, and their exodus from 'Scadanan' to inhabit places called *Golaida*, *Anthaib*, *Bainaib* and *Burgundaib*.[164] What follows is an annotated

---

[160] I have used the edition of Azzara, *Le leggi*, pp. 2–6, which is taken from Waitz, MGH SRL, pp. 2–6. A new edition is A. Bracciotti, *Origo gentis langobardorum: Introduzione, testo critico, commento*, Biblioteca di Cultura Romanobarbarica 2 (Rome, 1998), on which see below.

[161] Brothers Grimm, *Deutsche Sagen* (1816–19); K. Hauck, 'Lebensnormen und Kulturmythen in germanischen Stammes- und Herrschergenealogien', *Saeculum* 6 (1955), 182–223, at pp. 206–11; O. Gschwantler, 'Die Heldensage von Alboin und Rosamund', in H. Birkhan (ed.), *Festschrift für Otto Höfler zum 75. Geburtstag*, Philologia Germanica 3 (Vienna and Stuttgart, 1976), pp. 214–47; Gschwantler, 'Formen langobardischer mündlicher Überlieferung', *Jahrbücher für Internationale Germanistik* 11 (1979), 58–85; H. Moisl, 'Kingship and orally transmitted Stammestradition among the Lombards and the Franks', in H. Wolfram and A. Schwarcz (eds.), *Die Bayern und ihre Nachbarn* (Vienna, 1985), pp. 111–19. For harsh criticisms of such views, Goffart, *Narrators*, pp. 329–32; 'Germanic antiquity today'.

[162] E.g. W. Bruckner, *Der Sprache der Langobarden* (Strasburg, 1895), pp. 19–21. Similarly, A. Heusler, *Die altgermanische Dichtung* (Berlin, 1923), pp. 147–59; A. Bracciotti, 'La saga di Gambara e dei suoi figli nella *Origo gentis langobardorum*', *Romanobarbarica* 12 (1992–93), 81–6.

[163] *Origo*, 1: 'Est insula qui dicitur scadanan, quod interpretatur excidia, in partibus aquilonis, ubi multae gentes habitant; inter quos erat gens parva quae winnilis vocabatur.' Note the use of the word *interpretor*: a deponent verb in classical usage (Cicero, *De offic.* 1.142), its use as a passive can be found in the *Vetus latina* (e.g. Gen. 21.3) and in Jerome's Vulgate, John 20.16: see ThLL VII.1, 2257–8.

[164] Attempts have been made to identify these names with ancient, medieval and modern sites. Thus the *Origo gentis*' '*Bainaib*' (Paul, *HL* I.13, '*Bainthaib*') is thought to be the Germanicised form of

The early Lombards and their settlement in Italy

list of kings which includes the mention of victories over enemies, and of Lombard settlement in Rugiland, Pannonia and eventually Italy, where the famous story of Rosamund's treachery takes place. The *Origo* then swiftly runs through the kings up to Perctarit, thus providing us with a *terminus ante quem* (two of the three surviving recensions go this far, the other stops at Grimoald), and attaches titbits of information akin to headlines of seventh-century Lombard history.[165]

The legendary aspect of the text is therefore threefold: Lombard Scandinavian origins, the intervention of Woden and Frea, and the murder of Alboin by Rosamund and Helmichis. Of this last, the political intrigue of Rosamund's flight to Ravenna ensured its place in contemporary chronicles, and Paul coloured it with the elements of vendetta and skull-cup to create one of the highlights of the *HL*.[166] As for Scandinavian origins, the gloss that *Scadnan* means 'destruction' smacks of Greco-Roman ethnography, which tended to depict 'Scandinavia' as an island of wild environment and uninhabitability, a place where the people were made savage by necessity and from which they emigrated if they were to survive.[167] 'Scadanan' may indeed be related to the (modern) German word 'schaden', from an Old High German root of 'skaþan', meaning, 'destruction, damage'.[168] But more important is the use of the same topos in Jordanes' *Getica* as the place for Gothic origins, for it could easily have provided a model of *migratio gentis* that justified the presence of a northern people in the foreign land of Italy. The *Getica* emphasised cruelty of 'Scandza' to men and beasts alike, as well as its fecundity as a 'womb of nations', another topos of classical ethnography.[169] Was the *Origo* dependent on a knowledge of Jordanes' text?

---

the Latinate *Boiohaemium*, that is, Bohemia; *Golaida* (Paul 'Golanda') as lands previously held by the Goths (though exactly where remains even more speculative); '*Burgundaib*' (Paul, '*Vurgundaib*') as referring to former Burgundian lands between the middle Elbe and the Ober. '*Anthaib*' (Paul, '*Anthab*') defies identification altogether. See Bluhme, *Die Gens Langobardorum* (Bonn, 1874), pp. 22–30; Jarnut, 'Zur Frügeschichte der Langobarden', *Studi Medievali*, 3rd ser., 24:1 (1983), 1–16, at pp. 6–15; Christie, *The Lombards*, p. 14.

[165] Authari's and Agilulf's marriage to the Bavarian princess Theudelinda, Agilulf's victory over the rebellious dukes of Verona, Isola del S. Giuliano and Bergamo (erroneously reducing Agilulf's reign from twenty-six to six years), Rothari's victory over Romans on the Ligurian coast, and the expedition of Emperor Constans II to Campania and Sicily.

[166] John of Biclar, *Chron.*, anno 573; Marius, *Chron.*, anno 572; *Excerpta sangallensia* 717, anno 572 (MGH AA IX.1, p. 336); Gregory, *Historiae* IV.41; *Con. Prosp. Hav.* 5; Fredegar, *Chron.* III.66; Paul, *HL* II.28; Agnellus, *LPR*, 96; *HLGoth.* 5. See A. Bracciotti, 'Il ruolo del Peredeo, pp. 99–123. On the skull-cup, see Goffart, *Narrators*, pp. 391–2. Cf. Boccaccio, *Decameron*, 7.1.

[167] Cf. Paul, HL I.2, citing Pliny as his source.

[168] See J. Svennung, *Scandinavia und Scandia: lateinische-nordische Namenstudien* (Lund, 1963), pp. 52–64.

[169] *Getica*, 24; Goffart, *Narrators*, pp. 86–92.

Opinions are divided.[170] The *Getica* was composed in part for consumption by an Italian audience, so we should not be surprised to find it circulating in Italy a couple of centuries later. Paul the Deacon used it for his *Historia romana* (written towards 770) and therefore most probably for the *HL*, though he never acknowledged it. The Ravennate Geographer, in a text of the seventh or eighth century, openly acknowledged his use of the *Getica* for Scanza and Gothic origins.[171] Both the *Getica* and the *Origo* cast the Vandals as the subject-tribe's first opponents, and it has been claimed that both texts give a seventeen-king genealogy, presumably taken from the literary Roman myth that there were seventeen Roman kings between Aeneas and Romulus. For the *Getica* at least, we may suspect the lost Gothic history of Cassiodorus behind this erudite allusion, intended to help sway the sentiments of the Roman nobility to favour the Ostrogothic dynasty as a second *gens Iulia*.[172] But it is doubtful that the *Origo* consciously drew upon the same literary tradition, since it tallies up nineteen kings to Perctarit, and neither the intention nor the audience proposed for the seventeen-king allusion in the *Getica* makes much sense in the context of seventh-century Lombard Italy and the potted history of the *Origo*. Rothari's king list, however, does promote Rothari as the seventeenth king of the Lombards, and this is probably the more immediate source for the *Origo*: the two texts should not be confused. Whether Rothari was consciously imitating this Roman-cum-Gothic historiographical tradition is another matter. It is difficult to imagine any political mileage gained in cryptic allusions to ancient Roman kings or in any association with the Ostrogoths, whom the Lombards helped defeat.[173] There is nothing in the Latin of the *Origo* resembling a direct

---

[170] T. Mommsen, 'Die Quellen der Historia Langobardorum des Paulus Diaconus', *Neues Archiv* 5 (1880), 51–103, at p. 75; refuted by E. Bernheim, 'Über die *Origo gentis langobardorum*', *Neues Archiv* 21 (1896), 375–99, in favour of an independent oral tradition: so too B. Luiselli, *Storia culturale dei rapporti tra mondo romano e mondo germanico* (Rome, 1992), p. 758, and Wolfram, 'Origo et religio', p. 23. Cf. Goffart, *Narrators*, pp. 110, 384.

[171] *Ravennatis anonymi geographus*, ed. J. Schnetz, *Itineraria Romana*, II (Leipzig, 1940), I.1, 12, Scandza as 'antica scythia'.

[172] On the significance of this genealogy, H. Wolfram, *Intitulatio I* (Innsbruck, 1967), pp. 99–103; Wolfram, 'Methodische Fragen', pp. 473–90; Wolfram, 'Origo et religio', p. 31. On early medieval regnal lists, see D. Dumville, 'Kingship, genealogies and regnal lists', in P. Sawyer and I. Wood (eds.), *Early Medieval Kingship* (Leeds, 1977), pp. 72–104: also, H. Moisl, 'Anglo-Saxon royal genealogies and Germanic oral tradition', *Journal of Medieval History* 7 (1981), 215–48.

[173] *Contra* Wolfram, *Intitulatio*, p. 104, who argues that Rothari was deliberately combining the two images of early Roman 'Albanian' (Trojan-descent) kings and Amal kings 'an die Seite seiner italienischen Vörganger'. For the memory of the Ostrogoths in the late eighth century, see Paul, *HL* I.25; II.2, 5; III.11, 21, 27, 28; IV.21. Paul's knowledge of Ostrogothic history was, however, exceptional in that he wrote a continuation of Eutropius' *Historia romana*. The *HLCGoth*.(see below) added another king, *Pero*, between Godoin and Claffo: H. Wolfram, *Die Geburt Mitteleuropas* (Vienna and Berlin, 1987), p. 323, attributes the memory of this king

excerpt from Jordanes' text. But the anonymous author of the *Origo* need not have seen a copy of Jordanes' *Getica*. Stories of mysterious northern islands as the *Urheimat* of barbarians were popular in Jordanes' day (he declined to accept the alternative tale of the Goths' captivity in Britain), and Scandinavia, always considered an island by Greco-Romans, was Thule *par excellence*.[174]

As with the Goths, we should consign Lombard Scandinavian origins to the bin of ancient ethnography. Greco-Roman written traditions, however, will not serve as the source for the tale of Woden and Frea. The passage is terse enough to be given in full:

The Vandal dukes, Ambri and Assi, moved with their army against Winili, saying to them: 'Give us tribute, or prepare for war and fight us.' Then Ambri and Assi, dukes of the Vandals, asked Woden to grant them victory over the Winili. Woden responded, 'To whomever I see before the rising sun I shall grant the victory.' At the same time Gambara with her two sons, Ibor and Agio, who ruled the Winili as princes, implored Frea, the wife of Woden, to be favourable to the Winili. Frea advised them that, upon sunrise, the Winili women should comb their hair over their faces to look like beards and head out with their men. Then with the first rays of the rising sun, Frea, the wife of Woden, turned around the bed of her husband so that he faced the east, and woke him up. When he saw the Winili and their women with hair covering their faces he said, 'Who are these long-beards [langobardae]?' And Frea said to Woden, 'Just as you gave the name, now give them the victory.' And he gave them the victory, as it seemed that they could vindicate themselves if they obtained victory.[175] From that time onwards the Winili were called the Lombards.

Scholars of mythology have found traces of all sorts of murky meanings in the transvestite Winili women, including the symbolic representation of the shift from the Vanir to the Aesir pantheon of gods, representing the transition from a peace-loving, maternal society to a warrior, male-dominated existence for the *gens*.[176] 'Longbeard' is also one of Woden's epithets in later Scandinavian sources, and it would be unwise to dismiss the connection. Whatever its mythological significance, the story appears to have been popular. Paul, embarrassed by its paganism, dismissed the tale as a *ridicula fabula* of old, and explained it with learned euhemerism:

---

to Bohemian traditions, and reads its presence in the *HLCGoth.* as further proof that Rothari deliberately fashioned his genealogy to suit the Roman model by excising Pero from the list. This is possible, but the *HLCGoth.* contains other additional references (the Lombard stay in *Patespruna*, in Thrace, fights against the Bohemians, etc.) which may simply reflect an accumulation of legends over the centuries that were ignored by Paul.

[174] I follow here Heather, *The Goths*, pp. 26–30.
[175] Or so I render 'et dedit eis victoriam, ut ubi visum esset vindicarent se et victoriam haberent'.
[176] Wolfram, '*Origo et religio*', pp. 21–3. Cf. C. Eller, *The Myth of Matriarchal Prehistory* (Boston, 2000), pp. 31–9.

Woden is none other than the Greek god Mercury, worshipped by all Germanic peoples, and Mercury, like all pagan gods, was merely a man whom the deluded ancients thought to be a divinity.[177] For Paul, following Isidore of Seville (*Etym.*, IX.2.5), the Lombards earned their name from having long beards and not cutting their hair, nothing else. Nevertheless he felt compelled to include the tale in the *HL*, perhaps for fear of disappointing his readers. For already in the mid-seventh-century Fredegar chronicle the story appears in a slightly different form: Scandinavia is located in mainland Germany, and the Huns take the place of the Vandals as enemies, who would not allow the future Lombards to cross the Danube. Gone is the rapport between human beings and Germanic divinities: the Lombard women's disguise was merely a military ruse to frighten the Vandals by show of greater numbers, and Fredegar treated what followed with a degree of scepticism. As the troops lined up for battle, 'it is said that above both ranks [of Huns and Lombards] a voice said "these are the Lombards", and it is said by those people to have been the voice of their God, whom they madly (*fanatice*) call Wotan'.[178] The Fredegar version is the earliest we have, and the omission of Woden and Frea, and even of the name Winili, may be owed to the author's distance from Lombard Italy: it certainly rules out the presence of a copy of the *Origo* as we have it. Fredegar liked a good story, and that the *Origo*'s saga reached the ears of this Burgundian writer testifies to its popularity and circulation in the latter half of the seventh century.

ORIGO ET LEX?

Much importance accredited to the *Origo* stems from its supposed provenance as a preface attached to Rothari's Edict, thus endowing it with the character of an 'official' declaration of Lombard identity and past. Paul the Deacon, at two points in his narrative, tells us that his information can be corroborated 'in the prologue to Rothari's Edict' which can be found 'in all manuscripts of the Edict', and our three surviving recensions of the *Origo* come down to us attached to three manuscripts of the law code.[179] This would seem to provide a fairly straightforward

---

[177] Paul, *HL* I.9. Cf. Goffart, *Narrators*, p. 386.
[178] Fredegar, IV.65. Up to this point Fredegar had been following Gregory, IV.29, 40. 41. See S. M. Cingolani, *Le storie dei Longobardi: dall'origine a Paolo Diacono* (Rome, 1995), pp. 38–41; R. Collins, *Fredegar*, Authors of the Middle Ages 4.13 (Aldershot, 1996).
[179] *HL* I.21: 'Hoc si quis mendacium et non rei existimat veritatem, relegat prologum edicti, quem rex Rothari de Langobardorum legibus conposuit, et pene in omnibus hoc codicibus, sicut nos in hac historiola inseruimus, scriptum repperiet.' The point is made concerning King Waccho's subjugation of the Sueves: cf. Procopius, *Wars* VII.25.13–21; VIII.27. Elsewhere, *HL* IV.42, Paul refers to Rothari's 'prologue' to support his date for the year of the Edict's promulgation (643).

provenance for the text, were it not for two worrying factors. First, the internal evidence of the *Origo*, as we have it, demonstrates that it was written several decades after the promulgation of Rothari's Edict.[180] Second, neither the two earliest manuscripts of Lombard law contemporary with the Lombard kingdom (St Gall, Stiftsbibliothek 730; Vercelli, Biblioteca Capitolare 188), nor any of the six or so manuscripts written later in the ninth, tenth and eleventh centuries, contain the *Origo*.[181] The three manuscripts of Lombard law which contain the *Origo* date from no earlier than the tenth century. Of these, two can be shown as deriving from Beneventan-Lombard ethnic traditions and legal culture, while the third is attached to a collection of barbarian law which reflects Carolingian legal and ethnographic interests.

The question then arises: can the *Origo* which has come down to us be considered as a faithful copy of an earlier text written sometime prior to or contemporary with Rothari? Mommsen thought that both the author of the *Origo* and Paul the Deacon drew their information from an Ur-text embedded in Secundus' lost *historiola*, but we have no way of knowing.[182] Arguments for a more extensive Ur-*Origo* are further bolstered by seeing the *Historia langobardorum codicis gothani* (*HLCGoth*.), a text written at the court of King Pippin II *c.* 806 and surviving in one twelfth-century manuscript only (Gotha, Forschungsbibliothek 84), as dependent on the *Origo*, and therefore providing a witness to the circulation of the *Origo* some 150 years earlier than the manuscript evidence would allow.[183] But this argument is not convincing: the pro-Carolingian *HLCGoth*. has little resemblance here to the *Origo* (it mentions nothing of the Woden and Frea story, and claims Jerome as the source for the information that

---

[180] Modena, O.I.2, saec. X (possibly IX ex): Cava dei Tirreni, 4, saec. XI in.; Madrid, BN, 413 (D 117), saec. XI. On the date and provenance of these, see below. Opening phrases of the *Origo* are also found in two fifteenth-century manuscripts containing epitomes of Paul's *HL*: Vat. Urb. lat. 983; Paris, BN, lat. 6161, on which see Bracciotti, *Origo gentis*, pp. 76–8. The recension in the Codex Mutensis finishes in the reign of Grimoald (662–671): both the Cavensis and Matritensis end with the beginning of Perctarit's reign (672–688).

[181] On the date and provenance of these first, see p. 168. On the others, Ivrea, 34, saec. IX; Helmstedt, Ehemalige Universitätsbibliothek, 532, saec. X; Vat. lat. 5359, saec. IX–X; Blankoburg, 130.52, saec. X; Paris, BN, lat. 4613, saec. X; Paris, BN, lat. 4616, saec. X; Gotha, 84, saec. XI–XII (see below); Fulda, now lost, possibly saec. IX; Monte Cassino, 353, saec. X (*c.* 915–934); Vat. lat. 5001, saec. XIII. For description, see Bluhme, MGH Legum IV, pp. xii–xlvi. A study of the manuscripts of Lombard law is currently under preparation by W. Pohl, C. Radding and C. Meyer; W. Pohl, 'Memory, identity and power', in Y. Hen and M. Innes (eds.), *The Uses of the Past in the Early Middle Ages* (Cambridge, 2000), pp. 9–28, at p. 19 n. 26.

[182] T. Mommsen, 'Die Quellen der Historia Langobardorum', pp. 58–60 and 74; criticised by Waitz, 'Zur Frage nach den Quellen der *Historia Langobardorum*', ibid., 417–24, and W. Bruckner, 'Die Quellen der *Origo gentis langobardorum*', *Zeitschrift für Deutsches Altertum* 31 (1899), 47–58.

[183] Given in Azzara, *Le leggi*, pp. 282–91 (and see p. xxxv); and Bluhme, MGH Legum, pp. 641–6.

the Winili took their name from the *Vindilicus* river at the extremes of Gaul and changed their name because they were *ad barba prolixa et numquam tonsa* – both notions were taken *verbatim* from Isidore) and there is no reason why the author could not have taken his information from the text of Paul's *HL*.[184] As is suggested here, we do not know exactly what *Origo*-text(s) Paul may have been using to compile his account of Lombard origins.[185] In any case, the overwhelmingly classical tone and provenance of many of Paul's legends in the first book of the *HL* should warn us against using simple models of dependence and transmission here.[186]

Assessing the *Origo* as a legislative preface, it should be considered odd that a text intended to be attached to the code makes no mention of Lombard law or of Rothari and Grimoald as law-givers. Paul states that *antiquitas* tells the *ridicula fabula* of Woden and Frea, not Rothari's prologue. Rothari provides his king list, he says, because 'it seems useful to us for the memory of future times that we write on this parchment the names of our predecessor kings from the times when kings began to be designated for our Lombard people, as much as we have learned them from the elder men' (*in quantum per antiquos homines didicimus*): an unnecessary task if the *Origo* served as an official preface to the Edict. It might also be argued that Rothari, who proclaimed the Lombard settlement 'in the province of Italy' to be guided by divine power, who, mindful of the 'grace of God almighty', legislated 'in the name of God', and whose second law stated that the king's heart 'is in the hand of God' (Proverbs 20.1), would not have attached pagan folklore to the official copies of the code he was so careful to distribute to his judges.[187] After all, Arians were, among other things, extremely monotheistic.[188] It is even less likely that the pious King Liutprand permitted Germanic deities anywhere near his legislation. The failure of the *Origo* to be updated beyond Perctarit may well reflect its decline in popularity in this period, as the monarchy

---

[184] Noted by Goffart, *Narrators*, p. 382 n. 163. Cf. *Etym*. IX.2.95, with *HLCGoth.*, 2. The similarity of some passages of the *Origo* with *HLCGoth.* is best seen in the parallel layout of Bluhme, MGH Legum IV, p. xiv, esp. *Origo*, 3–4; *HLCGoth.*, 3–4. Cf. Cingolani, *Le storie*, pp. 35–36.

[185] Bracciotti, *Origo gentis*, p. 14 n. 41, hazards Paul's use of an *Origo* text 'belonging to the branch of the manuscripts of Modena and Gotha', for which she hypthothesises an eighth-century 'subarchetype' circulating in Italy (and further p. 184, 4.5 *regnum*).

[186] On Paul's debt to classical sources, see Müller, *Geschichte*, II, pp. 321–2, and Goffart, *Narrators*, chapter 5 *passim*.

[187] Rothari, *prol*. Cf. also Rothari 386, 'deo propitio . . . celestem faborem . . . divinam clementiam', and 376, 'quod christianis mentibus nullatenus credendum est nec possibilem'.

[188] Stressed by Meslin, *Les Ariens*, pp. 339–52. Grimoald legislated 'annuente domino', 'deo propitio' (*prol*.): that he constructed a church in Pavia dedicated to St Ambrose and was buried there would rule out his Arianism, if we can trust Paul, *HL* V.33. The church is not otherwise attested: Bullough, 'Urban change', p. 120.

increasingly promoted itself as a centre of Catholic orthodoxy in the late seventh and early eighth centuries.[189]

It is possible to locate the lack of manuscript evidence for the *Origo*'s attachment to the law code within the very same cultural milieu of Catholic intolerance at court. Our earliest witness to Rothari's code, St Gall 730, was most likely written at Bobbio, sometime in the third quarter of the seventh century.[190] Although grateful for royal patronage, Bobbiese monks may have drawn the line at redacting tales of pagan gods in a prefatory *Origo*. Our second-earliest recension, Vercelli 188, includes the legislation of Liutprand: from Perctarit's and certainly Liutprand's reign onward the *Origo* would no longer be welcome as a legislative preface, hence the lacuna in our manuscript evidence. In this light, we need to explain why the originally prefatory *Origo* was later reattached to law codes, providing us with our surviving recensions.

In the case of the Codex Mutensis (Modena O.I.2) we can see the Carolingian legal principle of personal law and a concomitant interest in ethnicity at work. Along with the text of Lombard law known as the *Concordia* (a reworking of Rothari's Edict in accordance with the legislation of later Lombard kings and organised by topic[191]), the manuscript also contains the range of Frankish barbarian law (*Lex salica, Lex ripuaria, Lex alamannorum, Lex baioariorum*), along with capitularies of Charlemagne, Pippin and Lothar, and extracts from the council of Paris (829) and the council of Pavia (850).[192] The Mutensis would appear be a copy of the (now lost) manuscript of law prepared for Count Eberhard of Friuli by Lupus of Ferrières copied at Fulda under Hrabanus Maurus, as we learn from the dedicatory verses of Lupus on folio 10.[193] It has been assumed that the Mutensis redaction of the *Origo* can be dated to 817–40, the period in which Lupus put together his manuscript for Eberhard

---

[189] Bracciotti, *Origo gentis*, pp. 14–21, argues that the *Origo* was the result of an 'estremo attaccamento nazionalistico', so that the text's paganism, its complete lack of reference to Christianity or even to 'god', and its attachment to the law code can be read as an appeal to Lombard 'nationalist' traditions, now threatened by Perctarit's Catholicism: at p. 21 n. 62, she proposes that the author was 'un funzionario della cancelleria regia di Grimoald'. Bracciotti's thesis needs to explain why, if Lombard legislation was such an important rallying point for 'nationalist' sentiment, it is not mentioned in the *Origo*, and why Grimoald receives such short shrift: the *Origo* merely records his reign, and the note of Constans II's presence in Italy is unassociated with Grimoald or Lombards: *Origo*, 7.

[190] See M. Tosi, 'L'Edictus Rothari nei manoscritti bobiensi', *Archivium Bobiese* 4 (1982), 11–72, and below, chapter 4.

[191] Ed. Bluhme, MGH Legum IV, pp. 235–88, and see below.

[192] The contents are set out by G. Russo, 'Le leggi longobarde nel Codice O.I.2 della Biblioteca Capitolare di Modena', *Atti VI CISAM* (Spoleto, 1975), 607–21; and H. Mordek, *Bibliotheca capitularium regum francorum manuscripta. Überlieferung und Traditionzusammenhang der fränkishen Herrschererlasse*, MGH Hilfsmittel 15 (Munich, 1995), pp. 256–68.

[193] Given by Russo, 'Leggi longobarde', p. 621; and K. Strecker (ed.), MGH Poetae IV.3, p. 1059.

(possibly 822–37: the work appears to have been completed before Lupus became abbot of Ferrières c. 837, and Hrabanus was abbot of Fulda from 822). But that Lupus inserted a copy of the *Origo gentis langobardorum* in his manuscript is extremely doubtful.[194] First, in his dedicatory verses, Lupus mentions that individual laws in his compilation are prefaced by *effigies* of the Franks, Alamanni and Lombards (this last *effigies* 'mirabile dictu'), but says nothing of *Origo* texts or the like. Second, the first quire of Modena O.I.2, in which the *Origo* is situated, contains other texts extraneous to Lupus' compilation (fragments of Isidore's *Etymologiae* IX.5–6, a capitulary from the council of Olonense (825)), followed by a blank folio, then the *Origo*, followed by another seven blank lines, before a list of emperors from Augustus to Louis the Pious which may or may not have been part of Lupus' original manuscript: the laws proper, with Lupus' dedicatory verses, begin the next quire.[195] It must be concluded that the *Origo gentis langobardorum* of the Codex Mutensis is part of a later addition to the manuscript and was not present in the (now lost) exemplar manuscript prepared by Lupus of Ferrières for Count Eberhard – a fact which is confirmed by the *Origo*'s absence in the other, though later, surviving copy of Lupus' manuscript, Gotha, Forschungsbibliothek I.84 (saec. XI–XII): the same manuscript in which we find the *HLCGoth.* serving as a preface to Rothari's code, but in a completely different part of the manuscript unrelated to Lupus' collection.[196] On the basis of the manuscript evidence alone, the earliest possible date for the *Origo* would

---

[194] W. Pohl, *Werkstätte der Erinnerung: Monte Cassino und die Gestaltung der langobardischer Vergangenheit* (Munich, 2001), pp. 117–29, draws the conclusion that Lupus did have the *Origo* before him and inserted it into the exemplar manuscript of the Mutensis: but he also seems to agree that the first quire of the Mutensis was not part of Lupus' original creation and seems extraneous to the collection.

[195] Mordek, *Bibliotheca*, pp. 257–8. The presence of the same list of emperors in the Codex Gothanus (see below, and Mordek, *ibid.*) suggests it may have been part of the original compilation, but equally it could have been added later. Both Lupus and Eberhard's will, ed. I. De Coussemaker, *Cartulaire de l'abbaye de Cysoing et de ses dépendances* (Lille, 1883), p. 3, mention only law.

[196] The Codex Gothanus also contains the *Concordia* of Lombard law found in the Mutensis, unique to these manuscripts, which would appear to have been what Lupus prepared for Eberhard by way of Lombard law: see K. Siewert, 'Neues zur Überlieferung der Leges Langobardorum', *Deutsches Archiv* 48 (1992), 166. Bracciotti uses the presence of the *HLCGoth.* in the Gotha manuscript to support further the idea that Lupus' original manuscript contained a copy of the *Origo gentis*, and further postulates a lost archetype (β) *Origo*- text for the authors of both the *Origo gentis* and the *HLCGoth.* But the presence of the *HLCGoth.* in the Codex Gothanus cannot be used to support the notion that the Lupus codex contained an *Origo* text of any sort: in fact it suggests quite the opposite. The Gotha manuscript is made up of four separate parts, redacted contemporaneously, of which the second part (fols. 147–223) contains exactly the same order of texts found in part two of the Codex Mutensis, that is, the legal manuscript prepared for Eberhard by Lupus: thus the absence of the *Origo* in both recensions demonstrates its extraneousness to Lupus' compilation. The *HLCGoth.* appears as a preface (fols. 335v–337v) to the fourth part of the Codex Gothanus which comprises a full recension of Rothari's Edict (fols. 338–74): see Bluhme, MGH Legum IV, p. 38; and Mordek, *Bibliotheca*, pp. 131–49. As said,

therefore be sometime during or after the reign of Lothar I as emperor (817–55); the latest would be 991, as suggested by the *Kalendarium* of the final quire (fols. 208–18), which is in a later hand and covers the period 991–1158.

For the two southern Italian manuscripts, the Codex Matritensis and Codex Cavensis, we may look to the particular culture of the principality of Benevento. A pagan origin-myth attached to the law code might more easily be accommodated in ninth- and tenth-century Benevento, where myths of Lombard military prowess could sit comfortably alongside pride in Lombard legislative traditions, in a time when 'it has pleased the celestial Piety that the duchy of the remaining tribe has been committed to us, who are gravely under threat from a multitude of peoples who do not cease to terrify and dispossess our fellow citizens, burning and sacking many of our villages and towns'.[197] For just as Duke Arichis had legislated for 'the salvation and justice of this country (*patria*)' in the 780s, so Duke Adelchis (853–78) looked to Lombard law as an 'enduring glory of this famous tribe'. What could be more complimentary than an origin-myth which recounted Lombard victories against overwhelming enemies and which promoted the unity of the *gens* in the face of adversity? It is perhaps more than a coincidence that the manuscript evidence for the Mutensis *Origo* and the *HLCGoth.* points to their circulation in the second half of the ninth century. In any case, both the Matritensis and Cavensis manuscripts date from nearly two centuries after Adelchis' reign, and the *Origo* may have been inserted anytime thereafter: in the case of the Codex Cavensis, Ibor, Agio, Frea and Woden were given a family snapshot in the form of a miniature, along with miniatures of Lombard kings.[198]

The internal evidence for the chronology of the *Origo*, and the negative evidence of its manuscript tradition, do not allow us to see a clear-cut relationship between the 'origin of the *Origo*' and the distribution of

---

the date of the Gotha manuscript is considerably late: dated by Bluhme and Waitz to the late tenth or early eleventh century, Bracciotti (*Origo gentis*, pp. 72–3), would push the date further (rightly, it seems) to the second half of the twelfth century. Hence, far from providing evidence for the early attachment of the *Origo* to Rothari's Edict, the attachment of the *HLCGoth.* to the Gotha manuscript further suggests that the addition of such texts to manuscripts of Lombard law was a later development that reflects Carolingian, or even post-Carolingian, concerns.

[197] Adelchis, *prol.* (866); Azzara, *Le leggi*, p. 273. Cingolani, *Le storie*, p. 33, suggests that the 'Beneventan tradition' of attaching the *Origo* to the law code dates from the late eighth century, when Paul was writing the *HL*.

[198] On the Matritensis, see G. Cavallo, 'Per l'origine e la data del cod. Matrit. 413 delle *leges Langobardorum*', *Studi di storia dell'arte in memoria di Mario Rotili* (Naples, 1984), I, pp. 135–42, who dates it from the mid-eleventh century. On the Cavensis, see M. Rotili, *La miniatura della Badia di Cava* (Cava dei Terreni, 1978), pp. 58–70, 81–3; M.L. Fobelli, 'Codici miniati dell'abbazia di Cava: le *leges Langobardorum* e il Beda', *Rassegna Storica Salernitana* 6:1 (1989), 35–63.

Lombard law, and therefore as some type of official statement by the Lombard kings concerning the identity of the *gens*. There can be little doubt that the tales recorded in the *Origo* were popular: they reached into Francia in the mid-seventh century, and their written version continued to delight Beneventans into the eleventh century. Exactly when they were first written down is impossible to pin down. The text itself suggests a date of composition sometime in the reign of Perctarit, though its legendary core, that of Lombard prehistory, may have been redacted much earlier, with annalistic entries later added until the project was abandoned, or suppressed.

CONCLUSION

Whatever the origin of the *Origo*, we should refrain from viewing it as the reflection of a culture that was necessarily antithetical to the late Roman and Christian influences present at the court of Agilulf and Theudelinda. The supposed 'paganism' of the Lombards in Italy has long been exaggerated, and needs to be measured against the more authoritative evidence of their early conversion to Christianity, the royal courts' involvement with the Three Chapters controversy, and the diversity of religious belief and practices throughout Italy at the time of Lombard settlement. Lombard Arianism should be seen in the same Italian context. Arianism had deep roots in Italy, so that its profession by some Lombard kings should not be surprising. But it never served as a badge of Lombard identity or political allegiance, and one gets the sense that it mattered less to contemporaries than the diatribes against Arianism by some churchmen would have us believe. Neither Arianism nor pagan practices seem to have hindered the success with which the Lombards established themselves as rulers of north and central Italy, a success owed in part to the ability of Lombard leaders to adapt themselves and the political system they implemented to the economic and cultural environment of a post-Roman Italy.

Precisely how that system worked remains obscure, but the evidence at our disposal suggests that the establishment of Lombard rule may have been less tumultuous and more organised than has been presumed. If the Lombards were invited to Italy, the experiment went woefully wrong for the Romans, as their previously esteemed and respected federates appropriated the means of government for themselves. This appears to have involved some maintenance of the late Roman framework for taxation and redistribution of resources, but our evidence is simply too scanty to allow any firm conclusions here, and by the middle of the seventh century Lombard government derived the greater part of its revenue and military resources through land-owning and vassalic relationships at the royal,

The early Lombards and their settlement in Italy

ducal and local levels. Taxes, tolls, levies and corvée work continued to be exacted by central government from local society throughout the period of the Lombard kingdom. These required a degree of bureaucratic procedure and functional literacy for their regulation and maintenance, as did the administration of justice, even if in both these spheres the Lombard system was considerably less sophisticated than the late Roman structure which provided its foundations. At the initial stages of conquest and settlement Lombard dukes and leaders quickly appropriated the means of literate communications for diplomacy with Byzantine and other (notably Frankish) powers, methods of negotiation which they doubtless encountered as federates of the Roman state in Noricum and Pannonia. But centralised government required a more voracious appropriation of literate culture. The success with which the royal court of Theudelinda and her two husbands established a court culture that could parry with Byzantine government on diplomacy, and with the papacy on doctrinal issues, demonstrates a considerable appreciation of the role of literacy in the cultural, religious and political life of the Italy they now controlled. By 613 the 'most excellent' King Agilulf could grant to 'his holy paternity', St Columbanus, the land necessary for the establishment of the monastery of Bobbio, 'through this our general diploma the licence of habitation and possession there in the name of God...given before all our dukes, gastalds and royal agents as an absolute command, so that none of them ever dares to go against the letter of our diploma'.[199] Brandishing both the pen and the sword, the Lombards had come to stay.

---

[199] CDL III.1: 'per hoc generalem nostrum praeceptum cedimus tuae sanct[a]e paternitati ibidem in Dei nomine licentia habitandi et possidendi... dantes quapropter omnibus ducibus, castaldiis, seu actionariis nostris omnimodis in mandatis ut nullus eorum contra hanc praecepti nostri pagina ire quandoque pr[a]esumat'.

3

LANGUAGE AND LITERACY

PART I: LOMBARD LANGUAGE

The existence of a native Lombard language, of a Germanic variety, has been posited as a cultural and social barrier to the assimilation of Latin, literate culture by the new barbarian overlords of Italy. The possession of a Germanic, native language is thought to have created a cultural gap between conquerors and conquered, and to have rendered the appropriation of both written and spoken Latin as a less important, auxiliary mode of communication, since the language of power inside the Lombard kingdom was essentially Germanic.[1] The evidence, however, suggests that this was not the case, and that even arguments for a considerable degree of bilingualism have little support in our sources. Unlike the example of the Gothic language, or other non-Latin vernacular languages which emerged in late antiquity from the increasingly tattered cultural umbrella of Roman imperial power, *Langobardic* (as I shall hereafter call a hypothetical Lombard language) never became a literary language. The reasons for this were manifold, but there were at least two main causes. The first is obvious: the overwhelming majority of the Italian population at the time of Lombard conquest were of Roman origin and spoke Latin. The Lombards, being a far smaller proportion of the population, although politically dominant, appropriated Latin as a necessary means to rule their subjects. The second reason is less obvious: a unified, widely diffused native Langobardic language may never have existed. That which has been identified as Langobardic speech, a western variety of Old High German closely akin to the Frankish language, may have been little more than a west Germanic dialect used among a small number of peoples prior to the conquest of Italy.

---

[1] This is a theme which runs throughout the work of many historical linguists, in particular: G. Restelli, *Goti, Tedeschi, Longobardi: rapporti di cultura e di lingua* (Brescia, 1984), esp. pp. 8–9; P. Scardigli, *Goti e Longobardi: studi di filologia germanica* (Rome, 1987); Scardigli, 'Appunti longobardi', in P. Chiarini *et al.* (eds.), *Filologia e critica: studi in onore di Vittorio Santoli* (Rome, 1976), I, pp. 91–131 (repr. in *Goti e Longobardi*, pp. 191–246); 'All'origine dei longobardismi in italiano', in H. Kolb and H. Lauffer (eds.), *Sprachliche Interferenz: Festschrift für Werner Betz zum 65. Geburtstag* (Tübingen, 1977), pp. 335–54. Also C.A. Mastrelli, 'Tracce linguistiche della dominazione longobarda nell'area del ducato di Spoleto', *Atti V CISAM* (Spoleto, 1983), 655–67.

Language and literacy

Despite this, we have evidence for the persistence of a Germanic language used by the Lombards after their settlement in Italy, and this needs to be explained. The sources are fourfold: onomastics, that is, names of both people and places; loan-words in Italian; comments from secondary sources, particularly Paul the Deacon; and most importantly, the presence of Germanic words and terms in the Lombard law code and in the charter evidence.[2] The following discussion will treat these topics in turn.

THE DEATH OF A LANGUAGE?

The Lombards themselves never referred to their once having possessed a homogeneous native language. Rothari recalled the 'ancient laws of our ancestors which were not written', and their memorization by 'ancient men' in the epilogue to his code (see next chapter), but no mention is made of an ancient language. The earliest certain statement we have on the existence of a Germanic, Langobardic language comes from the late tenth-century *Chronicon salernitanum*, which reminisces about the 'German language the Lombards once spoke' when explaining the office of *stolesazo*. The anonymous author (probably a monk of Salerno) was distant enough from Lombard court culture to translate Prince Grimoald IV's (804–17) previous position of *stolesazo* into a Latin equivalent ('in nostro eloquio') of 'one who governs the soldiers'. He seems to have got it wrong.[3] Sources from the later duchy of Benevento, which for reasons of political survival promoted nostalgic views of a glorious Lombard past and became a bastion of Lombard ethnic identity, cannot be taken as authoritative for early Lombard history and customs.[4] Confirmation of this can be seen in the Latin glosses on eleventh- and thirteenth-century southern Italian manuscripts of Lombard law. The glossators clearly had

---

[2] The existence of 'Langobardic' in 'Lombard runes' as evidence is not admissable, despite the suggestions of W. Krogman, *Das Hildesbrandslied in der langobardischen Urfassung hergestellt* (Berlin, 1959), pp. 34–6; K. Düwel, *Runenkunde*, Samlung Metzler M 72 (Stuttgart, 1968), p. 40; L. Musset, *Introduction à la runologie* (Paris, 1965), p. 370; W. Betz, 'Das Gegenwärtige des Althochdeutche', *Der Deutschunterricht* 5:6 (1953), 94–108, at pp. 97–8; W. Krause, *Die Runeninschriften im älteren Fithark: mit Beiträge von H. Jahnkuhn* (Göttingen, 1966), I, pp. 209–231; II, table 67, 71.

[3] *Chronicon Salernitanum*, c. 38: 'filius Grimoalt, quem lingua todesca, quod olim Langobardi loquebantur, stolesyz fuit appellatus, quod nos in nostro eloquio, qui ante obtutibus principis et regis milites hinc inde sedendo preordinat possumus vocitare, in principali dignitate est elevatus'. For *stolesaz* (*stolesayz*, *stolesyz*, etc.) Rothari, 150; F. Van der Rhee, *Die germanischen Wörter in den langobardischen Gesetzen* (Rotterdam, 1970), pp. 123–4 (hereafter *GWL*); as equivalent to a *thesaurarius*, Wickham, *EMI*, pp. 159, 160. Cf. *Gloss. cavens.* (n. 5): 'id est qui ordinat conventum'.

[4] See T. Brown, 'Ethnic independence and cultural deference: the attitude of the Lombard principalities', *Byzantinoslavica: Revue International des Etudes Byzantines* 54:1 (1993) 5–12: C.D. Fonseca, 'Longobardia minore e Longobardi nell'Italia meridionale', in P. Caratelli (ed.), *Magistra Barbaritas* (Milan, 1984), pp. 127–84; H. Taviani-Carozzi, *La Principauté lombarde de Salerne IXe–XIe siècle* (Rome, 1991), I, pp. 98–169.

little idea what the Germanic terms meant, but they were interested in finding out.[5]

Many modern scholars seem as constrained by the same preoccupation with an ethnically homogeneous Lombard people as the chronicler of Salerno. Scholars postulate a 'lost' ancient Langobardic language that seems to have quietly evaporated over time, though no one is exactly sure when or why such a process took place. Some scholars have suggested that groups persisted in speaking Langobardic into the eleventh century, whereas others argue that there was little knowledge of Langobardic language left by the time of King Liutprand.[6] Some philologists, armed with linguistic theories of 'enclavement', have gone so far as to argue that a last linguistic stronghold of spoken Langobardic (and Gothic) could be found in the dialects of the so-called Cimbrian enclave of the Tredici Communi north-east of Verona.[7] Historical linguists have applied modern theories of 'language death' to explain how 'Langobardian may well have been a mere cultural artefact, largely restricted to onomastic usage, after but one generation.'[8]

But abstract linguistic theories may not be necessary. The scholarly 'quest for the lost Lombard language' has largely ignored the complication of Lombard polyethnicity, for to do so admits an unfortunate degree of diversity and uncertainty which vitiates a search predicated on the ideal of a lost *Trümmersprache*. If there is some truth in the dictum that a dialect is a language without an army, then a Langobardic language might be said to

---

[5] A. Leoni, 'I glossari longobardi–latini', *Atti VI CISAM* (Spoleto, 1980), 267–76. The three manuscripts are: Cava dei Tirreni, Archivio della Badia della SS. Trinità, n. 4, ff. 167v–171v (saec. XI, probably written at Benevento); Madrid, Biblioteca Nazionale, 413, ff. 161r–162v (saec. XI, Benevento); Vatican, Biblioteca Apostolica, lat. 5001, ff. 139r–140v (saec. XIII, Salerno). It has been argued that such glossaries testify to an earlier northern Italian tradition of Old High German lexicography which had its epicentre in the heart of the Lombard kingdom: G. Baesecke, *Der deutsche Abrogans und die Herkunft des deutschen Schrifttums*, 2nd edn (Tübingen, 1969), pp. 148–55; A. Leoni, 'Vitalità della tradizione longobarda nell'Italia meridionale', *Medioevo Romanzo* 6:1 (1979), 3–21.

[6] For H. Pederson, *The Discovery of Language*, trans. J.W. Spargo (Indiana, 1962) (originally titled *Sprogvidenskaben i det Nittende Arhundrede: Metoder og Resultater*), p. 31, Langobardic 'finally died about the year 1000'. Cf. Bruckner, *Sprache*, p. 13, criticised by B. Migliorini, *Storia della lingua italiana* (Florence, 1960), p. 49. By the time of Liutprand: Bluhme, *Die Gens Langobardorum*, II, p. 3; Hartmann, *Geschichte Italiens*, I, p. 201; G. Bonfante, *Latini e Germani in Italia* (Brescia, 1965), p. 15; Van der Rhee, *GWL*, p. 148 n. 797.

[7] See G. Rapelli, 'L'onomastica personale e familiare nella Lessina Cimbra', and 'Per una storia dei Cimbri Tredicicomunignani', both in G. Volpato (ed.), *Civiltà Cimbra* (Verona, 1983), pp. 49–55, 75–83 respectively; Rapelli, *Testi Cimbri: gli scritti dei Cimbri dei Tredici Comuni Veronesi* (Verona, 1983); also R.L. Lencek, *Jan Baudouin de Courtenay on the Dialects Spoken in Venetian Slovenia and Rezija*, Documentation series 2, Society for Slovene Studies Newsletter (New York, 1977).

[8] E.g. T.L. Markey, 'Germanic in the Mediterranean: Lombards, Vandals, and Visigoths', in F.M. Clover and R.S. Humphreys (eds.), *Tradition and Innovation in Late Antiquity* (Madison, 1989), pp. 51–72, at p. 54.

Language and literacy

have existed. But the dictum also raises the question of what constituted the Lombards as a barbarian people, and how much their identity as a people was dependent upon military activity. Ethnic identity should not be confused with ethnic composition. Arguably the polyethnicity of the Lombards, and their military organisation, weakened the necessity of a native Langobardic language as a means of communication. The polyethnicity of the Lombards who invaded Italy meant that the only viable means of communication amongst such a diverse group of peoples, who had been living well within the orbit of the Roman empire, was the Latin language. Latin had been the official language of Pannonia for over six centuries. It was heard spoken amongst members of the army and civil administration; it appeared on documents and could be seen everywhere in the form of inscriptions.[9] Germanic languages no doubt existed in Pannonia and were used: in the 570s the Byzantine court required an interpreter for communications with the Gepids, and the Lombards appear to have had no problem communicating with them prior to their settlement in Italy.[10] During the time of their settlement in Pannonia, the Lombard war-lords were employed as mercenaries in the Roman army. If they had not already learned to communicate in Latin before this, they would certainly have learned to do so in Italy under Narses' command. There, too, they learned the efficacy of using the Latin language as an instrument which facilitated the exercise of power over a diverse group of peoples. With this proviso, I should like to turn now to assess the evidence of Germanic words associated with the Lombards which have been considered as proof of a native Langobardic language.

LANGOBARDIC LOAN-WORDS

The particularly 'Lombard' dialect of Old High German is usually identified by a linguistic rule known as the 'second consonantal shift' (Lombard *p* for the Germanic *b*, *t* for *d*, *s* for *t*) or the supposed distinctively Lombard

---

[9] See below, p. 242.
[10] See J.P. Wild, 'Loanwords and Roman expansion in north-west Europe', *World Archaeology* 8 (1976), 57–64. Lee, *Information and Frontiers*, p. 67. Gepids: Theophylact Simocatta, *Historiae* VI.10.6. We do not know what the Gepids spoke, cf. *HL* I.23, 'sermone barbarico', and below, n. 46; P. Lakatos, *Quellenbuch zur Geschichte der Gepiden* (Szeged, 1973), pp. 10–11; F. Wozniak, 'Byzantine diplomacy and the Lombard–Gepidic wars', *Balkan Studies* 20 (1979), 139–58. Negotiations between Romans and the Avars in the 570s–580s also required interpreters: Menander Protector, *Excerpta*, 8/11, 27.2/10. The Avars had their own language; Paul's comments are vague: *HL* IV.37. Diplomacy between the Lombards and the Avars, *HL* I.27; II.10; III.19; IV.4, 11, 20, 24, 26, 28, 37, 51; V.2, 19, 20, 21; VI.58. Nothing is mentioned about language differences, though diplomatic embassies may have acted as interpreters (cf. *HL* V.21). On language barriers in this period, see Pohl, 'Telling the difference', pp. 22–7.

initial '*a-*' with aspiration, both of which are thought to distinguish Langobardic from anything Alemannic or Frankish. The rules are vitiated, however, by their dependence on early medieval orthography as phonetically representative, and by the scant number of legal, military and agricultural terms that crept their way into Latin sources.[11] Whether a word is labelled Gothic, Frankish, Langobardic or something else often seems to depend on its sole use by one of these groups to the exclusion of the others. This is rare, and attempts at word-origin prance through the thickets of Old High German with little certainty, and sometimes with a little too much modern ideology. In his monumental work *Romania Germanica*, Ernst Gamillscheg 'revealed' that the Italian language contained no less than 300 loan-words of Lombard origin, compared to the paltry seventy or so that derived from 'Gothic'. The figures merely confirmed that the Goths were little more than pariahs feeding off Italian society: the Lombards, of course, were the stuff of real conquerors.[12] Gamillscheg found ancient German etymologies for all sorts of innocently Latinate words, and ascribed to the Lombards one loan-word after another without fussing too much about the date of their first appearance in documents.[13] Save for a few words, most of those thought to be Germanic loan-words in the Italian language do not appear in original

---

[11] On OHG in general see J. Bostock, *A Handbook on Old High German Literature*, 2nd edn (Oxford, 1976). I have consulted the following reference tools but only cited them where it seemed necessary or useful: E.G. Graff, *Althochdeutscher Sprachschatz oder Wörterbuch der althochdeutschen Sprache*, I–VI (Berlin, 1834–42), and W. Braune, *Althochdeutsche Grammatik* (Tübingen, 1966); J. Splett, *Althochdeutsches Wörterbuch*, 3 vols. (Berlin and New York, 1993) (hereafter *ADW*); A. Lloyd and O. Springer (eds.), *Etymologisches Wörterbuch des Althochdeutschen*, I (Göttingen, 1988); A. Lloyd and R. Lühr (eds.), *Etymologisches Wörterbuch des Althochdeutschen*, II (Göttingen, 1998) (herafter *EWA*). On the 'second consonantal shift' in OHG, see W. Mitzka, 'Das langobardisch und die althochdeutsche Dialektgeographie', *Zeitschrift für Mundartforschung* 20 (1951), 1–7; L.L. Hammerlich, 'Die germanischen und die hochdeutsch Lautverschiebung. I, Wie ensteht die germanischen Lautverschiebung? II. Worin besteht die hochdeutsche Lautverschiebung?', *Beiträge zur Geschichte der Deutschen Sprache und Literatur* (Tübingen) 77 (1955), 1–43, 165–93; O. Höflich, 'Die zweite Lautverschiebung bei Ostgermanen und Westgermanen', *Beiträge zur Geschichte der Deutschen Sprache und Literatur* (Tübingen) 79 (1957), 161–350. The problems of orthography are especially true for legal terms, all too apparent in Van der Rhee, *GWL*, and further G. Princi Bracini, 'Termini germanici per il diritto e la giustizia: sulle tracce dei significati autentici attraverso etimologie vecchie e nuove', *Settimane* 42 (Spoleto, 1995), 1053–1205. An attempt to reconcile orthographic differences with the geography of the manuscript tradition of Lombard law is P. Scardigli, 'Parole longobarde per l'ecdotica dell'editto di Rothari', in *Goti e Longobardi*, pp. 315–29.

[12] E. Gamillscheg, *Romania Germanica: Sprach- und Siedlungsgeschichte der Germanen auf dem Boden des alten Römerreichs*, 2 vols. (Berlin, 1934–36), II, p. 29, 'das Leben von Parias führte'. A good overview of Gamillscheg's thought on barbarians and Italy is his *Immigrazioni germaniche in Italia*, Veröffentlichungen der Abteilung für Kulturwissenschaft, Biblioteca Herziana in Rom 1:6 (Leipzig, 1937).

[13] Gamillscheg relied heavily on the work of C. Schneller, *Die romanischen Volksmundarten in Südtirol, nach ihren Zusammenhänge mit den romanischen und germanischen Sprachen, etymologisch und grammatisch Dargestellt* (Gera, 1870). On Schneller's influence on Gamillscheg, see C. Battisti,

Language and literacy

documents until the fourteenth century. Despite attempts at establishing discriminatory linguistic criteria such as sound-shifts (*Lautverschiebungen*), we do not really know if the word originated in Ostrogothic, Lombard, Frankish or Ottonian Italy.[14] Lists are compiled of 'Lombard' words that dovetail with the image of simple barbarians settling in a sophisticated Latin world; ground-level everyday words concerned with law, forestry, building activity, agriculture, technology, crafts, family life, household objects, military terms, animal names, etc.[15] When collected together and placed in a long list, these 'Lombard' words do indeed reflect the settlement of a considerable number of people, a true *Völkerwanderung*, rather than just that of warrior-bands. But these lists of 'Lombard' loan-words have been drawn from later documents spanning a chronological period of over 800 years, so that generally these documents containing words thought to have derived from a Langobardic language do not begin until at least three or four centuries after the fall of the Lombard kingdom. That these words nearly always refer to objects and manners of a 'primitive' pastoral or military life says more about the historiographical bias of some philologists than about the 'Germanic' people who supposedly used them.

PLACE-NAMES

The use of place-names as evidence for Germanic speakers entails similar methodological problems. When a predominance of place-names in the same region is coupled with archeological finds we can postulate a deeper and more concentrated settlement, such as around Friuli or in the Brescia region, but we cannot ascertain what the settlers spoke, exactly who they

---

Le valli dell'Alto Adige e il pensiero dei linguisti italiani sull'unità dei dialetti ladini (Florence, 1962), p. 25. One scholar has lamented the fact that in the realm of 'Lombard' philology, 'we all remain prisoners of his [Gamillscheg's] assertions': Scardigli, *Goti e Longobardi*, p. 293. It is difficult to see why this is necessary.

[14] See G. D'Arco Silvio Avalle, *Bassa latinità: il latino tra l'età tardo-antica e l'alto medioevo con particulare riguardo all'origine delle lingue romanze. Consonantismo* (Turin, 1969), esp. pp. 116–25; Bonfante, *Latini e Germani*, pp. 25–9. Hence in the Veronese dialect, 'Germanic' etymology is often attributed to words such as *fiàpo* (withered), *grùpia* (trough), *sbisigar* (rummage) and *slòdro* (dirty), although a Germanic etymology is only one of many other equally plausible etymologies; see M. Bondardo, *Il dialetto veronese* (Verona, 1972), pp. 52–5.

[15] E.g. P. Scardigli, 'Dalla cultura orale alla cultura scritta', in Menis (ed.), *I Longobardi*, pp. 152–7; and C.A. Mastrelli, 'La terminologia longobarda dei manufatti', *La civiltà dei longobardi in Europa, Accademia Nazionale dei Lincei: Problemi attuali di scienza e di cultura*, anno 371, qd. 189 (Rome, 1974), pp. 257–69. Langobardic words are invented, such as a hypothetical *wankja* to explain Mod. Ital. *guancia*: G. Bonfante, 'Note sui nomi della guancia e della mascella in Italia', *Biblios* 27 (1951), 361–96. Similarly, C.A. Mastrelli, 'L'origine longobarda dell'Ital. grugare (turbare "del piccione")', *Archivio Glottologico Italiano* 65 (1980), 19–29.

were, or indeed when they settled.[16] For example, the German suffix -*ing* found in many northern Italian place-names cannot be proven to derive from the Lombard language or the period of Lombard rule. Indeed a great number of them can be shown to derive from German intervention in Italian affairs during the Ottonian era, as with many Langobardic loan-word origins.[17] In the small number of cases where etymology can help us identify the ethnic origin of a place-name, it certainly cannot be used to infer the original date of that place-name in the absence of direct evidence.[18] Archaeology has offered little consolation to those wishing to identify Lombard place-names as indicative of Lombard settlement: of the ninety or so sites which have yielded 'Lombard' artefacts (itself a highly dubious attribution), only a few of these have, or are located near, place-names of supposed 'Lombard' origin.[19]

A good example is the problem of place-names that derive from the Lombard word *fara*. It is assumed that places such as Farra, Farra d'Isonzo, Fara di Soligo (it is most common in north-east Italy) are areas that experienced the settlement of a large number of Lombards grouped into *farae*, or clans.[20] These place-names undoubtedly derive from the term *fara*, but it needs to be remembered that the word was not used exclusively by the Lombards, who seem to have abandoned it for Latin terminology fairly quickly.[21] There is not mention of *farae*, or place-names deriving

---

[16] On place-names, the fundamental work was Gamillscheg, *Romania Germanica*, II, pp. 63–127. See also V. Grazi, 'Le parole lombarde di origine longobarda', *I Longobardi e la Lombardia*, pp. 45–53; C.A. Mastrelli, 'Toponomi di origine longobarda nel Trentino–Alto Adige', in G.C. Menis (ed.), *Italia Longobarda* (Venice, 1991), pp. 227–67; M.G. Arcamone, 'Reflexe des langobardischen Lautsystems in der italienischen Toponomastik', *Onoma* 21:2 (1977), 51–6. Mastrelli, 'L'elemento germanico nella toponomastica toscana', *Atti V CISAM* (Spoleto, 1973), 664–670; C. Battisti, 'L'elemento longobardo nella toponomastica umbra', *Atti del V Convegno di Studi Umbri* (Gubbio, 28 May – 1 June 1967) (Perugia, 1970), 235–48. For the south, F. Sabatini, *Riflessi linguistici della dominazione longobarda nell'Italia mediana e meridionale* (Florence, 1963).
[17] Stressed by D. Olivieri, *Toponomastica lombarda* (Milan, 1961), pp. 29–30.
[18] D.P. Blok, *Ortsnamen*, Typologie des Sources du Moyen Age Occidental 54 (Turnhout, 1988), pp. 21–25.
[19] One seriously doubts whether a more 'systematic archaeological survey' (Christie, *Lombards*, p. xvii) would solve the lack of correlation between the two types of data, artefacts and place-names, when the attribution of ethnicity to each is so fraught with methodological problems, and arguments remain circular.
[20] Other examples elsewhere: Fara Novarese (Novara), Fara d'Adda (Bergamo), Fara Olivana (Bergamo), Fara Vincentino (Vicenza), Fara Sabina (Chieti), Fara Filiorum Petri (Chieti), Fara San Martino (Chieti): see further the list in Mastrelli, 'La toponomastica lombarda', pp. 35–49, esp. pp. 37–8: and Gamillscheg, *Romania Germanica*, II, pp. 62–3; central and southern Italy, Sabatini, *Riflessi linguistici*, pp. 26–33.
[21] Our contemporary evidence is slight: Marius of Avrenches, *Chronicon*, MGH AA. XI, anno 569: Alboin 'in fara Italiam occupavit'; Paul the Deacon, *HL* II.9, who translated *faras* as 'generationes vel lineas'. *Fara* appears only once in Rothari's Edict (177), and elsewhere Rothari preferred to use the Latin *parentilla* to describe lineage in terms of a group of people from which a Lombard

Language and literacy

from the word, in the contemporary charter evidence. We have no way of knowing exactly what *farae* were for, or what size they were. Some historians see the *fara* as a type of actual lineage system, others believe *farae* were specifically military units made up of groups which may have been based on families.[22] In any case we are dealing with small numbers of people settling in those areas that consequently took on the term as a place-name, though exactly when this happened we cannot be sure. Moreover, the fact that a group was called a *fara* does not mean that the group comprised Lombards. *Farae* could have contained a mixture of ethnic identities, subsumed under a dominant core of *Langobardi* leaders who ensured their followers adhered to the *ius Langobardorum*. In short, place-names deriving from the word *fara* by no means indicate that the area experienced the settlement of a large number of ethnically homogeneous Lombards who spoke a native Langobardic language. The same can be said for those place-names based on other words associated with the Lombards, such as *arimanni*,[23] *sala*, *sunder* (see below, p. 122), *warder*, *wald*, *gahagi*,[24] and so on.

---

could claim inheritance rights, e.g. Rothari 153. It is not used in any later legislation. The word *faramannos* appears in the Burgundian code (*Lex Gundobada* 54), and other derivations elsewhere: see Van der Rhee, *GWL*, pp. 48–50.

[22] Cf. the definitions of G. Ausenda, 'The segmentary lineage in contemporary anthropology and among the Langobards', in Ausenda (ed.), *After Empire: Towards an Ethnology of Europe's Barbarians* (San Marino, 1995), pp. 15–45, at p. 39: 'residential groups comprising a lineage in its entirety or part thereof, with the possibility of affinal and even foreign admixtures, especially clients', contra A.C. Murray, *Germanic Kinship Structure: Studies in Law and Society in Antiquity and the Early Middle Ages* (Toronto, 1983), pp. 96–7, and J. Jarnut, *Bergamo 568–1098: Verfassung-, Sozial- und Wirtschaftsgeschichte einer langobardischen Stadt im Mittelalter* (Wiesbaden, 1979), pp. 133–40; Jarnut, *Geschichte der Langobarden*, pp. 47–48. Much of the 'migratory' case hinges on the indefinite etymology of *fara* deriving from OHG *faran* (mod. German *fahren*), meaning 'to go', 'to travel'.

[23] On the meaning of *arimanniae*, thought by some scholars to signify military settlements along the line of the Byzantine *limitanei*, see Brown, *Gentlemen and Officers*, pp. 88–9, and Harrison, *Early State*, pp. 69–72, 102–4. Thus the place-names which contained any number of letters thought to be derivative of *arimannia* (e.g. Armania [Sorgià], La Rimanna [L'Aquila], Colle Ramanna [near Vicovaro, Rome], Costermano, even Romagnano: see the lists in Gamillscheg, *Romania Germanica*, II, p. 66, and Sabatini, *Riflessi linguistici*, p. 38) were attributed to a sizeable Lombard settlement in the area, e.g., Bondardo, 'Il latino', p. 407; and C. Battisti, 'I nomi longobardi delle armi e le loro sopravvivenze nella lingua e nei dialetti italiani', *Settimane* 15 (Spoleto, 1968), 1067–1101 (cf. the criticisms of O. Bertolini, *ibid.*, pp. 1201–9).

[24] *Sala*: Sala Biellese (Novara), Sala al Barro (Como), Sala Comacina (Como), Sala Baganza (Parma) Sala Bolognese (Bologna), Sala Consilina (Salerno), Sala and San Pietro alla Sala (Benevento), Salaparuta (Trapani), etc.: Gamillscheg, *Romania Germanica*, II, p. 67; Sabatini, *Riflessi linguistici*, p. 33. *Sunder*: Sondrio, Sondalo (Sondrio), Sondrizza (Treviso), Sondra (pr. Montesano, Salerno): Gamillschegg, *Romania Germanica*, II, p. 68; Sabatini, *Riflessi linguistici*, p. 44. *Warda*: Garda and derivations: Gamillschegg, *Romania Germanica*, II, p. 68; Sabatini, *Riflessi linguistici*, p. 44. *Gahagi*: Gazzo, Gaggio, Gaggi, Gazzolo and many others, see Gamillscheg, *Romania Germanica*, II, p. 64; Sabatini, *Riflessi linguistici*, p. 78. Names relating to the word *Lombardi* (e.g. Lombardore [Alessandria], Masslombarda [Ravenna], Sant' Agata dei Lombardi [Benevento], etc.: see further, Gamillscheg, *Romania Germanica*, II, p. 69) should be attributed to a later period.

Literacy in Lombard Italy, c. 568–774

PERSONAL NAMES

Personal names are as hazardous as loan-words and place-names in constituting evidence for a spoken Langobardic language. The possession of a Germanic name is certainly no proof that a person spoke a Germanic language. Moreover, it is far from clear as to what was a specifically 'Lombard' name. As with the ethnic identification of loan-words in Italian and place-names in Italy, it is extremely difficult to determine whether a Germanic name is specifically Lombard or derives from one of the many west German dialects (Alemannic, Bavarian or Frankish), on the basis of the linguistic rule of the 'second consonantal shift' in Old High German. Names such as *Aupert, Arnoaldu, Ermifrid, Roadoaldus, Ratemund, Senoaldus* are considered Lombard.[25] But the rules underpinning the ethnic identification of such names are far from secure or certain, and rest on the assumptions that the orthography of the period when these names were written down was consistent or indeed corresponded to the way in which the name was pronounced. In fact there seem to be as many examples of the rules being broken as holding true.[26] Moreover, personal names of different origins were bestowed at baptism without regard to the nationality of the person being baptised. Christianity provided an onomastic culture that favoured the exchange of personal names from different ethnic backgrounds.

Just as the possession of a Germanic name does not indicate that the possessor spoke a Germanic language, there is no reason to assume that a change to a Roman name from a Germanic one entailed any correspondence with a switch from a Germanic language to Latin as the native tongue. The evidence we have before the eighth century is too sparse, and by then such practices as Lombard-named fathers giving their sons Roman names, or vice versa, or even Germanic-Roman onomastic

---

[25] Thus M.G. Arcamone, 'Antroponomia altomedievale nelle iscrizioni murali', in C. Carletti and G. Otranto (eds.), *Il Santuario di S. Michele sul Gargano dal VI al IX secolo* (Bari, 1980), pp. 255–318, at p. 257, asserts that the *Ansibertus*, who inscribed his name on the wall of the grotta at Gargano (see chapter 6 below), was Frankish or Gothic rather than Lombard, because of the *b* in his name. Cf. concerning the name *Nadigisi*: the suffix -*gisi* is thought to be of 'Gothic' or 'Frankish' origin, whereas -*chis* is the Lombard form, as in *Arichis*. Yet *Arichis* was also written as *Aregis, Arigis*, or *Arighis*: J. Jarnut, *Prosopographische und sozialgeschichtliche Studien zum Langobardenreich in Italien (568–774)* (Bonn, 1972), p. 63.

[26] E.g. that Frankish *b* becomes Langobardic *p*: but King Liutprand's name was spelled in more than one instance as *Leutbrandus* or *Liutbrandus*, as in the Corteolona inscription, see below, pp. 248–9; the name of Anselperga, daughter of King Desiderius and abbess of the monastery of San Salvatore in Brescia, written as *Anselberga, Ansilperga*, or even *Origperga*. CDL 151, 152, 155, 212, 217, 225, 226, 228, 257, 271; CDL III.31, 33, 36, 37, 38, 39, 40, 41, 44. It might be pointed out that all of these are later copies of the tenth, eleventh and twelfth centuries; but 226 ('Anselberga') is an original charter of 769. See also N. Wagner, 'Die Flexion des Langobardennamens *Ansefrida*', *Beiträge zur Namenforschung* 22:1 (1987), 47–52.

Language and literacy

amalgamations such as *Paulipert*, *Daviprand*, *Mauripert*, *Dulcipert*, and my favourite, *Floripert*, make ethnic identification by name almost impossible.[27] Up to and throughout the Ostrogothic period, Germanic personal names were usually an indication of that person's occupation as a professional soldier.[28] It has been pointed out that no person with a Germanic name appeared as a member of the Catholic clergy before the early seventh century, when a *Bernardus* is found as bishop of Vercelli.[29] The late antique church may have discriminated against people with Germanic names amongst its hierarchy, but if this were true it is important to remember that it was a *name* that they discriminated against, not ethnicity: Sigibuldus and Unigildus were the fathers of Popes Boniface II (530–2) and Pelagius II (579–90).[30] In the Lombard period, however, there appears to have been no discrimination against different types of names for different social status or functions.[31] In the early years of the kingdom, it may have been politically foolish for a war-leader or duke to use a Roman name, yet soon enough they did.[32] As an ethnic group, the Lombards were a minority of the population of Italy. Though legends proclaim their origins from lands fecund for procreation, they could not

---

[27] Dulcipert, CDL 210, 279: Mauripert, CDL 85, 113: Floripert, CDL 127, 220, 259, 260. Wickham, *EMI*, pp. 68–9 (Paulipert and Daviprand). Amalgamations could also be of a Germanic–Semitic combination: *Nazarimda*, daughter of *Nazarius*: CD 247. There are also numerous cases where one person had both a Germanic and a Greco-Roman name: Liutpert/Centulus, archdeacon of Pisa, and the deacon Richipertus/Maccio, CDL 93; Audepert/Argentio, CDL 183. See M.G. Arcamone, 'L'antroponomia germanica a Pisa durante l'età longobarda', in *Filologia e critica: studi in honore di V. Santoli*, Studi di Filologia Tedesca 6 (Rome, 1976), pp. 133–58. Elsewhere, Arcamone, 'Antroponomia longobarda in Lombardia', *Atti XII CISAM* (Spoleto, 1980), 277–82, claims that there were less hybrid names in the Po valley region than in other parts of Italy: 250 hybrid, 30 Germanic and 150 Semitic or Greco-Roman names. Jarnut's statistical analysis revealed that parents with 'Lombard' names gave Roman names to 40 per cent of their children: *Prosopographische*, pp. 404–5. The trend was equal in the other direction: parents with Roman names gave Lombard names to 40 per cent of their children. New directions of research into names and naming practices are set out in D. Geunich, W. Haubrichs and J. Jarnut (eds.), *Nomen et gens: zur geschichtlichen Aussagekraft frühmittelalterlicher Personennamen Ergänzungsbände zum Reallexicon der germanischen Altertumskunde* (Berlin, 1997), but even the editors note the difficulties and disappointments of such data (p. vi), as does Jarnut, 'Nobilis non vilis, cuius et nomen et genus scitur – a quotation from Isidore of Seville', in *ibid.*, pp. 116–26. See also M.G. Arcamone, 'Die langobardischen Personennamen in Italien. Nomen et gens der Sicht der linguistischen Analyse', in *ibid.*, pp. 56–76.

[28] A full account is in Amory, *People and Identity*.

[29] Lanzoni, *Le diocesi*, II, pp. 1041–2. Another possibility was Fredianus of Lucca, according to Lanzoni a Goth or a Lombard, *ibid.*, pp. 590–2. This overlooks the fact that members of the clergy could take a new name on consecration, as in the seventh century Anglo–Saxon examples of Winfrith (Boniface) and Willibrord (Clemens).

[30] *LP*, 57, 65, ed. Duchesne, I, pp. 281, 309.

[31] Possible exceptions are the names of the *magistri* who worked with stone, which are all Roman: see pp. 274–5.

[32] For example, Duke Lupus (Cividale, 662–663), Duke Gregorius (Benevento, 732–740), Duke Agatho (Perugia, c. 737); *HL* V.18–23; VI.55; VI.54.

have out-bred the native Italian population within a hundred-year period. We are then forced to conclude that a great number of Italians from Roman 'ethnic' background took Lombard names, and this certainly did not mean switching from Latin to a Germanic language.

Germanic personal names and place-names certainly testify to a Germanic element in the spoken language of the inhabitants of Italy, but these could derive from any number of different Germanic dialects. Italy had experienced the settlement of Germanic peoples for over 300 years by the seventh century. The province of Pannonia had experienced the settlement of an even greater number of various Germanic ethnic groups which had developed their own customs, languages, and systems of naming both people and places. The ceaseless acts of forming military alliances and peace treaties both with other barbarian groups and with the Roman empire testifies to a great deal of cultural fluidity and exchange between different barbarian groups. Part of that exchange was the borrowing of words and personal names from other groups that constituted allies or were considered as somehow akin through shared experiences as a group, such as in military campaigns, joint agricultural or pastoral enterprise, intermarriages between different tribes, joint celebration of festivities, and so on. To identify a word as specifically Langobardic is fraught with difficulties owing to this cultural-linguistic fluidity. More importantly, we cannot identify a Langobardic language for the simple reason that the Lombards themselves never did, as we shall now see.

PAUL THE DEACON

Following his source Gregory of Tours, Paul described how a group of Lombard dukes, having invaded Frankish Nissa during the interregnum, needed an 'interpretex' to communicate with the holy man Hospitius whom they found there in a disturbingly ascetic state.[33] Gregory's mention of an interpreter constitutes the only reference to the Lombards speaking anything other than Latin after their arrival in Italy. The implication is that the holy man spoke late Latin and the invading Lombards something utterly foreign to him. But it is difficult to imagine that none of the Lombard dukes, who had been living in Italy for at least six years by this time (574), nor any of their retainers, could manage enough Latin to ask Hospitius why he was chained to the roof. Hospitius' behaviour – he ate naught but bread and herbs and his manacled body was riddled with maggots – probably puzzled the marauding Lombard chieftains more than

---

[33] HL III.2. Gregory, *Historiae* VI.6: 'vocatumque interpraetem, [Langobardi] sciscitantur ab eo, quid male ficeret, ut tale supplitio artaretur'.

his language, but it is possible that the interpreter was needed for facilitating communication between different varieties of local vulgar Latin, or different dialects of Pannonian and Provençal Latin. Apart from correcting Gregory's grammar, Paul made no intervention here to explain the *interpretex*, and his silence on Lombards and language at this point needs to be measured against his comments elsewhere.

An example is his recording the use of the word *arga* (meaning 'coward') as an insult. Paul did not need to translate the word into Latin or mention that it was Lombard. It is found in the law code: it was an *iniuriosum verbum* not to be used lightly on pain of a duel or 12 *solidi* composition.[34] Although Paul's story and Rothari's law give us an insight into the nature of Lombard aristocratic culture, where courage was held in the highest esteem, the potency of the word *arga* is not solid evidence for a spoken Langobardic language, even among the Lombard nobility.[35] The word itself may even derive from the Greek *argos* ('inept', 'useless'), despite its possible appearance in the *Hildebrandslied*.[36] Indeed, Paul has the speaker, Argait, refer to the word *arga* as *vulgare verbum*, and characterises the whole exchange between the two litigants, redacted entirely in Latin, as *verba vulgaria*. The meaning here is of 'base' or 'coarse' language, and might even extend to a slang proto-Romance which Paul found distasteful.[37] Even if *arga* was considered by some to be a Langobardic word, the episode cannot be read as evidence of spoken Langobardic. Perhaps taking his cue from Rothari's law, Paul used the tale to denigrate what he saw as a dangerous and ultimately destructive Lombard custom, based on pride in warriorship which was too fickle and explosive to provide social cohesion, harmony, civil peace, and, more importantly, the strength of unity against the threat of invasion.[38]

---

[34] *HL* VI.24, where it is a play on words with the name 'Argait'. Rothari, 381.

[35] *Contra* Hartmann, *Geschichte Italiens*, II, p. 58.

[36] Greek etymology, see Zanella, *Storia*, p. 507 n. 34; Bruckner, *Sprache*, p. 202; also DuCange, *Glossarium*, I, p. 387. Van der Rhee, *GWL*, pp. 31–2, does not offer an etymology. Its presence in the *Hildebrandslied* (line 58), emended by more modern commentators to *argosto*, has been used to bolster theories of the 'Lombard recension' of the work, e.g. W. Krogmann, *Das Hildebrandslied in der langobardische Urfassung Hergestellt* (Berlin, 1958), pp. 34–8, but cf. H. Van der Kolk, *Das Hildebrandslied: ein forschungsgeschichtliche Darstellung* (Amsterdam, 1967), pp. 36, 116, and R. Lühr, *Studien zur Sprache des Hildebrandsliedes. Teil I. Herkunft und Sprache* B.22 (Frankfurt and Berne, 1982), I, pp. 364–8; II, pp. 682–5. Cf. Loyd and Springer, *EWA*, I, 322–3; Splett, *ADW*, p. 28.

[37] *HL* VI.24: 'Memento, dux Ferdulf, quod me esse inertem et inutilem dixeris et vulgari verbo arga vocaveris'. See M. Van Uytfanghe, 'Les expressions du type *quod vulgo vocant* dans des texts latins antérieurs au Concile de Tours et aux Serments de Strasbourg: témoinages lexicologiques et sociolinguistiques de la langue rustique romaine?', *Zeitschrift für Romanische Philologie* 105 (1989), 28–49.

[38] *HL* VI.24: 'Haec ideo vel maxime in hac posuimus historia, ne quid aliquid per contentionis malum simile contingat.'

In this same chapter Paul records a Slavic incursion (a 'sheep-raid') into the duchy of Friuli, and how the Lombard official (the above mentioned Argait) attempted to chase the Slavs.[39] Paul's gloss on Argait's status as 'the rector of that place, what they call in their own language *sculdahis*', raises serious questions about the intended audience for the *HL* and contemporary knowledge of Lombard office titles. The office of *sculdahis* is found in legislation and charters right throughout the Lombard period and beyond in the surviving duchy of Benevento, yet Paul felt the need to translate it into a Latin equivalent. Although it is only a small comment, it casts large shadows on the theory that the *HL*'s intended audience was the Beneventan court.[40] It may be overinterpretation, but the phrase *lingua propria dicunt* suggests that Paul was writing for people who are contemporary with, but outside, Lombard society: 'what *they* call in *their* language'. In the following gloss on *scaffardus* he uses the first person plural to qualify 'what we call in the common language'.[41] Paul's use of *vulgo* and the first person plural, in contrast to the above glosses recalling a language of the Lombards (*propria lingua*), suggests that it was simply a common word of no specific origin: *scaffardus* was certainly common to other Germanic languages.[42] For whom was Paul writing? Paul's career as a beneficiary of Frankish patronage suggests the possibility that the *HL* may have been intended for a Frankish audience as an historical guide to the Italy they had now conquered.[43] Yet Charlemagne's Franks would not have needed a Latin translation of *sculdahis*: they continued using the office in the administration of the kingdom.[44] Alternatively, Paul's comment was aimed at a general posterity without specific nationalities or ethnicities in mind. The same considerations apply when Paul refers to other Lombard offices, such as *marpahis* or *scilpor*.[45] As with *fara*, Paul felt the need to translate these terms which are considered by historians as fundamental to Lombard military culture. Yet Paul's own experience

[39] *HL* IV.24.
[40] Goffart, *Narrators*, chapter 5, though not the first to espouse this theory.
[41] *HL* V.2: 'Perctarit vero statim suo pincernae, quem vulgo scaffardum dicimus, praecepit'.
[42] Van der Rhee, 'Die germanischen Wörter in der *Historia Langobardorum* des Paulus Diaconus', *Romanobarbarica* 5 (1980), 271–96, at p. 288.
[43] See R. McKitterick, 'Paul the Deacon and the Franks', *EME* 8:3 (1999), 319–39.
[44] See E. Saracco Previdi, 'Lo *sculdahis* nel territorio longobardo di Rieti (sec. VIII e IX). Dall'amministrazione longobarda a quella franca', *Studi Medievali* 3:2 (1973), 219–75.
[45] Paul translates *marpahis* twice as *strator*, *HL* II.9: 'strator... quem lingua propria marpahis appellant', and VI.6. It, too, was still in use at the Beneventan court in the late eighth and early ninth centuries: see the references in J. Schütz, 'Langobardisch marphais', *Sprachwissenschaft* 14 (1989), 405–9. *Scilpor* receives a translation as *armiger* with no mention of language (*HL* II.28: 'hoc est armiger... erat'). Van der Rhee, 'Die germanischen Wörter', p. 283. Neither *marpahis* nor *scilpor* is mentioned in Lombard legislation. One royal charter of 674 refers to an 'Alfrit scildeporrus': CDL III.6. In the same document *stratores* is used instead of *marpahis*. Cf. *HL* V.36: 'cum comite Baioariorum, quem illi gravionem dicunt'.

proves otherwise. Langobardic language had died so long before that even the memory of it once existing needed to be revived.

Other references in Paul's *HL* suggest that Langobardic words were not specifically Langobardic at all but belonged to a larger Germanic linguistic realm shared by many different peoples, such as *bandum, lama, scala, lang,* and *bart*, words common to different dialects of Old High German.[46] Indeed, Paul shows an awareness of a larger common Germanic-linguistic realm when he referred to a *feld*: 'in campis patentis, qui sermone barbarico feld appellantur'.[47] *Feld* was likewise extremely common to western Old High German, hence Paul chose the adjective 'barbarico' to describe the word's commonality in Europe, for he used the same term to describe the peoples of northern Europe in the opening to the *HL*.[48] But Paul could be more precise. In another passage, often cited by scholars looking for vestiges of a 'Lombard oral culture', Paul reports how Alboin was so famous that songs are still sung about him amongst the Bavarians, Saxons, 'and other men of that same language' ('eiusdem linguae').[49] Hence Paul was aware of the linguistic affinities between Bavarians and Saxons, to which modern scholarship attests.[50] Paul may have been boasting, but he was not fabricating. The mid-seventh-century Anglo-Saxon poem *Widsith* mentions Audoin and Alboin in favourable terms.[51] What is striking about Paul's passage is the failure to mention that songs were sung about Alboin by the Lombards 'in their own language', or by the Lombards in any language at all. Paul does not explicitly say that the *eadem lingua* common to the Bavarians and Saxons was also common to the Lombards. No doubt songs were sung by the Lombards

---

[46] Paul possibly took *bandum* from the *Origo gentis langobardorum* (c. 4: 'tulit vando ipsius et capsidem'; or another, similar text: see above, pp. 87–98) which he translated as *vexillum, HL* I.20: 'vexillum, quod bandum appellant'. The subject of the verb *appellant* may be Lombards or Herulians. For *bandum*, possibly a Gothic word and common to other western dialects of Old High German such as Old Saxon and Frankish, see Van der Rhee, 'Die germanischen Wörter', pp. 275–6; *EWA*, I, pp. 465–8; Splett, *ADW*, I.1, p. 42. *Lama* (*HL* I.15: 'piscina, quae eorum lingua lama dicitur') is a word of north-east origin (Friulian) and should not be ascribed to the Lombards: Van der Rhee, 'Die germanischen Wörter', p. 285; Splett, *ADW*, I.1, p. 511. For *scala* (*HL* I.27: 'quod genus poculi apud eos scala dicitur, lingua vero Latina patera vocitatur') see Van der Rhee, 'Die germanischen Wörter', p. 289; Splett, *ADW*, I.2, p. 892. *Bard* and *lang, HL* I.9, from Isidore, *Etymologiae* IX.2.15. Cf. Van der Rhee, 'Die germanischen Wörter', p. 278; *EWA*, p. 465–6, 513; Splett, *ADW*, I.1, p. 42, 511–13.
[47] *HL* I.20.
[48] *HL* I.1: 'et aliae feroces et barbarae nationes e Germania prodierunt'. See L. Alfonsi, 'Romani e barbari nella *Historia langobardorum* di Paolo Diacono', *Romanobarbarica* 1 (1976), 7–24.
[49] *HL* I.27: 'Alboin vero ita praeclarum longe et lateque nomen percrebuit, ut hactenus etiam tam apud Baioariorum gentem quamque et Saxonum, sed et alios eiusdem linguae homines eius liberalita et gloria bellorumque felicitas et virtus in eorum carminibus celebretur.'
[50] Bostock, *Handbook*, pp. 10–13.
[51] Hodgkin, *Italy*, V, pp. 175–7. H. Munro Chadwick, *The Heroic Age* (Westport, CT, 1974), pp. 43–5.

themselves about the heroic king who conquered Italy. But one can only speculate in the light of Paul's silence in what language these were sung. In any case, Paul's silence indicates that songs in a Germanic language were not integral to Lombard culture, nor did they constitute an integral part of Lombard identity.

To conclude this excursus on the evidence of the *HL* for a native Langobardic language, we should note the interesting story of Bulgars who settled in Benevento under the direction of King Grimoald: 'The Bulgars have lived in these places we have mentioned down to this day, and although they speak Latin, they have still not lost the use of their own language.'[52] Two conclusions concerning the linguistic situation of late eighth-century Italy might be drawn from this comment. First, Latin was the spoken language of Italy, and people still recognised it as such, even Paul, who had an education in classical and patristic texts written in Latin centuries earlier. Second, the use of a second language was rare; if the Lombards still spoke a native Langobardic language at any point of their history in Italy, presumably Paul would have mentioned it. Indeed, his interest in bilingualism is attested in the above mentioned Bulgar story and in reference to one Lombard from Friuli who was fluent in Slavic.[53] Moreover, the story of the bilingual Bulgars seems tinged with a hint of nostalgia for a time when the Lombards spoke a language other than Latin, as does the *arga* episode. Paul's comments may indeed have been directed at a Beneventan audience already beginning to cultivate a strong nationalistic Lombard identity as the last bastion of a once great kingdom. The memory of a 'lost' national language was part of that constructed identity. That this thoroughly Latinised author, from a Lombard noble family, makes no comment on a Langobardic language in a 'history of his people' casts great shadows on any notions of Langobardic linguistic longevity.

LANGOBARDIC WORDS IN THE LAW CODE

As we shall see in the next chapter, Rothari's claim to present in his Edict the 'antiquas legis patrum nostrorum quae scriptae non erant', is not quite the full story: there is much in his Edict that is late Roman

---

[52] *HL* V.29: 'Qui usque hodie in his ut diximus locis habitantes, quamquam et Latine loquantur, linguae tamen propriae usum minime amiserunt'. The chronology of these events is unclear: Paul's narrative would date the events between 663 and 671, sometime after Grimoald had returned from Benevento, cf. the Byzantine chronicle of Theophanes, *sub anno* 6171 (that is 679/80) and Fredegar, *Chron.* IV.72. Grimoald granted the Bulgars *Sepinum* (Sepiano), *Bovianum* (Boiano), *Isernia*, land 'which was empty up until now'. See Hodgkin, *Italy*, VI, pp. 284–5. Grave sites with horse burials near Campochiaro, between Sepino and Boiano, have been identified with this settlement: see V. Ceglia, 'Lo scavo della necropoli di Vicenne', *Conoscenze* 4 (1988), 31–48.

[53] *HL* IV.44: 'Radulad . . . eisdem Sclavis propria illorum lingua locutus est'.

property law, and much that shares affinity with other barbarian law codes. The Lombard law code, in its entirety, from the legislation of Rothari to Aistulf, contains over eighty words that are of Germanic origin.[54] It is often assumed by linguists and historians alike that the use of these words in the law code is proof of Langobardic language and its linguistic relevance to a percentage of the population who were to adhere to the norms and values described by the code. The corrupt Latin of the law code is thought to mask a flourishing Langobardic oral culture.[55]

I should like to suggest here that rather than providing testimony to a living Langobardic language, the evidence of the code should be read to establish the contrary: the sparing and sometimes confusing nature of the use of such words is testimony to a continued use of Germanic terms within Lombard legal traditions, but not a living, spoken language. This is not to say these terms were irrelevant, or not used at the royal court or by judges in local courts. But as such they were part of Lombard juridical culture which became a flagship of Lombard government, and it is from this that they derive their importance in the Lombard period. Moreover, many Langobardic terms belonged to a wider Germanic linguistic sphere and can be found in other barbarian law codes, while many others have their origins in late Latin or Greek. But nearly all of those in the code are dependent in one way or another upon Latin for their explication. This can take the form either of a Latin gloss (that is, a Germanic word is rendered with an equivalent word or phrase) or of a Germanic gloss (a Latin word or expression is given an equivalent Germanic word) or by the general content of the law which postulates a particular circumstance in which the meaning of the Germanic word becomes obvious.

The Germanic terms used in the code can be broken down into the separate categories of social status and family law (thirty words or so), crimes and misdemeanours (seventeen), Lombard administrative positions (six), and everyday terms denoting agricultural phenomena or body parts (ten). Aside from these, there are some words which can be seen as belonging to a pan-Germanic linguistic culture (ten), and others that are possibly of late Latin or Greek origin (eight) – in both cases it is often impossible to know whether these terms were already in use in Italy, or whether the Lombards introduced them. The majority refer specifically to social status and family law, including some that derive from a pan-Germanic legal, linguistic culture reflected in other early Germanic legal codes, such as

---

[54] Conveniently listed by Azzara, *Le leggi*, pp. 305–9, and systematically by Van der Rhee, *GWL*, pp. 18–144. The discrepancy between the two lists (Azzara, 91 words, Van der Rhee 83) results from Azzara's inclusion of verbs from substantives (*fegang, fegangit*) and minor variants (*fulcfree, fulcfrea; gasindium, gasindius*).

[55] For example, Azzara, *Le leggi*, p. xxvii.

wergeld (social status by monetary value)[56] and *thinx* ('gift, donation, legal transaction' and related concepts of *gairethinx*, and the Latinised *thingare, thingatio*),[57] *fara* (kin-group), *faida* (feud or vendetta),[58] *morgingab* (morning gift),[59] *in pans* (king's protection/tutelage),[60] *baro* (freeman),[61] *mundium* (legal control over a woman, and related terms, *mundoald, selpmundia*),[62] *waregang* (foreigner)[63] and *trewas* (truce).[64] Others appear to pertain to an exclusively Lombard legal tradition (or we only know them from the Lombard evidence), though they may have legal equivalents or linguistic affinities with other Germanic peoples, such as *aldius/aldia* (half-free), *faderfio* (father's gift, akin to a dowry), *arimannus* (freeman, soldier), *fulcfree* (free status), *angargathungi* (worth of *wergeld*), *fulboran* (free woman), *gefand* (co-heir), *gamahalos* (relatives by marriage), *cawerfida* (tradition, custom), *launichild* (return-gift), *metfio* and *meta* (betrothal price, paid to bride's family), *threus* (natural, as opposed to legitimate, child), *wadia* (pledge) and *wirdibora* (status of freewoman). Many of these appear to be deeply rooted in pre-Italian Lombard social organisation, and some, such as *morgengab* and *mundium*, were maintained in Italy until the revival of Roman law in the twelfth and thirteenth centuries and beyond. One could expect that Germanic terms for 'co-heir' (*gefand*) and 'natural children' (*threus*) were used among Lombard aristocracy, but by the end of the eighth century we find the term *barba* for 'paternal uncle' being used in the funerary inscriptions of Jews in southern Italy. Although the word may be of Latin origin, the term is first found in the Lombard law code, and arguably it was

---

[56] Brunner, *Deutsche Rechtsgeschichte*, II, pp. 796–807; F. Genzmer, 'Rache, Wergeld und Klage in altgermanischen Rechtsleben', *Wissenschaftlich Akademie Tübingen des NSD-Dozentenbundes* (Tübingen, 1941), 280–97.

[57] *Thinx*: Rothari 171, 172, 174, Liutprand 65, 105, 140. *Gairethinx*: Rothari 167, 172, 174, 222, 224, 375, Liutprand 54. *Thingare*: Rothari 156, 157, 168, 170, 171, 172, 173, 176, 222, 224, 360, 367, Liutprand 9, 55, 77, 140, Aistulf 11, 12. *Thingatio*, Liutprand 73.

[58] Rothari 45, 74, 75, 138, 162, 188, 190, 214, 326, 387, Grimoald 8, Liutprand 13, 119, 127, 135, 136. Van der Rhee, *GWL*, pp. 46–8.

[59] Rothari 182, 199, 200, 216; Liutprand prolog. anno V, 7, 103, 117, Aistulf 14. *Lex. rib.* 37.2; *Lex alam.* 54.3; *Lex gund.* 42.2; G. Baesecke, 'Die deutschen Worte der germanischen Gesetze', *Beiträge zur Geschichte der deutschen Sprache und Literatur* 59 (Tübingen, 1935), 1–110, at pp. 32, 57, 64, 95. For use in charters, see pp. 185–6.

[60] Rothari 224. Cf. *bannum* (regis), etc. Brunner, *Deutsche Rechtsgeschichte*, I, pp. 201–13.

[61] *Pact. sal.* 31.1, 54.2.4; *Lex rib.* 61.12; *Lex alam.* 69, etc. Bruckner, *Sprache*, p. 40, 202; Van der Rhee, *GWL*, pp. 38–9; *EWA*, I, pp. 486–7.

[62] Rothari 204. Bruckner, *Sprache*, pp. 72, 191; Van der Rhee, *GWL*, pp. 114–15. See below, pp. 182–4.

[63] Rothari 367. Cf. *Ewa chamavorum* 9. Baesecke, 'Deutschen Worte', pp. 65, 95; Brunner, *Deutsche Rechtsgeschichte*, I, p. 400.

[64] Liutprand 42. Bruckner, *Sprache*, p. 133; Van der Rhee, *GWL*, pp. 128–9.

Language and literacy

from Lombard family law that this Jewish community borrowed the concept.[65]

Their use and placement in the law code can often be puzzling. Some words appear to mean the same thing, such as *fulcfrea* and *wirdibora* for 'woman of free status', and it is difficult to understand why different terms are being used, especially since both are Germanic glosses on Latin terms.[66] Moreover, Liutprand introduced the use of the adjective *frea* to describe a 'free woman', and cites Rothari's previous legislation for authority on the problem being addressed ('sicut gloriose memorie Rothari rex in anteriore edicto iussit'). Yet Rothari was content to use the Latin 'mulier libera' to render the same concept in those very same scenarios.[67] Likewise, interesting questions are raised by Liutprand's introduction into the code of the concept of *cawerfida*, or 'custom'.[68] It is first used in a law regarding succession to property, in which Liutprand states 'we have had this written down because, although it was not previously inserted into the Edict, all of our judges and *fideles* say that it has always been an ancient *cawerfida* until now'.[69] Legal historians have been quick to point out that such statements testify to Lombard law working within a dialectic of written law and social customs that have yet to be included in the code.[70] Whilst this is undoubtedly true, as it is for all written law, it is curious that the concept of custom was suddenly rendered with a Germanic word. In the same batch of legislation (that is, from the fourteenth year of Liutprand's reign, 726), Liutprand referred to the problem of unwritten custom in the same manner though without using the

---

[65] 'Hic requiesc[it benem]emori[us] / [S]amual filius Silani [cu]m ezih[i] / [e]l barbane suum qui vixit annos / [X]XXXII sit p[ax] sup[er] dormitor[ium] / [eorum amen]'. See D. Noy (ed.), *Jewish Inscriptions of Western Europe*, I, *Italy* (Cambridge, 1993), no. 121, pp. 157–60. I thank Mark Handley for bringing this to my attention and the reference. For *barba[s]*, *barbanis*: Rothari 163, 164, 186, Liutprand 145. Cf. Andreas of Bergamo, MGH SRL, p. 238. CDL 19 (715), p. 70, l.4. Also ChLA 831 (792). The *barba* of CDL 159 refers to its use in Rothari 382–3 as 'beard'. On the origin, Van der Rhee, *GWL*, pp. 36–8; Sabatini, *Riflessi linguistici*, pp. 237–8.

[66] Rothari 216, 'libera uxorem [sic], id est fulcfrea', and cf. 257: 'Si mulier libera fulcfrea super furtum comprehensa fuerit'. On *fulcfrea* see Princi Braccini, 'Termini germanici', pp. 1187–9. *Wirdibora*, Rothari 222: 'debeat eam [ancillam] libera thingare, sic libera, quod est wirdibora'. Cf. Liutprand 106. Reading the laws closely, the implication that *wirdibora* may refer to a process of being made free from previously servile or *aldia* status, in opposition to *fulcfrea* signifying a free-born woman, seems denied by the very etymology of *wirdibora* as 'free-born': Bruckner, *Sprache*, pp. 68, 189; but cf. Braune, *Althochdeutsche Grammatik*, p. 225; Van der Rhee, *GWL*, p. 143.

[67] Liutprand 194, 120, Rothari 186, 187.

[68] On the myriad possible etymologies and meanings for this word, see G. Princi Braccini, 'Un suggerimento da due glosse di Papia: cadarfida = "retaggio dei detti"?', *Romanobarbarica* 10 (1988–89), 309–66.

[69] Liutprand 77: 'quod cawerfida antiqua usque nunc sic fuissit'. Cf. Liutprand 133.

[70] For example, F. Calasso, *Medio evo del diritto*, Le Fonti 1 (Milan, 1954), p. 195.

word *cawerfida*.[71] Five years later he substituted the term *antiqua consuitudo* [*sic*] for *antiqua cawerfida* to describe the duel.[72] One gets the sense that Liutprand's introduction of the term *cawerfida* to Lombard legislation carried more ideological weight than practical use. In recalling an ancient word to denote ancient custom, Liutprand thus legitimised his enactment and excused Rothari's negligence all at once.

When we turn to our second-largest category, that of terms denoting particular crimes, we are likewise faced with both a formidable presence of a Germanic legal culture, and a degree of inconsistency in the use of the terms within the code. And as with many of the terms relating to social status or family law, many of the terms used for crimes find linguistic and legal parallels in other Germanic law codes, such as *marahworf* (throwing someone from their mount),[73] *haistan* (anger, violent behaviour),[74] *iderzon* (hedge breaking)[75] and *wifa* (unlawful occupation, possession).[76] Other terms we know only from the Lombard context, such as *anagrip* (abduction of woman),[77] *grapworf* (grave-robbing, or disturbing),[78] *fegangi* (theft caught 'red-handed', cf. Roman *furtum manifestum*),[79] *fraida* (illegal refuge, flight),[80] *harischild* (group sedition),[81] *haritraib* (penalty for

---

[71] Liutprand 73: 'Quia et sic specialiter in edictum non fuit institutum, tamen usque modo sic est iudicatum: ideo pro errore tollendum hoc scribere in edicti paginam iussimus.'

[72] Liutprand 118: *consuetudo antiqua* and settlement *per pugnam* as *consuitutinem gentis nostrae langobardorum*. Rothari 9 preferred the Germanic term *camfio* with a Latin gloss (*id est pugnam*): he did not say it was ancient custom. Cf. also Rothari 198, 202, 213, and esp. 368: 'De camphionibus'. On *camphio*, Princi Braccini, 'Termini germanici', pp. 1142, 1145.

[73] Rothari 30, 373. Also in *Lex bav.* 4.11 (*marach*), 4.18, (*marchfalli*), and *Lex alam.* 70.3, 72.1 (*marach*). Brunner, *Deutsche Rechtsgeschichte*, II, pp. 821–3; Baesecke, 'Deutschen Worte', pp. 17, 23; Bruckner, *Sprache*, pp. 141, 185; Van der Rhee, *GWL*, pp. 96–8.

[74] Rothari 277. *Lex alam.* 9; Van der Rhee, *GWL*, pp. 79–80; Bruckner, *Sprache*, pp. 99, 190; Brunner, *Deutsche Rechtsgeschichte*, II, p. 715.

[75] Rothari 285. Also in *Lex bav.* 10.16, and *Leges anglo-saxonum*, Aethelbert 27. Baesecke, 'Deutschen Worte', p. 23; Van der Rhee, *GWL*, pp. 89–90.

[76] Liutprand 134, 148. Cf. Ratchis 14 *wifa*, also in *Lex bav.* 10.18. Baesecke, 'Deutschen Worte', p. 160; Bruckner, *Sprache*, pp. 140–1; Van der Rhee, *GWL*, pp. 140–1. The meaning is obscure, despite philological attempts to discern it: G.B. Pellegrini, 'Terminologia agraria medievale in Italia', *Settimane* 13 (Spoleto, 1966), 647–60, 'fantoccio formato di spighe di grano'; cf. G. Fasoli, 'Considerazioni sul problema degli stanziamenti longobardi in Italia', *Atti del convegno di studi longobardi* (Udine, 1970), 49–59, at p. 54, 'manipolo di paglia o di canne incrociate'.

[77] Rothari 188, 189, 190, 214, Liutprand 127. Bruckner, *Sprache*, p. 202; Van der Rhee, *GWL*, pp. 27–9; *EWA*, I, p. 231 Note the *Gloss. mattrit*, 'id est mani arrigrippare carnem'. Parallel with *Lex bav.* 8.3 *horcrift*? Cf. Baesecke, 'Deutschen Worte', p. 23.

[78] Rothari 15. Van der Rhee, *GWL*, pp. 79–80.

[79] Rothari 253, 292, 372, Grimoald 9. Van der Rhee, *GWL*, pp. 50–2; Bruckner, *Sprache*, pp. 57–9; Splett, *ADW*, I.2, pp. 282–4. The meaning of Liutprand 147, that *servi, aldi* or *ancillae* who *stole* and were caught 'sint figanges', is not clear: see C. Calisse, *Storia del diritto italiano*, I, Le Fonti (Florence, 1930), pp. 342–3.

[80] Rothari 275. Bruckner, *Sprache*, p. 204; Van der Rhee, *GWL*, pp. 55–6.

[81] Liutprand 134, 141. Van der Rhee, *GWL*, p. 187; Bruckner, *Sprache*, p. 157.

Language and literacy

disturbing occupied house),[82] *hoberos* (breaking and entering),[83] *rairaub* (despoiling and hiding a dead body, especially one floating down the river),[84] and the crime of *morth*, that of homicide committed secretly, which seems to have greatly offended early Lombard sensibilities.[85]

As with the terms of social status, some inclusions are puzzling. Liutprand reasoned that the crime of a group of armed men expelling someone from their own home, or that of a group of violent women who did likewise, 'cannot be considered as *[h]arischild*', as though the matter had been thoroughly debated, but *[h]arschild* is mentioned nowhere else in the entire code.[86] Rothari did something similar when he decreed that *haritraib*, the sum of composition for disturbance to an occupied house, was to be paid 'just as recorded in this edict', which it was not.[87] Yet Liutprand's, and to a lesser extent Rothari's, legislative reasoning is testimony to the relevance of those terms in Lombard legal traditions cultivated at the royal court.

How well these terms were known and used by the majority of the populace is another matter. The fact that the terms were nearly always given a Latin equivalent could not have helped their dissemination among speakers of late Latin. Unfortunately we lack corroborative evidence of charters and *placita* for criminal cases or cases of personal injury, since charters deal almost exclusively with property law. There is, as far as I know, only one occasion in which a Germanic term for crime from the code is found in the charter evidence, that of *bluttare*, concerning a situation in which the boundaries of property law and criminal law were crossed. Introduced into the code by Liutprand and used only once, without a gloss, in a law against seditious activity, *bluttare* appears to mean specifically to deprive someone involved with the royal court, thus amounting to *lèse-majesté* rather than simply theft.[88] The word turns up in an ecclesiastical *placitum* from Lucca in 771, which records its use by the bishop, and

---

[82] Rothari 379. Bruckner, *Sprache*, pp. 182, 207; Van der Rhee, *GWL*, pp. 85–6, and see below.
[83] Rothari 278, 373, 380. Bruckner, *Sprache*, p. 79; Van der Rhee, *GWL*, pp. 86–8.
[84] Rothari 16. Van der Rhee, *GWL*, pp. 11–12. Cf. *Lex bav.* 19.4 *uualraupa*; Baesecke, 'Deutschen Worte', p. 23. Note the difference in penalty to *plodraub*.
[85] Rothari 14, 369, 370. Van der Rhee, *GWL*, pp. 104–5; Brunner, *Deutsche Rechtsgeschichte*, II, pp. 813–15.
[86] Liutprand 134, 141. On the latter see R. Balzaretti, '"These are things that men do, not women": the social regulation of female violence in Langobard Italy', in G. Halsall (ed.), *Violence and Society in Early Medieval Europe* (London, 1998), pp. 175–92, at pp. 186–8.
[87] Rothari 379; possibly ref. to Rothari 17 or 146.
[88] Liutprand 35: 'et si casam cuiuscumque bluttauerint aut res eorum tulerint qui cum palatio aut cum rege tenent et fidem suam cum iudice in palatio conservant'. Cf. Fischer-Drew trans. p. 161, restricts the meaning to those who hold property from the fisc or king, but the following example would extend it to those in negotation with state authorities. On the etymology, Bruckner, *Sprache*, p. 191; Van der Rhee, *GWL*, p. 41.

subsequently the plaintiffs, to mean precisely the same. However, close reading reveals that in using the term the bishop was merely reading the text of King Desiderius' royal order (called a *sacra iussio*), obtained by the plaintiffs from the court in Pavia, which directly accused Bishop Peredeo of having 'bluttated' the poor plaintiffs, a woman and her infant son, through his mismanagement: he had issued two separate charters granting the rights of habitation in a house owned by the church. Peredeo must have felt uneasy reading out the text of Desiderius' *iussio*: 'and therefore now we have expelled them unreasonably from [their home] for profit, we have *bluttated* them, removed them and some of their property from the premises, and we have taken from them everything which they possessed'.[89] The bishop did not hesitate to dispense justice. The penalty for having 'bluttated' someone was severe; their property was to be returned eightfold. The extra fine of *wergeld* might have been waived in Peredeo's case, but the tone of the royal *iussio* suggests that Desiderius might have easily found an alternative. Hence again we see the word's juridical dependency: it is impossible to know whether Bishop Peredeo, his clerics or the plaintiffs at the Lucchese court would have used the word at all if it were not for the king's writ. But that Desiderius used it as a term of accusation testifies to its importance and currency in centres of power and administration.

The better preservation of documents in Lucca furnishes us with glimpses of the use of Langobardic terms at the local level for which we otherwise lack testimony. An example is the use of the word *ferquidus*, restricted to charters of Lucchese origin, be they ecclesiastic or entirely secular. In the law code, the word is glossed 'id est similem' referring to the value of property, in terms of either composition for damages or the value of pledges.[90] In the charter evidence the term appears exclusively in the penalty clauses (the *stipulatio dupla*) concerning land in a strictly formulaic use, though here the term harkens back to its more etymological significance of 'in the place mentioned', in that it was used to signifiy the promise of compensation of land 'in the same place' should the vendor or donor fail to respect the terms of the transaction.[91]

---

[89] CDL 255. 'in qua [iussione] contenebatur... quod... nos dedissimus ecclesiam monasteri nostri Sancti Sauini per cartulam eidem Atriperto infantulo... similter per aliam cartam confirmassimus ipsum Petrum clericum in casa iamdicte ecclesiae... nos modo eos exinde foris expellissimus propter premium contra rationem, ut eos bluttassimus et de alias res eorum eos foris expellissimus et omnia eis tullissimus quantumcumque habuissent'. The plaintiff, Altitruda, later states: 'ut nos debluttare fecissitis'.

[90] Damages, Rothari 147, 330, 337, 349, Liutprand 151; the value of *launichild*, Rothari 175.

[91] CDL 68 (Jan. 739), is typical: 'si minime defensare non potuero ego Pettu aut mei heredis tibi qui supra Aloin aut tuis, repromitto adque spondeo me esset compunere in duppla meliorata terrula, de quo agitor, sub stemmationem in aferquede loco, et cartula venditionis in sua manea

Language and literacy

Another juridical term which made its way to the charter evidence was *uuadia*, a pan-Germanic term for pledge or surety, which in the Lombard context served as an equivalent for the Roman concept of *stipulatio* as found in many instances throughout the law code.[92] *Uuadia* could also be a problem. Both Liutprand and Ratchis repeatedly legislated that sureties in the form of *uuadia* needed witnesses as well a *fideiussor*: too many debtors (obviously in league with their *fideiussores*) were denying that such a transaction ever took place, and resorted to oath-taking or duels, as Rothari had stipulated.[93] We find caution in the charter evidence too, such as when Bonulus of Chiusi arranged to sell to Guntefrid some property in exchange for twelve days of manual labour. Without the clean receipt of price paid, a *charta promissionis* was drawn up, with both Bonulus and Guntefrid agreeing to a charge of 10 *solidi* should one of them default. Despite this, the scribe, Firmus *notarius*, noted at the foot of the charter that Guntefrid also gave to Bonulus 4 *solidi* as *uuadia*, and that Firmus himself acted as a surety (*fideiussor*) in the presence of four witnesses, only one of whom was a witness to the original transaction.[94] Bonulus was perhaps being unduly cautious: in any case, Firmus' footnote follows to the letter Liutprand's law on the presence of *fideiussores* and witnesses.[95] By the time of the end of the Lombard kingdom, we find even documents themselves being used as *uuadia*.[96]

As with *ferquidus*, the use of Langobardic terms was not restricted to the legal culture of the laity, but extended to ecclesiastics. In a dispute of 764 between two priests presided over by the bishop of Lucca, the accuser, Liutpert, stated that he could produce witnesses who had seen the defendant, Gundualt, pay for a private property with golden crosses from the altar of Gundualt's church of San Cassiano. Lucipert was asked *dare uuadia* to Gundualt as an assurance that Lucipert would furnish the court with the witnesses on an appointed day. Lucipert failed to do so, and the bishop had little choice but to judge the dispute on the basis of an examination of Gundualt's charter, which stated clearly that Gundualt had paid 20 gold *solidi*, and mentioned nothing of the gold

---

fermitatem'. Cf. CDL 84, 'in duplum res meliorata, de quod agitur, in frequede loco'. Note the scribe, Altipert, *vir devotus*, wrote another such charter, again for the church of S. Regolo in Gualdo, two years later, without using the same formula: CDL 87. Likewise, the scribe Teupert used the formula three times, CDL 91, 105, 134 (repeating the mistake of *sum* for *sub stimationem* which follows immediately after) but not in two earlier charters, CDL 74, 80. Other uses of *in ferquide loco*, CDL 108, 'tibi esse restauratur frequidem talem'; CDL 91, 'in ferquidem locum'. On the etymology, Van der Rhee, *GWL*, pp. 52–4.

[92] Rothari 360, 361, 362, 366, Liutprand 8, 15, 36, 37, 38, 39, 40, 61, 96, 128. Cf. Liutprand 15, *uuadiare*. Ratchis, prol., 5, 8. As *stipulatio*, Calasso, *Medio evo*, p. 186.
[93] Liutprand 36, 37, 38, 39, 40, Ratchis 8, Rothari 366.
[94] CDL 192 (Chiusi, 765).
[95] Liutprand 15, and cf. Ratchis 5.
[96] CDL 257 (Brescia, 773).

Literacy in Lombard Italy, c. 568–774

crosses in question. In closing the proceedings, the bishop reminded Gunduald to return the *uuadia* to Liutpert, prior to swearing five times on the Gospels.[97] The episode illustrates the complementary nature of oral procedure and written proofs which must have operated in secular courts also, and demonstrates the extent to which Langobardic legal terms penetrated local society.

But not only strictly legal terms. The better survival rate of Lucchese documents allows us to see the widespread use of the word *sala*, as an equivalent to the Latin *curtis*. It appears relatively often enough in the charter evidence for us to see its entry into later medieval terminology to designate seigneurial residence and eventually the modern Italian 'hall' or 'room'. But the word received no gloss in Rothari's Edict or in the *Memoratorio de mercedibus magistri commacinorum*, and was common to the west Germanic language-group (it appears in Alemannic law, for example), which throws its Langobardic origin into question: it may simply have been a Latinised Germanic word already in use in Italy.[98] The same can be said for *sundrius* (*-um*) (and its adjectival form *sundriale*), a related term exclusive to Lucchese charters and meaning independent estate or just simply 'property'. It does not appear in the law code at all, but has been attributed to the Lombards purely on the basis of chronology.[99] Philologists have traced numerous place-names to this term,[100] but whether this signifies the strong presence of a Germanic language in the area is another question.

MILITARY TERMS

It is not surprising that many of the words for social status, crimes and everyday objects belong to a military context. The crime of *astalin*, that of abandoning a fellow soldier (*collega*) in war, is listed among Rothari's 'top ten' in the Edict, all of which concern the security of king and state, and all of which incur capital punishment.[101] Other military terms

---

[97] CDL 184 (Lucca, 764). For another example of Lucchese priests giving *uuadia* and swearing on the Gospels, see CDL II, Appendix, a *placitum* of 786, pp. 448, 449. A slightly later example, CDL 262 (a placitum of 843).

[98] The meanings differ slightly between Rothari 133, 136, and *Memoratorio*, 1 (Azzara, *Le leggi*, p. 222), in which *sala* is used for 'roof' also. *Lex alamannica* 76. The etymology, Van der Rhee, *GWL*, p. 112; Sabatini, *Riflessi linguistici*, pp. 153–5. Examples: CDL 30 (Lucca, 722), 38 (Pistoia, 726), 90 (Lucca, 747), 105 (Lucca, 752), 155 'curte vel sala' (Pavia, 761), 161 (Lucca, 762), 178 (Lucca, 746), 214 (Lucca, 768), 229 (Lucca, 769), 237 (Lucca, 770), 269 (Lucca, 772), 286 (Lucca, 773), 87 (Lucca, 773).

[99] CDL 90 (747), 139 (759), 178 (764), 214 (768). *Sundriale* ('sala sundriale'): 105 (752), 161 (762), 250 (771), all Lucchese.

[100] See above, note 24.   [101] Rothari 7. Van der Rhee, *GWL*, pp. 33–4.

Language and literacy

possibly derive from late Latin military culture and were adapted to suit aspects of Germanic legal culture. *Camphio* (or *camfio*), from the Latin *campus*, to mean 'duel', also stars in Rothari's top ten and is glossed as 'pugna', which appears to have been the preferred word, despite *camphio's* survival in early Romance and modern Italian.[102] The word *sculca* was used by Rothari then later by Ratchis to mean some military duty akin to 'guard duty' or 'reconnaissance'. Germanic origins and etymologies have been proposed for it, but it is more probably a Latinised Greek word, ϛκούλκα, meaning a soldier in the service of guard duty or exploration, as found in the Pseudo-Maurice *Strategicon*.[103] The Greek origin is further supported by Rothari's use of another word of a similar meaning, *escaramas*, for 'explorers' or 'spies', which probably derives from the same root as the Middle Greek ϛκαμρις, meaning 'spies'.[104] We can only guess as to whether the Lombards picked up such words in Italy, or previously, in Pannonia or under Narses' command.[105]

AGRICULTURAL TERMS

Latinate origins can also be proposed for some of the agricultural terms used in the code and thought to be Langobardic. In a law against cutting down trees on someone else's property, Rothari gave four different Latin words for different types of oak-tree, *robur*, *cerrus*, *quercus* and *hisculum* ([h]*aesculus*), and glossed the last two with *modola* and *fagia*, both of which are unattested elsewhere, and probably derive from Greco-Roman usage.[106] The same can be said for *stupla*, 'a mowed field', as in the Eng. 'stubble' (mod. Ital. *stoppia*, mod. Germ. *Stoppel*), which probably derives from the Latin *stipula*, though we have no other attestation. It

---

[102] Rothari 9, 198, 202, 213, 368, Liutprand 118. On the question of late Latin, see Sabatini, *Riflessi linguistici*, pp. 236–9; Van der Rhee, *GWL*, pp. 90–2.
[103] See G. Frau, 'Contributo alla conoscenza dell'elemento longobardo nella toponomastica friuliana', *ibid.*, pp. 165–82, at pp. 175–6. For the Germanic etymologies (Got. *skalks*, ME *skulten*, etc.), see Sabatini, *Riflessi linguistici*, pp. 141–2; Van der Rhee, *GWL*, pp. 119–20.
[104] Rothari 5. Pointed out by Bognetti, 'S. Maria', p. 446.
[105] Some later words can be added to this category: e.g. *marca* (boundary, border) Ratchis 13. Also in *Lex. bav.* 13.9, *Lex. rib.* 60.5; Baesecke, 'Die deutschen Worte', pp. 19, 63, 67; *cuccura* (quiver), Aistulf 2, 3, from the Hunnic *kukur*? Van der Rhee, *GWL*, pp. 92–3; *zava* (insurrection, revolt) Ratchis 10. From OHG *gizawa*? See E. Graff, *Althochdeutscher Sprachschatz*, V, p. 713.
[106] Rothari 300, 'si quis rovore aut cerrum seu quercum, quod est modola, hisclo, quod est fagia'. On *modola*, Baesecke, 'Die deutschen Worte', p. 36; Bruckner, *Sprache*, p. 209; Van der Rhee, *GWL*, p. 101. The emendation of Bruckner, *Sprache*, p. 63, and Van der Rhee, *GWL*, pp. 54–5 to *fereha* from the readings of later manuscripts, and the proposed etymology from OGH *far[a]ha* (MHG *vorhe*, OS *furie*, OE *furh*, Mod. Germ. *föhre*) (Scots pine), seems strained: preferable is *fagia* from the Greek φάγειν as *aesculus* is from *esca, edo*.

is used in the same law in which Rothari coined another peculiar term, *fornaccar*, for the felony of denying another man fodder from an already mowed field.[107]

But not all Langobardic agricultural terms derive from Greco-Roman usage. Rothari's use of the word *plouus* (mod. Eng. 'plough') alongside the traditional Latin *aratrum* has caught the attention of economic historians.[108] The word is also used in Bavarian law in a manner suggesting it was taken from Rothari's code, yet the instrument itself may have first been used in Rhaetia.[109] Historians of technology have seized on the word as the first reference to the heavy-plough, as opposed to the more lightweight *aratrum*, as though the Lombards brought with them to Italy agricultural techniques from northern Europe which revolutionised agricultural production in the centuries to come.[110] But it is doubtful that Rothari saw any difference between the two words as representing two different types of plough,[111] and the appearance of *plouus* in the Edict may simply be due to it having been a common word on both sides of the Alps by this time. *Snaida* (cf. mod. Germ. *schneiden*) was a term employed by Rothari as gloss for the Latinate *ticlatura*, itself a little puzzling, and refers to the marking of trees to serve (presumably) as property markers. We find the word in a royal charter some twenty years prior to Rothari's Edict, suggesting that it may have been a word the Lombards brought with them.[112]

Some Germanic terms, however, are given a full explanation in Latin in a manner which suggests that their original meaning was far from clear to a contemporary Italian audience. Thus Rothari goes to great lengths to explain the meaning of *sonorpair* ('head boar') in a law concerning the theft of swine:

---

[107] Rothari 358. On *stupla*, see B. Löfstedt, *Studien über die Sprache der langobardischen Gesetze* (Stockholm, 1961), p. 346 n. 21. On *fornaccar*, Bruckner, *Sprache*, p. 40; Van der Rhee, *GWL*, pp. 56–8. The manuscript tradition of this word is problematic: see P. Scardigli, 'Fornaccar o fonsacar', in *Mille: il dibattiti del Circolo linguistico Fiorentino 1945–1970* (Florence, 1970), pp. 209–17 (repr. in *Goti e Longobardi*, pp. 295–302).

[108] Rothari 288: 'Si quis plouum aut aratram alienam [sic]'. See B. Kratz, 'Zu lateinischen *plovum* in den langobardischen Gesetzen', *Neuphilologische Mitteilungen* 66 (1965), 217–29.

[109] *Lex bav.* 31.2: Baesecke, 'Die deutschen Worte', p. 91; W. Mitzka, 'Pflügen und seine Wortgeographie. Der Pflüg in der Sprachgeschichte', *Zeitschrift für Agrargeschichte und Agrasoziologie* 6 (1958), 112–18.

[110] P. Jones, 'La storia economica. Dalla caduta dell'impero romano al secolo XIV', in R. Romano and C. Vivanti (eds.), *Storia d'Italia*, II, *Dalla caduta dell'impero romano al secolo XVIII* (Turin, 1974), pp. 1447–1810, at p. 1604; Pellegrini, 'Terminologia agraria', pp. 637–8.

[111] *Contra* Pellegrini, 'Terminologia argraria', pp. 637–8. On ploughing (*campo arato, araueri̇t, campo exarato*) cf. Rothari 354, 355.

[112] Rothari 240, 241. Van der Rhee, *GWL*, pp. 120–1; Bruckner, *Sprache*, p. 99; Sabatini, *Riflessi linguistici*, pp. 195–7. CDL III.2 (624), see p. 173.

Language and literacy

The boar which has fought and conquered all other boars is called a *sonorpair*. In one herd, however many pigs there may be, only one is regarded as the *sonorpair*. If the herd is less than 30 in number, there is no *sonorpair*, unless there are over 30 swine in the herd.[113]

The *sonorpair* has an unmistakably Germanic linguistic pedigree (lit. herd-boar), and its importance is no doubt linked with that of the higher value of a swineherder (*porcarius*) in the code (50 *solidi*) compared to cattle-, sheep- and goatherders (20 *solidi*). A glance at the multiple provisions of Salic law on different types of pig suggests that there is something quintessentially Germanic about Rothari's law, as though it might be taken as evidence of barbarian, northern European pastoral culture being grafted onto a predominantly agrarian Italian society. But as more recent studies have reminded us, pigs were the most common animal in early medieval Europe, and an unmistakable sign of an overwhelmingly agricultural economy.[114] But we may wonder about the point of including such words in the law code when their significance is limited and they required such a thorough explanation. Did it really matter what a head boar was *called* in the case of a dispute arising over the theft of swine? In view of the trouble taken to explain this term, the law appears to make little sense: the stolen *sonorpair* is to be compensated for by replacement with a similar animal, whereas if any (regular) swine are stolen, the compensation was eightfold the value of the animal taken. There are other equally baffling terms that required long-winded Latin explanations and could easily be dealt with in accordance to other laws.[115]

Elsewhere we find Germanic words used for body parts. One law stipulating sums of composition for blows to the limbs specified different sums for different parts of the limbs, the *murioth* ('the arm above the elbow') the *treno* ('arm below the elbow') and the *lagi* ('the leg above the knee').[116] Despite the long list of different types of injury, these

---

[113] Rothari 351.
[114] OGH *swanur* + *pair*, *bêr*. cf. *sonista*, *sonesti*, *Pactus sal.* 2.2, and 2.1–20 in general, *Lex rib.* 18.1. See Bruckner, *Sprache*, p. 79; Van der Rhee, *GWL*, pp. 121–2. *Porcarius*, Rothari 135; *armentarius, pecorarius, caprarius* 136. On pigs, Hartmann, *Geschichte Italiens*, II, p. 21; and Barnish, 'Pigs, plebeians and potentates'; C. Wickham, 'Pastoralism and underdevelopment in the early Middle Ages', *Settimane* 31 (Spoleto, 1983), pp. 401–55, reprinted in Wickham, *Land and Power*, pp. 121–55, at pp. 127–35, esp. pp. 130–2; M. Montanari, *L'alimentazione contadina nell'alto medioevo* (Naples, 1979), pp. 392–404; G. Clark, 'Stock economies in medieval Italy: a critical review of the archaeozoological evidence', *Archeologia Medievale* 14 (1987), 7–26. A. Giardina, 'Allevamenti ed economia della selva in Italia meridionale: trasformazioni e continuità', in A. Giardina and A. Schiavone (eds.), *Società romana e produzione schiavistica*, I (Bari, 1981), pp. 87–113.
[115] E.g. *walupaus*, Rothari 31, clearly of ideological importance to define; *fornaccar*, Rothari 358; *faritraib*, 379; *mahrworfin*, 30, 373; *rairaub*, 16; *plodraub*, 14.
[116] Rothari 384. See Van der Rhee, *GWL*, pp. 108–9, 127–8; Bonfante, *Latini e Germani*, p. 37 nn. 63, 66. R.B. ten Cate-Silfwerband, *Vlees, Bloed en Been* (Assen, 1958), p. 21.

are the only Germanic words for body parts used in the code, and even the same law reverts to Latin terminology for the leg beneath the knee (*tibia*) and the whole leggy ensemble (*coxa*). Again, it is possible that these words were adopted by the Lombards in Italy: *treno*, for example, may be a late Latin word.[117] For violent blows, only one law uses the Germanic *pulslahi*, a word common to other Germanic codes, but this is couched in terms of a gloss on the Latin *ferita* which is used throughout the code.[118]

VESTIGES OF LANGOBARDIC?

Some laws and Germanic terms carry vestiges of a Langobardic past. For example, when Rothari legislated against the retraction of what must be seen as the Lombard version of usufruct donations, he recalled an oral pronouncement that was an integral part of the ritual: 'If someone donates their property and says in that donation, *lid in laib*, that is, on the day of his death he will hand it over, let him not later maliciously dispose of that property, but let him enjoy it reasonably.'[119] The etymology of *lid* (Got. leiþan, OE liðan, OHG lidan, etc.) 'to go' and *laib* (OHG leiba, OE lâf, Got. laiba, etc.) 'death', 'otherworld', 'inheritance'[120] ('gehe ein in die Hinterlassenschaft', 'geh ins Erbe') matches Rothari's gloss, and we therefore have a snippet of oral Germanic legal culture. Yet the same law allows us to see how Latin orality replaced any vestiges of a Germanic language, as Rothari further stipulated that should the donor later need to sell that property, 'let him say to him whom he donated the property, "Look, you see that, driven by necessity, I am going to dispose of the property; but help me, if you can, and I shall preserve that property as yours". If he does not wish to help, let that which was given to another remain secure and permanent.'[121] The highly colloquial Latin expressions 'ecce vedis' and 'res istas uado dare'[122] may have replaced

---

[117] Van der Rhee, *GWL*, p. 128.

[118] Rothari 125, 'per unam feritam, id est pulslahi'. Cf. *Lex bav.* 4.1, 5.1, 6.1; *Lex alam.* 57 (pulislac); *Lex rib.* 20.1 (bunislegi). Baesecke, 'Die deutschen Worte', pp. 19, 61; Bruckner, *Sprache*, p. 96; Van der Rhee, *GWL*, pp. 41–3.

[119] Rothari 173: 'Si res suas alii thingauerit et dixerit in ipso thinx, lid in laib, id est, quod in die obitus sui relinquerit, non dispergat res ipsas postea doloso animo, nisi fruatur eas cum ratione.'

[120] Van de Rhee, *GWL*, pp. 92–3; Bruckner, *Sprache*, p. 91, Baesecke, 'Die deutchen Worte', p. 91; Restelli, *Goti*, p. 89. Cf. Fischer-Drew, trans., p. 260, who offers quite a different etymology.

[121] Rothari 173: 'Et si tales ei eueniret necessitas, ut terra cum mancipia aut sine mancipia uindere aut locum pigneris ponere debeat, dicat prius illi nobis cui thingauerit, "Ecce uedis, quia necessitate conpulsus res istas uado dare; si tibi uedetur, subueni mihi, et res istas conseruo in tuam proprietatem"'.

[122] For similar expressions, J. Herman, *Vulgar Latin*, trans. R. Wright (University Park, PA, 2000), pp. 72–4.

Language and literacy

what was originally phrased in a Germanic language and was of the same ceremonial character as *lid in laib*.

The ceremonial aspect is again present in Rothari's famous law on manumission which constitutes a *tour de force* of Germanic terms relating to the status of freedom and the decidedly non-Roman ritual of the 'four roads'.[123] The law contains no less than six Germanic terms (*fulcfree, amund, gairethinx, gaida et gisel, in pans*), nearly all of which are given as glosses on Latin terms or only after an equivalent Latin expression has been provided. The law opens with a Latin title and introduction to the subject, and qualifies the difference between full freedom and the retention of ties of loyalty or patronage by use of the term word, which constitutes a Germanic gloss on a Latin description.[124] A peculiar term, which receives no gloss, is the alliterative *et thingit in gaida et gisil* ('and he gives [to him/her that is being manumitted] a whip and an arrow'), thought to refer the symbolic use of objects to denote the manumitted person's new status as a free man or free woman.[125] The alliterative aspect of the term resembles that of *lid in laid*, as do some other expressions found in the code, such as *handegawerc et harigawerc* ('personal property'), which appears as a Germanic gloss in the law following that on manumission.[126] If the alliterative aspect of these terms derives from their originally oral transmission, it would further attest to the relatively poor standing of a Langobardic language in the middle of the seventh century, reduced to alliterative catch-phrases to denote what were complex social rituals, especially as regards the manumission procedure, or usufruct donations. Paul the Deacon refers to this very same manumission ritual when he recounts how the early Lombards sought to increase their numbers by manumitting slaves and prisoners 'per sagittam', then confirming their new status by 'murmuring some tribal words' (*quaedam patria uerba*).[127] Unfortunately we hear nothing of these words from Rothari himself. Instead he stipulated that the last act in the manumission ritual is that of the fourth person (acting as witness) pronouncing to the newly manumitted,

---

[123] Rothari 224.
[124] *Ibid.*: 'De Manomissionibus. Si quis servum suum proprium aut ancillam liberos dimittere voluerit, sit licentia, qualiter ei placeruit. Nam qui fulcfree et a se extraneum, id est amund, facere voluerit, sic debit facere.' On *[h]amund* (ha- mundium: also Rothari 235, Liutprand 23, 55, 98, Aistulf 11) see Van der Rhee, *GWL*, p. 28; Bruckner, *Sprache*, p. 201; Brunner, *Deutsche Rechtsgeschichte*, I, p. 144.
[125] See Van der Rhee, *GWL*, pp. 66–7; Brunner, *Deutsche Rechtsgeschichte*, I, p. 210; Princi Braccini, 'Termini germanici', p. 1156. *Gaida* is never substituted for *sagitta* in the code, e.g. Rothari 34.
[126] Rothari 225: 'res suas proprias, id est handegawerc et harigawerc'. Van der Rhee, *GWL*, pp. 81–2; Bruckner, *Sprache*, p. 41. Cf. also Aistulf 14: 'morgincap et meta'; G. Restelli, *Goti Tedeschi Langobardi* (Brescia, 1984), p. 89.
[127] *HL* I.13: 'sanciunt in more solito per sagittam., inmurmurantes nihilominus ob rei firmitatem quaedam patria uerba'.

Literacy in Lombard Italy, c. 568–774

'de quattuor vias, ubi volueris ambulare, liberam habeas postestatem'. If, by the seventh century, a past Langobardic language still carried a great deal of ceremonial and ritualistic force, one might expect to find it used here in the form of a stock phrase or pronouncement. But instead, as with the pronouncements prescribed for the retraction of *lid in laib* donations, a vulgar Latin phrase is invested with the ceremonial force necessary to carry the transaction. The manumission law was perhaps particularly aimed at a Latin-speaking audience, for such laws were of special importance to the agrarian peasant class, the bulk of the population, some of whom undoubtedly found more opportunity to acquire free status under Lombard rule than had been possible in late Roman society.

CONCLUSION

Patrick Wormald has asked of legislation by Germanic kings on the continent: 'if vernacular words and glosses were possible, why not whole clauses?'[128] 'Whole clauses' of Germanic words in the Lombard code were not viable, even possible, because of their irrelevance to the functionality of the law code and the administration of justice. Rothari did not choose to have a law code redacted in Latin because of its ideological significance or symbolism. He had no choice. The overwhelming majority of his subjects in Italy spoke only Latin and there was no coherent Germanic language amongst the Lombard hierarchy that could compete as a way of communicating something so important as a law for all to obey. It is indeed significant that whole clauses or phrases in Germanic never appear in the law code rather than just isolated words or the odd alliterative combination such as *lid in laib* or *gaida et gisil*. It is tempting to conclude that the Lombard kings and their retinues could come up with nothing more substantial. Paul the Deacon, raised and educated at the royal court of King Ratchis, could do no better. The introduction of Germanic words by Liutprand, not used in Rothari's legislation, further supports the idea that these words served a primarily ideological significance in constituting Lombard identity. Linguistic archaisms can be used to endow law with the aura of ancient authority – an obvious example is the use of Latin phrases in Anglophone courts, or the use of Norman French terms for legal concepts or misdemeanours.[129] In this way the Lombard regime could distinguish itself from the Romans, who threatened the very existence of

[128] '*Lex scripta*', p. 115.
[129] See P. Goodich, *Languages of Law: From Logic of Memory to Nomadic Masks* (London, 1990); C. Shranke, 'Rhetorical constructions of a national community: the role of the king's English in mid-Tudor writing', in A. Shepard and P. Withington (eds.), *Communities in Early Modern England* (Manchester, 2000), pp. 180–98.

the Lombard state and from whose legal culture the Lombards had borrowed heavily. It is possible that this use of the words was also political in another sense, that of placating hard-line traditionalist factions in the Lombard polity that saw themselves as guardians of ancient Lombard traditions and the embodiment of that which was the heart of the *gens*. These may have been men vehemently hostile to that which was Roman through the experience of embittered fighting against Byzantine forces and the consequent loss of friends, family and relatives. In this sense the inclusion of 'Langobardic' words in the law code was grounded in a political reality of appeasing a real desire to express Lombard identity with the use of non-Latin legal terms. The survival of Germanic terms in the Lombard law code has been largely considered the natural result of an existing degree of bilingualism among Lombard elites. But rather than view these Germanic terms as evidence for a homogeneous Langobardic language, their appearance might well be best understood as the result of a conscious attempt to construct Lombard national identity in the royal mirror of legislation.

PART II: LATIN

A 'Spanish' liturgical manuscript, written at Tarragona sometime in the early eighth century, somehow made its way across the seas and into the hands of Sergius, the *vicedominus* of the church of Cagliari in Sardinia. By 731/2, the manuscript had reached Pisa, where it was in the possession of Maurezius, the royal 'cellarer' (*canevaggio*) of King Liutprand. Before the century was out, the 'Mozarabic Orational', to use the anachronistic title later bestowed upon the manuscript, had reached Verona, where it has been preserved to the present day.[130] Besides the marginal additions to the manuscript which allow us to trace its itinerary, at the top of the third folio, in an unmistakable north Italian, eighth-century cursive hand, is the following note: '*Separebabovesalbapratoliaarabaetalboversoriotenebaetnegrosemenseminaba*' (He urged on the oxen, ploughed the white fields, held a white plough, and sowed black seed).

Known as the 'Indovinello veronese', the riddle of Verona was first thought to be a 'popular Italian quatrain' and earliest example of a proto-Romance, vernacular Italian, pre-dating the famous proto-Italian phrases found in recorded court cases (*placita*) of Campania by 150 years.[131] It was soon pointed out that the Veronese riddle was no innocent 'relic of popular pastoral poetry', but rather 'a scribal adage of erudite origin',

---

[130] Verona, Bib. cap. LXXXIX (84) (CLA IV.515). The Indovinello was discovered by L. Schiaparelli, 'Note paleografiche. Sulla data e provenienza del cod. LXXXIX della Biblioteca capitolare di Verona (l'Orazionale mozarabico)', *Archivio Storico Italiano* ser. 7, 1 (1924), 106–17.

[131] A. Schiaffini, 'I problemi dell'Indovinello veronese', in Schiaffini, *I mille anni della lingua italiana* (Milan, 1961), pp. 71–96; L. Cassata, 'Sul metro (e sul testo) dell'indovinello veronese', *Annali della Scuola Normale Superiore di Pisa*, cl. di lett. e fil., s.III, v.VIII fasc. (1978), 1229–36, suggests that the Indovinello is in hexameters; S. Mariotti, 'L'Indovinello veronese', in *Letterature comparate, problemi, metodi: studi in onore di Ettore Paratore* (Bologna, 1981), pp. 987–96; F. Guerra D'Antoni, 'A new perspective of the Veronese riddle', *Romance Philology* 36 (1982), 185–200; R. Di Virgilio, 'I buoi "dipari" dell'Indovinello veronese', *Giornale Italiano di Filologia* 15/36:1 (1984), 39–50. A. Bartoli Langeli, 'La mano e il libro', *Quaderni Veneti* 21 (1995), 66–97 would push the date of the Indovinello to the ninth century (following Schiaparelli), but cf. A. Petrucci and A. Romeo, 'L'orazionale visigotico di Verona. Aggiunte avventizie, indovinello grafico, tagli maffeiani', *Scrittura e Civiltà* 22 (1998), 13–30, who convincingly argue for *c.* 760s to 780s.

drawing upon the literary metaphor of ploughing as writing which goes back as far as Plato.¹³² The Indovinello, therefore, has much to do with scribal traditions and literary topoi, a point which is underlined by the fairly expert cursive hand in which it was written. Although primarily serving as a *probatio pennae*, the Indovinello is undeniably ludic. The person who had obtained that level of fluency in writing an intricate and well-practised script would have had a better acquaintance with classical orthography than the lines of the Indovinello suggest. As if to underline the point, another contemporary, slightly less cursive hand, wrote directly underneath, '+ gratias tibi agimus omnip[oten]s sempiterne d[eu]s'. The immediate purpose of this 'gara grafica' between the two hands is lost to us now.¹³³ But the resulting contrast between liturgical language and the proto-Romance orthography of the Indovinello further serves to highlight its use of metaphor to describe writing as labour intensive. Aside from the sheer physionomics of using pen and parchment, written Latin, a highly artificial language, required a knowledge of rules and regulations achieved through study and practice, for its form and structure differed substantially from those of spoken language, as we can see from evidence of the less learned – in epigraphy, letters, documents, graffiti, etc. – as early as the first century BC.

The Indovinello therefore raises many questions to be addressed in this chapter. How did the inhabitants of Lombard Italy actually speak in their day-to-day lives? If there was a divergence between spoken and written forms of language, how did this affect the use of written communication, and general levels of literacy, in this period? The fundamental question, however, which encapsulates all others and must be asked first of all is: what was the relationship between spoken and written language in this period? The corollary question to this, more frequently asked by historical linguists, of how Latin was spoken in this period, must take second place, for it is only through trying to understand how the surviving vestiges of written language may or may not reflect the spoken language of the period that we may begin to assess what the linguistic environment of Lombard Italy may have been.¹³⁴

---

¹³² E. Curtius, *European Literature in the Latin Middle Ages*, trans. W.R. Trask (Princeton, 1973), p. 313. Cf. Isidore, *Etym*.VI.9.2. For similar examples, see L. Bieler, 'Some remarks on the aenigmata laureshamensia', *Romanobarbarica* 2 (1977), 11–15; D. Ganz, 'Books and book production', in McKitterick (ed.), *NCMH* II, pp. 786–808, at p. 796; G. Sanga, 'Il bue e l'Indovinello', *Rivista Italiana di Dialettologia* 16 (1992), 9–18. The learned, ludic aspect is highlighted by O. Castellani Pollidoro, 'Per una pausa di riflessione sull'Indovinello veronese', *Studi Linguistici Italiani* 23 (1997), 153–79.

¹³³ Petrucci and Romeo, 'L'orazionale visigotico', p. 28.

¹³⁴ As recognised by R. Wright, 'Logographic script and assumptions of literacy in tenth-century Spain', in Wright, *Early Ibero-Romance* (Newark, 1994), pp. 165–80: Wright, 'The teaching of orthography in tenth-century Galicia', in *ibid*., pp. 181–208.

Literacy in Lombard Italic, c. 568–774

Surviving for the most part as originals, the charters of Lombard Italy demonstrate a mix of Romance forms and written traditions of Latin that place them at the forefront for discerning the relationship between orality and literacy in this period. The language of the charters has been characterised as vulgar Latin in the extreme or even a type of 'proto-Italian'.[135] But to use such terms ignores the very important element of written legal traditions within the texts, and how these may have influenced the scribes of the documents in their redaction of the less formulaic, early Romance elements. It has even been suggested that the vulgarised Latin in charters reflects an inferior level of command of the Latin language by Germanic-speaking Lombards:[136] but scribes with 'Roman' names, presumably native speakers of Latin (according to this erroneous ethnology), wrote even worse Latin.

In this chapter I shall explore the issues surrounding charters and other evidence from Lombard Italy first by offering a brief survey of the development of Latin in Italy in order to place the Lombard period in the historical perspective of the move from Latin to Romance. I shall then discuss briefly the language of the Lombard law code which serves as a useful introduction to the type of language found in Lombard charters, for both types of evidence are products of the same legal culture and linguistic environment. The charter evidence is particularly illuminating, for the language used demonstrates an interesting mix of scribal traditions and vernacular forms that provide insight into the relationship between written and oral culture, further revealed in the language of priests who demonstrated their familiarity with more 'correct' forms of Latin by citation of the Latin Vulgate but who chose to ignore it as a model for their own language. We then consider the recorded speech in some charters, and how this may have related to the orality of the proceedings they document. Finally we shall look at two examples of texts preserved in a Lucchese manuscript that demonstrate the types of non-religious and non-legal texts that have been lost to us from this period and which help to redress the imbalance caused by the predominance of legal sources as evidence.

FROM LATIN TO ITALIAN

The amount of scholarly literature on the development of late Latin and the emergence of Romance languages is enormous, and the amount of disagreement between scholars is nearly as much. We have long since

---

[135] G. Sanga and S. Baggio, 'Sul volgare in età longobarda', in E. Banfi *et al.* (eds.), *Italia settentrionale: Crocevia di idiomi romanzi* (Tübingen, 1995), pp. 247–60.
[136] G. Petracco Sicardi, 'Latino e romanzo di mano barbarica', *Romanobarbarica* 2 (1977), 183–208.

moved away from the deceptively simple questions: 'when did Latin since cease to be spoken?' and 'when did Romance language(s) commence?', to replace them with more sophisticated views concerning the different levels of Latin's intelligibility, its relationship to spoken language, and its astounding continuity as the only written language of early medieval continental Europe. In particular the contributions of Roger Wright force us to rethink the divisions between written and spoken language (still alive and well today), and challenge the assumption that a language need sound anything like the way it is written. Wright also pointed to the implementation of Alcuin's educational ideals concerning Latin orthography and phonetic pronunciation as the final blow which broke Latin's flexibility and ruptured its connection with the spoken languages of the populace.[137] There has been some dissent, particularly concerning the speed with which and extent to which Alcuin's reforms were put into practice, but Wright's arguments provide some of the best explanations for Latin remaining the language of church and state, institutions which maintained their dominant positions through consensus from, hence dialogue with, their subjects.[138] Michel Banniard similarly concluded that it is impossible to speak of an existing bilingualism (a spoken Latin and a spoken proto-Romance) or even diglossia (a written Latin and spoken proto-Romance) before the eighth century, for Latin retained a remarkable adaptability and flexibility in maintaining the interrelationship between the traditional written language and spoken language. In Francia at least, language spoken by illiterate people did not leave the 'diasystem' of late Latin until the mid-eighth century, when socio-linguistic development reached a critical stage in the complex relationship concerning the active and passive competence of speaker and listener respectively.[139]

In the light of this research, what are we to make of the situation in Lombard Italy? The longevity of Latin's intelligibility in Italy is often more assumed than discussed, and its relationship to a spoken language

---

[137] R. Wright, *Late Latin and Early Romance in Spain and Carolingian France* (Liverpool, 1982); Wright (ed.), *Latin and the Romance Languages in the Early Middle Ages* (London, 1991); Wright, *Early Ibero-Romance*.

[138] See J. Adams, [Review of Wright's *Late Latin*], *Liverpool Classical Monthly* 14 (1989), 14–16, 34–48; McKitterick, *Carolingians*, pp. 1–22; McKitterick, 'Latin and Romance: an historian's perspective', in Wright (ed.) *Latin*, pp. 130–45: K. Versteegh, 'The debate concerning Latin and early Romance', *Diachronica* 9 (1992), 259–85.

[139] M. Banniard, *Genèse culturelle de l'Europe: V–VII siècle* (Paris, 1989), pp. 178–214; Banniard, *Le Haut Moyen Age Occidental*, 3rd edn (Paris, 1991), pp. 96–120; Banniard, '*Vox Agrestis*: quelques problèmes d'élocution de Cassiodore à Alcuin', *Trames, Etudes Antiques* (Limoges, 1985), 195–208; and most thoroughly, Banniard, *Viva voce* (note the review of R. Wright, *Journal of Medieval Latin* 3 (1993), 78–94). See also Banniard, 'Diasystèmes et diachronie languagières du latin parlé tardif ou protofrançais (IIIe–VIIIe siècles)', in J. Herman (ed.), *La transizione dal latino alle lingue romanze* (Tübingen, 1998), pp. 131–54.

is rarely elaborated upon. Many scholars have been content to see the period prior to the Lombard presence as one of Latin linguistic unity. The degree of territorial homogeneity permitted 'l'intercommunication et l'intercompréhension sans obstacle entre latinophones appartenant à des régions diverses'.[140] Studies of Gregory the Great have confirmed that Gregory wrote sermons that were intelligible to a late sixth- and early seventh-century Italian audience of both clerics and laity, further confirming the impression of Latinate monolingualism.[141] The seventh century, however, is viewed as a period of 'undeniable decadence' for Latin, as the break up of the empire meant social fracture, localisation, and an acceleration of the process of 'dialectalisation' now that the evolution of speech was no longer curbed by written norms.[142] Dag Norberg suggested that the Italian language was born in the late seventh century, but posited a residual Latinity for the cities of Italy, where 'the deepest roots of the Carolingian Renaissance are to be found'.[143]

There are a few untenable assumptions buried within these views, which derive for the most part from the examination of more literary texts only. One is that urban environments somehow hold linguistic evolution in check, as though the inhabitants of cities spoke a more cultivated and archaicising language than the country bumpkins who fed them.[144] A more refined argument from the socio-linguistic point of view would suggest that the extensive inter-cultural and inter-class contacts found in cities create a more flexible, more sophisticated linguistic environment. Both this linguistic sophistication and the greater presence of written communication found in cities more easily bridged the gap between

---

[140] J. Herman, 'La situation linguistique en Italie au VI siècle', *Revue de Linguistique Romane* 52 (1988), 55–67, at pp. 65–6; Herman, 'Spoken and written Latin in the last centuries of the Roman empire. A contribution to the linguistic history of the western provinces', in Wright (ed.), *Latin*, pp. 29–43. Cf. Herman, *Vulgar Latin*, trans. Wright, pp. 115–20.

[141] See M. Banniard 'Iuxta uniuscuiusque qualitatem: l'écriture médiatrice chez Grégoire le Grand', in *Grégoire le Grand: Colloques internationaux du CNRS* (Paris, 1986), pp. 477–88; Banniard, *Viva voce*, pp. 105–80.

[142] A. Schiaffini, 'Problemi del passaggio del latino all'italiano (evoluzione, disgregazione, ricostruzione)', in *Studi in onore di Angelo Monteverdi*, 2 vols. (Modena, 1959), II, pp. 691–715, at p. 698.

[143] 'Le développement du latin en Italie de Saint Grégoire le Grand à Paul Diacre', *Settimane* 5 (Spoleto, 1958), 485–539, at pp. 495, 503. Similarly, L.J. Engels, *Observations sur le vocabulaire de Paul Diacre*, Latinitatis Christianorum Primaeva 16 (Nijmegen, 1961), p. 266, 'une sorte de protoitalien'. An eccentric view is G. Bonfante, 'Quando si è incominciato a parlare italiano? Criteri fonologici', in *Festschrift für W. von Wartburg* (Basel, 1969), pp. 21–46, and Bonfante, 'La lingua parlata nell'età imperiale', *Aufstieg und Niedergang der Römischen Welt* 29:1 (1983), 413–52, who argues that Italian language begins in the first century AD.

[144] *Contra* L. Versteegh, 'Latinitas, Hellenismos, Arabiyya', *Historiographia Linguistica* 12 (1986), 425–48; J. and M. Milroy, 'Linguistic change, social network, and speaker innovation', *Journal of Linguistics* 21 (1985), 339–84.

Language and literacy

written norms and spoken language.[145] Another assumption is that the presence of the Roman empire, even if a shadow of its former glory, helped to maintain a degree of linguistic continuity in Italy by its reliance upon a literate, if rudimentary, bureaucracy to function and the existence of schools or schooling systems to furnish that bureaucracy with new recruits. The evidence of the Ravennate papyri of the sixth and seventh century, however, demonstrates that both of these assumptions are misleading. The professionally trained and city-based *exceptores, forenses* and *tabelliones* who wrote these documents did so in a sophisticated and clear cursive script which was the official script of the period, and many of the documents which have come down to us emanated from the *curia* itself. Yet their orthography and grammar are far from classical and resemble those found in Lombard charters of the seventh and eighth century. Tjäder's long inventory of the orthographic phenomena found in the documents could just as easily be applied to Lombard Italy.[146] Moreover, changes in single letters are common, and again Tjäder's inventory serves to indicate the types of changes we commonly find in Lombard charters.[147] For some scholars, such phenomena could be interpreted

---

[145] See M. Richter, 'A socio-linguistic approach to the Latin middle ages', *Studies in Church History* 11 (1975), 69–82; Richter, '*Urbanitas–rusticitas*: linguistic aspects of a medieval dichotomy', *Studies in Church History* 16 (1979), 149–57; both repr. in Richter, *Studies in Medieval Language and Culture* (Dublin, 1995).

[146] To summarise from *Die nichtliterarischen lateinischen Papyri Italiens aus der Zeit 445–700*, 3 vols., ed. J.O. Tjäder (Lund, 1954/5–82), I, pp. 150–65 (Classical orthography of the word is given in square brackets where it seems necessary): anatyxe (*initegro* [*integro*]), *properiae* [*propriae*], *usumfrunctuarie* [*usumfructuarie*]; syncope (*cuticla* [*curticula*]), *tertorio* [*territorio*]; haplography (*actionariisce, conderit* [*condederit*]), *eodemonasterium* [*eodem monasterium*] *presentestis* [*presente testis*], *Paulacususcribsit* [*Paulacis subscribsit*]; dittography (*evavangelia, ininiugantur*); the doubling of consonants (*aeccclesiae, inllustrio, inn, legittur, uncciarum*); the reduction of double consonants (*aeclesia, aeglesia, cancelarius, oportunus, solemniter*); the doubling of vowels (*paatris, suub*); assimilation (*generari* [*generali*]); a lack of aspiration (*autenticus, carta/cartula, catolicus, swla/scolaris, spatarius*); the displacement of aspiration (*Anthiocia* [*Antiochia*]), *Crihsogonus* [*Chrisogonus*], *Micahelius* [*Michaelis*], *uhic/uih* [*huic*]; the elision of letters (*donatrem* [*donatorem*]), *pefecte* [*perfecte*], *qu* [*qui*]; the misuse of *i* and *ii* (*dominii, iudicii, petitorii, predii; Gregori, Theodosi, numerari*); the consistent misuses of prefixes *ad-*, *con-*, *in-* (*adfectione, adferatur, adfines, adlegare, adpellatur, adprobavit, ascripta, adtestatio; conpetere, conplere, conprehendo, conputo; industris, inmobilis, inmaculator, inplere, inprimo, inpulso, inrevocabilis, inrevocabiliter, inrigare*).

[147] Ibid. ae > e: *egritudo, seculo, precipio, presente, anime, carte, ecclesie, que* [*quae*]. au > u: *clusa*. b > v: *guvernantum, haveo, arvitrio, inbicillitatem*. c > g: *aeglesia, relegta, sagramenta*. c > q: *quoram, quur*. c lacking: *uih* [*huic*], or together with c and t, *santa, sante*. d > l: *polagrae*. d > t: *aput, at, it*. e > a: *cassante, marcatoris*. e > ae: *aecclesia, aedicere, aedidi, aelocutus, pariaete*; esp. after *pr*: *conpraehensem, depraessa, praetio*; and as case ending: *diae, gratae, mae, permissionae*. e > ei: *Baptistei, plateia*. e > i: *Arminiorum, Bilesarium*(!), *missuria* [*messoria*], *niquiverit, collictarius, cautilas, ecclisia, fecirunt, relictus, fuissit, adsolit*. g > c: *sacma*. h > ch: *nichilominus*. h omitted: (Greek words) *ebdomas, olografa, ypoteticae*, (Latin words) *ac* (*hac* or *hanc*), *ortus, orticellus*. h added: *hab, hac, his, hisdem, homnia, exhornatus, hostensa*. i > e: *possedet, reteneo, -ebus* (e.g. *legebus*), -*emus* (*possemus*). m > n: *principaliun, tanquam*. m lacking: *cora, circuissent*. mp > pp: *coppetit*. n > m: *comvocassent, imperpetuo, voluntatis*. n lacking: *hac* [*hanc*], *sacta* [*sancta*], *ostidimus* [*ostendimus*], *constituit*. o > u: *exurnatus, cunserbandis, muventibus, defensure*. ps >

as symptoms of a deep internal crisis within the Latin language itself throughout the fifth and sixth centuries.[148] This is doubtful, as the same orthographic phenomena can be found in inscriptions and documents dating from the earliest days of the empire. What both proponents of the 'crisis' view of Latin's development and those who link Latin's 'degeneracy' to the crumpling of empire have trouble explaining is why nobody who lived in the period seemed to mind. Scribes such as the Ravennate *tabelliones* and *forenses* were trained professionals who worked for court and other state offices, and who wrote documents for the highest-ranking members of their (still urban) society. Their grammar and orthography were at least acceptable to the magistrates and officials who employed them.[149]

The deviations from classical norms in the Ravennate papyri also raise the issue of proto-Romance, or to be more specific, proto-Italian. The Ravennate papyri demonstrate around eight basic rules of change fundamental for the development towards Romance which we find in Lombard charters also.[150] The implicit teleology in the concept of 'proto-Romance' can also be misleading. Carlton's study of the Ravennate papyri demonstrated that over half of the orthographical aberrations and tendencies away from classical Latin in the papyri were not predictive of Italian Romance, and some changes that are predictive of Romance (such as prosthesis) were poorly attested.[151] Similarly, Politzer's statistical analysis of Lombard charters sought to detect Romance trends in neatly divided categories (the fall of the final -s, the fall of the final -t, the voicing of intervocalic occlusives, the change of final -e, -i, -o, etc.) and to show dialectal divergences for charters from different regions. Politzer came up against the same anti-proto-Italian anomalies found in the Ravennate

---

s: *subscrisit*. s(s) > x: *inprexam, iuxiurandum*. s lacking: *petiti* [petisti], *subtantiae*. ti > ci: *donacio*. t > d: *sicud, dereliquid*. t lacking: *e* [et], *es* [est], *suscripsi* [subscripsit]. u > i: *sipraescripta*. u > o: *stipolatione, scotella, crocis, eondem, consule, rogatos*. u > b: *beneratione, cibitate, iubentatis, Rabennatis, reserbatione*. x > s: *misticia* [mixticia].

[148] A. Zamboni, 'Dal latino tardo agli albori romanzi: dinamiche linguistiche della transizione', *Settimane* 45 (Spoleto, 1998), 619–702.

[149] Tjäder, p. 147.

[150] (1) the diphthong *ae* is reduced to using the single letter *e*; (2) the *h* is omitted or added mistakenly; (3) the vowels *e* and *o* are often exchanged with *i* and *u* respectively; (4) the vowels *i* and *u* are often exchanged with *e* and *o* respectively; (5) the final *-m* is omitted; (6) other final consonants (especially *-s* and *-t*) are omitted; (7) the intervocalic *-b-* is rendered with *u* and vice versa; (8) the diagraph *qu* is substituted by *c*, and vice versa.

[151] C. Carlton, *A Linguistic Analysis of a Collection of Late Latin Documents Composed in Ravenna between A.D. 445–700: A Quantitative Approach*, Janua Linguarum Studia Memoriae Nicolai van Wijk Dedicata, Series Pratica 58 (The Hague and Paris, 1973). An earlier version was published as *Studies in Romance Lexicology, Based on a Collection of Latin Documents from Ravenna (A.D. 445–700)*, University of North Carolina Studies in the Romance Languages and Literature 54 (Chapel Hill, 1965).

Language and literacy

evidence, and did not demonstrate any clear-cut trends towards 'dialectalisation' in seventh- and eighth-century Italy, despite the tease of the evidence.[152] Both studies tended to ignore the important role played by scribal traditions in early medieval Italian evidence, which upset the picture of inevitable linguistic evolution. Moreover there is no acid-test with say, word order, that can demonstrate clearly the move from Latin to Romance forms.[153] The result is that neither proto-Romance nor proto-Italian, both categories from the reconstructionist school of linguistics, is an adequate description of the language found in legalistic evidence.[154]

When can we speak of 'early Italian'? Not until at least the tenth century, when we find evidence more solid than the Indovinello veronese for a conscious conceptual distinction between Latin and a vernacular language. But this does not mean the differences between the two languages were at all insurmountable. As Dante noted, *vulgare latinum*, the Romance language of *sì*, was to be preferred to those of *oc* and *oil*, for it leans more heavily on the system of grammar that is common to all, that of Latin.[155] Often cited as the demarcation point between Italian and Latin is a *placitum* of Capua of 960 in which three witnesses, all clerics from Monte Cassino, testified before a judge repeating the formula: 'sao ko kelle terre per kelle fini que ki contene, trenta anni le possette parte Sancti Benedicti'.[156] Linguists have done their best to explain the transition from Latin to Italianate forms.[157] But the phrase is by no means an innocent rendering of common speech: the presiding judge, Arichis, instructed the abbot of Monte Cassino to find three witnesses to pronounce this very phrase, and the rest of the court proceedings, including conversations between the judge and both parties, are redacted in Latin.

---

[152] R.L. Politzer, *A Study of the Language of the Eighth-Century Lombardic Documents: A Statistical Analysis of the Codice paleografico lombardo* (New York, 1949). Also, with F.N. Politzer, *Romance Trends in 7th and 8th century Latin Documents* (Chapel Hill, 1953), esp. p. 49.

[153] H. Pinkster, 'Evidence for SVO in Latin?', in Wright (ed.), *Latin*, pp. 69–82.

[154] R. Hall Jr, 'The reconstruction of Proto-Romance', *Language* 26 (1950), 6–27. cf. A. Vavaro, 'Latin and Romance: fragmentation or restructuring', in Wright (ed.), *Latin*, pp. 44–51, at p. 47: Banniard, *Vive voce*, pp. 29–37.

[155] See A. Schiaffini, *I mille anni della lingua italiana* (Milan, 1961), pp. 20, 23; cf. Curtius, *European literature*, p. 387; Migliorini, *Storia della lingua italiana* pp. 84–105.

[156] Given in full by Schiaffini, *I mille anni*, pp. 63–7. There are others: see A. Mancone (ed.), *Documenti cassinensi del secolo X con formule in volgare* (Rome, 1960).

[157] *sao* (Lat. *sapio*, mod. Ital. *so*), *kelle* (mod. Ital. *quelle*), *ki* (mod. Ital. *qui*), *contene* (Lat. *contenitur*), the definite article *le* (Lat. *illas*) and *ko* (from Lat. *quod*, med. Ital. *co*), the loss of intervocalic consonant (Lat. *possedete*) and the retention of the Latin genitive *Sancti Benedicti* with *parte* and without article as syntagmatic of toponyms for territory (as in *Monte Pauli*, etc.). See M. Bartoli, 'Sao ko kelle terre...', *Lingua nostra* 6 (1944–5), 1–6 ; S. Pellegrini, 'Ancora *Sao ko kelle terre*', *Lingua Nostra* 8 (1947), 33–8; P. Fiorelli, 'Marzo Novecentosessanta', *Lingua Nostra* 21 (1960), 1–12; G. Sanga and S. Baggio, 'Il volgare nei placiti Cassinesi: vecchie questioni e nuove acquisizioni', *Rivista Italiana di Dialettologia* 18 (1994), 7–30.

Although a linguistic landmark, the Capuan *placitum* highlights the complexity of using legal evidence to determine vernacular forms of speech in Italy, for the combination of written traditions, regional dialects and the social context of the transaction recorded need to be considered.[158] But the more important point to be made here is that a conscious conceptual distinction between Latin and vernacular is never made in the legal sources of Lombard Italy, and to these we now turn.

THE LANGUAGE OF THE LOMBARD LAW CODE

Löfstedt rigorously examined the language of the earliest manuscripts of Lombard law and carefully documented orthographic phenomena such as 'the use of e for i in stressed/unstressed syllables', 'the use of o for u long/short', 'the use of e for ae, ae for e', and so on. But as with Politzer's and Carlton's hunt for Romance, Löfstedt found as many cases when erroneous spelling or case usage was not predictive of early Romance.[159] More important, however, is to ask how the language of the code worked in terms of syntax and grammar, since it was read and consulted by judges, officials and the portions of the population at large, as we shall see in chapters 4 and 5. One reason for the code's success is the simplicity of the language used and the conservatism of its expression, particularly in Rothari's Edict, which rarely strays from the late Roman legislative formula of short, conditional constructions, with an initial 'if' clause governed by imperfect subjunctive verb ('si quis... fuerit/fecerit/haberet') followed by a 'then' clause in present subjunctive as imperative ('sit/faciat/ habeat/componat', etc.). The Edict employs active forms and synthetic passives without confusion, though occasionally passive or reflexive meanings seem a little strained, and deponents receive active forms.[160] There are some inventive verb-forms, such as the prepositions *super* and *inter* used both as prepositions and adverbs.[161] Other verbs such as *consentire*, *anteponere*, *antestare* received uneven treatment in taking dative or accusative case,[162] and it is in the irregularity of case usage that the greater part of the code's 'vulgarity' lies. There is some uncertainty surrounding the use of the dative, which occasionally

---

[158] Cf. R.M. Ruggieri, 'Tra storia della lingua e storia del diritto: elementi bizanti, longobardi e romanici nel placito capuano del 960', *Atti III CISAM* (Spoleto, 1959), 533–67.
[159] Löfstedt, *Studien*, esp. pp. 206–13.
[160] (References are to Rothari's laws unless indicated otherwise.) Strained: *spunsus . . . calumnia non requiratur* 192; deponent infinitive *sequere* 347.
[161] *si super fuerint, non numerentur* Liutprand 101; *si super quem dixerit* Aistulf 2; cf. Löfstedt, *Studien*, p. 328.
[162] Cf. 26, 28, 139, 217, 280, 155.

is substituted for an accusative, particularly with noun–verb constructions expressing violence to or towards someone, such as *plagam facere, violentiam facere, oculum excutere*, and *illius* is always used for *illi*.[163] But in many of these instances the intent is made clear by an easily recognisable subject (*si quis*), by the simplicity of the statement in itself, and by the word order, which sticks fairly close to subject–object–verb forms.[164] Elsewhere we see the types of confusion typical of later Latin texts. The final *-m* of the accusative in feminine nouns of the first declension is only rendered in half the occasions in which it should appear, and its appearance is more often connected to the designation of a person (*feminam, puellam*) rather than an inanimate object. This is a slightly better average than that gleaned from the charter evidence, in which *-am* endings after prepositions all but disappear. The neuter plural coalesces with the nominative feminine singular and, again common to late Latin texts, the third declension suffers even more. There is some confusion over prepositions which take the ablative in both genders (*cum, ex, ab*, etc.) but for the most part these are correct in about two thirds of the instances found, with *in* being something of a wild card.[165] Likewise with the charter evidence, the relative correctness of dative and ablative plural endings may result from their 'rein schriftsprachliche Erscheinung' ('purely literary use'),[166] unaffected by common speech, which abandoned them long before.[167] Despite this, the general impression from the imprecise use of the prepositions and their corresponding cases is that the different syntactic constrictions of prepositions were no longer relevant. The accusative and absolute cases were particularly confused when it came to absolute constructions, which are employed frequently throughout the code. These could take the accusative,[168] or a combination of accusative and ablative together.[169] Other lexical phenomena do suggest that the language of the text does reflect some spoken forms. As is common in late Latin texts, some words have switched gender, and *dies* enjoys its

---

[163] 150. Cf. Löfstedt, *Studien*, pp. 251–4.
[164] *si quis aldium alienum violentiam fecerit* 205; *si vir mulieri violentia fecerit* 186; *si quis homini libero violentia iniuste fecerit* 31; *si quis caballum alienum aurem aut oculum excusserit* 337, etc.
[165] *armam alterius tollere* 308; *de crimen* 195–8, 213; *cum nutrimen* 220; *ex ipso pignus* 252; *de ligamen* 264; *cum vimen* 303 (cf. the Lucca *Compositiones, cum cinos, cum medicamen*, below, and J. Svennung, *Compositiones lucenses: Studien zum Inhalt, zur Textkritik und Sprache* (Uppsala and Leipzig, 1941), p. 121). The declension fared better with the preposition *in* (*in tempore* 217; *in flumine* 16, 336; *in itinerare* 17, 148).
[166] Löfstedt, *Studien*, p. 233.
[167] On the correctness of *-ibus, -eorum* and *-iter* endings in Lombard charters as evidence of their 'fossilisation' in writing, see R.L. Politzer, 'The interpretation of correctness in late Latin texts', *Language* 37 (1961), 209–14; Politzer and Politzer, *Romance Trends*, pp. 21–2.
[168] *leges vivere; propriam mortem mori* 152; *casum facientem* 273; *necessitatem compulsus* 173.
[169] *Nam si casu facientem* 273; *sit sibi causa finita amicitia manentem* 74.

usual gender identity crisis.[170] The demonstrative pronouns *hic* and *iste* are for the most part interchangeable, but interestingly the nominative forms of *is*, *ea*, are never used, though other cases are (*eius, ei, eum, eam*, etc.). As with charters, *ipse* often acts as determinative adjective, and *ille* is primarily used as an anaphoric adjective in place of *is/ea*.[171]

In general the legislation of Liutprand contains longer sentences and more complex syntactical structures, and often includes a measure of legal argumentation in the text that is absent from Rothari's Edict. A good example of this type of 'jurisprudential analysis'[172] is the law promulgated in 733 concerning expulsion or victimisation, in which Liutprand seems concerned to justify the penalty and his classification of the crime:

Hoc autem ideo statuimus, ut nullus presumat malas causas in qualiscumque locum excitare aut facere; et non potuimus causam istam adsimilare neque ad arishcild neque ad consilium rusticanorum, neque ad rusticanorum seditione: et plus congruum nobis paruit esse de consilium malum, id est de consilio mortis. Quia quando se collegunt et super alius vadunt pro peccatis, ad id ipsum vadunt, ut malum faciant, aut si causas evenerit, hominem occidant et plagas aut feritas faciant: ideo, ut dixemus, adsimilavimus causam istam ad consilium mortis, quod sunt, sicut supra premisemus, solidi vigenti.

We establish this in order that no one may presume to incite or perform such evil deeds in any place and [since] we could not associate this crime as *arschild* (breach of the peace with an armed band: Rothari, 19, Liutprand, 35, 141) nor as the banding together of rustics (Rothari, 279), nor to the sedition of rustics (Rothari, 280) it seemed more fitting to us to consider it as the same as giving evil counsel, or plotting a death (Rothari, 11). For when [men], because of their sins, gather together and proceed against another man, they do this in order to commit some evil deed; they may even kill the man or inflict wounds or injuries upon him. Therefore, as we have said, we associate this crime with that of plotting someone's death, [the penalty for which] is twenty *solidi*, as we set forth above.[173]

With its longer phraseology and greater number of subordinate clauses, Liutprand's legislation demonstrates a more sophisticated use of written language, but it too contains the same types of errors in case usage and a reliance upon prepositions and word order (subject–object–verb) that we find in Rothari's Edict and in the charter evidence.

---

[170] *arbor*, now masc. 138, 319, 321; *grex*, now fem. 351; *tenor* now fem. *Dies: in eadem diae* 176; *in diae illa* 175; *inter istos dies* 252; *ab illo diae* L 90; *die isto* L 103.

[171] *sexta partem pretii ipsius, quod homo ipse adpraetiatus fuerint* 63; *iurit cum duodecim aidos suos . . . ita ut sex illi nominentur ab illo* 359.

[172] See P. Vinogradoff, *Roman Law in Medieval Europe* 2nd edn (London, 1929), pp. 212–24.

[173] Liutprand 134. Cf. trans. Fischer-Drew, p. 204.

Language and literacy

THE LANGUAGE OF LOMBARD CHARTERS

Charters were intended to be read aloud, both at the time of their redaction and when used in court to substantiate a claim. In the text of the charter itself, the scribe often states that he has reread the charter, so that the interested parties agree on its content and the witnesses may be sure the document to which they have subscribed records the transaction they witnessed.[174] Moreover, the structure of the charter was anchored in orality: the charter generally begins with an invocation to Christ, akin to a prayer; the *rogatores* (commissioners of the document) narrate their gift, sale or donation in the first person and address the recipient of the goods in the text of the charter; the objects involved in the transaction are listed in a linear fashion of a grammatical sentence, rather than in a vertical list of segmented typology; witnesses confirm their presence at the transaction in the first person, even if by marking a *signum crucis*; the scribe or notary confirms his redaction of the document in the first person.

Despite this emphasis on orality, Lombard charters contain highly formulaic legal language, sometimes very ill-fitted-out grammatically, that cannot have been easily understood, at least not initially, by persons other than those with a fair degree of familiarity with such language and the context in which it is used – the same can be said for legal documents in our own day. Were the orthographically correct and hence 'fossilised' endings *-ibus*, *-orum* and *-iter* read out phonetically, and if so did this constitute an obstacle to intelligibility? Arguably such 'archaisms' of written Latin could not have constituted tremendous barriers to comprehensibility for the very simple reason that there was not, nor ever had been, an alternative: the Latin language, in all its rigid precision and inflectional glory, had been the written language in Italy for over 1000 years. Upon such deep linguistic roots rested the edifice of an imperial language, used as *the* instrument of efficacious written communication in the exercise of power, which imbued Latin with vitality and vigour, and further surrounded it with cultural associations of status and prestige. Moreover, Latin was the language of both the law and the church. The rules governing secular and sacred life were framed in Latin. Within this cultural milieu and linguistic history, it is hard to imagine that the

---

[174] Court case: CDL 163 (762), 'fecemus [nos iudices] nobis relegere ipsa exemplar ordinationis'. Charters: e.g. CDL 112. 'Scripsit ego Godescalco notarius post tradita coram testibus relegi, complevi et dedit.' Confusion between the use of the first person and third person singular verb is common to Lombard charters. Witnesses: e.g. CDL 203, 'Signum manus Gaidualdi medici qui hanc cartulam fieri rogavit, et ei omnia relecta ut sunt complacuit'; 206, 'Angrafi, qui hanc cartula fieri rogavit et ipsorum relecta est.' An odd case is CDL 231, '[ego] rogatus a Gradone diacono testes subscripsi, me presente scripsit, et non est mihi relicto'.

preservation of archaisms in morphology, syntax and grammar in the written language constituted any insurmountable obstacles to comprehension by the general populace. People might have known how the synthetic passive worked within the semiological system of the written language without having to use it themselves in speech.[175] To put it another way, the move from spoken to written Latin from the sixth to the eighth century may have involved some forms of speech foreign to the tongue, but these forms were already familiar to eyes and ears.

Another approach to the charter evidence to determine the linguistic environment behind them is to focus on the details of the property or goods recorded in the transaction, which cannot rely on formulaic language in the same manner as the opening address (*invocatio*) and declaration (*pronuntio*), the subsequent legal stipulations (*stipulatio*) and the penalties listed for infringement of agreement (*sanctio*).[176] For example, the preference for the use of the preposition *de* when listing goods (*sex deminate de uino, de ipsa casa*) might suggest that the use of the genitive case was restricted to written tradition and was no longer used in speech. Yet the use of *de* in charters might just as easily be ascribed to written traditions also, since it is found in other, highly formulaic passages in which *de* is used for the genitive of value, source or description, followed by a long string of suspiciously correct ablatives.[177] Likewise, the description of goods often conforms to common formulae, particularly when it takes the form of measurement (*modium, caput, libra, iugerum*) with the ablative case or with a quantification of value in monetary terms.[178] Sometimes, however, a formula would not do, as when the priest Rixsolf wrote his own charter recording his donation to the family church and stipulated that part of the proceeds must go towards providing lunch three days a week for twenty-four poor people. Rixsolf specified what was to be eaten: 'and their lunch every week must be a bushel of corn, grain, baked bread, two *congia* (around twelve pints) of wine, and two *congia* of relish, beans and mixed millet, well thickened, and a condiment of fat or of

---

[175] *Contra*, H.F. Muller, 'The passive voice in vulgar Latin', *The Romanic Review* 12 (1921), 318–34. Cf. Politzer, 'Correctness in late Latin texts', pp. 213, 214.

[176] F. Sabatini, 'Dalla *scripta latina rustica* alle *scriptae Romanze*', *Studi Medievali* 9:1 (1961), 321–58, citing the examples of CDL 166, 167, 193.

[177] As in the common formula *ex omnibus rebus meis, tam de domo curtile quam de casis massaricis, terris, vineis, pratis, pascuis, siluis, cultum atque incultum, mobile vel immobile*, etc. Cf. the subscription of Maurezius in the Mozarabic orational (above, note 1): 'canevarius fidiiosor de anfora uino de Bonello in anno XX Liutprandi regis'. Maurezius coupled *anfora* and *uino* instead of using the genitive, but it is not surprising he has no trouble with using the genitive in regnal dating, which he probably saw all of the time.

[178] E.g. CDL 176, 'de ipsa res [*sic*] duo modia grano e dui modia farre, uino anforas quinque'; 166, 'reddere debeam porco uni ualente tremisse uno et uno pullo et quinque ouas et camisia una ualente tremisse uno'.

Language and literacy

oil'.[179] The most common and lengthiest descriptions, however, concern land, but even these were couched in terminology that demonstrates a certain uniformity across the board (*terrola de capite uno, casa cum curte, casa massicaria*). Noting the precise location of the land, however, required a little more compositional skill. An example of the type of non-Classical Latin employed for the task is a Sienese charter of 760, which records the sale of a forest:

hoc est silbula: ab uno latere de subtu curre fossatum, et ab a[lio] latere curre signa: da pede est tessaratu unu testuclu, et sup[er] ill[u] est alius testuclu tesseratu, et sup[er] ill[u] duo testucli sunt duo quercias, et sup[er] ipse una cerru tesseratu, et super ipsa cerru uade signa inter campu et silva; et de alia parte est terra emptori Possoni.[180]

While the precise meaning of *testuculus tesseratus* might escape us, the participants to the sale, Auduald and his neighbour Posso, had obviously ensured there would be no confusion by carefully marking trees, and ensuring that the *notarius* Gauspert noted the details they provided. In such clauses, then, we may hear vestiges of spoken forms in the use of prepositions with or without corresponding case *(da pede est, ab uno latere, super ipsa curru vade signa inter campu et silva)*, but on the whole the details of properties or goods are recorded in a recognisably Latinate manner, suggesting that the transition from spoken to written forms was not an arduous one.

The use of the abbreviation for *sup[er]* raises an important point that needs to be considered in weighing up the relationship between these texts and spoken language, and that is the possibility of visual, rather than phonetic, reception of the written word. Wright has proposed that early medieval scribes may have learned how to spell certain words in a logographic, rather than phonetic, fashion, much as is necessary in modern English, when the spelling of the word does not correspond to its pronunciation. Hence the teacher may have held up examples, written on parchment, wax tablets, a piece of wood, or any surface which could be written upon, of the word *SUPER*, explaining that this is the correct spelling of the word that was pronounced *sopra* (or *sobra*), or that *PETRUS* is the correct spelling of *Pietro*, and so on.[181] This would go some way to explaining the strange mix of Latin and Romance forms

---

[179] CDL 194, 'prandium eor[um] tali sit p[er] omnem septimana: scaphilo, grano, pane cocto et duo congia uino, et duo congia de pulmentario, faba et panico mixto, bene spisso et condito de uncto aut de oleo'.

[180] CDL 146. On *testuclus tesseratus*, see Schiaparelli, CDL II, pp. 55–6 nn. 2–3.

[181] Wright, 'Logographic script', pp. 174–5, using Spanish examples, and more fully in 'The teaching of orthography', p. 193, to the extent of advocating that 'every letter, every word, every phoneme, possibly every syllable, needs individual research'.

in our charter evidence, as scribes resorted to a 'learned' orthography for some terms, yet elsewhere improvised as best they could, navigating their own orthographic course between learned traditions and the contemporary pronunciation of the words. Logographic learning might also explain other phenomena: verbs with incorrect person endings, the correctness of suffixes such as *-ibus*, *-eorum*, *-iter* and *-itur* in contrast to the usual substitution and exchange of letters (e/i, o/u, t/d); and the high level of abbreviations found in the script of charters, which, if learned logographically also, saved the scribe the trouble of remembering the entire original, classical spelling of a word, instead of a simple, shortened version.

But the language of our documents is never that neat, being riddled with inconsistencies that logographic learning cannot explain. Besides the problem of determining why some words came with instructions and not others made up of similar phonetic components, we find scribes using different spellings for the same word across a range of charters over time. Orthographic incoherence is especially evident when the spelling changes for the one word within one document. A charter of 729, for example, renders *modius* three different ways, none of which is grammatically correct in terms of the correct case and number.[182] The Pisan *notarius* Teofrid wrote two documents thirteen years apart; in the second he spelt his name Teufrit.[183] The lack of respect for uniformity in orthography and grammar disturbs the modern reader, but it was obviously not a concern for the scribes of Lombard Italy, nor for those of Byzantine Ravenna.

PRIESTS AND THEIR BAD LATIN

The conscious rejection of classicising norms for grammar and spelling can best be seen in the charters of some ecclesiastics who wrote with a considerable degree of fluency and expertise. In 737 the priest Gaudentius, one of the chief scribes of the cathedral church of Lucca *c.* 737–50, and praised by palaeographers for his clear and sophisticated chancery script,[184] drew up a charter for his bishop, Walprand, which confirmed a grant of property to a certain cleric in reward for his father's service to the church.[185] Gaudentius' skill as a document writer is evident in the use of uncial script for the opening of the charter and his inclusion

---

[182] CDL 44, 'sex modius seminatura in trebus partebus... duo mudio in una uersuram, duo in alia, duo in tertia... fiaeri simul modio sex.'
[183] CDL 98, 171 (ChLA 804, 807).
[184] Petrucci, 'Il codice e i documenti', *Scriptores*, pp. 79–81.   [185] CDL 61.

Language and literacy

of a passage of scripture to set the theme.[186] But already in the grand uncial opening we find *saluaturi* (saluatori) and *cunserbato* (conservato), and the use of *u* instead of *o* is evident in several other passages, particularly in words beginning with *con-* (*cunsideraui, cunsequator, cunfermo te, cunquiset, cunquirere potuet, cumparare uisus fuet, cuncessa vel confermata sunt, cunquisitionem*), but also in words such as *timure, foturum*, and even for his own title of *sacerdus*.[187] In other places *o* and *u* are rendered correctly (*remedium seculi, seo, seditionem*), even if the case is not (*pro facinoris*). Three of the nine clerics who signed the document preferred *u* (*cunsensi*) in the formulaic *consensi et suscripsi*, but their bishop had no trouble (*una cum concesso omnium sacerdotum*).

Elsewhere in this same charter we see cases suffer. Take for example the bishops' declaration of intent, where the sense is clear, but the use of case is not in agreement:

Propterea aublactatum est meus animus et rememoratu sum eo quod multas et inumerauilis serbitias quas q[uon]d[am] Barucio pr[es]b[iter]o in eclesia Beati S[an]c[t]i Martini uel in obis in uita sua ostendere uisus fuet, ipse bona fedilitas adcomodauet meus animus, ut alico beneficio ostendere debuissim in filio eius.

Gaudentius employed the nominative *meus animus* in two occasions when he was unsure: as the object of the (obviously rare) verb *oblectatum est* (*aublactatum*), and again as object of *accommodauit* (*adcomdauet*), unless *meus animus* was meant as subject, which then exposes the confusion of *ipse bona fedilitas*. Elsewhere, inappropriate accusatives ring out as though learned from a formulary, or by rote.[188] On other occasions, formulaic phrases are close to, if not entirely, correct in case usage, despite orthographic deviation, but we find Gaudentius using the same formulaic language in later charters with slightly different deviations.[189]

If the priest Gaudentius, top scribe of the cathedral church, was as unconcerned with his grammar and as carefree about his spelling as to get even *eclesia* wrong, then it comes as no surprise that a bishop was equally unconcerned about his language. When the bishop of Pisa, John, drew up a document for two brothers, both clerics who had donated property to

---

[186] Matt. 16.26: 'quid prodeest hominis, si uniuersum mund[um] lugretor, et anime uero sue detrimentum patiator?'

[187] *nullus sacerdus Lucane huius eclesie*. But cf. *ego . . . una cum omnib[us] sacerdotib[us]* earlier on, and *una cum sacerdotib[us] meis*, and *et testibus nubilibus sacerdotarum*. Did the rhyme of *nullus sacerdus* lead him astray?

[188] 'ita ut a nullo hominem nulloq[ue] tempore'; 'in tua potestatem sine omnem inpedimentum inimici, iuuante d[omi]n[u]m Iesum Christum', etc.

[189] 'et ab ipso beato s[an]c[t]o Martino uel ab omnibus uertutibus sanctorum reatur recedat, et faciendi nulla aueat potestatem resubtrahendi'; 'set in omni tempore fermum et stauilitum p[er]maneat'. Cf. CDL 67, 73, 'sine omnem impedimento'; 'faciendi nulla aueas potestatem resubtrahendi'.

the church of Pisa, he used no less than seven different biblical references to raise the charter to an appropriate level of solemnity.[190] John appears to have had notes, or even a copy of the Vulgate before him, as his quotations from scripture are both orthographically and grammatically correct. Not so his own language. This shows an acquaintance with some classicising forms, such as the correct use of deponent verbs and the future tense.[191] But elsewhere John slips up, using ablatives for genitives, the ablative after *post* and *ad*, and *de* before nominatives and accusatives, all traits common in Lombard charters, yet the sense is clear when the case usage is not.[192] John's orthography is quite good, but words are spelled correctly in some occasions and not others: John uses the verb *rogabimus*, for *rogauimus*, but states in the *completio* that he wrote the charter 'rogitus a Liutpert'.

On the whole, John's orthography and grammar are a step above that of Gaudentius, and we might expect this of a bishop over a lowly priest. But striking in John's charter is the near perfect Latin of his scriptural citations. In same cases he appears to quote straight from scripture,[193] although he introduces a quotation from 1 John 2.15, as a statement of St Paul.[194] John paraphrased other passages, and his grammar began to waver, to the extent that some of his paraphrases are difficult to identify, but the bishop was obviously happy enough with them.[195]

John's charter testifies not only to the lack of concern for rigorously grammatical sentences and classical orthography, but also to the sense of inventiveness with biblical language that we find used by scribes elsewhere. Sicherad, priest of the Lucchese church and possibly a *magister* to Gaudentius, wrote a charter with the express permission of the bishop

---

[190] Schiaparelli, CDL 93, and p. 267, and 'Note paleografiche', pp. 111–13, identifies this John with the same who subscribed to a charter of 730, CDL 45.

[191] Deponent (despite the mistaken ablative of *voce*): *haec enim nobis est recordari beati Pauli apostoli uoce qui ait*. But cf. *debet unusquis eternis lauorari muneribus*. Future passive: *et ante tribunal eterni iudicis cum secura conscientia presentemur*.

[192] *ad ecclesia, ad parentibus nostris, ad marito ambolauerit, ad alio homine; . . . medietate de omnes res et substantia mea . . .; . . . postestate habeant heredes aut parentes de ipsi diacones prendere et tenere et defendere; unde pro memoranda futura tempora et anime nostre cautela . . .* etc.

[193] I Cor. 7.31–2, *preteri enim figura huius mundi. uolo uos sine sollicitudine esse*, with the exception of the lack of diphthong *ae* and final *-t* in *praeterit*. Cf. *facite uobis sacculos, que non uetescerent*, Luke 12.33; *nam et Dauid psalmigrafus uates cecinit ait: diuitie si affluent, nolite cor adponere*, Psalms 61.11.

[194] 'It[er]um Paulus egregius predicator dicit: *Nolite diligere mundum neq[ue] ea quae in mundo, et qui enim diligit mundum, non est caritas patris in eo*'. Less worrying is the suggestion that Zacche was a centurion: '*et centurio ait: D[omin]e, si aliquod defraudabi, reddo quadruplum*', Luke 19.8.

[195] E.g., 'interogatorius inquid: *adpropinquante mundi term[i]nus, cum signa [et] portenta conspicimus secundum ueritatis uoce leuare capita* (cf. Luke 21.7–28). *id est exhilarari corda et nostras mentes ad gaudia patriae celestis erigere*' seems to be culled from Prov. 15.13, *cor gaudiens exhilarat faciem in maerore animi deicitur spiritus*. Similarly obscure is 'q[uonia]m qui amat eum amatur ab eo quem amat, et p[er] hoc inimicus D[e]i esse conuincitur'. Both *convincitur* and *inimicus Dei* are found only once each, I Cor. 1.24, and I Ja. 4.

Language and literacy

and duke of Lucca.[196] The charter, written by a priest for a high-status client who had links with the secular and ecclesiastical power, opens with a rough quotation from Luke 2.14: 'In excellis gloria est omni[po]tenti D[e]i et in terra pax hominibus bone uoluntatis arbitrium addidit.' Sicherad then proceeded to build on the theme of preparation for the day of judgement with other citations of scripture which cannot be recognised and in which the sense becomes obscure.[197] Sicherad wrote another such charter ten years later, again concerning the foundation and endowment of a church by two brothers in the region around Lucca (Garfagnana) and again with the permission of the bishop of Lucca.[198] Again Sicherad rose to the occasion with a string of biblical quotations which demonstrate both his respect for the more correct orthography of the language of the scripture and his ability to paraphrase and elaborate upon its theme:

sicut euangelicam uox admonit dicens: fratris mei et amici mei, uenite ad regnum patris mei, possedite quod e[st] paratum uouis	Matt. 25.34: *regnum a consitutione mundi*
et aliui uendite que possedites et date aelimosinis et aueuetis tensaurum in celo et sequimini me	Luke 12.33: *Vendite quae possidetis et date elemoysenam, facite uobis sacculos qui non uetescerunt thesaurum non deficientem in caelis quo fur non adpropriat*, etc.
ut s[an]c[t]a Ier[usa]l[em] ad D[e]o transmissa descentem de celo	Ap. 21.2: *et ciuitatem sanctam Hierusalem nouam uidi descendentem de caelo a Deo paratam sicut sponsam ornatam uiro suo*
ubi lux indeficiens est	Ecc. 24.6: *Ego in caelis feci ut oriretur lumen indeficiens et sicut nebula texi omnem terram*
mereamor conlocari et mannam illam celestem angelicam	Ps. 77.24–5: *et pluit illis manna ad manducandum et panem caeli dedit eis panem angelorum manducauit homo cibaria misit eis in abundantiam*
c[um] s[an]c[t]i et iusti participes esse inueniamor.	

Some biblical citations appear in Lucchese charters well spaced apart chronologically, such as the adaptation of Matt. 6.19 and Luke 19.9,

---

[196] CDL 16 (713–14). This, a copy of the original, was also written by Sicherad. Cf. CDL 31 (723 Lucca), also by Sicherad.
[197] 'et declarat suoque arbitrio p[er]fectissime capiant homane mentis [a]bsq[ue] duuio [et] segreta Christi suscipere humilis esse propter se, sicut sta scriptura admonit dicens: gentiis, inquid, uia celestis intuentis, spiritalis uertute precingtis suauissime agentis hominis expectantis diei hore sexte adueniente D[omi]no i[. . .] inuocatus aduenturum. qua inutilis fama laudator qui seculum merca[tor] et siui nulla mansio fabricator, desiderans, mecum p[er]tractans, quamuis breuite', etc. Schiaparelli, CDL I, p. 43.
[198] CDL 31.

which must be owed to a formulary.[199] First found in a charter of 722, the same words are used *verbatim* in another Lucchese charter of 764. In both cases the charters record the donation of property by wealthy laymen to a church they had founded earlier and in which their daughters were to live 'chastely'. The scribe of the later charter, Prandulus, does not appear to have been a priest himself, but clearly worked for them.[200] Elsewhere we find lay scribes embroidering the donations of their pious clients with scriptural language.[201] It is tempting to draw the common-sense conclusion on the basis of these examples that the orthography and grammar of their biblical quotations was worse than that of their ecclesiastical contemporaries, who appear to have adhered more stringently to classical norms for passages of scripture. Clearly, however, ecclesiastical scribes wrote better, more classicising Latin when citing scripture, but they did not care to apply the same standards to the rest of their charters. Charters which have come down to us in later copies show a marked improvement in their orthography, and in verbatim quotations from the Vulgate, without the kind of experimentation or adventurous paraphrase we find in the charters preserved as originals.[202]

GRAMMAR AND AUTHORITY

When Benedict wrote his *Rule* in the early sixth century, he turned his back on Latin grammatical traditions of the late antique school and consciously sought to use a more accessible Latin, modelled on that of the Latin Bible, to set out the regulations of his monastic programme.[203] The priests and scribes of Lombard Italy appear to have followed Benedict's lead in ignoring the dictates of Latin grammatical tradition and attempting to write in a language that reflected the linguistic environment in which they lived and worked. But not only in Lombard Italy: Rome too appears to have had little concern for classical norms of orthography and grammar, as is clear from ninth-century papyrus documents issued from the papal

---

[199] 'Nolite thesaurizare uobis sup[er] terram, ubi furis effodiunt et furantur, sed thensaurizate uobis thesaurum in caelum, ubi fur, id est diabolus, non adpropinquat. et iterum dicens: facite uobis amic[us] de mamone iniquitatis, ut cum defeceretis recipiam uos in aeterna tabernacula'. On formularies, see below, pp. 221–9.

[200] CDL 30, 178. Prandulus, cf. CDL 227.

[201] CDL 59: 'sicut nos divina eloquia intruet dicens: qui in hoc secolo date parua, in s[an]c[t]a diae remissionis accepit magna, pro terrena celestia, et pro temporalia sempiterna'. Cf. Matt. 19.21, Mark 10.29–30, Luke 18.30. The biblical passage appears in the charters of Maurace's successor, Audoald, CDL 291, 774. See below, pp. 223–4; CDL 234 (769). 'quidquid homo in loca uenera uia contulerit, centubl[um] acepiet, et insup[er] uitam hedernam possedeuit'. Cf. Matt. 19.29.

[202] E.g. CDL 18.   [203] See pp. 45–9.

curia.²⁰⁴ The contrast between Italian and northern European attitudes towards Latin can be seen in Boniface's visit to Rome in 719 to seek papal approval for his planned missionary activity in Germany. When Pope Gregory II began to ask questions, Boniface excused himself from answering on the grounds that he was inexperienced with the pope's usual manner of speech (*vestrae familiaritatis sermone*), and asked that he be allowed to respond in writing. Permission was granted, and Boniface presented a tract written in high literary style (*urbana eloquentiae scientie conscripta*).²⁰⁵ For Boniface, a native Anglo-Saxon speaker who had already written a Latin grammar, Latin was a language of written texts, a learned language in which each letter on the page represented a particular sound in accordance with the rules of late antique grammarians. In contrast, the pope's Latin was a living language that had evolved over centuries of linguistic development.²⁰⁶ Gregory had been director of the papal library prior to his election and was steeped in a world of texts, yet he used the common speech of his day to converse over theological matters, because of its affinity to the written tradition, notwithstanding the changes in pronunciation and, probably, grammar, which threw Boniface. The contemporary recensions of the *Life* of Gregory II in the *Liber pontificalis* confirm the picture that eighth-century papal Rome shared none of the enthusiasm for classicising Latin that the Carolingians were to promote in the following century.²⁰⁷ More 'bookish' attitudes towards Latin could certainly be found in Lombard Italy. The anonymous seventh-century grammatical text known as the *Appendix Probi*, found attached to the grammatical works of Ps. Probus in a palimpsest manuscript from Bobbio, consists of a long list of different forms of spelling particular words (227 in all).²⁰⁸ The *Appendix* rejected forms of words which appeared perfectly respectable to classical authors such as Plautus, Horace, Martial, Pliny, Seneca, Martial, Phaedrus and Servius, and even words acceptable to Jerome for his Vulgate were compared to more classical forms.²⁰⁹ We find the same attitude in Italy when we look back to Cassiodorus, whose

---

²⁰⁴ See ChLA, L (2nd series, ninth century) (Zurich, 1999), ed. R. Cosma, no. 1, p. 16: 'una lingua grammaticalmente più che incerta'. The rough Latin was noted by Bresslau, *Handbuch*, II, p. 330.
²⁰⁵ *Vita Bonifatii*, ed. W. Levison (Hanover, 1905), pp. 28, 29. See Wright, 'Latino e Romanzo: Bonifazio e il Papa Gregorio II', in J. Herman and L. Mondin (eds.), *La preistoria dell'Italiano* (Tübingen, 2000), pp. 219–29; Law, *Grammar and Grammarians*, p. 189.
²⁰⁶ See J. Herman, 'Sur un exemple de la langue parlée à Rome au VIe siècle', in G. Calbioli and S. Guartiero (eds.), *Latin vulgaire–Latin tardif II* (Tübingen, 1990), pp. 145–57.
²⁰⁷ See Duchesne, *LP* I, pp. ccxx–ccxxiii; Wright, 'Latino e Romanzo', pp. 216–17.
²⁰⁸ Naples, lat. 1 (Vindobon. 17) (CLA IV.388–90). See C. Robson, 'L'Appendix Probi et la philologie latine', *Moyen Age* 69 (1963), 37–54, at pp. 39, 41.
²⁰⁹ Some examples: *catellus*, corrected to *catulus*; *butro* to *botruus*; *cocus* to *coquus*; *calda* to *calida*; *gruis* to *grus*. Jerome: *formunsus* to *formosus*.

Literacy in Lombard Italic, c. 568–774

uncritical obsequience to grammatical tradition in his *De orthographia* led him to make some puzzling recommendations concerning the spelling of words, some of which he unconsciously contradicted immediately.[210] Cassiodorus' reverence for scholarly tradition was not unique: Priscian grafted the rules of ancient Greek grammarians onto contemporary Latin usage.[211] Divorced from these antiquarian and irrelevant traditions, seventh- and eighth-century Italian scribes struck out in new directions to find a compromise between the written legal traditions they inherited and the linguistic environment of their day.

THE LANGUAGE OF THE COURTS

One method of moving away from the formulaic aspect of the language of charters in order to detect elements of vernacular speech behind literate traditions is to examine the speech recorded in some documented court cases (*placita*). There are only a few documented *placita* prior to 774; many of them are brief and tend to paraphrase the plaintiffs' speeches given before judges. An exception is the document recording the royal inquiry into the dispute between the dioceses of Siena and Arezzo, which comes down to us in a ninth- or tenth-century copy made, it seems, at the church of Arezzo, where it has been preserved to the present day. It is probable, therefore, that the Latin of those interviewed has been tidied up a little, both by the royal agent Gunteram's staff or by the late ninth-, early tenth-century Aretine copyist.[212] But we should not dismiss the document outright as evidence too tainted by later correction. A royal *inquisitio* was an official matter, and the procedures were probably enveloped in a considerable degree of ceremony.[213] In any case, the language is similar

---

[210] *Tamtus, quamtus* rather than *tantus quantus* (PL 70, 1245 C); *narare* (1249 B: also *Inst.*, I.15.10), contradicted 1251 B; *samguis* for *sanguis* in nominative case (1268 D).

[211] R. Wright, 'Even Priscian nods', *Acts of the Sixth International Conference on Late and Vulgar Latin* (Helsinki, forthcoming). See also M. Passalacqua, 'Priscian's *Institutio de nomine et pronomine et verbo* in the ninth century', in V. Law (ed.), *History of Linguistic Thought in the Early Middle Ages* (Amsterdam, 1993), pp. 193–204; A. Luhtala, 'Syntax and dialectic in Carolingian commentaries on Priscian's *Institutiones grammaticae*', in *ibid.*, pp. 145–91.

[212] CDL 19. Throughout the following I give page and line numbers for Schiaparelli's text. That this was a copy of the original royal document, rather than a purely Aretine record of events and final victory, seems confirmed by Gunteram's speech in first person singular and plural, and by its separate transmission from the other documents recording the dispute (CDL 4, 17, 20) which were originally preserved on papyrus and were copied in the eleventh century by Gezo, *notarius* of the Aretine church. See Schiaparelli, CDL I, p. 8, 78; and below, pp. 189–90. One word used throughout the *placitum* has received individual attention: P. Aebischer, 'Latin longobard *diocia*, "ressort ecclésiastique"', *Le Moyen Age* 69 (1963), 55–65.

[213] See A. Petrucci and C. Romeo, 'Scrivere in iudicio: modi soggetti e funzioni di scrittura nei placiti del regnum italiae (sec. IX–XI)', *Scrittura e Civiltà* 13 (1989), 5–48.

Language and literacy

to those *placita* that have come down to us in original and which were written by lay scribes at the command of state officials.[214]

Some responses have a distinctly colloquial ring to them. To Gunteram's question, the old priest Semeris, of the monastery of San Ansano, responded in perfectly grammatical fashion: 'Iam Ambrosio misso domno regi de causa ista professionem feci, et uobis ueritatem dico, quia ab antiquo tempore oraculus fuit de sub ecclesia Sanctae Mariae in Pacena...' [62.2]. When asked if there was a bishop in Siena at the time of his consecration in Arezzo, Semeris responded: 'Memoro quia erat bone memoriae Magnus episcopus', and went on to give an account of Magnus' ministrations, again in near perfectly correct Latin. The term *memoro* has a decidedly vulgar ring; though it is not found in Italian texts until Bartolomeo da San Concordio (Pisa, 1262–1347), we can safely assume it readily took the place of the learned deponent *memor* + genitive much earlier. Both the judges' and Semeris' speech occasionally slips into the types of mistakes we find throughout Lombard charters, such as the confusion over the correct case with prepositions *de* and *post* [215] and the loss of the accusative case when the object appears to be emphasised. Elsewhere in direct speech we see similar confusion over prepositions and corresponding case,[216] although *iuxta* + accusative seems to have caused no confusion, perhaps owing to its frequency in ecclesiastical texts and canon law.[217] One finds the use of *ad* + accusative to express motion or direction[218] and the use of *iste* as the preferred form for the definite article.[219]

We also see the use of prepositions in what appear to have been common expressions, such as *per rogo* [66.25; 70.10, 14, 17; 72.18], *per nocte* [72.25], *de sub* to express possession or authority [71.9], and the adverbial *postea* [70.7; 73.1] to indicate time or sequence. There is a glimpse at some Romance words, such as the preferred use of *toti* (mod. Ital. *tutti*)

---

[214] Cf. ChLA 1098 (Manaresi 6), a court case of 785. Also ChLA, 1084, 1071.

[215] 'interrogauimus eum ... de qualem chrisma accipiebat?' [63.4], though cf. 'ad qualem episcopum obediebas?' [62.20]; Gunteram, 'de diocesas illas et monasteria de quibus intentio' [61.5], 'ego post eius decesso' [63.6].

[216] 'ad illo tempore' [63.13], 'nisi si de seculares causes nobis oppressio fiebat' [63.20], 'per isto pallio sancti Quirici et evangelia que hic lecta sunt' [67.23], 'cum istas diocias' [73.27], 'per ... ista crucem' [66.30], 'dum ipsa ecclesia tenui' [63.5].

[217] E.g. 'obediui iuxta canonicam institutionem' [66.17], similar perhaps to the correct use of *secundum* + accusative [e.g. 66.1]. Cf. CDL 20, 'sicut santis patris Nicei et Affessani adque Calcedonensis conciliis statuerunt' [82.15].

[218] 'ambolaui ad Lupercianum episcopum ... et obedientia sicut deuet ad episcopum suum' [65.14, 17] or similarly, 'nam semper obedientia ad episcopum Aretine ecclesiae habui' [64.21], 'ambolaui ad Aritio' [64.29].

[219] 'per ista sancta quattuor Dei euangelia' [63.24; 64.14, 28; 65.13, *et passim*); also common in the related *notitia iudicati* of 714, CDL 17], 'usque in anno isto' [70.19, 24], 'iste Ursus sagratus fuet' [70.2], 'istas diocias' [72.18], 'istas diocias sed it ipso baptisterio' [73.1], 'isti homines'.

over *omnes* (*fuemus toti tres* [69.28]); one cannot help wonder about the old cleric Dominicus also known as *Tutto* [68.4]. What appear to have been colourful colloquialisms escape.[220] The use of verbs remained fairly elementary, and subordinate clauses taking imperfect or perfect subjunctive are rare. The use of passive forms for active deponent verbs seems for the most part limited to first person expression and deponents are otherwise avoided.[221] Likewise the occasional gerundive turns up,[222] but on the whole these are rare, as is the use of the passive infinitive.[223] Verbs which used to take the dative *ob[o]edire* [62.20], *imperare* [63.15] now take the accusative. Yet there are some surprising classicising remnants: the past tense (*tuli*) of the irregular verb *fero*, which did not survive into modern Italian, is used throughout [e.g. 64.9; 65.19; 66.6, 15; 67.1; and *passim*], and some correct case usage, including retention of neuter gender (*ad ipsum corpus sanctum* [62.16]), the use of *pro* with ablative (*pro sacratione mea* [62.22]) and, not suprisingly, nearly always correct case and gender in the formulaic *manu mea scripsi/feci* [66.7,15].

We might expect fundamental familiarity with Latin, even if slightly deviating from classical rules, from the clerics interviewed by Gunteram. But we find soldiers expressing themselves in similar language, such as the *exercitalis* Gundoald, who testified to support the church of Arezzo:

scio ab infantia mea, et parentes meos dicentes audiui, et per me posteas natus sum scio, istas diocias sed et ipso baptisterio Sanctae Restitutae semper sagrationem apud episcopo Aredino habe[re] et consi[gna]tionem in populo facere, et presbiteros sagrare et altaria. [72.30–73.4]

I know that from an early age, because I heard my relatives saying so, and well after I was born, that those churches and especially the baptistry of of S. Restituta have always been held by the bishop of Arezzo, and that he always performed services among the people, and consecrated their priests and altars.

Unfortunately, the majority of responses by laymen are recorded with brief phrases or more often the simple formula 'Item [name and title] similiter dixit', leaving us to wonder whether their responses were so colloquial or so vulgarised that Gunteram or the scribe responsible for

---

[220] Colloquialisms [?]: 'Quia in eclesia Senense ad calica militaui' [66.20], 'ueritatem dico coram Deo, quia tribui munera episcopo Aredine ecclesiae, ut ipse misit missus suos, qui mihi de ipso santo corpus patrocias dederunt' [72.10], 'Quia ab infantia mea usque modo, habeo pene annos quinquaginta, semper diocias istas, unde mihi breue ostendis' [73.20]; and to the interrogative *tu ubi tonsus?* the priest Aufrit responded: 'In Roma, et ab infantia mea, posteas tonsus fui, in Cosona militaui in diocia Sancti Donati, et hic ueniebam cotidie et faciebam officio' [69.15ff].
[221] 'quia omnia ueritatem locutus sum' [70.2], 'ueritatem dico et non mentior' [63.10, 25].
[222] 'propter santuaria ad ipsa ecclesia sanctificandum misit me ut pergere et adducere reliquias santi Ampsani' [72.9]
[223] 'intra plebe nostra sacrari fuit oportunum' [63.16].

recording the proceedings found it difficult to render their speech in writing, though the same formula was used for many clerics' responses also.[224] Yet some responses step outside the bounds of formulaic language and have a realistic ring to them, such as when the cleric Romanus of Montepulciano (*castrum Policianum*) recalled before Gunteram how the gastald of Siena had threatened him to keep quiet should he be summoned to court:

Uuarnefrit gastaldius mihi dicebat: Ecce missus uenit inquirere causa ista, et tu, si interrogatus fueris, quomodo dicere habes? Ego respondi ei: Caue ut non interroget, nam si interrogatus fuero, ueritatem dicere habeo. Sic respondit mihi: Ergo taci tu uiro, qui est missus domni regi. modo me inuenisti, et non te posso contendere, Deo teste, quod ueritatem scio: tibi dico, quia diocias istas fines Messolas et castello Pulliciani usque in Sancti Angilo fine Pisana cum oraculis suis unde modo mihi breue legis, semper Sancti Donati diocias esse scio ab infantia mea usque in die isto. [74.13–22]

Warnefrit the gastald said to me, 'So, the *missus* is coming to inquire into this case; but you, what will you have to say, if you are questioned?' I replied to him: 'Look out that he does not ask me, for if I'm asked, I'll have to tell the truth.' He then said to me: 'Therefore you be silent before him who is the lord king's *missus*.' But now you have found me here, and I cannot struggle against you, as God is my witness, because I know the truth: I say to you that those churches between the boundaries of Messola and Montepulciano, including S. Angelus within the territory of Pisa, along with its parish churches which you have read out to me from the list – I know that all of these, from the time of my childhood right up to this very day, belong to the church of S. Donatus [in Arezzo].

Romanus probably had a lot more to say, and that which he did say probably differed from the way it was recorded: his verbs were not so perfectly tensed or suffixes pronounced as such (*dicebat, uenit, interroget, interrogatus fuero, inuenisti*). But other expressions are well attested in vulgar Latin texts (and mod. Italian), such as the auxiliary *habeo* + infinitive (*dicere*) to express obligation or future, or the syntax of *tibi dico, taci tu, non te posso contendere*, so that the flavour of Romanus' speech is not entirely smothered by officialdom.

We find the same lively sense of the vernacular in other court cases, such the *placitum* held in the royal palace in Pavia in 762, when the two plaintiffs refute each others arguments by beginning with 'non/nihil mihi impedit' and present their charters as proof with a triumphant 'ecce exempla'.[225] In this and other cases, certainly much that was said or later deemed to

---

[224] Cf. the responses of Allerad, 'centenario [*sic*] de uico Pantano', [73.6–9], and Landoari, 'exercitalis de Consona' [73.20–4].
[225] CDL 163.

have been irrelevant to the judges' decision has been left out.[226] But the very diversity of the *placita* of the eighth and ninth centuries, in contrast with the highly formulaic cases documented from the end of the ninth century onwards, suggests that the speeches attributed to the participants strongly resembled at least elements of that which was said on the day, and this was said in a manner that could be rendered in simple Latin by the scribe.

The same strong whiff of vernacular can be found in charters which record an agreement or settlement between two parties. In a Piacentine charter of 762, a local landowner, Ansoald, *vir honestus*, promised to pay his nephew Lopoald, priest of the church of San Pietro at Varsi, two tremisses and a piece of land for damages done to the property of the church.[227] Throughout the course of the document we learn that Ansoald was initially under obligation to pay a fine of 20 *solidi*, a penalty in accordance with Liutprand's 134rd law (though the law code is not mentioned), but owing to Lopoald's 'parentalis caritas' and the entreaties by friends and family, Lopoald lowered the amount owed. Apart from the *invocatio* and *datatio* at the opening of the document, and the *admonitio*, witness list and scribal *completio* at the end, there is nothing formulaic about the content of the charter, which has something of an oral flavour, despite a degree of formal rhetoric. Ansoald's words are rendered in clear and simple speech:

eo quod cecidi tibi Lopoald presbitero nepoti meo in culpa de solidus uiginti, pro eo quod res tuas habui et possedi contra rationem; sed tu iam nominato Lopoald presbiter considerasti parentalis caritas, et una cum amicis et parentis nostris concesserunt mihi cui supra Ansoaldi ipsa calomnia vel culpa, tantum dedi tibi exinde tremisse duos in auro et petiola una de terrola cum vite.

and so I fell into a debt of 20 *solidi* owed to you priest Lopoald, my nephew, for my offence, because I unjustly held and took possession of your property. But you, Lopoald, the above mentioned priest, mindful of familial charity together with our relatives and friends, you have all lowered the penalty which I, the abovesaid Ansoald, owe for my crime and villainy, so that I have now given two gold tremisses and a plot of land with vines.

The relative simplicity of the Latin should not lead us to think that this is the reported speech of Ansoald. This charter is the result of collaboration between three parties: Ansoald, Lopoald and the scribe Maurace, the *vir clarissimus* who wrote eight of the eleven charters extant from Piacenza in a neat and elegant cursive hand.[228] His orthography is fairly classicising for the times, and he is at least consistent in his deviancies. Maurace knew

---

[226] Cf. Wickham, in 'Land disputes', in *Land and Power*, pp. 231–2.   [227] CDL 159.
[228] ChLA 816–23, 825 (CDL 52, 54, 59, 60, 64, 79, 109, 129, 159).

what to write to prevent Ansoald from seeming utterly humiliated, and he knew that Lopoald required a document that would stand up in any court. In other Piacentine charters, he demonstrated his awareness of the ancient Roman *mancipatio* formulae by including it (quite unnecessarily) in land transactions.[229] There, his language is of a more formal nature. In this charter, he chose his language accordingly, and dropped the archaisms, which were unnecessary for the informal arrangement prescribed in the document. Hence the language retains a sense of informality also, and one gets the sense that this only contributed to its legal validity.

THE *COMPOSITIONES* AND THE *ARS NUMERI PITACORICI* OF LUCCA 490

So far in this chapter we have been discussing the language of laws and charters, each infused with its own written tradition that can mask the relationship of their language with that spoken in the Lombard period. We shall now consider briefly two further examples of non-literary Latin texts found in the famous manuscript 490 of the Biblioteca Capitolare of Lucca which throw further light on the linguistic situation in Italy in this period and the use of written texts in spheres otherwise unattested.

Redacted at the same time as the renowned recension of the *Liber pontificalis* and by four of the same scribes, a small text, comprising only twenty-nine pages (fols. 211v, 217r–231r) and containing some 120 or so technical recipes for the preparation of mosaics, paints, inks, parchment and the like, was inserted into the same manuscript, for reasons that are not entirely clear.[230] The text, written in a mixture of uncial and cursive scripts, generally goes under the name *Compositiones*, after the description of Muratori. There are some indications that it was copied

---

[229] A. Solmi, 'La formula della *mancipatio* nei documenti piacentini del secolo VIII', *Archivio Storico Italiano* 71:2 (1913), 225–70; see below, chapter 5.

[230] First published by Muratori in *Antiquitates Italicae* IV (1734), cols. 674–717. Better editions are J. Burnam, *A Classical Technology Edited from Codex Lucensis 490* (Boston, 1920); H. Hedfors, *Compositiones ad tigenda musiva: herausgegeben, übersetzt und philologish Erklärt* (Uppsala, 1932). I have used Burnam's edition, which is directly transcribed from Lucca 490 only: Hedfors' edition incorporates later source and manuscript readings, and is therefore a superior version of the text, but not for our purposes. As with Burnam, I cite the column numbers of Muratori's edition, since Burnam's is rare. See Duchesne, *LP* I, pp. clxiv–clxvi, for earlier bibliography on the text. On the content, see R.P. Johnson, *Compositiones variae, from Codex 490, Biblioteca Capitolare, Lucca, Italy*, Illinois Studies in Language and Literature 23, no.3 (Urbana, 1939); G. Arrighi, 'Tecnica delle costruzioni del secolo VIII: Il *De fabrica in acqua* e il *De Malta* nel Cod. 490 della Biblioteca Capitolare di Lucca', *Automazione e Automatismi* 3 (1962), 26–9; Arrighi, 'Ricette di colorazione e tintura del vetro dell'epoca di Carlo Magno', in *Actes des VIImes Journées Internationales de la Couleur* (Paris, 1963), pp. 365–71. On language, Svennung, *Compositiones lucenses*. On the date of the manuscript, see below, pp. 283–4.

from a Spanish exemplar,[231] but there are also grounds for the original text to have been of Greco-Italian provenance. Many of the recipes have Greek antecedents, some dating back to the third century.[232] One recipe, 'On the gold-varnisher', was transcribed directly from Greek into Latin characters, another recipe mentions *aurum bizantium* and *tremisses bizantii* (687 D), and the language of others shows signs of direct translation or word-forms that derive from a rough adaptation of Greek terms.[233] Far more exotic for this period, however, is the presence of words from the eastern Mediterranean, such as Syriac *luza* (almond), Persian *lulachin* (lilac), Arabic *gebel/-al* (rock). These, along with the occasional mention of *Alexandrini* and *alumen Asianum*, suggest Alexandria or at least Egypt as a place of origin.[234] Whatever its origin, the *Compositiones* of Lucca 490 is one of the earliest surviving Latin documents in the tradition of Greco-Roman technical-chemical recipes.[235]

The text is precise in its descriptions and recommendations. It eschews digressions of any sort, and lacks the type of material usually included in such works, such as mystic notes on the significance of numbers and symbols, or discussion of the fabrication of artificial precious stones, both prevalent in later medieval Latin treatises of a similar type. Two recipes on the preparation of parchment provide as good examples as any of the nature of the text. The directives come in the middle of a series of recipes for making dyes and dying hides and other objects yellow, red and 'onion green':

---

[231] The 'Spanish exemplar' theory of Burnham, *Classical Technology*, pp. 5–12, rests on some highly contestable linguistic observations: the scribe often adds a prosthetic *h*, the frequent use of *ipse* as article, the confusion of *b/v*, the occurrence of *calentem* instead of *cal[i]dum* to mean 'warm', and the appearance of the early Spanish *denante* (688 D). The theories pile up: Burnam suggests that the parent of the Lucchese version was a Spanish archetype written in cursive sometime around 725, which in turn derived from a Roman semi-uncial text of around 650, although Burnam admits that there is no reason why it could not be earlier or later than this. Against this, some linguistic forms point to Italy, which Burnam would attribute to the Italian copyist: adding an initial *g* to *lillium* (697 D), the word *banga* for 'spade' (707 A), expressions such as *post tote bullite* (690 B), the use of *pensionem*, 'a weighing' (716 C). For arguments against the Spanish exemplar, see Johnson, *Compositiones, passim*, esp. p. 22, 84.

[232] See Johnson, *Compositiones*, pp. 35–44.

[233] 714 E: 'Crisorantista crisorcatarios. [s]ana. me<mi>gminos. meta ydr[os]. argiros. [et] chetes. cinion[chetis] chete. [y] spureorum. [i]psi<mi>ion. ydr[os.] argyros. che[t]matha. aut a<na>baleti(s). sceugn(s)ias. d(a corr. ex u) u(f)fira. [h]ecnamix(s) an<tes>. chisimon. p. diati. te(h)reu pulea sibuli'. Cf. trans. Burnam, *Classical Technology*, p. 73.

[234] *luza* (678 E), *gebel* (698 D), *lulacin* (713 A). Note also Arabo-Persian *lazurizon* for 'blue' (699). The retention of the 'l' suggests a Greek source, since it is dropped in medieval Latin and Romance (*azur*, from λαζούριον), as also in the form *lazurizonta* in *zebelazuri zonta*. See Svennung, *Compositiones*, pp. 15–17.

[235] See Hersford, *Compositiones*, pp. xvii–viii; but cf. Johnson, *Compositiones*, p. 81; and now M. Clark, *The Art of All Colours: Medieval Recipe Books for Painters and Illuminators* (London, 2001).

De parga(mina).
  Parga(mina ex bobina). quomodo fieri debet. mitte. illam. in calcem. et temperas. iaceat. ibi. per dies. iii. et tende illam. in cantiro. et rade illa. cum nobacula de ambas partes. et laxas desicare. deinde quodquod uolueris. scalipitura. facere. fac. et post pingue. cum colorib(us).

How parchment from bovines should be made. Put it (a hide) in lime and let it remain there for three days. And stretch it on a horse [clothes horse?] and scrape it with a knife on both sides and let dry. Then, do as much scraping as you see fit; afterwards paint with colours.[236]

Colours are extensively treated throughout the text, such as in the recipe 'On dying hides green', which in itself is quite colourful:

De tinctio pellis prasini[s].
  Tincto pellis prasini(s) tolle(s) pellem. depellatam. et mitte stercos. caninus. et colombinus. et gallinacium. et solbes. ea in iot(t)a. et mittis. in ipsa pelles et conficis. eas ibi. p[er] dies. iii. et posthec eice illas exinde. et labas. hutiliter. demitte desiccar(e). et post hec tolles. alumen. asianum. et secundu[m]. quod superius docuimus. de ali(tina). et tolle post egluza. et pisas decoques utiliter. cum urina. dimittis. refridare. et cu(s)e ipsas pellas sicut. hutres. quomodo dixim[us] de alithina. et coctione mittis in ipsos. Et confrica bene. et jsufflas modicum. abeat. uent[um]. et confice bene. donec conbibat. ipsum medicamen. et posthec refundis. ex ipsis. et tolles. ipsas. pelles. laba semel. et postea. tolle de lulacin ÷ [= *unciae*] iiii. p[er] pell[em]. et hurinam dispumata. libras. vi. et comisce. ipsut lulacin mittis. in ipsos utrem sicut. iota luze. et conficis bene donec sumatur. ipse umore. confectionis. et refundis. q[uo]d. superat. inpecorina. iota luza <e> et lulacin. sicut p[re]diximus. in alithina. et exiet. pecorina[s] (se)cundu[m] prasinum.

Dyeing hides green: take a hide from which the hair has been removed and put on it dog's dung, and that of doves and fowls, and melt in the liquid and put in there the skins and treat them there for three days and then take them out and wash suitably, let dry: then take Asiatic alum just as had been said above about the genuine, then take almonds and crush and boil with urine; let it cool off. And pound the skins like bellows, as we have said about the genuine. And you put the mixture into the skins. And rub well, and you blow it moderately that it may have wind and mix thoroughly until the compound sets and next pour out some of them and you take the skins; wash once and afterwards take some indigo, four pounds to a skin, and simmered urine six pounds and mix the indigo and put it into the skins as you do the almond liquid and mingle till the liquid part of the mixture is taken up and you pour out the remainder on the sheep hide, that is the almond liquor and the indigo as we have stated before regarding the genuine, and the sheep hide will come out green.[237]

---

[236] 683 A, cf. trans. Burnam, *Classical Technology*, p. 93. For the transcription, text within ( ) = correction in manuscript, usually in cursive, [ ] = abbreviated, < > = Burnam's restoration. For purple parchment, cf. 703 A.

[237] 678 E–679 C. Trans. Burnam, *Classical Technology*, pp. 88–9.

Some recipes required ingredients less easily attainable. Four different recipes concerned writing in gold (*crisografia*): one offered advice on how to eke out the ink if you 'wish to write more abundantly', while another concentrated on achieving the same effect without having to use real gold, a deceit which involved concocting a potion of crushed rosin, Cilician saffron, orpiment and tortoise gall *(fel testudinis)*, among other things.[238]

The language of the *Compositiones* has been called 'Low Latin with a vengeance',[239] but for all its faults and failures to live up to a classicist's expectations it remains simple and clear in its intent. The simplicity of the language lies in the short, sharp instructions, the unsophisticated word order and the use of prepositions to express time or relationship *(et post pingue, posthec eice)*, even when the case is mistaken, such as *de* + accusative *(de ambas partes)*, which is common throughout the text, as is the use of *ex* + genitive. Otherwise the genitive case can be rendered with ablative endings, and *de* can even be used with nominatives. The present indicative, future, present subjunctive, imperative and even present participle plus the gerund are all used interchangeably. Early Romance forms include the use of *donec* + subjective *(donec sumatur, donec conbibat)*, the use of the auxiliary *habere (quod habes inaurare*, 'that which you want to gild', 709 C), and the loss of final -*t* in some verbs *(confla* 716 E, *da* 715 E, *dimitta* 699 B extr., *remanea* 710 C). Simple third person imperatives are often complemented with or substituted by second person present indicatives, the use of infinitives *(dessicare*, or *sufflare ad ignem*, 700 E) or subjunctives *(iaceat)*. *Ne* does not occur at all, while the negative for the imperative is nearly always expressed with a prefatory *non (non demittas*, 713 D).[240] The text has a strong preference for verbs ending in -*izare (metallizare*, 'harden like metal', 684 E), for compounds beginning with *ex-* which are intensive *(exmodice*, 'to a very moderate degree', 682 D; *exalbidus*, 'very white', 676 C), and for adjectives ending in -*inus (caninus, columbinus)*. The definite article is employed frequently and is more often signified by *ille/illa* (despite use of *ea* in the above example), though often by *ipse* in nominative (cf. *unum*, 714 D). *Quod* assumes the function of a general relative, and there are some plain odd expressions (e.g. *perut*, 'exactly as', 683 D). With respect to orthography we find the usual late Latin confusion over *b/v (labas)*, *i/e (dispumata)* (but *o/u*, for some reason, is rare), the loss of *a* in the dipthong *ae (hec, posthec)*, missing or misplaced aspiration *(abeat, hutiliter, hurina, hutres)*, and so on.

[238] 693 A–D. Cf. 692 C–E, 710 A–D.
[239] Burnam, *Classical Technology*, p. 10. At length, Svennung, *Compositiones*, pp. 100–75.
[240] On one instance a future imperative is used *(addito*, 703 C), and elsewhere we find what looks like early examples of the Italian i- type *(triti*, 'crush', 715 A; *frangi*, 'break', 713 C). Cf. Burnam, *Classical Technology*, p. 168.

Language and literacy

The grammar of the *Compositiones*, therefore, presents us with no great surprises for the study of vulgar Latin texts. But its vocabulary is another matter. Besides the above mentioned Arabic, Persian and Syrian words, there are around ninety Latin words which are not found in any other sources, some of which are owed to some inventive uses of language. Most of these derive from the workshop,[241] others derive from descriptions of technical phenomena,[242] while many are trade or technical terms deriving from Greek antecedents.[243] Others may have easily been used outside the workshop,[244] and while some survived into modern Italian,[245] many simply disappeared.[246]

In comparison with high literary or legal evidence, the stark clarity of the Latin language of this functional text is striking and serves as a sharp reminder of the many other different types of texts of practical and applied information that are lost to us, such as manuals on animal husbandry, agriculture, construction, cookbooks and school books. This includes texts of a not so practical nature, such as the odd numerological text found on fol. 235 of the Lucca 490 manuscript entitled 'Incipit ars numeri pitacoricis de con[venientibus] et non conuenientibus numerum littere', which concerns the signification of certain letters and corresponding numbers to determine the success of a man and woman in amorous relations.[247] Texts such as these have a long pedigree from classical antiquity,[248] but why it appears in the Lucchese manuscript remains unknown.[249] The *Ars numeri* begins by establishing a numerical significance of each letter (A i, B ii, C iii, E v, F i, G viiii, H vi, I iiii, K v, L vii, M vi, N v and so on),

---

[241] E.g. *adluminentur* ('take on a bright colour', 691 A, from *alumen*), *crisopetala* ('gold foil', 704 C), *deliquatio* ('straining off', 713 E), *dessicatio* ('powder', 715 A), *interrationem* ('putting in the ground', 710 B), *coloridietur* ('colour', 675 E), *deauratura* ('gilding', 689 D), *excalifacias* ('heat', 708 C), *lamnizas* ('cut into strips', 693 E), *intrantem* ('ingredient', 700 E), *queiussans* ('applying whitelead', 675 E), *mutuosa* ('friable', 676 A), *scapilatura* ('clipping', 683 A).

[242] *oligine* ('oily', 686 E), *plumbinus* ('leaden', 675 B), *sceugnasias* ('painting, sketch', 714 E), *subaurosum* ('Of somewhat golden colour', 683 D), *subporphira* ('purplish', 715 E), *sulfuritantum* ('sulphurous', 685 D), *taurotica* ('of an ox', 689 D).

[243] *matiola* ('small hammer', 690 E), *stripterea* ('alum', στυπτηρία, 699 C), *tricas* ('filaments', τρίχας, 696 C), *tricorelinon* ('hairy filaments', τρίχος ἔλιον, 696 A), *pofirizontam* ('of porphory', 712 D).

[244] *excaliscente* ('grow hot', 706 E), *albidiante* ('white', 696 D), *calitudo* ('heat', 767 E), *crepidinosus* ('full of cracks' or 'making a crackling sound', 716 E), *lixare* ('smooth, polish', 689 A, C), *turbale* ('grow turbid', 699 C), *vetrissimo* ('very old', 710 A).

[245] *radus* ('thin', 692 A, *rado*).

[246] *scara* ('wild' or 'rosemary', 696 D); *tritare* ('to crush' or 'to bruise', 699 E, cf. *tritura* 697 C).

[247] See G. Arrighi, 'Un inedito di aritmosofia nel Codice 490 (saec. VIII–IX) della Biblioteca Capitolare Feliniana di Lucca', *Atti V CISAM* (Spoleto, 1973), 675–769.

[248] Similar texts are the 'Ludum pittagoricum' and 'Segreto do Pittagora' included in Cortona, Biblioteca del Comune e dell'Accademia Etrusca, 214 (296), cf. *Inventari dei manoscritti delle biblioteche d'Italia*, XVIII, p. 87. On the types of text, see P.-H. Michel, *De Pythagore à Euclide: contribution à l'histoire des mathématiques préeuclidiennes* (Paris, 1950), p. 683.

[249] On the writer, Schiaparelli, *Il Codice 490*, p. 50.

then runs down a long list of outcomes according to a particular number from i to viiii, for the most part in numerical order, but beginning again abruptly or repeating the same number. We can only guess at how the initial stage of the divination took place – perhaps using some combination of the letters which make up the couple's names or similar – but the language of the text is clear. To quote some examples:

i. They will come together,[250] the man will be more loving than the woman, and she will offend the man with her tongue, and he will often be offended.
(*Convenientes erunt, vir mulieri diligentior erit et illa offendit lingua ideo virum sepe offendit.*)

iii. They will be partners,[251] and the man will be very caring and very loving but she will be quite insolent.
(*Communicatores erunt, vir mulieri indulgentior et diligentior erit et illa procacior.*)

v. The woman will love the man [but] he will ignore her and therefore [the relationship] will not work.
(*Mulier virum amabit et illi eam neglegit ideo non convenit.*)

vi. They will be partners, the woman will be better than the man, but he will ignore her.
(*Communicatores erunt, mulier viro melior erit sed vir eam neglegit.*)

vii. They will come together and they will share money and the woman will despise him.
(*Convenientes erunt et communicatores pecunie et mulier eum contemnet.*)

viii. The woman will love the man well [but] they will have doubts.
(*Mulier virum obtime amabit et erunt in dubitationem.*)

ii. They will be curious enough to become lovers.
(*Procuriosi adque amantes erunt.*)

iiii. Jealous women will be between them and they will scarcely be together.
(*Zeliotipias inter eos erit adque vix conveniet.*)

And so on. The theme of disturbance by a third party occurs frequently, or a third person will 'come between them and cause fights', and this is especially dangerous for the woman, who when confronted with rivals 'will feel herself to be defeated and will remain longing'.[252] Neighbours could be a problem, and there are always those who plot against the

---

[250] That is, 'be married'.
[251] The meaning of the term *communicatores* as 'partners' (lit. sharers), rather than referring simply to sexual relations (common in late antique usage) is revealed in other sections where the word is coupled with a qualifying noun, such as that of 'communicatores pecunie', and elsewhere 'amantes erunt adque communicatores peculii'.
[252] 'ii. rivales inter se convenient, duo mulieres eum continebant'. The possibility holds for the woman: 'ii. 'Rivales duo convenient et mulier eos continebit'. 'iiii. Mulier viro melior erit et erit tertia persona que inter eos faciet rixa'; 'vii. Ex rivalibus erit rixa, que a se illa se substernit et erit multivola.'

couple.²⁵³ Domestic arrangements need to be in order, but there is no hope if either dreams of greener pastures.²⁵⁴ We can only wonder at how often the clerics of Lucca consulted the *Ars numeri pitacoricis*. Even less homogeneous to the collection of texts in Lucca 490 than the *Compositiones*, the preservation of both texts in that manuscript raises more questions about the church of Lucca than it does answers. Nevertheless both texts reflect the diverse range of information that circulated in written form. The language of these texts can be considered popular in the sense that it was intended to be understood without extensive recourse to learned, literary traditions.

CONCLUSION

Although the language of the evidence discussed here shows strong traces of Romance forms, the linguistic environment of Lombard Italy was fundamentally Latinate, and this has important implications for understanding the place of literacy in early medieval Italian society. Arguably the gap between written and spoken forms of language was narrower than anywhere else in Europe in the seventh and eighth centuries, and this facilitated a greater degree of accessibility to written traditions and forms of communication – to read a law code, to write a charter, to have one written which expresses your intent, to make your claim in court, to read the Bible, to learn how to dye a parchment green, to determine who should and who should not marry. Written Latin, in its simplest inflexional form of verb suffixes to indicate person, and five cases to indicate syntactic function, with or without the correct use of prepositions, was more easily intelligible to Romance-speakers who already used a Latinate vocabulary. The morphological changes that needed to be learned in the transition from spoken to traditional written forms were certainly as easy to learn as the letter-forms and intricate ligatures and abbreviations found in the cursive script of Lombard charters. On this issue we need to reckon with the confidence and inventiveness of Lombard scribes when they turned to written forms of communication that were anchored in long-standing traditions. Scribes within Lombard Italy did not write grammatically and orthographically imperfect Latin because they could do no better. They chose to write the way they did, without unblinking respect for classical norms, for these were no longer relevant,

---

[253] 'viii. Non convenient propter propinquos et vir eam non soffert', *bis*: 'vi. Insidiosi erunt et inter utrumque non convenient.'
[254] 'vii. Non convenie propter domesticitate'; 'viii. Non convenient, vir aut mulier alibi animum habet'.

no longer buoyed by sustained schooling at the hands of the grammarian in the laborious process of *enarratio* applied to a canon of classical texts. As scribes facilitating the legality of transactions by recording them in the appropriate fashion, the primary requisite of their language was its comprehensibility to both parties of the transaction, and its intelligibility was rooted in the recognition of the authority it invoked and local traditions of speech, as we shall see further in chapter 5.

4
LAW AND GOVERNMENT

We promulgate the present Edict, as we have organised it, under God's guidance with the utmost care and scrutiny granted by heavenly favour. Investigating thoroughly and recalling the ancient laws of our ancestors which were not written, we have ordered that they be written down in these pages (*in hoc membranum*), with both the counsel and consent of our highest judges, and with all those we have established as the strength of our most fortunate army, because these laws benefit all of our people in common. We have examined and preserved [the laws] in this tome (*sub hoc capitulo*), with divine clemency assisting, through both the careful scrutiny of the ancient laws of the Lombards and through that which we were able to determine through the memory of our elders, so that we may add them to this Edict. Furthermore we now confirm [this Edict] in assembly (*gairethinx*) according to the custom of our people, in order that this law be steadfast and enduring, and be preserved entirely and inviolably by all of our subjects in our most fortunate times and those of the future.[1]

Earlier Lombard kings had presided over royal courts founded upon Roman administrative culture and had issued charters.[2] Yet in 643 King Rothari promulgated his 'Edict', a relatively humble Roman legal term for an ambitious act of legislation which carefully set out 388 previously unwritten laws with the intention of circumscribing an impressive range of behaviours and customs in Lombard society. A transition from oral to

---

[1] Rothari [law] 386. For Lombard law I have mainly relied on the edition of Azzara and Gasparri, *Le leggi dei Longobardi*, which used the text established by F. Beyerle, *Die Gesetze der Langobarden* III (Wizenhausen, 1962–63), and which is an improvement on that of F. Bluhme, MGH Leges IV (Hanover, 1868: repr. Stuttgart 1965), though both have been consulted. The English translation of K. Fischer-Drew, *The Lombard Laws* (Philadelphia, 1973), although useful, is too often misleading: translations are mine unless otherwise noted. Throughout the following, the term 'Edict' refers specifically to the legislation of Rothari, and 'law code' to Lombard legislation in general, excluding that of the Beneventan dukes.

[2] Royal charters: C. Brühl (ed.) CDL III.1, Fonti per la Storia d'Italia 64 (Rome, 1973). On their transmission and protocol, Brühl, *Studien zu den langobardischen Königsurkunden*, Bibliothek des deutschen historischen Instituts in Rom 33 (Tübingen, 1970); Brühl, 'Langobardische Königsurkunden als Geschichtsquelle', in *Studi storici in onore di O. Bertolini* (Pisa, 1972), pp. 47–72. Only four charters issued prior to Rothari's reign have survived (CDL III.1, 613; III.2, 624(?); III.3, 625–6; III.4, 626–36), and none issued by Rothari himself, though his son Rodoald referred to one: CDL III.5.

Literacy in Lombard Italy, c. 568–774

written law, legal prehistory to history, is indeed a momentous change and warrants attention in a study of literacy: but the focus here is historical, not anthropological, and the subject Lombard Italy, not Lombards *per se*. The first part of this chapter examines why Rothari turned to the written word as an instrument of rule, and what the redaction and promulgation of the Edict can tell us about the place of literacy in the cultural milieu of the period. Thereafter I turn to examine the Lombard law code, which comprises Rothari's Edict and the legislation of later kings, for evidence of literate practices in Italo-Lombard society, beginning with references to the use of charters, then turning to discuss two subjects, manumission and the legal status of women, both of which allow us to gauge the effectiveness of written law and the close correlation between the code and the use of charters. Finally I discuss the evidence within the code and charters for the uses of writing in the administrative hierarchy of the kingdom. The chapter is concerned throughout with understanding the connection between government and literate practices.

ROTHARI AND THE PROMULGATION OF THE EDICT

Despite Rothari's solemn declaration towards the end of his Edict that Lombard laws had not been written down, legal historians have found traces of classical Roman, Bavarian, Alemannic, Visigothic and even Byzantine law in the text.[3] Moreover, the allusions to 'ancient laws of the Lombards' contrast with the snappy tone of legislative experience in the prologue, in which Rothari sets out his reasons for having the Edict redacted:

We have perceived it necessary to correct the law, which renews and amends all past laws, adds that which was lacking, and eliminates that which was superfluous. We wish to have all law collected in one volume, so that everyone may live peacefully under a secure law and with justice, and so that everyone will willingly work against enemies and defend themselves and their territory (*contra inimicos laborare seque suosque defendere fines*).[4]

---

[3] The tradition of 'uncovering' the written 'sources' behind Rothari's Edict is a long one, beginning with G. Tamassia, *Le fonti dell'editto di Rotari* (Pisa, 1889) and P. Del Giudice, 'Le tracce di diritto romano nelle leggi longobarde', in *Studi di storia e diritto* (Milan, 1889), pp. 262–409. See E. Besta, 'Le fonti del editto di Rotari', *Atti I CISAM* (Spoleto, 1952), 51–69; and G. Astuti, 'Influssi romanistici nelle fonti del diritto longobardo', *Settimane* 22 (Spoleto, 1975), 653–96. G.P. Bognetti, 'Caratteri del secolo VII in Occidente', *L'età* IV, pp. 137–88, at p. 150, stressed the similarity of the Edict's language to Roman military regulations. A. Cavanna, 'Nuovi problemi intorno alle fonti dell'editto di Rothari', *Studia et Documenta Historiae et Iuris* 34 (1968), 269–361, unconvincingly argued that the principal influences were the *Edictum Theoderici* and the *Fragmenta Gaudenziana*: but only two laws of Rothari's (156, 219) can be seen as directly deriving from these sources (ET 65, FG 69, and ET 65, FG 20, respectively). See also E. Levy, *West Roman Vulgar Law: The Law of Property* (Philadelphia, 1951), pp. 54, 94–6.

[4] Rothari, *prol.*, Azzara, *Le leggi*, p. 12.

Law and government

References to 'correcting the law', 'adding that which was lacking' and 'eliminating that which was superfluous' certainly suggest a pre-existing body of written law, and it has been argued that Rothari merely revised a previous legal compilation of some sort as part of his programme to centralise political power and enhance the prestige of the monarchy.[5] But the phrase itself is a legislative topos taken from Justinian's Novel VIII, and hence further throws into relief the mixed quality of the Lombard law code as a combination of various influences and sources. Some historians have seen similarities with Anglo-Saxon or Scandinavian law and therefore stress the antiquity of the Edict's contents, dating back to a remote pre-Italian and pre-literate past, as a key to Lombard culture and identity.[6] A favoured interpretative paradigm of past scholarship has been to juxtapose this pristine 'Germanic' content of the Edict with its Latin, hence 'Roman' form. From this perspective the Edict is seen as marking the Lombards' 'passage towards another kind of civilisation',[7] or the gauge with which we can measure their 'Romanisation', along the scale of legislation by subsequent and less Germanic kings, often pictured as a continuous triumph of Roman law over Germanic custom.[8] There are undoubtedly elements of non-Roman custom in the Edict, such as the institution of the feud (*faida*), the use of compositions for injuries, and inheritance laws. But as we shall see, there is much that is Roman too. The German–Roman dichotomy can easily lead to circular arguments over what is 'German' and 'Roman'. It has even been suggested that Lombard legal concepts such as *mundium, gairethinx, wadia* and *launichild* are the result of an imperfect 'Germanisation' of ancient Roman concepts.[9]

While certainly valid, this line of enquiry is unhelpful for understanding the purpose of Rothari's Edict and its possible effects. Besides the

---

[5] B. Paradisi, 'Il prologo e l'epilogo dell'Editto di Rotari', *Studia et Documenta Historiae et Iuris* 34 (1968), 1–31.
[6] For example: Brunner, *Deutsche Rechtsgeschichte*, I, p. 417. Rothari's code was a 'legislative Schöpfung aus der Zeit der Volksrechte'; Anglo-Saxon connection, *ibid.*, pp. 536–9; also T. Hodgkin, 'Sulla relazione ethnologica fra i Longobardi e gli Angli', in *XI Centenario di Paolo Diacono: Atti e memorie del Congresso storico* (Cividale, 1900), pp. 150–63; Buchner 'Die römischen und die germanischen Wesenszüge in der neuen politischen Ordnung des Abendlandes', *Settimane* 5 (Spoleto, 1958), 247–78, at pp. 258, 262–3. L. Hartmann, *The Cambridge Medieval History*, II (Cambridge, 1911), p. 204: 'the Lombards preserved their law unchanged in essential matters since their departure from the Lower Elbe'.
[7] Riché, *Education*, p. 340.
[8] A theme often found in historical surveys of Italian law, e.g. E. Besta, *Fonti del diritto italiano dalla caduta dell'impero sino ai tempi nostri* (Padua, 1938), pp. 47–8; Calasso, *Medio evo del diritto*, pp. 220–5, 249–53. See also F. Sinatti D'Amico, *Le prove giudizarie nel diritto longobardo: legislazione e prassi da Rotari ad Astolfo*, Fondazione Guglielmo Castelli 40 (Milan, 1968), pp. 203–344; Gasparri, *La cultura*, pp. 101–33.
[9] E. Cortese, 'Il processo longobardo tra romanità e germanismo', *Settimana* 42 (Spoleto, 1994), 621–47; cf Wickham, *EMI*, p. 36.

king's concern for justice and the welfare of his people, Rothari's choice of words in the prologue and epilogue suggests more immediate political motivations behind the transition to written law. A compilation of law 'in one volume' was thought to inspire his subjects to 'work against enemies' and 'defend themselves and their territory', and at the close of the Edict the king makes clear reference to the involvement and approval of members of 'our most fortunate army'. Less than two weeks after the promulgation of the Edict (22 November), Rothari launched the first wars of aggression against the Byzantines in four decades.[10] If the Edict sprung from a need to centralise and consolidate the Lombard monarchy against external pressures and centrifugal political forces, as Bognetti has argued, it appears to have been successful: Rothari conquered Emilia and all of the Ligurian coast, and pushed further into Veneto, leaving only a strip of coastline to the Byzantines. The circumstances behind the compilation and promulgation of the Edict remind us to consider the important question of 'not what [early medieval] kings did for legislation, so much as what legislation did for kings'.[11] Bognetti's analysis of Lombard political factions behind the Edict's promulgation, in which Rothari and the Edict represent national 'Germanist' reactions to the Romanising Agilulfing dynasty, remains necessarily speculative owing to lack of evidence. The ideological significance of promulgating the Edict, as a means for the king to emulate the literary legal culture of the Roman and Judeo-Christian civilisation and reinforce the political and cultural links of the monarchy with its people, is only part of the picture. As we shall see, the code's practical use in regulating Italo-Lombard society is clearly demonstrated by the charter evidence.

Moreover, the miscellany of legal sources behind the redaction of the Edict further highlights Rothari's practical purpose of putting 'all law collected in one volume'. Rothari's Edict filled a vacuum created by the confused condition of Roman law in the west, a confusion which resulted from the practice of imperial rescripts and the circulation of different compilations of classical law. This is a theme well known to modern legal historians, but even Paul the Deacon, in praising Justinian's efforts at codification, lamented the previous state of affairs in the west.[12]

---

[10] *HL* IV.45. For the date, O. Bertolini, 'Il patriarco Isacio esarca d'Italia (625–643)', in *Scritti scelti di storia medievale di O. Bertolini*, ed. O. Banta, 2 vols. (Livorno, 1968), I, pp. 65–8. Bognetti, 'L'Editto di Rotari come espediente politico di una monarchia barbarica', *L'età* IV, pp. 114–35; Bognetti, 'Frammenti di uno studio sulla composizione dell'Editto di Rotari', *L'età* IV, pp. 585–609.
[11] Wormald, '*Lex scripta*', p. 105. But. cf. McKitterick, *Carolingians*, pp. 38–9.
[12] 'Leges quoque Romanorum, quarum prolixitas nimia erat et inutilis dissonantia ... Nam omnes constitutiones principum, quae utique multis in voluminibus habebantur ... Rursumque singulorum magistratuum sive iudicum leges, quae usque ad duo milia pene libros erant extensae'. *HL* I.25.

Law and government

Ernst Levy has methodically documented how such a state of affairs created the amorphous legal culture of Roman vulgar law: that is, law not deriving from a single text but from the practice of interpreting a collection of different texts for application in Roman provincial courts. Many barbarian codes drew from this legal culture for inspiration, particularly in order to establish property laws.[13] Post-Roman and post-Ostrogothic Italy was undoubtedly fertile ground for the reception of a number of legal influences, including elements of orally transmitted law or custom which Rothari cites in his epilogue and which is continually referred to in the legislation of later Lombard kings.[14] The selection of different legal sources available to Rothari and his *primati iudices* for consultation certainly speaks in favour of a highly literate legal milieu at the Lombard royal court, though we need not posit the existence of a Pavese 'school of law' that laid the foundations for later medieval centres of legal studies in north Italy.[15] The internal organisation of the Edict, divided into homogeneous sections, testifies to its redaction by people with some experience in putting legislation together. The Edict may be divided thus.[16]

Laws 1–13, crimes against public authority;
14–145, crimes amongst private individuals;
146–52, damage to property;
153–77, laws of succession;
178–223, marriage laws;
224–6, manumission;
227–44, property laws;
245–52, obligations;
253–358, minor crimes and damages;
359–66, oaths, pledges, legal procedures;
367–88, miscellaneous affairs and epilogue.

The organisation is not perfect, some laws appear completely out of place, and the heterogeneous character of the last section (359–66) suggests that

---

[13] E. Levy, 'Reflections of the first "Reception" of Roman law in Germanic states', *American Historical Review* 48 (1942), 20–9; Levy, 'The vulgarisation of Roman law in the early middle ages', *Medievalia et Humanistica* 1 (1943), 14–40; and more fully Levy's magisterial monograph, *West Roman Vulgar Law*. Levy's work has not been without criticism; see the discussion by C. Schott, 'Der Stand der Leges-Forschung', *Frühmittelalterliche Studien* 13 (1979), 29–55, at pp. 43–6.

[14] E.g. Liutprand 73, 77, 119, 133.

[15] E.g. G. Mengozzi, *Ricerche sull'attività della scuola di Pavia nell'altomedievo* (Pavia, 1924); A. Viscardi, *Le origini. Storia letteraria d'Italia*, I, 3rd edn (London, 1929), pp. 198–201. Cf. the more cautious accounts of C.H. Radding, *The Origins of Medieval Jurisprudence: Pavia and Bologna 850–1150* (New Haven and London, 1988), and Gualazzini, 'La scuola pavese con particulare riguardo all'insegnamento del diritto', *Atti IV CISAM* (Spoleto, 1969), 35–73.

[16] Legal historians have seen slightly different divisions in the Edict's structure. I follow here Azzara, *Le leggi*, pp. xxviii–xxix.

Literacy in Lombard Italy, c. 568–774

laws were constantly being added after the process of redaction had already begun.

As we shall see below and in the following chapter, the charter evidence provides secure testimony to the practical application of the law code. An alternative method for discerning the application of the law code is to monitor its manuscript tradition as a guide to its reception and transmission.[17] Unfortunately, the manuscript evidence from the Lombard period itself is a poor indicator of the code's contemporary use. While later ninth-, tenth- and eleventh-century manuscripts of Lombard law contain marginalia and cross-referencing that indicate close consultation of the code,[18] only two manuscripts can be dated to the Lombard period, and these yield little information about the transmission and reception of the text. The oldest manuscript, St Gall 730, written around 700, containing only Rothari's legislation without a prologue or chapter titles, is suggestive of connections between Pavia and the monastery of Bobbio, but we cannot determine any more than that.[19] The second manuscript, the Vercellensis 188, is of an indeterminable eighth- or ninth-century date and was written somewhere in northern Italy.[20] It contains the laws of Rothari, Grimoald and Liutprand, and, interestingly, numbers them in a continuous fashion; hence Liutprand's first law was numbered 398. This is the only evidence concerning the code's original format that is remotely suggestive of a consultative use, yet its significance is limited by the fact that no reference to the number of a law is made in any other source: neither in the charters which explicitly cite the code as an authority, nor in the legislation of successive kings as they refer back to the laws 'which have been established in this Edict'.

---

[17] For such an analyisis of Salic law, McKitterick, *Carolingians*, pp. 40–60, *contra* the arguments of H. Nehlsen, 'Zur Aktualität und Effectivität germanischer Rechtsaufzeichnungen', in P. Classen (ed.), *Recht und Schrift im Mittelalter* (Sigmaringen, 1977), pp. 449–502. The Carolingian evidence presents an almost directly opposite situation to that of the Lombard period: an abundance of contemporary legal manuscripts and a dearth of evidence for direct references to written law in contemporary charters and *placita*.

[18] See G. Moschetti, *Primordi esegetici sulla legislazione longobarda nel secolo IX a Verona secondo il Codice Vat. lat. 5359* (Spoleto, 1954); also G. Barni, 'Il diritto longobardo nel *Liber consuetudinum Mediolani*', *Atti I CISAM* (Spoleto, 1952), 205–18; Radding, *Origins*, pp. 24–46.

[19] CLA VII.949. On its date and origin: A. Dold, *Zur ältesten Handschrift des Edictus Rothari* (Stuttgart, 1955), p. 25 (Bobbio); Bischoff, *Latin Palaeography: Antiquity and the Middle Ages*, trans. D. Ó Cróinín and D. Ganz (Cambridge, 1993), p. 191, 'typically Lombard and probably written at Pavia', yet pointing out Irish influence in the large initial letters; Tosi, 'L'Edictus Rothari', argues for Bobbio on palaeographical grounds, but also draws attention to the curious coincidence of the date of the Edict coming into effect (23 Nov., Rothari 388) being the feast day of Columbanus (BHL 1898). Bluhme, MGH Leges IV, pp. xii–vi, xvi, suggested the manuscript originally contained a prologue.

[20] CLA IV.469 ('late eighth century'). Bluhme, MGH Leges IV, pp. xvi–xix, dated it to the ninth century. Successive scholars have dated it earlier: see Azzara, *Le leggi*, pp. xxxv–xxxvii.

Law and government

There is, however, another aspect of the Edict's 'manuscript tradition' that is suggestive of its circulation for the administration of justice, namely the reference to the Edict's transmission within the Edict itself. At the end of the Edict, Rothari reaffirmed royal control over the Edict's contents by making them copyright:

> We also add and decree, that disputes which have been settled may not be reopened. Those disputes, however, which have not been settled or have been brought forwards after this date, 22 November 643, must be resolved and settled according to this Edict. We also give this general order lest any fraud be applied to this Edict through the fault of the scribes: if any contention arises, no other copies of this code shall be accredited or received except those which have been written or certified by the hand of our notary Ansoald, or obtained directly from him, who wrote [this Edict] in accordance with our command.[21]

The precise dating of the legislation's applicability is thoroughly Roman protocol.[22] What is more, only officially authorised copies were to be used, presumably by judges, though the absence of any specified reception suggests that Rothari expected his 'official' Edict to be circulated on a much wider scale.[23] The measures taken to counteract *fraus* also suggest that there were people ready to exploit the authority associated with the written word for their own purposes. The Edict was launched into a literate social environment where the use of written law was no novelty but an established part of Italian legal culture. Unfortunately, the paucity of manuscript evidence provides us with little idea of what an 'official' court copy may have looked like, but we possibly know what to look for. Amongst the archaeological finds at the Lombard warrior-graves at Trezzo d'Adda (some 12 km south-west of Bergamo) was a seal-ring with the inscription 'ANSU [cross] ALDO' written above the portrait of a bearded figure, comparable in style to the portrait of Agilulf on the Valdinievole helmet.[24] The ring can be dated to the mid-seventh century, and there are no other attestations of the name Ansoald in this period.[25] It is impossible to say whether the two names denote the same person, or whether official copies of the Edict would have contained this or a similar mark. Although Rothari's law did not specifically mention a seal or seal-ring, the wording of 'aut recognitum seu requisitum' is sufficiently indeterminate to render it plausible.

---

[21] Rothari 388.   [22] Wormald, '*Lex scripta*' p. 118.
[23] *Contra* Wormald, '*Lex scripta*', p. 115; judges who were 'presumably illiterate'. Cf. Burgundian code, McKitterick *Carolingians*, p. 62.
[24] See plate IV.7 in Menis (ed.), *I Longobardi*, p. 161.
[25] Jarnut, *Prosographische*, pp. 53–4. Most begin to appear in the eighth century, though this is undoubtedly due to the increase in surviving evidence.

Literacy in Lombard Italy, c. 568–774

Did Lombard rulers use seal-rings? Scholars have ignored their significance as part of literate culture of Lombard government, but there is sufficient evidence for their use. Three actual rings have been found: besides that of Ansoald (whether or not Rothari's notary), another from the graves of Trezzo d'Adda was that of 'Rodchis', about whom we know nothing, and more recently that of a Lombard duke, Anso, was found in the Crypta Balbi excavations at Rome.[26] Two royal charters mention seal-rings, and two private charters from the duchy of Benevento record a request for the duke to furnish their charter with the mark of his seal-ring for authentification.[27] As we shall see below, the Lombard law code possibly alludes to seal-rings in several instances, and Ratchis explicitly required their use for the issuing of passports. No doubt not all kings, dukes or officials used seal-rings, but some obviously did. Whether the court of Rothari, or that of an earlier king, introduced the use of seal-rings for administrative purposes remains speculative, but by the time of Ratchis they were part of the administrative culture of the court. Admittedly, seal-rings are not much evidence of literacy *per se* – the use of seals may even be termed 'sub-literacy'[28] – but they are a visual counterpart to written communication, icons which help to validate the message, and thus are part of the message itself. Their existence presupposes a literate stratum of communication and testifies to the tenacity of Roman traditions of government.[29]

By promulgating his Edict, Rothari ensured his place in Lombard history, forever after remembered by his own *gens* and others as the law-giving king.[30] Rothari's awareness of his own historicity seems confirmed by his attachment of a regnal list to the beginning of the code and, perhaps, the potted history of the *Origo gentis langobardorum*, or a text similar to it. The exploitation of Old Testament imagery, a chosen people and their divinely chosen king, is made explicit in Rothari's self-allusion

---

[26] P. Delogu et al., *Crypta Balbi* (Catalogue) (Rome, 2000), p. 61.
[27] CDL III.5, Rodoald (Rothari's son), 652: 'Pro perpetem firmitatem anuli nostri sigillum subter adfigi praecepimus'; CDL III.13, Liutprand (715): 'ut verius credatur de anulo nostro insigniri iussimus.' Brühl, *Studien*, pp. 32–45, argues that these passages were interpolations, and against seal rings, 'unthinkable' in the Lombard period. Benevento: CDL V.2: 'ut effigiem anuli sui affigi precepit', and similarly CDL V.4. Cf. CDL V.13 (781), for the seal ring of the bishop of Benevento. Beneventan dukes of the ninth century appear to have used seal rings. For the Lombard period, Zielinski, *ibid.*, pp. 350–1, remains wisely undecided.
[28] See M. Mullet, 'Writing in early medieval Byzantium', in McKitterick (ed.) *Uses of Literacy*, p. 183.
[29] E. James, *The Franks* (Oxford, 1988), p. 61.
[30] Paul forgave Rothari for his Arianism because of the Edict: *HL* IV.42, 47 (Paul was a fan of legislators: cf. *HL* I.25 on Justinian). The Carolingian *Codex Gothani*, 7, was more than laudatory: 'Istius rothari regis temporibus ortum est lumen in tenebris; per quem supradicti langobardi ad cannonicam tenderunt certamina.' The last epithet is curiously Carolingian: 'et [Langobardi] sacerdotum facti sunt adiutores'.

Law and government

to King Solomon in the second law as a means of justifying the king's absolute right to kill whomsoever he pleases, imagery and allusion which Liutprand also used in his legislation, and other kings followed suit.[31] This forces us to acknowledge another ingredient of the literate background which informs the Edict, the influence of Christianity, a religion of the book. Rothari made the act of swearing oaths upon the Gospels an integral element of Lombard law, and valued it more highly than oaths sworn upon arms.[32] Later legislation appears to have dropped oaths sworn upon arms as an option,[33] and Aistulf specifically required judges who professed innocence in failing to attend to matters of national security to 'purify' themselves by swearing on the Gospels that they were ignorant of the illegal actions of the freemen in their districts.[34] Biblical quotations, oaths sworn upon the Gospels, and even letters from the pope advising on family law,[35] all testify to the permeating influence of a literate Christian culture within the code. This should not be surprising. The ideology of kingship in the early middle ages included the notion that kings were responsible for the spiritual welfare of their subjects and the orthodoxy of their kingdom. The Lombard royal court at Pavia was no exception, as can be seen in the activities of the Synod of Pavia in 698. As we saw in chapter 2, royal intervention in matters of religious doctrine goes back to the earliest kings. Contact with, and concession to, a literate, ecclesiastical milieu was unavoidable for the governing of Italy.

THE USE OF CHARTERS IN LOMBARD LEGISLATION

There are far fewer references in Rothari's Edict to the use of writing in the legal process in comparison with the legislation of eighth-century kings, particularly that of Liutprand and Ratchis. The lower quantity of references suggests that the use of writing was a less important part of the legal culture in which Rothari's Edict was launched. The quality of the

---

[31] Rothari 2: 'because the hearts of kings are in the hand of God' (Prov. 21.1). Cf. Liutprand, prologues of years V and XVI, and laws 30, 33, 34, 76, 84, 85, 100, 133, 140, 144. *Notitia de actoribus regis*, 5. See also below, p. 250. Cf. Ratchis 12 (Tobias 12.7), Aistulf 12 (St Paul *iubet*).

[32] Rothari 359. Cases involving 20 *solidi* or more required twelve oathhelpers (*aidos*) or oathtakers (*sacramentales*) to 'swear upon the Sacred Gospels'; cases involving 12–20 *solidi* required six men (three men for cases under 12 *solidi*) to swear oaths in consecrated arms (*arma sacrata*). In disputes between creditors and debtors, Rothari gave the choice of oaths over Gospels or arms (366), but the law implies reference to the same value-scale of 359.

[33] Liutprand 61.   [34] Aistulf 4: 'purificet se ad sancta dei evangelia'.

[35] Liutprand 33: 'Hoc autem ideo afiximus, quia deo teste papa urbis romae, qui in omni mundo caput ecclesiarum dei et sacerdotum est, per suam epistolam nos adortavit.' The 'letter' may refer to the decrees of the Roman synod of 721: the chronology matches. See O. Bertolini, 'Le chiese longobarde dopo la conversione al cattolicesimo ed i loro rapporti con il papato', *Settimane* 7 (Spoleto, 1960), 62–94; repr. in *Scritti scelti*, p. 98.

references, however, suggests something else. Aside from the mention of charters of manumission, which I shall discuss below, the first reference in Rothari's Edict to the use of documents is a royal affirmation of the need for those who have leased land to keep written documents (*libellus scriptus*) which record the terms of the lease and therefore may be used in court as proof against the occupier of the land who claims to have bought the property outright.[36] The law's heading, 'De emptionibus et vinditionibus', is somewhat misleading, as its primary concern is with leases. Yet the law also implies that, without the existence of a document to the contrary, the tenant who has built upon the property or established a *casa mancipiata*, and can produce witnesses to testify that he has held the property for at least five years, shall own the land outright. The law suggests that although oral means of proof in the form of oath-helping were certainly valid in property disputes, a document could be used as *prima facie* evidence that overruled oral testimony.[37] The corollary of this law is Rothari's legislation 'De cartola falsa aut quolibet membranum' to ensure the validity of the document by prescribing the punishment for writing a false document: 'He who forges a charter or any other kind of document shall have his hand cut off.'[38] This punishment, undoubtedly effective, was the same for minting coins without the king's permission.[39] While perhaps offending modern sensibilities, we cannot see this as a particularly 'barbarian' practice limited to primitive Germans: it was also a Byzantine custom made law by Heraclius.[40] The Visigothic code shares the same law, but Rothari pre-dates the Visigothic effort and also makes no distinction between either the status of the perpetrators (the first time in the history of this law), or between public and private documents, as does the Visigothic code.[41] Yet mutilation penalties were extremely rare in Lombard law. With the exception of capital punishment, this is as rough as it gets, and Rothari's only such penalties: the king wanted a system of compositions, not of violence.[42]

---

[36] Rothari 227. Possibly taken from the legislation of Honorius and Theodosius; Levy, *West Roman Vulgar Law*, pp. 183ff. Also Paradisi, 'Il prologo', p. 17; Riché, *Education*, p. 340 n. 224; Wickham, *EMI*, p. 124. The term *libellus* occurs nowhere else in the Lombard laws, except for the *libellarius* land-contract of Liutprand 92 (see below).
[37] Wickham, *EMI*, p. 124; cf. Riché, *Education*, p. 340 n. 224.
[38] Rothari 243. 'manus ei incidatur', not 'manu incisione multetur', Lopez, 'Byzantine law', pp. 451, 456 (n. 55).
[39] Rothari 242.   [40] Lopez, 'Byzantine law'.
[41] *Lex visig.* VII.5, 1, 2, and 6.2. See Lopez, 'Byzantine law', pp. 450–1, 465; S. Lear, 'The public law of the Visigothic code', *Speculum* 26 (1951), 1–23 Appendix C; King, 'Law', pp. 92, 110–11; Schott, 'Der Stand', pp. 32–5. Cf. *Lex ribuaria* (59) on the *cancellarius*' loss of right thumb for a false charter.
[42] But see Liutprand 141, Ratchis 2. The interpretation of Gasparri, *La cultura*, pp. 140–51, is unconvincing. On the issues of private feud and public authority, see Calisse, *A History of Italian Law*,

Law and government

The position of these two laws within the structure of the Edict raises some points concerning the legal position of writing in regard to contractual agreements. The laws concerning the use of *libelli* (227) and the punishment for false charters (243) bridge a sub-section regarding property. Within this sub-section, eight laws concerning transactions involving movable property (slaves, produce, horses) make no mention of the use of documents, and another six are concerned with boundary markers.[43] The following sub-section (245–52) defines the correct procedures of contractual agreements, particularly sales, in terms of pledges, oaths and sureties, though without mentioning documents. The use of documents was, then, classified under the rubric of immovable property, and a separate section was needed for specifying how oral agreements were to be made in the absence of documents. Although the tenor of Rothari's legislation was far from making writing a necessity, the important point here is that correct procedures for oral forms of contractual obligation were redacted in writing as a means by which to measure their legitimacy.[44]

Liutprand changed the punishment for writing false charters to composition of one's *wergeld*. He went even further in defining what constituted a legally valid document: charters should be written either 'according to Lombard law, which is well known and open to all, or according to Roman law'.[45] The reference to Roman law has often been cited as proof of the existence of the principle of the personality of the law in Italy, and as a corollary, a fundamental division in Lombard society between Germanic conquerors, who used Lombard law, and their subjects, who continued to use Roman law.[46] There is some evidence within the code itself of an ethnic division, but this is minor.[47] All other factors suggest

---

trans. L.B. Register, Continental Legal History Series 8 (Boston, 1928), p. 95; Wickham, *EMI*, pp. 117–19; G. Halsall in Halsall (ed.), *Violence and Society in the Early Medieval West* (Woodbridge and Rochester, 1998), pp 1–45, esp. pp. 19–29; R. Balzaretti, ' "These are things that men do, not women": the social regulation of female violence in Langobard Italy', in *ibid.*, pp. 175–92.

[43] Exactly what was used for 'signs' and 'marked trees' ('arbor signatus' [*sic*] with 'teclatura inter fines decernendas signata est' [238, 239], or 'nova signa, id est ticlatura aut snaida' [240, 241]) is unclear. Cf. Bluhme, MGH Leges IV, p. 59 n. 33; DuCange, *Glossarium*, VIII, p. 95; F. Arnaldi, *Lexicon latinitatis italicae medii aevi* (Brussels, 1939), II (ed. P. Smiraglia, Brussels, 1957–64), p. 253. *Snaida* (*sinaida, senaida, signaida, schneiden*) appears before the Edict in CDL III.2 (624). See Van der Rhee, *GWL*, pp. 120–1. Boundaries are often referred to in charters as marked by *signa*: e.g. CDL 161, 'latere tenente in vinea...fini signa posite'. Cf. CDL III.4, 22.

[44] See P. Classen, 'Fortleben und Wandel spätromischen Urkundenwesens im frühen Mittelalter', in Classen (ed.), *Recht und Schrift im Mittelalter*, Vorträge und Forschungen 23 (Sigmaringen, 1977), pp. 13–54, at pp. 14–15.

[45] Liutprand 91.

[46] I address this issue more fully in 'How territorial was Lombard law?', in P. Erhart and W. Pohl, *Die Langobarden: Herrschaft und Identität* (Vienna, forthcoming).

[47] Only one law of Rothari (194) mentions Romans (fornicating with a Roman *serva*: same fine as a Lombard) and two of Liutprand (91, and 127 concerning Roman–Lombard marriages). One

that the cultural fusion between Lombards and 'Romans' (whoever these may be) also entailed the fusion of legal systems, so that it is impossible to 'distinguish between a Lombard and Roman legal tradition in the actions of Italians at any social level in our sources'.[48] To what, then, was Liutprand referring?

There are a number of possibilities. First, the term 'Roman law' could generally refer to the legal culture of late Roman vulgar law in relation to property, which in any case formed the basis for property law in the Lombard code. Second, the term 'Roman law' may have been reserved for sections of the population that, for different reasons, did not, or had not yet, acknowledged Lombard law, such as the church, or the inhabitants of regions recently conquered by the king's military campaigns against the Byzantines.[49] A third possibility is that to write charters 'according to Roman law' refers to the use of ancient Roman legal formulae in the text of the charter, such as the *mancipatio* formulae found in Piacentine charters.[50] The most probable answer, however, is given by the remainder of the law. Liutprand further gave permission for pacts and agreements between two parties to go outside the law (*subdiscendere*), provided that the agreement was ratified in the form of a charter. The exception to this was any matter pertaining to inheritance, which must be 'written according to law'. Although the wording does not specifically state the redaction of a charter is required in the case of such agreements, it is implied by the following phrase exonerating scribes from possible blame.[51] Liutprand's first acts of legislation fourteen years earlier substantially revised Lombard inheritance laws along more Roman lines by extending the inheritance rights of women and legitimating gifts to

---

Pistoiese charter of 767 refers to tenants as *romani*, CDL 206; see Wickham, *EMI*, p. 71. Rothari's law on *waregang* (367) was addressed to 'foreigners' ('qui de exteras fines in regni nostri finibus advenerit' and does not mention Romans, but cf. Delogu, 'Longobardi e Romani', pp. 129–34. See B. Pohl-Resl, 'Legal practice and ethnic identity in Lombard Italy', in W. Pohl and H. Reimitz (eds.), *Strategies of Distinction: The Construction of Ethnic Communities, 300–800* (Leiden, Boston and Cologne), pp. 205–19.

[48] Wickham, *EMI*, p. 69, citing a charter of 780 which refers to use of a *launichild* ('countergift') as 'in accordance with Roman law'.

[49] See Gasparri, 'Il regno e la legge', p. 253.

[50] N. Everett, 'Scribes and charters in Lombard Italy', *Studi Medievali* 3rd ser., 41:1 (2000), 39–83, at pp. 66–7; and below, pp. 221–2.

[51] Liutprand 91: 'Nam quod ad hereditandum pertinet, per legem scribant. Et quia de cartola falsa in anteriore edictum adfixum est, sic permaneat.' The last phrase 'de cartola falsa' refers not to Rothari 243 concerning amputation of the hand (Fischer-Drew trans., p. 84), but to Liutprand 63 on knowingly subscribing to a false charter (discussed below), since this present law (91) has changed the penalty to composition of the scribe's wergeld. Liutprand's law on women and charters (22, c.a. 721), however, must refer to Rothari 243 on the basis of chronology.

the church.⁵² Thus Liutprand's phrase 'according to Roman or Lombard law' was intended as a generic statement to the effect that all charters recording matters which pertained to inheritance must be in accordance with written law, regardless of its ethnic associations. The similarities between inheritance laws in Roman vulgar law and Liutprandic legislation permitted the comparison.⁵³ The phrase 'according to Lombard law or Roman law' was intended to highlight the parallels between the two, not to contrast them.

For the purpose of understanding the role of the written word in the legal sphere, however, the important point to note is the power of the charter to legitimate agreements between individuals that were outside the precepts of any written law. Such agreements were undoubtedly common, particularly as a means of resolving disputes, but Liutprand required them to be recorded in writing in order to be legally valid.⁵⁴ This, in turn, explains Liutprand's earlier prescriptions to ensure the legality of the charter. Aside from the punishment inflicted on scribes for writing false charters, the witness who knowingly subscribed to a false charter was required to pay his *wergeld* as composition, as was the person who requested their subscription, for false subscription was equal to giving false oral testimony.⁵⁵ Moreover, Liutprand required that any agreement in the form of a written *cautio* must specify the objects that were pledged from the property and note how much the property was worth, in order that the person who pledged the property might not (deviously) sell it before they had fulfilled their obligations.⁵⁶ The king further conceded the right for children without guardians to sell land to avoid starvation. The whole process was to be closely supervised by a judge or king's representative to prevent injustice, but importantly, 'In the charter of sale it should be noted that this sale was made on account of the necessity created by hunger.'⁵⁷

The laws of Liutprand often prescribed both the content and the format that charters were to assume, as we shall see below in relation to women.

---

⁵² Liutprand 1–6, which revises Rothari's laws of rightful succession (Rothari 153–77). See Calasso, *Medio evo del diritto*, pp. 220–5, 249–53; Sinatti D'Amico, *Le prove*, pp. 203–30, and below on women and legal literacy.
⁵³ On herditary rural tenure see Levy, *West Roman Vulgar Law*, pp. 91–4.
⁵⁴ Further evident in Liutprand 107 on *cartolae convenientiae*; cf. P. Geary, 'Extrajudicial means of conflict resolution', *Settimane* 42 (Spoleto, 1994), 569–602, at p. 578.
⁵⁵ Liutprand 63.
⁵⁶ Liutprand 67. Admittedly, *cautio* can refer to an oral or written agreement, and the phrases 'nisi dixerit in ipsa cautionem' and 'faciat in ipsa cautionem de tantis rebus' could be read either way. The form of agreement is essentially Roman; Bluhme, MGH Leges IV, p. 134.
⁵⁷ Liutprand 149. Not 'so that the sale could later be annulled' (Radding, *Origins*, p. 25), but rather to legitimate the sale made by a minor.

Further information concerning the procedure behind charters must be gleaned from indirect comments in the law. For example, in upholding the primacy of thirty-year possession of property against challenges made by claimants who possess a charter of gift, Liutprand described such charters as 'per gairethinx facta aut per susceptum launichild', although Rothari's laws concerning gifts made with *gairethinx* or *launichild* did not mention charters, nor did Liutprand's later re-endorsement of Rothari's laws.[58] Oddly, Liutprand declares that he is legislating for customs which have yet to be recorded in the code, yet Rothari's laws seem perfectly clear. That charters were redacted in the context of such social rituals is confirmed by a *placitum* of 762 held in Pavia, in which the judges decided that a charter offered as proof of a claim was invalid 'quia nec per garetihinx [sic] nec per launichild factam non erat, sicut edicti contenit textus'.[59] Ratchis specified that charters of sale must be written by a 'public scribe' or subscribed by suitable witnesses testifying that the price mentioned in the charter had been paid by the purchaser.[60] Moreover, Ratchis' law testifies to the supremacy of written evidence over oral testimony, for 'evil men' were prepared to swear that a sales price had not yet been fully paid even though the purchaser had a charter confirming the sale: 'this seems harsh to us and our judges... men may be ruined by such an accusation since anything can be taken away by such an oath'. As Wickham noted, 'henceforth, no oath could invalidate a properly drawn up charter'.[61]

The requirement of witnesses to testify that the price had been paid derived directly from Roman vulgar law, as did the primacy of thirty-year possession as proof of ownership.[62] In one sense, the supremacy of the thirty-year possession rule demonstrates the limitations of the legal force of charters in Lombard law: they were not omnipotent against other forms of proof, but were subject to rules and regulations circumscribing their use and validity. In another sense, their superiority was potentially dangerous: hence Liutprand legislated that, anybody who possessed movable or immovable property by means of a forged charter lost that property, *despite* their possession of that property for thirty years or more.[63]

Most of the laws referring to the use of documents discussed so far have concerned the possession of land or movable property. This is hardly surprising. The law of property in the Lombard code was essentially Roman,[64] and Roman law privileged writing as the best form of proof

---

[58] Rothari 172–5. Liutprand 73 (726).   [59] CDL 163.
[60] Ratchis 8. See pp. 203–4 below.   [61] Wickham, *EMI*, p. 124.
[62] Levy, *West Roman Vulgar Law*, p. 137, and pp. 184–90, esp. p. 188.
[63] Liutprand 114.
[64] G. Diurni, *Le situazioni possessorie nel medievo: età longobardo-franca* (Milan, 1988), pp. 8–27.

for recording rights of possession and ownership. One of the few methods of land-holding specifically called by name in the Lombard law code is the *livellarium*, possession by 'book' or charter, of the free tenant.[65] The reference is made in passing, for the real concern of the law is with homicide committed by a free tenant on his land held by *livellarium*. Yet the etymology is a powerful reminder of the importance of written legal norms that underpinned late Roman and early medieval Italian society, a society in which the economic basis for wealth and status was control over agricultural production. Land-owners, then, had great incentive to know written law and to use documents in accordance with its precepts, as had their tenants. Whether they themselves could read the law code and documents is another matter; if they could not, they could certainly have found someone who did. I turn now to discuss two subjects which demonstrate that the use of written law and charters extended well beyond male land-owners into Italo-Lombard society, namely, the manumission of slaves and the legal position of women.

MANUMISSION

One area in which a close relationship between law and charters can be seen is in the manumission of slaves. As we have seen, Rothari's legislation attempted to be thoroughly comprehensive in providing the correct procedures to be observed by dividing the subject into four different methods of manumission according to different levels of 'free status'.[66] The 'four roads' ritual and the use of symbolic objects, the *gaida et gisil* ('whip and arrow') to signify the manumitted person's new status seem a far cry from the civilities of manumission in Roman law. The use of no less than six Germanic terms in this law serves to reinforce the impression that Rothari's concern was to preserve a uniquely 'Germanic' custom. The impression, however, is somewhat undermined by a late Roman exhortation to follow up the proceedings with the redaction of a charter:

These are the four types of manumission. The possibility of future difficulty requires that the manner in which the man or woman has been freed should be recorded in a charter of freedom. If the charter has not been executed, however, nevertheless the former slave's freedom remains in effect.[67]

---

[65] Liutprand 92.
[66] Rothari 224. Above, pp. 127–8. Both Bluhme, MGH Leges IV, p. 55 n. 28, and Paradisi, 'Il prologo', p. 16, see the division of the law into four separate sub-chapters as evidence of its earlier or initially separate redaction.
[67] Cf. A. Watson, *The Roman Slave* (London, 1987), pp. 23–34; K. Bradley, *Slavery and Society in Ancient Rome* (Cambridge, 1994), pp. 145–56.

Rothari recommended that a charter be drawn up as an expedient to avoid possible disputes over the slave's status, though he did not make it a requirement. To be legal, a manumission was performed in a ritualistic social context (*gairethinx*) that was witnessed by several people. Liutprand later recognised the ritual of leading the slave around a church altar as equally valid to that of the 'four roads'. In a manner similar to Rothari's legislation, he drew a line regarding manumissions to half-free status, stipulating that these should be done in some 'other manner, by means of a charter or whatever manner pleases him'.[68] In the legislation of both Rothari and Liutprand, the redaction of a charter is the preferred procedure for raising the status of a slave to half-free: full freedom required a symbolic ritual act before witnesses. The two levels of status were not to be confused. The charter, then, served as an instrument of precision to define the terms of the manumission. Aistulf was also concerned with precision when he legislated against ungrateful *manumitti* who were not willing to serve their benefactors once they had been granted their freedom. The result, lamented the king, was that free men were no longer willing to grant freedom to their servants. The solution proposed was that the lord give the manumitted slave 'a charter and thus reserve the service of that one so long as he lives; after his lord's death the servant shall be completely free. This shall be observed as noted in the text of that charter.'[69]

Proof of the application of law code with respect to manumission can be found in some surviving charters. An outstanding example of judges applying the letter of the law is a *placitum* dating to the second quarter of the eighth century. It records a judgement concerning the legal status of Lucio, who claimed to have been manumitted 'circa altario' by the ancestors of Toto of Campione, who was now pressing Lucio for labour services as an *aldius*.[70] In his defence, Lucio presented a charter 'de tempore Cuniperti' which stated that Toto's ancestors had fixed the price of Lucio's *mundium*, and that of his heirs, at 3 *solidi*, and that Lucio had been manumitted by means of the 'altar method'. The judges responded that Lucio's charter pre-dated Liutprand's law of 721 which legitimated the 'altar method' of manumission. Lucio was, therefore, 'not a freeman but an *aldius*'.[71] Lucio was given a few more chances to prove his

---

[68] Liutprand 23. See C.G. Mor, 'La manumissione in ecclesia', *Rivista di Storia del Diritto Italiano* 1 (1928), 80–150, esp. pp. 116–27.
[69] Aistulf 11: 'stabilem debeat permanere secundum textu cartule quam ei fecerit'.
[70] CDL 81. On the date: Schiaparelli, CDL I, pp. 236–7.
[71] *Ibid.*: 'set ante erant ipsas cartolas quam domnus Liutprand in edecto adfixeset, cot sic esset liuerus qui cerca altare esset ductus, comoto qui in quattrouio esset thingatus. et paruet nouis ut non

freedom by answering questions concerning his reasons for providing the contended labour services for the last thirty years (Lucio claimed to have done so 'pro bona voluntas') and whether he could provide witnesses who could testify to his free status, but Lucio could not. His presentation of a *monimen*, despite its legal invalidity, may have bought him the benefit of the doubt among the judges, who then resorted to oral interrogation. What is beyond doubt, however, was the judges' knowledge of the law code and its direct application in a court of law.

Despite the discrepancy between the dates of Lucio's *monimen* and the law regarding manumission 'circa altario', the text of the *monimen* demonstrates adherence to Liutprand's earlier legislation in another respect, that of the right of the lord to maintain the *mundium* of the manumitted slave, provided that 'this amount be confirmed in a charter for him or her [manumitted]', and this is precisely what Lucio's *monimen* stated.[72] Although we have no other examples in which the manumitted persons themselves received a charter specifying the value of their *mundium*, there is a sufficient number of charters concerning the purchase of women and women slaves, within which the price of the woman's *mundium* is explicitly stated. In these cases the charters remained in the possession of the women's *mundoald* or legal guardian.[73]

If Lombard law did not specify that a charter was essential to confirm manumission, there is evidence to suggest that person who was manumitted required a document for security. In a Piacentine *charta absolutionis* of 753, a certain Ambrosius stated that, although he and his brother Autharene had already manumitted Domoald 'years ago', Domoald, who had since entered the church of San Pietro di Varsi to live as a monk, now requested a charter confirming his freedom 'from every bond of servitude' and his possessions.[74] Two wills by wealthy laymen included the manumission of their slaves 'circa altario' as part of their stipulations. The will of Tassilo of Lucca instructed that it was the responsibility of the priests to whom he left his property to provide twelve former slaves with charters confirming their manumission and the property bequeathed to them as a reward for their services.[75] The will of Taido, *gasindius regis*, a

---

poteret esse liuerus, nisi aldius'. Liutprand (9) had already decreed in 717 that manumission *circa altario* was acceptable if the slave had been handed over directly to the king, who then handed the slave over to a priest for the ritual manumission. This 'royal exemption' seems to have paved the way for the legislation of four years later (Liutprand 23).

[72] Liutprand 10 (717). Lucio's judges: 'et ipso monimen contineuat, cot cesseset ei parentes Totuni tres solidos mundium et tres reseruaset ad heredibus suis'.

[73] For example, CDL 29, 53, 233, 252.   [74] CDL 109.

[75] CDL 214 (768): 'et uolo ut omnis hominis meis mihi pertinentis uos liueris circa altario demettere deueatis, et eorum cartulam absolutionis emettere diueatis'.

pious and patriotic servant of the state, does not mention the redaction of charters, but instead stipulates that the slaves were to be manumitted by the bishop of Bergamo himself, and explicitly mentions the Lombard law code.[76] Both of these wills post-date Aistulf's law of 755 which specifically ordered that such arrangements made 'per cartola' were to be respected by ecclesiastics and relatives of the dead man.[77] Liutprand even instituted that servile couples mistreated by lecherous owners were to receive a written *praeceptum* from local or royal authorities to confirm their freedom, since the traditional rituals of *gairethinx* and the four roads or the *circa altarium* method might somehow be prevented by their disgraced, yet still potentially coercive, previous owner.[78]

The charter evidence confirms that manumission, and indeed the regulation of the social hierarchy itself, was carried out in strict accordance with written law. Conversely, the laws and the surviving charters confirm the importance of charters themselves as constituting a primary means of proof to the slave's free status. The correspondence between the two forms of text testifies to the penetration of the written word down to the lowest levels of Italo-Lombard society. No doubt many of these slaves were unable to read the texts for themselves.[79] But they would certainly, and easily, have found someone to read for them. As we saw in chapter 3, although formulaic legal language may have baffled the uninitiated (as it does now), the vulgar Latin of the charters of this period was rooted in vernacular expression and syntactic simplicity: it was not at a learned remove from those who appeared in the courts, nor, judging from the language of the *placita*, those who administered them. As Aistulf decreed, the conditions of the slave's freedom was 'to be noted in the text of the charter'.[80] No matter how the information contained in the text reached them, slaves and free men alike were certainly aware of the importance of such texts for maintaining or changing their social status, as well as the importance of written law in regulating such status. The evidence for manumission in Italo-Lombard society suggests that there was great incentive for members of even the lowest class to learn to read and use texts to their advantage, and that not doing so was a disadvantage they could ill afford.

---

[76] CDL 293 (Bergamo, 774): 'uolo adque instituto ut omnes fiant deducti erga altario beastissimi Christi martyris Sancti Alexandri sito Bergomate... per manus pontifici sancte Bergomensis... et ubi illo die omnis permaneant liberi et absoluti, sicut a principalibus huius gentis catholice Langubardorum in aedicti pagina est institutum'.
[77] Aistulf 12. [78] Liutprand 140.
[79] R. Balzaretti, 'The monastery of Sant'Ambrogio and dispute settlement in early medieval Milan', *EME* 3:1 (1994), 1–18, at pp. 16–18.
[80] Aistulf 11, as above.

Law and government

WOMEN AND LEGAL LITERACY

Assessments of the position of women in early medieval Italy have, not without reason, been fairly negative.[81] Yet a comparative study of the position of women in barbarian legislation found that women were valued more highly in Lombard society than in any other of the barbarian successor kingdoms.[82] Historical analyses that attempt to discern the 'value' of women, however, are often based on extra-empirical evaluations of the concept of the 'value of women'.[83] Recent work on women and literacy in the early middle ages has revealed the extent to which women participated in literate practices and literary culture in this period.[84] There is little evidence from Lombard Italy for women's involvement with the world of books and literacy, though that which we have is suggestive of a great deal more activity than has survived. We have discussed the royal court of Queen Theudelinda and her involvement in the Three Chapters dispute. Courtly literate traditions are also evident in the eighth-century epitaphs of queens and other women, including nuns with royal connections.[85] For women of the religious life, the convent of San Salvatore in Brescia is suggestive of practices in female monasteries elsewhere,[86] and Paul the

---

[81] Wickham, *EMI*, pp. 124–5. Useful overviews, generally concerned with a later period, are: D. Owen Hughes, 'Invisible madonnas? The Italian historiographical and the women of medieval Italy', in S. Mosher Stuard (ed.), *Women in Medieval History and Historiography* (Philadelphia, 1987), pp. 25–57; G. Piccinni, 'Le donne nella vita dell'Italia medievale', in A. Groppi (ed.), *Il lavoro delle donne. Storia delle donne in Italia* 2 (Rome and Bari, 1996), pp. 5–46. P. Skinner, *Women in Medieval Italian Society 500–1200* (Harlow, 2001) reached me only after this book had gone to press.

[82] M.T. Guerra-Medici, *I diritti delle donne nella società altomedievale*, Ius nostrum serie 2a:4 (Naples, 1986), esp. pp. 224–7, 305–13. Cf. S. Wemple, *Women in Frankish Society: Marriage and the Cloister 500–900* (Philadelphia, 1981); R.V. Colman, 'The abduction of women in barbarian law', *Florilegium* 5 (1983), 62–75.

[83] M.W. Kaufman, 'Spare ribs: the conception of women in the middle ages and the Renaissance', *Soundings* 56:2 (1973), 135–61, esp. pp. 139–40; N. Damsholt, 'Theories of patriarchy in women's history', in K. Glente and K. Jensen (eds.), *Female Power in the Middle Ages* (Copenhagen, 1989), pp. 55–76; J.M. Bennett, 'Feminism and history', *Gender and History* 1 (1989), 251–72.

[84] McKitterick, *Carolingians*, pp. 219, 223–7; R. McKitterick, 'Frauen und Schriftlichkeit im Frühmittelalter', in H.W. Goetz (ed.), *Weibliche Lebensgestaltung im frühen Mittelalter* (Cologne and Vienna, 1991), pp. 65–118 (Eng. version in McKitterick, *Books, Scribes and Learning in the Frankish Kingdoms: Sixth to Ninth Centuries* (Aldershot, 1994), ch. 8); R. McKitterick, 'Nuns' scriptoria in England and Francia in the eighth century', *Francia* 19:1 (1992), 1–35 (repr. in *Books, Scribes*, ch. 7); J. Nelson, 'Women and the word in the earlier middle ages', in W. Sheils and D. Wood (eds.), *Women in the Church* (Oxford, 1990), pp. 53–87; J. Nelson, 'Gender and genre in women historians of the early middle ages', in *L'Historiographie médiévale en Europe* (Paris, 1991), pp. 149–63.

[85] Theudelinda, above, pp. 85–6: Epitaphs of Theodota (by Theodota), Cunincperga and Ragintruda, below, pp. 254–8. Paul the Deacon's epitaph of Queen Ansa: MGH SRL, pp. 191–2.

[86] The later inventory (*c*. 879–907) of the nunnery of San Salvatore, which records the possession of gospels, missals, psalters, liturgical books and patristic works, doubtless reflects an earlier period, as do manuscripts now in Brescia's Biblioteca Queriniana (CLA III.282–4), but preserved at San

Deacon's work for the duchess Adelperga is testimony to her interest in literary matters, particularly narrative history.[87] But perhaps more importantly, in terms of greater numbers of women and a more common experience of literacy, our legal sources demonstrate that written law and charters directly concerned women, and that women were directly concerned to understand and exploit legal literacy to protect their interests.

The absence of autograph subscriptions by women in Lombard charters led Petrucci to conclude that in the eighth century 'there existed amongst the middle and upper classes of society a certain diffusion of the knowledge of script which, however, completely excluded women'.[88] This is due as much to Roman legal traditions (or more precisely, customs) as to Lombard law, in which women were legally dependent upon men to act as legal guardians in giving consent.[89] This meant that women did not autograph charters with formulaic phrases, not that reading and understanding laws and charters had little or no significance for them. Far from it. In his second year as king, Liutprand devoted no less than five out of his first six acts of legislation to the position of women by increasing their rights to the inheritance of property, a process that can be seen throughout all Lombard legislation from Rothari to Aistulf. By his ninth year as king (721), Liutprand needed to specify how women could sell property, which included the use of charters:

Salvatore from an early age, and in one case (CLA 283: A.III.14, Jerome, *In Isaiam*, saec. VIII) possibly written there. See G. Pasquali (ed.), 'San Salvatore di Brescia', in A. Castagnetti *et al.* (eds.), *Inventari altomedievali di terre, coloni e reddite*, Fonti per la Storia d'Italia 104 (Rome, 1979), pp. 41–94.

[87] MGH AA. II, ed. H. Droysen, esp. Paul's prefatory letter to Anselperga, pp. 4–5: 'ipsa [Adelperga] quoque subtili ingenio et sagacissimo studio prudentium arcana rimeris, ita ut philosophorum aurata eloquia poetarumque gemmea dicta tibi in promptu sint, historiis etiam seu commentis tam divinis inhaereas quam mundanis'.

[88] Petrucci, 'Alle origini', *Scriptores*, p. 23.

[89] Rothari 204. See E. Cortese, 'Per la storia del mundio in Italia', *Rivista Italiana per le Scienze Giuridiche* 8 (1955–56), 323–474. An odd exception is the autograph subscription of Theodelinda, wife of Senatur, CDL 18. The charter comes down to us in a twelfth-century cartulary, and is perhaps the result of scribal tradition. Women and signatures in late Roman law: J. Beaucamp, *Le Statut de la femme à Byzance (4e–7e siècle)*, II, *Les Pratiques sociales* (Paris, 1992), pp. 28–31; A. Arjava, *Women and Law in Late Antiquity* (Oxford, 1996), pp. 235–7. Note the perceptive comments of J. Nelson, 'Literacy in Carolingian government', in McKitterick (ed.), *Uses*, p. 272. On the practice of Lombard law for women, see B. Pohl-Resl, 'Quod me legibus contanget auere. Rechtsfähigkeit und Landbesitz langobardischer Frauen', *MIÖG* 101 (1993), 201–27. For a slightly later period, see P. Skinner, 'Women, literacy and invisibility in southern Italy 900–1200', in L. Smith and J. Taylor (eds.), *Women, the Book and the Worldly*, II (Cambridge, 1995), pp. 1–11; Skinner, 'Women, wills and wealth in medieval southern Italy', *EME* 2 (1993), 133–52; Skinner, 'Disputes and disparity: women in court in medieval southern Italy', *Reading Medieval Studies* 22 (1996), 85–104.

Law and government

If a woman wishes to sell her property with the consent of her husband, or in community with him, he who wishes to buy from her, or those who wish to sell to her, shall notify two or three relatives of the woman who are nearest in relationship to her. If in the presence of these relatives the woman says that she has acted under compulsion, then that which she sold shall not be valid. But if in the presence of her relatives, or of the judge who presides in that place, she claims that she did not act under compulsion but voluntarily sold her property, then that which she sold ought to remain valid from that day forth, provided that the relatives who were present or the judge subscribed the charter.[90]

Liutprand added further that the scribe who prepared the charter shall write it only with the consent of the relatives or of the judge: failure to do so rendered the sale invalid and the scribe's hand was to be amputated in accordance with Rothari's law on forgeries.[91] One of our earliest original charters demonstrates Liutprand's law in action only four years after its promulgation. In 725, Ermedruda sold a Gallic slave boy by the name of Satrelanus to a certain Toto for the price of 12 *solidi*. The language of Ermedruda's charter, written by Faustinus *notarius regis postestatis*, neatly conforms to the language of Liutprand's law code, which is perhaps not surprising given the scribe's title. In the opening *pronuntio* of the charter, Faustinus stated that Ermedruda was selling the slave 'una cum consenso et uolontate ipsius genitori suo'. Ermedruda's subscription likewise stated that she made the sale of her own free will ('bona voluntate sua') and the witnesses all repeat similar *consentienti eius genitori* formulae in their subscriptions (she had inherited the slave 'ei de paterna successione' in the first place). Only one of the witnesses stated that Ermedruda had suffered no violence, in a phrase that echoes the law code. Other charters involving women similarly echo the law code or cite it explicitly.[92] The use of written instruments as a means of safeguarding women against violent expropriation was not new: the Theodosian code likewise made similar provisions.[93] If the muddle of late Roman law obscured the legal position of women with respect to transactions, Liutprand's legislation

---

[90] Liutprand 22. Cf. Fischer-Drew trans., pp. 154–5. In another law, which can be attributed either to Liutprand (law 29 of 722, as recorded in the three later Beneventan manuscripts of Lombard law which preserve it), or to later Beneventan legislation (see Moschetti, *Primordi esegetici*, p. 27), the option of having judges *or* relatives present was dropped: the presence of both was necessary.
[91] Liutprand 29. Cf. Guerra-Medici, *I diritti*, p. 75.
[92] *Ibid.*: 'in cuius presentia se nullas uiolentas patire clamauit'. Cf. Liutprand 22: 'in presentia de ipsis parentibus suis mulier illa violentas aliquas se dixerit pati'. Cf. CDL 131, and 226 which cites the code: Schiaparelli notes that 'nullius cogentis imperii' is an echo of *CTh* 22.9.3. For further examples, Pohl-Resl, 'Rechtsfähigkeit', pp. 207–19. Such clauses are common into the eleventh century.
[93] *CTh*. 2.29.2.

made it clear: to do business with women in the buying or selling of land required pen, parchment and a knowledge of the law code.

We have seen above that charters of manumission were the same for women as for men. Further confirmation of the direct application of the law code in relation to women can be seen in two charters that record the purchase of a woman's *mundium*. In a Piacentine charter of 721, the brothers Sigirad and Arochis, *viri devoti* of Castelseprio (Sepriasca), purchase the *mundium* of Anstruda for 3 *solidi* owing to her having married their servant.[94] A later Comascan charter of 735 records that the same two brothers purchased the *mundium* of another woman, Scolastica, because she too had married one of their servants.[95] Amongst the many laws in the code that concern possession of women's *mundii*, none stipulated that the purchase of a *mundium* needed to be recorded in a charter, yet the new servile status of the women meant that the price and possession of their *mundium* was to be recorded in accordance with Liutprand's law on manumission, even though no manumission had taken place.[96] Here we can see that the use of documentation had gone beyond the requirements of the law code as part of the general practice of recording the possession of property (here servile women and their children) in charters.

The legislation of both Rothari and Liutprand allowed for direct royal intervention in disputes over the legal position of women with respect to property, inheritance or manumission by having the case brought before the royal court for resolution. Two Milanese charters demonstrate royal intervention in action. The first charter, a *notitia traditionis*, dating sometime prior to 769, is a small document consisting of six lines of script which confirmed that a certain Arichis had handed over his niece Magnerata in marriage to Anscauso, along with all her possessions, including those which were owed to her by her sisters and aunts. The charter reveals that the king himself had decided upon the division of property and had appointed a royal *missus* to oversee the procedure.[97] Just why Desiderius (or by this stage his co-regent son Adelchis) needed to intervene in dividing the spoils amongst the women is unknown, but another later charter of 769 by Magnerata, now widowed and *ancilla dei*, suggests that the stakes were probably high, as Magnerata donated an olive-grove and vineyard, which she specifies as set amongst other family plots of

---

[94] CDL 29. [95] CDL 53.
[96] Liutprand 10, cited above. Laws concerning a woman's *mundium*: Rothari 26, 160–1, 165, 182, 184, 186–91, 195–201, 204, 214–16, 369, 385; Grimoald 6; Liutprand 9–10, 14, 30, 57, 60, 93, 100, 114, 119, 127, 139, 145.
[97] CDL 233 (ChLA 851). Cf. Rothari 183, Liutprand 103. On Magnerata's family, see G. Rossetti, 'I ceti proprietari et professionali: stato sociale, funzioni e prestigio a Milano nei secoli VIII–IX: l'età longobarda', *Atti X CISAM* (Spoleto, 1986), 165–207.

Law and government

her uncle and niece, to the church of San Zeno in Campione that her relatives had founded.[98] The second charter of 771, titled by the scribe as a 'Notitia brevis memoratio pro foturis temporibus', confirmed that Autpert, *actor domni regis*, had received 3 *solidi* from Toto for the *mundium* of Ermetruda, daughter of Antoninus and *aldia regia*, because of her marriage to Toto's *aldius* Theutodoin. Hence the *Notitia* is in direct concordance with the laws of Rothari and Liutprand concerning the legal status of *aldii* and their children, as noted in the text of the charter by the scribe Uualpert *indignus presbiter*.[99]

Liutprand's legislation also introduced the use of documents into the realm of Lombard family law in stipulating the conditions for the correct employment of the *morgengab* or 'morning gift' as part of the marriage contract.[100] As well as specifying that the *morgengab* given to the woman should be no more than one quarter of the husband's property, Liutprand also decreed that, prior to the marriage, and in the presence of friends and relatives, the husband must 'announce the gift by means of a written instrument, confirmed by witnesses, which states "observe that which I gave as a morning gift to my wife", so that in the future she may not lose the gift by any perjury'.[101] Moreover, the use of documents in order to certify the conditions of a marriage contract are hinted at in Liutprand's later provision which allowed a minor (that is, under eighteen years old) to arrange his betrothal prior to becoming legally independent: should the minor desire to marry a woman, 'he shall have the right to provide the marriage portion (*meta*), and to give the morning gift as the Edict provides, and to incur obligations and to offer surety and to have charters written for these if he so desires. The man who acts as a surety or the scribe who prepares a charter for such things shall not incur condemnation for doing so'.[102] Unfortunately, no *morgengab* charters which stipulate marriage arrangements survive, aside from those cited above which demonstrate royal intervention. There are, however, some charters which record the succession of property given to women as *morgengab*,[103] and one brief 'memoratorium de morganicapu' (here perhaps getting closer to the type of document envisaged by Liutprand) in which the wealthy Lucchese land-owner Ursus, acting as executor, divided up the *morgengab*

---

[98] CDL 235 (ChLA 852). Note the *arengae*, partially reproducing Matt. 19.29.
[99] CDL 252 (ChLA 853): 'unde ab hac die in tua qui supra Totoni uel ad heredibus tuis permaneat potestatem saluua libertatem suam una cum agnotione sua quanti in tempore ex ea nati fuerit qualiter lex est', cf. Rothari 218, Liutprand 126.
[100] Liutprand 7. On *morgengabe*, Calisse, *History of Italian Law*, pp. 574–5; cf. J. Rabinowitz, 'Jewish and Lombard Law', *Jewish Social Studies* 12 (1950), 299–328.
[101] 'ostendat per scriptum a testibus rouoratum et dicat: "quia ecce quod coniugi meae morgingab dedi"'.
[102] Liutprand 117. [103] CDL 30, 67, 120 (cf. 115).

Literacy in Lombard Italy, c. 568–774

of his (presumably dead) sister amongst her children.[104] The great number of surviving charters that mirror the law code, as demonstrated througout this chapter, suggests that Liutprand's legislation was not merely ideal abstraction but was firmly rooted in observing the uses of, and the needs for, documentary practices in Italo-Lombard society.

ADMINISTRATION AND COMMUNICATION

Oral communication, references to which can be found throughout the entire code and in the charters and *placita* recording how decisions were deliberated upon, was, of course, of vital importance in the administration of the kingdom. Yet the literate–oral dichotomy has far less force for a society in which the language written was essentially a formalised version of that which was spoken. There was no great leap between the physical presence of a messenger giving an oral report and the presence of a letter or communiqué relaying the same information. In the execution of governmental directives and orders, oral and literate forms coexisted and complemented one another.[105] I now turn to consider the use of written communication in Lombard government from the top levels of administration, for which we must rely on charter evidence, down to the lesser officials and their functions as mentioned in the law code.

The Lombard royal court at Pavia, and the ducal courts of Spoleto and Benevento, all possessed writing offices which issued diplomas to various parties. Surviving royal charters begin as early as 613. Our run of ducal charters, however, does not begin until the eighth century, though there is little reason to doubt that active 'chanceries' existed in those duchies before then.[106] Indeed the greatest problem for understanding how royal and ducal writing offices functioned in the period is the poor rate of survival. Only thirty-three royal charters have survived, though we know of over 150 others that have perished.[107] Moreover, no original royal or ducal charter has survived. This may have been because they were written on papyrus, in accordance with Italian practices at the time, though

---

[104] CDL 70. Ursus: CDL 69, 30.
[105] Cf. Nelson, 'Literacy in Carolingian government', pp. 267, 274.
[106] For royal charters, Brühl (above, note 2). Spoletan ducal charters Brühl, CDL IV.1, Fonti per la Storia d'Italia 65 (Rome, 1981): Brühl, 'Überlegungen zur Diplomatik der spoletischen Herzogsurkunden', *Atti IX CISAM* (Spoleto, 1983), 124–63. The Beneventan ducal charters, proposed for CDL IV.2 have yet to be published, though one (no. 8) appears in H. Zielinski's edition of Beneventan private charters, CDL V, Fonti per la Storia d'Italia 66 (Rome, 1986). One must sift through the generally unsatisfactory and very dated edition of C. Troya, *Codice diplomatico longobardo* I–V (Naples, 1852–55).
[107] Brühl provides a comprehensive list of the lost royal charters in CDL III, pp. 267–312, but these are only those mentioned in surviving royal charters. Private charters refer to other lost royal charters; e.g. CDL 30, 295 (at least 13).

Law and government

there are certainly a number of other reasons to do with inadequate archival practices.[108] We can only make educated guesses about the physical form of royal and ducal charters. The existence of *probatio pennae* on the back of a private charter of Chiusi, consisting of the standard *intitulatio* of Lombard royal charters ('Fl[avius] Desiderius vir excell[entissimus] rex'), in elongated cursive script, led Schiaparelli to argue that Lombard royal charters must have looked like Merovingian and (early) Carolingian royal diplomas.[109] But the same practice is standard in Roman imperial edicts and documents of provincial offices, and this is probably what the Lombard chanceries inherited. Very little information about how the chanceries operated can be gleaned from the documents themselves, and we shall tackle the subject of who wrote royal and private charters in the following chapter.

Royal and ducal charters testify to the role of literacy in maintaining connections between central and local authorities in the duchies. One example from each of the southern duchies will suffice. The first example is a *placitum* held in Spoleto in 747 concerning several disputes over land between citizens of Rieti and the monastery of Farfa. The document, concerning eight different *causae* pertaining to the same territory of the *gualdum publicum* of S. Iacintus, not only provides details concerning the administration of justice and types of land-holding, but also bears witness to a comparable degree of acceptance of monarchial superiority by a duke of Spoleto.[110] At the request of the monastery of Farfa, King Ratchis had to intervene in the dispute by sending a royal *missus* armed with a written order (*praeceptum*) to settle the case. While seven of the eight cases heard involved strictly oral forms of proof in the form of oaths, one involved the close scrutiny of royal and ducal charters: the royal charter held by the monastery pre-dated the ducal charter of the layman Theodices, and the monastery won the case. Moreover, the results of the hearing were reported back to Duke Lupo in Spoleto, who then ordered a notary to make four copies of the results to be given out to the royal court, to the

---

[108] On use of papyrus, see C.R. Brühl, 'Chronologie und Urkunden der Herzöge von Spoleto im 8. Jahrhundert', *Quellen und Forschungen aus Italienischen Archiven und Bibliotheken* 51 (1972), 1–92, at, pp. 31–3; Zielinski, *Studien*, pp. 48–9. See below, chapter 5, n. 123. The burning of the royal palace in Pavia in 1024 may have played a part in the loss of royal documents and records: the fires of 1071 and 1075 certainly destroyed the documentary reserves of Milan: *Storia di Milano* (Milan, 1954), II, p. 182 and III, p. 193. Cf. CDL III.18 and 19 (744, 746): 'Placentia est urbs in ignis incendio con-cremata et omnes munimina ecclesiae ... ab eodem incendio sunt combusta.'

[109] Schiaparelli, 'Note diplomatiche', in G. Cencetti (ed.), *Note paleografiche e diplomatiche*, pp. 357–61. CDL 185 (765).

[110] CDL V.8. See discussion and bibiography in Zielinski, CDL V, pp. 33–4, and Zielinski, *Studien*, pp. 124–7, 238; C.J. Wickham, 'European forests in the early middle ages' in *Land and Power*, pp. 162–5.

ducal court, to the monastery of Farfa, and to the officials of Rieti who participated in the case as judges.[111] The *notitia* provides a rare glimpse of the use of literate communication between the royal, ducal and local administrations, as well as the importance of written documents as proof in local, ducal and royal courts.

The second example, a charter of 766 from the duchy of Benevento, records a dispute between the monastery of San Vincenzo al Volturno and a group of private land-owners, represented by the gastald Radoald, concerning land in Isernia. Duke Godescalc (739/40–42) donated 'per cartolam' the land in question to the monastery, but his enemy and successor, Duke Gisulf II (742–51), confiscated the land and donated it to his own supporters (*fidelibus suis*). Complaints ensued, and Duke Liutprand (715–57/8) and his mother Scauniperge gave some of the land back to the monastery. But the trouble was far from over. A certain landowner, Alahis, took the case to the royal court of King Aistulf, showing the ducal charter of Gisulf II confirming his ownership, and the monastery did likewise. Aistulf appears to have attempted to settle the issue by dividing up the lands between the two parties, and issued a charter to confirm his decision.[112] Some land-owners were not content with the decision, and petitioned the gastald Radoald to defend their case against the monastery at the court of Duke Arichis II (757/8–87). What followed was a series of compromises between the two opposing parties, decided upon by the duke and confirmed in a 'cartola convenientiae', of which two copies were made, one for each party, that of the monastery being our surviving document. The whole affair demonstrates the importance attached to ducal charters as a means of confirming ownership: both parties had charters, and neither was prepared to give up the case on the strength of those proofs. More interesting, however, is the disregard for the royal charter expressed by the land-owners. Duke Arichis II likewise appears to have dismissed the authority of Aistulf's charter, for the eschatacol of the surviving *cartola convenientiae* declares that nothing shall break the agreement decided upon, 'not even any document or royal charter issued by King Aistulf from when he judged the case, but let

---

[111] Examination of charters: 'Et dum relegissemus precepta ipsa, illud regale preceptum continebatur quod mense iunio, indictione .xii, anno primo predicti domni regis, et illlus predicti Luponis ducis legebatur posterior, idest mense octobris, indictione .xiii', etc. Zielinski, CDL V, p. 36, argues that scribe, Petrus, was from the court at Pavia.

[112] CDL V.7: 'Pro quas vero res surrexit Alahis adversus monasterium cum precepto Gysulfi quondam ducis et depit agere contra monasterium... Et dum multe exinde cause emersissent, convenerat inter Alahis et monasterium, quid quisque per scriptas habere debuisset.' King Aistulf: 'et ipse [rex] per suum iudicium confirmaverat manum illam, quam Alahis consignaverat, qualiter inter ipsum et monasterium convenerat'. *Manus* must mean the document.

those things which are written [in this document] remain immutable and inviolable'.[113]

Both of these examples raise numerous issues concerning ducal independence from the central government of Pavia, in terms of both political reality and administrative culture, which cannot be dealt with here.[114] The problem is complicated by the preservation of these documents as copies made by less than trustworthy monks of the late eleventh and early twelfth centuries, intent on recording the long history of their monasteries' landed wealth.[115] Both examples serve, however, to highlight the importance of documents to the general administrative culture of the *regnum*, and how the literate practices of government facilitated links between power at the local, ducal and royal level.

The dispute between the dioceses of Arezzo and Siena affords a further glimpse into the machinations of government, in terms of direct royal intervention into local affairs – seemingly necessary in the absence of any ducal authority in the region.[116] In this case the proceedings, and the documents that accompanied them, appear to have failed to fulfil their purpose. The king's *missus* and *maiordomus*, Ambrose, was sent to clear up the matter at a hearing held at Siena 'in curte domno regis [*sic*]'.[117] Eight months after having secured a favourable *iudicatum* from Ambrose, the bishop of Arezzo, Lupertianus, took Ambrose's *iudicatum* to the royal court, and Liutprand duly issued to him a confirmatory charter.[118] Even this was not enough to curb the bishop of Siena, Adeodatus, who had the support of the local Sienese gastalds. Only three months later another *missus*, the *notarius regis* Gunteram, was sent by Liutprand to judge again

---

[113] Ibid.: 'Similiter et sint amodo cassate vel corrupte, nullum in se habentes roborem, neque manusconscriptas nec per iudicata nec vel precepta, quae Aystulfus rex emisit de suprascripta convenientia, sed tantum iste amodo conscriptae stabiles et inviolate suum debeant conservare roborem.'

[114] D. Bullough, 'The writing office of the Dukes of Spoleto in the eighth century', in D. Bullough and R.L. Stony (eds.) *The Study of Medieval Records: Essays in Honour of Kathleen Major* (Oxford, 1971), pp. 1–21, at pp. 18–21.

[115] Brühl, 'Überlegungen zur Diplomatik'; Zielinski, *Studien*; W. Kurze, 'Zur Kopiertätikeit Gregors von Catino', *Quellen und Forschungen aus Italienischen Archiven und Bibliotheken* 53 (1973), 409–65.

[116] Most Tuscan cities, with the exception of Lucca and Chiusi, never seem to have had dukes: P.M. Conti, 'La Tuscia e i suoi ordinamenti territoriali nell'alto medioevo', *Atti V CISAM* (Spoleto, 1973), 61–116; C.J. Wickham, 'Economic and social institutions in northern Tuscany in the eighth century', in A. Spicciani (ed.), *Istituzioni ecclesiastiche della Toscana medievale* (Galtina, 1980), pp. 7–34. Co-operation between royal and ducal authority with respect to the use of documents in court: CDL 113 (754); between royal and episcopal authority, CDL 255 (771).

[117] CDL 17 (714, August). We first learn of the dispute from a charter of 650, CDL 4. See above, chapter 3, n. 82.

[118] CDL III.12 (715, 6 March): 'sicut textus idicati noscitus contineri vel a supradicto Ambrosium difinitum atque sanccitum est [*sic*]'.

the issue. Gunteram was thorough: he questioned no less than eighty people, half of them lay, half of them ecclesiastics. The responses of every one of them were recorded in writing, and we sampled some of these in chapter 3.[119] A month later, an ecclesiastical court was held in which four Tuscan bishops and Gunteram presided as judges, who once again, having examined clerical letters of ordination brought before the court, decided in favour of Arezzo. A document was issued to Lupertianus, but again Adeodatus must have ignored the sentence, for three months later the case was again heard at the royal court in Pavia, where it ended, at least until it was reopened again in 850, to continue for several centuries.[120]

The proceedings of the Siena–Arezzo dispute demonstrate how royal authority could founder when confronted with the tight nexus of local political alliances – in this case between the bishop and gastalds of Siena. Yet it is also clear that the mechanics of royal intervention generated some paperwork in the form of records of proceedings and the conclusions of the judges, as can be seen in other examples of the *missi* or *actores* in action.[121]

So far the discussion has centred on the uses of charters issued, either from the centres of government or by private individuals, and the attitude of the courts and judges towards charters as proof of a claim. What evidence is there for other forms of communication used amongst the hierarchy of Lombard administration? The *Liber pontificalis* records that Liutprand, after his summit-meeting with Pope Zachary in Terni (*c.* 742), 'sent his letters' to Tuscany and the Po plain to order the release of captives from Roman towns.[122] The Lombard law code, and in particular eighth-century legislation, provides further information concerning the literate practices of government in the *regnum*.

When disputes involved people from the same judicial district but under the administration of different *sculdahis*, the accuser must go 'cum

---

[119] CDL 19 (715, 20 June). This *inquisitio* of Gunteram was preserved separately from the other five documents concerning this dispute (CDL 4, 17, 20: CDL III.12, 13), recorded on a parchment roll and dated by Bischoff from the second half of the ninth century to the first third of the tenth: Brühl, CDL III, p. 52. We learn from CDL 20 that Gunteram interrogated the Sienese gastald Tagipert also. Siena appears to have had two gastalds simultaneously: Tagipert and Warnefrit (on the latter see also CDL 50).

[120] Ecclesiastical court, CDL 20 (July 15, 'in vico qui dicitur Uualari'). Royal court, CDL III.13 (14 Oct.). This last is not merely the confirmation of a judgement of a *maiordomus*, as with CDL III.12, but a complete rehearing. On the dispute's history, Gasparri, 'Il regno longobardo in Italia. Struttura e funzionamento di uno stato altomedievale', in Cammarosano and Gasparri (eds.), *Langobardia*, pp. 237–305, at pp. 241–9.

[121] See CDL 21 (716): 'Ultianus notarius et missus domni regis'; CDL 113 (754); CDL 233 (769): 'qualiter rex inter eas diuisione fecet per misso suo'; CDL 252 (771): 'Notitia brevis memoratio . . . in corum presentia . . . Autpert actor domini regi'.

[122] LP 93.9.

misso aut epistola de suo sculdahi' to the defendant's regional *sculdahis* and notify him of the charge, forcing that *sculdahis* to render a decision within four to six days.[123] We should note that communication between the *sculdaheis* took place with the use of a messenger (*missus*) or by letter, for in the following law concerning disputes between people from different judicial districts (*civitates*), Liutprand requested that the higher administrative office of judges in both districts arrange the case to be heard, and dropped the option of a messenger: the plaintiff must take with him a letter from his judge to the judge of the defendant.[124] Likewise, Ratchis decreed that judges must warn a *gasindus* 'aut per epistola aut proprio ore' of his misconduct towards any *arrimanus*.[125]

Further evidence of the literate environment in which the office of judge functioned can be seen in Ratchis' first act of legislation concerning the failure of judges to fulfil their duties. The law would appear to be 'reactive' in responding to fundamental problems and dissatisfaction with the system, for Ratchis stated that he and his retinue 'cannot go anywhere' without being besieged by complaints and appeals. The king reminded judges of their obligations to preside over their courts themselves and not take bribes: 'sicut iam per manum scriptam nobis promiserunt'.[126] The meaning here is difficult: *scriptam* would appear to agree with *manum*, though an implied *cartolam* is possible. The sense of the phrase is something akin to 'as the judges promised to us by means of writing (or a written contract) with their own hand'. The judges possibly had some form of written contract with the king. Was it a letter, a substantially long promise of good conduct listing the duties and obligations to be fulfilled, or was it merely subscription (autographed formula or *signum manus*) to a document already drawn up by the king's court? The formulae used to describe a subscription elsewhere in the code (*ponere manum*), particularly that used in the legislation of Ratchis,[127] tend to suggest that it was something more, but we can only guess as to its form, or how far down the administrative ladder the use of these mysterious *scriptae* reached. In the same law Ratchis also exhorted judges to admonish other local officials ('schudahis, centini, locopositi, vel quos sub se habent ordinatos'), so that these latter act righteously 'and promise thus to their judge, just as (*sicut*) the judges themselves have promised us'. The *sicut* would appear to refer to the promise made *per manum scriptam* mentioned previously in the law, and if so it suggests that Ratchis was

---

[123] Liutprand 26.   [124] Liutprand 27.   [125] Ratchis 14.   [126] Ratchis 1.
[127] For example, Liutprand 22: 'ut ipso parentes, qui inter fuerent, aut iudex in cartola ipsa manum ponant'. Ratchis, 8, made a distinction between autographs and *signum manus* formula: 'et testes in ipsa cartola subscripserint aut manus posuerint et manifestaverint in ipsa cartola quod pretium inter eos statutum suscepisset'.

Literacy in Lombard Italy, c. 568–774

urging (or describing) the use of written contracts between judges and the lesser officials under their jurisdiction.

For regulating the management of royal estates, around 733 Liutprand issued a special series of six *praecepta*, the *Notitia de actoribus regis*, essentially a forerunner of the Carolingian capitulary, which detailed the duties and responsibilities of the men selected to administer the royal *curtes*. The first requirement of the king was that the *actor* swear upon the Gospels that 'If I should learn of anything that is against the regulations, I will make this known (*facio notitiam*) to the king, so that the matter will be resolved.'[128] Given the choice of the word *notitia* to describe the royal decrees themselves, it is plausible that the *notitia* to be supplied by the *actor* was a written document. Moreover, Liutprand warned his agents that the royal court possessed a 'list (*breve*) of all the territories that pertained to those estates' in case any royal property be bought from the *aldii* or servants attached to those estates; composition to be paid for doing so was to be in accordance with that 'which was written... in the Edict'. To avoid confusion, any purchases of royal property were to be confirmed in a royal charter.[129]

Whether it was a reflection of an increasingly hostile political environment in the mid-eighth century, or the logical development of Liutprand's state-centralising initiatives, Ratchis tightened the controls on those crossing the frontiers of his kingdom, 'so that neither our enemies nor our people can send spies through [the boundaries] or allow fugitives to go out, and so that no man can enter [our kingdom] without a royal seal or royal letter'.[130] Ratchis further added that, in the case of pilgrims heading for Rome, the judge should question the pilgrims to ascertain their origins and if their motives are true. If the judge be satisfied with their response, he should then:

issue a passport (*clusarius syngraphus*), placing it on a wax tablet and setting his seal upon it, so that afterwards the travellers may show this notice to our appointed agents. After this notice has been sent to us, our agents shall give the travellers a letter to enable them to go to Rome; when they return from Rome, they shall receive the mark of the king's seal ring.[131]

---

[128] *Notitia* 1.
[129] *Notitia* 5: 'per omnes curtes nostras brebi facimus de omni territuria de ipsas pertinentes'. Confusion: 'praeceptum fecimus aut feceremus'. Cf. Nelson, 'Literacy in Carolingian government', pp. 273–8.
[130] Ratchis 13: 'sine signo aut epistola regis'. Fisher-Drew trans., p. 223–4, translates as 'without a letter sealed by the king', but *aut* suggests an option of two different objects.
[131] Ratchis 13: 'faciat iudex aut clusarius syngraphus et mittat in cera et ponant sibi sigillum suum, ut ipsi postea ostendant ipsum signum missis nostris quos nos ordaenaverimus. Signum post hoc missus nostri faciant eis epistola ad romam ambulandi; et con venerent da romo, accipiant signo de anolo regis.' Again, Fischer-Drew trans., pp. 223–4, 'the judges shall collect these letters that

Law and government

While no doubt the need for tight border controls was directed towards curbing Frankish incursions, the use of the term *syngraphus* may also point towards the Byzantine areas, as do the similar laws of Aistulf requiring 'Roman' merchants to have letters of regal authority prior to entering Lombard territory and conducting business.[132] We can only speculate as to the ideological motives behind the requirement that pilgrims returning from Rome receive the mark of the king's seal-ring. In any case, the legislation of Liutprand, Ratchis and Aistulf portrays a bureaucratic system of checks and balances centred around the power of royal *signa* and *litterae*. The failure of a judge or *sculdahis* to adhere to these measures meant death and confiscation of his property; if the judge or *sculdahis* was deceived or unaware, he had the chance of clearing himself, but was still fined his *wergeld* for incompetence.[133]

What of the other offices in the kingdom that we know so little about, such as the *maiordomus*, *vestarius*, *camerarius*, *actionarius*, or those with more Germanic titles such as the *maraphis*, *scilpor*, *scaffard*, *antepor*, *stolesaz*, or even *gastald*? The code does not mention them in relation to literate practices. Yet the concentration on the offices of *iudex*, *sculdahis*, *missus* and *gasindus* covers a lot of administrative ground. Dukes and gastalds are often simply called *iudices* in charters.[134] Aside from their judicial function, dukes and gastalds controlled the local circumscriptions, based on the Roman city-territories and ecclesiastical dioceses.[135] The *sculdahis* was a regional officer within that territory commanded by the gastald or duke, though we have no idea how many there were in one territory. Naturally, the law code only refers to the use of letters amongst these officials in relation to judicial matters. We can only speculate upon the uses of other

---

bear the seal of the king's ring' is misleading: the *peregrini* (those who come '*da romo* [sic!]') are the subject of *accipiant*, not the judges. The specific mention of a seal ring (*signo de anolo regis*) should not be equated with the previous phrase (*sine signo aut epistola regis*) used in relation to those crossing the borders. See G. Tangl, 'Die Passvorschrift des Königs Ratchis und ihre Beziehung zu dem Verhältnis zwischen Franken und Langobarden vom 6.–8. Jahrhundert', *Quellen und Forschungen aus Italienischen Archiven und Bibliotheken* 38 (1958), 1–66. Walter Pohl has pointed out to me that the manuscript tradition of Ratchis 13 and 14 (found only in Vat. lat. 5535 9, and Cava dei Tirreni 4) suggests that these two laws were issued separately as *capitularia*, possibly in the same manner of the *Memoratio de mercedes commacinorum*. They were certainly accepted as law by the time of Aistulf 5.

[132] Aistulf 4, 5, 6. Only this last law, 'De navigio et terreno negotio', explicitly mentions a letter ('sine epistula regis aut sine voluntate iudicis sui'), but the use of 'sine voluntate regis' in the others implies the use of some type of letter or seal in the context of the previous laws of Ratchis.
[133] Ratchis 13, Aistulf 4, 5, 6, 7.
[134] E.g. CDL 21. Ratchis 4 clearly demonstrates the use of *iudex* in a military context. On the titles and offices, see Delogu, 'Lombard and Carolingian Italy', in R. McKitterick (ed.), *NCMH*, II (Cambridge, 1995), pp. 290–319, at pp. 291–3; Barnwell, *Kings, Courtiers*, pp. 54–96.
[135] Wickham, *EMI*, p. 41; Tabacco, *The Struggle*, pp. 99–116; Harrison, *Early State*, pp. 54–96; Gasparri, 'Il regno longobardo', pp. 237–305.

forms of literacy that such officials might have used: registers for military service, accounts, letters of military command, archives of proceedings in the judicial or military sphere, etc. In the Siena–Arezzo dispute, clerics who lived within the boundaries of the territory of Siena took with them a letter from their *gastaldius* when they went to find the bishop of Arezzo in order to be consecrated.[136] The *placita* and royal charters demonstrate *maiordomi* and *notarii regis* in action as the king's *missi*, going off to various parts of the kingdom to hear cases along with *gastaldi*, issuing documents recording their decisions.[137] Whether or not the court cases were arranged by an exchange of letters between the local administration and central government is unknown, but certainly plausible given the evidence of the code.

CONCLUSION

The Lombard law code was not simply an expression of royal ideology without practical purpose or effect. Lombard kings attempted to regulate the activities of Italo-Lombard society by the use of written law. The acts of legislation alone presuppose a literate audience to understand the content of the laws and to live by their precepts. The adherence to written law concerning property, inheritance, manumission and the economic activities of women is amply demonstrated by the charter evidence, as is the adherence to laws concerning the form and function of charters themselves. The direct correspondence between the precepts of the law and the contents of charters demonstrates the effectiveness of the law code and its circulation amongst a considerable proportion of the population. This went beyond judges who were expected to know, and did know, the content of the law code prescribing correct forms of conduct for themselves and for those under their authority. Explicit references to the law code in charters or the borrowings of its language are common.[138]

---

[136] CDL 19, p. 65, line 14; likewise, Florentinus, p. 67, line 7; Firmolus, p. 67, line 15; Teodald, p. 72, line l; Aufrit and friends, p. 69, line 26. *Litterae rogatoriae* went the other way, from the *vicedominus* of Arezzo to the bishop of Siena, p. 68, line 22. This appears to be a slight variation on Liutprand 27: the letter should also be delivered to a *iudex* of the neighbouring district, rather than to the bishop.

[137] As with the Siena–Arezzo dispute (CDL 17, 19, 20, 21; CDL III.4) so too with the dispute between the gastalds of Parma and Piacenza (CDL III.6) which, as the king discovered, had already been settled by his predecessor Arioald (626–636). See G.P. Bognetti, 'Il gastaldato longobardo e i giudicati di Adaloaldo, Arioaldo e Pertarido nella lite tra Parma e Piacenza', *L'età*, I, pp. 219–74; Sinatti d'Amico, *Le prove*, pp. 176–9. Cf. CDL III.22 (747), Ratchis confirmed previous privileges granted by Liutprand and those now administered by his *missi*.

[138] For more examples, see F. Sinatti d'Amico, 'L'applicazione dell'Edictum in Tuscia', *Atti V CISAM* (Spoleto, 1973), 745–81; Pohl-Resl, 'Rechtsfähigkeit'.

Law and government

The charter evidence forces us to consider the effectiveness of the code in those areas of law for which we have no confirmatory sources, such as criminal or personal law. Laws which define the precise sound of head-bones being broken at a distance of 12 feet, or which protect women crouching to relieve themselves, may be attributed to either *ad hoc* reactive legislation addressing a particular case, or to ancient customs (Liutprand's *cawerfeda antiqua*), or to some combination of these.[139] The impression one gains is of a precise and ambitious use of the written word to circumscribe a vast array of social mores and customs. The code not only meticulously fixed sums of composition as penalties for crimes and misdemeanours. It also fixed prices for labour costs of specialists in construction work.[140] The attempt to cover such extensive grounds under the umbrella of written law would not, and could not, have been undertaken by kings unless there was an audience for it. But the influence must work both ways. Written law was used because there was a sufficient amount of people who were sufficiently literate to make it work. Conversely, people learned literate skills partly in order to know right from wrong as defined by those who governed the society in which they lived, to protect themselves and their freedom under the umbrella of written law.[141] The corollary to the use of written law was adherence to the ideal of the state which produced that law.

The Lombard state and written law worked together in a partnership that was founded upon an established base of legal literacy that owed much to the tenacity of late Roman property law and its preference for written instruments. But more than that, adherence to written law was esteemed, and Lombard rulers, at least from Liutprand onwards, sought to associate themselves with written law as a source of prestige. It was precisely his capacity for legislative reform that earned Liutprand the unique epithet from Paul the Deacon of *nutritor gentis*.[142] Both Ratchis and Aistulf were sure to follow suit in promulgating law. Desiderius' legislative silence is difficult to explain, though his submission to both Frankish and papal demands to secure the throne may have played a large part, at least initially.

---

[139] Rothari 47, Liutprand 125. Cf. Grimoald 6, Ratchis 12, Aistulf 15. *Cawarfeda antiqua*, Liutprand 77, 133.

[140] *Memoratio de mercedes commacinorum*, to be attributed to either Grimoald or Liutprand: Azzara (ed.), *Le leggi*, pp. 221–6. Cf. the *Pactus Commacinus*, ed. in L.M. Hartmann, *Zur Wirtschaftsgeschichte Italiens im frühen Mittelalter* (Gotha, 1904), pp. 123–4; Eng. trans. R. Balzaretti, 'Cities, emporia and monasteries: local economies of the Po Valley 700–875', in N. Christie and S. Loseby (eds.), *Towns in Transition: Urban Evolution in Late Antiquity and the Early Middle Ages* (Aldershot, 1996) pp. 213–34, at pp. 219–20.

[141] See E.W. Stevens Jr., *Literacy, Law, and the Social Order* (Dekalb, 1988).

[142] *HL* VI.58. Cf. Rothari, *HL* IV.42, 47; Grimoald and Perctarit V.33; other kings II.29, 31; III.35; IV.41, 42, 48, 51; VI.17.

He certainly issued charters, as did his co-regent son, independently of his father.¹⁴³ Kings legislated for different reasons, and we need not see any necessary connection between the issue of legislation and greater appreciation or experience of literacy in the person of the king or at his court. Liutprand, we are told by Paul, was illiterate.¹⁴⁴ Cunincpert awarded prizes to grammar teachers, and Aripert II, whose concern for justice was renowned, issued a royal charter written in gold letters to the pope.¹⁴⁵ Neither king legislated. To expect them to have done so as 'proof' of their appreciation of literacy, or their exploitation of literacy to govern, is anachronistic. More important than individual kings, however, were the institutions that maintained this legal literacy in Lombard Italy. They are taken for granted in the sources, and are obscured from out view: Lombard legislation does not mention the names or qualifications of the anonymous jurists who composed it, nor do the scribes of charters ever tell us how and where they learned their trade. But both found employment in the society ruled by Lombard government. It is time now to look a little more closely at the scribes and their handiwork.

---

¹⁴³ CDL III.31, 33, 34, 35, 36, 39 40, 41, 43; Adelchis 37, 38, 42, 44.
¹⁴⁴ *HL* VI.58: 'litterarum quidem ignarus, sed philosophis aequandus'. As topos, see B. Baldwin, 'Illiterate emperors', *Historia* 38 (1998), 124–6; Moorhead, *Theoderic*, pp. 104–6; as reference to classical literary culture, Grundmann, '*Litteratus–illiteratus*', pp. 15–16, 24–6.
¹⁴⁵ Cunincpert *HL* VI.7; Aripert II, *LP* 88:3, ed. Duchesne, I, p. 385 (John VII), the source for Paul's mention of same, *HL* VI.28 (or Bede, *Chron*. 575). On Aripert II, see below, p. 288.

5

CHARTERS

There are over 370 'private' charters which survive from the Lombard period. Most of these are originals, and we know that many more were written. In the introduction to this study I briefly discussed the way in which Petrucci has examined the Italian charters for evidence of literacy by concentrating on the percentage of autograph subscriptions to charters by witnesses. This type of analysis can yield interesting results, particularly with respect to determining the extent of a person's familiarity with writing by the fluency of their hand, as we shall see below. But in focusing solely upon the act of writing as a definition of literacy, we can also lose sight of the sociological, even anthropological, aspect of the function of written modes of communication in a given society. We need to ask not only how people subscribed to charters, but what they thought about charters when they did so. Chris Wickham's study of recorded court cases (*placita*) examined attitudes towards written documents as evidence in Lombard and Carolingian Italy.[1] The authority of a charter as evidence went beyond mere symbolic significance; charters were read out in court, examined for authenticity and signs of proper notarial forms, and judged as to whether they had been drawn up in accordance to written norms or not. The court procedures recorded revealed 'the attachment of early medieval Italians to written legal norms', for 'written evidence was of supreme importance... Charters had force, and people felt it.'[2]

The examination of court cases has done much to show how charters reflect social relations and the currents of political and economic power that bind groups together for common purposes and action. But the emphasis is firmly on the end product; that is, how the charter testifies to an act that has happened. Such an approach risks neglecting how a

---

[1] 'Land disputes', in Davies and Fouracre (eds.), *The Settlement of Disputes*.Cf. R. Collins, 'Visigothic law and regional custom in disputes in early medieval Spain', in *ibid.*, pp. 207–14. Wickham's article is reprinted, with revisions and additions, in his *Land and Power*, pp. 229–57.
[2] Wickham, 'Land disputes', in *Land and Power*, pp. 239–40.

charter itself 'happened', or how, as an end product, it came into being.[3] That is to say, we cannot understand the role of charters as instruments of written communication unless we know something of the social and historical processes at work that created the *loca* for the use of charters, and how such forces determined their form and structure.

In this chapter I should like to examine Lombard charters as evidence for literate practices along the following lines of enquiry: who wrote charters, how and where did they learn to do so, what type of training was required, how were charters written, and finally where and how were they preserved? Asking such questions raises many issues concerning the development of documentary practices in this period, and throughout the following the attempt will be made to place the Lombard material in its historical setting. Lombard charters have, on the whole, been seen by scholars of diplomatics and law as further confirmation of a type of 'privatisation' of the modes of documentary proof in the early medieval west.[4] As I have tried to show elsewhere, this characterisation of developments is misleading.[5] The form and content of Lombard charters suggest that, far from being products of a less organised and less literate post-Roman political order, the charters of Lombard Italy have deep Roman roots in a legal culture of property law and practice that changed little, if at all, with the arrival of the new barbarian overlords.

Royal or ducal charters were discussed in the previous chapter in relation to law and government. The focus of this chapter is on 'private' charters, and I have concentrated on the collection of 295 private charters from Tuscany and northern Italy edited in Luigi Schiaparelli's *Codice diplomatico longobardo*, of which 80 per cent or more were transcribed from surviving originals. The originality of these documents permits palaeographical analyses, either by first-hand examination of the document, or by consultation with the excellent facsimiles contained in the *Chartae latinae antiquiores* collection, as a means of ascertaining or clarifying certain issues that relate to the script-culture in which this type of 'documentary'

---

[3] See P. Rück, 'Die Urkunde als Kunstwerk', in A. von Euw and P. Schreiner (eds.), *Kaiserin Theophanu*, 2 vols. (Cologne, 1991), pp. 311–33; and note the comments of K. Heidecker (ed.), *Charters and the Written Word in Medieval Society* (Turnhout, 2000), pp. 10–12.
[4] The best survey is P. Classen, 'Fortleben und Wandel'; also Classen, *Kaiserreskript und Königsurkunde: Diplomatische Studien zum Problem der Kontinuität zwischen Altertum und Mittelalter*, Byzantine Texts and Studies 15 (Thessalonika, 1977); building on the work of H. Steinacker, *Die antiken Grundlagen der frühmittelalterlichen Privaturkunden* (Leipzig and Berlin, 1927). Still fundamental is H. Bresslau, *Handbuch der Urkundenlehre für Deutschland und Italien*, 2 vols. (Leipzig and Berlin, 1889/1931).
[5] Everett, 'Scribes and charters'.

Charters

or 'pragmatic' literacy operated.[6] In contrast, the charters from the duchies of Spoleto or Benevento mostly concern a small number of ecclesiastical institutions (as the Spoletan collection relates exclusively to the monastery of Farfa) and do not come down to us in their original form. They were transmitted, moreover, in cartularies or later copies, and are best left aside for my purposes here. They will be referred to only when they throw some light on questions relating to charters of Schiaparelli's CDL collection.[7]

NOTARIES AND SCRIBES

Who wrote Lombard charters, and what authority, if any, did they have to do so? An expedient method for attempting to answer such questions is to concentrate on the qualificatory titles scribes gave themselves in their work and to ask whether these titles represent any particular office or occupation whose specific function was the writing of documents. In particular, the use of the title *notarius* by many scribes of Lombard documents raises a series of issues concerning the continuity of late Roman administration and documentary practices, and the existence of a social hierarchy centred on the function of writing.[8] One particular strain of Italian historiography has concentrated on finding the 'origins' of the modern Italian 'notariato' in the *notarii* who penned Lombard charters.[9]

---

[6] For the terms in relation to later periods, see H. Keller, C. Meier and T. Scharff (eds.), *Schriftlichkeit und Lebenspraxis im Mittelalter: Erfassen, Bewahren, Verändern* (Munich, 1999); R. Britnell (ed.), *Pragmatic Literacy: East and West, 1200–1300* (Woodbridge, 1997).

[7] See above, p. 189.

[8] See E. Durando, *Il tabellionato o notariato nelle leggi romane, nelle leggi medievali italiane e posteriori* (Turin, 1897), pp. 24–60; O. Redlich, 'Die Privaturkunden des Mittelalters', in G. von Below and F. Meinecke (eds.), *Handbuch der mittelalterlichen und neueren Geschichte* (Berlin, 1911), p. 19: Bresslau, *Handbuch*, pp. 127, 560; Viscardi, *Le origini*, pp. 212ff. G. Mengozzi, *La città italiana nell'altomedievo*, 2nd edn, ed. A. Solmi (Florence, 1931), pp. 254–5; Mengozzi, *Ricerche sull'attività della scuola di Pavia nell'altomedioevo* (Pavia, 1924), pp. 198ff. Contra Mengozzi, Riché, *Education*, p. 413. Petrucci, *Notarii*, p. 6. More recently, Radding, *Origins*, pp. 1–44. On general history of the term *notarius*, Leclercq, 'Notaire', *Dictionnaire*, XII, 2, coll. 1623–24. The best overall survey of the history of the Italian notariate is A. Petrucci, *Notarii: documenti per la storia del notariato italiano* (Milan, 1958). On the earlier period, see M. Amelloti, 'L' età romana', in part I of M. Amelloti and G. Costamagna, *Alle origini del notariato Italiano*, Studi Storici sul Notariato Italiano 2 (Rome, 1974), pp. 1–142. Also Jones, *Later Roman Empire*, I, pp. 515–16, 691–2. Still fundamental, Bresslau *Handbuch*, I, 2, pp. 187–91.

[9] Numerous examples of this can be found in the series Studi Storici sul Notariato Italiano, esp.: no. 4, A. Liva, *Notariato e documento notarile a Milano, dall'altomedioevale alla fine del Settecento* (Rome, 1979), pp. 5–33; no. 6, M. Amelotti et al., *Per una storia del notariato meridionale* (Rome, 1982), in particular M. Galante, 'Il notaio e il documento notarile a Salerno in epoca longobarda', pp. 71–94; no. 8, *Il notariato nella civiltà Toscana* (Rome, 1985), esp. A. Petrucci, 'Modello notarile e testualità', pp. 123–47, and M. Montorzi, 'Il notaio di tribunale come pubblico funzionario: un primo quadro di problemi e qualche spunto analitico', pp. 5–60.

This line of enquiry seeks to determine whether the *notarii* of the Lombard period, like their Roman predecessors and later medieval successors, enjoyed *fides publica*, that is, recognition by the state of their authority to draw up valid legal documents, an authority enshrined in the laws of the state and in the establishment of an institutionalised profession. Thus, the debates over the Italian evidence are similar to those concerning the concept of the *Gerichtsschreiber* or 'public notary' in Carolingian Francia,[10] with the exception that the Italian debates weigh much more heavily the concept of 'public', owing to Italian historical development and the existence of the modern Italian institution of 'il notariato' and 'i notai' as a cornerstone of the Italian legal system.[11] We need to move away from preoccupations with the origins of modern institutions and examine the evidence.

To break down the different titles used amongst the 175 charters in which the scribe gives some type of title, fifty-five scribes used *notarius* to define themselves, clearly the largest proportion of the titles given, seconded by *clericus* (twenty-six) then *diaconus* (twenty-three) and *presbiter* (twenty); the rest are quite lowly numbers, except for *vir clarissimus* and *scriptor* with twelve each. The low number of fifty-five *notarii* out of 175 titles, however, diminishes even more when compared to the eighty-five or so writers who gave themselves no title whatsoever. To obfuscate the position of *notarius* even more, we rarely have more than one, two, or at most three charters written by the same *notarius* with which we could follow his work or draw conclusions about the professionalism of his office. The scribe who gives us the greatest number of original charters, nine, is Maurace of Piacenza, who defined himself only as *vir clarissimus*. His record is followed by five or six each for two Lucchese scribes, Prandulus and the *presbiter* Gaudentius, both of whom were in service of the Lucchese church.[12] Hence the redactors of Lombard charters were in no way a monopoly of *notarii*, for the title of *notarius* was given by only 25 per cent of those who wrote charters and qualified themselves in some way. It seems an even less impressive figure when we consider that a higher 30 per cent of writers felt no need to qualify themselves in any way whatsoever. Quantitative reckonings can never give us certainties.[13] But a total

---

[10] See McKitterick, *Carolingians*, pp. 118–20.

[11] For discussion on Italian historiography of this period, see Tabacco, *The Struggle*, pp. 1–36; C.J. Wickham, *The Mountains and the City: The Tuscan Apennines in the Early Middle Ages* (Oxford, 1988), pp. xiii–xxvii.

[12] On Maurace, see below. Prandulus, CDL 135, 136, 178, 227, 286. Gaudentius 61, 67, 73, 76, 95, 99. This does not include Stephanus, the Spoletan scribe who wrote nineteen private charters.

[13] See A. Petrucci's review of David Cressy's *Literacy and the Social Order: Reading and Writing in Tudor and Stuart England* (Cambridge, 1980), 'David Cressy: sull'alfabetismo in Inghilterra', *Quaderni Storici* 51/a. Dec. (1982), 1129–33.

Charters

of 25 per cent, combined with the fact that the writers qualified themselves with *notarius* twice as often as any other title, is sufficient evidence to suggest the importance of the title to those who wrote charters or wanted them written. The reason *why* the title was important requires further analysis.

An examination of the law code yields interesting clues, if not definite answers. The first thing that strikes us is that not once do we find the word *notarius*; instead 'scriba' is the noun preferred by royal legislation, 'scrivane' being used on one occasion by Ratchis.[14] To exaggerate the discorrelation even more, not one of our 290 or so documents from the Lombard kingdom mentions the word *scriba*. There is sufficient evidence, however, that the Lombard kings both knew of and used *notarii* for administrative purposes at the royal court from the very beginnings of the *regnum*. Narrative sources testify to *notarii* in direct service of the kings Agilulf (590–616) and Adaloald (616–26). Rothari defined his legislative notary in the laws as 'Ansoald notarius noster', and a diploma of Perctarit (674) also refers to 'Ausone notario nostro'.[15] The only reference we have to an actual *notarius sacri palatii* comes in the eighth century from Liutprand's first act of legislation (713).[16] This was probably the same 'Poto' who appears simply as 'notarius' in Liutprand's diploma of 715.[17] Again, in the eighth century, when our evidence is more ample, private charters refer to a *notarius regiae postestatis*, though three of these actually refer to men with the title acting as witnesses.[18] In addition, the combination of *notarius et missus* is used twice to describe Gunteram's position in the Siena–Arezzo dispute in the early eighth century. The term is also used to describe the role of king's representative, Ultianus, in a dispute

---

[14] Liutprand 22, 91, Ratchis 8.
[15] Rothari 388, perhaps looking back to the *Marcianus notarius regis / sedis regiae* of Odovacer in 489, L. Schiaparelli, *Raccolta di documenti latini*, I, *Documenti romani* (Como, 1923), p. 120. Paul the Deacon, *HL* IV. 35: 'Stabilicianum notarium suum [i.e. Agilulfi]'; Jonas, *Vita Columbani* 2.7 (ed. Krusch, p. 247): 'Aureus Adalualdi regis Langobardorum notarium'; Perctarit, CDL III.6. The references to *notarii* in the two charters of Adaloald (CDL III.2, 3, of 624 and 625–626 respectively) are possibly later interpolations: see Brühl, *Studien*, p. 13.
[16] Liutprand 6. Fisher-Drew trans., pp. 146–7, fails to include this law.
[17] CDL III.12.
[18] CDL 17, Siena 714, copy saec. XI, *notitia iudicati*, *Sichifredus notarius regis*, writer: CDL 18, Pavia 714, copy saec. XII, *Auferat notarius regis* and *Todo notarius regiae postestatis* witnesses: CDL 21, Pieve a Nievole 716, copy saec. XVII, *notitiia iudicati*, *Ebregausus notarius regiae postestatis*, writer: CDL 36, Milan 725, orig., *Faustinus notarius regiae postestatis*, writer: CDL 137, Pavia 759, orig., *Audo notarius regiae postestatis*, writer: CDL 155, Pavia 761, copy XII, *Gumpert notarius regiae postestatis*, writer: CDL 226, Pavia 769, orig., *Gunpert notarius regiae postestatis*, witness: CDL 225, 768 (prob. Pavia), copy saec. VII, *Aufret notarius regis*, writer. The term *notarius regis*, though found frequently, is not present in any original document. Schiaparelli, 'Note diplomatiche, 1. I notai', p. 19, argued that it was the result of a mistake on the part of copyists for *regiae potestatis*.

of 716. The document recording the *placitum publicum* was redacted by Ebregausus *notarius regie potestatis*.[19]

The ample evidence for the title *notarius* being well known and used at the royal court and by royal authorities themselves in the eighth century begs the question of why *notarius* never appears in royal legislative acts and the word *scriba* (or later *scrivane*) was preferred. I should like to suggest that *scriba*, 'writer',[20] was a deliberate choice of neutral terminology that would encompass the wide variety of document-writers who existed throughout the kingdom, without attempting to designate any particular qualifications or social status as necessary prerequisites for the ability to write a legally valid document. In other words, the purpose of *scriba* may have been to encourage the use of charters in the juridical system and not confine such activities to certain groups or individuals in a tightly defined hierarchy. Further, the deliberate use of *scriba* presupposes a fairly widespread critical mass of writing ability amongst the Italo-Lombard population ready to be pooled for occasions when the inhabitants of the *regnum* needed to document their transactions with one another. Indeed the often emphasised *reactive* quality of Lombard legislation suggests that the royal court is merely trying to curtail the abuses of a system in which there was a plethora of writers and documentary activity already at work.

The situation was not novel. We should not be too alarmed by the lack of specificity in Lombard legislation with respect to the titles scribes were to use. Late Roman imperial legislation was just as carefree. The word *notarius* is not used in the Theodosian or Justinianic codes, *tabellio* being the preferred expression for someone who writes documents for the general public.[21] The specification of a certain type of writer is rare. In fourth- and fifth-century legislation the term *scriba* is used in a manner which suggests that the term could be applied equally to those who wrote for some type of public office or for the general public when they wished to record private transactions.[22] In late Roman law, the status of the scribe does not appear to have been an issue for the creation of a legally valid

---

[19] Gunteram, CDL 19, 20; CDL 21, 'Ultianus notarius et missus'.

[20] Semantic differences in late antiquity: 'clerk or poet', Harris, *Ancient Literacy*, p. 159; 'scholar', Richter, *Formation*, p. 51. The same ambiguity can be seen in modern English's use of 'writer', see A. Gaur, *A History of Writing*, rev. edn (London, 1992). Our best guide is perhaps Isidore: 'ab scribendo autem scriba nomen accepit', *Etym.*, VI.14, 9, repeated by Paul the Deacon in his epitome of Festus, *Sexti Pompei Festi: De verborum significatu cum Pauli epitome*, ed. W.M. Lindsay (Leipzig, 1933), pp. 446–8.

[21] CTh 9.19.1 (316) (= CJ 9.22, Brev. 9.15.1). Note the *interpretatio*'s qualification of *tabellio*, 'qui admanuensis nunc dicitur'; CTh 12.1.3 (316), on *tabelliones* and the decurionate; cf. *NVal*. 15.1 (445), on sales tax.

[22] CTh 8.2.1 (= CJ 10.71) (341) prohibiting *tabularii* and *scribi* from performing imperial service in lieu of duties at municipal or provincial level; cf. CTh 8.9.1 (335); 11.8.3 (409) (= CJ 1.55.9).

document.²³ Legislative language of imperial edicts often refers to 'vera et sollemnis scriptura', 'scriptas iure ac sollemniter voluntates' and 'legitimas scripturas', but the qualities of *legitima* and *sollemnitas* did not derive from the status of the scribe. The emphasis was upon two other factors of equal importance. First, the correct number (five or seven) witnesses must testify to the transaction, and, in cases where the transaction was incomplete, to the intent of the person making the transaction, that is, the author of the document.²⁴ Second, that the price agreed upon be recorded in the document.²⁵ Both of these requirements, and indeed the redaction of a document itself, were part of the trend towards public performance in the development of Roman law, a trend evident in the legislation from Constantine onwards and one which reflects the practices of 'vulgar law' so methodically documented by Ernst Levy.²⁶ To the extent that property law in the Lombard code was based upon the Roman legal culture of vulgar law, the language of Ratchis' law cited above similarly refers to the need of the *scripta* to be 'ad testibus idoneis rovorata' and that the witnesses testify 'quod pretium inter eos statutum suscepisset'. The same principles extend to donations and other transactions, both in late Roman legislation and Lombard law. The socio-cultural phenomenon of creating a probative text for legitimating property rights over land-ownership was a well-established tradition that needed little, if any, regulation from a centralised government to make it legally valid and recognised by state authority.

These last twin concepts of legal validity and state recognition lead us straight into another conundrum posed by the evidence. In 746 King Ratchis legislated that:

if anyone has negotiated a charter of sale concerning any property, and the charter has been written by a public scribe (*ad scrivane publico scripta*), and confirmed by suitable witnesses, and the witnesses subscribe to the charter or place their hand upon it (to make the sign of the cross) to confirm that the vendor has received the price agreed upon by the parties concerned; and if the purchaser is afterward accused of not having paid the full price, he shall not be required to give an

---

²³ Some telling examples: *CTh* 2.27 (= *CJ* 4.2; *Brev.* 2.27), 'si certum petatur de chirographis'. Honorius (421) required the creditor to prove the authenticity of the document by the handwriting of the deceased and 'by many other proofs'; identifying and questioning the scribe are not mentioned. *CTh* 11.39.4 (= *CJ* 4.20.2; *Brev.* 11.14,), 'De fide testium et instrumentorum' (346), where *scriptura* is shown to be 'falso conscribta', or conversely 'veritate subnixa', without recourse to the scribe. Likewise *NTh* 16, 'De testamentis', recalls ancient practice wherein the testator may 'proferre scripturam vel ipsius testatoris vel cuiuslibet alterius manu conscriptam'.

²⁴ *CTh* 4.4, 'de testamentis et codicillis' (cf. *Brev.* 4.4; *CJ* 6.23; 6.36), esp. 4.4.5, and 4.4.7 (424). Note also the *interpretatio* concerning 'legitimas scripturas'.

²⁵ *NVal.* 32 (451). See also *CTh* 5.10.1.

²⁶ Levy, *West Roman Vulgar Law*, esp. pp. 128–37.

oath, unless he has obligated himself by pledges; the seller may then take pledges from the surety.[27]

What is the significance of Ratchis' use of the adjective *publicus* with *scriva*? Elsewhere in the Lombard law code, the word *publicus* as an adjective generally refers to the royal fisc or to some type of state official.[28] The choice of *publicus* by Ratchis, therefore, would appear to refer to something more than accessibility or availability of scribes, as Schiaparelli concluded.[29] Does the use of *publicus* refer to a writer somehow attached to an official of the state, such as a judge, gastald or *sculdahis*?

The charter evidence is equally inconclusive. One charter was redacted by a certain 'Gaff clericus notarius publico Bergomates'.[30] The additional use of *clericus* would appear to denote some type of association with an ecclesiastical institution, but there is no reference to such in the charter which, in terms of content, witnesses and place of redaction, is otherwise a document concerning affairs amongst the laity.[31] A *placitum* of 750, preserved in the Farfa *regestrum*, refers to a charter presented in court which was considered by the judges as 'fraudelentia pro qua re nec notarium verum nec habebant testimonia'.[32] To use this single reference as secure evidence of a publicly recognised office[33] is fraught with problems. First and foremost, it does not state *publicus* but the much looser definition of *verus*. Second, as a document from Gregorio di Catino's twelfth-century cartulary, it is less than trustworthy. It may reflect, therefore, the institutions of Gregorio's time rather than those of the eighth century. The wording of the judges also implies that the negation of the charter's validity was because of its failure to observe correct socio-legal procedure. In this case, the procedure involved the procuring of valid witnesses (*testimonia*) which would have rooted the document in a social environment so that the claims of its contents could have been tested by interrogation of the witnesses who subscribed. This is the same emphasis on the social context of the charter's redaction that can be seen in Ratchis'

---

[27] Ratchis 8. Cf. Fischer-Drew trans., p. 221.
[28] Liutprand 35, 57, 63, 121, 148, 152. Also used as a substantive for 'official' (*publicus loci*), Liutprand 141, 142. *Notitia* 5. DuCange, *Glossarium*, VI–VII, p. 587. In the case of wild women attacking weak men, the 'publicus... conprehendat ipsas mulieres' of Liutprand 141 seems to mean judge, but could mean any of the recognised authorities that might be in that place, such as a *sculdaheis* or *gastaldus* – our knowledge on how these positions relate to that of judge is indeed sketchy, Delogu, 'Lombard and Carolingian Italy', pp. 291–3; Barnwell, *Kings, Courtiers and Imperium*, pp. 109–23. Costamagna and Amellot; *Alle origini*, pp. 163–4, insists on 'judge', but *iudices* are specifically named when necessary throughout the law code.
[29] Schiaparelli, 'Note diplomatiche', I, p. 32.   [30] CDL 285.
[31] The *rogator* of the document, Agepertus *vir venerabilis*, also defined himself as *clericus*. The witnesses are all *viri devoti*. The charter was 'Actum in vico Castellis', which remains unidentified. The combination of Gaff's titles is similar to the *exceptores* found in our charters: see below.
[32] CDL IV.1.12.   [33] *Pace* Costamagna and Amelotti, *Alle origini*, p. 176.

Charters

law mentioned above. Clear reference to a charter written by a 'public notary' can be found in a *placitum* of 887, though the charter was also contested because it was not 'written according to the law' nor signed by witnesses.[34] Hence the lack of reference to a *notarius* in the law code and its adequate attestation, both in private charters and in the context of some type of investment of royal authority (*regiae potestatis*), forces us to ask the same question that Bullough asked thirty years ago in relation to the *notarius ducis* of the Spoletan charters:[35] was there a specifically defined office or position located within the sphere of the royal entourage or palace, or did *regiae potestatis* simply refer to a writer contracted to write a royal document, commissioned from a pool of professional lay notaries or writers already practising their craft for private individuals, be it inside or outside Pavia? Other similar uses of the term *regiae potestatis* for various offices suggest a circle of people centred around the Pavese court, as do the contents and location of the documents.[36] Since we know almost nothing of the specific offices to which these titles seem to be referring (that is, the duration of the position or the terms of appointment), we can say nothing more as to whether the notaries *regiae postestatis* were in fact a publicly recognised group of professionals deriving their authority from royal appointment.[37] We are left with sketchy impressions of high-status functionaries who in one way or another belong to an established court administrative culture, but we lack details.

The lack of detail similarly frustrates interpretation of the few (in fact, only three) references to *exceptores* as writers of Lombard documents.[38]

[34] Manaresi, *I Placiti*, 96; Cf. Wickham, 'Land disputes', in *Land and Power*, p. 240.
[35] Bullough, 'The writing office'.
[36] 'vesterarius regiae potestatis', CDL 48, see also CDL 257, 'Liutfret vesterarius', with no other qualification: 'maiescarius regiae potestatis', CDL 18: 'medicus regiae potestatis', CDL 38: similar expressions, 'gasindius regis', CDL 48 (Pavia), 155 (Pavia), 163 (Pistoia), 226 (Pavia), 228 (Leno, Brescia), 293 (Bergamo): 'gasindius domnae reginae', CDL 155, 226: 'antepor domnae reginae', CDL 226, 257 (Brescia): 'scafardo domae reginae', CDL 257: 'marcarius domnis regis', CDL 228, perhaps 'marsalc', as in CDL 257. See A. Solmi, *L'amministrazione finanzaria del regno italico nell'alto medioevo* (Pavia, 1932), pp. 32–4.
[37] See P. Vigo, 'Ricerche su notai e notabili longobardi del Sacro Palazzo di Pavia', *Ricerche Medievali* 4 (1969–70), 94–143, esp. p. 101; Schiaparelli, 'Note diplomatiche 1', p. 21.
[38] CDL 29, in the *eschatacol* of the charter, 'scripsi ego Uitalis v[ir] r[eligiosus] subdiac[onus] except[or] ciuitatis Placentinae', left out of the *completio*. CDL 48, 'Benedictus v[ir] r[eligiosus] subdiac[onus] et except[or] Ticinensis', who 'dictated' a Pavian charter of 730 (surviving in a contemporary Lucchese copy) to a certain 'Magnus notar[ius] s[an]ct[ae] Tic[inensis] eccl[esiae]'. The charter demonstrates interesting links between the Lucchese church and the Pavian court, the *rogatori* being Sigemund 'archpriest' of Lucca and his three brothers 'vir magnifici gasindi regis'. The copy was written by Osprand, whose career and script-type links him with a chancellery writing tradition of Lucca, see Petrucci, 'Il codice e i documenti', *Scriptores*, pp. 80–5. Bresslau, *Handbuch*, I, 2, pp. 355–7, identified the witnessing notary 'Teutpert' as the *illustris referendarius* of King Aistulf (CDL III.25, 26, 28), but these documents are dubious or simply falsifications (as in 26). CDL 82, 'Deusdedit exceptore' (there follows a frustrating lacuna in the charter); the *completio* lacks the qualification. On *exceptores* see Jones, *Later Roman Empire*, pp. 587–9.

A close look at the circumstances of the charters, however, negates any simplistic interpretation of continuity or that the use of such titles 'gives us no reason to doubt that these eighth century municipal officials fulfilled the same role as the functionaries in the antique *curia*'.[39] In two cases, the *exceptores* were also clerics ('subdiaconi'), and in two cases also the title of *exceptor* was coupled with the qualification of a place or city ('exceptor Ticinensis', 'exceptor civitatis Piacentinae'), as can be seen in two examples of the title *notarius*.[40] The few examples of ecclesiastics who write charters and take the title *notarius ecclesiae* do not clarify matters. The writing careers of two Lucchese clerics, the priest Gaudentius and the subdeacon Osprand (later a deacon), are well known.[41] However, they take the title *notarius ecclesiae* only once each in their output, on both occasions when they have copied a charter originally redacted by a *notarius*.[42] It is possible that these church notaries were fulfilling the same role of the *notarii civitatis*. That is to say, as a grand proprietor the church offered solid institutional support for documentary activity within that territory or city, but the recognition of their authority was, as with the lay *notarii civitatis*, dependent on the surviving civic sense of community. The *notarius ecclesiae* may have been an office to which the people of that region, or, when necessary, authoritative outsiders such as royal *missi*, could have appealed when challenging or defending claims that rested upon charter evidence. Petrucci has suggested that the origin of the Lombard title *notarius* lay in the continuity of the use of the term from Roman times within the church.[43] The argument is intriguing; there is certainly no evidence to refute it. But it does not explain what the title meant in the secular sphere, and paints too neat a picture of a

---

[39] Riché, *Education*, p. 405. Cf. Bognetti, 'L'*exceptor civitatis* ed il problema della continuità', *L'età*, IV, pp. 669–708, suggesting continuity of Roman nomenclature rather than curial administrative functions.

[40] CDL 284, 'Gaff cl[ericus] notar[ius] publico Bergomates' (mentioned above) and the less trustworthy 'notarius civitatis Asisinate' (Assisi) of the Farfa collection, CDL V.36. It remains uncertain, however, whether these last two referred to a distinctly separate office; that is, a qualitative difference between *exceptores* and *notarii*. Later references of the Carolingian period to indicate a particular *notarius comitatus* (such as *Brixiensis*, *Mediolanensis* or *Parmensis*) would suggest we are dealing with the same antique institution of a *notarius civitatis*, but we cannot be certain. The scenario painted by Mengozzi, *Ricerche*, pp. 308–11 (misreading a capitulary of Pippin c. 790, MGH Cap. I, c. 15. p. 201), that a 'citizen scribe' elected suitable candidates who practised their trade as *notarii civitatis* in the *forum*, has no support in the evidence.

[41] See Petrucci, 'Il codice e i documenti', *Scriptores*, pp. 80–84, and references cited.

[42] CDL 40 (727–8). The charter was originally dictated by the *rogator*, the abbot Radchis, to 'Eoin notario et in Christo filio meo', suggesting Eoin was *notarius ecclesiae*, but Gaudentius does not mention it: 'Ego Gaudentius idignus presbiter notarius sanctee eclesiae Lucane ciuitatis quantum in autentico inuenire potui, sine fraude uel dolo exeplaui, nec plus atdedi, nec minime scribsi.' Osprand, CDL 48 (730), his original drawn up by 'Magnus notarius sancte Ticinensis ecclesie scriptor'.

[43] Petrucci, *Notarii*, p. 19.

Charters

Roman office or title taking refuge in the shelter of the church only to re-emerge as a secular title centuries later when the dust from the Gothic wars and Lombard invasions settled. It also does not consider the extent to which the church was merely adopting and extending practices that already existed in the community.[44]

The evidence of the Lombard charters, and indeed Lombard legislation, does not permit any identification of the title of *notarius* as designating a writer of documents who enjoyed *fides publica*, that is, as an official whose licence to write documents was recognised and endorsed by the state in any way. Just what the title did represent remains uncertain. No doubt many of our Lombard *notarii*, such as Gaff the 'clericus notarius publico Bergomates', or the many *notarii regiae potestatis* in our sources, fulfilled some role as 'public' scribes whose professionalism was recognised by the community in which they worked. The same could be said for other titles, such as Vitalis, 'vir religiosus subdiaconus exceptor ciuitatis Piacentinae', or Maurace the *vir clarissimus* who wrote charters in an exquisite cursive script for the church of San Pietro in Varsi. Indeed, there appears to have been no strict division between writers who used lay titles and those who used ecclesiastical titles: *notarii* who wrote for churches as clients, *notarii ecclesiae*, or simply *presbiteri*, had lay clientele: they could even work for the government.[45] As with the debates concerning the existence of the *Gerichtsschreiber* in Carolingian Francia, there is the danger of 'letting the separate case studies determine the issue in terms of the existence or non-existence of public notaries. The reality was clearly much more complex.'[46] The wide variety of titles used by the writers of Lombard charters suggests that there was a diverse stratum of persons who were capable of drawing up a charter and that their status as professional or semi-professional writers was irrelevant to the validity of the charter itself.

To place this in historical and diplomatic perspective, the contrast with the evidence of the Ravennate papyri of the fifth to the seventh century is startling.[47] There, nearly all documents, with a few exceptions, were

---

[44] Cf. McKitterick, *Carolingians*, p. 125, and T. Noble, 'Literacy and the papal government in late antiquity and the early middle ages', in McKitterick (ed.), *Uses of Literacy*, pp. 82–108, at pp. 92–5.

[45] For example: CDL 252 (771 = ChLA 853), a 'Notitia brevis memoratio pro foturis temporibus [sic]', written by the *indignus presbiter* Ualpert for Autpert, *actor domni regis*, for the sale of the *mundium* of an *aldia regis*. The document refers to Lombard law ('qualiter lex est', cf. Rothari 218, Liutprand 126, on children of *aldii*), and was witnessed by *viri devoti exercitales*. Ualpert's expert cursive script demonstrates considerable 'padronanza grafica' (Magistrale, ChLA XXVIII, p. 49), but we know nothing else about him.

[46] *Carolingians*, pp. 119–20.

[47] See Everett, 'Scribes and charters', pp. 56–7, which gives references to Tjäder, *Die nichtliterarischen lateinischen Papyri*. Tjäder's excellent edition, however, is less user-friendly than the still better

redacted by *tabelliones* or *forenses*, seemingly interchangeable terms, whether they were later redacted by *exceptores* for registration before the *defensor civitatis* or *curia* for depositing in the municipal archives (*gesta municipalia*) or not.[48] Most of the *notarii* who appear belong to the church of Ravenna, the notable exceptions being King Odovacer's *notarius regiae sedis* and a *notarius sacri vesterarii*. The correspondence between the description of the office of *tabellio* in Justinian's 44th Novel, aimed at the city of Constantinople, and the evidence of the Ravennate papyri suggest that *tabelliones* and the *stationes* in which they worked had to be licensed or registered with the state in some way.[49] Moreover, the Ravennate papyri testify to the existence of a *schola tabellionum/forensium civitatis* in Ravenna and Rome in the seventh century, although their antiquity and purpose, as corporations or educational institutions, are unclear.

Fragmentary references to documentary practices in Ravenna, Rome and Constantinople, however, should not constitute the benchmark by which we measure developments in Lombard Italy. Nor do the papyri of Ravenna offer the most instructive comparison with which to understand the form and function of Lombard charters. Ravenna was the imperial administrative capital of the Roman west from the early fifth century onwards, and remained an imperial outpost in an increasingly Lombard Italian peninsula. The majority of documents preserved in the Ravennate collection reflect the activities of a powerful archiepiscopal church that had merged with the chief centre of civil administration in Italy.[50] Arguably the survival of a *schola forensium civitatis* into the seventh century, and the monopoly of *forenses* and *tabelliones* as writers of documents which have survived, are a further reflection of this administrative symbiosis.

A better understanding of the form and function of Lombard charters can be gained from a comparison with other documentation surviving from the post-Roman West. In particular, the *Tablettes Albertini*[51] from Vandal Africa, consisting of forty-five wooden tablets containing thirty-four documents which date to the period 493–6, demonstrate many characteristics similar to Lombard charters. The scribes who redacted the

---

editions he prepared with A. Petrucci for ChLA: see the concordance in ChLA XXIX, p. 10. On Ravenna, see W. Steinhoff, 'Origins and development of the notariate at Ravenna (sixth through thirteenth centuries)', unpubl. PhD thesis, New York University 1976, University Microfilms International (Ann Arbor, 1980).

[48] I discuss the issue of the preservation of charters below.
[49] Novel 44.1. Cf. Jones, *Later Roman Empire*, pp. 515–16.
[50] See T.S. Brown, 'The Church of Ravenna and the imperial administration in the seventh century', *English Historical Review* 94 (1979), 1–28; Brown, *Gentlemen and Officers*, pp. 15–20.
[51] The definitive edition is C. Courtois et al. (eds.), *Tablettes Albertini: actes privés de l'époque vandale* (Paris, 1952). Full references given in Everett, 'Scribes and charters', pp. 59–61.

Charters

Tablettes appear to have held no professional or publicly recognised status. Their grammar and orthography is far from classical, suggesting adaptative interplay with the linguistic environment in which they worked, as we suggested in chapter 3 for Lombard charters. The scribes wrote in a practised, cursive script, full of ligatures and abbreviated forms, which demonstrate fluency and competence with the medium.[52] The use of formulaic language varies enough from document to document to suggest that the scribes did not slavishly copy models provided by a formulary but instead possessed a sound degree of familiarity with the correct formulae that they could then apply to the specific circumstances of the transaction at hand. Witnesses, who usually consisted of relatives or friends who lived in the same area, testified to the transaction having taken place. Finally, the scribe states that he was a witness to the transaction and wrote the document at the request of the vendor.

We find strikingly similar formulae and structure in other early medieval lay documents in other post-Roman provinces such as Merovingian Gaul and Visigothic Spain.[53] Within the legal culture of Roman vulgar law, private transactions did not need to be registered in public archives, nor do they mention any other procedures stipulated in statutary or imperial law, such as the introduction of the purchaser into the estate or the assumption of tax obligations. The parties to the transaction were satisfied to establish that the price was paid, the land handed over and the liability for eviction assumed.[54] Recording this process did not require the skills of a professional scribe (*notarius* or *tabellio*) whose licence to write valid documents was dependent upon recognition of his profession by the authority of the state. This type of lay, private documentary activity stemmed from what we may call the 'proprietorial culture' of late

---

[52] See C. Perrat, 'L'écriture et la langue', in Courtois *et al.* (eds.), *Tablettes Albertini*, pp. 22–49.

[53] For Francia, see ChLA 592, will of Erminthrude, saec. VI–VII; ChLA 679 (762); ChLA 609 (769). For Spain, see M. C. Diaz y Diaz, 'Un document privé de l'Espagne wisigothique sur ardoise', *Studi Medievali* 3rd ser., 1 (1960), 52–71; I. Sorino Velázquez, *Las pizzaras visigodas: edición crítica y estudio* (Madrid, 1989), nos. 4, 8, 9, 12,13, 14, 15, 19, 22, 26, 39, 40, 42, 44, 60, 61, 62, 63, 64, 65, 66, 67, 80, 92, 94. Cf. Classen, 'Fortleben und Wandel', p. 29–30.

[54] The structure can be broken down easily enough: (a) initial *datatio* protocol; (b) the *emptio-venditio* formulae, introducing the identity of vendor and buyer, their consent, the object of sale and the price agreed upon; (c) obligation or *stipulatio* formulae, recording delivery of price by the buyer and the transference of both object and legal rights pertaining to the object by the vendor (that is, *traditio rei* and *traditio iuris*); (d) guarantees of the vendor, one stating the penalty to be paid (double the price of object of sale) for any infringement of agreement in future by the vendor or his heirs, and another guarantee stipulating the vendor's liability to reimburse the buyer the sum paid for the object against successful contestation of vendor's ownership by a third party; (e) the eschatocol, in which the scribe states that he was a witness to the transaction and wrote the document at the request of the vendor; (f) the subscriptions of witnesses to the transaction.

antiquity, or simply the everyday world of the land-owner. The business of land-owning required the service of those with legal literate skills for the redaction of documents recording the rightful possession of land. This proprietorial culture drew upon a pool of literate skills that could be found in local communities in which writing held a central place in the ordering and regulation of the distribution of wealth. The desire to obtain written proofs for property rights was deeply embedded in Roman vulgar law, the law of property. The resultant documentation demonstrates remarkable uniformity in structure and formulae in addressing the primary concerns of Roman property law.

Imperial legislation, the use of public notaries and the public registration of documents had little place in the local African society glimpsed behind the *Tablettes Albertini*, or in the communities behind Merovingian wills and Visigothic slate-texts, even if the empire had still existed. Likewise, the documentary activity of Lombard Italy, as seen in the charters, would have been the same if the Lombards had never left Pannonia. In the context of the this proprietorial culture, the lack of any publicly recognised office for the redaction or preservation of private documents in Lombard Italy should not surprise us. Nor should the plethora of different titles used (*notarius*, *scriptor*, *vir clarissimus*, *clericus*, *presbiter*, *diaconus*, *subdiaconus*, and so on), nor indeed the lack of one, be considered in terms of discontinuity from the late Roman world outside of major cities or centres of imperial administration. Lombard charters should instead be viewed in the context of continuity of the type of 'ground-level' documentation we see in the *Tablettes Albertini* and elsewhere in the late and post-Roman world. Less than thirty years before the Lombard invasion Cassiodorus waxed lyrical on the *securitas* afforded by the *scribarum officium* of Ravenna, an office that seems to have disappeared along with the Ostrogoths. Cassiodorus was perhaps closer to the mark when extolling the supreme probative power of the documents themselves: the *vox antiqua chartarum* constituted *indisputabile testimonium*.[55] But Lombard charters were not indisputable. The evidence of the *placita* reveals that their legal validity could be and was questioned on other grounds – authenticity, correct procedure observed, concordance with Lombard law – rather than the narrow criteria of who wrote it and what authority they had to do so. In this sense, the charters of Lombard Italy can be seen as a development, and refinement, of both the principles and practices of late Roman legal culture and the place of literacy within it.

---

[55] *Var.* XII.21: 'scribarum officium securitas solet esse cunctorum quoniam ius omnium eius solicitudine custoditur'; 'hoc honorabile decus, indisputabile testimonium, vox antiqua chartarum'.

Charters

REDACTION AND DISPOSITIVITY

The redaction of the document, on the basis of an examination of the charters, appears to have taken place on the one, pre-arranged occasion when the 'commissioner' (*rogator*) of the document and all witnesses were present, as is suggested by the tenor of the scribes' eschatocol.[56] This does not exclude the possibility that the main body of the charter, with details of the transaction, may have been prepared previously, after initial consultation between scribe and *rogator*, in the form of notes on scraps of parchment or on wax tablets. A Milanese charter demonstrates how one scribe, the *notarius* Alfrit, took down the important and non-formulaic parts of transaction (the lands, their size and what type they were, where they were situated, names of people involved, etc.), in syllabic tachigraphy on the back of the piece of parchment to be used for the formal document.[57] The lack of evidence for a temporal gap between the body of the charter and the opening *datatio*, in the form of either poor use of spacing or different coloured ink, suggests that, no matter how the content was prepared, the whole of the charter was written out on one occasion. Certainly this was not always the case. The witness lists appearing as dorsal notes on some Lucchese charters suggest that the process of redaction may have been more protracted.[58] Lucchese charters may be a special case, and it would be unwise to draw general conclusions from such evidence: Lucchese bishops made their own rules when it came to charters.[59]

Determining the process of redaction relates to another subject that lies at the heart of understanding the social function of charters as instruments of written communication and as records, namely, the questions surrounding dispositivity. Did the charter merely record a transaction signified by ritual acts or did it actually constitute the transaction by its own symbolism? That is, was the parchment equivalent to the ritual of giving a clod of earth? To what were the witnesses testifying: the ritual of transfer, the redaction of the charter itself and correct procedure observed, or

---

[56] E.g. CDL 29: 'scripsi ego Vitalis... rogatus et petitus ad Anstruda muliere ipsa tamen praesentem mihique dictantem et praesentia testium mano sua propria subter sign[um] s[an]c[t]e crucis facientem'. 'Commissioner': there is no good English equivalent for *rogator*, lit. 'proposer', hence I use the Latin term. 'Author' is feasible but possibly confusing in this context.

[57] CDL 234. See L. Schiaparelli, 'Tachigrafia sillabica nelle carte Italiane', *Bullettino dell'Istituto Storico Italiano* 33 (1928), 10–35. Cf. McKitterick, *Carolingians*, pp. 94–8, on the charters of St Gall.

[58] P. Supino Martini, 'Le sottoscrizioni testimoniali al documento italiano del secolo VIII: le carte di Lucca', *Bullettino dell'Istituto Storico Italiano* 98 (1992), 87–108.

[59] See L. Bertini, 'Peredeo, vescovo di Lucca', in *Studi storici in onore di O. Bertolini*, I (Pisa, 1972), pp. 21–46; Wickham, 'Land disputes', pp. 241–2.

both?[60] As discussed in the previous chapter, Lombard laws seem to indicate that the signing of charters, though not the making of them, included a symbolic ritual.[61] Schiaparelli tackled such problems for the Italian material by focusing on the formula *post traditam* in both Ravennate papyri and Lombard charters. He argued that the common formula of *post tradita complevi et dedi* and its variants found in the *completiones* of the Lombard documents referred to the charter having been *tradita* on or over a copy of the Gospels or an altar accompanied by a sworn oath from the giver, receiver and witnesses present to the transaction.[62] Schiaparelli's purpose was to complement Brunner's argument that the actual handing over of the charter by the issuer to the receiver was a symbolic act which constituted the finality of the transaction: that is, the *traditio rei* and *traditio cartae* became merged into a single act, *traditio per cartam*. Although intriguing, the evidence for Schiaparelli's theory is lacking. Only two Lombard charters actually mention an altar, and no attempt was made by Schiaparelli to explain the evidence that opposes such a theory in the Ravennate papyri.[63] Amongst the documents recording transactions where a church was the beneficiary, there may indeed have been cases when the charter was placed upon the altar in a symbolic ritual signifying the transferral of property which the charter fails to mention explicitly, as would have been the case of an *offersio* to a monastery living under Benedictine rule.[64] Schiaparelli's theory does serve, however, to highlight the original context of the formulaic language used in Lombard charters, and reminds us of the ideological baggage that such language carried. The 'intrusions' of Christianity into the actual format of the document do not seem, at a glance, to constitute more than minor changes: the inclusion of Christ's name in the *invocatio* which begins the document, or the use of some charmingly inventive biblical allusion in the *arengae* or *sanctio*.[65] Behind

---

[60] Brunner, *Deutsche Rechtsgeschichte*, pp. 563–74; Classen, 'Fortleben und Wandel', pp. 42–7.
[61] Gifts, Liutprand 54; marriage gifts, Liutprand 29; manumission, Rothari 224; women selling property, Liutprand 22.
[62] 'Note diplomatiche, 3. La formula *post traditam (chartam)*', *Archivio Storico Italiano*, ser. 7, 19 (1933), 34–51; Brunner, *Zur Rechtsgeschichte der römischen und germanischen Urkunde*, I (Berlin, 1880), pp. 87–96, and a host of later commentators (see Schiaparelli, p. 34 n. 1).
[63] Tjäder, P. 12 (555); also PP. 13, 14, 15.   [64] RB 58, 59. See above, p. 48.
[65] The invocation to Christ at the beginning of documents to record transactions between lay people seems to date from around the mid-seventh century, judging from the evidence of the Ravennate papyri and Visigothic slate texts: cf. Tjäder, II, pp. 159 and n. 56, 288 n. 1, 293 n. 1; Velázquez Soriano, *Las pizarras*, nos. 62, 94, in contrast to those which begin with a Chi-Rho-type symbol, as in nos. 40, 41. See further, L. Santifaller, 'Über die Verbal-Invokation in der älteren Papsturkunden', *Römische Historische Mitteilungen* 3 (1958/59 and 1959/60), 17–113; P. Rabikauskas, 'Zur Verbal-Invokation in römischen Privaturkunden', *Römische Historische Mitteilungen* 4 (1960/61), 23–5; P. Rück, 'Beiträge zur diplomatischen Semiotik', in Rück (ed.), *Graphische Symbole in mittelalterlichen Urkunden* (Sigmaringen, 1996), pp. 13–48, at pp. 24–8. Examples of inventive *arengae*: CDL 82, 78, 123. Cf. Liva, *Notariato*, p. 17.

Charters

these theological touch-ups lies the *mentalité* of the sacrality of writing as part of the Judeo-Christian heritage. The pervasive secular influence of Roman vulgar law had found a religious ally in promoting the solemnity of the written word.

LOMBARD CURSIVE

Palaeographers generally agree that a 'new Roman cursive' script, with distinctly different elements from 'late Roman cursive', can first be seen in the fifth-century texts of the *Tablettes Albertini* and the earliest papyri of Ravenna, continuing with slight changes until around the seventh century. From the beginning of the seventh century onwards the script of the Ravennate papyri demonstrates changes in letter forms and the use of ligatures. This script in turn has been dubbed 'new Italian' cursive and is the basis of that which we find used in Lombard charters, with irregular and capricious letter-forms and ligatures that are distinctively 'north Italian'.[66] It is important to underline the fact that all original Lombard charters were written in a cursive script which is immediately recognisable, even to a half-trained palaeographic eye, and is significantly uniform, despite the range of variation.[67] This suggests that script-type, as much as correct formulae, concordance with the law and observing the correct procedure of procuring witnesses and their subscriptions, was considered an essential element of a legitimate and legally valid charter. Yet there is no direct evidence to confirm this. Both the Theodosian and the Justinianic Codes refer to the use of palaeography to check the authenticity of a charter, as does Visigothic law, yet Lombard legislation is silent.[68] The closest we come to a direct statement on what was considered the correct form of a charter is that of a *placitum* held in Piacenza in 854, when a charter of the 620s was read out in court and accepted as valid by the judges because it was set out 'propter barbarico exempla'.[69] It is uncertain whether this was a recognition of the charter's script, its structure or the formulaic language it contained. It was probably a mixture of all three. But the correct script, a sophisticated cursive, undoubtedly played

---

[66] Excellent discussions of this script are Tjäder and Petrucci, introduction to ChLA XXIII, pp. vii–viii (here dubbed 'new Italian'); and E. Cau, 'Scrittura e cultura a Novara (secoli VIII–X)', *Ricerche Medievali* 6–9 (1971–74), 1–87, at pp. 9–14. See also J.O. Tjäder, 'Some ancient letter-forms in the later Roman cursive and early medieval script of the *notarii*', *Scrittura e Civiltà* 6 (1982), 5–21. Cf. Schiaparelli, 'Note paleografiche. Intorno all'origine della scrittura curiale romana', *Archivio Storico Italiano* ser. 7, 6 (1926), 165–82. On the problem of palaeographic nomenclature: F. Bartolini, 'La nomenclatura della scritture documentarie', *X Congresso Internazionale di Scienze Storiche, Roma 1955*, I (Florence, 1955), 434–76.

[67] Cf. Bischoff, *Latin Palaeography*, pp. 101–2.

[68] *CTh* 2.27.1, 9.12.2. For Merovingian Gaul, see Gregory of Tours, *Historiae* x. 19.

[69] CDL III.4. Cf. Wickham, 'Land disputes', in *Land and power*, p. 240.

a role in conferring legitimacy on a charter. As I shall demonstrate below, in learning to write one moved from uncial to cursive forms, not the other way around. The scribes who wrote Lombard charters could certainly have written them in more minuscule or even uncial letter-forms and without ligatures, but they never did. Caroline minuscule was not used for documents in many areas of north Italy until well beyond the eleventh century, and in Ravenna never at all.[70] Such practice testifies to the deep roots of Roman documentary culture in early medieval Italian society.

There is, however, another, simpler, reason for the exclusive use of cursive script for the redaction of charters, namely, the increased speed with which it allowed the scribe to write the document. T.A.M. Bishop commented that the development of cursive script in twelfth-century England did not result from any special training but 'something far simpler and historically significant: the common pressure of urgent business'.[71] In Lombard Italy certainly a degree of special training in the correct use of ligatures and abbreviations was required, but Bishop's point concerning the pressure of urgent business is a salient one. The average size of a Lombard charter was around 42 × 25 cm. The average number of lines of script per text was thirty-three (exclusive of the witnesses list and the scribe's *completio*).[72] If writing took, say, twenty-five seconds per line (at maximum), then a charter would have taken the scribe around fourteen minutes to write the main text. The redaction of the entire charter, of course, would have taken much longer. If the document was redacted 'on the day', that is, if the scribe arrived at the appointed place where the two parties of the exchange and witnesses had gathered, the scribe would have had to take down details of the transaction and then translate them into the appropriate legal language. In addition, the recitation of the document's contents and the collection of subscriptions were done prior to the scribe's final *completio* clause and *traditio* of the charter. This process may have required two to three hours of the scribe's time. A more calligraphic script of course, such as the uncials and half-uncials and

---

[70] See Petrucci, 'Scritture e scriventi', *Scriptores*, pp. 57–76.
[71] Cited by Clanchy, *From Memory to Written Record*, p. 129.
[72] This average is taken from a survey of four collections of original documents: Siena, Archivio di Stato, ChLA XXIII (nos. 730–50). Average size: 35.45 × 26.49 cm. Average number of lines of script per text: 25.76. Pisa, Archivio arcivescovile, ChLA XXVI (nos. 799–812). Average size: 50.57 × 27.5. Average number of lines of script per text: 41.35. Piacenza, Archivo Capitolare, ChLA XXVII (nos. 816–33). Average size: 42.3 × 23.7 cm. Average number of lines per text: 31.8. Milan, Archivio di Stato, ChLA XXVIII (nos. 844–61). Average size: 33.94 × 25.77. Average number of lines of script per text: 27.27. The size (and indeed the shape) of Lombard charters can vary greatly, from say 24 × 16 cm to 60 × 50 cm (ChLA 856, 803), and can contain anything from six to sixty-five lines of script per charter (Cf. ChLA 851 and 812). The average number of pieces of parchment used suggests a ratio of six to seven charters per goat, and five to six charters *per pecus*. See R. Reed, *Ancient Skins, Parchments and Leathers* (London and New York, 1972).

minuscules of Anglo-Saxon charters, would have taken much longer.[73] Hence the exclusive use of cursive script of Lombard charters derives not only from the ideological importance of time-honoured authority, but also from the practicalities of the 'business world' of land-owning, an activity that was far more busy than is perhaps suggested by the solemnity that surrounds a 1300-year-old document.

THREE CHARTERS AND THE 'ELEMENTARY SCRIPT'

The type of cursive script used by scribes in Lombard charters required a good measure of calligraphic skill and a great deal of practice. It is a specialised script that demonstrates a person's full immersion in the 'graphic culture' of the late Roman world. How did one learn to write such a script? Leaving aside for the moment the highly competent cursives of those scribes who wrote charters, we can see the process of how one learned to write, and as a corollary read, cursive script by monitoring the autograph subscriptions of witness at the bottom of some charters. My intention here is to complement Petrucci's theory concerning the primary levels of instruction in writing, the product of which he calls an 'elementary script' (*grafico elementare* or *grafico di base*), a type of minuscule script, rarely employing connecting strokes between letters or ligatures of any sort.[74] This seems entirely sound, and similar to modern schooling practices in which children learn to 'print' their letters before learning how to link them together. But the model is a little misleading, for in our charters scribal intricacies such as abbreviations and suprascript letters appear to have been taught, or learned at the same time. Three examples will suffice.

The first example is a charter of 756 in which the widow Uualderata of Campione donates an olive-grove to the church of San Zeno (see Plate I).[75] Interesting for our purposes are the three autographs given by the witnesses, but particularly that of Agelmund, Uualderata's son, who acted as legal consent for his mother's transaction. Agelmund's script shows a very unpractised hand, compared to that of his uncle Arochis below it, with large blotchy, separated letters of slightly uneven size.[76] We

---

[73] See P. Wormald, 'Bede and the conversion of England: the charter evidence', Jarrow Lecture 1984, pp. 10–13.

[74] First proposed in Petrucci, 'Libro, scrittura, e scuola', and restated with some revision in 'Alle origini', *Scriptores*, pp. 13–34.

[75] ChLA 849. CDL 123, Natale 16. On the scribe, see A.R. Natale, 'Note paleografiche sulle carte private della Svizzera italiana nell'alto medioevo. II. La corsiva di Orso *scriptor* in Campione nel 756', *Bollettino Storico della Svizzera Italiana* ser. 4, 25 (1950), 135–43.

[76] Most of the letter-forms are a pre-minuscule deriving from half-uncial: 'a', 'u', 'n' with bowed arch, and 't', a clearly uncial 'g' remaining.

Literacy in Lombard Italy, c. 568–774

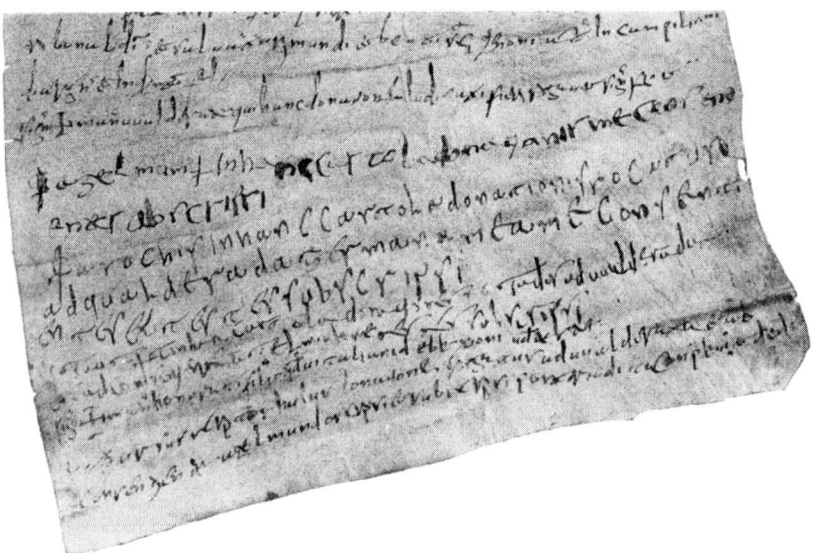

Plate I Elementary script. Milan, Archivio di Stato, Museo Diplomatico, no. 14 (from ChLA XXVIII, no. 849, p. 39)

should note the largely unsuccessful attempts to connect certain letters.[77] Further interconnection of letters and examples of a nascent cursive can be clearly seen in the 'e' of Agelmund, which moves from an uncial form towards the characteristic 'figure 8' form of late Roman 'new cursive' and which is common in Lombard Italy. Also indicative of nascent cursive are the 'ti' and 'te' ligatures found in *donationis* and *consentiente*. Agelmund must have been at least over eighteen to be a legal guardian,[78] but one wonders if the unpractised hand witnessed here is not that of someone learning to write. The script of his uncle Arochis is far neater and more precise, in generic terms sitting somewhere in that thorny distinction between half-cursive and pre-Caroline minuscule scripts in Lombard Italy.[79] Yet the clear letter-separation of the first line becomes increasingly challenged by the emergence in the second of tentative connections between the 'e' and 'r' in *Qualderata* (*sic*), the 'e's becoming more daringly tactile via the centre horizontal stroke connecting with 'n', 't' and 's' in *consentientes* and *testis*, culminating in a ligatured cross-like 'et'. Hence one can glimpse the process of an elementary minuscule script based on new cursive forms developing towards a more cursive hand by the intrepid yet

[77] 'a' with 'r' in *cartola*, 'c' with 'o' and 'e' with 'n' in *consentiente*, 'u' with 'b' in *subscripsi*.
[78] Rothari 204.   [79] As above, note 66 and below, pp. 310ff.

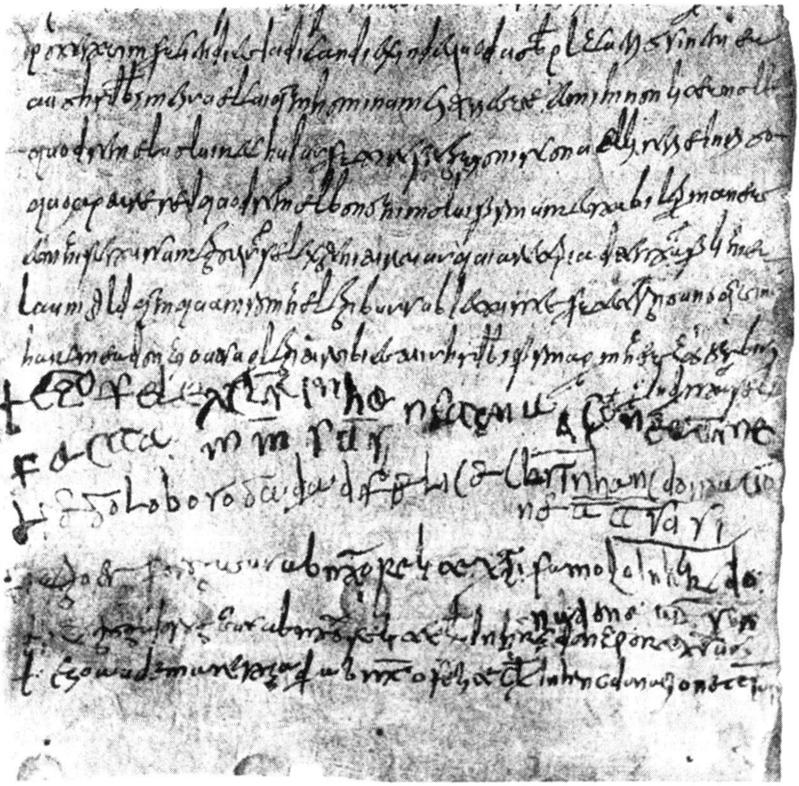

Charters

Plate II Elementary script. Verona, Archivio di Stato, Ospitale Civico, no. 3
(from ChLA XXXIX, no. 873, p. 59)

increasing use of connecting strokes between letters, particularly with the letter 'e' used as a starting point.[80]

Another 'elementary script' very similar to that of Agelmund can be seen in a Veronese charter of 780, in which Felex *clericus*, the *rogator* of the charter, also writes a blotchy, unconfident minuscule hand that seems embarrassingly wayward among the scribal expertise that surrounds it (see Plate II). Yet Felex manages to include simple abbreviated forms for

---

[80] The practised cursive of the following witness, Gautpert, contrasts sharply with Arochis' pre-Caroline minuscule in its relatively frequent use of connected forms ('a' with 'h' in *hanc* and with 'n' in *donationis*, which uses 'ti' ligature, etc.). Noticeable is the strange t-like 'g' and the extremely ligatured and elaborate strokes in *testis*. Natale, 'Note paleografiche', pp. 139–42, argued that the 't' and 'e' in both Arichis and Agelmund have Merovingian forms, but such types are merely coincidental variations from a common late Roman cursive base.

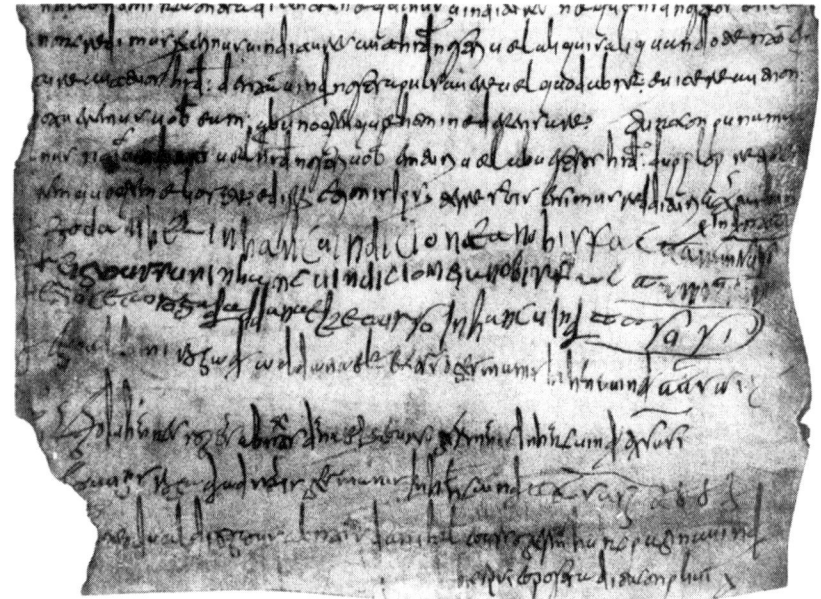

Plate III Elementary script. Verona, Biblioteca Capitolare, III.3–3v
(from ChLA XXXIX, no. 876, p. 71)

m[anu] m[ea] and *subs[crips]i*.[81] More chronologically relevant, however, is another Veronese charter from 772 that shows similar phenomena – one of the very few charters in which all those involved in the transaction provide autograph subscriptions (see Plate III).[82] The *rogatores* of the document, the brothers Daniele and Ursus, write a disconnected minuscule, tentatively extending the horizontal stroke of the 'e' to join following letters, both finishing with abbreviated forms of *m[anu] m[ea]* and *subs[crips]i*. Yet a variety of expert cursives can be found in the autograph subscriptions of the witnesses Ceto, Albini, Iuhannes and Augis, all of whom use such cursive traits as superscript letters, the same abbreviations for *vind[itione]*, 'tt' for *testis*, and individualistically inventive forms of *subscripsi*.[83]

---

[81] ChLA 873. Cipolla 11. Noticeable also are the separated minuscule forms combined, with innovative *sigla* for *testis* and *subscripsi*, of the witness Lobo, similarly found in the practised cursives of Erfo and Gaio below him.

[82] ChLA 876; CDL 277.

[83] Further observations: Ceto, tail of 'g' linking with following 'a' and extended looped tail of 'd' to abbreviate '-us' in *rogadus*; the fantastically elaborate *subscripsi* abbreviation involving an encompassing bracket; Albini, similar forms to Ceto though a straighter, smaller and more disciplined

Charters

Other subscriptions to charters furnish us with numerous examples of similar palaeographic phenomena found in the above three examples,[84] but enough has been said to permit two general conclusions. First, the above examples confirm Petrucci's thesis regarding the processes by which one moved from the 'elementary script' of a minuscule-based script to more elaborated cursive. Second, even those witnesses who wrote at the level of the elementary script included some abbreviations and ligatures (most notably the connection of 'e' to following letters) common to highly competent cursives in their use of formulaic phrases of subscription. We see a similar phenomenon in the Visigothic slate-texts of the sixth and seventh centuries, in which large, rounded minuscule letters are used in school exercises and by the witnesses to some charters, with some minor use of ligatures and abbreviations, even at an early stage of competence.[85] In particular, two slate-texts show someone practising the letters of the alphabet in the same manner as a piece of Italian evidence, a seventh- or eighth-century brick from Crema (some 45 km south-east of Milan) that is inscribed (seemingly by finger) with the name *Garipaldus* and which proceeds to trace the letters 'A B C D E F G H' up to the brick's broken edge (suggesting it continued).[86] Interesting is the alternation of A from a late cursive 'u' form to a more closed half-uncial then back again, and the late cursive G, both of which contrast with the rustic capitalis quadrata used for the remaining letters. This appears to reflect both writing and reading practice, and to constitute an attempt at fostering familiarity with the alphabet.

How did a person advance from such introductory levels of graphic capacity to the competence required to write an entire charter? With respect to our *notarii* and the secular sphere, Schiaparelli hypothesised a series of levels: from the *discipulus* under the instruction of a *magister*; the *scriptor*, that is, one who is authorised to write documents, but always *ex*

---

hand: Iuhannes, superscript 'a' (*hanc*) and 'd' (*rogadus*) including a superscript abbreviation form for s[upra]s[crip]tus, 'tt' for *testis* and a snazzy abbreviated *subscripsi* with horizontal bar above; Augis, similar to Ceto, with noticeable three figure-8 connected loops at end akin to many notarial hands.

[84] Other instructive examples: CDL 93, ChLA 803 (Pisa 748), the autographs of Liutpert and Alpert; CDL 124, ChLA 805 (Pisa 753), the autographs of Andreas (*episcopus*!), Aunemund, and Barunta; CDL 45, ChLA 800 (Pisa 730), the autograph of Aloari; CDL 284, ChLA 868 (Bergamo 773), the autograph of Agepertus; CDL 168, ChLA 871 (Verona 762), the autograph of Alfre; CDL 234, ChLA 852 (Milan 769), the autograph of Aunefrit: CDL 252, ChLA 853 (Milan 771), the autograph of Gisefrit.

[85] For example, Velázquez Soriano, *Las pizarras*, nos.7, 20, 26, 27 (and 100, *probationes pennae*?), and discussion, pp. 65–103.

[86] See A. Caretta, 'Note sulle epigrafi longobarde di Laus Pompeia del Cremasco', *Archivio Storico Lombardo* 9:3 (1963), 174–5, at pp. 193–5. The dating is mainly on palaeographical and onomastic grounds – we know of no 'Garipaldus' before the seventh century. Alphabets in Spain: Velázquez Soriano, *Las pizarras*, nos. 25, 57.

dictato of a *notarius*; and finally the *notarius*.[87] The evidence of distinction between *scriptor* and *notarius* in terms of promotion or more professional status, such as has been argued for the Farfa and Lucchese documents, also contains examples that contradict any possible conclusions.[88] The only references we have to *magistri* and *discipuli* are those from two original Lucchese charters, where we know a writing school of sorts existed at the cathedral.[89] But it would be unwise to use this as evidence for 'schools' of notarial training elsewhere in the kingdom, especially from outside the church.[90] Besides the reference to a *schola forensium*, the Ravennate papyri also contain one will drawn up by a certain Julian, an 'assistant' (*adiutor*) to John, *forensis huius civitatis Ravennatis*, who approved Julian's work, which suggests an apprenticeship system.[91] This was probably the case for many of our Lombard scribes, but we have no such testimony in the charters.[92] That expert legal training was required to write charters is cast into doubt by Liutprand's law of 727 which decrees that those writing charters, if they are not fully acquainted with Roman or Lombard law, should ask 'others' who do know.[93] As we have seen, there is no evidence in the law code or in the charters themselves that the capacity and authority to write charters was limited to specific persons or groups that have recognisable characteristics or social status. Yet despite this 'free market'

---

[87] Schiaparelli, 'Note diplomatiche I', pp. 25–8.

[88] The Farfa examples: Stefano, *scriptor* of charters of 761 and 764 (May) CDL IV.1, 15 and CDL V.39, should not necessarily be identified with the Stefano *notarius* of Rieti, 764 – 773; see Zielinski, *Studien*, p. 133 and Brühl, *Studien*, pp. 49–51. Lucca: Radalpert writes a charter of 752 without title, becomes *notarius* in 754 and 755, but then drops the title again in 765 (CDL 102, 113, 121, 189); likewise the priest Tanipert is *presbitero notario* [sic] *scriptor* in 757 and simply *presbitero* in 759 (CDL 126, 133). Liva, *Notariato*, p. 9, cites the case of Ambrosius, *notarius* in 848, *scriptor* two years later. The relationship between the person who wrote the documents 'ex dictato' and the person who was dictating is equally inconclusive; see Schiaparelli, 'Note diplomatiche VI. Dictare, ex dictato, ex dicto, dictator', *Archivio Storico Italiano* ser. 7, 21 (1934), 21–37.

[89] CDL 85, 'Ego Perteradu clericus ex dectato Gaudentio presbitero magistro meo iscripsi, complevi, relegi et dedi', followed by Gaudentius' approval, 'propria manus mea suscripsi et confirmaui'; likewise, CDL 86, 'Quam meis repromessionis pagina Gaudentius presbiter una cum Perteradu clerico discipuli eius iscriuere rogaui ex dectato suprascripto Gaudentio magistro meo scripsi ego Perterad', followed again by Gaudentius' approval as above.

[90] Petrucci, 'Il codice e i documenti', *Scriptores*, pp. 77–108.

[91] Tjäder, P. 6. 'Iulianus vir honestus scribtor huius cartulae et adiutor Iohannis forensis habens stationem apud sanctum Iohannem Baptista . . . suscriptum complevi.' John's subscription of approval: 'Iohanis vir honestus, forensis huius civitatis Ravennatis, hunc testamentum . . . scribtum a Iuliano viro honesto adiutore meo, et testibus roboratum et traditum, conplevi et dedi.' John also appears to have had a *statio* under the portico of Theoderic's palace.

[92] A possibility is CDL 136 (ChLA 953) redacted in Lucca by Prandulo, 'detantem Alpert', and the charter finishes, after the witnesses' formulaic subscriptions, with 'Ego Alpert subscripsi' in Alpert's own hand, instead of Prandulo's *completio*. Yet Prandulo wrote a *completio* in a document of the same year, CDL 135 (a late eighth-century copy). He is not the same Prandulo who wrote CDL 178, 227, nor 220, 286.

[93] Liutprand 19. Cf. Justinian, *Nov.* 66, granting a two-month period of grace for new laws in order that *tabelliones* may learn them.

Charters

of documentary practice, the charters that have come down to us have a recognisable consistency and uniformity, especially in regard to their purpose or particular genre. That is to say, *chartae donationis, venditionis, de accepto mundio, promissionis, cambiationis,* and so on, contain a high degree of homogeneity that transcends the differences which particularity of time, place, persons involved and purpose may impose upon the form and content of the document. But how was such uniformity maintained?

FORMULARIES AND FORMULAE

Unlike that which we have for the Visigothic, Merovingian and Carolingian kingdoms, there are no surviving formularies from Italy in this period, nor were there for centuries to come.[94] Nor can any influences or traces of such *oltrealpe* formularies be found in the charters of Lombard Italy. The work of Leicht, and after him, more thoroughly, Schiaparelli, on late Roman and Ravennate *formulae* in Lombard charters, revealed two important conclusions.[95] First, Lombard charters use formulaic language common to both Roman and late Roman documents, though these two are often mixed in a way that does not permit any clear division that allows us to envisage separate strands of development. Second, though there are certainly some examples of shared formulae among the charters of a particular region which suggest local traditions and preferences, there are no rigid or clear-cut regional divisions for the use of set formulae here and not there, as though they developed in isolation. There are, however, two particular cases which afford some insight into regional documentary culture and raise issues that help fill out the picture of legal literacy in a local setting, namely, the documents of Piacenza and of Lucca.

PIACENZA

The charters preserved at the Archivio capitolare in Piacenza are unique in their use of the ancient Roman formulae of *mancipatio–emptio*, found

---

[94] *Formulae Merovingici et Karolini Aevi*, ed. K. Zeumer, MGH Form. On their use, Wood, 'Administration', pp. 64–6. On the *Liber Diurnus* as a formulary for the papal chancery: L. Santifaller in H. Zimmermann (ed.), *Liber Diurnus: Studien und Forschungen von Leo Santifaller*, Päpste und Papsttum 10 (Stuttgart, 1976); cf. Noble, 'Literacy and the papal government', pp. 95–6. Cassiodorus' two books of *formulae* in the *Variae* pertain to public documents, not private. The first known Italian formulary for private charters is the (now lost) early twelfth-century 'Formularium tabellionum' of Irnerius: Brunner, *Rechtsgeschichte*, I, p. 567; Bresslau, *Handbuch*, I, p. 623.

[95] P.S. Leicht, *Formulari notarili nell'Italia settentrionale*, excerpt of *Mélanges Fitting*, II (Montpellier, 1908); Schiaparelli, 'Note diplomatiche sulle carte longobarde, 2. Tracce di antichi formulari nelle carte longobarde', *Archivio Storico Italiano* ser. 7, 19 (1933), 3–34.

nowhere else in the charters of the *regnum*.⁹⁶ The concept of *mancipatio* belongs to ancient Roman civil law, where it was used to describe the formal acceptance of the rights of ownership as distinct from possession.⁹⁷ From the third century onwards, however, such 'classical niceties' (as Ernst Levy puts it) ceased to be relevant to the late Roman world, as a sale moved back to the status of a cash transaction where sale and conveyance or transferal of ownership merged together into a single transaction.⁹⁸ It is generally agreed by legal historians, however, that the use of this term in the Ravennate papyri and the Piacentine charters constituted nothing less than an antiquated use of formulae devoid of any legal sense.⁹⁹ What is significant, for our purposes, is its survival in Lombard charters as evidence of a rarely detected link between Ravennate papyri and Lombard charters. As I have suggested elsewhere, the presence of the *mancipatio–emptio* formulae in some Piacentine charters may well be one of the causes behind Liutprand's well-known imperative of 727 that charters must be written 'according to the Roman or Lombard law'.¹⁰⁰ Liutprand was perhaps trying to legitimize the various different *formulae chartarum* in use throughout the kingdom, particularly those with such strong Roman legal remnants as the Piacentine, in the same way that the the word *scriba* in Lombard legislation attempted to encompass the variety of document writers. Moreover, a link between the documentary practices of Ravenna and Piacenza can be seen in another Piacentine charter that contains the remarkable use of a formulaic phrase found in a document of Ravenna. In 774, on the eve of the Frankish conquest of Pavia, Petronia, *honesta femina*, donated some land to the church of San Pietro in Varsi. The opening *datatio* clause of the charters is striking: 'In Christi nomine facta cartola donationis tempore barbarici anno dominorum nostrorum Desiderius et Adelchis regis.'¹⁰¹ This 'barbarous time'

---

⁹⁶ ChLA 816–23, 825. CDL 52, 54, 59, 60, 64, 79, 109, 129, 159. The usual form of the *receptio* clause of Lombard charters runs along the lines of 'pro que pretium . . . accepisse et habere se dixit **A** (*venditor*) a **B** (*emptor*)', or something similar. That found in the Piacentine charters resembles the form of sixth-century Ravennate papyri where the 'mancipationes emptionis causa pretio accepto' formula is used, that is, stating that the price has been agreed upon, but it does not state that the price has actually been received from the purchaser: 'Expensum prediis rustecis, id est terra . . . eam emit mancipioque accepit **A** . . . Petit enim **A** . . . vinditor et omnem pretium placitum et definitum in presenti accepit, sicut inter eos convenit . . . facta hanc mancipationem **A** . . .'.

⁹⁷ See A. Solmi, 'La formula'; V. Arangio-Ruiz, 'Mancipatio e documenti contabili da Ercolano a Piacenza', *La Parola del Passato* 12 (1957), 35–56.

⁹⁸ *West Roman Vulgar Law*, pp. 128, 135, 137, 141, 178; Solmi, 'La formula'.

⁹⁹ Tjäder, I, pp. 14–15 n. 8; P.S. Leicht, 'Ultime vicende della *mancipatio* in Italia', *Atti del II Congresso nazionale di studi romani* 3 (Rome, 1931), 13–19.

¹⁰⁰ Liutprand 91; Everett, 'Scribes and charters', pp. 67–8; cf. above, p. 174.

¹⁰¹ CDL 291. ChLA 827. 6 May. The Franks took the city on 5 June: R. Davis, *Lives*, p. 142 n. 70. The formula is not used in any other of the six charters of 774 (CDL 289–94).

Charters

is doubtless a reference to wars with the Franks, and the same phrase is found in a Ravennate charter of 553, when Ranilo, *sublimis femina*, donated land to the church of Ravenna 'tempore hoc barbarici', also at time of war and conquest by a foreign power.[102] To be sure, the usage of this phrase as a temporal indicator of war may be consigned to common parlance or mere coincidence.[103] But the similarity of the transactions — both donations by women, retaining usufruct rights for themselves and their husbands, at a time of civil unrest — and the rarity of the dating formula tend to suggest some link between the documentary traditions of the two regions, the two Italies. The Piacentine church was, after all, under the archepiscopal jurisdiction of Ravenna, and Piacenza was linked with Ravenna via the Po river.[104]

While the strength of Piacentine legal culture can be seen in the court cases of the ninth and tenth centuries,[105] the charters from the Lombard period permit a view of the tenacity of documentary tradition. The scribe who wrote the document in 'barbaric times', Audoald, wrote a clear, regular cursive, and titled himself *vir clarissimus* in the manner of his predecessor, the scribe Maurace, whose professional presence dominates the Piacentine collection. The evidence for Maurace's twenty-seven-year career (735–63) as a writer comes exclusively from the documents he wrote for the church of San Pietro in Varsi, which included donations and sales of land and, as we have seen, the settlement of disputes.[106] His script is a highly cursive, individual, but regular charter-hand, with small lettering and a noticeable enthusiasm for ligatures, sometimes linking up to seven letters in one word, as well as using word ligatures.[107] The *notarius* who autographed Audoald's charter as a witness, Labari, wrote in a similar script. Hence palaeographically the charter is rooted in the same local traditions as Maurace's handiwork. Moreover, the *arengae* Audoald used in the charter written in 'barbaric times' are also found in an earlier charter

---

[102] Tjäder, P. 13.
[103] Justinian referred to the 'decursio barbarici temporis' in his 'Lex quae data est pro debitoribus' of c. 557, CJ III.803. Cf. Paul the Deacon, *HL* VI.35, 'tempora fuerunt barbarica'. Goffart, *Narrators*, p. 419, as a guide to Paul's prejudices and narrative design, but Paul simply means the period was troubled with war.
[104] See F. Lanzoni, *Le diocesi d'Italia dalle origini al principio del secolo VII*, Studi e Testi (Faenza, 1927), pp. 815–16; R. Schumann, 'Le fondazioni ecclesiastiche e il disegno urbano di Piacenza tra il tardo romano (350) e la Signoria (1313)', *Bollettino Storico Piacentino* 71 (1976), 159–71; J.C. Picard, *Le souvenir des évêques* (Rome, 1988), pp. 275–7 313–16; G.P. Bognetti, 'La navigazione padana e il sopravvivere della civiltà antica', *L'età*, IV, pp. 539–56.
[105] Wickham 'Land disputes', in *Land and Power*, p. 246.
[106] Above, pp. 154–5.
[107] Maurace: ChLA 816–23, 825 (CDL 52, 54, 59, 60, 64, 79, 109, 129, 159). Ligature: c*[ontractum]*, line 23, ChLA 816. See Schiaparelli, 'Ricerche sulle carte. I', p. 50. Audoald wrote with less use of ligatures, artifices, some odd letter-forms and orthography. See Tjäder, ChLA XXVII, 827, p. 69.

(736) of Maurace: exactly the same formulae, with only slight modifications, are used both to introduce the *arengae* and in the *arengae* itself.[108] Was Audoald working from a formulary, or a copy of the earlier charter? The deviations differ enough between the two charters, including the common *arengae*, to suggest that the scribes were working from memory, but ultimately we cannot know. The replication of formulae, and the consistency of form and content of Piacentine charters throughout the Lombard period and beyond, are testimony to the strength of firmly established local traditions of documentary practice, and further suggest that the charters which survive are only a fraction of that which was produced there.[109]

LUCCA

The abundance of surviving charter evidence from the archiepiscopal archive of Lucca allows us to see how the cathedral church took a singularly active role in the development of literate traditions in the region. A few examples of the use of formulae among the collection are instructive. Two *chartae dotis*, both redacted 'in vico Gurgite' (in Capannori, Lucca), both in October 757 (on the same day?), and both commissioned by the same land-owner, Eonand, *vir devotus*, contain exactly the same formulae, yet were written by two different scribes, the priests Deusdona and Tanipert respectively.[110] The lands offered by Eonand to the two different churches of Santa Maria (in Gurgite) and San Paolo (Capannori) are both situated near Treponzio (also in Capannori, Lucca). The priests Deusdona and Tanipert (the latter endowing himself with the title *presbiterio notario* in the *completio*) appear to belong to one or both of these churches, and use of the same formulae suggests they shared a common administrative culture. Tanipert wrote another *charta dotis* 'in Gurgite' two years later for another donation, from a different land-owner to a different church (San Prospero), yet he employed similar formulae and the same *arengae* as the two charters of 757.[111] Tanipert could not, however, rely entirely on the model of his earlier charter, for the property and usufruct terms differed considerably.[112] From the identical passages

---

[108] CDL 59 (736) (ChLA 818); CDL 291 (774) (ChLA 827).
[109] For charters post 774–800 (previously unedited), ChLA 828–33. See further: P. Galetti, *Una campagna e la sua città: Piacenza e territorio nei secoli VIII–X* (Bologna, 1994).
[110] CDL 125, 126 (ChLA 944, 945). The date: Schiaparelli, CDL II, p. 5.
[111] CDL 133.
[112] 'Set tamen sit complacuet animum meum ut ipsa sup[er]scripta res, dum aduiuere meruero ego Radualdu una cum guge mea Auderada uel filia mea Sunderada, sit potestatem tantum usufructuandi, nam non fragendi, non donandi, non uendendi, nec p[er] ullo ingenio ad alio

Charters

found in both of Tanipert's charters and that of Deusdona, we can reconstruct the template or formulary they had before them:

In di. nomine regnante dno. no. name *rege*
anno regni eius year *mense* month
p. ind. number of indiction
fel.
Ideoque ego name and title, *filio qd.* name
tibi eclesie di. adque beatissime sci. name of church, genitive case *pp. salutem d.*

[The *arengae*]

rerum omnium creaturarum creator ds. fecit hominem ad imaginem sue similitudinis dans ei intellectum ut ea que futura sunt agnoscat et de animabis suis a longe prodentur prevideant.
et ideoque ego name and title *offero et tibi eclesie beatissimi sci.* name of church, genitive case
type of property *(uno fuscione de terra mea) (omnes res medietatem)*
its location *(as in a) uno caput tenet in via publica, alio caput...uno latere tenet... alio latere tenet...*
its attributes *(as in b) casa cum structura case fundmento curte orto uineas terris cultum uel incultum arboribus fructiferas uel infructiferas mobile vel inmobile seomounetibus*

[A re-statement of *traditio*]

(a) *terra quomodo circumdata est, tradedi tibi do. ecclesie sci* name of church, genitive case *in integrum*
(b) *omnia et in omnibus iam dicxit medietatem sci* name of church, genitive case *sit potestatem in integrum.*

[Usufruct clause]

set tamen sit placuet animum meum ut ispa sup.scripta property [*res/terra*] *dum aduiuere meruero ego* name. If others *una cum* names *sit postestatem tantum usufractandi*
nam pos viro obitum meum/nostrum reuertatur ipsa sup.scripta property [*res/terra*] *ad ipsa di. eclesia sci.* name of church, genitive case *sit potestatem.*
et ipse sacerdos qui inuidem fueret ordinatus pro nostris facinoribus die noctuque laudem do. precare deueas.
et qui contra hac decretionem seo dotalium mei paginola aliqui agi presumere in omnipotenti di. incurra iudicium et cum ipso abea portionem qui tradedet (tradide) salvatore (-ure).
et pro confermationem name of priest/scribe *prbo. scriuere rogaui. actum in uico corgite renum et ind. sup.scripta. fel.*

> homine faciendi nec adhuc ad alia eclesia faciendi. Et si ipsa sup[er]scripta filia mea nomine Sunderada caste et munde uoluere in ispa res resedere, tantum, dicxit, usufructuandi i nostra sit potestatem. Nam pos viro obitum nostrum revertatur ipsa sup[er]scripta res ad ipsa D[e]I eclesia S[anct]i Prosperi sit potestatem'.

Literacy in Lombard Italy, c. 568–774

But Tanipert's fellow-priest Deusdona chose not to use this same formula again four years later for another *charta dotis* to the same church of San Paolo, and again written in Gurgite.[113] This was probably due to the choice of the *rogator* of the document, Pettula, but her choice of *arengae* was not unique: the same *arengae* are found in two other Lucchese charters of 759 and 772 written for different Lucchese churches by what appear to be lay scribes.[114] Similarly, we find the *arengae* given in the two above mentioned charters commissioned by Eonand in another Lucchese charter of 748 written by the Lucchese priest-scribe Gaudentius.[115]

The Lucchese evidence provides numerous similar examples of shared formulae and *arengae* which attest to the influence, and effectiveness, of the writing 'school' at the cathedral of Lucca, the palaeographical traces of which have been identified by Petrucci in the hands of Lucchese writers across the last three quarters of the eighth century and into the mid-ninth.[116] Tracing the use of formulae further confirms the palaeographical evidence for a distinction between urban and rural settings, between cathedral clergy and parish priests. Situated in Capannori, around 10 km from the city centre, Tanipert and Deusdona administered semi-rural parishes outside the immediate influence of the cathedral. Even if they were not trained to write charters at the cathedral school, as their use of common formulae suggests, they were certainly not of the same graphic capacity as the cathedral clerics Gaudentius or Osprand (see Plate IVa–c). Nor were they of the same capability when it came to manipulating formulaic language to the client's needs and the exigencies of the transaction. A good example of such proficiency among the cathedral clergy is the priest Fratellus, from whose hand we have a short string of surviving charters across the years 759–62, and whose speciality appears to have been drawing up leases for his bishop.[117] Fratellus' orthography and grammar are far from classical, but they are still clearly a cut above those of many of his Lucchese contemporaries and other scribes elsewhere in the *regnum*. In the leases, Fratellus needed to accommodate a series of

---

[113] CDL 157. It appears that Pettula's husband never possessed her *mundium*: cf. Liutprand 114 and 139.

[114] CDL 136 (S. Angelo, 759), 269 (S. Giuliano, 772). The *arengae*: 'Dum super isti futuri seculi hauitare meruerimor, oportum est nobis de illa aeterna vita cogitare, qui peccata pondera nostrorum subleuare possint, quia aliut tensauro non est simile illi, qualis est ille suauis, qui meritis est habere vitam eternam.' Variations in 136: *meruermur, de illa eterna cogitare vita, peccata pondorum nostrorum relevare possit*; in 269, *avitarem meruerimor, quogitare, quia alium temsaurum non est similis ille soauis qui bene meritum est auire vitam eterna*.

[115] CDL 94.

[116] Petrucci, 'Il codice e i documenti', *Scriptores*, pp. 77–86.

[117] CDL 139 (lease), 145, 160, 166 (lease), 167 (lease) (and 156). Subdeacon in 759 (139), he was priest within the year (145). (ChLA 955, 960, 968, 974, 973 [966]). On his script ('abile e personale'), G. Nicolaj, ChLA XXXII, p. 77.

Charters

specific and highly individual requirements to a formulaic model, and this he does successfully, owing to his grasp of the language. Although he leans on formulae common to many Lombard charters for the obligation clauses, as the bishop and his tenants relay a series of promises to maintain the terms of the contract, Fratellus was on his own for the terms themselves, and for listing the particulars of the property leased. His precision is impressive, even to the extent of giving an address for the annual delivery of an autumnal pig as rent.[118] His precision of expression is achieved not so much by adherence to classical grammar, but rather by his consistency in deploying verb-forms and case endings well on their way to Romance.[119]

The recurrence of common formulae and *arengae* across the range of Lucchese charters, often very distant from one another in terms of place and time of redaction, is testimony to the strength of the documentary tradition cultivated at the cathedral, the largest land-owner in the region, situated in the Lombard capital of Tuscany.[120] In the following century Lucchese clergy were to lose their predominance as document writers to lay *notarii* of the region.[121] But for the eighth century, the often exquisitely executed charters they wrote for individuals who endowed the churches and monasteries of the city and surrounding countryside demonstrate a continuity of documentary tradition, and a professionalism in writing, that is unrivalled in the collection of charters from the Lombard period.

While there are other examples of shared formulae among charters from other regions, the evidence is too scant to allow any solid

---

[118] CDL 167: 'per omnem annum de ipsa casa uel res reddere debeam uno animale annutino in mense maggio porco in annutino in octummio, sex decimate de uino, grano siligine bono modia quattuor, angaria quantas utilitas fuerit in curte uestra in Lusciano et ipse animale et porco a nos usque a Rosellas minare debeam'. Rosellas identified as Roselle, Grosseto: Schiaparelli, CDL I, p. 104 n. 1.

[119] Interesting is Fratellus' preference to the gerund in ablative case instead of a gerundive or infinitive form. While not strictly correct, the sense remains clear, and corresponds to its use in modern Italian: 'ut sacerdos . . . uolo ut s[upra]s[crip]ta res in eius sit potestatem dispensando'; 'et luminaria s[an]c[t]orum faciendo'; 'nam non in aliquo subtrahendo uel in alia ecl[esia] faciendo'; 'et quis de redib[us] meis in ipso monasterio capite tonso caste uiuendo', CDL 145. Occasionally the gerund in genitive case is used correctly to express purpose: 'uolo ut in ipso monasterio uel eius res nulla licentia habeat inperandi', yet the gerundive in ablative case is generally preferred even when used with preposition *ad* to express obligation: 'non exeam alibi ad habitando', CDL 166; '[terra, casa, res] mihi ad resendendo et laborando et meliorando dedisti', CDL 167. Cf. Politzer, *A Study of the Language*, p. 118. The same is observed in some Ravennate papyri: Carlton, *A Linguistic Analysis*, p. 141.

[120] See H. Scharzmaier, *Lucca und das Reich bis zum Ende des 11. Jahrhunderts: Studien zur Sozialstruktur einer Herzogstadt in der Toscana* (Tübingen, 1972), pp. 140–70.

[121] H. Keller, 'Der Gerichtsort in oberitalienischen und toskanischen Städten', *Quellen und Forschungen aus Italienischen Archiven und Bibliotheken* 49 (1969), 5–62, at pp. 9–14, and chart p. 13.

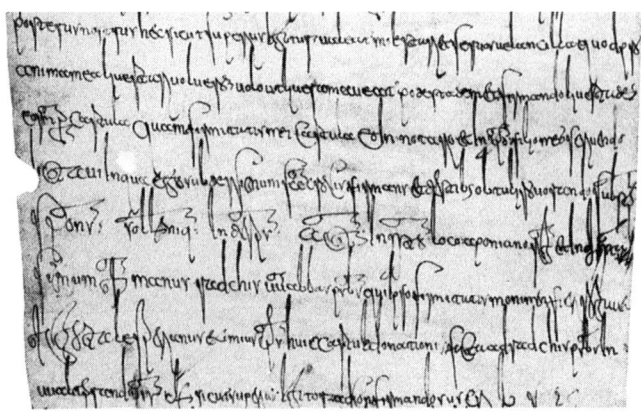

Plate IVa Gaudentius. Lucca, Archivio arcivescovile, Diplomatico no. 13 (from ChLA XXX, no. 905, p. 63)

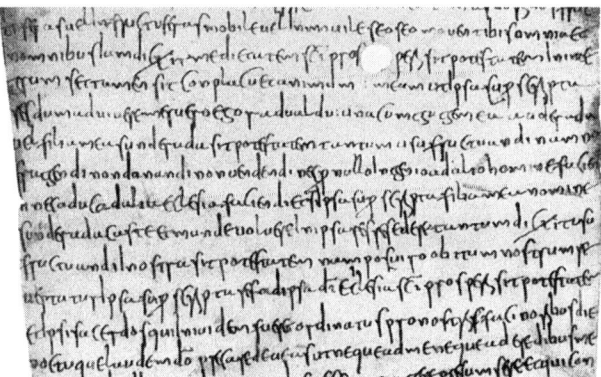

Plate IVb Tanipert. Lucca, Archivio arcivescovile, Diplomatico no. 57 [++M3] (from ChLA XXXII, no. 950, p. 60).

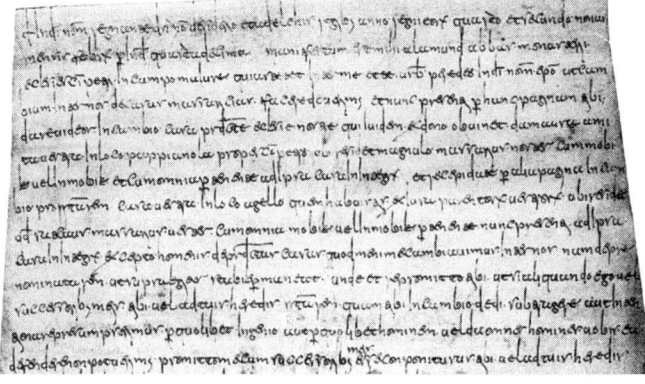

Plate IVc Osprand. Lucca, Archivio arcivescovile, Diplomatico no. 71 [+M, 65] (from ChLA XXXIII, no. 963, p. 15)

Charters

conclusions.[122] It is clear, however, that there were no set rules or rigid traditions concerning the particular formulae which scribes used. The similarities found in the language of some charters point to common sources of instruction which may have taken the form of using formularies or simply the use of past documents as models. When Liutprand legislated that 'those who do not know how [to write documents according to the law] should ask others', he assumed that there was a sufficient pool of knowledge of law and of formulae among the inhabitants of Lombard Italy that enabled anyone wishing to write a charter to learn the appropriate forms.

THE PRESERVATION OF CHARTERS

It has been suggested by some scholars that the demise of the *gesta municipalia* and the decline of public registration in the medieval west are reasons for the survival of individual charters from the seventh century onwards.[123] This would appear to dovetail nicely with the pattern of surviving evidence, particularly that of Merovingian Gaul.[124] For Lombard Italy, however, such a theory must grapple with the 'darkness' of the seventh century; our run of surviving charters does not really get under way until the dawn of the eighth century. This may have been partly due to the continued use of papyrus in Italy (as in Gaul too) for recording transactions, though poor archival practices may have played a part also.[125] Liutprand's legitimation of gifts to the church in 713, in his first acts of legislation, certainly explains the better survival rate of all types of charters, as ecclesiastical institutions kept records of sales or agreements between laity that related to land which the institution latter possessed, and this is the only manner in which lay documents have come

---

[122] Some interesting cases: three charters of Treviso (CDL 216 [768], 277 [772], 289 [773]), redacted four or five years apart and recording sales of land to the gastald Ermuald; the 'constat me accepisse' formulae common to Milan (CDL 36), Pavia (226), Brescia (128) and Asti (119), as compared to the use of 'constat me vendisse' in Tuscany, Lazio, Verona (CDL 290) and Treviso (37, 216); Lombardia, Piedmonte, Liguria and Pavia have a characteristic introduction to a *charta donationis* in which the donor exhorts 'presens presentibus dixi' (for example, CDL 18). Is the common Lucchese formula 'ego ... tibi salutem dixi' (CDL 22, 24, 42, 62, 67, 73, 77, 94, 125, 126, 133, 186, 189 and Pisa 183) a remnant of classical letter-address?

[123] Classen, 'Fortleben und Wandel', pp. 48–9. W. Bergmann, 'Untersuchungen zu den Gerichtsurkunden der Merowingerzeit', *Archiv für Diplomatik* 22 (1976), 1–186, at pp. 105–6.

[124] See D. Ganz and W. Goffart, 'Charters earlier than 800 from French collections', *Speculum* 65 (1990), 906–32.

[125] On papyrus for royal and ducal documents, see above, chapter 4, note 108, pp. 186–7. For private charters: see Schiaparelli, CDL I, p. 9; cf. Bischoff, *Latin Palaeography*, pp. 34–5; Noble, 'Literacy and the papal government', pp. 82–108. Use of papyrus in Merovingian Gaul, Ganz and Goffart, 'Charters earlier than 800', p. 912.

down to us.¹²⁶ It makes little sense to attribute the poor survival rate for seventh-century Italy to any continued existence of *gesta municipalia*, as though their presence, questionable enough in Byzantine Italy in this period, slowed down the cultural transition to the preservation of private documents by individuals, for the use of *gesta municipalia* was probably very limited in the first place.¹²⁷

In a similar vein, it has also been suggested that the demise of the *gesta municipalia* contributed to the emergence of a new form of document in seventh-century Gaul, the *placitum*, as though decisions made by the royal court fulfilled the same role as the court of the *curia municipalis* in the late Roman period, by providing an authoritative document that records the rightful ownership of a possessor.¹²⁸ Boüard suggested that the judicial origin of the authentic notarial act, that is, one with *fides publica*, lay in the fusion of notariate and judicature in Lombard Italy which, he argued, could constitute 'confessiones in iure'.¹²⁹ But there is no evidence in our period of any fusion between those who presided over the court cases and those who recorded their outcomes. Moreover the evidence we have suggests that the courts may have been reluctant to issue a document recording their proceedings: the responsibility for documentation appears to have lain with private individuals. A charter of 770 recording an exchange of lands between members of the same family reveals that the terms of the exchange had been already decided upon at the royal court, which seems to have advised them to have documents drawn up. This they did with the help of a local Piacentine *vir clarissimus*, who wrote a copy for each party, whether independently or under the auspices of local authority is unclear.¹³⁰ Copies of original charters, however, could be approved by the royal court, thus conferring a degree of public authority upon the document. A *placitum* of 763 held in Pavia records a dispute between the *gasindius* of Pistoia, Tasso, on behalf of the woman Rottruda, against a certain Auripert. Both parties presented

---

¹²⁶ Liutprand 6. Our first lay document, a sale, dates from 720, CDL 23 (Pisa). Gifts: CDL 14 (710), 16 (713), 18 (714). See P. Wormald, in Davies and Fouracre (eds.), *Settlement of Disputes*, pp. 1–2, 4.
¹²⁷ Everett, 'Scribes and charters', pp. 73–7.
¹²⁸ Classen, 'Fortleben und Wandel', pp. 48–9; and Fouracre, ' "Placita" and the settlement of disputes in later Merovingian francia', in Davies and Fouracre (eds.), *Settlement of Disputes*, pp. 23–44, at pp. 26, 42; Bergmann, 'Untersuchen zu der Gerichtsurkunden', pp. 153–80.
¹²⁹ Boüard, *L'Acte privé*, pp. 19, 170–4.
¹³⁰ CDL 249 (ChLA 826): 'et repromettemus nos suprascripti ... quod in corte domno regi dare *deuemus*, ut nos te [Audepert] exinde securo facere *deueamus*. Unde duae cartole conuinentiae pari tinore conscripte sunt, et sibi per manibus inuicem tradiderunt.' Italics mine. We know nothing more about this scribe, Ermenfrit; the document was redacted 'in Teuolario' (probably Tolarolo, on the Ceno river) where one of the parties lived. On court cases in general, see L.Y. Bruyning, 'Lawcourt proceedings in the Lombard kingdom before and after the Frankish conquest', *Journal of Medieval History* 11 (1985), 193–214; and Radding, *Origins*, pp. 37–67.

Charters

charters which were copies of the original documents to support their claims. The copy of the winning party, Tasso and Rottruda, had been signed by King Aistulf himself. How or why Rottruda had obtained royal approval of her copy remains unknown, although it is possible that the bishop of Pisa played a role in securing the *iudicatum*, since the charter concerned property donated for the establishment of a *xenodochium* which was to be administered under the auspices of the bishop. According to the judges, their decision was based on the legal deficiencies of the losing party's charter, not because the winning charter had been confirmed by the king.[131] As we saw in the previous chapter in relation to ducal charters, a document issued by Lombard rulers or their courts did not necessarily provide irrefutable proof of a claim, but rather was to be examined to determine its legitimacy according to the requirements of Lombard law.

Although there is abundant evidence that the laity had charters redacted and used them to substantiate claims to property rights, we have no idea of how or where they stored them. Kings, dukes and other officials, such as *missi regis* or gastalds, presumably had their chanceries or notaries draw up copies of the documents they issued for preservation in an archive attached to the courts. Is there any evidence for private archives of the laity? A suggestive piece of evidence is a *breve de moniminas*, preserved at the Archivio arcivescovile of Pisa among the ten pre-Carolingian original charters dating to our period. The *breve* lists over 100 documents, including charters, royal diplomas, letters, *brevi*, *iudicata*, *livellaria* (leases). The list ended up in the hands of the Pisan bishop Domnucianus, though it was headed with the title 'Breve de moniminas quem reddidet Teuspert Ghittie Deo ancille et ad filie eius'. We do not know who Teuspert was, why he gave the nun Ghittia and her daughters the list, or why the list (and presumably the documents it records) ended up with the bishop. The different types of the sixty-four *cartulae* are carefully listed, and some of the other persons mentioned in the list in relation to the documents appear in other Tuscan charters.[132] Of documents listed, thirty-eight

---

[131] CDL 163.
[132] CDL 295 (ChLA 808). For the dating, see editors' comments, ChLA XXVI, p. 55. To break down the list: fifty documents concern 'Alahis'; sixteen (twelve charters, four diplomas) concern the church of San Pietro ai Sette Pini and/or the archdeacon Alateo (whom we know from ChLA 806, CDL 171) and the priest Liufrido (mentioned in CDL 230); twelve issued in favour of other people; seven in which the beneficiaries are not mentioned; five for which nothing is mentioned. The list also mentions *precepta* from kings Liutprand and Ratchis that confirm other charters, as well as non-informative phrases such as 'brevi decem' and 'epistule tris'. Similarly the 'livellaria' is not elaborated upon. The different types of document listed: *venditio* 34, *donatio/offersio* 5, *dispensatio* 3, *de mundio accepto* 3, *conventiae* 2, *cautio* 1, *cauto cappilato* 2, *traditio* 1, *de morte* 1, *tingatio* 1, *promissio* 1, *de affeduciato* 1, *precepta* 20 (varied types: *confirmatio* 9, *tingatio* 2, *renovatio* 1, *de finibus* 1, *de salinas* 1). There are also eleven more *brevi*, three *epistulae* and two *iudicata*.

Literacy in Lombard Italy, c. 568–774

charters and six royal diplomas from King Liutprand (one of which mentions another six royal diplomas) record the purchases and possessions of Alahis, certainly a wealthy layman, and possibly the same Alahis, *vir magnificus*, who subscribed to a Lucchese charter of 722.[133] Alahis had preserved over forty-two documents recording his rightful possessions, and it seems reasonable to suppose that he did so in some sort of private archive.

The fact that Alahis' charters ended up in the hands of the nun Ghittia, and then transferred to the bishop of Pisa, is another reminder that all of our charters from this period survived owing to their preservation in an ecclesiastical institution, as can be seen in the Milanese, Sienese, Pisan and Piacentine collections which contain lay documents.[134] There is, however, very little evidence as to the location and organisation of these archives in this period. Some examples of dorsal notes from the Lucchese collection suggest that the charters were filed in a system based upon recognising the witnesses who subscribed.[135] Similarly, a charter from the collection of the church of San Pietro in Varsi contains the dorsal note in the hand of the scribe Peredeo, 'test[is] autoravele Unp[er]tus de Veriano'.[136] No Lombard charters included a *notitia testium* at the foot of the document, a post-Justinianic innovation found in the papyri of Ravenna, which perhaps facilitated quick reference when searching for a particular witness.[137] An original charter from Novara reveals that a layman could employ a non-clerical scribe to redact a charter inside the church itself. Radoald from 'Gausingo' (probably near San Pietro in Mosezzo), donated some land to the bishop of Novara, Gratiosus, on the condition that the bishop dedicate the altar of the church in the name of St Michael and that *luminaria* were maintained for the salvation of Radoald's soul.[138] Radoald stated that he reread the charter written by the *notarius* Lautchis, signed it, and handed it over 'to be conserved by you [Gratiosus] in the *scrineum* [sic] of the holy church'. It is difficult to determine whether the acts of rereading and signing the charter took place in the church or elsewhere, but it is certain that the charter, from

---

[133] CDL 30. The chronology matches, as does the social range of those involved: Orso, *rogator*, was wealthy, and had received gifts of land from King Aripert (701–712), and alongside Alahis in the witnesses list were the Lucchese bishop and Walpert, 'vir gloriosissimus dux'.

[134] ChLA XXVIII, XXIII–IV, XXVI, XXII, respectively.

[135] In a charter of 772, CDL 259 (ChLA 1027) the dorsal notes name the witnesses who subscribed to the charter, as well as giving the date, in abbreviated form. Likewise, CDL 195 (766) (ChLA 990), although without the date.

[136] CDL 130 (758). Why Unpertus of Veriano should have been singled out amongst the other six witnesses remains a mystery. Not all dorsal notes pertain to archival usage: cf. CDL 234; 58 157 (both Lucchese).

[137] See Tjäder, I, p. 276.

[138] CDL 149: 'et uobis vel in scrineo sancte heclecia tradedi conservandum'. The transaction was 'Actum in civitatem Novaria'. Rotpert, defined himself as a 'ciuis Novariensis'.

its conception, was intended to be stored in the *scrinium* of the church of St Martin, a rare reference to some type of official archive.

CONCLUSION

Being a Lombard *notarius* was not a 'profession' which depended on regulation or recognition by the Lombard state, but was rather an occupation or profession for which the authority to write legally valid documents was dependent upon the adherence of the document to a set of rules and procedures that were firmly established in the late Roman legal culture of vulgar law. These conditions were reiterated, with some innovations, in Lombard legislation. The 'private' status of the Lombard *notarius* was nothing new: it was merely a continuation of the type of ground-level documentary culture we see in the ideals of late Roman legislation and in the practice of the redaction of documents such as the *Tablettes Albertini* and other lay documents of the early medieval west, in which the writer of a document did not need to be licensed or even recognised by the state. Moreover, use of the word 'private' to describe charters that record transactions between individuals in the Lombard period is a little misleading, for all charters depended upon their adherence to 'public' laws for their validity. Any legally valid document was a public document, otherwise it was pointless.

The mechanics of how the profession, or trade, of document writing was maintained is obscured from our view. There were certainly *scholae*, corporations or guilds of writers, in administrative cities such as Ravenna or Rome, but we know little about them. In Lombard Italy, as elsewhere, the script and formulae of the documents, as well as the references to *magistri* and *discipuli*, demonstrate the strength of documentary traditions and hint at the existence of some type of professional hierarchy for document-writers. This is evident in the *viri clarissimi* of the Piacentine collection, who allow us to see continuity of local traditions not simply throughout the Lombard period but also stretching back to pre-Lombard Italy. The Lucchese collection demonstrates how a powerful and somewhat enterprising episcopal church cultivated and maintained chancery traditions to protect its own interests and whose influence extended throughout the entire region. Elsewhere, the obscurity that surrounds the institutional aspect of writing documents merely reflects the insignificance of such institutions to the dictates of late Roman law. In late Roman as much as post-Roman Italy, a document could be considered valid evidence of ownership in the case of dispute so long as it had been written according to law and correct procedures, and with the appropriate formulaic language, regardless of who wrote it. We are still a long way from the later medieval institution of the established notariate enjoying *fides publica*. Charlemagne's decree of 805, in which he declared 'every bishop, abbot and count should have his own notary',[139] may have been a step towards governmental recognition, and hence control, over documentary practice which resulted in development of a licensed notariate. It also may have recognised a situation that already existed in Lombard Italy. But it is important to realise how such a decree was foreign to Lombard legislative tradition. Lombard kings did not need to stipulate that ecclesiastical or governmental institutions be manned with personnel trained in legal literate traditions: it is taken for granted. It seems telling that all four statutes of Charlemagne's first act of legislation in Italy concerned charters. The sense behind his legislation is that there was much activity going on, and Charlemagne needed to make his mark upon it as another means of securing recognition of his authority.[140]

Though literary luminaries in Lombard Italy are few in comparison with ninth-century Carolingian Europe, one gets the sense that Italians continued to rely on Roman traditions of functional literacy, such as the redaction of charters to record transactions: the increase in surviving documentation of the ninth century merely confirms the picture.[141] These traditions were not limited to an elite but extended to the majority of the population for whom the adherence to *lex scripta* and the use of *cartae* were no novelties but an integral part of their society and culture. This type of functional literacy was capillary in early medieval Italy, and continued to be so throughout the Frankish period. But in terms of legal literacy, the Lombard period witnessed a degree of synthesis between the central authority and local practice which would have pleased and impressed ancient Romans as much as it escaped the grasp of the Franks.

---

[139] MGH Cap. I, 43.4, p. 121.   [140] MGH Cap. I, 88, pp. 187–8.
[141] F. Bougard, *La Justice dans la Royaume d'Italie* (Rome, 1995), p. 76, and *passim*.

6

INSCRIPTIONS

There are many different types of inscriptions that served different purposes and used different types of materials which can be dated to the Lombard period, such as dedicatory inscriptions in stone, painted inscriptions, graffiti and coins. This chapter will concentrate on epigraphy, or inscriptions in stone, for two reasons. The first reason is that they provide texts sufficient in length to allow us to delve further into the literate culture of Lombard Italy. The second reason is that, in comparison with other early medieval successor kingdoms in the west, such as Frankish Gaul or Visigothic Spain,[1] Lombard Italy has furnished us with evidence of a rich epigraphic culture that merits attention. McKitterick regretted the omission of inscriptions from her study of literacy in Carolingian Francia owing to problems with source collections.[2] The problem is different for Lombard Italy, in fact often tending towards antiquarian overkill.[3] The implications for literacy of this surviving corpus of inscriptions remain unclear.

---

[1] For the Merovingian evidence, see E. Le Blant (ed.), *Inscriptions chrétiennes de la Gaule antérieures au VIIIe siècle*, 2 vols. (Paris, 1856–65) and E. Salin, *La Civilisation mérovingienne: d'après les sépultures, les textes, et la laboratoire*, II, *Les sépultures* (Paris, 1952). More recently, *Recueil des inscriptions chrétiennes de la Gaule, antérieures à la Renaissance carolingienne*, I, *Première Belgique*, ed. N. Gauthier (Paris, 1975), and *ibid.*, XV, *Viennoise du Nord*, ed. F. Descombes (Paris, 1985). R. Favreau, 'Les commanditaires dans les inscriptions du haut moyen âge occidental', *Settimane* 39.2 (Spoleto, 1992), 681–722. For Visigothic Spain, see E. Hübner, *Inscriptiones Hispaniae Christianae*, 2 vols. (CIL II) (Berlin, 1871–1900). Hübner is often, but certainly not always, superceded by J. Vives, *Inscripciones cristianas de la España romana y visigoda*, Monumenta Hispaniae Sacra, Serie Patristica 2 (Barcelona, 1969). For the Rhineland see W. Boppert, *Die frühchristlichen Inschriften des Mittelrheingebietes* (Mainz am Rhein, 1971).

[2] *Carolingians*, p. 271, although the situation has improved since.

[3] I have generally consulted the following: A. Silvagni, *Monumenta epigraphica christiana*, 3 vols. (Vatican City, 1943); G.B. De Rossi, *Inscriptiones christianae urbis Romae septimo saeculo antiquiores* (Rome, 1857/61–88); G. Panazza, *Lapidi e sculture paleocristiane e pre-romaniche di Pavia*, Arte del Primo Millenio. Atti del II Convegno per lo studio dell'arte dell'alto medioevo, tenuto presso l'Università di Pavia nel Settembre 1950 (Turin, 1953), pp. 209–302; MGH Poetae IV, 'Rhythmi langobardici' (ed. Duemmler), pp. 718–31; P. Rugo, *Le iscrizioni del sec. VI–VII–VII esistenti in Italia*, vols. 1–5 (Citadella, 1974–78); C. Troya, *Codice diplomatico longobardo*, I–V, con note storiche, osservazioni e dissertazioni (Naples, 1852–55). Where necessary: *Insriptiones Italicae*, Unione accademica

Literacy in Lombard Italy, c. 568–774

In this chapter I shall first briefly explore some of the problems of using inscriptions as evidence for literacy, before moving on to discuss the importance of the epigraphic heritage of ancient Rome and its survival in Italy as a key to understanding the role of inscriptions in Lombard Italy. I then proceed to discuss various examples of 'lost' inscriptions from the *syllogae* collections and explore the idea of an epigraphic renewal in the eighth century during the reign of Liutprand, using the examples of the 'Theodota school' inscriptions as representative of a specifically 'Lombard style'. Finally, I turn to the unique evidence of the graffiti at Gargano as it further fills out the picture of epigraphic culture of early medieval Italy, before making a few comments on the form of Italian epigraphy which dates from prior to the eighth-century evidence. The material under discussion is predominantly from northern Italy, and evidence from the duchy of Benevento will not be discussed, except for that of the graffiti at Gargano. Apart from the major problem of space, the main reason for excluding the Beneventan material is that it post-dates the period of the Lombard kingdom, though it developed a strong and homogeneous epigraphic style in the ninth century that continued throughout the later history of the principality. I hope that the following discussion contributes to our understanding of the later Beneventan material by further uncovering its foundations in the extraordinarily rich epigraphic culture found in Lombard north Italy.[4]

The emphasis here is on examining a more public display of literacy. The evidence challenges the suspicion that the use of literate communication was limited to the higher-status members of society. A discussion of literacy should attempt to understand the effect of inscriptions that could be seen by a larger number of people than the documentary

---

nazionale, Istituto poligrafico e zecca dello stato, 13 vols. (Rome, 1888–), and the *Supplementa Italica, Nuova serie* to the CIL, 12 vols. (Rome, 1981–94); C. Cecchelli, *I monumenti di Friuli dal sec. IV all'XI*, vol. I (Milan and Rome, 1943); U. Monneret de Villard, 'Iscrizioni cristiane della Provincia di Como anteriori al secolo XI, *Rivista archeologica della provincia e antica diocesi di Como* 65–6, anno 12 (Como, 1912).

[4] On the Beneventan material, see Gray, 'Palaeography', pp. 1123–138, p. 165; Rugo, *Iscrizioni esistenti*, IV, nos. 13–128; C. Russo Mailler, *Il senso medievale della morte nei carmini epitaffici dell'Italia meridionale fra VI e XI secolo* (Naples, 1981). For the uses of script at the monasteries of San Vincenzo and Monte Cassino in the mid to late eighth century, see J. Mitchell, 'Display of script'; Mitchell, 'Literacy displayed: the use of inscriptions at the monastery of San Vincenzo al Volturno in the early ninth century in McKitterick (ed.), *Uses*, pp. 186–225. The problem of viewing the evidence of San Vincenzo as pertaining to Lombard Italy is complicated by Frankish involvement and patronage of the monastery: R. Hodges and J. Mitchell (eds.), *San Vincenzo al Volturno: The Archeology, Art and Territory of an Early Medieval Monastery*, BAR Int. Ser. 252 (Oxford, 1985); R. Hodges (ed.), *San Vincenzo al Volturno I: The 1980–86 Excavations*, Archaeological Monographs of the British School at Rome 7 (London, 1993); but see G. West, 'Charlemagne's involvement in central and southern Italy: power and the limits of authority', *EME* 8.3 (1999), 341–67, and R. Balzaretti, 'San Vincenzo al Volturno. History rewritten?', *ibid.*, 387–99.

evidence of charters, written laws and manuscripts. Who were these inscriptions directed towards? Who could read them? What was the relationship between the commissioner of an inscription, the artisan who produced it and the expected audience? What is the evidence for understanding epigraphic production as an industry centred upon the use of the inscribed word? Although such questions concerning inscriptions as evidence for literacy have rarely been applied to the early middle ages, they have been well tackled by historians of antiquity. In his study of literacy in the ancient world Harris considered inscriptions in predominantly quantitative terms, arguing that the 'density' of surviving inscriptions in a given region serves as a 'rough indication of the level of literacy', and that chronological fluctuations in the numbers of surviving inscriptions provide evidence for the rise and decline of literacy.[5] The critical response to Harris' approach has well pointed out the deficiencies of merely quantitative considerations in the Roman world, in spite of Harris' slant on inscriptions, and literacy in general, as pertaining only to an elite.[6]

In searching for vestiges of a literate world in Merovingian Gaul, Riché believed that 'an inscription is, in effect, the best manifestation of a written civilisation; why would it have been engraved if not to be read?'[7] The question must be asked for Lombard Italy, despite the fewer numbers in comparison with the ancient Roman world. There are around fifteen or so lengthy inscriptions in rhythmic verse that survive, although only half of these are in lapidary form; the other half are recorded in *syllogae*. These may possibly be just the tip of the iceberg, for several fragments of inscriptions preserved in the Casa Anelli in Pavia suggest that there

---

[5] *Ancient Literacy*, pp. 265–7, 287–8, 314–15, which builds on the views Harris put forward in 'Literacy and epigraphy, I', *Zeitschrift für Papyrologie und Epigraphik* 52 (1983), 87–111. Cf. R. MacMullen, 'The epigraphic habit in the Roman empire', *American Journal of Philology* 103 (1982), 233–46; and F. Meyer, 'Explaining the epigraphic habit in the Roman Empire', *Journal of Roman Studies* 80 (1990), 74–96.

[6] See J.H. Humphreys (ed.), *Literacy in the Roman World*, Journal of Roman Archaeology Suppl. Ser. 3 (Ann Arbor, 1991), esp. T. Cornell, 'The tyranny of evidence: a discussion of the possible uses of literacy in Etruria and Latium in the Archaic age', pp. 7–34; A. Bowman, 'Literacy in the Roman empire: mass and mode', pp. 119–31, esp. p. 122; N. Horsfall, 'Statistics and states of mind', pp. 59–76. J.L. Franklin Jr., 'Literacy and the parietal inscriptions of Pompei', in *ibid.*, pp. 77–98. Harris has been unrepentant: see his '*Instrumentum domesticum* and Roman literacy', in *Acta Colloqui Epigraphici Latini* (Sept. 1991), Commentationes humanarum litterarum 104 (Rome, 1995), pp. 19–27. The 'decline' of surviving epigraphy is well documented by K. Randsborg, *The First Millenium AD in Europe and the Mediterranean: An Archaeological Essay* (Cambridge, 1991), pp. 108–15; see esp. figs. 62 (Noricum), 63 (Pannonia and Cologne), 65 (Rome and vicinity), 66 (Antioch), 67 (Christian gravestones with inscriptions from Rome, Spain and northern Gaul). Cf. Harris, *Ancient Literacy*, pp. 287–8, 298.

[7] *Education*, p. 181. Cf. P. Wormald, 'The uses of literacy in Anglo-Saxon England and its neighbours', *Transactions of the Royal Historical Society* 5 ser., 27 (1977), 95–114; S. Kelly, 'Anglo-Saxon lay society and the written word', in McKitterick (ed.), *Uses*, pp. 37–8.

was a far greater number of 'Pavese' style inscriptions produced in this period.[8] There is also a substantial number of short dedicatory or funerary inscriptions, say around fifty, that merit attention for different reasons. The use of this evidence in the following discussion will be, therefore, necessarily selective.

In many cases the attribution of a particular inscription to the period and locations of the Lombard *regnum* remains speculative. One of the greatest difficulties of using this evidence for a study of literacy is the loss of the inscriptions' original location. Very few, if any, of our inscriptions remain *in situ*, and their history is often completely unknown prior to the beginning of antiquarian interest in describing and transcribing inscriptions 'de aetate vetustissima' that commences in the fifteenth century or later.[9] In cases where we do have some record of an inscription's history by antiquarian or museum reports, the history is a discouraging one of constant relocation of the inscription, or worse still, of its damage or disappearance.[10] In promoting the prestige of the city or diocese, many inscriptions were suddenly discovered and set up for public viewing, some of them of highly dubious authenticity.[11] Overcoming such problems requires assistance from the disciplines of history, palaeography, art history and linguistics, as well as epigraphy itself, which has its own internal debates on method and interpretation.[12]

---

[8] Panazza, nos. 67–73.

[9] L. Keppie, *Understanding Roman Inscriptions* (London, 1991), pp. 30–7.

[10] Panazza's catalogue, *Lapidi e sculture*, provides an account, where possible, of each inscription's history. Damage need not be attributed to humans only; see M.R.D. Seaward and C. Giacobini, 'Lichen-induced biodeterioration of Italian monuments, frescoes and other archaeological materials', *Studia Geobotanica* 8 (1988), 3–11.

[11] See C. La Rocca, 'Using the Roman past. Abandoned towns and local power in eleventh century Piemonte', *EME* 5:1 (1996), 45–69; C. Maccabruni, *Pavia: la tradizione dell'antico nella città medievale* (Pavia, 1990); see M. Greenhalgh, *The Survival of Roman Antiquities in the Middle Ages* (London, 1989), pp. 172–82. Ward-Perkins, *Classical Antiquity*, p. 32. Further on inscriptions in Pavia, see the references to inscriptions by Ennodius, *Carmina* 2.8 and 2.9 (MGH AA. VII, p. 120), 2.20 (p. 134), 2.10–15 (p. 122), 2.17 (p. 127), 2.18 (p. 134), 2.37–45 (pp. 147–9).

[12] Good introductory guides to the Roman material are A.E. Gordon, *Illustrated Introduction to Ancient Roman Epigraphy* (Berkeley and London, 1983) and G.C. Susini, *Il lapicida romano: introduzione all'epigrafia latina* (Bologna, 1966), trans. A.M. Dabrowski and intro. E. Badian, *The Roman Stonecutter: An Introduction to Latin Epigraphy* (Oxford, 1973); more recently, G.C. Susini, *Epigrafia Romana* (Rome, 1982). For medieval epigraphy in particular: R. Favreau, *Epigraphie médiévale*, L'Atelier du Médiéviste 5 (Turnhout, 1997); Favreau, *Inscriptions médiévales*, Typologie des sources du moyen âge occidental (Turnhout, 1979); Favreau, *Etudes d'épigraphie médiévale*, 2 vols. (Limoges, 1995). On the relationship between the disciplines of palaeography and epigraphy, see Susini, *Roman Stonecutter*, pp. 1–9, and Petrucci's survey of opinions (R. Favreau, M. Guarducci, J. Mallon, S. Panciera, A. Prosdocimi, G. Scalia, H. Solin, G. Susini) in 'Epigrafia e paleografia. Inchiesta sui rapporti fra due discipline', *Scrittura e Civiltà* 5 (1981), 265–312. See also, A. Campana, 'Tutela dei beni epigrafici', *Epigrafica* 30 (1968), 5–8; R.M. Kloos, 'Methoden und Möglichkeiten der lateinischen Epigraphik des Mittelalters', in *Actes du VII e Congrès international d'épigraphie grecque et latine* (Bucharest and Paris, 1979), pp. 91–103.

Inscriptions

The content and preservation of nearly all of our surviving inscriptions from Lombard Italy testify to an ecclesiastical milieu of commissioners and audience. The significance of this for discerning their original reception remains unclear. The immediate assumptions are, first, of a reduction in the number of people who were exposed to the display of script in epigraphic form and, second, a diminution of its importance in everyday life. Thus it is thought that the interior of a church somehow conceals an inscription from the larger reception which the more public display of ancient Roman monuments enjoyed. Petrucci has argued that the 'ubiquitous presence of writing' found in the cities of the empire was inseparable from the ancient use and appreciation of public space. For him, the middle ages constituted a rupture in the 'connective tissue' of the daily use of writing by private individuals and its official use in public open space by lay authorities. The narrow, winding streets of the early middle ages, the intentional closing of spaces, and the 'dizzying vertical perspectives of the city walls, interrupted here and there by architraves and protuberances', were not conducive to the public acts of communication transmitted and received by an urban literate milieu.[13] The debates over the relative urbanism of early medieval Italian towns do not need to be repeated here, but Petrucci's emphasis on 'public space' as an integral component of the impetus behind epigraphic display must be considered if we are to understand the communicative role of inscriptions in early medieval Italy. We also need to consider how much a church could have constituted a type of 'public space' that facilitated the display of inscriptions to be read by a more attentive audience than that of passers-by: a space that was designated for meditation on a religion of the book; a quiet space where more time might be spent comprehending an inscribed text than a busy street allows.[14]

ANCIENT ROMAN EPIGRAPHY IN MEDIEVAL ITALY

Italy's Roman epigraphic heritage is of the utmost importance if we are to consider the attitude of the inhabitants of Lombard Italy towards script and written communication. For the ancient world, the inscription was a means for solemn expression of social values, of imperial ideology and aristocratic class-dominance. The use of language was literal and figural, a sentence had a chain of resonances that placed the deed or the dead

---

[13] A. Petrucci, *La scrittura: ideologia e rappresentazione* (Turin, 1980), trans. L. Lapin, *Public Lettering: Script, Power, and Culture* (Chicago and London, 1993), pp. 1–3.

[14] Most studies of Christianisation of city spaces have centred on Rome: but see P. Testini, G. Cantino Wataghin and L. Pani Ermini, 'La cattedrale in Italia', in *Actes du XI Congrès international d'archéologie chrétienne*, I (Vatican City, 1989), pp. 5–57.

in a long tradition of Roman superiority and exaltation of achievement. By their physical existence, inscriptions affected all those who saw them, not just the commissioners of the work or the highly literate, but also the semi-literate and illiterate who were confronted with a set of symbols that were construed together to convey meanings and to imbue society with a certain code of values. The text may contain a verbal message, but the whole figural design that accompanies it has an associative set of significations that can work on numerous levels. Susini pointed out the pedagogical aspect of inscriptions in the ancient Roman world:

> inscriptions were a permanent element of the daily visual environment of the citizen... [inscriptions] could not fail to exercise an educational influence; honorary and votive inscriptions, inscriptions on the pediments of buildings and especially on sepulchral stelae, probably constituted the best reading practice, intentional or otherwise, for many adults and children alike.[15]

The satire of a certain freedman's declaration 'lapidarias litteras scio' in Petronius' *Satyricon* (58.7) serves to remind us of the public nature of inscriptions, as well as the need of elites to distinguish their brand of literacy, based on a rhetorical education, from that of the common folk, based on the interpretation of texts in their everyday life.[16] Just how many Roman inscriptions survived *in situ* as part of the 'daily visual environment' of Lombard Italy is difficult to determine. The 'regional density of monumental inscriptions' calculated from the *Corpus inscriptionum latinarum* suggests that northern Italy was less furnished with inscriptions than central Italy and Campania in particular.[17] There are many deficiencies with such a method of calculation, not least that the CIL is severely out of date, and only contains between half and two thirds of the texts published for most regions.

One aspect that helped keep Roman inscriptions before the 'eyes of generations ever on the move' was the '*frontality*' of all Roman monuments: the predomination of the frontal view in addressing an 'endless posterity'.[18] Funeral monuments lined the highways with *tituli loquentes*.

---

[15] *Roman Stonecutter*, p. 52.
[16] On the meaning of *lapidarias litteras*, see R.W. Daniel, 'Liberal education and semi-literacy in Petronius', *Zeitschrift für Papyrologie und Epigraphik* 40 (1980), 153–9; P. Veyne, *A History of Private Life from Pagan Rome to Byzantium*, trans. A. Goldhammer (Cambridge, MA and London, 1987), p. 18. Horsfall, 'Statistics or states of mind', p. 62, confesses that this was how he learned himself.
[17] From Harris, *Ancient Literacy*, pp. 265–71, and table 3, p. 266. On the basis of the number of inscriptions per 1000 square kilometres, Harris suggests that Campania, with a figure of 410.9, was the 'most literate' part of Italy, whilst Liguria (42.9) and Lucania (18.5) were the 'least literate'. Other figures: Umbria (275.7), Picenum (205.1), Samnium (156.6), Venetia (119.9), Etruria (118.0), Apulia (73.6), Transpadana (70.8), Aemilia (69.5).
[18] *Roman Stonecutter*, pp. 22ff.

Inscriptions

Many of these were the *Siste viator et lege* variety that address the reader directly, like the epitaph of a certain Claudia: 'Stranger, what I have to say is little, stand near and read it through...I have spoken, go your way.'[19] The commissioner's objectives and the stonemason's task combine to ensure legibility of an inscription addressed to diverse peoples along highways, not some obscure message to God(s), as has been argued for ancient Egyptian or Assyrian monuments.[20] That Lombard inscriptions worked within the same tradition of addressing the reader directly is testimony to the continuity of 'frontality' in the display of inscribed messages. But one also wonders about the effect of a visible display of ancient Roman monuments and inscriptions on the inhabitants of Lombard Italy in terms of the preservation of historical memory. In contemporary Constantinople, both pagan and Christian inscriptions could inspire awe and terror, and were used as evidence to validate popular accounts of the past.[21] When commissioned by Duke Arichis to write dedicatory verses to be displayed on the walls of Salerno, Paul the Deacon contrasts the construction of such monuments under Lombard, Christian rule with the 'Aemula romuleis...moenia templis' of Italy's pagan past. The past Paul knows is not just from his reading of Eutropius, but also from the present world that he sees around him.[22]

Leaving aside the more substantial monuments with script, many of which must have been visible in the Lombard period, one type of monument that calls attention to the more functional aspects of the physical presence of script is the milestone. Over 4000 Roman milestones are known to us, although it is difficult to know how many of these may have survived *in situ* in the eighth century.[23] Quintilian commented on the soothing effect on weary legs of the ever-reducing tally on milestones

---

[19] 'Hospes, quod deico paullum est: asta ac pellege...dixi. abei', Gordon, *Illustrated Introduction*, p. 34.

[20] See J. Baines, 'Literacy and ancient Egyptian society', *Man* 81 (1983), 572–99. Cf. E.S. Meltzer, 'Remarks on ancient Egyptian writing with emphasis on its mnemonic aspects', in P. Kolers *et al.* (ed.), *Processing of Visible Language*, II (New York and London, 1980), pp. 22–45.

[21] See the references to inscriptions in the eighth-century Byzantine text, *Constantinople in the Early Eighth Century: The Parastaseis Syntomoi Chronikai*, ed. and trans. J. Herrin and A. Cameron (Leiden, 1984), cc. 7, 16, 17, 24, 26, 34, 40, 41, 49, 61, 64–5, 80, 81. The language of these inscriptions has been described as 'subliterary...representing the uneasy balance between the purist ideal and the speech of the people'; R. Browning, *Medieval and Modern Greek* (London, 1969), p. 61. The same may be said for the Lombard inscriptions, see below.

[22] The poem in Neff, *Die Gedichte*, IV, p. 15. Paul and Eutropius, see Goffart, *Narrators*, c. 5 *passim*. On the poem and its context, see N. Acocella, 'Le origini di Salerno medievale negli scritti di Paolo Diacono', in *Salerno medievale e altri saggi* (Naples, 1971), pp. 513–63.

[23] The CIL vol. 17.1 (ed. G. Walser) on milestones in Italy is still in preparation (forthcoming with Walter de Gruyter and Co.), though vol. 17.2, *Milliaria provinciarum narbonensis galliarum germaniarum* has been published (Berlin, 1986). Harris, *Ancient Literacy*, excluded milestones.

Literacy in Lombard Italy, c. 568–774

as the long-suffering traveller passed them.[24] Milestones were designed so that the traveller with horse and cart could read and comprehend the whole ten- to fifteen-line text without stopping.[25] Milestones lined the roads in and out of Aquileia, perhaps often seen by the Lombards as they passed back and forth from Pannonia to Italy, or elsewhere along the main roads of the peninsula.[26] Roman milestones not only measured the distance along the road from its starting point, they sometimes also reported construction work and who had been responsible for it. The Acephalous Elogium, which probably dates to the second or first century BC, not only gives accurate distances to various cities, but also recounts, in first person, the achievements of the road builder, including his retrieval of 917 runaway Italian slaves from Sicily, and records his claim to be 'the first to drive sheep herders to withdraw from public land in favour of ploughmen'.[27] How long such markers remained visible is another question: the Elogium was reported in the fifteenth century to be in the same place where it stands today, now immured in a monument on the Italian state highway no. 19 near Lucania. The continuity of the use of Roman roads in Italy during the Lombard period suggests that milestones would still have been of indispensable use to merchants, traders, pilgrims, not to mention the Lombard armies and travelling officials (the *missi regis* for example) in the administration of the kingdom.[28] The brief texts and numerals of milestones did not require a wealth of literate skills to interpret, but they may have provided some incentive to obtain such skills and perhaps further testify to the use of literate forms of communication in the 'everyday visual environment' of Lombard Italy.

---

[24] *Inst. orat.* 4.5.22.   [25] Susini, *Roman Stonecutter*, p. 22.
[26] G. Brusin, 'Epigrafi aquileisei in funzione di pietre miliari', *Atti dell'Istituto Veneto di Scienze, Lettere e Arti* 1.14 (1955–56), 281–90 (Via Gemina, Via Annia, Via Postumia). On the Roman inscriptions and milestones of Pannonia, see D. Arpad, *Inscriptiones ad res pannonicas pertinentes extra provinciae fines repertae*, dissertationes Pannonicae (Budapest, 1932), and A. Brelich, *Aspetti della morte nelle iscrizioni sepolcro dell'impero romano* (Budapest, 1937); A. Legnyel and G.T.B. Radan (eds.), *The Archaeology of Roman Pannonia* (Budapest, 1980), esp. pp. 116–20, 404–6, and plates viii, ix, xi, xxxviii, lix, xc, xci, xcii, xciii, cii, cxvi, cxxxvi, cxlvi, cxlvii, cxviii, cxcviii, cxlix, clviii; milestones in particular, pp. 104, 138, 208–9. See also T. Kolnik, 'Q. Atilius Primus – *interprex, centurio* und *negotiator*', *Acta Archaeologica Academiae Scientiae Hungaricae* 30 (1978), 61–75; P.M. Bersanetti, 'Massimino il Trace e la rete stradale dell'impero', *Atti del III Congresso di Studi Romani* (1934), 593–506. Also L. Pitmada, 'S. Onofrio (Catanzaro) – rinvenimento di cippo miliare', *Notizie degli scavi di Antichità* 6, *Atti dell'Accademia dei Lincei*, ser. 8 (1952–53), 343–4. An example of one carved into the natural cliff-face is found at Donnaz, Aosta Valley (CIL V.8074), Susini, *Roman Stonecutter*, p. 21.
[27] Gordon, *Illustrated Introduction*, no. 12.
[28] See G. Schmiedt, 'Città scomparse e città di nuova formazione in Italia in relazione al sistema di communicazione', *Settimane* 21 (Spoleto, 1974), 503–607; Harrison, *Early State*, pp. 54–86.

Inscriptions

THE *SYLLOGAE* INSCRIPTIONS: LOST TEXTS, LOST IMAGES

To return to the more substantial inscriptions, we can gauge some sense of what was left standing (or lying) to be seen in this period from the several collections of inscriptions of Rome and Italy jotted down in manuscripts, often with itineraries of the *loca sanctorum*, mostly by Anglo-Saxons, in the seventh, eighth and ninth centuries, called a *sylloge*.[29] The impression one gets from De Rossi's transcription of these manuscripts' contents is that there was a considerable number of inscriptions on display not only in and around Rome (where clearly the bulk of the travellers'/authors' interest lay) but also all along the Via Flaminia, and in Spoleto, Ravenna, Pavia and Milan. Judging by the content of these *syllogae*, the authors' reasons for copying these down vary. Some are interested in noting classical-pagan inscriptions full of abbreviations and references to emperors, elites and titles of civil offices long past as well as the inscriptions on Christian churches and monuments. Other *syllogae* are only interested in the latter and combine them with an itinerary of places to visit or a 'report' on ceremonial and liturgical practices of the *patria sancti petri*.[30] A particularly interesting *sylloge* that demonstrates the presence of, and interest in, the epigraphy on display in Italy is the *Laureshamensis*. Written in the eighth or ninth century, it is one of our earliest 'itinerary' texts recording Roman-pagan and Christian monuments in Italy, and it includes inscriptions from in and around Rome, Ravenna, Spoleto, Milan, Pavia, Piacenza, Vercelli and Ivrea.[31] The author appears to have travelled up the peninsula from

---

[29] De Rossi put them together in *Inscriptiones christianae urbis Romae septimo saeculo antiquiores* (*ICR*), II.1 (Rome, 1857/61–88). See also A. Silvagni, 'The *Sylloge* of Cambridge', *Rivista di Archeologia Cristiana* 20 (1943), 74–95. I have therefore relied on De Rossi's arguments for dating, with the exception of the *Laureshamensis*. On seventh- and eighth-century *itineraria* for Rome, see R. Valentini and G. Zucchetti, *Codice topografico della città di Roma*, II (Rome, 1942), pp. 72–99, esp. p. 75; J. Wilkinson, *Jerusalem Pilgrims before the Crusades* (Warminster, 1977). The *Sylloge ensiedlensis* is available in facsimile: G. Walser (ed.), *Die Einsiedler Inschriftensammlung und der Pilgerführer durch Rom (Codex einsiedlensis 326): Facsimile, Umschrift, Übersetzung und Kommentar* (Stuttgart, 1987).
[30] Such as the *Einsidlensis*, possibly dating from the time of Charlemagne and Pope Hadrian: De Rossi, *ICR* II, pp. 9–33.
[31] De Rossi's transcription does not make for clarity. He divided up the text into four different parts on the basis of palaeographical differences in the manuscript, Vat. Pal. lat. 833; *Sylloge laureshamensis, pars prima, secunda, tertia, quarta*, *ICR* II, pp. 142–53, 124–30, 159–73, 95–118, respectively. Having examined the manuscript, however, I do not believe that the changes in (minuscule) script necessarily indicate different periods of redaction. Fols. 27–35, which focus on Rome, seem contemporaneous with 35v–54v, the *circumpadana et subalpina* section (the subtitle is De Rossi's invention), despite the change of ink evident on fol. 32v, which appears to be in the same hand as the previous folios, until fol. 34. Some letter forms of the *circumpadana* section differ, such as the more half-uncial 'g', the long tail on the 'x' and the use of the diagonal stroke above the middle letter of a word to indicate a contraction (s p̄ r super, dī domini, x p̄ e Christe,

Literacy in Lombard Italy, c. 568–774

Rome to Ivrea (or perhaps vice versa), visiting churches in search of worthy inscriptions, and showed a particular interest in metres, although a conscious indication of such only begins with the Piacentine epigraphy on folio 49 of the manuscript, prefaced by the abbreviation in capitals 'RITHM' or 'RITM' indicating rhythmic metres, and 'METR' for hexameters – we shall return to some of these 'lost' Lombard inscriptions in a moment. Another interesting collection is that of the *Sylloge centulensis*, written in a Corvey manuscript of the eighth or ninth century.[32] Beginning with Rome, it proceeds to Spoleto then Ravenna and seems only interested in the heights of what we might term Petrean poetry. These are the types of truly accomplished works that Riché described as 'religious poetry in classic vocabulary and form', a mark of the transitional period from ancient to medieval literary expression, where Virgilian reminiscences on Christian themes ensured that 'not even dogma escaped the laws of poetry'.[33] These literary compositions set in stone may have played some role in providing models for the ones we find associated with the ecclesiastical and secular elites of Pavia and Milan in the late seventh and eighth centuries. We now turn to a few examples of these which also only survive in *sylloge* form.

In the *Sylloge lauresbamensis* there exists a group of inscriptions that are associated in diverse ways with the bishop of Pavia, Damian (d. 711). His own twenty-six-line epitaph in rhythmic metre is testimony to the existence of a high literary culture, and attributes to Damian himself the

---

etc.). However the constant use of the 'e-t' ligature ('&') and diagonal stroke indicating omission of a consonant or vowel (ae' á, etc.) throughout the text serves to confirm that the two sections were contemporaneously composed as part of one enterprise. The same problem occurs on fols. 53v and 54, where De Rossi perceived a change of hand and a later redaction of epigraphy found in Rome (on the basis of the use of words such as *vestiarius* or *tenuiarius* in the texts copied), but there is no reason why these monuments could not have been found in Ivrea and redacted as a continuation of that on fol. 53. Fols. 55–82 appear to be a separate collection (pertaining to Rome only), as De Rossi suggests. Hence fols. 27–53/4 appear to make up a whole 'Italian collection' that included Rome, Spoleto, Ravenna and the northern cities.

[32] Preserved from the twelfth century in St Petersburg, MS Leningrad F. XIV.1. De Rossi, *ICR* II, pp. 72–97. Also of interest here is the *Sylloge turonensis*, probably compiled in the seventh century on the monuments of Rome: De Rossi, *ICR* II, pp. 58–72. Other, later collections of Roman inscriptions: *Sylloge parisina* (MS Paris BN lat. 8071; De Rossi, *ICR* II, pp. 244ff; *Sylloge virdunensis*, MS Verdun 45; De Rossi, *ICR* II, pp. 131ff; *Sylloge wirceburgensis*, MS Würzburg Mp. m. f.2; De Rossi, *ICR* II, pp. 154ff).

[33] *Education*, p. 82. His examples are the metrical inscriptions on the Via Salaria (*ICR* II, pp. 100, 137), Ennodius of Pavia's poems for the Milan baptistry (*Carm.* 2.56, MGH AA. VII, p. 157) and those decorating the effigies of Milan's bishops (*Carm.* 2.77–8), the epitaphs of the bishops of Spoleto (*CIL* V.6722ff), the poem in honour of Pope Hormisdas by his son (*ICR* I, p. 108), and the 'De Maria virgine ad Rusticianam' (*ICR* II, p. 109). Amongst the better known are the epitaphs of Pope Gregory the Great (*consul dei*), Elpis (wife of Boethius?), Catula, the martyrs Hypolitus and Laurence, the Anglo-Saxon king Caedwalla, and Drotculf of Ravenna – the last two of which Paul the Deacon incorporated into his *HL*.

Inscriptions

'GLORIA VATUM'.[34] Paul the Deacon mentioned him only briefly in the *HL*, yet noted that he was 'liberalibus artibus sufficienter instructus'.[35] The epitaph extols his virtues and wisdom, his building and decorating of churches and, interestingly, restoring the thermal baths at Pavia[36] (we shall see what Liutprand thought of baths below).

Similarly, there are four lengthy poems, three being epitaphs, in rhythmic verse that can be linked to a 'deacon Thomas', most probably the same deacon Thomas mentioned by Paul the Deacon as serving under Bishop Damian, and who is also mentioned in the *Carmen de synodo ticinensi*. Thomas' own sixteen-line epitaph records his chastity,[37] an attribute that would explain the significance of the somewhat strange and distasteful exchange reported in the *HL* between Thomas and the usurper Alahis concerning clean underpants.[38] The twenty-nine-line epitaph of a certain 'Barionas', caretaker (*custos*) of the church of San Michele in Pavia, concludes that a 'germanus Thomas' was responsible for the epitaph's composition and the construction of the tomb, possibly the same Thomas with clean underpants mentioned above, although we cannot be certain.[39] The poem begins by beseeching the reader to help stave off the 'rustic muse' so that the author may compose a poem worthy of Baronias' earned praises, and then ends with a 'literary compositional' topos that laments the impossible task of composing verses worthy enough for the task, so that Pan's rustic pipe must eventually triumph:

---

[34] Panazza, no. 61. Text also in MGH Poetae IV, pp. 719–20, CXXXIV. Also line 13: 'QUAM PRAEROGATIVA VATIS DIVINO MUNERE DATA'. Bognetti thought the lines 'QUOS SINUS ENUTRIT/LIGURIE ET GIGNUNT QUOSQUOS ATHENEA RURA' testified to Damian's Greek origin, and thus saw him as one of the many eastern missionaries combating paganism and Arianism in Pavia and Milan: 'S. Maria', pp. 237ff, and subsequently, E. Cattaneo, 'Missionari orientali a Milano nell'età longobarda', *Archivio Storico Lombardo*, ser. 9.3 (1963), 216–45.

[35] *HL* V.58. A surviving letter of Damianus to the emperor Constantine IV and the Sixth Oecumenical Council (680–681) testifies to his literary competence, *PL* 87, 1264; see Riché, *Education*, p. 410, and below, p. 285. Damian had not yet been appointed as bishop of Pavia at the time of the council: Waitz, MGH SRL, p. 166 n. 3.

[36] 'THERMARUMQUE VAPORES/UT GEMINAS DILUERET CULTU PROPRIO SORDES CORPORUM PER AQUAS ANIMAE PLACABILIA SACRA'.

[37] Panazza, no. 49. Text also given in MGH Poetae IV, p. 722, CXXXVII. (*Carmen de synodo ticinensi*, *ibid.*, p. 730). 'TE MUNDA ACTIO THOMAS MOSTRABAT HONESTUM/TECUM VIRGINITAS AB INCUNABILIS VIXIT/TECUMQUE VERITAS ADVITARINE TAM PERMANSIT/TU CASTO LABIO PUDICA VERBAPROMEBAS'. Cf. 'Thomas' (bishop of Milan, *c.* 759–783), Rugo, *Iscrizioni esistenti*, V, no. 31.

[38] *HL* V.38. An odd story: cf. *HL* V.40.

[39] Panazza, no. 52. 'FUNERIS OFFICUM THOMAS HOC SOLVIT AMANTER/GERMANUS DULCIS MERITIS ET MUNERE COMPAR'. C. Merkel, 'L'epitaffio di Ennodio e la basilica di S. Michele in Pavia', *Atti della Reale Accademia dei Lincei* 292 (Rome, 1896), 83–134, noted some derivations from the epitaph of Ennodius which was, of course, also in the church of San Michele, but they are minor similarities and the whole epitaph of Baronias stands as an original and accomplished piece of poetry.

I shall rely on poor Baronias, just minister of Christ, to help set forth this poem, written to be pronounced for ever. Alas, reader, I ask the rustic muse forbid to me to dwell on this man's noble heritage and rather that I sing the song of his merits... we cannot express everything [concerning this man] in verse worthy enough, a task that causes the pipe to silence my tongue.[40]

This Baronias, who is attested by no other source, was responsible for yet another literary and lyrical tomb, that of the 'twice widowed' Columba, a woman of high status in the upper echelons of Lombard society. As with Baronias, we have no other documentation of this elusive 'dove', but, similar to the Baronias epitaph, Columba's addresses the reader and refers to the act of composing verse and, what is more, setting it into stone:

whose [i.e. Columba's] life, reader, the chisel could scarcely relate to you, for pressed against the petty marble like a weak stylus it could not even touch upon how she was a mother to those in need, and how the stars shone with her strength and gay voice.[41]

Yet another verse inscription associated with a 'Thomas', which follows from the epitaph of Columba on the next folio of the manuscript containing the *Sylloge laureshamensis*, is that written by John, nephew of the above mentioned Thomas. Here the poem indicates its association with depictions (frescoes?) of events from the Apocalypse:

John, the guardian of this venerable church and successor to his uncle Thomas, who completed this holy and beautiful work which the minister of God, Thomas, began with a devoted heart, is driven to write these little verses, so that if you, reader, desire to understand all these things/deeds (*gesta*) you might seek the answers in the wonderful book of Holy John. There you will find indeed what is written about how the master revealed to his disciples that which shines forth in the holy atrium.[42]

[40] 'NITAR PERSPICUI XPR CELEBRANDA MINISTRI/BARONIAE PARVO DEPROMERE POEMATE FACTA/LECTOR HEU POSCO DICENTIS RUSTICA MUSA/PROHIBEAT MERITE RIMARI INSIGNIA LAUDIS/STEMMATE QUO CLUERIT GENERIS QUID CARMINA PANGAM...IAM QUAM DIGNE NON POSSUMUS OMNIA VERSU/PROMERE CONTICEAT NOSTRAE FISTULA LINGUAE'. On this often clumsy use of the *brevitas loqui* topos, see Curtius, *European Literature*, pp. 489–94, as found in Paul the Deacon's epitaph for Queen Ansa. The same topos is found in the Theodota epitaph; see below.

[41] My rendering of a difficult passage, probably due to scribal tradition: 'SCAPTOR/QUOD CALIBI STILO ARTATUS MARMORE PARVO/SI TETIGISSE SATIS FUERIT QUOD MATER EGENTUM/HUIUS OPE ALACRI PULSABANT SIDERA VOCE'. Panazza, p. 247, records the proposed emendations of Mommsen (*prodere possum quod calibi stilus artatur*) and Duemmler (*scalptor quit calibi stilo aratur*).

[42] Another difficult text: 'SCRIBERE VERSICVLOS IOHANNIS COMPVLIT ISTOS/SVCCESSOR PATRVI CVSTVS VENERABILIS AVLAE/HVIVS ET EXPLETOR SCI PVLCHRIQ. LABORIS/QVEM COEPIT THOMAS DNI DEVOTO CORDE MINISTER/AVT SI TOTA CVPIS LECTOR COGNOSCERE GESTA/EGREGIVM SCI LIBRV SCRVTVRE IOHANNIS/ILLIC INVENIES VERO REVELANTE MAGISTRO/DISCIPVLV SCRIPSISSE SACRIS QUOD FULGET IN ATRIIS'. See De Rossi, *ICR* II, pp. 167–8 n. 18. Panazza, no. 51.

Inscriptions

The temptation is to identify Thomas as the same man of the two other inscriptions (the epitaph of Thomas, Baronias' 'brother Thomas', who would then of course be associated with the Columba for whom Baronias composed an epitaph), the deacon Thomas in the *HL* and the *Carmen de synodo ticinensi*, but nothing confirms the identification.[43]

Whoever the Thomas and John of this inscription were, the interesting element is the reference to the use of text and images together and the exhortation to the reader to further his or her understanding of the images by reading the text of the Apocalypse. This is precisely the type of education by image that is referred to by Gregory the Great in his famous passage on the use of images in churches in his letter to the bishop of Marseilles. In that letter Gregory the Great advocated the use of images for the religious instruction of the illiterate who could at least 'read the pictures', a passage that became of the utmost importance for the defence of the use of images in the west against the proponents of Iconoclasm in the east.[44] The inscription, however, seems to be aimed at one level higher than that with which Gregory was concerned, in that it addresses a *lector* already literate enough to read the inscribed (or perhaps painted) text. The inscription has therefore combined four functions: the commemoration of the person initially responsible (Thomas) for the procuring and sponsoring of the art-work; self-advertisement by John for his continuation and completion of the initial work; proclamation of John's authorship of the *versiculi* that commemorate the completion of the work; and the exhortation to read the scriptures in order to enlighten the reader about the artistic merit of the images and their meaning. Unfortunately the inscription does not say if there were already words accompanying the images for educational purposes.

Testimonies are scarce for the use of inscriptions as a pedagogical device for practice in reading. Gregory of Tours tells us how the slave Brachio learned to read by copying down in a notebook the letters he saw next to the portraits of the Apostles and saints in the church; he later went to ask the younger clerics what they were called. Gregory commented that the boy 'both read and wrote before he knew his alphabet'.[45] If the images commemorated by John's verses were accompanied by words, they could

---

[43] Its position in the manuscript (Vat. Pal. lat. 833 f.47) and the abbreviated 'item versus' as heading, the inscription before having 'versus in quaedam ecclesiae', suggest Pavia but not any church in particular; De Rossi, *ICR* II, p. 169. Robolini suggested that it was a church dedicated to St John the Evangelist, see Panazza, p. 247.

[44] Ep. XI.10, MGH Ep. II, p. 271. See C.M. Chazelle, 'Pictures, books and the illiterate: Pope Gregory I's letters to Serenus of Marseilles', *Word and Image* 6 (1990), 138–63. For Gregory's authority in the *Libri carolini* (I.19, II.28), see H.L. Kessler, '*Facies bibliothecae revelata*: Carolingian art as spiritual seeing', *Settimane* 41.2 (Spoleto, 1993), 533–94.

[45] *Vitae patrum* XII, MGH, SRM, I.2, p. 713.

Literacy in Lombard Italy, c. 568–774

undoubtedly have been used to the same effect. Unfortunately, we have no such direct evidence for this type of learning activity in Italy. Several other inscriptions from the *Sylloge laureshamensis* provide evidence of the use of text and image in the churches of Lombard Italy.[46] This use could be directed didactically by facilitating familiarity with script as the first steps to the attainment of literate skills, and as a way of communicating to the populace the message of Christ and the holy scriptures.

CORTEOLONA AND THE EPIGRAPHIC CULTURE OF LIUTPRANDIAN PAVIA

Sometime a little after 729 Liutprand founded a palace with a basilica and monastery dedicated to S. Anastasius at Corteolona, around 20 km south of Pavia towards Cremona, along the Olona river, which runs on further to meet up with the Po.[47] Very little of the construction remains, but two dedicatory inscriptions, presumably positioned in the church or cloister, have come down to us through the anonymously written *Sylloge laureshamensis*. Deconstructing the content of the inscriptions takes us much further into the cultural ambience of Liutprand's reign. It serves to justify the choice of the term 'Liutprandian' epigraphy for the surviving corpus of inscriptions which date to the period of Liutprand's reign. Therefore a full translation of the two inscriptions follows:[48]

Behold the house of the Lord, built with beautiful materials, it shines forth and glistens, decorated with various metals. Rome, the capital of the faith, has given it its precious marble, mosaics and columns, how these give light to the eyes of the world! Hooray for prince Liutprand, the author of this holy work! Your deeds will proclaim you fortunate throughout time, you, who desiring to decorate the triumphs of your people, have stamped the whole country with these inscriptions.

---

[46] De Rossi, *ICR* II, p. 168 n. 20. Panazza, no. 87, which calls attention to a picture of Jesus trampling a lion. As to its location, the heading of 'in quaedam ecclesiae' in the manuscript is unhelpful, but the poem's position in the manuscript suggests Pavia or its environs. Likewise De Rossi, *ICR* II, p. 169 n. 18. Panazza, no. 88, a cross that speaks to the reader: and De Rossi, *ICR* II, p. 33 n. 82, Panazza, no. 60, inscription in Greek capitals which was accompanied by an image of S. Peter, from the *Sylloge einsiedlensis*. I cannot agree with the thesis of M.P. Billanovich, 'Le tradizioni sull'apostolicità di S. Siro', *Rendiconti dell'Istituto Lombardo di Scienze e Lettere: Classe di Lettere* 127 (1993), 139–59, at p. 142, that this inscription was accompanied by a statue of St Sirus of Pavia.

[47] The earliest testimony is Paul, *HL* VI.58. See A. Riccardi, *Le vicende, l'area, e gli avanzi, del Regium Palatium e della cappella e monastero di S. Anastasio dei Re Longobardi, Carolingi e Re d'Italia nella corte regia ed imperiale di Corte Olona, provincia di Pavia* (Milan, 1889), and more recently, C. Calderini, 'Il palazzo di Liutprando a Corteolona', *Contributi dell'Istituto di Archeologia* 5 (1975), 174–225.

[48] I have used the text of De Rossi, *ICR* II, pp. 168–9, which is closest to the manuscript. There are some minor variations in Duemmler's version, MGH Poetae I, pp. 105ff, and even more in Calderini, 'Il palazzo', p. 179.

Inscriptions

When the emperor Leo fell into the pit of schism from the heights of the just, persuaded by a wretched philosopher, then I, King Liutprand, decided to build for myself baths with this beautiful marble and these columns. Then later I hastened as a devoted man to Rome itself, and when I reached it, I kissed the holy head of S. Anastasius, and suddenly you, Christ, show to me, your servant of the ancestral place, in this heart of mine, that I am to build this house in which I pray, holding the palms of my hands towards the stars, 'Son of God, on behalf of a faithful people, you who rule the angelic assembly and govern all things, I pray that you make the Catholic faith grow with me, and that you favour this temple, just as was said unto Solomon himself'.

ECCE DOMUS DNI P[ER] PULCHRO CONDITA TEXTU
EMICAT & UARIO FULG & DISTINCTA M & ALLO
MARMORA CUI PTIOSA DEDIT MUSEUMQ. COLUMNAS
ROMA CAPUT FIDEI ILLUSTRANT QUALUMINA MUNDI
EUGE AUCTOR SACRI PRINCEPS LEUTBRANDO LABORIS
TE TUA FELICEM CLAMABANT ACTA PER AEUUM
QUI PROPRIE GENTIS CUPIENS ORNARE TRIUMPHOS
HIS TITULIS PATRIAM SIGNASTJ DENIQ. TOTUM.[49]

QUANDO LEO CECEDIT MISERO DOCTORE SUASAS
SCISMATIS IN FOUEAM RECTO DE CULMINE CAESAR
TUNC EGO REGALES STATUI HIS MIHI CONDERE TERMAS
MARMORIBUS PULCHRIS LEUDBRANT REX ATQ. COLUNIS
SED ROMA P(RO)PERANS POSTQUA DEVOTUS AD IPSAM
PERVENI ATQ. SACRO CAPITI MEA BASIA FIXI
SCI ANASTASII SERUUS TUUS ECCE REPENTE
PATERNA DE SEDE MEO HANC PECTORE XPE
PRAECLAR FUNDARE DOMU SUB CULMINE MONSTRAS
TALIBUS UNDE MEAS TENDENS AD SIDERA PALMAS
UOCIBUS ORO DI FILI PRO PLEBE FIDELJ
QUI REGIS ANGELICOS CO & US QUI CUNCTA GUBERNAS
FAC PCOR UT CRESCAT MECUM CATHOLICUS ORDO
ET TEMPLO CONCEDE ISTI UT SALOMONI LOCUTUS.

My interpretation of 'his titulis' as meaning 'with these inscriptions' is not free of problems. In late antique parlance, *titulus* could refer to a number of things, including a parish church. The context of the poem, however, tends to deny other interpretations.[50]

---

[49] Cf. Paul the Deacon in his epitaph for Duke Arichis of Benevento: 'Ornasti patriam doctrinis moenibus aulis/ hinc in perpetuum laus tua semper erit'. Neff, *Die Gedichte*, p. 147.

[50] See DuCange, *Glossarium*, VII, pp. 114–16, and the comments of R. Davis (trans.), *Liber pontificalis: The Lives of the Eighth Century Popes* (Liverpool, 1992), glossary. Niermeyer's *Lexicon*, pp. 1029–31, lists no fewer than twenty-two definitions that range from tombstones to choirs: the *LP* frequently used *titulus* as 'monument', its use for 'parish church' being rare after the fifth century. In the works of Ennodius of Pavia and Cassiodorus the word can refer to an inscription, title, church

The implication that Liutprand is behind a programme of inscriptions to be set up throughout the Italy of his kingdom may be a slight exaggeration, but there is evidence of his strong involvement with epigraphic production. We have over ten surviving inscriptions that record his name, albeit sometimes in a form that is no more than a dating clause (*tempore regis Liutprandi*, etc.),[51] yet the previous kings do not appear very often, if at all, on inscriptions.[52] It is therefore all the more remarkable that Liutprand's name was inscribed so often.

The rest of the Corteolona inscription helps place Liutprand's reign in a broader cultural context. The king favourably compares himself to the emperor Leo, who had fallen into the depths of schism because his spiritual weakness allowed him to be charmed by a heretical *doctor*. Liutprand further 'one-ups' the empire by stating that though he too is powerful enough to build baths like a Roman emperor, his love of Christ and respect for Rome compels him to build a church instead with beautiful materials he had acquired. The dedication of the church to S. Anastasius, and more importantly the analogy of Solomon, reaffirms the image Liutprand promoted in his legislation of the king as the mediating instrument of the divine for his people and as guardian of the faith – Old Testament imagery fairly common in the early middle ages in the context of royal power.[53] Paul the Deacon used the comparison with Solomon for Arichis and the palace chapel at Salerno, perhaps in imitation of Liutprand's self-analogy.[54]

---

office, honour, tax or document: see, for example, Ennodius, *Opera*, MGH AA. VII, ed. F. Vogel (Berlin, 1885), pp. 2, 7, 22, 40, 61, 67, 101, 103; Cassiodorus, *Variae*, MGH AA. XII, ed. T. Mommsen (Berlin, 1894), pp. 120, 147, 283, 90, and esp. pp. 51, 49, 180. Note also Pope Gregory I's use of the term, MGH Ep. I, pp. 85, 325, 364; II, p. 35, esp. editors' comments, I, p. 54 n. 2. The use of *signare*, to 'seal', 'sign' or 'stamp' is more suggestive of literate communication via inscriptions: Lewis and Short (Oxford, 1984), p. 1697; Niermeyer, *Lexicon*, p. 970; DuCange, *Glossarium*, p. 480.

[51] Gray, nos. 25, 28, 29, 30, 33, 34, 48, and Panazza, nos. 62, 63. Though note the epitaph of Peter, bishop of Pavia, who was 'inclytus prosapia regis', yet Liutprand is not mentioned.

[52] The exceptions are: Agilulf, on the laminia di Valdinievole, see R. Elze, 'Die Agilulfkrone des Schatzes von Monza', in H. Beumann (ed.), *Historische Forschungen für W. Schlesinger* (Cologne and Vienna, 1974), pp. 167–84: Agilulf and Adaloald on the the stamped tile at San Simpliciano; Mitchell, 'Display of script', p. 893; Cunincpert, on Cunincperga' epitaph and his own, if the latter is authentic, Panazza, nos. 58, 75 (and below); one inscription from the *Sylloge lauresheamenis* refers to King Desiderius, De Rossi, ICR II, p. 167 n. 17; and Aistulf, in the Luni epitaph, Mazzini, 'L'epitaffio di Leodegar'; Rugo, *Inscrizione esitenti*, III, no. 81.

[53] See V.F. Ohly, 'Halbbiblische und ausserbiblische typologie', *Settimane* 23 (Spoleto, 1976), 429–72, at p. 464. See also J. McClure, 'Bede's Old Testament Kings', in P. Wormald et al. (eds.) *Ideal and Reality*, pp. 76–98. We also have a text that may be connected to some type of visual monument that was also in Liutprand's church of San Anastasius in Corteolona: 'CONTINET ISTA MANUS MUNDU PROSTERNIT ELATOS/ET HUMILES ERIGIT IUSTE MISERATA ROGANTI'.

[54] 'Regnator tibi, summe decus, trinominis ille Hebreae gentis Solymis construxit asylum', Neff, *Die Gedichte*, IV, ii, p. 18.

Inscriptions

The emphasis on 'faith', of the people to their king and therefore to God, can be seen in much of Liutprand's legislation.[55] The point here is that the two forms of literate communication (that is, laws and epitaphs) are used in conjunction to propagate court ideology.[56]

Liutprand's propaganda went beyond the palace and into the cloister. The tombstone of Cumianus of Bobbio (died *c.* 736) provides an example of Liutprand's patronage of epigraphic production.[57] The 180 × 90 cm tombstone was originally part of a sarcophagus for which another ornamental slab survives, decorated with high-quality reliefs of rope-pattern, rosettes, crosses and vegetal designs (see Plate V). The twin-border decoration that surrounds the text is suggestive of both earlier and later models: the initial border of deep incisions to form squared flower-shapes with a medial point resembles that of the Aldo epitaph of Milan, whilst the secondary border of vine-scrolls in circular patterns with motifs of flowers, leaves and *grappole* becomes a recurring form of decoration that designates the aulic Pavese style that we see in later examples such as the Theodota and Cunincperga epitaphs (see below). The lengthy nineteen-line text, in neatly cut capitals 3.8 cm high,[58] relates how Cumianus left Ireland at the sprightly age of seventy-four to live at Bobbio *dogma columbani servando* for twenty-one years before he died there when he was ninety-five. The language used to provide the dates is of a rhetorical, even poetic nature.[59] The invocation at the end of the inscription testifies to

---

[55] Some examples: the prologues of years V and XVI, and Liutprand 30, 33, 34, 76, 84, 85, 100, 133, 140, 144, *Notitia*, c. 5. The emphasis on 'defence' in the prologue to the legislation of 727 had its secular significance: that same year Liutprand recommenced offensives against the Byzantine territories. See Bertolini, *Roma e i Longobardi*, pp. 34ff.

[56] The words *sede paterna* and comparison with Solomon may be read further: Liutprand was possibly propagating an ideology of hereditary kingship and dynastic continuity needed to secure the throne for his nephew Hildeprand to succeed him, as the curious 'divinitory' story of Paul the Deacon suggests, *HL* VI.5. See C.G. Mor, 'La successione al trono nel diritto pubblico', in *Scritti di storia giuridica altomedievale* (Pisa, 1977), pp. 437–64. Solomon was also alluded to in Liutprand's first act of legislation (cf. III Kings 2. 26–7): a reflection on his relationship with the papacy?

[57] Menis (ed.), *I Longobardi*, IX.18, and photograph, p. 350. Gray, no. 33. R.M. Kloos, 'Zum Stil der langobardischen Steininschriften des achten Jahrhunderts', *Atti VI CISAM* (Spoleto, 1980), 169–82, p. 178. Complete text given in MGH Poetae IV, p. 723, CXXXVIII.

[58] The lettering belongs to Gray's 'second school', which features the 'G ending in a curl, the M with a short drop and all the apices tipped with serifs, N with a short diagonal and pronounced serif, an egg-shaped O pointed at the top, Q with the tail inside and the R with the curved and aggressive leg', p. 62, also found in the Vitalis epitaph and two fragments from the *Casa Anelli* (nos. 35, 41, 42, respectively). All of these have similar border-decoration.

[59] His time at Bobbio: 'Olimpiadis quattuor uniuque circolo anni / sic vixit feliciter'. His age at death: 'huic [Cumiano] aetatis anni fuerunt novies deni / lustrun quoque unum mensesque quattuor simul'. Gray reads *Olimpias* as a four-year period and so calculates Cumianus' time at Bobbio to be seventy years, 'Palaeography', p. 70. But in the Latin West *Olimpias* became synonymous with the Latin *lustrum* and denoted a five-year period: Lewis and Short, p. 1263.

Plate V   Epitaph of Cummianus. Bobbio, Museo dell'Abbazia (from
P. Caratelli (ed.), *Magistra Barbaritas* (Milan, 1984), no. 183, p. 271)

Inscriptions

Liutprand's involvement: 'but excellent father, be a powerful intercessor on behalf of the most glorious king Liutprand, who in his devotion has decorated your tomb with beautiful stone-work so that it might be known where your sweet corpse lies covered'.[60] The Cumianus tombstone is a reminder of the strong links between the Lombard royal court and the famous monastery, which was founded with the support and patronage of King Agilulf and Queen Theudelinda in the early seventh century. The earliest surviving royal Lombard charter (613) records this donation, and links between Lombard rulers and Bobbio continued throughout the seventh century. We have no contemporary charters from Liutprand that testify to his patronage of this monastery;[61] instead we have this inscription, and a mere fragment of another.[62] The craftsman who executed the work was proud enough to include his name in the last line of Cumianus' epitaph: 'FECIT IOHANNES MAGISTER'. Unfortunately we have no way of knowing whether this *magister* was attached to the monastery or to the Pavese court as a royally appointed artisan, or indeed worked freelance for commissions: his name does not recur in any other of the inscriptions of similar style. Liutprand's interest in the affairs of *magistri* can be seen in his legislative attempts to regulate prices and the workers' wages. 'Marble-workers' are mentioned and accounted for, and nearly all of our surviving examples are in marble.[63] The literary culture of Bobbio must be understood as being sponsored to some extent by royal Lombard patronage. The Cumianus epitaph permits us to include epigraphy as part of that literary culture.

The Corteolona inscription and Cumianus' epitaph are two examples of how Liutprand was using epigraphy as a means of royal propaganda, advertising his benevolence and piety for all to see. This raises the question of audience, for the two examples belong to an ecclesiastical context, perhaps suggesting a more restricted, monastic reception – the Corteolona

---

Gray also calculates Cumianus' death at ninety years of age, but the phrase 'lustrun [*sic*] quoque unum menses quattuor simul' is clearly 'one term of five years and four months': the use of *lustrum* here further suggests that it was interchangeable with *Olimpias*, as does the use of *lustrum* in the inscriptions of S. Mustiola mentioned above, and in the Luni epitaph, Mazzini, 'L'epitaffio'.

[60] 'AT PATER EGREGIE, POTENS INTERCESSOR EXSISTE/PRO GLORIOSISSIMO LIUTPRANDO REGE, QUI TUUM/PRAETIOSO LAPIDE TYMBUM DECORAVIT DEVOTUS/SIT UT MANIFESTUM, ALMUM UBI TEGITUR CORPUS'.

[61] A diploma of the emperor Louis II in 860, however, refers to 'praeceptiones et privilegia regum Langobardorum' for Bobbio and lists all Lombard kings, including Liutprand, and a concession of his that allowed the monastery to fish within his *curtis* at Lake Garda for 10 *solidi* a year. See Brühl, CDL III, p. 272; and Cipolla, *Codice diplomatico di Bobbio*, I.60, pp. 181–2.

[62] Gray, no. 34. The inscription, '+ D. LIUTPRAND REXV', carved in fine capitals around 5 cm high, was discovered during restoration of the crypt of the abbey church in 1910. See Cipolla, *Codice diplomatico di Bobbio*, p. 135.

[63] *Memoratio de mercedes commacinorum*, ed. Azzara, *Le leggi*, pp. 221–5, c. 7. Could *axes marmoreas* refer to the preparation of marble slabs to be inscribed?

inscriptions may have been situated in the adjoining monastery rather than in the palatial basilica. The inscription was prominent enough, however, to be copied down by one of the many visitors to Italy in the eighth century. Paul the Deacon describes the palatial church as a 'domicilium', that is, a place where pilgrims would stay.[64] As with the Cumianus epitaph, these inscriptions advertising royal favour were intended to impress and reaffirm the links between the secular and ecclesiastical hierarchies.[65]

Two other examples exemplify Liutprand's politico-epigraphic strategy. A damaged verse inscription, now preserved at the Museo Civico in Modena, records how Liutprand established '...SECURITAS ET PAX...' in what was formerly a place of dangers: 'HIC UBI INSIDIAE PRIUS PARABANTUR P...'[66] The poem stresses the unity of all people and common purpose in the 'TRANQUILL[US] et FLORENTISSIM[US]' reign of Liutprand, king of the highest virtue.[67] Another inscription, recording the king's involvement in the restoration of the church of Santa Mustiola, Chiusi, demonstrates Liutprand's attempt to establish alliances between the duke and bishop of Chiusi and the royal court.[68]

THE THEODOTA GROUP

The evidence from Liutprand's reign, therefore, testifies to royal patronage of epigraphic production to promote the political and ideological concerns of the royal court. It appears as more than a coincidence, therefore, that there is an increase in the number of inscriptions surviving in lapidary form both during and after his reign. Aside from the many fragments preserved at the Casa Anelli, other inscriptions of eighth-century date survive, including a group representative of a distinctive 'Lombard

---

[64] HL VI.58. DuCange, Glossarium, III, p. 163.
[65] Gray, 'Palaeography', p. 70, notes that the back of the slab has been carved with interlacings that are crude in comparison with the border decoration and suggests a date of the ninth or tenth century, in which case the tomb must have been dismembered very early. 'Crudeness', however, is a weak criterion for dating.
[66] Text in MGH Poetae IV, p. 723, CXXXIX. Rugo, Iscrizioni esistenti, V, no. 179. Gray, no. 28: 'the letters are pleasantly but rudely cut. The squareness suggests the Ravennate tradition', p. 67. Letter height 5.5 cm. Although the end of every line is missing, making interpretation difficult, it is usually considered as referring to the foundation of the city of Cittanova, where the inscription was found walled into the façade of the parish church in 1559.
[67] The text is damaged and the Latin corrupt: 'SIC VIRTUS ALTISSIMI FECIT LONGIBARDO {...} / TEMPORE TRANQUILLI ET FLORENTISSIMI {...} / OMNES UT UNANIMES [sic] INPLENTES PRINC {...}'.
[68] Gray, no. 25. Text in A. Mai, Scriptorum veterum nova collectio, V (Rome, 1831), p. 144; and in Rugo, Iscrizioni esistenti, III, no. 91. It is possible that the 'Duke Gregory' mentioned in the inscription was Liutprand's nephew, whom Liutprand later installed as duke of Benevento (732) to stave off possible rebellions, according to Paul the Deacon, HL VI.55, 56. Cf. Gasparri, I duchi, p. 93.

style', those which Gray dubbed the 'Theodota group'.[69] Let us begin with the namesake of Gray's category, followed by the example of yet another woman who, like Theodota, moved in royal circles and who became a nun in Pavia.

The Theodota epitaph, inscribed on the top slab of a sarcophagus also using sculptured representations of animals and vegetation, is seen as one of the highlights of Lombard epigraphy in its style, and as the first true example of the 'Pavian school'.[70] It contains a rhythmic inscription in two columns of straight and high majuscule letters (height 4.5 cm). Though now fragmentary, the full text was, luckily, transcribed by Bossi in 1604, for since then it has had a rough history, including being used as a doorstep for nearly two centuries.[71] The subject of the inscription would appear to be the extremely long-haired Roman girl Theodota, whom Paul the Deacon mentions in the *HL*.[72] A date of around 750 for the inscription seems acceptable on palaeographical and historical grounds, and in terms of style it appears to have been a precursor for a string of later epitaphs executed in a similar fashion.[73] Theodota's Roman heritage may have been a factor for the design and decoration of the sarcophagus. The poetic epitaph seems to emphasise her *genus Romanum*,[74] and the figurative sculpture of the sarcophagus uses classical and Byzantine pictorial symbols that match the message of Theodota's eternal life in death. The style in which the symbols are portrayed, that of 'static asymmetry', is characteristic of a mature 'Lombard' style that was to predominate in Italy in the late eighth and early ninth centuries and extend its influence throughout Christian Europe.[75]

The epitaph was composed by Theodota's disciple, who received her mistress' 'name, office and position', meaning she became a second Abbess

---

[69] Gray, 'Palaeography', pp. 60–1.
[70] On the Pavese 'school' or 'style', see R.M. Kloos, 'Die frühmittelalterliche lateinische Epigraphik', in *La cultura in Italia fra tardo antico e alto medioevo*, II (Rome, 1981), pp. 103–32; Kloos, 'Zum Stil'. Also A. Peroni, 'Pavia *capitale longobarda*. Testimonianze archeologiche e manufatti artistici', in *I Longobardi e la Lombardia: Saggi*. (Milan, 1978), pp. 73–81.
[71] Panazza, no. 66, giving illustration of slab with text. Rugo, *Iscrizioni esistenti*, V, no. 105. Good colour plates of the sarcophagus in Menis (ed.), *I Longobardi*, p. 311, vii.16. Full text in MGH Poetae IV, pp. 724–5, CXL.
[72] 'puella ex nobilissimo Romanorum genere orta, eleganti corpore et flavis prolixisque capillis pene usque ad pedes decorata', V.38.
[73] Gray, 'Palaeography', pp. 74–5. Cf. Kloos, 'Zum Stil', pp. 170–1.
[74] Particularly lines 12–15: 'DECEBAT SIC DENIQUE TALO CUM EX STIRPE VENIRET / .{...}. EX NOVILI CRESCENS UT FLUVIUS FONTE/.{...}. EXTRA SA. A GENITIORUM EXTITIT MAGNA'. The poem opens emphasising 'EIUS PROSAPIAM'.
[75] The starting-point for discussions of 'Lombard' sculptural style is G. De Francovich, 'Il problema delle origini della scultura cosiddetta "Longobarda"', *Atti I CISAM* (Spoleto, 1952), 255–76. On 'static asymmetry', see C. Sheppard, 'Subtleties of Lombard marble sculpture of the seventh and eighth centuries', *Gazette des Beaux Arts* 63 (1964), 193–206, esp. p. 198.

Theodota, causing some confusion with the dating.[76] The text itself is not without literary merit. The opening lines refer to the art of composition, and the second half includes a *brevitas loqui* topos, quite wordy in itself.[77] The language of the poems includes some nice classicisms (such as *caeliculae*) and rhetorical tricks, such as the homonymic play in 'in tribuendo dapes aegenis [*sic*] dapsiles', juxtaposing *dapes* and *dapsiles* with *aegenis*, or the use of anthropomorphic Christianisms: 'she nourished the little lambettes in her Lordly flock'.[78] The poem reveals something of her character: the little lambs she 'taught, censured, corrected and loved' giving us the suspicion that she may have been a little harsh, for she maintained a 'wrinkled brow, though she was pure of heart with them'. We are relieved to hear that her 'gentle hands refrained from using the whip'.[79]

From the two Theodotas we move to discuss another nun, Cunincperga, 'mater dei ancillarum suavis', daughter of King Cunincpert and abbess of the monastery of S. Agata in Pavia, which was founded by her grandfather King Perctarit, and whose epitaph dates to around 750–60[80] (see Plate VI). Her life and deeds are commemorated in an epitaph similar to that of Theodota's in style and layout. It is a rhythmic poem in two columns of eleven lines (the contents of the second column are rendered indecipherable by the loss of nearly the whole second half of the slab, leaving only one or two words of the second column).[81] The poem is of the 'siste et lege' or *titulus loquens* genre that addresses the reader directly: 'Learn, you, who wishes to know what this little tomb covers, and what figure is shut inside this decorative stone.'[82] As in the Theodota epitaph, we learn something of Cunincperga's character, which stresses her likeness to her father in comportment and behaviour. Striking, however, is the description, unparalleled in this period, of her

---

[76] 'HOC ERGO THEODOTA, ALUMNIS TUA, THEODATAE/CUI RELINQUISTI NOMEN, DIGNITATEM, CATHETRAM'.

[77] 'SI AD CURSUS RERUM ET PRAEENTIS STUDIA SAECLI / TENDATUR ORATIO, MULTA SUNT QUAE POSSOMUS DICI'. The topos sounds awkward and stilted, as it often does: see Curtius, *European Literature*, pp. 487–94. The opening: 'CUM DESCRIBERE NON POSSIM THEODOTAE TERRENAE CAELICULAE SIC DEMUM EIUS PROSAPIAM TEXAM'.

[78] 'IN GREGE DOMINICO PASCENS OVICULAS CHRISTI'.

[79] 'FOVENS DOCVIT, ARGVIT, CORREXIT, AMAVIT…FRONTEM RUGATAM TENENS ERAT QUIBUS PECTORE PURA/CUIUS ABSTINEBANT A FLAGELLIS PLACIDAE MANUS'.

[80] Panazza, no. 57. Gray, no. 45. Colour plate in Menis (ed.), *I Longobardi*, p. 162, iv.8. Text in MGH Poetae IV, p. 727, CXLIV. Santa Agata was part of the same foundation as Santa Maria di Theodota, therefore Cunincperga could have become abbess only after the death of Theodota: Gray, 'Palaeography', p. 76.

[81] On the style of letters, Gray, 'Palaeography', p. 60.

[82] 'DISCE QUI VELLIS NOSSE, QUID TEGIT TOMULUS ISTE/QUALIS ET IMAGO PRETIOSO CLAUDITUR SAXO'.

Inscriptions

Plate VI Epitaph of Cunincperga. Pavia, Museo Civico Malaspina B21 (from G.C. Menis (ed.), *I Longobardi* (Milan, 1990), IV.8, p. 162)

beauty: 'she was of a beauty distinguished among the likes of other beautiful women, with her serene face, her youthful eyes, her brow innocent of gloom, her lips flowing with honey. She was truly the offspring of her father, the excellent king Cunincpert.'[83] The vertical alignment of the final letter of each line, achieved by various uses of superscript letters and creative ligatures, and near perfect layout of the text in the script-space, betrays careful consideration and planning behind this epigraphic monument prior to its execution in stone, although the smaller letters of the last line (2.5 cm high) cast some shadows on perceiving it as perfectly proportioned.[84] The last lines of the first column, 'what is witnessed now

---

[83] 'HAEC FVIT SPECIE PVLCHRAS INTER FEMINAS PVLCHRA / FACIE SERENA, OCVLIS VERNANTIBVS QVIDEM / FRONTE NVBIS INSCIA, LABIIS FLVENTIBVS MELLA. / VERE PATRIS NATA CVNINCPERTI OPTIMI REGIS / CVIVS IN SE TOTVM GESTAVIT FILIA VVLTVM'. On descriptions in this period, see P. Squatriti, 'Personal appearance and physiognomics in early medieval Italy', *Journal of Medieval History* 14 (1988), 191–202.

[84] The creative use of superscript letters and ligatures, comparable to that found in the dedicatory inscription on the font of Callixtus in Cividale, are well brought out in Gray's illustration of the letter forms, 'Palaeography', p. 63.

Literacy in Lombard Italy, c. 568–774

[that is, Cunincperga's pious character] in the sacred college of virgins' suggests that the inscription was not originally situated in the monastery. As with the Audoald epitaph (below), we can only speculate as to where it may have been placed initially.[85]

The Theodota and Cunincperga epitaphs are examples of how those associated with the elite Pavese world, whose origins and social positions represent the link between the upper echelons of the secular and ecclesiastical hierarchy in the Lombard capital, were commemorated with the use of the inscribed word.[86] The examples also serve as the tangible evidence with which we can imagine the original lapidary form of the lengthy rhythmic inscriptions that come to us in manuscript form such as those of the *Sylloge laureshamensis*.

Nearly all of the epigraphic evidence which survives from this period across Europe derives from an ecclesiastical milieu. The term 'clericalisation'[87] to describe the shift in both authorship and audience of epigraphy in the early middle ages is perhaps little more than a simplifying buzz word, but it does point to a significant change in epigraphic production and reception. From the late sixth to the ninth century, only two sectors of society seem to have commissioned funerary inscriptions: the clerical and monastic part of the population who used inscriptions to celebrate the church hierarchy and the holy presence of the saints that protect their church and city; and the ruling local lay elites, kings, territorial rulers, who were also the benefactors and founders of churches and monasteries. This description would cover all of the inscriptions datable to Lombard Italy, except for one curious example. The eighth-century epitaph of Audoald (*c.* 763), duke of Liguria, should caution us against applying the grandiose term of 'clericalisation' too stringently. There is nothing ecclesiastical, even Christian, about the inscription at all: it simply boasted of Audoald's military prowess and his fame throughout the duchy (see Plate VII):[88]

+SVB REGIBVS LIGVRIAE DVCATVM TENVIT AVDAX
AVDOALD ARMIPOTENS, CLARIS NATALIBVS ORTVS
VICTRIX CVIVIS DEXTERA SVBEGIT NAVITER HOSTES

---

[85] 'QUOD TESTATUR MODO VIRGINUM COLLEGIUM SACRUM'. On the history of the slab, which was walled into the entry of the monastery between 1791 and 1823, see Panazza, p. 264.

[86] The fragment of another 'mater virginum' (that is, abbess) epitaph survives walled into the Casa Anelli: Gray, no. 42. Panazza, no. 69. It uses similar language to the Theodota and Cunincperga inscription, has the characteristic Pavese border decoration, and was found on the site of the monastery of Santa Agata al Monte, as were the fragments of another inscription of similar style, Gray, no. 41.

[87] A. Petrucci in his 'Scrittura e figura nella memoria funeraria', *Settimane* 41 (Spoleto, 1994), 277–97, at p. 279.

[88] Gray, no. 46; Rugo, *Iscrizioni esistenti*, V, no. 107; Panazza, no. 80.

Plate VII Epitaph of Audoald. Pavia, Museo Civico Malaspina, B20 (from P. Caratelli (ed.), *Magistra Barbaritas* (Milan, 1984), no. 164, p. 270).

FINITIMOS ET CVUNCTOS LONGEQVE LATEQVAE DEGENTES
BELLIGERAS DOMAVIT ACIES ET HOSTILIA CASTRA
MAXIMA CVM LAVDE PROSTRAVIT DIDYMVS[89] ISTE
CVIVS LICET CORPVS HVIVS SVB TEGMINE CAVTIS
LATEAT NON FAMA SILET VVLGATIS PLENA TRIVMPHIS
QVAE VIRVM QVALIS FVERIT QVANTVSQVE PER VRBEM
INNOTVIT LAVRIGERVM ET VIRTVS BELLICA DVCEM
SEXIES QVI DENIS PERACTIS CIRCITER ANNIS
SPIRITVM AD AETHERA MISIT ET MEMBRA SEPVLCHRO
HVMANDA DEDIT PRIMA CVM INDICTIO ESSET
DIE NONARVM IVLIARVM FERIA QVINTA.

In the time of [two] kings brave Audoald held the dukedom, mighty in arms and raised from noble stock, whose enemies he assiduously and bravely conquered, and all those who lived within and along the borders of his territory. He broke through dangerous battle-lines, and with the greatest glory this Apollo vanquished enemy camps. His repute of triumph is known amongst the people, a fame which speaks throughout the town of what type of man he was, a victorious duke, skilled in war, so that he is more than the body that lies hidden under the cover of a crag. Having lived around sixty years he surrendered his spirit to heaven and resigned his body to be buried in the tomb, at the time of the first indiction, fifth day of the nones of July.

We know of Audoald from no other source, and the dates of his epitaph are uncertain. The reference to 7 July and indiction leave us with four possibilities (628, 673, 718, 763) which the reference to fighting at the 'time of two kings' limits down to two: the reign of Perctarit and Cunincpert (680–8), or of Liutprand and Hildeprand (735–44). The latter date gains more weight as the vague references to wars and vanquishing *hostes finitimos* most likely refer to major military operations such as Liutprand's expedition against the exarchate in 743 or his assistance to Charles Martel against the Saracens in Provence in 739.[90] Although Muratori found the inscription in the atrium of Santa Maria in Pertica in 1717, we can be fairly confident that it was originally positioned somewhere else, though we can only guess where: perhaps Audoald's quarters or the royal palace in Pavia or Corteolona. Audoald's epitaph is certainly slight evidence for a secular epigraphic market of commissioners and audience, but it does serve as a warning against accepting too easily generalisations such as 'clericalisation'. Moreover, the recording of the noble victories

---

[89] I read this as *Didymeus*, the Didymean (Apollo): Lewis and Short, p. 573. Cf. Gray, 'Palaeography', p. 77, 'didimus', but the letter is clearly cut as Y, which is not substituted for I anywhere in the poem.

[90] Here I follow Gray, no. 46: most previous scholars followed Muratori's date of 718. See Panazza, no. 80.

Inscriptions

of this 'Didymean' suggests a degree of continuity with the epigraphic culture from the ancient world to the medieval – a continuity of practices which clerics borrowed from and imitated, rather than saved from extinction.

The Pavese evidence leads me to make two observations that need to be considered in the context of literacy. The first thing to note is that none of the surviving lengthier, more literary, inscriptions uses word-spacing. This raises the question of how these inscriptions were actually read. It appears that Lombard epigraphy assumes an audience that would have construed meanings from combinations of syllables prior to the recognition of individual words in the reader's minds: that is to say, the viewer was reading with his/her ears as well as eyes.[91] Also suggestive of the inscriptions' recitation when read is the use of punctuation marks, usually *virgulae* or little leafy flourishes at the end of a phrase or where there is a sense-end. On the whole, a phrase can be up to three or four lines long without punctuation. In general, the monumental Roman inscriptions, particularly from the late first century AD onwards, always used a medial point between words.[92] It is possible that the use of the medial point to achieve word-separation enabled Roman inscriptions to communicate to an incredibly diverse range of people in an official language spoken with a diversity of accents. In an inflected language, accentuation of mispronunciation could seriously hamper effective communication. This raises the question whether the lack of word-separation in Lombard inscriptions is an indication that they were aimed at a more restricted audience of native late Latin speakers. For those not accustomed to an inflected language, word-separation was a device that facilitated comprehension, especially for non-Latin native speakers. The Lombard inscriptions, however, with their lack of word-separation, seem to have assumed that the audience was sufficiently familiar with the Latin language to decipher meaning without the ocular assistance of segmentising typography.

The second observation to make concerns the use of rhythmic metres in the north Italian material. Although we have no eighth-century Beneventan inscriptions, the ninth-century inscriptions demonstrate a homogeneous epigraphic style and at all times the texts retain classical quantification of metre, although sometimes in an erroneous fashion.[93] It has been suggested that rhythmic verse grew out of the musical chants of the church of late antiquity and the need for a written mnemonic language. This mnemonic language needed to correspond with the cadence

---

[91] See P. Saenger, 'The separation of words and the order of words: the genesis of medieval reading', *Scrittura e Civiltà* 14 (1990), 49–74, esp. pp. 53–4; and below, pp. 308–9.
[92] Gordon, *Illustrated Introduction*, p. 13.   [93] Russo Mailler, *Il senso*, pp. 10–15.

of spoken Latin that was no longer related to the ancient pronunciation which quantified syllabification represented. The correspondence of rhythmic verse to the spoken language is a much debated subject amongst scholars of Latin literature and poetics. Rhythmic metre also had its own rules which derived from the scholastic study of rhetoric and grammar.[94] We have from the Lombard period, however, secure testimony of the correspondence of rhythmic metre to the spoken Latin in the *Carmen de synodo ticinensi*. At the end of this rhythmic poem the author sought pardon from the king for his incapacity to write in the 'appropriate' metre and described his work as 'prose':

> Mihi ignosce, rex, quaeso, piissime,
> Tua qui iussa nequivi, ut condecet,
> Pangere ore styloque contexere
> Recte, ut valent edissere medrici.
> Scripsi per prosa ut oratiunculam.[95]

Pardon me for my ignorance, most pious king, for I was not able to sing of your deeds with a worthy voice or render them with the appropriate style, as the prosodians might do. Instead I wrote prose, in the manner of a little oration.

Whatever its precise meaning, the references in the *Carmen de synodo ticinensi* to 'prose', 'a little speech/oration', and the irregularity of the accentuation indicate the poem's proximity to the language spoken at the time and, therefore, the proximity of its rhythmic metre to spoken language also. Ernst Curtius noted that this was the earliest application of the term *prosa* to a poem, yet he believed the author only used it 'to escape from his dilemma' of not knowing how to write in any metre at all. Norberg viewed 'la difformité' of the *Carmen* as 'typique de l'époque', and argued that regularity of accentuation in rhythmic metre only emerges a little later with the *Versus de Mediolano* (c. 725–39).[96] But the argument that regularity in accentuation emerged in the twenty-year or so period between the composition of the two texts is seriously challenged by the presence of regular and irregular accentuated metre in Lombard inscriptions, in both *syllogae* and lapidary forms. Irrespective of regularity of accentuation, it appears that the authors (and commissioners) of the Lombard

---

[94] The classic guide is D. Norberg, *Introduction à l'étude de la versification latine médiévale*, Acta Universitatis Stockholmiensis, Studia Latina Stockholmiensia 5 (Stockholm, 1958), pp. 87–161. Cf. D.S. Avalle, 'Dalla metrica alla ritmica', in G. Cavallo, C. Leonardi and E. Menestò (eds.), *Lo spazio letterario del medioevo. Medioevo latino*, I:1, *La produzione del testo* (Rome, 1993), pp. 383–420, and G. Ropa, *ibid.*, II, *I testi liturgici*, pp. 391–476.

[95] MGH Poetae IV, p. 731.

[96] Curtius, *European Literature*, p. 150. D. Norberg, 'Le développement du latin en Italie de S. Grégoire le Grand à Paul Diacre', *Settimane* 5 (Spoleto, 1958), 485–539, at p. 501.

Inscriptions

epigraphic poems have deliberately chosen a style of language that was more accessible to its audience, a style which had more of a mnemonic effect for the preservation of the inscribed message in the minds of those that read it.

The *Carmen de synodo ticinensi* also demonstrates an awareness of a 'superior' form of versification (*medrici*), presumably quantitative verse, more appropriate for the composition of panegyrics for the king, and the contemporary incapacity for doing so. It is difficult to believe that Cunincpert could not find someone capable of composing a panegyric in quantified metre: Paul tells us how Felix, uncle of his own teacher Flavianus, 'eo tempore floruit in arte grammatica', and how King Cunincpert rewarded him with gifts.[97] One should not take the anonymous author of the *Carmen de synodo ticinensi* too seriously: perhaps his statements of incompetence should be taken in the same manner as Gregory of Tours' professions of ineptitude – crafty statements hidden in the guise of humility that draw attention to their innovative use of language. As is demonstrated by the charter evidence, with its 'innovative' orthography and grammar, the writers and readers of Lombard Italy were not content merely to follow the examples of the past, but confidently strove to mould a written language with a long history both to suit the needs of the times and to correspond more closely with vernacular idiom and expression. The permanence of carving poetic texts in stone that did so demonstrates just how serious about achieving these aims they were.

To compare the eighth-century evidence with what came before not only highlights the extraordinary quality of the Lombard achievement in this area, but also emphasises how this epigraphy served as an expression of cultural values among which literacy was esteemed. From around the fourth century we see a tendency to abandon the V-shaped cut when carving letters in favour of the less elegant 'a cordone' technique, that is, with the incision perpendicular to the groove, already well evident in palaeochristian funerary epigraphy.[98] The letter-carving of inscriptions in fifth- and sixth-century Rome demonstrates that, despite some papal epitaphs with some innovative letter-forms, the *urbs aeterna* was not exempt from the decline of the V-cut.[99] This was a phenomenon not

---

[97] *HL* VI.7.
[98] Susini, *Roman Stonecutter*, p. 39. N. Gray, 'The Filocalian letter', *Papers of the British School at Rome* 24 (1956), 1–23, at pp. 9–10. On the practicalities of epigraphy see D. Kindersley and L. Lopes Cardozo, *Letters Slate Cut: Workshop Philosophy and Practice* (Cambridge, 1990). I must thank Lida Lopes Cardozo for discussions about, and even demonstrations of, epigraphic practice.
[99] See C. Carletti, *Iscrizioni cristiane a Roma: testimonianze di vita cristiana, sec. III–VII*, Biblioteca Patristica 7 (Florence, 1986), pp. 15–20.

limited to Italy but common to the whole late empire. This has not prevented some scholars from attributing a Dark Age in Italian epigraphy to the effect of the Lombard invasion.[100]

But perhaps more important than poor workshop practices as a sign of major decline in epigraphy was the increasing preponderance of iconic signification over the use of the inscribed word. We have little epigraphy from the late sixth and first three quarters of the seventh century, and that which we have demonstrates a preponderance of the figurative signification in the text-space of the monument. For example, in the altar slab at Monza, dated to the early seventh century, the roughly inscribed letters running along the inside top margin of the engraved space are divided by the top section of a cross flanked by attentive sheep; their attention directs ours to the centre of the cross. The inscription (RESPECE ET EXAUDVI ME DOMENE DS MEUS) (cf. Psalms 12.4) is important but complementary to the overall figurative design (see Plate VIII).[101] The Milanese epitaphs of Aldo, Manefridus and Odelbertus, all dated to the seventh century, similarly have figurative crosses which divide up the text.[102] The epitaph of Aldo, however, with its well-carved letters, extensive text and domineering cross seems to stand at a juncture for what follows in the eighth-century Pavese epigraphy: a resurgence of the primacy of the text (see Plate IX).[103] In the Pavese inscriptions, figurative signs and decorations are reduced to the margins which serve to highlight the text of considerable artistic merit or funereal solemnity. As with charters, so with inscriptions, the seventh century remains an enigmatic vacuum of evidence which inspires hypotheses of decline and renaissance. One would hesitate to use such scant evidence as indicative of any

---

[100] Bognetti, 'Storia, archeologia, e diritto nel problema dei Longobardi', *L'età*, III, pp. 176–266, esp. pp. 204–9, 213–15.

[101] A.M. Romanini, ' "Committenza regia e pluralismo culturale nella "Longobardia major" ' ', *Settimane* 39 (Spoleto, 1992), 57–92, at pp. 76–7, fig. 27, table xxvii; Rugo, *Iscrizioni esistenti*, V, no. 62.

[102] Aldo (originally at San Giovanni in Conca, now preserved at the Castello Sforzesco, Milan), Manefridus (San Vincenzo, Galliano [Cantù]) and Odelbertus. See A.M. Romanini, 'Problemi di scultura e plastica altomedievali', *Settimane* 12 (Spoleto, 1971), 426–67, esp. pp. 450–61; the epitaph of the brothers Grauso and Aldo has also been considered as belonging to this Milanese group by the similarity of its form and lettering, see O. Banti 'Considerazioni a proposito di alcune epigrafi dei secoli VIII–IX conservate a Brescia', in *S. Giulia di Brescia: archeologia, arte, storia di un monastero regio dai Longobardi al Barbarossa* (Brescia, 1992), pp. 163–77.

[103] The Aldo epitaph is by far the longest text, which has been reconstructed by A. Lusuardi Siena, '*Pium super amnem iter*: riflessioni sull'epigrafe di Aldo da S. Giovanni in Conca a Milano', *Arte Medievale* 2nd ser., 4:1 (1990), 1–12. It has been suggested that the tombstone inscription in San Abbondius, Como, is in fact of the same date as the Aldo inscription and perhaps of the same workshop: see S. Lomartire, 'L'iscrizione della lastra n.12', in *S. Abbondio, lo spazio e il tempo* (Como, 1984), pp. 235–9.

Inscriptions

Plate VIII   RESPECE ET AUDI. Monza, Museo del Duomo (from P. Caratelli (ed.), *Magistra Barbaritas* (Milan, 1984), no. 161, p. 269)

major patterns or trends in the use of epigraphy in this period, but the chronology of the pieces we do have suggests that the eighth century witnessed a remarkable renewal in the use of epigraphy for the monumental display of text.

GRAFFITI AT GARGANO

Graffiti are a rarity in the early middle ages. The 159 or so individual inscriptions found on the walls of the grotta di San Michele at Monte Sant'Angelo in the Gargano peninsula constitute one of the few surviving examples of such activity in the early medieval west.[104] It is worth, therefore, asking, why graffiti are found in Lombard Italy, and what they might tell us about the script-culture of the period.

---

[104] Collected in C. Carletti and G. Otranto (eds.), *Il Santuario di San Michele sul Gargano dal VI al IX secolo: contributo alla storia della Longobardia meridionale* (Bari, 1980), whose numeration of inscriptions I use here. Graffiti are also found in a cave at Olevano sul Tusciano, in the hills behind Salerno. A study of these is much needed: see P. Peduto, 'Insediamenti longobardi del ducato di Benevento (sec. VI–VIII)', in Cammarosano and Gasparri (eds.), *Langobardia*, pp. 307–73; G. Kalby, 'La cripta eremetica di Olevano sul Tusciano I', *Napoli Nobilissima* 3 (1963–64), 205–27; Kalby, '*ibid*., II', *ibid*., 4 (1964–65), 22–41; M. D'Onofrio and V. Pace, *La campania: Italia romanica* (Milan, 1981), pp. 343–5. A few examples from Spoleto: C. Tedeschi, 'Graffiti altomedievali del Tempietto sul Clitunno. A proposito della recente edizione di Carola Jäggi', *Scrittura e Civiltà* 24 (2000), 413–19. On the graffiti at Trani, see below, note 132.

Plate IX Epitaph of Aldo. Milan, Castello Sforzesco (from P. Caratelli (ed.), *Magistra Barbaritas* (Milan, 1984), no. 163, p. 268).

Inscriptions

The chronology of the inscriptions at Gargano ranges from the seventh century to no later than 869–75.[105] As is well known, the close connection of the Lombard regime with the cult of St Michael began in the seventh century with Grimoald's victory over the (possibly) Byzantine invasion of the promontory in 650.[106] Paul the Deacon tells us that the Byzantines had come 'ut oraculum sancti archangeli in monte Gargano situm depraedarent', though this has been questioned: Paul was sufficiently anti-Byzantine and pro-Grimoald to colour his information concerning the event.[107] It has been long been argued that Grimoald used the cult of the archangel as a political tool to unite the Arian–Catholic divisions and help foster a sense of Lombard unity, especially between Benevento and Pavia.[108] There is an inscription in the cave that may attest to Grimoald's patronage of the site, but various interpretations are possible.[109]

Whenever and however the site began, and whoever first sponsored it, it soon became a popular point of pilgrimage. In the epitaph he wrote for Queen Ansa, Paul the Deacon assured travellers that, thanks to this queen and her endowments, they can be confident of being received at

---

[105] Our earliest inscriptions include those of the Lombard Beneventan dukes Grimoald I (647–662, king 662–671) and his son Romoald I (663–687). In 869 a Saracen attack destroyed the site according to Hincmar of Rheims: see G. Musca, *L'emirato di Bari 847–871* (Bari, 1964), p. 164. Confirmation is found in a diploma of emperor Louis II (871–875); Carletti, 'Iscrizioni murali', pp. 11–13.

[106] The definitive source on the beginnings of the cult in Italy is the short *Liber de apparitione S. Michaelis in monte Gargano*, MGH SRL, pp. 540–3. The text has been variously dated from the sixth to the ninth century: see G. Otranto 'Il *Liber de apparitione* e il culto di San Michele sul Gargano nella documentazione liturgica altomedievale', *Vetera Christianorum* 18 (1981), 377–401, who dates it between 750 and 800. For an earlier dating (from c. 670), N. Everett, 'The *Liber de apparitione* S. *Michaelis de Gargano* and the hagiography of dispossession', *Analecta Bollandiana* 120 (2002), 364–91.

[107] Paul, *HL* IV.46. Followed by Erchempert, c. 27, MGH SRL, p. 224, and the *Chronica sancti Benedicti cassinensis*, ibid., p. 475. But cf. Gasparri, *I duchi*, p. 89 n. 231: simply pirates.

[108] Bognetti was the first to espouse it. See 'S. Maria', *L'età*, II, p. 333 and 'I "Loca sanctorum" e la storia della Chiesa nel regno dei Longobardi', *L'età*, III, pp 334–5. Bognetti's claim that Grimoald built a church dedicated to the archangel in Pavia has been disputed (it may have already been there). See Otranto, 'Il *regnum* longobardo e il santuario micaelico del Gargano: note epigrafia e storia', *Vetera Christianorum* 22 (1985), 165–80, at p. 166. Theories abound on the Lombard appropriation of the cult of Michael as exterminating or placating their rampant paganism: G. Fischetti, *Mercurio Mithra Michael: magia, mito e misteri nella grotta dell'Arcangelo* (Monte Sant'Angelo, 1973); Gasparri, *La cultura*, pp. 155–61.

[109] Carletti and Otranto, *Il Santuario*, no. 44. 'h[i]c patri eius [r]egni [c]umsor[t]ior/ e[re]ctor sic terre[n]a su[m]tsit/ [c]elestia n[u]m[q]ua[m] relinqui[t]'. Carletti identifies the *pater* and *consortior regni* with Grimoald and son Romoald respectively ('Iscrizioni murali', pp. 14–15); Otranto, 'Il *regnum*', prefers to identify Perctarit and Cunincpert for more convincing reasons: Grimoald's lack of religious fervour, Cunincpert's exile in Benevento during Grimoald's reign, his use of Michael on Lombard coins and (possibly) shields, and palaeographic correspondence with the 'Pavese school'. One inscription, no. 82, suggests that Duke Romoald I of Benevento sponsored the building of staircases and a gallery in the grotta; see M. Trotta and A. Renzulli, 'I luoghi del *Liber de apparitione di S. Michele al Gargano*: l'ecclesia beati Petri', *Vetera Christianorum* 35 (1998), 335–59.

Literacy in Lombard Italy, c. 568–774

Gargano: 'All you pilgrims who come from the west, take to the road in safety when you come to venerate shrines of St Peter's land or when you seek the the venerable cave amongst Garganian rock.'[110] Who were these *peregrini* who visited the site, and what did they write there? The inscriptions are mostly just names and do not tell us much in themselves, but they tell us about Beneventan-Lombard history and its cultural contacts. Of the 182 names they record (168 men, fourteen identifiable as women), ninety-seven seem securely Germanic, though one would hesitate to call them 'Lombard'.[111] There are also thirty-nine Roman and early Christian names that are attributable to sixty-five different people.[112] A few pilgrims tell us where they came from. 'Arricus' (no. 8) included in his inscription that he was 'de Marsica', that is, near Fucino, then inside the duchy of Benevento. Northern Italian presence is testified by *Leo de Bergamo* (no. 163). Moving across the Alps, some names appear to be Frankish,[113] and we know from narrative sources, albeit later, that Frankish visitors came, such as Obertus, bishop of Avranches, who came in 709;[114] Wolfang, the founder of the monastery of St Michael at Verdun, in 722;[115] and in 765 the bishop of Verdun, Magdalveus, paid a visit.[116] Coming from even further afield were Anglo-Saxon pilgrims. Their presence is testified by runic inscriptions, the earliest found in Italy,[117] and by one fellow, *Eadrhid v[ir] h[onestus]* (no. 56), who even recorded his nationality ('saxso') alongside his name.[118] A possibly celebrity inscription is that of *Petrunace* (no. 35), who may have been the Brescian monk who refounded Monte Cassino with Pope Gregory II's support.[119]

The use of acclamations written with the visitors' names provides a glimpse of how the graffiti at Gargano are part of a larger culture of devotional practices. Most common is the formula *biba in deo (vivas in deo) semper*, showing exchange of the usual labial 'b' with 'v' and the fall of final consonant that is found in charters. It may be expressing a funerary

---

[110] Neff, *Die Gedichte*, p. 48, IX: 'Securus iam carpe viam, peregrinus ab oris / Occiduis quisquis venerandi culmina Petri / Garganiamque petis rupem venerabilis antri'.
[111] Pace Arcamone, 'Antroponomia altomedievale'.
[112] 12 *Iohannis* (4, 6, 13, 20, 26, 38, 74, 98, 108, 110, 140 × 2), 6 *Petrus* (14, 16, 17, 27, 50, 97), 3 *Maurus* (80, 131, 148), 3 *Leo* (126, 132, 163), 2 of *Paulus, Dominicus* and *Paschalis* (4, 78, 36, 39, 107, 109).
[113] Carletti and Otranto, *Il Santuario*, nos. 8, 15, 29, 30, 31, 57, 89, 103, 162.
[114] *Apparitio in Monte Tumbae auct. an.* 7, in AA.SS., Sept., iii, p. 77.
[115] *Chronicon S. Michaelis monasterii in pago virdunensi*, MGH SS IV, pp. 79–80.
[116] *Vita S. Magdalvei ep. conf.* 24, in AA.SS., Oct., ii, p. 538.
[117] C.A. Mastrelli, 'Le iscrizioni runiche', in Carletti and Otranto (eds.), *Il Santuario*, pp. 319–36.
[118] Arcamone, 'Antroponomia altomedievale', p. 275.
[119] Paul, *HL* VI.40. His inscription is in the same section as Romoald II and the chronology of the dukedom (706–731) and re-establishment of Monte Cassino (*c.* 718) matches. See P. Vaccari, 'S. Benedetto e i Longobardi', *Atti II CISAM* (Spoleto, 1953), 297–315.

Inscriptions

or penitential function. It is also found in numerous examples of fibulae and rings found in Lombard graves dating to the seventh and eighth centuries, as well as cultural contact with other sacred sites, including Rome. A similar example is *tu qui legis ora pro me* (or just *ora pro me*), also found in Rome in this period.[120]

Though most of the inscriptions are executed in a rough, unpractised hand, some testify to a solid acquaintance with writing skills. The inscriptions of Grimoald (no. 44), Romoald I (no. 82) and Romoald II (no. 52) show traces of an expert hand in their use of space and the formation of the letters (see Plate X). They share the same characteristics of vertically elongated letters as found in the capital in Pavia, which we shall discuss below, especially the elongated P, R, E, F, the triangular D, and the small rhomboid O in four strokes. They are also palaeographically compatible with the funerary inscriptions found at Monte Cassino.[121] The inscription of Romoald II seems to have used ruled lines for the horizontal alignment of the script.[122] Many inscriptions share sufficient common characteristics to suggest that a particular group was inscribed by the same hand. It is possible that the custodians of the grotta performed these services for faithful pilgrims, or the work may have been by a hired hand.[123] We have two groups of inscriptions where the inscriber may have been a professional, or at least practised, stone-carver. One group is that carved by Sabilo, whose name comes at the end of a list of five names (one a *c[larissimus] v[ir]*) with *fec[it]* (no. 72). Sabilo's script is of uniform capitals in a relatively deep V-cut and runs neatly and along six straight lines. His rhomboid O, triangular D, and ligatures of A with U and T with E demonstrate a considerable degree of epigraphic skill. Another practised hand is that of *Gaidemari*, whose inscriptions include only people of a high social status: one inscription of four lines for Duke Romoald and another for four *viri honesti* (as above, no. 82, Plate X). His clientele suggests his close association with the Beneventan ducal court, though we cannot be certain in what capacity. The script sits neatly on straight, horizontal lines which are cut as deeply as the carved capital letters,

---

[120] M. Salvatore, 'Fibule con iscrizione dell'Italia meridionale', *Vetera Christianorum* 14 (1977), 339–56. Also, A. Melucco-Vaccaro, 'Il restauro delle decorazioni ageminate "multiple" di Nocera Umbra e di Castel Trosino: un'occasione per un riesame metodologico', *Archeologia Medievale* 5 (1978), 41–3. The same expression is also found in other pilgrimage centres, such as Commodilla, the crypt of SS. Pietro e Marcellino at Rome and the south church at Treviri – all dating to the seventh and eighth centuries: see Carletti, *Iscrizioni cristiane*, p. 14.

[121] A. Pantoni, 'Documenti epigrafici sulla presenza di settentrionali a Monte Cassino', *Benedictina* 12 (1958), 205–38.

[122] Carletti, 'Iscrizioni murali', p. 25.

[123] A. Petrucci, 'Aspetti del culto e del pellegrinaggio di S. Michele Arcangelo sul Monte Gargano', *Atti del IV Convegno di studi sul tema 'Pellegrinaggio e culto dei Santi in Europa fino alla fine della I Crociata'* (Todi, 1963), 154–95, at p. 169.

Literacy in Lombard Italy, c. 568–774

Plate X   Inscriptions of Grimoald, Romoald and Romoald II. Gargano,
Grotta di San Michele (from P. Caratelli (ed.), *Magistra Barbaritas*
(Milan, 1984), nos. 48 and 49, p. 133)

and which demonstrate characteristics common to seventh- and eighth-
century epigraphy: elongation of letters and horizontal lines instead of
curved bowls at tops and bottoms of letter. As with the script of Sabilo, the
D is triangular and the O rhomboid, and ligatures are used (D with U, T

Inscriptions

with E, D with E). Gaidemari's hand seems less adept than that of Sabilo, but the two 'professionals' testify to the acceptability of commissioning others to carve one's name as an act of devotion at the site.

The high-status clients of Gaidemari are evidence of lay presence, or at least interests, at the site, and this seems further attested by those who did not qualify themselves with epithets such as *servi dei, in deo umilis* or *serbus Petri*, epithets which suggest ecclesiastic or monastic vocations.[124] Out of the ten *v[iri] h[onesti]* that appear, seven have Germanic, possibly Lombard, names.[125] Only two (*Maurus*, no. 131, and *Justu*, no. 143, interestingly using *bh* instead of *vh*) seem definitely to have inscribed their own names, while the others possibly hired more experienced carvers, as was the case with the inscriptions of Gaidemari and Sabilo. But can we infer a measure of lay literacy by such results? Seven of the 14 *viri clarissimi* who appear in Schiaparelli's charters were indeed notaries who wrote charters (including one *Benedictus vc* who was a ducal notary). The fact that the *vir clarissimus* at Gargano had his name carved by a more practised, professional hand reminds us of the enormous problems in equating titles with a person's attainment of literary skills.[126] That the Beneventan court used lapidaries also to inscribe their names further suggests that scratching your own name on a wall is an unreliable test of literacy, and possibly reflects levels of wealth rather than education or familiarity with script. The wealthier one was, the less likely the need to write.[127] The same question confronts us when we consider the inscriptions of women's names at the grotta. The well-carved uncial letters in the inscriptions of *Rumildi* (no. 7) and *Varnetruda* (no. 34) suggest they may haved obtained the services of a local lapidary. This, however, can be taken as indicative not of their illiteracy, as Carletti suggests, but rather of their wealth and ability to pay, not only craftsmen, but also for the maintenance of protection on their journey to the site. At least three of the fourteen women recorded seem to have inscribed their own names (nos. 15, 47, 54), or at least do not seem to have used the more practised hand of another.

One might also ask about the ecclesiastical presence at the site in comparison with lay. At least eighteen inscriptions can be identified as those of priests by the qualification of *pbr* or *prb*, three of which add *peccator*.[128] We also have the inscriptions of five *monachi*, two with seemingly Lombard

---

[124] Nos. 97, 15, 85, respectively.
[125] Nos. 56, 81, 98. On the meaning of the title, P.M. Conti, 'L'uso dei titoli onorari ed aulici nel regno longobardo', in *Studi storici in onore di Ottorino Bertolini* I (Pisa, 1971), p. 170, on the basis of seventy-eight references.
[126] Schiaparelli, CDL 45 (Benedict), 52, 58, 71, 142, 249, 291. Conti, 'L'uso dei titoli', p. 169.
[127] *Contra* Carletti, 'Iscrizioni murali', p. 30.
[128] *pbr* nos. 27, 33, 46, 77, 86, 112, 119, 120, 127: *prb* nos. 36, 42, 74, 113, 138, 155. Another, *Burgu*, added *dni presbyter*, no. 100. The deacon *Iuane* carved his name in rough capitals, no. 108.

names.[129] The four acclamations of *peregrinus* are an early example of the changed meaning of the term from 'foreigner, visitor/traveller' to 'visitor for devotional purposes', a definition not firmly established until the first Crusade.[130] But as regards the ability to write, it seems that all these inscribed their name with their own hand. Their script alternates between an atypical capitalis and uncial type, perhaps reflecting their experience of an ecclesiastical 'book-culture'. Petrucci has suggested that the script-type matches that of primary instruction in writing at Rome in the first half of the ninth century – that which he has elsewhere characterised as the 'patrimony of the semi-literate'.[131] One would hesitate to judge an individual's level of literacy on the basis of how well they inscribe their name on a wall of solid rock. More important, however, was their participation in a cultural milieu (that of pilgrimage to devotional sites) which used literate activity as a means of demonstrating their affiliation with that culture. Belief in Christianity entailed acts of worship where the written word was of central importance. The graffiti at Gargano were another manifestation of faith and devotion, and inscribing one's name in the grotta was an act that extended beyond the clergy into lay society.

Evidence of the extension of such practices into lay society can be sen in the graffiti found on a tomb slab under the cathedral church at Trani. Excavations revealed several tombs dating to the period between the foundation of the earlier structure of the church of Santa Maria (itself founded upon an earlier structure, dated to 350–400 on the basis of late imperial coins found there) at the end of the fifth or beginning of the sixth century, and the later construction of the Romanesque church of S. Nicola Pellegrino in 1097. A slab of local stone, now seriously deteriorated, was used for the lid of one tomb and was incised with graffiti of both figures and script, of which eighty-three are still visible, some requiring technical assistance, others irrecoverable. Twenty incisions are short inscriptions of a type similar to that which we find in Gargano (*vivas in deo*). Inside the tomb was found a gold-laminated cross of the type found in the Lombard graves of Castel Trosino and elsewhere, but the lid was not originally part of the same tomb, as can be determined by its greater size and the fact that the graffiti are found on the interior side of the lid, facing downwards. The original destination for the tomb lid is therefore unknown, but the palaeography of its inscriptions and the contemporarily incised figures of, among other things, warriors

---

[129] Nos. 11, 49 (Ansipertus), 69 (Afridus), 78, 107.   [130] Carletti, 'Iscrizioni murali', pp. 22–33.
[131] P. Supino Martini and A. Petrucci, 'Materiali e ipotesi per una storia della cultura scritta nella Roma del IX secolo', *Scrittura e Civiltà* 2 (1978), 100–1; Petrucci, 'Alle origini', *Scriptores*, pp. 25–6.

or soldiers in Lombard-style dress place the date of its original execution and use squarely in the Lombard period, and probably the seventh century.[132]

The inscriptions, consisting of names and short epithets of the variety we find at Gargano (*biba in deo [vivas in deo]*), also reveal the name of the deceased, 'Forte', who is addressed at least five times (65, 67, 68, 69, 70). Two other Latinate names appear (*Bonesso* 72, 81, *Petrus* 73), another two names are indeterminable (*Nimx.me n* 77, *Iamnel* ? 80) and only one Germanic, and possibly Langobardic, name can be traced among the overlapping incisions (*Raddelchisi* 83). The palaeography of the inscriptions differs somewhat from that which we find at Gargano. The greater part of the graffiti at Trani was roughly executed in what Carletti identifies as 'new cursive' letters, well spaced and rarely connected, interspersed with some atypical capitals. There is no trace of uncial script whatsoever. The lack of uncial forms may or may not further reflect the essentially lay character of the well-wishers who incised Forte's tomb, none of whom qualified himself by any religious title, unlike those at Gargano. Combined with the rough portraits of Lombard-style warriors with shields and swords and on horseback, the overall impression is one of a small-scale yet public commemoration of an individual of Christian faith and who was involved in military activity of one sort or another, and who was probably successful, as his name suggests. Placed at the centre of the tombstone among the various figurative incisions is the figure of a winged angel (Michael?) holding a closed book on his right with his left hand (46). Whatever the precise meaning intended, the warrior Forte was accompanied to the next world by his angelic guardian armed with the book of life.

We cannot know how many people visited Gargano throughout the Lombard period, and therefore cannot ascertain what percentage of visitors the 159 inscriptions represent. The overall impression is that clearly many of the visitors to the grotta possessed a minimum degree of the ability to write. If they could not write themselves, they had the option of finding someone to do it for them. As a devotional site, Gargano operated within a sphere of literacy and written testimonials that was, arguably, peculiarly Italian. Gargano's fame as a devotional site certainly extended beyond the peninsula, but its patronage was owed to Lombard rulers, initially those of the Beneventan ducal court, and soon after directly sponsored by Pavia. The graffiti at the site, the act of

---

[132] Edited and reproduced by C. Carletti, 'Graffiti di Trani', *Vetera Christianorum* 25 (1988), 585–604, and numeration given there. On the excavations (1970–71), see R. Mola, 'Scavi e ricerche sotto la cattedrale di Trani', *Puglia Paleocristiana* 2 (1974), 189–214; R. Moreno Cassano, 'Mosaici paleocristiani di Puglia', *Mélanges de l'Ecole Française du Rome, Antiquité* 88 (1976), 315–17.

commemorating one's name in stone, owed something of its cultural setting to the epigraphic heritage of both ancient and Lombard Italy.

CONCLUSION

There are many other types of inscription that further demonstrate the 'script culture' of Lombard Italy which are not considered here, such as coin legends, painted script, or the monumental display of script at Spoleto and Salerno.[133] The wealth of epigraphic evidence from Lombard Italy, in comparison with other early medieval kingdoms, testifies to the continuity of the industry of epigraphy from the Roman period, an industry centred around the public display of the written word. The references to *magistri* and *discipuli* in some works, rare in the ancient world, demonstrate pride in a profession with a hierarchy of instruction.[134] We even have the sculptured portrait of a *magister* with *scalptrum* and mallet in hand.[135] Interestingly, the names of the *magistri* recorded as having executed the works are exclusively Roman. The names of the bishops, priests and functionaries that appear alongside them can be Latinate or Germanic. The division seems all the more ominous in the light of other

---

[133] On coin legends see E.A. Arslan, 'Emissioni monetarie e segni del potere', *Settimane* 39 (Spoleto, 1992), 791–847. Painted script at Brescia, see F. Mütherich and A. Peroni (eds.), *Seminario internazionale sulla decorazione pittorica del San Salvatore di Brescia* (Pavia, 1983), esp. pp. 80–1. Spoleto, H.P. L'Orange and H. Thorp, *Il tempietto longobardo di Cividale*, Acta ad archaeologiam et artium historiam pertinentia VII.3 (Rome, 1977), plates cliv–clvii. Mitchell, 'Display of script', p. 13 n. 33. The displays of monumental script at Salerno, P. Peduto and M. Romito, 'Chiesa di San Pietro a Corte', *Passeggiate Salernitane* 3 (1988), 20–7. Peduto et al. (eds.), 'Un accesso alla storia di Salerno: stratigrafie e materiali dell'area palaziale longobarda', *Rassegna Storica Salernitana* V/2:10 (1988), 2–28; Peduto, 'Insediamenti longobardi', pp. 321–5. The Callixtus canopy at Cividale: Mitchell, 'Display of script', p. 6, fig. 5. The Senatur monogram slab: Panazza, no. 64. Also Menis (ed.), *Longobardi*, p. 312, vii.18. Commentary: Bognetti, 'S. Maria', pp. 397–8; Kloos 'Zum Stil', pp. 169–82.

[134] Cf. *magister Iohannis* on Cummian's epitaph at Bobbio (discussed above). On the tombstone found at Savigliano ('ego gennarius fici qui in tempore fui magester marmorarius'), see S. Casartelli Novelli, 'L'immagine della croce nella scultura longobarda e nell'*entrelacs* carolingio della diocesi di Torino', in A.A. Schmid (ed.), *Riforma religiosa e arti nell'epoca carolingia. Atti del XXIV Congresso internazionale di storia dell'arte* (Bologna, 1983), pp. 109–15. In type it matches the Milanese tombstones of Manifred, Odelbertus and Aldo, and is therefore probably early seventh century. 'Ursus magister . . . cum discepolis [sic]', Iventinus and Iuventianus, on the ciborium at San Giorgio di Valpolicella (again with the presence of Liutprand, 'nosto lioprande rege'), see Ward-Perkins, *Classical Antiquity*, p. 54. The same 'Ursus magester' of the Ferentillo altar? (See note 135.)

[135] The 'Ursus magester' on the altar slab at Ferentillo: see S. Casartelli Novelli, 'Committenza e produzione scultorea "bassa"', *Settimane* 39:2 (Spoleto, 1992), 531–67, esp. p. 549. Excellent close-up photographs are found in M. Brozzi, C. Calderini and M. Rotili, *L'Italia dei Longbardi* (Milan, 1980), no. 4; E. Herzig, 'Die langobardische Fragmente in der Abtei S. Pietro in Ferentillo', *Römische Quartalschrift für christlichen Altertumskunde und für Kirchengeschichte* 20 (1906), 49–81; J. Serra, *La diocesi di Spoleto: corpus della scultura altomedievale*, II (Spoleto, 1961), cat. no. 12, pp. 19–24 table 5. See also C. Pietrangeli, 'I sarcofagi romani dell'abbazia longobarda di Ferentillo', *Atti I CISAM* (Spoleto, 1952), 451–6.

evidence which suggests that the use of Roman or Germanic names did not correspond to any divisions in Italo-Lombard society in terms of a person's status, occupation or function. We can only speculate as to whether the use of only Roman names for the *magistri marmorai* in Italy is indicative of some elusive aspect of the industry that escapes us or is merely a false impression due to the lack of further surviving evidence.

The importance of the Roman epigraphic heritage in Italy cannot be underestimated. The survival of Roman inscriptions provided a daily visual environment in which the public display of script not only facilitated reading practice and a familiarity with written forms of communication, but also imparted a strong sense of history to the culture of Lombard Italy. Arguably, these vestiges of the Roman past contributed to the creation of a distinctly 'Lombard style' of epigraphy, with its use of rhythmic metres and ornamental border-decoration, which we find in eighth-century Pavia and elsewhere. That is to say, the uniformity of style amongst these surviving inscriptions suggests a conscious and deliberate attempt by the Lombard ruling elite to use forms that were recognisable to an audience, of both Italians and visitors, as belonging to the new regime, in contradistinction to the presence of the Roman past in the physical world that surrounded them. Indeed, the originality of the Lombard material is also evident when compared with contemporary Roman and Ravennate epigraphy.[136] Liutprand grasped the potential of inscriptions as a means of propagating the ideology of a unified and Christian *regnum* under his rulership. The elites of Pavia appear to have developed his methods further. The surviving 'Lombard style' inscriptions are also suggestive of the original form of those preserved in *syllogae*.

The career of Paul the Deacon should be considered in the cultural context of the epigraphy of Italy. Paul was commissioned to compose epigraphic works, funerary and dedicatory, for the members of the Lombard, Frankish and Beneventan courts, as well as incorporating the epitaphs of Drotculf, King Caedwalla and Venantius Fortunatus in his *HL* – the last of which he composed himself. His reasons for incorporating Fortunatus' epitaph into the *HL* are revealing: 'we have added these few words about such a great man so that his fellow-citizens might not remain ignorant of his life'.[137] Not one of Fortunatus' epigraphic commissions has survived

---

[136] On Rome, note the negative assessments of Gray, 'Palaeography', p. 158, and Riché, *Education*, p. 419. Similarly on Ravennate epigraphy, Gray, 'Palaeography', p. 55 (who interestingly suggests Lombard influence on Ravenna, p. 58: a rare turning of the tables in art history). Cavallo's study of the Ravenna material, 'Le iscrizioni di Ravenna dei secoli VI–VIII. Tracce per uno studio grafico-culturale', *Corso di Cultura sull'Arte Ravennate e Bizantina* 31 (1984), 109–36, is likewise less than complimentary.

[137] *HL* II.14.

in lapidary form. Paul had learned from his predecessor's example: write as much on parchment as you like, people still forget: poems in stone endure to be read. The epigraphic culture of Paul's Pavia undoubtedly played a part in his education, not only by furnishing the young scholar with the visible presence of poetic texts to ensure a deep familiarity with poetic language and style, but also by providing models of inscribed dedicatory and funerary texts from which he could have drawn inspiration for the composition and configuration of inscribed texts commissioned by his patrons. Paul, a highly literate individual, may have been exceptional in his interaction with, and consumption of, the visual environment afforded by inscriptions. We can only speculate upon the extent to which this interaction with inscriptions, as artefacts of a literate culture, worked at lower levels of literacy and affected the population of Lombard Italy.

7

MANUSCRIPTS

The Gothic wars unleashed by Justinian put an end to whatever vestiges of Roman, secular book culture had survived in Italy under Ostrogothic rule. For scholars interested in the transmission of classical literature, by the mid-sixth century in Italy 'the Dark Ages had come, and they seem to have come with a vengeance'.[1] Of the 135 extant sixth-century codices that can be attributed to Italy, only ten are works of classical literature, with similar figures for practical texts of a legal or scientific nature, compared to over 100 reflecting religious interests – a pattern of survival that becomes common in Italy, and elsewhere, for many centuries to come.[2] Famous palimpsest manuscripts preserved in Italy, in which classical works were erased to copy out the text of the Bible or the works of the Fathers, seem further evidence of a materially poor and increasingly intolerant culture that had no interest in preserving the literary traditions of the pagan past.[3]

The unhappy fate of classical literature has had the unfortunate effect of casting the Lombards in the role of accomplices in the destruction of literate traditions. After all, as far as we know, early Lombard rulers did not espouse literary culture as a virtue, or patronise the production of books. Despite this, possibly one quarter to one third of the 1811 or so items catalogued in the volumes of *Codices Latini Antiquiores* that date from the

---

[1] L. D. Reynolds (ed.), *Texts and Transmission: A Survey of the Latin Classics* (Oxford, 1983), p. xv. See G. Cavallo, 'La circolazione libraria dell'età di Giustiniano', in *L'imperatore Giustiniano: storia e mito* (Milan, 1978), pp. 201–36; Cavallo, 'Libri e continuità della cultura antica in età barbarica', in Caratelli (ed.), *Magistra Barbaritas*, pp. 603–61, esp. pp. 632–3 on the Lombards; 'Scrittura, alfabetismo e produzione libraria nel tardo antico', in *La cultura in Italia fra tardo antico e alto medioevo*, II (Rome, 1981), pp. 523–38; C. Nordenfolk, *Die spätantiken Zierbuchstaben* (Stockholm, 1970); J.O. Tjäder, 'Der Codex Argentius in Uppsala und der Buchmeister Viliaric in Ravenna', *Studia Gotica* (Stockholm, 1972), 144–64.

[2] A. Petrucci, 'Scrittura e libro nell'Italia altomedievale. Il sesto secolo', *Studi Medievali* 3rd ser., 10 (1969), 157–212, figures at p. 173: forty biblical texts, gospels, biblical commentaries or liturgical books; sixty-eight Christian authors and fathers of the church; nine legal texts; eight scientific works (mostly medicine). See also Petrucci, 'La concezione cristiana del libro fra VI e VII secolo', *Studi Medievali* 14 (1973), 961–84, repr. in Cavallo (ed.), *Libri e lettori*, pp. 5–25, 233–8.

[3] E.A. Lowe, '*Codices rescripti*: a list of the oldest Latin palimpsests with stray observations on their origin', *Mélanges Eugène Tisserant*, V, Studi e Testi 235 (Rome, 1934), pp. 67–81, at pp. 69–70.

period of the sixth to the end of the eighth century can be attributed to Italy.[4] The achievement this represents is somewhat diminished by the fact that this figure does not tally the creation of new works in this period, but rather the transmission and augmentation of existing knowledge. Yet it is precisely this type of literary activity that preserved and transformed literate traditions of the past to lay the foundations for the future. Its importance should not be underestimated.[5] When we look across the range of extant manuscripts from the Lombard period, we find a certain vitality in the development and dissemination of skills centred on the cultivation of the written word that merits attention, and which further throws some light on the place of literacy in Italo-Lombard society.

In this chapter I shall survey the extant evidence by concentrating on some particular themes. First, I shall briefly discuss the nature of the Italian manuscript evidence and the interpretative problems involved in dating and attributing manuscripts to particular centres in this period. Since the principal collections are those of Verona and Bobbio, I divide the discussion into clerical schools and monastic centres, which allows us to explore the institutional background of manuscript production in this period and place these institutions in the historical context of the Lombard kingdom. Two themes in particular emerge from the division: the relative silence of the clergy and the flowering of monasticism. The discussion then turns briefly to the preservation of classical literature, before exploring the issue of pre-Caroline minuscule scripts in Italy, the various types found, and the relationship of this development to the question of literacy. At the recent exhibition concerning the 'Future of the Lombards', an eminent palaeographer called attention to the fact that we still lack a comprehensive study of the production of manuscripts in seventh- and eighth-century Italy which would help place the surviving corpus in various contexts of palaeography, codicology, the internal organisation and arrangement of texts and their textual tradition, and how book production relates to the written culture in general in this period.[6] The following pages make no claim to fulfilling this *desideratum*,

---

[4] The percentage is based on the 'statistics' reluctantly given by Lowe in the prefaces to each volume of CLA (except vols. II, VIII, and I, III and IV; these last two are mostly 'codici italici', IV, p. v), and impressions gained from my own experience in compiling a handlist of Italian manuscripts for this period currently in preparation. Lowe's subjectivity in attributing items 'written doubtless in Italy' for what he perceived as productions of higher quality has been criticised: see R. McKitterick, 'Frankish uncial: a new context for the Echternach scriptorium', in P. Bange and A.G. Weiler (eds.), *Willibrord zijn Wereld en zijn Werk* (Nijmegen, 1990), pp. 374–88, at p. 376 (repr. in McKitterick, *Books, Scribes and Learning*, ch. 5).

[5] McKitterick, 'Eighth-century foundations', in McKitterick (ed.), *NCMH*, II, p. 682.

[6] G. Cavallo, 'Libri e cultura nelle due Italie longobarde', in C. Bertelli and G.P. Brogiolo (eds.), *Il futuro dei Longobardi: l'Italia e la costruzione dell'Europa di Carlo Magno. Saggi* (Milan, 2000), pp. 85–104, at p. 100.

but merely sketch out some lines of development, and hopefully suggest future areas for research.

THE ITALIAN COLLECTION: VERONA AND BOBBIO

The variety of scripts used and diversity of texts copied in the Lombard period make attribution of a particular manuscript to any one writing centre or scriptorium extremely tenuous. For we lack homogeneous groups of styles or types of book that might allow us to discern specific traditions in practice and locate them in time and place, or which permit us to confirm that their origin is the same place as their later provenance.[7] Palaeography, for all its philological knowledge, precision and legitimate claims to the use of scientific methods, also depends upon fairly subjective aesthetic considerations and a sense of intuition. It is not an exact science, nor should it pretend to be.[8] Most of our hypotheses rest heavily upon consideration of the two outstanding collections at the cathedral chapter library in Verona and that once preserved at the monastery of Bobbio, now dispersed among the libraries of Milan, Turin, Rome, Naples and Vienna.[9] These collections furnish us with some of our most important palaeographical landmarks. At Verona, the famous manuscript of the works of Sulpicius Severus, subscribed by a certain Ursicinus, *lector* of the Veronese church, in 517, not only testifies to the existence of an active scriptorium at the Veronese church at this time, but also provides us with a chronological point of reference for the development of half-uncial.[10] For Bobbio, the inscription at the bottom of a palimpsest manuscript of Ulfilas assures us that it belonged to the cupboard (*arca*) of the Abbot Atala (615–22) who succeeded Columbanus. The manuscript therefore gives us some idea of what contemporary half-uncial looks like, and confirms that the monastery had an active scriptorium, possibly with a strong presence of insular scribal traditions at an early date. Jonas of Bobbio mentions that Atala restored the bindings on the books of the monastery, but tells us nothing of the abbey's scriptorium.[11] But even these two centres, for

---

[7] See M. Angrisani, 'Materiali per uno studio della produzione libraria latina antica e medievale in Italia', *Bollettino del Comitato per la Preparazione dell'Edizione Nazionale dei Classici Greci e Latini* nuov. ser. 24 (1978), 87–112; 26 (1978), 113–37; 27 (1979), 139–51.

[8] See G. Costamagna, 'Paleografia: scienza o estetica?', *Scrittura e Civiltà* 22 (1998), 409–18, and A. Pratesi and J. Gumpert, *ibid.*, pp. 397–409.

[9] On the later history of the abbey and its codices, see P. Verrua, *Bobbio e Padua: S. Columbano e S. Giustina, codici e monaci* (Padua, 1938); M. Ferrari, 'Le scoperte a Bobbio nel 1493: vicende di codici e fortuna di testi', *Italia Medievale e Umanistica* 13 (1970), 144–51; 'Spigolature bobbiesi', *Italia Medievale e Umanistica* 16 (1973), 9–30.

[10] Verona, XXXVIII (36) (CLA IV.494).

[11] Milan, Ambr. S. 45 sup. (CLA III.365). 'L[iber] de arca domno atalani'. Cf. Turin, Arch. Stat., IB, II. 27 (CLA IV.438) and Vat. lat. 5758 (CLA I.36). Cavallo, 'Libri e cultura', p. 86.

which we have certain evidence of a scriptorium and complementary library, demonstrate a great deal of diversity in the scripts used, page layout, manuscript size and techniques of preparation, so that it is far from clear-cut as to which manuscripts were written there or in another centre and imported later: the Bangor antiphonary is a telling case in point.[12] Early medieval manuscripts preserved in the library of Bobbio, sometimes identified in a tenth-century (possibly earlier) catalogue or in the more systematic catalogue drawn up in 1461,[13] and often corroborated by a tell-tale *ex libris* on the frontispiece of the manuscript, show such a bewildering variety of Insular, Merovingian, Spanish, Byzantine and native Italian influences that it is far from clear exactly which books were written there.[14] The same variety of influences, with the exception of an almost complete absence of Insular 'symptoms', is found among the manuscripts preserved at Verona. The half a dozen half-uncial manuscripts that resemble the Ursicinus codex point to certain stylistic preferences in the sixth century, but no recognisable 'house style' of production can

L. Schiaparelli, *Influenze straniere, nella scrittura italiana dei secoli VIII e IX*, studi e Testi 47 (Rome, 1927) p. 32; Lowe, 'Codices rescripti', nos. 128, 222. Jonas, *Vita Columbani*, II.25. On the history of the abbey and scriptorium in this period, the starting-point is G. Mercati, *Prolegomena de fatis bibliothecae monasterii S. Columbani Bobiensis*, in his *M. Tulli Ciceronis de re publica libri et codice rescripto Vat. lat. 5757 phototypice expressi et de codice ipso Vat. lat. 5757*, 3 vols., Codices et Vaticanis selecti XXII–XXIV (Vatican City, 1934); P. Engelbert, 'Zur Frühgeschichte des bobbieser Skriptoriums', *Revue Bénédictine* 78 (1968), 220–60; C. Cipolla, *Codici bobbiesi della Biblioteca Nazionale dell'Università di Torino* (Milan, 1936–39), pp. vii–xii. Unfairly dismissed by Lowe (CLA IV, p. xv, and omitted from the bibliography), the study by P. Collura, *Studi paleografici: la precarolina e la carolina a Bobbio*, Fontes Ambrosiani 22 (Milan, 1943, repr. 1968) (on the above MS at pp. 79ff, tables 26–27) is fundamental. On the political and economic history of the monastery in this period, V. Polonio, *Il monastero di S. Colombano di Bobbio dalla fondazione all'epoca carolingia* (Genua, 1962); and C. G. Mor, 'Excerpta bobbiensa saec. X', in *Contributi alla storia dell'Università di Pavia* (Pavia, 1925), pp. 43–114, at pp. 45–51.

[12] E.g. M. Van der Hout, 'Gothic palimpsests of Bobbio', *Scriptorium* 6 (1952), 87–98. An excellent attempt to sort out types and symptoms is Tosi, 'L'Edictus Rothari'.Bangor antiphonary: Milan, Ambr. C 5 inf (CLA III.311). Cf. Turin, F.IV.1 fasc. 9 (CLA IV.454). See A.R. Natale, 'Esercizi di calligrafia insulare in codici del sec. VIII: note paleografiche', *Archivio Storico Italiano* 116 (1958), 54–74.

[13] The catologue has been reprinted several times since Muratori, *Antiquitates Italicae Medii Aevi*, III (Milan, 1740), Diss. XLIII, cols. 817–23, including G. Becker, *Catologi bibliothecarum antiqui* (Bonn, 1885), pp. 489–97; Collura, *Studi*, pp. 219–24. The most recent edition, with discussion of its discovery and loss, and additional index of manuscripts, is M. Tosi, 'Il governo abbaziale di Gerberto di Bobbio', in *Gerberto: scienza, storia e mito. Atti del Gerberti Symposium* (Bobbio 25–27 July 1983), Archivium Bobiense Studia II (Piacenza, 1985), pp. 71–107, 130–9, 197–223; repr. Tosi, 'Documenti riguardanti l'abbaziato di Gerbert a Bobbio: riedizioni', *Archivium Bobiense* 6–7 (1984–85), pp. 135–61. On the problematic dating of the catalogue, see, M. Esposito, 'The ancient Bobbio catalogue', *Journal of Theological Studies* 32 (1931), 337–41; and Collura, *Studi*, pp. 7–11.

[14] A.R. Natale, 'Influenze merovingiche e studi calligrafici nello scriptorium di Bobbio', in *Miscellanea G. Galbiati*, II, Fontes Ambrosiani 26 (Milan, 1951), pp. 1–23; Natale, *Studi paleografici: arte e imitazione della scrittura insulare in codici bobbiesi* (Milan, 1964); A. Themelly, 'Note sulla decorazione di alcuni manoscritti bobbiensi VII e VIII secoli', *Romanobarbarica* 12 (1993), 101–22.

Manuscripts

be determined from the extant manuscripts for the following period.[15] The later characteristic cursive hands in the margins may help prove a manuscript's presence there in the seventh or eighth century, but not its origin, and many books probably came in from neighbouring libraries and scriptoria, including Bobbio.

The problem of attribution extends beyond the regional. For example, the manuscript Ivrea 1,[16] a copy of Gregory's *Pastoral Care*, was written in a half-cursive minuscule script strikingly akin to what has become known as the 'Luxeuil type', characterised by slender, leftward-leaning letters and particular ligatures (*g*- and *t*-), and named after Luxeuil, the monastery founded by Columbanus, thought to be the 'mother house' of this particular style. The acrostics written on the first folio, by the same hand that wrote the main text, read 'Desiderius Papa' and 'Vivat Deo', and we know of a Bishop Desiderius who held the see of of Ivrea towards the end of the seventh century (*c*. 669), which is entirely consistent with the date of the script. To complicate the picture further, we find 'Luxeuil type' script used at Bobbio in the seventh century,[17] and not surprisingly it appears to have been used at Luxeuil's daughter houses.[18] Yet the characteristics of 'Luxeuil type' are also found in works written in places outside the Columbanian sphere of influence, hence the association of the script with this particular location in nomenclature has perhaps been misleading.[19]

---

[15] For introduction and discussion of collection, Schiaparelli, *Influenze*, pp. 20–5, and 'L'Orazionale Mozarabico', *passim*; Lowe, CLA IV, pp. xix–xx; K. Christ, *The Handbook of Medieval Library History*, rev. A. Kern, trans. T.M. Otto (Meteuchen, NJ and London, 1984), pp. 77–8. For plates, E. Carusi and W.M. Lindsay, *Monumenti palaeographici veronesi*, 2 vols. (Rome, 1928–34), and A. Piazzi (ed.), *Biblioteca Capitolare Verona* (Fiesole, 1994). G. Turrini, *Indice dei codici capitolari di Verona redatto 1625 dal canonico Agostino Rezzani: testo critico rapportato al Catalogo di Antonio Spagnolo* (Verona, 1965), and Turini, *Millennium scriptorii veronensis dal IV al XV* (Verona, 1967), provide good plates, but as catalogues are now superceded by A. Spagnolo, *I manoscritti della Biblioteca Capitolare di Verona: catalogo descrittivo*, ed. Silvia Marchio (Verona, 1996). On the variety, see V.B. Pagnin, 'Espressioni scrittorie dell'ambiente culturale veronese dal V al VII secolo', *Ricerche Medievali* 13–14 (1978–80), 5–18.

[16] CLA III.300. Cavallo (ed.), *Libri e lettori*, tav. 10.

[17] Ambr. C. 105 inf. fols. 1–135, 137–9, 150, 154–7 (CLA III.323b), Hegesippus, *De bello iudaico*. Italian, and probably Bobbiese, origin seems confirmed by the presence of *Carmen de synodo ticinensi* inserted on blank portion of fol. 121–121v, as with Ambr. E. 147 sup. (CLA 26b + c). Collura, *Studi*, pp. 46, 49, 54–9 and tables 6–8; Lowe, *Codices rescripti*, no. 42. Turin A II.2 (now lost, CLA IV.444); Vat. lat. 5763 (CLA I.39); see further Schiaparelli, *Influenze*, pp. 30–6, and Natale, 'Influenze merovingiche', pp. 15–16.

[18] See D. Ganz, 'The Luxeuil Prophets and Merovingian Missionary Strategies', *Yale University Library Gazette* 66 (1991), supplement (= R. Babcock (ed.), Beinecke Studies in Early Manuscripts), pp. 105–16; M. Ferrari, 'Libri e testi prima del Mille', in G. Cracco (ed.), *Storia della Chiesa di Ivrea: dalle origini al XV secolo* (Rome, 1998), pp. 511–17.

[19] *Contra* Lowe, 'The script of Luxeuil, a title vindicated', *Revue Bénédictine* 63 (1953), 132–42 (repr. in E.A. Lowe, *Palaeographical Papers, 1907–1965*, ed. L. Bielart, 2 vols. (Oxford, 1972), II, pp. 389–98). For example, the minuscule scripts of Verona LV (53) (CLA IV.507), and LXII (60) (CLA IV.512) (on which see below), clearly written in Verona or a north Italian centre,

Literacy in Lombard Italy, c. 568–774

When we break down the characteristics lumped together by Lowe, and consider the individual manuscripts, and what we know of manuscripts securely attributable to Luxeuil in this period, it is equally possible that the 'Luxeuil script' originated in Italy.[20] It has also been claimed, less convincingly, for Lyons.[21] We are still left with the question: was this earliest copy of Gregory's work written at the monastery of Luxeuil (after all, Columbanus himself called the *Pastoral Care* 'sweeter than honey'), one of its daughter houses, or Bobbio, and then sent to the bishop of Ivrea? Or was it written in another centre in northern Italy, perhaps in Ivrea itself? The question may never be answered satisfactorily, but the conundrum highlights difficulties of attribution when one or more writing centres share a similar style, a common religious culture, and literary interests, all of which transcend regional, to say nothing of 'national' boundaries in the cultivation of Christ's kingdom on earth.[22]

The rich collections housed at Bobbio and Verona serve to dispel rigid conceptual divisions we might entertain between monastic and clerical centres in terms of scriptorial activity. Each could function as a preserve of literary culture in this period, as is confirmed by the references to education of a similar type taking place in each, and by the often interchangeable use of the terms *monasterium* and *ecclesia* in our charter evidence for the smaller, private foundations.[23] Nevertheless, a distinction between secular clerical office and monastic vocation was maintained, and for the sake of convenience the following discussion is divided into

---

are said to have traces of Luxeuil influence (Schiaparelli, *Influenze*, pp. 17, 25; Bischoff, *Latin Palaeography*, p. 103), but the similarities are extremely superficial, and assessment appears to be confused by a manuscript of Gregory's *Moralia*, Verona XL (38) (CLA IV.438), written in a clearly 'Luxeuil-type' minuscule, which arrived at Verona by the ninth century. Ganz, 'Luxeuil Prophets', pp. 115–16 n. 8, would attribute Verona XL (38) and Ivrea 1, along with several other 'Luxeuil-type' manuscripts, including the famous 'Luxeuil lectionary' (Paris lat. 9427, CLA V.579), to the same scriptorium. Cf. P. Salmon, *Le Lectionnaire de Luxeuil* (Rome, 1953), II, pp. 23–6.

[20] See M.C. Putnam, 'Evidence for the origin of the script of Luxeuil', *Speculum* 38 (1963), 256–66.

[21] C. Chartier, 'Note sur les origines de l'écriture dite de Luxeuil', *Revue Bénédictine* 58 (1948), 149–57.

[22] Other examples of the 'French connection' include: Milan, Ambr. F. 84 sup. CLA III.341, *Vitae Patrum*. Uncial, saec. VIII. Collura, *Studi*, p. 75, tables 24, 25. Cf. K. Holter 'Der Buchschmuck in Süddeutsch land und Oberitalien', in W. Brownfels and H. Schnitzler (eds.), *Karl der Grosse: Lebenswerk und Nachleben*, III, *Karolingische Kunst* (Dusseldorf, 1968), pp. 74–115, at p. 95; Monte Cassino, 523, pp. 201–4 (CLA III.380). Augustine, *Tractatus in evangelium Iohannis* (cxii, cxiii). Uncial, saec. VII–VIII. B. Bischoff, *Manuscripts and Libraries in the Age of Charlemagne*, ed. and trans. M. Gorman (Cambridge, 1994), p. 48 n. 139; Vat. Reg. lat. 1040 (CLA I.112). *Acta Concili Oecumenici Sexti*. Uncial, saec. VIII. Written in north-east France, probably at St Amand, but was at Rome soon after, where additions and corrections were made in Roman uncial, saec. VIII–IX. See Bischoff, *Manuscripts*, p. 51 and 27 n. 34.

[23] See C. Violante, 'Le strutture organizzative della cura d'anime nelle campagne dell'Italia centro-settentrionale', *Settimane* 28 (Spoleto, 1982), 936–1157, revised and reprinted in Violante, *Ricerche sulle istituzioni ecclesiastiche dell'Italia centro-settentrionale nel medioevo* (Palermo, 1986), pp. 105–262, esp. pp. 145–59, 164–8, 170, 180–2.

Manuscripts

clerical schools and monasteries in order to gain some idea of the network of writing centres active in this period.

CLERICAL SCHOOLS

With respect to clerical or cathedral schools, there are signs of active scriptoria at Vercelli, Ivrea, Monza, Milan, Pavia, Brescia, Novara, Perugia, Ancona and Lucca in this period, but the extant evidence is not sufficient, nor are the attributions secure enough, to determine any particulars that help fill out an impressionistic picture too open to speculation.[24] One would like to know, for instance, why the bishop of Novara arranged for the copying of Julian Antecessor's *Epitome* of Justinian's *Codex*,[25] whether the copies of patristic works and Lombard law preserved at Vercelli were actually written there,[26] and to what extent these reflect common practices in cathedral churches.

The same should be asked of the famous Lucca 490 codex, which we met in chapter 3. Lauded for its diversity of texts and scripts by Schiaparelli as a 'library in one little volume', it was roundly condemned by Petrucci as an 'antibook' for its heterogeneous character.[27] It nevertheless presents us with the picture of over thirty scribes working side-by-side, in highly individualistic scripts ranging from uncials to cursives, with no sign of any attempt to create a degree of homogeneity of form: 'a babel of scripts', somehow considered as evidence that Italy 'lagged behind' the rest of Europe at this time.[28] The contents of the manuscript reveals a range of texts, assembled from various different sources, including ecclesiastical history (*Liber pontificalis*, Eusebius–Rufinus *Historia ecclesiastica*), canon law (*Samblasiana*, *Collectio Hispana*, *Decretum Gelasianum*), patristic excerpts and biblical commentary (Ambrose, Augustine, Gregory, Alcuin), extracts from Isidore's *Etymologiae* and *Liber de officiis ecclesiasticis*, treatises

---

[24] See G. Billanovich and M. Ferrari, 'La trasmissione dei testi nell'Italia nord-occidentale: I. Monza, Pavia, Milano, Bobbio. II. Milano, Nonantola, Brescia', *Settimane* 22 (Spoleto, 1975), 303–55; Petrucci, 'Scritture e scriventi a padania: Milano e Bergamo', *Scriptores*, pp. 57–75.

[25] Milan, Arch. civ. stor., Trivulziano 688 (CLA III.366). Cf. Novara, 2 (LXXXIV) (CLA III.406). Cau, 'Scrittura e cultura', pp. 9–14, 27–34.

[26] Vercelli, CLVIII, fols. 360–3 (CLA IV.668b), CLXXXII (IV.469), CLXXXIII and fols. 107v–111v (IV.469–70), CLXXXVIII (IV.471). See P. Levine, 'Historical evidence for calligraphic activity in Vercelli from St Eusebius to Atto', *Speculum* 30 (1950), 561–80, who claims, p. 579, that we have no secure evidence of a manuscript written at Vercelli until the tenth century (MS XXXIX).

[27] CLA III.330. The definitive palaeographic study remains L. Schiaparelli, *Il Codice 490 della Biblioteca capitolare di Lucca e la scuola scrittoria Lucchese (secoli VIII–IX)*, Studi e Testi 36 (Rome, 1924) and the companion volume of plates *Il Codice CCCCXC della Biblioteca capitolare di Lucca*, 2 vols. (Rome, 1924); Petrucci, 'Il codice e i documenti', p. 92. On the text of the *LP*, see *LP* I, ed. Duchesne pp. clxiv–vi *et passim*; McKitterick, 'The audience', pp. 108–10.

[28] Lowe, CLA VI, p. xii.

on computus and Easter tables, recipes for goldsmiths, painters and, as we have seen, for the preparation of parchments and the manufacture of ink. The compilation appears to have been designed to serve the practical purpose of providing a solid grounding in the principles of the faith, the definition of doctrinal orthodoxy, behavioural norms for the clergy and the history and tradition of the church since its inception. While the date of the manuscript's compilation (787–96, 800–16, for parts one and two) is firmly within the Carolingian period, both palaeographical considerations and the question of exemplars suggest the overall configuration of the codex was rooted in a pre-Carolingian context. The various compilations of *patristica* containing many of the same texts collected together in Lucca 490 suggest that this particular manuscript was no radical departure from Italian ecclesiastical traditions of the seventh and eighth centuries.[29] The existence of a writing school attached to the cathedral at Lucca, as we have seen in chapter 5, may go some way towards explaining the heterogeneous quality of the script of manuscript 490. Rather than seeing its variety as 'a pathetic example of scribal incompetence',[30] the manuscript instead might be better understood as the result of a didactic experiment to facilitate reading (let alone writing) in different types of book-script, a useful and somewhat necessary exercise for an Italian cleric, at the same time as providing a handbook of key-texts to define orthodoxy and the principles of pastoral care. The bishop himself seems to have had a hand in it.[31] Whatever the reasons behind the 'babel of scripts' of 490, we should refrain from seeing it as an example of scribal decadence in Italy, and perhaps see in its diversity of scripts and texts a certain vitality and confidence. Lucca in this period was the ecclesiastical and political capital of Lombard Tuscany, and was well located to provide a place of rest for weary pilgrims on their way to and from the *lumina Petri et Pauli*.[32] Unfortunately, the absence of extant manuscript evidence from Lucca earlier than that of 490 prevents us from placing this particular manuscript in the larger context of scribal traditions there.

Even more disconcerting is the absence of surviving codices which can be attributed to the ecclesiastical capitals of the north, particularly

---

[29] E.g. Milan, Ambr. H. 78 sup. + Turin, G.V.15 (CLA III.347), saec. VIex; Ambr. O. 212 sup. (CLA III.361), Naples, lat. 2 (Vindobon. 16) (CLA III.391–6), fols. 1–41, secondary script, saec. VIII; Vercelli, CLXXXIII (CLA III.469, as above). C. Bertelli, 'Stato degli studi sulla miniatura fra il VII e il IX secolo in Italia', *Studi Medievali* 3rd ser., 9 (1968), p. 114, suggests that the miniature on fol. 348 (in 490) was dependent upon Roman models and Carolingian concern for them.

[30] E.A. Lowe, 'Handwriting', in C.G. Crump and E.F. Jacob (eds.), *The Legacy of the Middle Ages* (Oxford, 1948), pp. 197–226, at p. 214 (repr. as Lowe, *Handwriting: Our Medieval Legacy* (Rome, 1969).

[31] Schiaparelli, *Il Codice*, pp. 30–3, identifies one (Visigothic) hand as that of Bishop John I (780–800), on the basis of a comparison with John's subscriptions to some charters.

[32] CDL 48, 140, 194, 96; Schwarzmaier, *Lucca und das Reich*, pp. 4–15.

the metropolitan see of Milan and its rival Pavia, though some liturgical texts demonstrate local liturgy of the former.³³ As we have seen in chapter 6, the epigraphy of Milan and Pavia at the end of the seventh and beginning of the eighth centuries reflects a learned ecclesiastical culture there, which must have relied on the production and preservation of books. Our sources hint at their existence. At the Synod of Pavia in 698 the reformers, gathered in the palace of King Cunincpert, 'read the holy books of the fathers' to the schismatic Aquileiese clerics to convince them of their errors, in sharp contrast to the strategy of Pope Sergius, who simply ordered the 'manuscripts of the perverse sect' to be burned.³⁴ But already in 680, in preparation for the Sixth Oecumenical Council at Constantinople, the bishop of Pavia, Damian, then deacon at Milan, wrote a letter to the emperor in the archbishop of Milan's name condemning the Monothelite heresy, and claimed as his authorities the writings of Gregory Nazianzus, Basil of Cappadocia, Cyril and Athanasius of Alexandria, John of Constantinople, Hilary of Poitiers, Augustine, Ambrose, Jerome and Leo the Great: 'for whatever they taught, knew, and defended with their lives and writings, we now take up in all devotion'.³⁵ We might expect a metropolitan see of Milan's stature to be well furnished with such texts, but the books themselves elude us. Damian's testimony of Milan's resources receives further confirmation in the anonymous *Versus in laudem mediolanensis civitatis* (c. 730). The poem was possibly written in response to the upstart pretensions of the Pavese church in this period, and reflects both clerical and civic pride: 'She is the queen of towns, mother of the realm, whom all nations of this world now praise together, and who bears the eminent title of metropolis. The immense dignity of her power endures, so that all the bishops (*presules*) of ancient Italy (*Ausonia*) come to her to be instructed according to the dictates of canon law.'³⁶

Collections of canon law, along with Bibles, Gospels, Psalters, sacramentaries, and other liturgical and patristic texts, were part of the stock set that each cathedral church and many parish churches under their jurisdiction would have possessed. When the bishops of Tuscany met in the parish church of San Genesio in Vallari (near San Miniato) to decide on the dispute between the churches of Arezzo and Siena, they consulted the decrees of the councils of Nicaea, Ephesus and Chalcedon, before making

---

[33] Billanovich and Ferrari, 'La trasmissione', pp. 305–10; Petrucci, 'Scritture e scriventi', *Scriptores*, pp. 57–62. Milan possibly used liturgical rolls: T.F. Kelly, *The Exultet in Southern Italy* (Oxford, 1996), pp. 26–8.
[34] MGH SRL, p. 190: 'aulam ingressi ortodoxi pariter/adversus prabos coeperunt contendere, libros legentes sancitos a patribus', 'pastor apostolicus/digni quae erant sectae pravae codices/quos antefati conscripserunt auctores/iussit conburi'.
[35] PL 87, 1265A.   [36] MGH Poetae I, p. 24.

their decision.[37] The *Concordia canonum cresconii*, a derivative of the *Collectio dionysiana*, enjoyed a wider circulation in Italy than elsewhere, and appears to have been the preferred collection in the Lombard period. Though poor in quantity, the manuscript evidence prior to 800 suggests active interest in different canon law collections and an attempt to organise canonical precepts into a more coherent whole.[38] In fact the *Carmen de synodo ticinensi*, our principal source for the Synod of Pavia, comes down to us written in a contemporary, cursive hand on to some blank pages of a manuscript containing the acts of the council of Chalcedon which may have been used at the Synod, and which therefore corroborates the poet's claim to reformers and schismatics poring over ancient texts.[39]

CLERICS ON THE MARGINS

The *Carmen de synodo* draws attention to the lack of the composition of new works by the clergy in this period, and to where we might look for signs of literate life among these manuscripts of past works. Many of the manuscripts contain *marginalia* – often in cursive but sometimes uncial, half-uncial and even Tironian notes, in a very wide range of scribal competence – that testify to the readers' responses and interests. This is particularly true for the manuscripts preserved at Verona. For example, one of the earliest manuscripts of Verona's collection is a sixth- or seventh-century Greek–Latin Psalter, also containing some hymns and canticles.[40] The Greek text suggests the manuscript was originally written in an area where Greek was still spoken and perhaps taught, possibly in

---

[37] CDL 20.
[38] Text, PL 88, 830–942; K. Zechiel-Eckes, *Die Concordia canonum des Creconius: studien und edition*, Freiburger Beiträge zur mittelalterlichen Geschichte 5, 2 vols. (Frankfurt am Main, 1992). See R. Kottje, 'Einheit und Vielfalt des kirchlichen Lebens in der Karolingerzeit', *Zeitschrift für Kirchengeschichte* 76 (1965), 323–42. Italian manuscripts of canon law datable to the Lombard period are: Verona, LXII (CLA IV.512: see Zechiel-Eckes, *Concordia*, II, 349–51) , saec. VII–VIII (*Concordia canonum Cresconii*: Zechiel-Eckes, II, pp. 348–9); LIX (CLA IV.509: Zechiel-Eckes, ibid), saec. VI/VII. (*idem*); LXI (CLA III.511), saec. VII/VIII (*Collectio canonum* and *Epitome hispana*); LX (CLA III.510), saec. VIII (*Collectio canonum africana Theodosii diaconi*). See W. Telfer, 'The Codex Verona LX (58)', *Harvard Theological Review* 36 (1943), 169–246; Erfurt, Stadtbucherei Ampl. 2.74. (CLA VIII.1190), saec. VI. (fragment of the Council of Grangras); Modena, O.I.12 (CLA III.369), saec. VIII (*Acta synodi chalcedonensis*); Novara, 2 (lxxxi) (CLA III.406), saec. VIII (*idem*); S. Paul in Carinthia Stiftsbibliothek, 7. I (CLA X.1457), saec. VIII (*Collectio sanblasiana*); Oxford, Bodleian Library, 100 + 101 + 102 (CLA.II 255), saec. VI/VII (*Collectio canonum africana Theodosii diaconi*) most likely written in the same place as Paris Bib. nat. 11326 (CLA V.609). R. McKitterick, 'Knowledge of canon law in the Frankish kingdoms before 789: the manuscript evidence', *Journal of Theological Studies* 36 (1985), 96–117, at p. 100 n. 23, sees this last as Merovingian in origin.
[39] Milan, Ambr. E. 147 sup + Vat. lat. 5750, fols. 114, 116. (CLA I.26b + c). The same hand also wrote out the *Carmen* in Ambr. C. 105 inf. (CLA III.232b), fol. 121–121v.
[40] Verona I (1) (CLA IV.472).

Ravenna. Sometime in the seventh or eighth century, an expert cursive hand, identifiably north Italian, copied out on folios 403v and 404v, originally left blank, the text of a letter written by Jesus to the Apostle Thomas. 'In the last days', the Lord warned Thomas, 'there shall be war, famine and earthquakes.' Pride, vanity and blasphemy will flourish among the people, 'and anyone shall say what he pleases'. Priests will fight among themselves, will perform the Eucharist in false spirit, and will become forces of subversion, just as they were before, 'by selling the tax books of the cities for gold and silver, and the leaders of the town shall be condemned'.[41] Just why a north Italian scribe thought to copy out this highly apocryphal text, roundly condemned in the pseudo-Gelasian *Decretum de libris recipiendis et non recipiendis*,[42] into a Greco-Latin Psalter, remains unknown. Perhaps the scribe thought the passage had some relevance to his own period, or was simply attracted by its apocalyptic language. The only other copy of this letter, or one very similar to it, also surfaces in Italy: it survives as a late fifth-century fragment in a palimpsest manuscript from Bobbio and was erased in the eighth century to make way for grammatical works.[43]

Other manuscripts preserved at Verona testify to a considerable degree of clerical, literate activity 'on the margins' in seventh- and eighth-century Italy, well before the more famous examples of *marginalia* attributed to Bishop Pacificus and his *schola sacerdotium*, both of which appear to belong more to the realm of myth than history.[44] A good example is the famous and unique 'Leonine sacramentary' of late sixth-century date, which contains many seventh-century liturgical additions of an ascetical or doctrinal nature, in uncial and half-uncial script. Both the nature of the sacramentary itself and the marginal notes added later

---

[41] Alluded to by Scipio Maffei, *Opera*, X (Venice, 1790), p. 92, it was printed by C.G. Dionisi, *Apologetiche Riflessioni* (1755), appendix, and was transcribed by Dom Antonio Spagnolo for M.R. James, who published it in *JTS* 11 (1910), 288–90. '[sacerdotes] erunt sub[vertitores] sicut et ante fuerant, dantes capitularia ciuitates auri et argenti, et condemnabuntur priores urbium'. On this last I read *civitatum* for *civitates*. For *capitularia*, cf. *CTh* 11, 16, 14.

[42] E.V. Dobschütz, *Das Decretum Gelasianum de libris recipiendis in kritischem Text*, Texte und Untersuchungen zur Geschichte der altchristlichen Literatur 38.8, Heft 4 (Leipzig, 1912), suggested the origin of the *Decretum* in early sixth-century Italy, but cf. McKitterick, *Carolingians*, pp. 202–5, who posits its origin in seventh-century Burgundy. The issue warrants further attention.

[43] Naples, lat. 2 (Vindobon. 16), fols. 60, 67 (CLA IV.396). The lower script is barely legible. See J. Bick, 'Wiener Palimpseste', *Sitzungsberichte der Kaiserliche Akademia der Wissenschaft in Wien* (Phil. Hist. Kl.) 159 (1908), pp. 90–7 and table IV. The letter is referred to in the Berlin-Phillips recension (saec. VIII–IX) of Jerome's *Chronicon*: see James, *JTS*, p. 288.

[44] See C. La Rocca, *Pacifico di Verona: il passato carolingio nella costruzione della memoria urbana* (Rome, 1995), esp. pp. 173–84; La Rocca, 'A man for all seasons: Pacificus of Verona and the creation of a local Carolingian past', in Hen and Innes (eds.), *Uses of the Past*, pp. 250–77. Cf. T. Venturini, *Ricerche paleografiche intorno'all arcidiacono Pacifico di Verona* (Verona, 1929); V. Lazzarini, *Scuola calligrafica veronese del s. IX* (Venice, 1904).

suggest it was designed for private study and not liturgical use.[45] In the section 'everyday prayers' (*orationes et praeces diurnae*), one commentator appears to have been concerned with creating marginal rubrics of introductory phrases for quick reference to a particular prayer.[46] At the bottom of one folio (24v), a note is added in a rough cursive hand: 'Preces populi tui, quaesumus Domine, clementer adsume, ut nos servos tuos custodias ab omni malo adque defendas.' We can date the effort of this particular anonymous reader owing to his scribbling in the margin of yet another manuscript preserved in Verona, a graceful fifth-century copy of Hilary of Poitiers' commentary on the Psalms, where he wrote 'in none [*scil.* nomine] d[omi]ni nostri I[e]h[s]um xpi ariperto rege fuit vera iustitia et sincera'.[47] What caused this seemingly spontaneous bout of approbation for King Aripert II (701–12) is unknown. A little further down the page, after an erasure of three lines, he writes '+ uilius abbas monastirium s[an]c[t]i tohme apostoli cuit uocapulo est pineolo', which would appear to refer to Pignolo, now a part of the city of Verona, although we know nothing of this abbot and his monastery. Nor is it certain whether it was Vilius who wrote the entries, though the prayer in the Leonine sacramentary, and the nature of the sacramentary itself, would suggest that it was, and perhaps provide an important clue to the manuscript's mysterious and much-debated origins, as well as providing a cautionary reminder of the diverse origins of the Veronese collection. In any case the marginal nod to Aripert II provides an interesting and near contemporary counterpoint to the mixed picture painted by Paul of this colourful king. Ruthlessly murdering potential opposition, and a mutilator of women's faces, Aripert gave back the patrimony of the Cottian Alps to the papacy, confirmed it in a charter written in gold letters, exiled the bishop of Pavia to Spoleto, and used to go about the cities of his kingdom at night in disguise, carefully asking questions to find out if anyone was plotting against him, or which judges were corrupt. During his reign the Italian economy enjoyed tremendous prosperity, 'but the times were barbaric'. Aripert II drowned trying to carry the state's coffers across the Ticino

---

[45] Verona, LXXXV (80) (CLA IV.514). Facsimile editions of the sacramentary were published by A. Dold and M. Wolfe (Beuron, 1957) and F. Sauer (Graz, 1960). See L.C. Mohlberg *et al.* (eds.), *Sacramentarium Veronense* (Rome, 1956), pp. lxiv–lxix, and A.D Hope, *The Leonine Sacramentary: A Reassessment of Its Nature and Purpose* (Oxford, 1971). On the *marginalia*, see A. Spagnolo, 'Il sacramentario veronese e Scipio Maffei', *Atti della Reale Accademia delle Scienze di Torino* 33 (1897), 231–52.

[46] E.g. fol. 46, 'contra lacerantes vel adulantes', 'pro duplici corde', 'orandum pro persequentibus'; fol. 47v, 'in periculis vel prosperitate gratias referendas deo'; fol. 56, 'humilibus adesse deum in cunctis operibus eorum'.

[47] Verona XIII (11) (CLA IV.484), fol. 48ov.

river and flee to Francia.⁴⁸ Yet Paul conceded that the king was a pious man and a 'lover of justice', an epithet that finds confirmation in the margins of an ecclesiastical manuscript.

Other marginal additions were more ambitious. In a seventh-century manuscript containing the text of I–II Kings and Julius Honorius' *Cosmographia*, on the first folio, originally left blank, a slightly later hand, in large, crude uncial script, wrote out the Pseudo-Augustine sermon *De die iudicii*, otherwise known as the Doomsday sermon,⁴⁹ which consists of an excessively morbid reflection on Judgement Day. On the verso of this same folio, another hand, a local cursive minuscule of eighth-century date, wrote out a lesson from Ezechiel (36.22–8). The same cursive minuscule hand is found on yet another Veronese manuscript, a fifth-century copy of Pseudo-Clemens, *Recognitiones*. Here, too, where he could find blank folios, the same scribe inserted a liturgical lesson entitled 'Lectio Danielis prophetae cum cantico',⁵⁰ and three similar entries are made by the same hand, or one very similar to it, in the 'Ursicinus' manuscript. These further demonstrate the prevalence of a pre-Jerome Vulgate in Italian churches, and its rich texture, including a variation on Isaiah 33.18, wherein the prophet asks 'where are the grammarians?'⁵¹

The Veronese collection manuscripts, therefore, provide testimony to active engagement of clerics with the books at their disposal, occasionally correcting the original text, sometimes adding material in the margins

---

⁴⁸ *HL* VI.19–21, 28, 35. Palaeographical considerations, and Paul's portrait, tend to rule out Aripert I (653–661) as the referee, though it is not impossible.

⁴⁹ Verona II (2) (CLA IV.477). Sermo app. 251: *PL* 39, 2210. C.D. Wright, *The Irish Tradition in Old English Literature* (Cambridge, 1993), p. 218 n. 17. The sermon has by default, and erroneously, been attributed to Irish exegetical culture: see N. Everett and M. Gorman, 'The *Interrogationes de littera et de vetere testamento*: an eighth-century school text from northeastern Italy (Verona?)', in M. Gorman (ed.), *Lo studio della Bibbia nell'alto medioevo* (forthcoming), concerning MS Cesena S.XXI.5. At the foot of this first folio of Verona II (2), a Latin note in Greek capitals was made by the same hand that entered similar material on fol. 24v of Verona LXXXV (80) (CLA IV.514), which appears to comprise a dedication to Bishop Egino *(in dei nomine Ratpert clericus indus Eginoni)*.

⁵⁰ Verona XXXVII (35), fols. 169v, 231, 231v, and fol. 6 (formerly a single leaf known as Verona IV (4)) (CLA IV.493).

⁵¹ See XXXVIII (36) (CLA IV.494) fols. 117v, Isa. 27.11–13, Jer. 4.3–5; fol. 118. Isa. 33.9–19; 'ubi sunt grammatici? 'ubi sunt consularii?', cf. Jerome, 'ubi est litteratus, ubi legis verba ponderans'. Edited by A. Spagnolo, 'Tre frammenti biblici', *Atti e Memorie dell'Accademia di Verona* ser. IV, vol. X (1910), pp. 1–5 and plates, who saw two separate hands at work here. Cf. LI (49) (CLA IV.504), fol. 132v. The appearance on the last page of the Ursicinus manuscript, in eighth-century uncial, of the opening verses of the poem on the canons later attributed to Ailerannus raises all sorts of questions that cannot be answered here: see M. Gorman, 'The myth of Hiberno-Latin exegesis', *RB* 110 (2000), 42–85, at pp. 67, 70–2; D. Ó Cróinín, 'Hiberno-Latin', *Revue Bénédictine* 110 (2000), 221; D. Howlett, 'Seven studies in seventh-century texts', *Peritia* 10 (1996), 1–70, at pp. 11–20.

to complement it, other times simply filling up the space of blank pages. Marginal entries are not limited to Verona. An elegant sixth-century manuscript of the Gospels, preserved at Cividale and probably written there, caught the attention of many: seventh- and eighth-century readers offered interesting liturgical comments next to the main text, and from the ninth century famous (and not so famous) visitors to Aquileia and Cividale wrote their names in the margins.[52] In a manuscript of Maximus of Turin's *Sermons*, civic pride seems to have spurred an annotator to mark out the passages that refer to St Eusebius, noting several times that the saint was the patron of Vercelli, hence suggesting that the manuscript was written there or at least preserved there. He even admired Maximus' rhetoric, noting 'eleganter' next to passages such as 'et proditur proditor, antequam prodat'.[53]

Marginal comments testify to the literate activity of some clergy in Lombard Italy as they perused and pondered the meanings of the texts before them. Yet this raises the question as to why this did not extend to composition in this period, the absence of which cannot be entirely attributed to a loss of evidence. As I have tried to show elsewhere, the corpus of hagiographic texts that can be dated to this period shows that some clerics were eminently capable of writing prose texts of considerably quality and artistry.[54] They also show a keen awareness of the antiquity of their particular church or region, and attempt to refashion its contemporary identity by drawing on its pre-Christian and palaeochristian past. Hagiographic traditions remained strong in Italy, and throughout the seventh and eighth centuries hagiographic texts were composed that expressed the fears, hopes and aspirations of a particular community. Elsewhere we have little more than hints. The *Carmen de synodo ticinensi* demonstrates both an awareness of literary traditions (in this case quantitative poetry) and an ability to adapt them to new subjects, and the *Versus in laudem mediolensis civitatis* shows that such skills were not limited to Pavia. For all the suggestive promise contained in the epitaphs of Pavese and Milanese clerics of the late seventh and eighth centuries, none of them has left us a biblical commentary or theological treatise, with the exception of Damian, and one gets the sense that Paul noted his efforts

---

[52] Cividale, Museo archeologico S.N. + Prague, Biblitheca Metropolitan. CIM 1 + Venice, S. Marco, S.N. (CLA III.285). See D. De Bruyne, 'Les notes liturgiques du codex Forojuliensis', *Revue Bénédictine* 30 (1913), 208–24.

[53] Milan, Ambr. C. 98 inf. + M. 77 sup. (fol. 93) (CLA III.322). Has features common with Vercelli 183 (Jerome, *De viris ill.*) Later belonged to Bobbio; 'proditor', fol. 6, Sermo 36. *De eadem Paschatis solemnitate VIII*. PL 57, 607B. For Eusebius–Vercelli, see fols. 97v, 98, 108v, 109. Cf. also 21v, 26, 36, 80, 92v, 106, 116v.

[54] 'The hagiography of Lombard Italy', *Hagiographica* 6 (2000), 49–126.

precisely because they were rare.⁵⁵ There are, however, a number of texts now coming to light that show some clerics were composing works of biblical commentary, and chronicles which combined secular and ecclesiastical historiographical traditions.⁵⁶ They also compiled question-and-answer texts for instruction on the origins of the alphabet, who wrote the individual books of the Bible, what they contain, and which were canonical, as well as introducing the student to the art of biblical exegesis by teaching them to read scripture historically and allegorically.⁵⁷

As with the hagiographic texts, the combination of the anonymity of these works and scholarly bias has removed them from the field of vision, and only now are they receiving the attention they deserve. An anonymous commentary on Genesis which appears to have been written sometime in the first half of the eighth century explains how the use of different tenses in the opening words of Genesis (*terra erat, tenebrae erant, ferebatur super aquas*, etc.) correspond to different stages in the formation of the world, and these are best understood by reference to writing and grammar:

for just as the grammarians say, we use the perfect [tense] for things that have been done, such as 'I wrote', and if it were said, that the thing done was finished long before, so that it is more than 'perfect', such as 'he had written', then it is equivalent to 'long ago I completed something'. This is not said unless it happened a long time before. We use the imperfect when we have left something so that we have not finished it, such as 'I was writing'. For whoever says 'I was writing' demonstrates that he has given himself to the act of writing, but he has not finished all of it'.⁵⁸

Analogies with writing helped make sense of the creation of the world. As Contreni commented for the Carolingian period: 'Most Carolingian biblical exegesis . . . was inspired precisely by pedagogical concerns, not by a desire to advance the cause of scholarship, nor by any impulse to

---

⁵⁵ *HL* VI.4.
⁵⁶ The *Chronica Sancti Hieronymi*, in Karlsruhe CXXXIX. See C. Munier, 'Pseudo-Hiéronymienne de Sélestat. Un schéma de catéchèse baptismale?', *RB* 104 (1994), 106–22.
⁵⁷ For the question-and-answer text of Paris lat. 10616 (+ 10457; CLA V.601), see Everett and Gorman, '*Interrogationes de littera*'. Likewise in the same manuscript, the *Commemoratio Geneseos*: M. Gorman, 'A Critique of Bischoff's theory of Irish exegesis: the commentary on Genesis in Munich Clm 6302 (Wendepunkte 2)', *Journal of Medieval Latin* 7 (1997), 178–211, at pp. 207–11.
⁵⁸ Vercelli, 121 fol. 8v. 'Ideo Grammatici dicunt, perfectum dicimus de re perfecta ut scripsi, ac si diceret, modo defini finita re, plusquam perfectum, ut scripserat, id est rem olim compleui. Non dicitur enim nisi de antiquo tempore factum. Inperfectum dicimus ubi omisimus, necdum compleuimus, ut scribebam. Qui enim dicit scribebam, monstrat se dedisse ad scribendum, nec complesse per totum. Sic erat mundi materia incepta per substantium, nec dum consummata per formam.' I thank Michael Gorman, who is preparing a critical edition of this interesting text, for providing me with a transcription.

push on to new exegetical frontiers.'⁵⁹ As more exegetical texts of this nature turn up, we have reason to suspect that the case was the same in Lombard Italy. It has been suggested that the commentary on Daniel attributed to Peter of Pisa, for example, may be a version of the debate between Peter and the Jew called Lull which Alcuin heard while he was in Pavia, and which he knew 'had been written down' although no copy in Tours could be found.⁶⁰ Indeed at one point Peter seems to have mixed his genres: when King Belshazzar offered to provide purple clothing and a gold neck-chain (*torquis*) to anyone who can interpret the mysterious writing that appeared on the palace wall, Peter pointed out the neck-chain's ambiguous gender.⁶¹ Compositions such as this draw attention to the increasing alliance between grammatical and biblical studies in the eighth and ninth centuries. Peter, Paul the Deacon and Paulinus of Aquileia may have been exceptional students, but the schools and techniques which equipped these Italian clerics, and those of lesser or latent literary talent, must have relied on a great many more books than have come down to us.

MONASTERIES AND MONASTIC CULTURE

We can safely assume a great deal more scriptorial activity took place than has survived from the great abbeys of Monte Cassino, Farfa, Monte Amiata, Novalesa, Nonantola and San Vincenzo al Volturno – all of which were founded, or refounded in the case of Monte Cassino, in the Lombard period and under the patronage of Lombard nobility. We have less than a dozen manuscripts of Monte Cassino which can be securely dated from the eighth century, but know much more was written.⁶² For all the signs of 'literacy displayed' on tiles, on tombs and in wall-paintings revealed by the excavations of the site of San Vincenzo al Vulturno, no scriptorium has been located there. Nor can we attribute any eighth- or ninth-century manuscripts with any certainty to the abbey, except perhaps for one

---

⁵⁹ J. Contreni, 'Carolingian biblical studies', in U.-R. Blumenthal (ed.), *Carolingian Essays* (Washington, DC, 1983), pp. 71–98 at p. 79.

⁶⁰ D. Bullough, 'Reminiscence and reality: text, translation and testimony of an Alcuin letter', *Journal of Medieval Latin* 5 (1995), 174–201. The text is *PL* 96, 1347–62. Alcuin, Ep. 172, MGH Ep. IV, p. 285.

⁶¹ *PL* 96, 1350. Q.18 'Quaeritur cur legatur, purpura vestietur et torquem aream habebit in collo? cur torquem feminino genere translator protulerit? Exemplo doctus fecit. Nam Cicero in Mario torquem genere feminino posuit, sed Titus Libius masculino dixit.'

⁶² E.A. Lowe, *The Beneventan Script: A History of the South Italian Minuscule* (Oxford, 1914), pp. 6–10; H. Bloch, 'Monte Cassino's teachers in the high Middle Ages', *Settimane* 19 (Spoleto, 1972), 562–603, at pp. 567–70; S. La Rocca, 'Versus in Benedicti laudem', *Romanobarbarica* 3 (1978), 335–63.

Gospel book.⁶³ But the life and work of Ambrosius Autpert (d. 784), who wrote his monumental commentary on the apocalypse there (758–67), prove that the monastery was equipped with a solid stock of patristic sources at least.⁶⁴ Likewise, although we are told the abbey of Farfa's famous homilist, Alan (761–70), 'magnificently copied out many codices', and Alan's own *Homilarium* seems to have circulated quickly and widely, we have few, if any, products from that abbey's scriptorium.⁶⁵

The extent of these losses can perhaps in part be measured against the notice of book production at the monastery of Novalesa, founded in the Alpine pass near Susa by Abbo, the supposed son of the bishop of Turin.⁶⁶ By *c.* 906, at the time of its (supposed) destruction by Saracens, the monastery boasted over 6666 volumes in its library, though the source for this suspicious figure, the eleventh-century *Chronicon novalicensis*, is notorious for its historical inaccuracy and the technical problems involved in reconstructing the parts of the chronicle from later antiquarian sources.⁶⁷ The *Chronicon* also singles out for praise one scribe of the monastery, Attepert, who seems to have been active in the period prior

---

⁶³ London, British Library, Add. 5463 (CLA II.162). D.H. Wright, 'The canon tables of the Codex Beneventanus and related decoration', *Dumbarton Oaks Papers* 33 (1979), 133–55, and now E. Condello, *Una scrittura e un territorio: l'onciale dei secoli V–VIII nell'Italia meridionale* (Spoleto, 1994), pp. 89–93. Cf. Mitchell, 'Literacy displayed', pp. 217–19.

⁶⁴ See S. Bovo, 'Le fonti del Commento di Ambrogio Autperto sull'Apocalisse', *Studi Anselmiani* 27–8 (1951), 372–403: primarily Ambrose, Gregory, Jerome and Tyconius, but also Primasius Adrumetanus, Victorinus di Petau and Augustine. See further C. Leonardi, 'Spiritualità di Ambrogio Autpert', *Studi Medievali* 9 (1968), 1–131, and R. Weber (ed.), *Ambrosi Autperti opera*, CCCM 27 (Turnhout, 1975), I, pp. v–vi.

⁶⁵ Gregorio di Catino, *Chronicon*, ed. Balzani, I, p. 122. Grégoire, *Homéliares*, pp. 17–23. See P. Supino Martini, 'La produzione libraria negli "scriptoria" delle abbazie di Farfa e di S. Eutizio', *Atti IX CISAM* (Spoleto, 1970), 581–607.

⁶⁶ The foundation documents are collected in C. Cipolla (ed.), *Monumenta novaliciensia vetustiora: raccolta degli atti e delle chronache riguardanti l'abbazia della Novalesa*, Fonti per la Storia d'Italia 31–2 (Rome, 1898–1901). See P. Geary, *Aristocracy in Provence in the early Middle Ages* (Vienna, 1985), pp. 12–35; edition and Eng. trans. of Abbo's will, pp. 38–79. Cf I. Gulli, 'A proposito della più antica tradizione novalicense', *Archivio Storico Italiano* 117 (1959), 306–18. Although the monastery belonged politically to Carolingian Francia, the material remains of the abbey point to Pavia: see S. Casartelli Novelli, 'Confini e bottega provinciale delle Marittime nel divenire della scultura longobarda dai primi del VIII secolo all'anno 774', *Storia dell'Arte* 32 (1978), 11–22; G. Cantino Wataghin, 'Ricerche archeologiche all'abbazia di Novalesa (1978–81)', in *La Novalesa: ricerche, fonti documentarie, restauri* (Susa, 1988), pp. 329–357; Cantino Wataghin, 'L'abbazia di Novalesa alla luce delle indagini archeologiche: verifiche e problemi', in *Dal Piemonte all'Europa: esperienze monastiche nella società medievale. XXXIV Congresso storico subalpino, Torino 1985* (Turin, 1988), pp. 569–85.

⁶⁷ Ed. C. Cipolla in *Monumenta*, II, *Chron.* IV: frag. xix–xx, pp. 230–2. Cipolla's edition does not make for clarity: better is G.C. Alessio (ed.), *Cronaca di Novalesa* (Turin, 1982), pp. 231–6. The figure, reminiscent of the legend of the martyrs of the Theban legion, was changed to 6000 and 600 by the different antiquarian sources which record this fragment. On the manuscripts – gospels, psalters and missals, liturgical, hagiographic and patristic works, monastic rules, narrative history (Paul the Deacon, Bede, Josephus) and grammar (Donatus) – and the inventory, see Alessio, *Cronica*, pp. lv–lx, with refs.; inventory in Cipolla, *Monumenta*, II, p. 312. On more typical figures from library catalogues of the period, D. Ganz, 'Books and book production', in

to the Frankish conquest of Italy. Not only 'scientia litterarum valde imbutus', Attepert was also a highly accomplished and extremely fast copier of texts, so that his exquisite hand could still be recognised at a glance in the eleventh century.[68] None of these manuscripts survive today. The twenty or so manuscripts of possible Novalese origin that survive from the tenth and eleventh centuries, and the fragments of an eleventh-century inventory of the monastery's library (listing twenty-six or so items), suggest a more modest collection of books in the service of monastic reading habits not unusual for the period, as does the literary culture of the anonymous chronicler. But the story of Attepert's expert hand does testify to an active scriptorium manned with accomplished personnel in the Lombard period.

One northern Italian monastery which has left us books and hence some idea of its literary interests and activity is that of Nonantola, founded in 752 by the Lombard noble Anselm (d. 803), its first abbot and one-time duke of Friuli and brother-in-law to King Aistulf.[69] We know little about Anselm himself, but he appears to have been an important political figure. He was exiled to Monte Cassino in 762 by King Desiderius, only to return to northern Italy after the Carolingian conquest, when he seems quickly to have secured the allegiance of the new regime to uphold the monastery's rights and property.[70] The abbey was rich: it controlled some 400 sq. km of the surrounding countryside, the greater part of it donated by Lombard kings and dukes of Persiceta.[71] Unfortunately, owing to fire and sacking in the 890s, little of the original structure remains. Written sources concentrate on the property of the monastery and provide scant

McKitterick (ed.), *NCMH*, II, pp. 786–808, at pp. 791–2. Literary embellishment and culture: G. Penco, 'Tradizione mediolatina e fonti romanze nel *Chronicon Novaliciense*', *Benedictina* 12 (1958), 1–14.

[68] *Chron.* III.20.

[69] The principal documents are the (ninth- or tenth-century) *Vita Anselmi*, ed. Waitz, MGH SRL, pp. 567–70, and the (eleventh-century) *Catalogi abbatum nonantulorum*, ibid., pp. 570–3. The falsified royal charters, CDL III.20, 25, 26, 32, contain almost nothing trustworthy. See Brühl, *Studien*, pp. 153–60.

[70] Knowledge of Anselm's exile, it seems, is owed exclusively to the eleventh-century *Catalogus*, which records a seven-year exile at Monte Cassino, and adds the vague notice 'sicut multorum seniorum relatione didicimus, pro eo quod nescio quid deliquit in desiderio', MGH SRL, p. 571. The absence of such information in the *Vita Anselmi*, written, it seems, before the catalogue, suggests the exile is legendary, or was simply forgotten, which is doubtful. Cf. K. Schmidt, 'Anselm von Nonantola. Olim dux militum – nunc dux monachorum', *Quellen und Forschungen aus Italienischen Archiven und Bibliotheken* 47 (1967), 1–122.

[71] A. Gaudenzi, 'Il monastero di Nonantola, il ducato di Persiceta, e la chiesa di Bologna', *Bullettino dell'Istituto Storico Italiano* 22 (1901), 77–214; G. Spinelli, 'San Silvestro di Nonantola', in Spinelli (ed.), *Monasteri Benedettini in Emilia Romagna* (Milan, 1980), pp. 33–51. On the topography, see P. Bonacini, 'Regno ed episcopato a Modena nei secoli VII e VIII. Il periodo longobardo', *Studi Medievali* 33 (1992), 73–108, at p. 102.

information on architectural elements and the material culture of the abbey.[72]

The earliest catalogues of the monastery's library would appear to reflect the poorer state the abbey was in after the disasters at the end of the ninth century.[73] The *Catalogue of Nonantolan Abbots* (written *c.* 1038) tells us that while Anselm was in Monte Cassino 'he lived blessedly and acquired many codices',[74] and there has been much speculation as to which of the fifteen or so Nonantolan manuscripts that may date from the eighth century may have been originally products of the scriptorium at Monte Cassino.[75] In the absence of any indication in the manuscript itself, in the form of a dedication or colophon, attribution to one or the other centre must remain speculative. Indeed, it would seem that this connection with Monte Cassino goes some way to explaining the development of the distinctive minuscule script of Nonantola. This script has much in common with the Beneventan script that emerges in southern Italy in this period.[76] A further factor which supports the connection is the later Nonantolan manuscript attestations of liturgical chants which have much in common with those of Monte Cassino and Benevento.[77]

But Anselm did not need to rely on Monte Cassino for books. While he was away from his abbey his second-in-charge, the priest Vigilantius, managed the monastery most adequately, acquiring 'much wealth for the abbey in books and in many other things'.[78] To search for classical literature across the range of books that survive from this early period might lead to the conclusion that Nonantola was 'culturally insignificant'.[79] But the transmission of classical texts is a fairly limited definition of

---

[72] F. Zuliani, 'L'abbazia di Nonantola', in F. Zuliani and C. Segre Montel (eds.), *La pittura nell'Abbazia di Nonantola: un refettorio affrescato di età romanica* (Nonantola, 1991), pp. 5–28.

[73] There are five principal catalogues: that which lists forty codices acquired by Abbot Rodulf (1002–35); that of 1166, which lists only six codices; that of 1331, which lists 185; that of 1464, which lists 255; and that of 1464–90, which lists 237. See G. Gullotta, *Gli antichi cataloghi e i codici della Abbazia di Nonantola*, Studi e Testi 181 (Vatican City, 1955); J. Russychaert, *Les Manuscrits de l'abbaye de Nonantola: table de concordance annotée et index des manuscrits*, Studi e Testi 182 (Vatican City, 1955). B. Bischoff, 'Manoscritti nonantoli dispersi dell'epoca carolingia', *La Bibliofilia* 85 (1983), 99–124.

[74] MGH SRL, p. 571: 'beate vixit et multos codices adquisivit'.

[75] The most likely candidates are Rome, BN, 1006 (CLA IV.428), 1378, and Sessor. 590 (CLA IV.427). See M. Palma, 'Nonantola e il Sud. Contributo alla storia della scrittura libraria nell'Italia dell'ottavo secolo', *Scrittura e Civiltà* 3 (1979), 77–88; Palma, 'Alle origini del tipo di Nonantola: nuove testimonianze meridionali', *Scrittura e Civiltà* 7 (1983), 141–9.

[76] The classic study was G. Cencetti, 'Scriptoria e scritture nel monachesimo benedettino', *Settimane* 4 (Spoleto, 1957), 187–219, repr. in Cavallo (ed.), *Libri e lettori*, pp. 73–129.

[77] See T. Bailey, 'Ambrosian chant in southern Italy', *Journal of the Plainsong and Medieval Music Society* 6 (1983), 1–7; Bailey, *The Ambrosian Alleluias* (Egham, Surrey, 1983), pp. 51–2.

[78] MGH SRL, p. 571: 'et multa commoda ibidem adquisivit in libris et in aliis multis rebus'.

[79] Riché, *Education*, p. 401.

culture. In terms of Christian literate culture the abbey was far from negligent. To Nonantola we owe our earliest surviving copy of Augustine's *Confessions*.[80] Although written two centuries earlier than the foundation of the abbey, the manuscript found a safe home in Nonantola, where it was partly restored in the eighth or ninth century, and it is the only copy of the text to come down to us from before the ninth century. Our oldest copy of Augustine's *De genesi ad litteram*, of similar vintage, also found refuge there.[81] Judging from the manuscripts that can be dated to the eighth century, patristic scholarship was Anselm's and Vigilantius' main concern.[82] While it is certainly true that the manuscripts of the ninth century are more elaborately decorated and perhaps reflect wider interests of a more developed literary culture in terms of Christian and classical content,[83] it would be unwise to assume that these interests and skills were not present from the very foundation of the monastery.

What is important to recognise, however, is that Nonantola was founded by a member of the Lombard aristocracy of the highest level, with the direct support of the Lombard King Aistulf. But this was the king's second act of generosity. Already, two years earlier, in the very first year of his reign, Aistulf had given Anselm territory in Fanano to build a monastery and hospice on the road to Tuscany for pilgrims and 'guests'.[84] The *Vita Anselmi* proudly chronicles this, the following foundation of Nonantola and its subsequent dedication by the bishop of Reggio, according to the year of Aistulf's reign, and notes that it was both the king and Anselm who persuaded the archbishop of Ravenna, Sergius (744–69), to come to Nonantola to consecrate the church and its altar. At this point, the author goes overboard in his concern for artistry over historical accuracy: in 753 both Aistulf and Anselm go together to Rome to seek and obtain the relics of St Silvester for the abbey from none other

---

[80] Rome, BN, Sessor. 55 (CLA IV.420a–b), also containing Cassian's *Collationes*, and sermons of Ambrose and Maximus of Turin. See M. Gorman, 'The earliest manuscript tradition of St Augustine's Confessions', *Journal of Theological Studies* 34 (1983), 114–45.

[81] Sessor. 13 (CLA IV.418). See E.A. Lowe, 'More facts about our oldest Latin manuscripts', in his *Palaeogaphical Papers*, I, pp. 260–1.

[82] Among the collection is: Gregory, *Homiliae in evangelia* (Rome, BN, Sessor. 39; CLA IV.419), Eucherius, *Formulae spiritalis intellegentiae* and *Instructionum ad Salonem libri duo* (Sessor. 77; CLA IV.423), Jerome, *Adversus Iovinianum* (Jerome, Sessor. 128; CLA IV.426); Pseudo-Chrysostom, commentary on Mark and Matthew; the real Chrysostom, *De reparatione lapsi* (Sessor. 94; CLA IV.425), Eugippius, *Excerpta ex operibus Augustini* (Sessor. 590; CLA IV.427); Fulgentius, *De fide* and the *Epistula datiani* (Fuglentius, Rome, BN, 1006; CLA IV.28); (Pseudo-) Augustine, *Speculum*, Cyprian, *Opera* (Sessor. 58; CLA IV.422); a volume of Augustine's sermons (London, Chester Beatty 5; CLA II.161); and another Augustine miscellany (London, Add. 43460; CLA II.180–1).

[83] The more celebrated examples are Paris, Mazarine 660, Cassiodorus, *Institutiones*; Modena, O.I 11, Hypocrates, *Aphorismi*; Vat. lat. 5951, Celsus, *De medicina*.

[84] *Vita Anselmi*, 2–3, MGH SRL, p. 567.

than Pope Hadrian (772–85). By contrast, the rule of 'Charlemagne the emperor' is only briefly mentioned as a means of dating Anselm's death (803). When Nonantola wished to remember the origins of its holy establishment, it proudly associated them with the most hated king in early medieval papal history.[85]

Lombard royalty also became associated with the foundation of the abbey of San Salvatore at Monte Amiata, which later legend ascribed to the retirement there of Aistulf's brother and royal predecessor, Ratchis, who in fact retired to Monte Cassino in 749.[86] The true founders of Monte Amiata are revealed in a charter of 762, recording the foundation of another two monasteries in Friuli, namely, Santa Maria di Sesto (Udine) and Salto (Povoletto, Cividale). With this we can unravel the legend of Ratchis' involvement.[87] The charter of 762 records that Erfo, and his brothers Marco and Anto, had earlier heard the voice of Psalm 44.11 ('hear o daughter, consider and incline your ear. Forget your people and your father's house'). The boys subsequently 'left our homeland and family and decided to live in Tuscany',[88] where they founded Monte Amiata, before returning to their native Friuli, where they owned a lot of land. Despite the wealth of detail contained in the foundation charter concerning the property the boys donated, and the fact that the charter was drawn up at the monastery of Nonantola, we know nothing of any educational or scriptorial activity there.[89] Nor do we know of any such activity at Monte Amiata in this period, though a possible product of the monastery's scriptorium is a copy of the collection of canon law by Cresconius, written in a combination of uncial and pre-Caroline minuscule scripts which betray some Anglo-Saxon influence in the use of sharp triangular ascenders, long pointed descenders and highly decorative initials.[90]

---

[85] *LP* 94, ed. Duchesne, I, pp. 440–55.

[86] The eleventh-century *Fundatio monasterii sancto salvatoris montisamiati*, MGH SRL, pp. 564–5. See W. Kurze, 'Die langobardische Königsurkunden für S. Salvatore am Monte Amiata', *Quellen und Forschungen aus Italienischen Archiven und Bibliotheken* 57 (1977), 315–31.

[87] R. Della Torre, *L'abbazia di Sesto in Sylvis* (Udine, 1979), pp. 8–12.

[88] CDL 162, of 762 (Nonantola), 'hanc nos secuti uocem, eximus de terra et de cognatione nostra, et disposuimus habitare in Tusciae partibus', which appears to refer to Monte Amiata. Cf. CDL 248, of 770 (Chiusi).

[89] CDL 162. G. Cantino Wataghin, 'Monasterium in locum qui vocatur Sexto. L'archeologia per la storia dell'abbazia di S. Maria di Sesto', in G.C. Menis and A. Tilatti (eds.), *L'abbazia di S. Maria di Sesto fra archeologia e storia* (Pordenone, 1999), pp. 3–51; and G. Spinelli, 'Origine e primi sviluppi della fondazione monastica sestense (762–967)', in *ibid.*, pp. 97–121. On the charter and properties mentioned, see H. Krahwinkler, *Friaul im Frühmittelalter: Geschichte einer Region vom Ende des fünften bis zum Ende des zehnten Jahrhunderts* (Vienna, 1992), pp. 87–118.

[90] Vat. Barb. lat. 679 (XIV.52) (CLA I.65). Uncial and pre-Caroline minuscule. Saec. VIII–IX. Central Italy. Belonged to monastery of Monte Amiata in saec. XI. Text; *PL* 56 135. Bischoff, *Panorama*, p. 252 (= *Manuscripts*, p. 49); Mordek, *Bibliotheca*, pp. 751–7. Suggestive of the richness

Literacy in Lombard Italy, c. 568–774

While the monasteries of Bobbio and Monte Cassino might be considered as special cases owing to their association with famous monastic holy men, their subsequent history and their surviving manuscripts, the more modest achievements of Nonantola could constitute the yardstick by which we should measure the now lost efforts of Novalesa, Farfa, Monte Amiata and San Vincenzo al Volturno as centres of manuscript production and preservation, and therefore as repositories of literary culture in the eighth century. The foundation of these larger abbeys also draws attention to the part played by Lombard nobility in providing the material wealth supporting these efforts to create spiritual refuges for the cultivation of Christ's kingdom on earth wherein those who entered engaged with Christ's message as written in the Gospels. We know that kings Perctarit, Cunincpert and Liutprand founded monasteries in Pavia (Sant' Agata, San Giorgio, San Pietro in Ciel d'Oro) and endowed them with property.[91] The splendid physical remains of the complex of San Salvatore in Brescia, morevoer, provides some idea of the beneficence of royal patronage. We see the same initiatives at the ducal level with Duke Faroald II of Spoleto (c. 700), who re-established the abbey of Ferentillo.[92] We have no surviving testimony of the production of manuscripts in these centres, although they must have required, at the least, Bibles, Gospels, Psalters, sacramentaries, liturgical books and prayer books for the daily observance of religious services and feasts, let alone patristic works or biblical commentaries for private study. These, moreover, are just the larger establishments: from the charter evidence we know of over forty-one monasteries founded in the Lombard period, but we know next to nothing else about them.[93] Not all of these need to have been furnished

---

of the library there are Vat. lat. 3314, Porphyrio's commentary on Horace, and the rare Firmicus Maternus, *De errore profanarum religionum*, Vat. Pal. lat. 165, both saec. IX². It is tempting to conjecture that the insular influences are somehow related to the presence of the famous Codex Amiatinus at the abbey, or vice versa, but we have no information concerning how Abbot Coelfred's pandect Bible ended up with the monks of San Salvatore more than thirty years after Coelfred's death (717–718), and possibly much later than that: P. Meyvaert, 'Bede, Cassiodorus and the Codex Amiatinus', *Speculum* 71 (1996), 827–83.

[91] Paul, *HL* V.34, VI.17, 48, 58.

[92] *HL* VI.44. On Ferentillo, see C. Pietrangeli 'I sarcofagi romani', and chapter 6, note 135. Dukes of Benevento were also involved in San Vincenzo and Monte Cassino in this period: P. Bertolini, 'I duchi di Benevento e San Vincenzo al Volturno. Le origini', in F. Avagliano (ed.), *Una grande abbazia altomedievale nel Molise: San Vincenzo al Volturno, Atti del I Convegno di studi sul medioevo meridionale, Venafro–San Vincenzo al Volturno 19–22 maggio 1982* (Monte Cassino, 1985), pp. 85–177; Bertolini, 'I Longobardi di Benevento e Monte Cassino', in F. Avagliano (ed.), *Montecassino: dalla prima alla seconda destruzione. Momenti e aspetti di storia cassinese (sec. VI–IX), Atti del II Convegno di studi sul medioevo meridionale, Cassino–Montecassino 27–31 maggio 1984* (Monte Cassino, 1987), pp. 55–100.

[93] G. Cantino Wataghin, 'Monasteri di età longobarda: spunti per una ricerca', *Corso di Cultura dell'Arte Ravennate e Bizantina* 36 (1989), 73–100.

Manuscripts

with the means of producing books. As the Frankish evidence suggests, monastic establishments, irrespective of gender, could acquire books from writing centres that specialised in particular texts and writing styles.[94] But the very presence of monastic communities created a demand, or consumptive market, for the production of texts. It has been suggested that the foundation of these small, proprietary monasteries or *Eigenklöster* in the Lombard period, particularly in Tuscany and the north, constituted a break in monastic traditions established in Italy in the fourth, fifth and sixth centuries. But this underestimates the degree of diversity already existent in late antique Italy.[95] It would be more appropriate to see these Lombard monasteries as a development of previous traditions, parallel to the foundation of larger abbeys and communities, to suit new social conditions. In other words, the small proprietary church or monastery was established to fulfil the spiritual and material needs of family members, supported by the relatively modest and more evenly distributed reserves of wealth among Lombard land-owners.[96] These monasteries would certainly have used and preserved texts, but it is far from axiomatic that they had the means to create them.

Some insight into one of these *Eigenklöster* is offered by the *Life of Walfred*, a late eighth-century hagiographic work recording the foundation of the monastery of San Pietro di Monteverdi by two Pisan nobles in 754.[97] Walfred himself, we are told, was 'sapiens in verbis, litteris imbutus', his son and successor, Gunfred, 'sapientia doctus'. When Gunfred attempted to write some laudatory verses over his father's tomb in the monastery, his father's ghost intervened and struck Gunfred down with fever: Walfred had always shunned such worldly vanities, and his son never dared to write again. We hear of charters being preserved there (Gunfred tried to steal them), and that a copy of Benedict's *Rule* was brought in by a monk from San Vincenzo al Volturno, but there is no mention of books used or produced there, and the composition of the *Vita Walfredi* does not reflect a learned, literary environment or a well-stocked library.[98] The secular clergy of rural parishes could at least draw upon the resources of the cathedral churches and their scriptoria for

---

[94] The example of Chelles: McKitterick, 'Nuns' scriptoria'.
[95] Jenal, *Italia ascetica*, II, pp. 943–9.   [96] Wickham, 'Aristocratic power', pp. 159–64.
[97] BHL 8792. Re-edited with a collection of studies in K. Schmidt, *Vita Walfredi und Kloster Monteverdi: toskanisches Mönchtum zwischen langobardischer und fränkischer Herrschaft* (Tübingen, 1991).
[98] *Vita Walfredi*, c. 5, p. 46. On sources see U. Eigler, 'Die *Vita Walfredi*. Ein spätes Zeugnis "langobardischer" Literatur', in Schmidt (ed.) *Vita Walfredi*, pp. 64–74, who suggests that beyond the Vulgate, ancient sources may have been used for the knowledge of the names *Cyrnus* for Corsica (c. 2) and the confused *Alfea* for Pisa (c. 1), as well as knowledge of the herb *nerbago* (plantain) as a remedy for toothaches. The similarities to the *Vita Sturmi* (Eigler, *Vita Walfredi*, p. 68) are just that.

books: an archpriest at the cathedral church of Lucca, Sichimund, donated his property, including his books, to the church of San Pietro where he was brought up.[99] Likewise, the monasteries may have drawn upon the resources of the secular clergy to whose jurisdiction they were subject: or perhaps they sought books from the larger abbeys with active scriptoria, as with the copy of Benedict's *Rule* at San Pietro di Monteverdi supplied by San Vincenzo al Volturno.[100] But there were clearly no fixed rules or customs as to what a monastery should possess beyond these necessities. When he refounded Monte Cassino, the Lombard noble Petronax asked Pope Zachary 'for books of holy scripture and whatever else is useful to a monastery'. Zachary promptly gave him the copy of Benedict's *Rule* written by the holy abbot himself.[101] No other books are mentioned, but copies of scripture may also have been acquired.

So far we have talked only of ecclesiastical or monastic establishments. Is there any evidence for lay production and preservation of books such as that found in the Carolingian period? No there is not, but it would be unwise to dismiss the possibility. We have seen that Rothari made provision for the dissemination of 'official' copies of his edict, and that judges were expected to know, and did know, Lombard law. The subscription of the Pisan royal 'cellarer' (*canevaggio regis*) Maurezius, on the frontipiece of the Spanish 'Mozarabic Orational' manuscript, in which Maurezius states his role as a guarantor for an amphora of wine, cannot be taken as evidence that Maurezius owned the manuscript, but it does testify to its circulation in a lay environment, and therefore to the access of laity to such objects.[102]

THE PRESERVATION OF CLASSICAL LITERATURE

Italy's importance as the repository of literature from the classical world throughout the middle ages in the west is well known and unquestionable.[103] What has been questioned, however, is the degree to which the period of the Lombard kingdom played any active part in the preservation of classical texts, and the amount of interest these texts

---

[99] CDL 73 (740): 'Omnia usitilia, seo scherpa meam, tam pannis, eramen, uel auricalco, codicis uel omnia quidquid in dominio esset uidetor'. The location of the church of San Pietro is uncertain, but Sichimund's title of archpriest suggests he served as an important member of the Lucchese cathedral clergy: corroborated by the fact that the charter was redacted by none other than the well-known Lucchese scribe and presbiter Gaudentius. See Petrucci, 'Il codice e i documenti', *Scriptores*, pp. 77–84.

[100] Cf. CDL 116.   [101] *HL* IV.40.

[102] Schiaparelli, 'Sulla data e provenienza', pp. 106–17, and above, p. 130. Carolingian evidence: McKitterick, *Carolingians*, pp. 238–41.

[103] Reynolds, *Texts and Transmission*, pp. xv, xviii–ix, and esp. xxii–iv.

generated in comparison with the documented enthusiasm for classical literature found in the Carolingian world of the ninth century. Manuscripts of classical works are few before then, and the crucial question of exemplars for the Carolingian manuscripts has always turned easily to Italy but uncomfortably to the Lombards. The common approach is to bypass them altogether by geographical and chronological excursion. Hence a standard handbook asks:

> Where did all the books that have salvaged so much of Latin literature come from? As far as we can tell from the evidence available, the total contribution of Ireland and England, Spain and Gaul, was small in comparison with what came from Italy itself, from Rome and Campania and particularly, it would seem, from Ravenna after its capture by the forces of Charlemagne.[104]

Rome, its hinterland and route to Naples, and Ravenna must have provided the goods, for there were no Lombards there.[105] Even Bernard Bischoff, who was prepared to postulate an Italian antecedent or exemplar when no such trace survives, and whose scholarly contributions have done much to differentiate regional styles of writing in eighth- and ninth-century Italy, often referred to a phantom 'shipment of books' from Ravenna to Aachen when Charlemagne stripped the city to furnish his royal palace, for which there is not a shred of manuscript evidence, nor evidence of any other sort.[106]

Doubtless the libraries of Rome and Ravenna preserved manuscripts of classical literature and provided the Carolingian world with copies of texts hitherto unknown on the other side of the Alps. There is, however, sufficient evidence for the copying and cultivation of classical literature in centres located in Lombard Italy, though much of it, like the careers of the Italians at Charlemagne's court, seems only to surface after the demise of the Lombard kingdom. An example is the copy of Seneca's

---

[104] L.D. Reynolds and N.G. Wilson, *Scribes and Scholars: A Guide to the Transmission of Greek and Latin Literature*, 3rd edn (Oxford, 1991), p. 97. Likewise, Reynolds, *Texts and Transmission*, p. xxiii. Cf. J. Brown, 'Historical introduction to the use of classical Latin authors in the British Isles from the fifth to the eleventh century', repr. in Brown, *A Palaeographer's View: Selected Writings of Julian Brown*, ed. J. Bately et al. (London, 1993), pp. 141–78, at p. 148.

[105] E.g. A. Pertusi, 'Bisanzio e l'irradiazione della sua civiltà in Occidente nell'alto medioevo', *Setttimane* 11 (Spoleto, 1964), 119–31.

[106] *Manuscripts*, p. 131 (exemplars), 140–1 ('treasure-trove', 'massive shipment of books', etc.). See also his 'Italienische Handschriften des neunten bis elften Jahrhunderts in frühmittelalterlichen Bibliotheken ausserhalb Italiens', in C. Questa and R. Rafaelli (eds.), *il libro e il testo. Atti del convegno internazionale, Urbino 20–23 Settembre 1982* (Urbino, 1984), pp. 169–94. Bischoff's citation of Wigbod's dedication verses *(Manuscripts*, pp. 138, 141) is misleading: cf. M. Gorman, 'Wigbod and biblical studies under Charlemagne', *RB* 107 (1997), 40–76. Vat. lat. 4929, written in Auxerre from a possibly sixth-century exemplar written in Ravenna, cannot be used as evidence for the phantom 'shipment' in Charlemagne's day: G. Billanovich, 'Dall'antica Ravenna alle biblioteche umanistiche', *Aevum* 30 (1956), 316–62.

De beneficiis and his *De clementia*, written in an early, pre-Caroline minuscule script by at least ten different hands at a centre somewhere near Milan, or where the Ambrosian rite was still in use.[107] The manuscript ('Codex Nazarianus') is often cited as the earliest Carolingian classical text, and therefore lauded as a symbol of the renewed interest in secular Latin literature of the ancient world. But there is the possibility that the manuscript dates even earlier; its rough and unpolished minuscule and inconsistency – with some hands employing sweeping, cursive forms containing a wealth of ligatures, while others wrote in short, stunted letters – speaks more of pre-Carolingian Italian scribal traditions. There is, moreover, always the question of its exemplar.[108] Another early ninth-century manuscript preserved and probably written at Brescia contains the letters of Seneca. The monastery of San Faustino there became a centre for the study of classical texts and for their transmission from Carolingian Milan to east and west Francia, and there are signs that such activity built upon earlier traditions.[109] The famous Codex Salmasianus, which contains the eclectic collection of classical texts known as the *Anthologia Latina*, dates from the late eighth century. Its origin has been ascribed to Spain, southern France and northern Italy, but Bischoff has drawn attention to the similarity of its script to that found in an Evangeliary preserved at Perugia, hence the Salmasianus probably originated somewhere in southern Tuscany or Umbria, possibly Perugia itself.[110]

We gain a tantalising glimpse of the classical literary heritage that was preserved in Lombard Italy in the famous list of classical works recorded in the late eighth-century manuscript, Berlin Diez. B. 66.[111] Among those listed are Lucan's *De bello civili*, Statius' *Thebaid*, four plays of Terence *(Andria, Eunuchus, Hecyra, Heauton)*, Juvenal's *Satires*, the poetry of Horace (*Ars poetica*), Tibullus and Martial, the works of Claudian *(De raptu Proserpinae, In Eutropium, De bello gothico, De bello Gildonico)*, Cicero (*In Catilinam, Pro Deiotaro, In Verrem*), Sallust (*In Catilinam, Iugurtha*), among other rarities such as Alcimus' *Controversiae*, and the works of Arusianus Messius and Julius Victor on rhetoric.[112] The list

---

[107] Vat. Pal. lat. 1547. Bischoff, *Manuscripts*, p. 48, who points to similarities with St Gall 908 (CLA 953–65), and pp. 129, 147. It was listed in a catalogue of books at Lorsch *c.* 850; Bischoff, *Lorsch im Spiegel seiner Handschriften* (Munich, 1974), pp. 52, 80 (2nd edn, pp. 60, 89). Cavallo, 'Libri e cultura', p. 90, entertains an earlier, firmly eighth-century date for the manuscript.
[108] See the comments of A. Petrucci, 'Scrivere il testo', in *La critica del testo. Atti del Convegno di Lecce, 22–26 Oct. 1984* (Rome, 1985), pp. 215–17.
[109] Brescia, Quer. B.II.6. See Billanovich, 'La trasmissione', pp. 346–8.
[110] Paris lat. 10318 (CLA V.593). Perugia 2 (CLA III.408). Bischoff, *Manuscripts*, pp. 131, 152.
[111] CLA VIII.1044.
[112] The list has been edited several times: M. Haupt, *Hermes* 3 (1869), 221, Becker, *Catalogi*, no. 20; B.L. Ullman, 'A list of classical manuscripts (in an eighth-century codex) perhaps from Corbie',

was publicised by Bernard Bischoff as a library catalogue, or at least a list of titles, of rare classical works which he suggests were preserved at Charlemagne's palace; it thus provides us with precious insight 'for our knowledge of the court library from around 790'.[113] There is, however, no concrete evidence that can link this list, or the manuscript which contains it, to the court of Charlemagne. In fact all considerations of the evidence point to Verona as a place of origin: the most telling sign being that the Greek-Latin text of the *Magnificat* contained in Diez. B. 66 (p. 116) was copied by the second scribe (Bischoff's scribe B[114]), an Italian, directly from a sixth-century manuscript that is still in Verona today, and was certainly there in the seventh and eighth centuries, when it was annotated.[115] Moreover, the contents of the manuscript are connected with Peter of Pisa in several ways: we find poems from Charlemagne, Angilbert and Paul the Deacon to Peter, and another poem of Fiducia, Peter's friend, to Angilram of Metz, and the miscellany of grammatical works within the manuscript (pp. 3–66, 68–116, 129–216) has been attributed to Peter's handiwork. It must be admitted that, beyond being an Italian who worked for Charlemagne, nothing we know about Peter of Pisa would link him to Verona, and he appears to have returned to his native Pisa by 796, if we accept that the subscriptions to a Pisan charter by Petrus *diaconus* and Fiducia *clericus*, are by the same people.[116] But it is in this manuscript that we also find the sole copy of the poem celebrating King Pippin's victory over the Avars in 796, providing us with a *terminus post quem* for the compilation of the manuscript, and once again suggesting that it derives from the circle of Pippin's court at Verona, and that the list of classical works made by scribe B resulted from some type of survey, made hastily, of one or several libraries in or around Verona. Arguing against the attribution to Verona, however, is the fact that no such grammatical or classical works have been located there, nor does

---

Scriptorium 8 (1954), 24–37; and now M. Gorman, 'Peter of Pisa and the *Quaestiunculae* copied for Charlemagne in Brussels II 2572, with a note on the Codex Diezianus from Verona', *RB* 110 (2000), 238–60, at p. 260.

[113] *Manuscripts*, pp. 67–75, at p. 73. See also Bischoff, 'Hadoard und die klassiker Handschriften aus Corbie', MS I, pp. 49–63, and the facsimile edition of the text, Bischoff, *Sammelhandschrift Diez. B. Sant. 66. Grammatici Latini et Catalogus librorum*, Codices selecti phototypice impressi 42 (Graz, 1973). Cf. McKitterick, *Carolingians*, pp. 17, 172–3.

[114] *Sammelhandschrift Diez. B. Sant. 66*, pp. 21–3, where he distinguishes between the two scribes: A, a Frank, who wrote pp. 3–116, 7; and B, an Italian, who wrote pp. 116, 7–128, and 217–363.

[115] Verona, I (1), CLA IV.472. The discovery was made by C. Villa, 'Die Horazüberlieferung und die "Bibliothek Karls des Grossen"', *Deutsches Archiv für Erforschung des Mittelalters* 51:1 (1995), 29–52; and 'La tradizione di Orazio e la "biblioteca di Carlo Magno": per l'elenco di opere nel codice Berlin Diez B. 66', in *Formative Stages of Classical Traditions: Latin Texts from Antiquity to the Renaissance, Proceedings of a Conference held at Erice, 16–22 October 1993* (Spoleto, 1996), pp. 299–322.

[116] ChLA 812.

the textual history point to Verona in any significant way, whereas we know of the transmission of classics at Corbie, Tours, St Denis and Fleury, which has prompted some scholars to look to France as the source for the list.[117]

But there are Italian manuscripts of classical works which do share affinities with Berlin Diez. B. 66 and confirm that an Italian origin for the manuscript and its 'list of classics' is more likely. For example, Verona CLXIII, a late eighth-century manuscript in Italian minuscule script, contains an anthology of classical poems, as well as those of Claudian and the *Disticha catonis*.[118] Its Veronese provenance, if not origin, is assured by the marginalia in the same hand as some of the codices mentioned above.[119] Later Italian manuscripts further confirm the identification of an Italian tradition behind the Berlin compilation. Paris lat. 7900a, written in or near Milan sometime in the second half of the ninth century, contains the complete works of Terence, Horace, Lucan and Juvenal, and appears to derive from a tradition similar to the text of these authors in Diez. B. 66. This manuscript appears to have direct connections with another late ninth-century miscellany of classical and Christian works, Berne 363, again probably written in or near Milan, which contains the commentary of Servius and the poetry of Horace, and the rare Fortunatianus, who was not found again until the discovery of a manuscript at Bobbio in 1493.[120] Also important in this regard is a late eighth-century Cassinese manuscript which Paul the Deacon may have consulted, Paris lat. 7530.[121] Found in Benevento by Lorenzo Valla in 1441, it contains

---

[117] Ullman, 'A list', pp. 36–7. Overlooked by Ullmann and others in this sense is the comment concerning scripts that occurs in the treatise 'De voce et litteris', towards the end of the manuscript, p. 346 (that is, scribe B). The question and response: 'Apud Latinos quod genera scribendi esse uidentur? Resp. IIII. Coaequaria et antiquaria manus et virgilica manus, qua nunc Romani utuntur, et epistularis; cui adiacet Schothica manus et Brithanica manus, quae versa dicitur.' As Bischoff noted in his facsimile edition, *Sammelhandschrift Diez. B*, pp. 32–3, a shorter version of such appears in an early ninth-century manuscript from Corbie containing a similar *Interrogatio de grammatica*, Paris. lat. 13025, fol. 62v: 'Sed de figuris litterarum nemo interpretari potest, quia apud Latinos multa genera sunt scribendi, Quattuor genera sunt: antiquaria manus, Virgiliaca, iactiaca, coaequaria.' For the term 'Virgiliaca/virgiliana' as rustic capitals, see Bischoff, 'Die alten Namen der lateinischen Schriftarten', *Philologus* 89 (1934), 461–5, repr. in Bischoff, MS I, pp. 1–5. The whole issue warrants further attention than can be given here.

[118] CLA IV.516.

[119] In particular Verona XIII (11) and LXXV (80) (CLA IV.484, 514).

[120] F. Munari, *Catalogue of MSS of Ovid's Metamorphoses* (London, 1957), no. 37; Ferrari, 'Centri di trasmissione', pp. 312–13; C. Villa, *La lectura Terentii, da Ildemao a Francesco Petrarca*, Studi sul Petrarca 17 (Padua, 1984), pp. 24–61. A full facsimile edition exists: H. Hagen, *Codex bernensis 363 phototypice editus* (Leiden, 1897).

[121] CLA V.569. See L. Holtz, 'Le Parisinus Latinus 7530, synthèse cassinense des art libéraux', *Studi Medievali* 16 (1975), 97–152; F. Newton, *The Scriptorium at Monte Cassino 1058–1105* (Cambridge, 1999), pp. 133 n. 66, 184, n. 318.

one of Paul's poems, as well as a range of classical works. But more importantly, like the Diez. B. 66 and Paris 7900a manuscripts, it also contains the commentary of Servius and the glossary known as the *Poeta i. vates*. Moreover, both these manuscripts contain excerpts from the works of Malleus Theodorus, with the text of the Paris lat. 7530 closely resembling the version of Malleus' work attached to the famous Bamberg manuscript of Cassiodorus' *Institutiones*, likewise written in an Italian centre somewhere towards the end of the eighth century.[122] These manuscripts are witnesses to a tradition of the preservation of classical literature in Lombard Italy, and further support the possibility of a Veronese origin for the books referred to in the list of Berlin Diez. B. 66. Beyond this, the palaeographical evidence, the content of the manuscript and the association with Peter of Pisa suggest that the Codex Diez. B. 66 was indeed compiled in north Italy as a grammatical and poetical miscellany for a scholar or school which cultivated the study of grammar and had a demonstrable interest in secular classical literature. In any case, the notion that the list represents the interests, or indeed a part, of the court library of Charlemagne, may no longer be tenable.

Apart from classical literature, there were also the more functional texts of grammar and medicine used in schools and monasteries. Grammatical works preserved in manuscripts from Bobbio, Verona and elsewhere have been well discussed by others.[123] Ninth- or tenth-century manuscripts of medical works hint at earlier traditions, such as the manuscript of Celsus, a work not known outside northern Italy in this period.[124] Evidence of interest in medical works is found in the fragments that have come down to us, such as of Pseudo-Apulius *De herbarum virtutibus* preserved at Ivrea, Berlin and Hildesheim.[125] Unfortunately, many of the medical recipes, often found on one folio or so in manuscripts of an unrelated character or which survive as palimpsests, are difficult to read owing to damage and their highly cursive scripts, but they warrant proper investigation.[126]

---

[122] Bamberg, Patr. 61 (CLA VIII.1029).   [123] Law, *Grammar*; Holtz, *Donat*.
[124] Vat. lat. 5951. See A. Beccaria, *I codici di medicina del periodo presalernitano (secoli IX, X, XI)* (Rome, 1956), pp. 10–13.
[125] Berlin, Staatsbibliothek, Lat. fol. 381 no. 1 + Hildersheim, Beverinische Bibliothek, 658 (offset) (CLA VIII.1050). Uncial, saec. VI–VII: Ivrea, 94 (CLA III.301). These fragments are possibly from the same manuscript.
[126] Some examples: Vat. Pal. lat. 187 (CLA I.80a–b, 81), fol. 7, *recepta medica*, north Italian cursive, saec. VIII; Vat. Urb. lat. 293 (CLA I.116), fols. 95–6, *Fragmentum de re medica*, uncial, saec. VIII. Cf. G. Carbonelli, *Frammento medico del secolo VII: Cod. Vat. Urb. Lat. 293*, Istituto nazionale medico farmacologico (Rome, 1921); Milan, Ambr. C. 105 inf. (CLA 323a and b; CLA 324), fols. 1 and 9 (lower script) *recepta medica*, cursive minuscule, saec. VI; Modena, O. I. 11. (CLA III.368) *Medica varia*; Apuleius, etc., Italian minuscule, AD 801. Schiaparelli, *Influenze straniere*, p. 22, D. Fava, *Tesori della bibliotheche d'Italia: Emilia e Romagna* (Milan, 1932) p. 137.

Literacy in Lombard Italy, c. 568–774

ITALIAN MINUSCULE AND THE QUESTION OF 'LEGIBILITY'

The fewer manuscripts prior to the ninth century and the diversity of their script-types is often noted as an interesting yet ultimately disturbing state of affairs for the history of literacy. Manuscripts in capricious uncial or wildly cursive minuscule demonstrate not only what might have been without the ascension of Carolingian power, but also how 'elaborate calligraphic virtuosity and very poor levels of orthography and Latinity go hand in hand with libraries that seldom owned as many as fifty volumes'.[127] Valuations of quality can often go hand in hand with the appreciation of quantity; in a search for evidence of literate activity the greater quantity of material suggests more literacy and a greater appreciation of it. In this sense, the eighth century resembles an exciting cultural experiment that may have grown out of control, luckily shelved before it became too harmful to the onward march of literacy in medieval Europe. In the following section I should like to consider the 'elaborate calligraphic virtuosity' found in the manuscript evidence of Lombard Italy and explore its implications for literacy. The overriding theme of the history of script in this period, be it in Italy or elsewhere, is the development and triumph of minuscule forms of script. I should like, therefore, to pause to consider this before surveying some of the more interesting examples of Italian scribal virtuosity from Lombard Italy.

The triumph of minuscule script is an important development in this period, yet the phenomenon remains unexplained, and its significance in the history of literacy remains unclear. We still need to account for the general move towards minuscule-type scripts which 'crop up on all sides'[128] of Europe in the late seventh and throughout the eighth century. While we might attribute the development of Visigothic minuscule, which first appears in the early eighth century, to the zeal of the seventh-century Spanish church, similar motivations could not account for the increasing use of minuscule forms in Merovingian Gaul,[129] nor for Lombard Italy. There appears to have been a tendency towards the use of less wildly cursive scripts and more rounded minuscule letter-forms in the charter evidence as we move across the eighth century. This, too, seems concomitant with an attempt by some scribes in Lucca and elsewhere to use more classical norms and standards in orthography and syntax.

There is a danger, however, of equating the move to minuscule forms as simply springing from a desire for legibility, for the very notion of

---

[127] Ganz, 'Books and book production', p. 787.   [128] Lowe, CLA VI, p. xi.
[129] Bischoff, *Latin Palaeography*, pp. 104–9.

legibility is historically relative and highly subjective. Minuscule letter-forms may well seem legible to us, since Caroline minuscule pleased the aesthetic sensibilities of humanist scholars in the fifteenth century, who used it to develop their own version, which subsequently became the basis of the Roman type developed by the earliest printers and which we still use today. The fact that Caroline minuscule was superseded for centuries all over Europe from the tenth century onwards is a pertinent reminder of the historical relativity of its assumed legibility.[130] Moreover, studies in psychology of reading have shown that letter-forms in themselves are not especially conducive to facilitating reading.[131] Their recognition, and the speed with which they are cognitively processed, depends on familiarity and practice. Far more important in this respect is the uniformity and consistency of the letter-forms, and the way in which they are set out on the page. The importance of this last for legibility is also relative to specific times and places. Through the study of insular manuscript culture, Malcolm Parkes has coined the phrase 'grammar of legibility' to describe the complementary processes of punctuation and layout of text used by insular scribes to facilitate the reading of Latin, for them a foreign language with no direct relation to their everyday vernacular speech.[132] In order to facilitate comprehension of a text according to the grammatical rules of the language, Irish and Anglo-Saxons invented a range of techniques of punctuation, and the use of differently shaped and sized letters, to divide up the text and signify to the reader unfamiliar with the sound of the language before them the beginnings and ends of phrases, sentences, paragraphs, chapters, books and so on.

The need for this type of 'legibility', as Parkes has defined it, is mostly absent from the Italian manuscript and charter evidence of the Lombard period and well beyond. Punctuation is kept to a minimum, usually consisting of no more than medial point placed here or there to signify a sense ending, and blank spaces are often used to mark the end of the sentence. This is sometimes followed by a *littera notabilior* (a letter larger or taller than the others, sometimes a capital) to indicate a new sentence, but not always. The use of simple points to mark *subdistinctiones* for pauses and to

---

[130] See esp. R. McKitterick, 'Carolingian book production: some problems', *The Library*, ser. 6, 12 (1990), 1–33; S. Morison, *First Principles of Typography* (Cambridge, 1951); Morison, *Politics and Script: Aspects of Authority and Freedom in the Development of Graeco-Latin Script from the Sixth Century B.C. to the Twentieth Century A.D.* (Oxford, 1972).

[131] B. Zachrisson, *Studies in the Legibility of Printed Text* (Stockholm, 1965); I. and M.M. Taylor, *The Psychology of Reading* (New York, 1983).

[132] M. Parkes, 'The contribution of insular scribes in the seventh and eighth centuries to the grammar of legibility', repr. in Parkes, *Scribes, Scripts and Readers: Studies in the Communication, Presentation, and Dissemination of Medieval Texts* (London, 1991), pp. 1–18, and Parkes, *Pause and Effect: An Introduction to the History of Punctuation in the West* (Aldershot, 1993), pp. 20–9.

identify lesser disjunctions within the sentence appears to increase gradually over time, becoming the norm only into the eighth century. We are still a long way from the 'emblematic punctuation' we use to distinguish the grammatical structure of a text by a series of encoded signs (commas, full stops, colons, semicolons, question marks, etc.).[133] The haphazard use of punctuation in early medieval Italian manuscripts has contributed to its neglect as a subject worthy of study, the heterogeneity and inconsistency suspected of yielding little insight worthy of the effort.[134] In this sense, then, the notion of legibility needs to be redefined, if only so that we may dispense with it altogether as an anachronistic and fairly useless term for understanding the development of writing in Italy on its own terms. For the very proximity of the spoken language to that written out in manuscripts places the redaction of text firmly in an aural environment. Legibility, then, does not come so much from visual signification alone, but is intricately linked with the intelligibility of what the text says, how it says it, and how this relates to both the linguistic environment of the readers and their experience in reading such texts. On the whole Italian scribes seem to have distinguished units of speech, usually a phrase or sentence, with the use of punctuation inherited from the ancient world (*positurae, prosodiae*, in the terminology of the grammarians), and these were, by modern or even medieval Irish standards, quite minimal.[135] It depended also on the type of text: biblical and liturgical texts are often set out *per cola et commata* (each constituent element of a period begins on a new line) in accordance with an authoritative late antique tradition, while canon law or scholarly texts like Isidore's *Etymologiae* rely on page layout to signify where and when new sections, chapters and subjects begin, and the use of different coloured inks (usually alternating black and red) and only occasionally a hierarchy of scripts in titles, subtitles and colophons. As with other continental manuscripts of this period, the setting out of text varied greatly, without obvious regional or 'writing-school' styles of *mise en page*, and there was a great deal of experimentation with styles of layout within one writing centre, as the manuscripts from Bobbio attest.[136]

The dangers of anachronism become apparent when we consider word-separation, seen by some scholars to be a key development in the history of reading, and by implication a victory for intelligibility. For it is thought that modern modes of reading, being highly visual and geared

---

[133] P. Saenger, *Space between Words: The Origins of Silent Reading* (Stanford, 1997), p. 73.
[134] A. Petrucci, 'Lire au moyen âge', *Mélanges de l'Ecole Française de Rome. Moyen Age, Temps Modernes* 96 (1984), 603–16, at pp. 605–6.
[135] Parkes, *Pause and Effect*, pp. 9–18.
[136] See further, J. Vezin and H.J. Martin (eds.), *Mise-en-page et mise en texte dans les manuscrit du moyen âge* (Paris, 1990).

Manuscripts

towards speed in finding and selecting information from a greater variety of texts ('reference reading'), demands a higher degree of legibility, and our optical physiology is greatly aided by graphic representation for rapid lexical access. Word-separation provides this extra graphic dimension to the cognitive processing of script. While word-separation may have played a large part in the origin and development of silent reading into the modern era, it is irrelevant to considerations of legibility in the Lombard period, for word-separation does not really get underway in Italy until the second half of the eleventh century, and only becomes standard in the thirteenth century.[137] The unseparated *scriptura continua* of the ancient world, or sometimes 'aerated' script, which employs spacing here and there to break up the text into passages of, say, five to fifteen words, is standard practice in Italian manuscripts of this era. Once again the reason is principally linguistic: the Latin which Italian scribes wrote out in manuscripts, or indeed in charters, was familiar enough to them from their common, everyday speech, or at least familiar enough to detect individual words and sense-endings by ear when they read it aloud. The same must be said for continental centres, for word-separation does not get underway in the Carolingian world until the ninth century, and even then the evidence presents no clear chronology or patterns of development. Monosyllabic prepositions, for example, were not separated from the words they govern until the tenth century, and it has been argued that word-separation is not the norm in French manuscripts until the eleventh century.[138]

In the absence of contemporary comments or complaints, such as Jerome on letters too small for his bad eyesight, or Boniface having trouble with ligatures and varied letter-forms,[139] legibility can only constitute an ascetic or value judgement on behalf of the historian. Yet the common move towards minuscule script throughout the eighth century must have been a response to a perceived need to make script more accessible to those with less expertise in reading. I shall return to this theme below, but first it is necessary to define what is minuscule script in the early medieval Italian context.

The term 'minuscule-type' is necessarily imprecise, for the various minuscule scripts which emerge demonstrate diverse characteristics which

---

[137] A. Petrucci, 'Lire au moyen âge'; P. Saenger, *Space*, 'The separation of words'.

[138] Bischoff, *Latin Palaeography*, p. 173; Saenger, *Space*, pp. 18–26. It should be noted that even insular scribes, supposedly the pioneers of word-separation, were by no means consistent in this period, and demonstrate a considerable degree of precociousness in practice: Saenger, *Space*, p. 306 n. 13.

[139] Kelly, *Jerome*, p. 308; P. Meyvaert, 'Uncial letters: Jerome's meaning of the term', *Journal of Theological Studies* 34 (1983), 185–8; Parkes, *Pause and Effect*, p. 26. Boniface: 'clare discretis et absolutis letteris' must also refer to [the lack of] ligatures.

seem to have sprung from different origins. In the search for the 'rise of minuscule', palaeographers are in general agreement that the minuscule forms were generated primarily from the elementary 'private' or 'domestic' used in everday life in the ancient and late Roman west, essentially a cursive script, in which letter-forms initially designed for attachment to a following letter in a ligature gave way to creating new letter-forms.[140] At the same time, however, calligraphic script had been moving in the same direction. Later half-uncial scripts of the sixth and seventh centuries show a similar concern for economy and a greater degree of speed: it is a fine line between later half-uncial and early minuscule scripts.[141] Cursive script saved time and space.[142] Minuscule scripts, as a result, are smaller and more economical, yet keep the letter forms distinct and aligned. The compromise in Italy, as elsewhere, was the development of what has been loosely termed either 'cursive minuscule', 'Italian minuscule' or 'pre-Caroline minuscule', depending on less than objective considerations.[143] 'Cursive minuscule' simply refers to minuscule-based letter-forms in which many cursive elements are employed, such as intricate ligatures, much use of abbreviation, and a rapid execution of the ductus that results in prolonged ascenders, descenders and the odd scribal flourish. For less rapid and more calligraphic minuscule, the adjectives 'Italian' or 'pre-Caroline' are often used indiscriminately, neither of which is completely satisfactory, though the former's nationalism is preferable to the fatal teleology of the latter.[144] In the following I should like to survey the array of Italian minuscule scripts, to use the more appropriate term, from the more cursive to the less so, to gain some idea of the variety of scripts and their uses, before returning to the question of their relationship to literacy.

CURSIVE AND MINUSCULE BOOK SCRIPTS

An early example of the use of a cursive minuscule for a book-hand is the sixth-century papyrus manuscript of Josephus' *De antiquitatibus iudaicis* (Lib. v–xiii), written in north Italy, probably in or near Milan, where it

---

[140] J.O. Tjäder, 'Considerazioni e proposte sulla scrittura latina nell'età romana', *Palaeographica, diplomatica et archivistica: studi in onore di G. Batelli*, Storia e Letteratura. Raccolta di Studi e Testi 139 (Rome, 1979), I, pp. 31–62; G. Cencetti, 'Postilla nuova a un problema paleografico vecchio: l'origine della minuscola carolina', *Nuova Historia* 7 (1952), 9–32; Bischoff, *Latin Palaeography*, pp. 100–15.
[141] Lowe, CLA IV, p. vi. [142] See, for example, Turin, G.V.26 (CLA IV.463), fol. 5v.
[143] B. Pagnin,'Studio sulla formazione della precarolina italiana', in *Scritti di paleografia e diplomatica in onore di Vincenzo Federici* (Florence, 1944), pp. 19–46; Bartolini, 'Semicorsiva o precarolina?'; 'Note paleografiche'; 'La nomenclatura delle scritture'.
[144] Cf. Schiaparelli: Italian cursive minuscule developed completely 'independently from any foreign influence'; *Influenze straniere*, p. 64.

Manuscripts

was later preserved at the monastery of San Ambrogio.[145] The script is a flowing, forward-leaning cursive akin to the type we find in fifth- and sixth-century papyri, and many features of the manuscript point backwards rather than forwards in time: the ligatures are of the older, pre-'new cursive' type, abbreviations are restricted to *nomina sacra*, the text is set out in *scriptura continua* with little punctuation, the i-longa is used initially, medially and mid-word after r- or t-, the spelling is highly classicised.[146]

Also somewhat antiquated is the use of a papyrus codex, and it is worth considering this in the context of writing materials used in this period. Papyrus books can be found in use up to the late seventh, possibly early eighth, century, but on the whole are fairly rare in our surviving collection, so that it is difficult to know how much this rarity is owed to subsequent destruction (papyrus is said to last about 300–400 years, but much less in a European climate), or to a preference for parchment.[147] As is suggested by the charter evidence, there is good reason to think that papyrus was still a commonly used writing material in seventh-century Italy. The early medieval Italian manuscripts that have survived from the sixth to the eleventh century were nearly always made from goat-skins, infrequently sheep-skins, and seldom from the skin of a calf.[148] While this is by no means unusual in continental Europe and lands around the Mediterranean, it does contrast with the Italian charter evidence, in which the parchments are predominately made of sheep-skin.[149] Why this is so – goats for books, sheep for charters – remains unclear. In any case, the script of the papyrus Josephus also seems to point forward towards the development of cursive minuscule scripts in Italy during the Lombard period, as witnessed in a palimpsest manuscript of Bobbio, wherein a Gothic text of Ulfilas was erased in the early seventh century for Jerome's commentary on Isaiah, written in a compressed, half-uncial script that verges on minuscule, and in which Irish and Merovingian

---

[145] Milan, Ambr. Cimelio ms. 1 (CLA III.304). Tjäder, I, p. 40. F. Troncarelli, *Vivarium: i libri, il destino*, Instrumenta Patristica 33 (Turnhout, 1998), pp. 12–14, lists this manuscript among seventeen that may have been written at Cassiodorus' Vivarium or possibly belonged there at some stage.

[146] Cf. Milan, Ambr., C. 105 inf., fols. 1 and 9, lower script (CLA III.323a).

[147] Tjäder, I, pp. 37–42. Bischoff, *Latin Palaeography*, pp. 7–8. Note the eighth-century parchment roll of Mombello di Imbersago, Archivio del Principe, S.N. (CLA III.371), presumably written in Ravenna. In general, C.H. Roberts and T.C. Skeat, *Birth of the Codex*, 2nd edn (Oxford, 1983); and the review of M. McCormick, *Scriptorium* 39 (1985), 151–8.

[148] See A. Di Majo, C. Federici and M. Palma, 'La pergamena dei codici altomedievali italiani', *Scriptorium* 39 (1985), 3–12. Cf. P. Schreiner, 'Zur Pergamentherstellung im byzantinischen Osten', *Codices Manuscripti* 9 (1983), 93–127, at p. 126; P. Rück (ed.), *Pergament: Geschichte, Struktur, Restaurierung, Herstellung* (Sigmaringen, 1991).

[149] On charter skins, see the tables of M. Palma, ChLA XXXVIII pp. vi–viii; ChLA XL, pp. v–vi.

Literacy in Lombard Italy, c. 568–774

influences were clearly at work.[150] The many and varied hands of the manuscripts from Bobbio, with their eclectic combination of different styles and influences, demonstrate the diversity of scribal practice there, which perhaps resulted in an unconscious experimentalism with cursive and minuscule forms. A copy of Ambrose' *De spiritu sancto* written there in the early eighth century reflects a curious mix of Italian and 'celtic' elements that inspired a little multiculturalism in the editor of CLA : 'a rather rapid uncalligraphic North Italian cursive minuscule penned by an Irish hand under French influence'.[151]

A superb example of (a more) cursive minuscule is the canon law collection of Cresconius preserved at Verona.[152] Heavily ligatured – up to six letters at a time – and abbreviated in insular fashion, yet with practised and clear formation of letters, the script was penned by an expert hand that shows further traces of insular influence in the bent shafts of some letters (*b, l*), yet is typically north Italian in others, such as the forward-leaning shoulder of *r*, the '2'-shaped *z*, the omnipresent ligatures for *ti, te, it* and *et*, and the highly mobile superscript *a*. The script runs merrily along straight, evenly spaced lines, red uncials are used for titles (canons) and some splendid ornamental initials are employed (sadly most have been destroyed by reagent), so that the overall effect is a sense of efficiency in time and resources and an initiated professionalism on behalf of both scribe and reader. The later minuscule corrections and additions by various readers prove that not all who consulted this book found its script so comely. But the manuscript itself as artefact also signifies profound cultural change: it is in fact a palimpsest of Justinian's *Code*, its stately sixth-century uncial script duly erased and the well-prepared leaves economically folded to make bifolia for Cresconius' *Concordia canonum*, a far more relevant collection of laws for the times.[153] At least two other manuscripts of canon law from this period demonstrate a preference for a less cursive but equally native minuscule. One, another copy of Cresconius' collection, possibly written at the monastery of Monte Amiata, was redacted in a curious mix of minuscule and uncial forms, best seen in its eccentric and somewhat zippy *g*.[154] The 'Codex Ingilrammi', a collection of canon law

---

[150] Milan, Ambr. S. 45 sup. (CLA III.365), above, n. 11. Schiaparelli, *Influenze straniere*, p. 32; Collura, *Studi*, pp. 79 ff and tables 26–7; Lowe, 'Codices rescripti', nos. 128, 222; Cavallo, 'Libri e cultura', p. 86.

[151] Milan, Ambr. D. 268 inf. (CLA III.334). Cf. Ambr. I. 61 sup. (CLA III.350), and [Turin, A.II.2] (CLA IV.444b).

[152] Verona, LXII (60). CLA IV.512. Bischoff, *Latin Palaeography*, plate 9.

[153] CLA IV.513. The overall style has much in common with Florentine Laurenziana *Digest*, S. N. (CLA III.295), and Gaius' *Institutiones* in Verona, IV [3] (CLA IV.488).

[154] Vat. Barb. lat. 679 (XIV.52) (CLA I.65). Both Lowe and Bischoff, *Panorama*, p. 252 (= *Manuscripts*, p. 49), point to insular influence in some letter-forms. Cf. Modena, Archivio capitolare,

Manuscripts

initially redacted, as we learn from the first part of the colophon, by the scribe Sicipertus for the bishop of Metz, Ingilrammus (768–91), and later copied at Chieti in the Abruzzi, as we learn from the second part of the colophon, is further testimony to the movement of manuscripts across the Alps in this period.[155] The script is a much more harmonious and orderly minuscule, keeping ligatures to a minimum (*ae, ti, te*), with some delightful decoration of initials, and lots of snakes to fill up space in the titles.

Italian minuscule scripts were by no means limited to the redaction of canon law. Other texts of an ecclesiastical nature such as Gregory's *Moralia*,[156] and the *Homiliae in evangelia*,[157] Maximus of Turin's *Homiliae*,[158] and Junilius' *Instituta divinae legis*,[159] were written out in individualistic minuscule scripts with varying degrees of cursive elements. Occasionally, one detects an effort to tone down the cursive, as with a Gospel book attributed to central Italy, in which the scribe employs ligatures for *en, ra* and *ri*, then perhaps guiltily drops here and there into copying the uncial of his exemplar for this text of texts.[160] Other times it was simply a question of space: the scribe of the *Anthologia Latina* or Codex Salmasianus switched from uncial to cursive minuscule forms

---

O. I. 12 *Collectio canonum* (CLA IIII.369), uncial, saec. VIII. Written in north Italy. Marginal entries suggest Nonatola as origin. Fava, *Tesori*, p. 137; *LP* I, ed. Duchesne, pp. cxcvi ff.

[155] Vat. Reg. lat. 1997 (CLA I.113). Colophon on fol. 153. Schiaparelli, *Influenze*, pp. 55–9; Bischoff, *Panorama*, p. 253 (= *Manuscripts*, p. 52); P. Supino Martini, 'Per lo studio delle scritture altomedievali italiane: la collezione canonica chietina (Vat. Reg. lat. 1997)', *Scrittura e Civiltà* 1 (1977), 133, dates it to the mid-ninth century.

[156] Berlin, Deutsche Staatsbibliothek, Frag. 48 (CLA 1046). Gregory, *Moralia in Job*. (xxxiv.15–18). Cursive minuscule, saec. VIII. One folio only.

[157] Karlsruhe, Aug. CC (CLA VIII.1093). Gregory, *Homiliae in evangelia* (Lib. II). Lowe would assign its origin to a scriptorium in south-western Germany or Switzerland (possibly Reichenau, where the manuscript was later). But north Italy is just as likely, particularly given the use of typically Veronese abbreviations for *misericordia* (*ma* with horizontal stroke above) and *noster*, and the confluence of characteristics and interests that surround this manuscript and others later preserved at Reichenau: cf. St Gall 108 and 207 (CLA VII.905 and 920); Karlsruhe, Aug. CCXXII (CLA VIII.1096) and CCLXI (CLA VIII.1111).

[158] Milan, Ambr. C. 98 inf. + M. 77 sup. (fol. 93) (CLA III.322). Maximus of Turin, *Homiliae*. Possibly written at Vercelli, as suggested by features common with Vercelli 183 (Jerome, *De viris ill*.) and *marginalia* which call attention to Vercelli and S. Eusebius. Later belonged to Bobbio.

[159] Milan, Ambr. I.1 sup. (CLA III.348). Junilius, *Instituta divinae legis; de proprietate nominum*. Perhaps written at Bobbio, as it later belonged there. Collura, *Studi*, p. 90 and table 31, notes that some letter-forms and abbreviations suggest insular influence: Bischoff, *Manuscripts*, p. 51 n. 151, suggests central Italy as provenance.

[160] Perugia, Biblioteca capitolare, 2 (CLA IV. 408). *Evangelia*. The (seemingly contemporary or slightly later) musical notation in the lesson of the passion shows it was used liturgically: P. McGurk, *Latin Gospel Books from A.D. 400 to A.D. 800* (Paris, 1961), pp. 89–91; Bischoff, *Panorama*, p. 253 (= *Manuscripts*, pp. 50, 131), points to similarities of Paris lat. 10318 (CLA V. 593).

Literacy in Lombard Italy, c. 568–774

the closer he got to the end of the page in order to finish off a line at an appropriate point in the text.[161]

But this type of reserve was dropped when it came to more educational or 'scholastic' texts, such as the works of Isidore, which furnish us with some of the best examples of Italian minuscule.[162] One such is the Bobbio recension of Isidore's *Etymologiae* (I–X),[163] written by several hands of varying degrees of calligraphic competence and cursiveness, some demonstrating an expert's acquaintance with ligatures, abbreviations and the elegant chancery-script flourishes we find in the best north Italian charter-hands, and nearly all showing some signs of insular influence common to products of the Bobbio scriptorium. Other educational texts written there, such as the palimpsest collection of grammatical works preserved in Naples, show similar styles of pennmanship,[164] but we also find rapid minuscules used to copy texts of a less directly didactic nature, such as our earliest copy of the *Liber pontificalis*,[165] or Julius Valerius' *Res Gestae Alexandri*.[166] A miniscule similar to the Bobbio hands but much neater in execution and arrangement of text on the page is found in another, slightly defective copy of the *Etymologiae*, written c. 760–78 somewhere in north Italy, later at Nonantola.[167] Continuity in the use of capricious and quirky minuscule forms can be seen in many north

---

[161] Paris, lat. 10318 (CLA V.593). M. Spallone, 'Il Par. lat. 10318 (Salmasiano): dal manoscritto altomedievale ad una reccolta enciclopedica tardo-antica', *Italia Medioevale e Umanistica* 25 (1982), 1–71.

[162] Apart from those mentioned here and below, I include Milan, Ambr. B 31 sup. (CLA III.308), *Liber differentiarum; glossarium*; Vercelli, CCII (not in CLA); Paris, lat. 5730. (CLA V.562); Karlsruhe, Aug. LVII (CLA VIII.1077); Wolfenbüttel Weiss. 64, and its twin Vat. lat. 5763 (CLA 39); Berlin, Phillips 1831.

[163] Milan, Ambr. L. 99 sup. (CLA III.353). Isidore, *Etymologiae* I–X. North Italian pre-Caroline minuscule, saec. VIII. MS not to be confused with Wolfenbüttel Weiss. 64 and its twin Vat. lat. 5763 (as above), which is no. 104 in the inventory of 1461 and was therefore at Bobbio by the tenth century. Bischoff, *Panorama*, p. 252n. (= *Manuscripts*, p. 50 n. 149) dates the manuscript to Lombard period proper (pre-Charlemagne). Schiaparelli, *Influenze straniere*, pp. 16–23; Lindsay, *Etym.*, p. vii. Collura, *Studi*, pp. 60–5, and tables 9–13.

[164] Naples, lat. 1 (Vindobon. 17) (CLA III.388, 389, 390). Secondary script, *Grammatica varia*; *De verbo ad Severum*; Probus, *Ars minor*; *Appendix probi*: primary script, *Libri regum* (frag.), and *Genesis* (frag.) (both Vetus Latina) uncial, saec. V. Collura, *Studi*, pp. 52ff and table 5. Lowe, *Codices rescripti*, nos. 53, 98, 99; Cf. A. Dold, in *Anzeiger der Akademie der Wissenschaften in Wien* (phil.-hist. Klass.) 79 (1942), pp. 51–63.

[165] Naples IV.A.8, fols. 40–7 (CLA III.403). The recension stops at pontificate of Conon (d. 687), suggesting its redaction soon after. Lowe, 'Codices rescripti', nos. 61, 62, 104–6; Bischoff, *Studien*, II, p. 319; Collura, *Studi*, pp. 50ff and table 4; Duchesne, *LP* I, p. clxxvi. Cipolla, *Cod. bob.*, p. 28 and plates I, XI, XXXVI, XLII, p. 63, plate XI, pp. 60ff., plate X.

[166] [Turin, A. II. 2] (CLA IV.440). Lowe, *Codices rescripti*, no. 167.

[167] Modena, Arch. cap. O.I.17 (CLA III.370). The date is deduced from the contents of fols. 104v–105v, the first of a series of nineteen-year cycles. Contains marginal entries in ninth-century minuscule of the Nonantola type. Many of its 123 folios are fragmentary: Fava, *Tesori*, p. 137.

Manuscripts

Italian manuscripts that date from the end of the eighth and early ninth centuries.[168]

CONCLUSION

The sturdy lines and symmetric loops of carefully executed uncial or minuscule scripts impart an impression of appropriate solemnity behind the handiwork. It has been argued that Caroline minuscule could only have come about in a cultural environment that stressed a correctness in forms of orthography and grammar according to a set of fixed norms. The concern for the legibility of the text, and the subsequent uniformity of script, corresponds to the reform of language and the pronunciation of Latin, which turned to the rules of ancient grammarians for authority.[169] In this sense the uniformity of Caroline minuscule is reassuringly modern. It suggests that people in the Carolingian period, like us, were sophisticated enough to appreciate that effective communication necessitates some sacrifice of individualistic forms for a greater degree of regulation which renders the message more accessible to an unknown recipient. It is, therefore, this very public element of Carolingian manuscripts, their adherence to a common calligraphic code, in line with the attempt at uniformity of orthography, and the lack of such in Lombard Italy that underscore the achievements of book production in the Lombard period.

But we are entitled to ask whether this 'elaborate calligraphic virtuosity' may, to some extent, reflect a higher level of familiarity with the culture of the written word and an overarching confidence in writing and reading various scripts, rather than the careful solemnity and public accountability of Caroline minuscule. Bischoff remarked that the uniformity of the minuscule 'probably had the ground prepared for it where calligraphic skill was less developed, where the less dynamic and perhaps more deliberate script becomes simpler, and where the habit of forming ligatures becomes less frequent'. Such phenomena were more likely as 'the level of literacy declined'.[170] Following this line of argument, it might be said that minuscule, for all its legibility, appealed to a lower

---

[168] Some examples: Milan, Arch. civico storico, trivulziano 688 (CLA III.366); Modena, Arch Cap. O.I.11 (CLA III.368); Karlsruhe, Aug. CLXXXI (CLA VIII.1086); Aug. CCLI, fols. 72–213 (CLA VIII.1110); London, Cotton Nero A. II, fols. 14–45 (CLA II.186); Vienna, Nationalbibliothek, 945 (CLA X.1492); Paris, lat. 10318 (CLA V.593); Paris. Baluze 270, fols. 76–94; Princeton, W.H. Scheide coll. (CLA XI.1665); St Gall, 1399 a.3 (CLA VII.997), 108 (CLA VII.905), 227 (CLA VII.930); 908 (CLA VII.953–65); St Petersburg, F.V.I.7 (CLA XI.1603).

[169] D. Ganz, 'The preconditions for Caroline minuscule', *Viator* 18 (1987), 23–43, esp. pp. 38–43; Bischoff, *Latin Palaeography*, p. 112, Charlemagne's reforms 'strengthened the tendency towards discipline, order and harmony that was present in the script'.

[170] Bischoff, *Latin Palaeography*, p. 107.

common denominator in both scribes and readers. But the waning of cursive, as a calligraphic script, does not necessarily mean a less literate society: whatever may have been lost in sophistication of script was more than compensated for by accessibility, so that a greater number of readers, encompassing a greater variety of levels in reading skills, could participate in the transmission of information in the form of a book. To put it another way: the more elite literacy of cursive script could not compete against the strength of numbers behind the more accessible minuscule. On top of this, the use of the smaller minuscule letter-forms, as opposed to capitalis or uncial, had immediate economic and ergonomic advantages in saving parchment and the scribe's time. But whatever the complex causes for the move to minuscule, the diversity of form and richness in variation found in Italian manuscripts is testimony to a degree of calligraphic confidence and expertise in Lombard Italy that is further reflected in the charter evidence, an expertise that should not be undervalued or veiled by modern notions of legibility. That Italian scribes could choose to write in a more uniform style of minuscule is amply proven by the development of Beneventan script in the south, but this seems to have required the ideological and economic pull of a revitalised and flourishing Monte Cassino, and perhaps a degree of *campanilismo* against the Frankish north and its own minuscule.[171]

[171] Lowe, *Beneventan Script*, pp. 10–14; Cencetti, 'Scritture e circolazione', pp. 97–8. Cf. P. Supino Martini, 'Carolina romana e minuscola romanesca. Appunti per una storia della scrittura latina in Rome tra IX e XI secolo', *Scrittura e Civiltà* 2 (1978), 45–101.

CONCLUSION

οἷοί ἐσμεν τῷ λόγῳ δι' ἐπιστολῶν ἀπόντες, τοιοῦτοι καὶ παρόντες τῷ ἔργῳ.

II Cor. 10.11.

Some time in the first half of the ninth century, a priest who lived among the Slavs wrote to fellow-priests who had been staying too long in Italy and needed reminding of their pastoral responsibilities. As a means of justifying his own epistolary effort, he began his exhortatory letter with a learned allusion to Italy's history of literacy:

> For even the primitive Italians who lived in ancient times, as Cicero said in *On rhetoric*, used to send each other messages on the bark of a tree, well before the use of charters, parchment or writing tablets carved from smoothly hewn wood. Therefore they called the bearers of these missives *tabellarii*, and those who wrote them *librarii* after the bark of the tree. How much more, therefore, that we who live in a world polished by those arts ought not to forget how they distinguished themselves, although they lived in crude rusticity and knew nothing of civilisation.[1]

Italy's long history of literacy under Roman rule left an enduring idea of the peninsula as a legendary land of letters, the *fons civilitatis*. This study has sought to unravel this legend for a period in which Italy was conquered and ruled by a barbarian people for over 200 years, a period

---

[1] MGH Ep. IV, pp. 484–90, at p. 484. T. von Sickel, *Alcuinstudien*, Sitzungsberichte der philosophisch-historischen Klasse der kaiserlichen Akademie der Wissenschaften in Wien 79 (1875), pp. 461–550, at p. 535, argued that the author of this letter was Alcuin's disciple Wizo (Candidus). Refuted by H. Löwe, 'Zur Geschichte Wizos', *Deutsches Archiv* 6 (1943), 363–73, without presenting arguments; but see J. Marenbon, *From the Circle of Alcuin to the School of Auxerre: Logic, Theology and Philosophy in the Early Middle Ages* (Cambridge, 1981), p. 42 n. 59. The date of the letter falls between the composition of Alcuin's *Liber de anima* (c. 801), which the letter uses, and that of the manuscripts, Munich, Clm 14510 and Clm 13581, both saec. IX$^{2/4}$: Bischoff, *Die südostdeutschen Schreibschulen und Bibliotheken in der Karolingerzeit*, I, *Die bayerischen Diözesen* (Wiesbaden, 1960), p. 232. *On rhetoric* ('de rhetoricis') was a title often used for Cicero's *De inventione* (e.g. Cassiodorus, *Inst.* II.2.10), but it contains nothing concerning *rudes Italici*. The source for *tabellarii* is Isidore, *Etym.* V.24.4; *librarii*, ibid. VI.13.3, or Cassiodorus, *Inst.* II, praef.

that falls between the end of the Roman empire in the west and the so-called Carolingian Renaissance of the ninth century.

The study of literacy in Lombard Italy presents something of a paradox. The lack of surviving testimony for compositional or, for want of a better term, 'literary' literacy – narrative history, poetry, moral or theological treatises, biography – is offset by the relative abundance, in early medieval terms at least, of functional and administrative literacy in the form of charters and adherence to written law, evidence which testifies to the importance of the written word and the frequency with which people encountered it in their everyday lives. But just how frequently, and how many people did so, is impossible to answer. If this study has often taken a tone, at once speculative and admonitory, which stresses the amount of evidence that has been lost, or that the amount of literacy in Lombard Italy was much greater than has hitherto been realised, it is hoped that the reader may understand why this is necessary. Often characterised as Italy's Dark Ages, the Lombard period has been traditionally viewed as a low point in Italian history, when the peninsula was split in two, the last remnants of Roman civilisation were extinguished, and native Italians were subjected to the rule of foreign, Germanic overlords, a warrior caste who governed by the sword rather than through civil institutions. Literacy, it is assumed, barely survived in such an environment, or was restricted to the sphere of a beleaguered and disorganised church. I hope to have shown that this was not the case.

It is impossible to estimate meaningfully either how many people in Lombard Italy were literate, or, of course, how literate they were, when the surviving evidence is a fraction of that which once existed. 'We work on fragments', lamented Luigi Schiaparelli at the end of his edition of 296 charters from Lombard northern Italy and Tuscany, a quantity of surviving documents that is unparalleled in the early medieval world.[2] But quantification, as much as qualification, of literacy in this period is also impossible because of the absence of direct evidence. No surviving author of the period specifically discussed the acquisition of literate skills, or defined it in terms of degrees of literacy and illiteracy, whether in accordance with some ideal or in relation to others. Unfortunately, survival of evidence is the key here. On the basis of the surviving laws, charters and inscriptions, we might conclude that Lombard Italy was the most literate society in the west in this period. It would be just as erroneous to conclude that Merovingian Gaul was the most piously Christian region because of its greater amount of surviving hagiography. But the evidence at our disposal does permit us to conclude that literacy was capillary in Italo-Lombard

[2] CDL, II, p. 440.

Conclusion

society. It helped form and maintain links between rulers and ruled, central and local authority, secular and ecclesiastical powers. This owed much to the Roman heritage in Italy, but Italians under Lombard rule in the seventh and eighth centuries developed further literate traditions of government, administration and commemoration to suit their own needs and that of a society whose political and economic axes were fundamentally different from the structures which had underpinned the late Roman world.

In chapters 1 and 2 it was shown that Lombard rule had little to do with the displacement and subsequent disintegration of late Roman education and its emphasis on rhetoric. The increasing militarisation of Roman society in the sixth century and shifts in the economic organisation of the empire altered the institutional framework within which this type of literacy was cultivated. Theoderic's concern to paint the machinery of his government in Roman colours meant support for activities considered to be traditionally Roman. The cultivation of rhetoric under the banner of *litterae* or the 'liberal arts' appealed to such sentiments, but we should not fail to consider critically the achievements of those who engaged in this type of literary activity. By their own standards, authors such as Cassiodorus and Ennodius failed to live up to the traditions with which they associated themselves. They cite Cicero and Quintilian as role models, but their often impenetrable prose shows that they have not imbibed the teachings of these authorities.[3] That there was none after them to carry this spluttering torch should come as no surprise, especially as traditional 'praise of letters' was under attack from a non-aristocratic, and hence more socially persuasive, egalitarian ethos that extolled the supremacy of simple language to convey the highest of truths. The Christian polemic against rhetoric found a wider audience than could isolated elites justifying their importance and defending their interests to one another. In the desecularised world of the second half of the sixth century, the cultivation of rhetoric, almost the sole purpose of the late Roman education system, no longer offered rewards to be enjoyed in this life, let alone the next. The new heroes of Gregory the Great's Italy were semi-literate or illiterate holy men, men who read (or had read for them) the holy scriptures but little else. This, then, was the model of behaviour handed down to Italian churches, a model in which the medium was deemed less important than the message. Having turned their backs on Latin rhetoric, Italian clerics failed to develop an

---

[3] E.g. Ennodius, *Op.* 40, pp. 38, 46, 49, 50; *Op.* 9, p. 14; *Op.* 80, p. 101; cf. 'Quintilian' in *Op.* 363, p. 260; Cassiodorus, *Var.* I.3, VI.5 (*magister eloquentiae*): VIII.12; VIII.19; XI praef. (*fons eloquentiae*); *Inst.* II.2.4, 7; II.2.10, 13; II.3.8, 14.

educational programme of their own that might have invested the acquisition of literate skills for composition with the type of prestige they held in ninth-century Carolingian Francia.

The Lombards did not bring about any reversal of cultural values and prestige. As was set out in chapter 2, their ability to adopt the cultural trappings expected of them as rulers of Italy, and to adapt their designs to the administrative infrastructure that Italian cities afforded, contributed significantly to their success. The question of their accommodation, whether by allocation of tax revenues, by their appropriation of land or by some combination of the two, will never be satisfactorily answered on the basis of the evidence we have. But it is clear that elements of Roman administration, and particularly the articulation of centralised power through the network of cities, were maintained. This probably included mechanisms for the collection of taxes and tolls by governmental personnel, be they king's agents, gastalds, dukes, 'judges' or their retainers, with the economic power necessary to perform their functions and maintain social order. All this required a degree of functional literacy for administrative purposes – creating and keeping records of sums paid or owing, transfers of possession of fiscal property, lists of personnel and their responsibilities, commands and reports from one office to another – that has been lost to us. There is every good reason to assume this material once existed in profusion, and that it was a fundamental feature in the settlement of the Lombard rulers, whether adhering to the authority of a centralised monarchy or not. The notion of a Lombard 'invasion' is misleading; there are good grounds for understanding their initial entry into Italy in terms of a Roman invitation. But if so, it was an experiment that went disastrously wrong for Lombard as well as Roman unity in Italy. When Lombard dukes finally did settle for a centralised monarchy, a confident court culture emerged in which literary activity held an esteemed place. So, significantly, did schismatic clerics who found refuge and a sympathetic hearing for their views on the Three Chapters dispute. The importance of the schism in facilitating links between Lombard rulers and local society, through the support lent to the new regime by prelates now under its protection, should not be underestimated. It helps to explain the consolidation and continued success of the Lombard monarchy as much as military might and organisational ability.

The profession of pagan beliefs, not unusual in Italy, by some Lombards is outweighed in significance by the evidence for their early conversion to Catholic Christianity or the flirting of some rulers with predominantly native Italian Arianism. Far too much emphasis has been placed on the image of the Lombards gleaned from the *Origo gentis langobardorum*: hardy pagans who ferried their ancestral Germanic religion and cosmology into

Conclusion

Italy as a means of maintaining group identity. Undoubtedly, the popular tale, or origin-myth, of how the Winili became 'Long-beards' with the help of Woden and Frea reflects a pre-Italian and pre-Christian past. The notion that it circulated as an attachment to Rothari's Edict, an understandable assumption given Paul the Deacon's comments and its later manuscript tradition, has placed undue emphasis on the text, as though it constituted some sort of official statement of Lombard identity. But the *Origo*, as we have it, was not attached to the Lombard law code in our period; that is a subsequent development which reflects later ethnographic concerns. The circulation of an origin-myth containing pagan mythology, in the form of a Latin text, should not be considered as necessarily antithetical to or irreconcilable with Agilulf and Theudelinda's patronage of Columbanus and the foundation of Bobbio, Rothari's Arianism, or Perctarit's extremist piety against the Jews. The *Origo*'s survival is testimony to tolerance of an entertaining origin-myth involving Germanic deities, not to paganism.

Determining the nature of the relationship between the Lombard state and the church, an institution grounded in a religion of the book and which harboured literate activity, is crucial for our understanding of literacy in this period. One of the themes that has emerged from this study is that this relationship was much more complex and more congenial than has been previously thought. In his letter of 680 to the emperor, Damian, then deacon at Milan and writing on behalf of the archbishop, drew a contrast between the piety of Lombard rulers and the demented minds at the imperial court: 'we ... live under the most fortunate and most Christian of rulers protected by God, our lords Perctarit and Cunincpert, most excellent kings of the Lombards, devotees of the Christian faith, whose holy devotion and reverence is of equal strength to that of the holy apostles or the most revered fathers'.[4] The first Lombard king mentioned in the *Liber pontificalis* is Aripert II (701–12) and the royal charter written in gold which he sent to the pope. As for Liutprand, his religiosity and recognition of Rome's authority cannot be in doubt. Not only did he save the pope from imperial assassins in the 720s, when 'Romans and Lombards bound themselves together like brothers in the tie of faith, all of them willing to undergo a glorious death in the pontiff's defence', he was also instrumental in reconciling the pope and the exarch. In the 740s, Liutprand forgave Pope Hadrian for his meddling alliances with the southern duchies and upon request gave back the territories he had conquered in the Pentapolis and around Ravenna, though clearly the capture

---

[4] *PL* 87, 1261–5, at 1246D.

of the imperial capital was well within the king's grasp.[5] Papal hatred of the Lombards was based on more than mere territorial concerns, but it is difficult to determine the ideological or cultural component of the prejudice which Rome continued to hold throughout the life of the kingdom, despite periods of highly amicable *detente*. Caution is needed to avoid infecting our understanding of church–state relations within the *regnum* with the same prejudice. A re-examination of the sources from the perspective of literacy points in a very different direction from that which is implied by the high politics of the Franco–papal alliance.

The question of Lombard identity was tackled further in chapter 3, by examining the Germanic words that appear either as place-names, personal names and loan-words in Italian or as legal terms in the Lombard law code, and asking whether these can be considered as evidence for a native Germanic, Langobardic language which faded out of use during the period of the *regnum*. None of these categories of evidence demonstrates the existence of a spoken, native Langobardic language. The methodological uncertainties that surround the first three of the aforementioned categories – in terms of chronology of use, whether they were specifically 'Langobardic' as opposed to deriving from some other variety of Old High German dialect, and whether they need reflect the continued presence of a spoken Germanic language at all – together limit their usefulness as evidence. The same can be said for many of the Germanic terms in the Lombard law code, but here the evidence points in another direction: the use of Germanic terms in Lombard legislation was primarily of ideological import rather than any linguistic necessity. The use of archaic, 'Langobardic' words for legal terms and concepts reinforced the identity of the *gens langobardorum* in the royal mirror of legislation. The use of archaic legalisms to endow Lombard law with an aura of ancient authority was a necessary counterbalance to the redaction of the entire code in Latin. Many of the terms which denoted crimes or legal concepts were certainly used in everyday speech and especially in the courts. But this does not mean that the Lombards consistently employed a native Langobardic language. Paul the Deacon's comments tend to suggest they ceased to do so quite quickly, possibly soon after their arrival in Italy. Lombard Italy did not experience a Germanic–Latin bilingualism on any significant scale, and certainly not in a manner that pitted any linguistic, political or cultural obstacles against the acquisition of literate skills in Latin. Instead, the use of Germanic terms in the law code is more significant in further highlighting the importance of law in the construction of Lombard identity.

[5] *LP* 91,16–17; 93,2–16.

Conclusion

Directly relevant to the question of literacy in this period is the development of Latin as both a spoken and a written language, and the relationship between the two. Despite its formulaic quality, the language of charters reveals something of linguistic changes on the road to Romance, including the breakdown of correct case-usage or verb-forms, the increasing use of prepositions, the simplification of word order, and the morphology of words. But even given these moves away from classical Latin towards Romance forms, the language of the charters is still firmly Latinate in form and structure. The overall impression is that the vernacular, spoken language of the period was, at least in terms of vocabulary, morphology and pronunciation, close to written traditions of Latin, so that the proximity of written to spoken language made Latin literacy much more accessible than anywhere else in contemporary Europe, except perhaps Visigothic Spain, where the situation was probably similar. In terms of determining attitudes towards literacy, it is interesting that Lombard scribes preferred to chart their own linguistic waters between the Charybdis of vernacular forms and the Scylla of formulaic legal language. The level of (calli-)graphic skill revealed in the cursive script of their charters, and the employment of formulaic legal language, demonstrate that a higher degree of classically 'correct' Latinity was certainly possible, but scribes and their clients chose otherwise. As with the Ravennate papyri of the fifth and sixth centuries, Italian scribes wrote documents that would stand up in court, for which classical standards of orthography or grammar did not matter. We see the same with the charters of priests, whose use of more classically correct orthography and grammar in their scriptural quotations shows knowledge of such forms, but they chose to write a language that reflected the linguistic environment of their day, rather than an artificial, ideal language. One gets the sense that among the inhabitants of Lombard Italy, as within papal Rome, there was a pervasive recognition that time and language had indeed moved on since Roman days. There was little point in classicising Latin, whether culturally or for the purposes of effective communication. The rough or 'vulgar' quality of the Latin of Lombard charters reflects the very vitality of a literate, legal culture in Italy. The artisan recipes and *ars numeri* text from the Lucca 490 manuscript show that a simple but clear vulgar Latin was used for other types of texts. They also serve as a reminder of how much writing outside the legal sphere has been lost.

The proximity of spoken and written forms of communication goes a long way to explaining the effectiveness of written traditions in government and in the legal life of Lombard Italy, witnessed in the application of the law code and in the use of charters. But that is only one cause: the late Roman legal heritage, which privileged writing over other forms of proof, is certainly another, particularly with respect to property law. The law code itself testifies to the use of written communication in government at central and local levels, although the letters and lists referred to there have not survived. The charter evidence confirms that legislation was followed by scribes and enforced in the courts. Only documentation concerning property and personal status is extant, but its concordance with the precepts of Lombard legislation suggests that matters of criminal and family law were likewise deliberated upon and judged according to an interpretation of written law. Adherence to the law code also demonstrates the strength of the ideology of the state in Italy. While this owes much to the inherited political culture of late Roman Italy, Lombard rulers adopted and developed this legacy to the requirements of a monarchical government which promoted the ideal of a people unified by common law. The social diversity of the scribes who wrote charters, and the often rough and ready products of their handiwork, seem *ad hoc* and disorganised in comparison with later medieval documentation and the organised, state-recognised offices of *notarii* in high medieval Italy. Yet the very lack of a specialised and tightly organised profession of charter writers does not automatically mean that either charters, or those who wrote them, were less important or integral to the functioning of society. As with private documents in the late Roman world, the status of the writer was unimportant: what mattered was the adherence to the stipulations of written law, correct procedure, formulae, and requisite number of witnesses. In fact the charter evidence of Lombard Italy can be seen as an aspect of direct continuity with the late Roman world, and affords us a glance both backwards and sideways to the type of documentation that became increasingly common throughout the late Roman and post-Roman Mediterranean but which has elsewhere mostly been lost. In the corpus of Lombard charters we can detect elements of regional documentary culture, as was seen in relation to the evidence of *viri clarissimi* at Piacenza and the cathedral church of Lucca. But more striking is the overall degree of uniformity in format and formulae across the range of charters separated by time and geography, a uniformity that demonstrates a widespread continuity of legal traditions.

In chapters 6 and 7 we moved away from legal evidence to discuss two types of artefact of a more literary nature, namely, inscriptions and manuscripts. Consideration of the epigraphic heritage of Roman Italy is important for understanding not only the development of inscriptions during the Lombard period but also the experience of literacy at an everyday visual level. The physical environment of Lombard Italy, at least in the towns, was littered with letters: inscriptions recording the public munificence of an individual or family, statues and stelae alongside roads

Conclusion

with carved messages for passers-by, milestones which gave distances to the nearest towns and occasionally told stories, funerary epigraphy of varying levels of sophistication for the commemoration of the dead. The *syllogae* or collections of (frequently now lost) inscriptions put together by visitors to Italy demonstrate the attention such visual display attracted. Many of the more poetic compositions were copied as models of literary expression in epigraphic form. Such display was a feature of the physical and mental world of the young Paul the Deacon. Its effect on others of less literary inclination can only be surmised. The epigraphic 'flowering' of late seventh- and eighth-century Lombard Italy is testimony not just to the increasing links between secular and ecclesiastical elites in Pavia and Milan, but also to a revival of epigraphic funerary traditions unrivalled elsewhere in early medieval Europe. The use of rhythmic metres for poetic commemoration of the dead, carved in intricate and innovative letter-forms and framed by decorative borders, presents a certain homogeneity that allows us to identify a 'Lombard' style of inscription. The extent to which this style emerged in conscious contradistinction to surviving displays of Roman epigraphy is difficult to determine, but it is important to recognise that Lombard epigraphy offered no slavish imitation of Roman forms. King Liutprand in particular seems to have been aware of the communicative power of inscriptions to advertise his benevolence and bolster his prestige. Undoubtedly the young Pippin III saw much more at Liutprand's court than has survived,[6] but it appears to have made little impression. The Frankish conquest, for reasons difficult to determine, put an end to the development of epigraphy in Lombard Italy.

There has been a misguided tendency to dismiss the production of manuscripts in Lombard Italy as paltry or insignificant in comparison with the ninth-century explosion in numbers of surviving manuscripts. The same could be said for the subsequent decline of the tenth century, although books were no less prized or important for the development of literate traditions and intellectual pursuits.[7] The difficulty of assessing manuscript production in Italy as evidence for literacy stems from the diversity of writing styles and the uncertainties of attribution to any

---

[6] Paul, *HL* VI.53.
[7] See C. Bozzolo and E. Ornato, *Pour une Histoire du livre manuscrit au moyen âge: trois essais de codicologie quantitative*, 2nd edn (Paris, 1983); M. Ferrari, 'La biblioteca del monastero di S. Ambrogio', in *Il monastero di S. Ambrogio: episodi per una storia. Convegno di Studi nel XII centenario 784–1984*, Biblioteca Erudita. Studi, Documenti di Storia e di Filologia 3 (Milan, 1988), pp. 82–164; Ferrari, 'Manoscritti e testi fra Lombardia e Germania nel secolo X', in W. Berschin (ed.), *Lateinische Kultur im zehnten Jahrhundert. Akten des I. internationalen Mittellateinerkongresses* (Stuttgart, 1991), pp. 105–15; N. Daniel, *Handschriften des zehnten Jahrhunderts aus der Freisinger Dombibliothek* (Munich, 1973).

one centre within, and sometimes outside, Lombard Italy. The major collections of Bobbio and Verona, a monastery and cathedral church respectively, give us some insight into two centres of book production and preservation. But not all of the manuscripts preserved in those centres were necessarily written there, and it is difficult to know whether these centres were typical of other monasteries or churches where books were produced and preserved. There is no concrete evidence for lay production or ownership of books in Lombard Italy, but it would be unwise to dismiss the possibility, given the pretensions of the royal court and the evidence for literacy among lay scribes who wrote charters. Gerbert of Aurillac remarked (c. 988) to his friend, a monk at Bobbio whom Gerbert commissioned to find some rare books at any expense, 'for you know how many writers there are in both the cities and the countryside of Italy everywhere'.[8] From the diversity of writing styles found in the manuscripts that can be dated to our period one gets the sense that three centuries earlier Lombard Italy, too, had its fair share of writers. Further palaeographic and codicological studies are needed to identify the products of particular writing centres and possible connections between them, and to develop more precise criteria for the dating of manuscripts in this period. This would also help us to determine more clearly the important role played by Lombard Italy, both pre and post 774, in furnishing the Carolingian world with exemplars and manuscripts of classical literature, as well as works of religious inspiration and purpose.

The history of scripts in this period has often been cast in the mould of a period of calligraphic disorder and disorganisation until the eventual triumph of Caroline minuscule in the late eighth and ninth centuries. The very diversity of book-scripts used in Lombard Italy should be viewed as testimony to a vibrant and active scriptorial culture in which experimentation and a range of competencies could be accommodated. Even so, it is clear that among the diversity of scripts in use for book production in Lombard Italy a native minuscule was emerging in the second half of the eighth century, as it was in other parts of Europe. More importantly for the history of literacy, the very notions of 'legibility' we ascribe to minuscule scripts reflect our own familiarity with them rather than any objective criteria for clarity or comprehensibility in written communication. Similarly, the turn away from the use of more elaborate cursive scripts could be viewed as marking a decline in standards of literacy, for

---

[8] 'Nosti quanto studio librorum exemplaria undique conquiram, nosti quot scriptores in urbibus ac in agris Italiae passim habeantur.' A. Olleris (ed.), *Œuvres de Gerbert* (Paris, 1867), Ep. 78 (CXXX), pp. 45–6. On the date, M. Uhlirz, *Untersuchungen über Inhalt und Datierung der Briefe Gerberts von Aurillac, Papst Sylvesters II* (Göttingen, 1957), p. 108.

Conclusion

such scripts, with their use of intricate ligatures and density of abbreviation, required a greater familiarity with the written word than a regular and uniform minuscule. But if minuscule is not as intrinsically superior as is sometimes implied, the move to minuscule may well represent a 'democratisation' of literacy in rendering the written message accessible to a wider audience with less experience of reading and writing. The elitism of cursive book-scripts may reflect a higher degree of literacy, not to mention a more urgent need for a finished product, but the restricted accessibility of cursive script could point to a less literate society.

In the absence of evidence many aspects of Lombard Italy will remain an enigma – the nature of the initial settlement of the Lombards, the relationship between rulers and ruled, the machinery of government, the functioning of the courts, the connections between church and state, economic life, and so on. A study of literacy must necessarily suffer from the same deficiency. Nevertheless, by focusing upon that which does survive, I hope to have provided some idea of the role of the written word in Lombard Italy, and to have recaptured something of the background from which Paul the Deacon, Peter of Pisa and Paulinus of Aquileia emerged to take centre stage in the Carolingian Renaissance, only to return to the land where they learned their letters.

BIBLIOGRAPHY

PRIMARY SOURCES

NARRATIVE SOURCES

Listed by author or, when unknown, by title.

Agathias. *Agathiae Mytiniaei Historiarum libri quinque*, ed. R. Keydell, Corpus Fontium Historiae Byzantinae 2 (Berlin, 1967).

Agnellus, Andreas. *Liber pontificalis ecclesiae ravennatis*, ed. O. Holder-Egger, MGH SRL, pp. 265–391.

Alcuin. MGH Poetae I, ed. E. Duemmler, pp. 160–351.

Alcuin. MGH, Ep. IV, pp. 153–210.

Arator. *Arator's Acts of the Apostles (De actibus apostolorum)*, ed. and trans. R. J. Schrader (Atlanta, 1987).

Augustine. *Confessions*. CCSL 27, ed. L. Verheijen (Turnhout, 1981).

Augustine. *De doctrina christiana*. CCSL 32, ed. K.-D. Daur (Turnhout, 1972).

Barbatus, St, bishop of Benevento. *Vita Barbati*, ed. G. Waitz, MGH SRL, pp. 555–63.

Bede. *Baedae Opera historica*, 2 vols., ed. J.E. King, Loeb edn (Cambridge, MA, 1954).

Bede. *Chronica*, ed. G. Waitz, MGH AA. III.

Benedict. *The Rule of St Benedict 1980*, ed. and trans. T. Frye *et al.*, (Collegeville, MN, 1981); text taken from J. Neufville and A. De Vogüe (eds.), *La Règle de Saint Benoît*, 6 vols., Sources Chrétiennes 181–6 (Paris, 1971–72).

Caesarius of Arles, Life of. In, *Caesarius of Arles: Life, Testament, Letters*, trans. W. Klingshirn (Liverpool, 1994).

Cassiodorus. *Institutiones*, ed. R.A.B. Mynors (Oxford, 1937); trans. L. Webber Jones, *An Introduction to Divine and Human Readings* (New York, 1966).

Cassiodorus. *Variae*, ed. T. Mommsen, MGH AA. XII. Selected translations: S. Barnish, Translated Texts for Historians 12 (Liverpool, 1992).

Cassius Dio. *History of Rome*, ed. and trans. E. Cary, Loeb edn (London and New York, 1927).

Chronica S. Benedicti cassinensis, ed. G. Waitz, MGH SRL, pp. 364–489.

Chronicon S. Michaelis monasterii in pago virdunensi, ed. G. Waitz, MGH SS. IV, pp. 78–86.

Codex Gothani, ed. G. Waitz, MGH SRL, pp. 7–11, and *Le Leggi*, ed. C. Azzara (Milan, 1992), pp. 281–92.

Columbanus. *Sancti Columbani Opera*, ed. and trans. G.S.M. Walker (Dublin, 1970).

Continuatio haveniensis Prosperii, ed. T. Mommsen, MGH AA. IX, pp. 305–54; trans. S. Muhlberger, 'Heroic kings and unruly generals', *Florilegium* 6 (1984), 71–95.

Bibliography

Einhard. *Vita Karoli Magni* post G. Pertz recensuit G. Waitz, MGH, *Scriptores rerum germanicarum in usum scholarum ex monumentis germaniae historicis separatim editi*; trans. L. Thorpe, with Notker's *De Carolo Magno*, in *Two Lives of Charlemagne: Einhard and Notker the Stammerer* (Harmondsworth, 1969).
Ennodius of Pavia. *Ennodi Opera*, ed. F. Vogel, MGH AA. VII.
Epistulae langobardicae collectae, ed. W. Grundlach, MGH Ep. III, pp. 691–715.
Erchempert. *Erchemperti Historia langobardorum beneventorum*, ed. E. Holder-Egger, MGH SRL, pp. 231–64.
Fortunatus, Venantius. *Opera poetica*, ed. F. Leo, MGH AA. IV.
Fredegar. *Chronicarum quae dicuntur Fredegarii scholastici libri IV cum continuationibus*, ed. B. Krusch, MGH SRM II, pp. 1–193.
Fredegar. *Fredegarii Chronicorum liber quartus cum continuationibus*, ed. and Eng. trans. J.M. Wallace-Hadrill (Oxford, 1960).
Gregory the Great. *Dialogues*, 3 vols., ed. A. de Vogüe (Paris, 1979), and trans. O.J. Zimmermann, *The Dialogues of St. Gregory the Great*, Fathers of the Church 39 (New York, 1959).
Gregory the Great (Pope). *Registrum epistolarum*, ed. P. Ewald and L. Hartmann, MGH Ep. I–II.
Gregory of Tours. *History of the Franks*, trans. L. Thorpe (London, 1974).
Gregory of Tours. *Opera omnia*, ed. B. Krusch and W. Arndt, MGH SRM I.
Isidore, bishop of Seville. *Chronica*, ed. T. Mommsen, MGH AA. XIII, pp. 247–327.
Isidore, bishop of Seville. *Historia gothorum vandalorum sueborum*, ed. T. Mommsen, MGH AA. XI, pp. 267–303.
Isidore, bishop of Seville. *Isidori hispalensis episcopi Etymologiarum sive originum libri XX*, ed. W.M. Lindsay (Oxford, 1956).
Jerome. *Apologie contre Rufin*, ed. P. Lardet, Sources Chrétiennes 303 (Paris, 1983).
John of Biclar. *Chronica Iohannis abbatis monasterii biclarensis*, ed. T. Mommsen, MGH AA. XI, pp. 205–20.
John of Ephesus. *Historiae ecclesiasticae pars tertia*, ed. E. Brooks, *Corpus scriptorum christianorum orientalum. Scriptores syri, series tertia*, III (Versio Latina) (Louvain, 1936).
John Lydus. *De magistratibus* III.54.1–3, trans. T.F. Carney, in *Bureaucracy in Traditional Society: Romano-Byzantine Bureaucracies Viewed from Within*, III (Kansas, 1971).
Jonas. *Vita Columbani abbatis discipulorumque eius*, ed. B. Krusch, MGH SRM IV, pp. 61–152.
Jordanes. *Getica*, ed. T. Mommsen, MGH AA. V.1, pp. 53–138; also *The Gothic History of Jordanes*, ed. and trans. C.C. Mierow, with introduction and notes (Cambridge and New York, 1966).
Jordanes. *Romana*, ed. T. Mommsen, MGH AA. V.1, pp. 1–52.
Julianus Pomerius, *De vita contemplativa*. PL 59, 411–520.
Liber de apparitione S. Michaelis in Monte Gargano, ed. G. Waitz, MGH SRL, pp. 541–5.
Liber pontificalis, ed. L. Duchesne, 3 vols. (Paris, 1981). Also ed. T. Mommsen, MGH, *Gesta pontificum romanorum*, I.1 (Pars prior) (Munich, 1982). Eng. trans. R. Davis, *The Book of Pontiffs* (*Liber pontificalis*): *The Ancient Biographies of the First Ninety Roman Bishops to AD 715* (Liverpool, 1989); *The Lives of the Eighth Century Popes* (*Liber pontificalis*): *The Ancient Biographies of Nine Popes from A.D. 715 to 817*, ed. and trans. R. Davis (Liverpool, 1992).

Bibliography

Marius of Avenches. *Chronica minora*, ed. T. Mommsen, in MGH AA. XI, pp. 37–105.
Master, The. *Rule*, ed. A. De Vogüe, *La Règle du Maître*, Sources Chrétiennes 105–7 (Paris, 1964–67).
Menander Protector. *Excerpta*, ed. and trans. R.C. Blockley, *The History of Menander the Guardsman: Introductory Essay, Text, Translation and Historiographical Notes* (Liverpool, 1985).
Menander Protector. *Fragmenta historicorum graecorum*, I–IV, ed. E. Mullerus (Paris, 1851).
Origo gentis langobardorum, ed. G. Waitz, MGH SRL, pp. 1–6, and in *Le leggi*, ed. C. Azzara, pp. 1–10; *Origo gentis langobardorum*, ed. A. Bracciotti (Rome, 1998).
Parastaseis syntomoi chronikai, in A. Cameron and J. Herrin (eds.), *Constantinople in the Early Eighth Century: The Parastaseis syntomoi chronikai* (Leiden, 1984).
Paul the Deacon. *Collectio Pauli*, ed. D. Norberg, *In Registrum Gregorii Magni studia critica* (Uppsala, 1937–39).
Paul the Deacon. MGH Ep. IV, pp. 505–16.
Paul the Deacon. *Gesta episcoporum mettensium*, PL 95, 699–715.
Paul the Deacon. *Historia langobardorum*, ed. G. Waitz in MGH SRL, pp. 7–156.
Other editions of the *HL*:
  Paul the Deacon's History of the Lombards, trans. W. Dudley Foulke (Philadelphia, 1907).
  Storia dei Longobardi, intro. B. Luiselli; Italian trans. and notes Antonio Zanella, BUR (Milan, 1991). Latin text in MGH.
  ed. E. Bartolini, TEA Series (Milan, 1988).
  ed. Lidia Capo, Series Fondazione Lorenzo Valla/ A. Mondatori editore (Milan, 1992).
  Intro. L. Leonardi; App. crit. R. Cassarelli, Electa series (Milan, 1991).
Paul the Deacon. *Historia romana* (*Breviarium ab urbe condita*), ed. H. Droysen, MGH AA. II; and ed. A. Crivelluci, Fonti per la Storia d'Italia 51 (Rome, 1913).
Paul the Deacon. *Sexti Pompei Festi De verborum significatu cum Pauli epitome*, ed. W.M. Lindsay (Leipzig, 1933).
Paul the Deacon. *Vita beatissimi Gregorii Magni urbis Romae papa*, PL 85, 41–59.
Paul the Deacon. Poetry: K. Neff, *Die Gedichte des Paulus Diaconus: Kritiche und erklärende Ausgabe*, Quellen und Untersuchungen zur lateinischen Philologie des Mittelalters 3. IV (Munich, 1908).
Pelagius II, Pope. MGH Ep. II, Appendices II and III, pp. 437–67.
Pelagius II, Pope. MGH Ep. III, pp. 448–50.
Peter Chrysologus. *Opera*, CCSL 24 a–b, ed. A. Olivar (Turnhout, 1975–82).
Pliny, The Elder. *Natural History*, ed. H. Rackham, W.H.S. Jones and D.E. Eichholz, Loeb edn (London and New York, 1949).
Procopius of Caeserea. *De bello gothico*, ed. and trans. H.B. Dewing, vols. III–V, Loeb edn (London and New York, 1919–28).
Ptolemy, Claudius. *Geographica*, ed. C. Nobbe (Leipzig, 1966).
Ravennatis anonymi geographus, ed. J. Schnetz, *Itineraria romana*, II (Leipzig, 1940).
Sidonius Apollinaris. *Works*, ed. and trans. W.B. Anderson, Loeb edn, 2 vols. (Cambridge, 1936, 1965).

Bibliography

Strabo. *Geographica*, ed. and trans. H.L. Jones, Loeb edn (London and New York, 1944).
Tacitus, Cornelius. *Agricola, Germania et Dialogus*, ed. and trans. M. Hutton, Loeb edn (Cambridge, 1970).
Tacitus, Cornelius. *La vita di Agricola. La Germania*, Latin with Italian trans. B. Ceva, BUR (Milan, 1995).
Theophylact Simocatta. *Theophylacti Simocattae Historiae*, ed. C. de Boor (Leipzig, 1887).
Velleius Paterculus. *Res gestae divi Augusti*, ed. and trans. F.W. Shipley, Loeb edn (London and Cambridge MA, 1967).
Zeno, bishop of Verona (*c.* 360–380). *Tractatus*, ed. B. Löfsted (Turnhout, 1971), reprinted with Italian trans. and ed. G. Banterle (Milan and Rome, 1987).

INSCRIPTIONS

Listed by editor in alphabetical order.
Boppert, W. *Die frühchristlichen Inschriften des Mittelrheingebietes* (Mainz am Rhein, 1971).
Carletti, C. *Iscrizioni cristiane a Roma: testimonianze di vita cristiana, sec. III–VIII*, Biblioteca Patristica 7 (Florence, 1986).
'Iscrizioni murali', in C. Carletti and G. Otranto (eds.), *Il Santuario di San Michele sul Gargano dal VI al IX secolo: contributo all storia della Longobardia meridionale* (Bari, 1980).
Cecchelli, C. *I monumenti di Friuli dal sec. IV all'XI*, I (Milan and Rome, 1943).
De Rossi, G.B. *Inscriptiones christianae urbis Romae septimo saeculo antiquiores* (Rome, 1857/61–88).
Descombes, F. *Viennoise du Nord*, Recueil des Inscriptions Chrétiennes de la Gaule, antérieures à la Renaissance Carolingienne 15 (Paris, 1985).
Dümmler, E. (ed.). MGH Poetae IV, ii, 'Rhythmi langobardici', pp. 718–31.
Gautier, N. *Première Belgique*, Recueil des Inscriptions Chrétiennes de la Gaule, antérieures à la Renaissance Carolingienne 1 (Paris, 1975).
Hübner, E. *Inscriptiones Hispaniae christianae*, 2 vols. (CIL II) (Berlin, 1871–1900).
Le Blant, E. *Inscriptions chrétiennes de la Gaule antérieures au VIIIe siècle*, 2 vols. (Paris, 1856–65).
Monneret de Villard, U. 'Iscrizioni cristiane della Provincia di Como anteriori al secolo XI', *Rivista archeologica della provincia e antica diocesi di Como* 65–66, anno 12 (Como, 1912).
Panazza, G. *Lapidi e sculture paleocristiane e pre-romaniche di Pavia, Arte del Primo Millenio. Atti del II Convegno per lo studio dell'arte dell'alto medioevo, tenuto presso l'Università di Pavia nel Settembre 1950* (Turin, 1953).
Rugo, P. *Le iscrizioni del sec. VI–VII–VII esistenti in Italia*, 5 vols. (Citadella, 1974–78).
Salin, E. *La Civilisation mérovingienne: d'après les sépultures, les textes et la laboratoire*, II, *Les sépultures* (Paris, 1952).
Silvagni, A. *Monumenta epigraphica christiana*, 3 vols. (Vatican City, 1943).
Troya, C. *Codice diplomatico longobardo*, I–V (Naples, 1852–55).

Bibliography

Vives, J. *Inscripciones cristianas de la España romana y visigoda*, Monumenta Hispaniae Sacra, Serie Patristica 2 (Barcelona, 1969).

DOCUMENTS AND CHARTERS

Codice diplomatico longobardo:
Codice diplomatico longobardo, vols. I–V, ed. C. Troya (Naples, 1852–55).
Codice diplomatico longobardo, vols. I and II, ed. L. Schiaparelli, Fonti per la Storia d'Italia 62 and 63 (Rome, 1929, 1933).
Codice diplomatico longobardo, vol. III, ed. C. Brühl, Fonti per la Storia d'Italia 64 (Rome, 1973).
Codice diplomatico longobardo, vol. IV:1, ed. C. Brühl, Fonti per la Storia d'Italia 65 (Rome, 1981).
Codice diplomatico longobardo, vol. V, ed. H. Zielinski, Fonti per la Storia d'Italia 66 (Rome, 1986).
Codice diplomatico del monastero di S. Colombano di Bobbio, ed. C. Cipolla and G. Buzzi, Fonti per la Storia d'Italia 52–4 (Rome, 1918).
Chartae latinae antiquiores, ed. A. Bruckner and R. Marichal (Olten, 1954–).
Formulae Merovingici et Karolini aevi, ed. K. Zeumer, MGH Form.
Il museo diplomatico dell'Archivio di Stato di Milano, ed. A.R. Natale (Milan, 1971).
Die nichtliterarischen lateinischen Papyri italiens aus der Zeit 445–700, 3 vols., ed. J.O. Tjäder (Lund, 1954/55–82).
I Placiti del 'Regnum Italiae', 3 vols., ed. C. Manaresi, Fonti per la Storia d'Italia 92, 96, 97 (Rome, 1955–60).
Regesto di Farfa, 5 vols., ed. I. Giorgio and U. Balzani (Rome, 1879–1914).
Tablettes Albertini: actes privés de l'époque vandale, ed. C. Courtois *et al.* (Paris, 1952).
Velázquez Soriano, I. (ed.). *El Latín de las pizarras visigóticas*, 2 vols. (Madrid, 1989).

LAWS

Azzara, C. and S. Gasparri (eds.). *Le leggi dei Longobardi: storia, memoria e diritto di un popolo germanico*, Le Fonti 1 (Milan, 1992), with Italian trans. by C. Azzara.
Beyerle, F. (ed.). *Die Gesetze der Langobarden*, Schriften der Akademie für deutsches Recht, Gruppe 5: Rechtsgechichte; Germanenrecht 3 (Weimar, 1947); reprinted as *Die Gesetze der Langobarden*, III (Wizenhausen, 1962–63), with German trans.
Bluhme, F. (ed.). *Leges langobardorum*, MGH Leges IV (Hanover, 1868: repr. Stuttgart, 1965).
Bluhme, F. (ed.). *Edictum Theoderici regis*, MGH Leges V (Hanover, 1875–89), pp. 154–79.
Fischer-Drew, K. (trans.). *The Lombard Laws* (Philadelphia, 1973).
Pharr, C. (ed. and trans.). *Theodosius II, Emperor of the East: The Theodosian Code and Novels and the Sirmondian Constitutions*, Corpus of Roman Law 1 (Princeton, 1952).
Salis, L.R. de (ed.). *Lex burgundiorum*, MGH Leges II, pp. 2–122; trans. K. Fischer-Drew, *The Burgundian Code* (Philadelphia, 1949).
Zeumer, K. (ed.). *Leges visigothorum*, MGH Leges n.g. I, (Hanover, 1902).

Bibliography

SECONDARY SOURCES

Excluded are some of the more specialised works on archaeology, palaeography, epigraphy, etc., that have been used to illuminate a particular point. Full references have been given in the notes to the text where relevant.

Acocella, N. 'Le origini di Salerno medievale negli scritti di Paolo Diacono', in *Salerno medievale e altri saggi* (Naples, 1971), pp. 513–63.

Alföldy, G. *Noricum*, trans. A. Birley (London and Boston, 1974).

Alfonsi, L. 'Romani e barbari nella *Historia langobardorum* di Paolo Diacono', *Romanobarbarica* 1 (1976), 7–24.

Amory, P. 'The meaning and purpose of ethnic terminology in the Burgundian laws', *EME* 2:1 (1993), 1–28.

People and Identity in Ostrogothic Italy, 489–554 A.D. (Cambridge, 1997).

Arangio-Ruiz, V. '*Mancipatio* e documenti contabili da Ercolano a Piacenza', *La Parola del Passato* 12 (1957), 35–56.

Arcamone, M.G. 'L'antroponimia germanica a Pisa durante l'età longobarda', in *Filologia e critica: studi in honore di V. Santoli*, Studia di Filologia Tedesca 6 (Rome, 1976), pp. 133–58.

'Reflexe des langobardischen Lautsystems in der italienischen Toponomastik', *Onoma* 21:2 (1977), 51–6.

'Antroponimia longobarda in Lombardia', *Atti XII CISAM* (Spoleto, 1980), 277–82.

'Antroponimia altomedievale nelle iscrizioni murali', in C. Carletti and G. Otranto (eds.), *Il Santuario di S. Michele sul Gargano, dal VI al IX secolo* (Bari, 1980), pp. 255–318.

'Die langobardischen Personnennamen in Italien. Nomen et gens der Sicht der linguistischen Analyse', in D. Geunich et al. (eds.), *Nomen et gens* (Berlin, 1997), pp. 56–76.

Arnaldi, F. *Lexicon latinitatis italicae medii aevi* (Brussels, 1939), I (Vol. II ed. P. Smiraglia (Brussels, 1957–64)).

Arpad, D. *Inscriptiones ad res pannonicas pertinentes extra provinciae fines repertae*, Dissertationes Pannonicae (Budapest, 1932).

Arrighi, G. 'Un inedito di aritmosofia nel Codice 490 (saec. VIII–IX) della Biblioteca Capitolare Feliniana di Lucca', *Atti V CISAM* (Spoleto, 1973), 675–769.

Arslan, E.A. 'La monetazione', in P. Caratelli (ed.), *Magistra Barbaritas* (Milan, 1984), pp. 413–44.

'Una riforma monetaria di Cuniperto, re dei Longobardi (668–700)', *Numismatica e antichità classiche* 15 (1986), 249–75.

'Le monete', in G.C. Menis (ed.), *I Longobardi* (Milan, 1990), pp. 164–5, table pp. 166–77.

'Emissioni monetarie e segni del potere', *Settimane* 39 (Spoleto, 1992), 791–847.

Arthur, P. and D. Whitehouse. 'Appunti sulla produzione laterizia nell'Italia centro-meridionale tra il VI e XII secolo', *Archeologia Medievale* 10 (1983), 525–37.

Astuti, G. 'Spirito del diritto longobardo: il processo oralico', in *La civiltà dei Longobardi in Europa, problemi attuali di scienza e storia* 189, Accademia Nazionale dei Lincei (Rome, 1974), pp. 85–100.

'Influssi romanistici nelle fonti del diritto longobardo', *Settimane* 22 (Spoleto, 1975), 653–96.

Bibliography

Auerbach, E. *Literary Language and Its Public in Late Antiquity and in the Middle Ages*, trans. Ralph Manheim (New York, 1965).
Ausenda, G. 'The segmentary lineage in contemporary anthropology and among the Langobards', in G. Ausenda (ed.), *After Empire: Towards an Ethnology of Europe's Barbarians* (San Marino, 1995), pp. 15–45.
Bachrach, B. *The Anatomy of a Little War: The Gundovald Affair* (Boulder, 1994).
Baesecke, G. *Der deutsche Abrogans und die Herkunft des deutschen Schriftums*, 2nd edn (Tübingen, 1969).
Baines, J. 'Literacy and ancient Egyptian society', *Man* 81 (1983), 572–99.
Balogh, J. '*Voces paginarum*: Beiträge zur Geschichte des lauten Lesens und Schreibens', *Philologus* 82 (1927), 84–109, 202–40.
Balsdon, J.P. *Romans and Aliens* (London, 1979).
Balzaretti, R. 'History, archaeology and early medieval urbanism: the north Italian debate', *The Journal of the Accordia Research Centre* 2 (1991), 87–104.
'The monastery of Sant'Ambrogio and dispute settlement in early medieval Milan', *EME* 3:1 (1994), 1–18.
'Cities, emporia and monasteries: local economies of the Po Valley 700–875', in N. Christie and S. Loseby (eds.), *Towns in Transition: Urban Evolution in Late Antiquity and the Early Middle Ages* (Aldershot, 1996), pp. 213–34.
'"These are things that men do, not women": the social regulation of female violence in Langobard Italy', in G. Halsall (ed.), *Violence and Society in Early Medieval Europe* (Woodbridge and Rochester, 1998), pp. 175–92.
The Lands of Saint Ambrose: Monks and Society in Early Medieval Milan (Leiden, Cologne and Boston, 2000).
Banniard, M. '*Vox agrestis*: quelques problèmes d'élocution de Cassiodorre à Alcuin', *Trames, Etudes, Antiques* (Limoges, 1985), 195–208.
'*Iuxta uniuscuiusque qualitatem*: l'écriture médiatrice chez Grégoire le Grand', in J. Fantaine, R. Gillet and S. Pellistrandi (eds.), *Grégoire le Grand*, Colloques internationaux du CNRS (Paris, 1986), pp. 477–88.
Genèse culturelle de l'Europe: V–VII siècle (Paris, 1989).
Le Haut Moyen Age Occidental, 3rd edn (Paris, 1991).
Viva voce: communication écrite et communication orale du IV au IX siècle en Occident latin, Collection des Etudes Augustiniennes (Paris, 1992).
'diasystèmes et diachronie languagières du latin parlé tardif ou protofrançais (IIIe–VIIIe siècles)', in J. Herman (ed.), *La transizione dal latino alle lingue romanze* (Tübingen, 1998), pp. 131–54.
Banti, O. 'Considerazioni a proposito di alcune epigrafi dei secoli VIII–IX conservate a Brescia', in *S. Giulia di Brescia: archeologia, arte, storia di un monastero regio dai Longobardi al Barbarossa* (Brescia, 1992), pp. 163–77.
Barni, G. 'Il diritto longobardo nel Liber consuetudinum Mediolani', *Atti I CISAM* (Spoleto, 1952), 205–18.
Bartolini, F. 'Semicorsiva o precarolina?', *Bullettino dell'Archeologia e Paleografia Italiana* 12 (1943), 2–33.
'Note paleografiche. Ancora sulle scritture precaroline', *Bullettino dell'Istituto Storico Italiano* 62 (1950), 139–72.
'La nomenclatura della scrittura documentarie', *X Congresso Internazionale di Scienze Storiche, Roma 1955*, I (Florence, 1955), 434–76.

Bibliography

Battisti, C. *Avviamento allo studio del latino volgare* (Bari, 1949).
  Le valli dell'Alto Adige e il pensiero dei linguisti italiani sull'unità dei dialetti ladini (Florence, 1962).
  'I nomi longobardi delle armi e le loro sopravvivenze nella lingua e nei dialetti italiani', *Settimane* 15 (Spoleto, 1968), 1067–1101.
  'L'elemento longobardo nella toponomastica umbra', *Atti del V Convegno di Studi Umbri* (Gubbio, 28 May – 1 June 1967) (Perugia, 1970), 235–48.
Bäuml, F. 'Varieties and consequences of medieval literacy and illiteracy', *Speculum* 55:2 (1980), 237–65.
Belting, H. 'Studien zum beneventanischen Hof im 8. Jahrhundert', *Dumbarton Oaks Papers* 16 (1962), 141–93.
Bernareggi, E. *Moneta Langobardorum* (Milan, 1983).
Berschin, W. *Biographie und Epochenstil in lateinischen Mittelalter*, Quellen und Untersuchungen zur lateinischen Philolologie des Mittelalters I.VIII (Stuttgart, 1986).
  Greek Letters and the Latin Middle Ages: from Jerome to Nicholas of Cusa, trans. J.C. Frakes (Washington, 1988).
  Merovingische Biographie: Italien, Spanien und die Inseln im frühen Mittelalter, Quellen und Untersuchungen zur lateinischen Philolologie des Mittelalters II.IX (Stuttgart, 1988).
Bertini, L. 'Peredeo, vescovo di Lucca', in *Studi storici in onore di Ottorino Bertolini*, I (Pisa, 1972), pp. 21–46.
Bertolini, O. *Roma di fronte a Bisanzio e ai Longobardi*, Storia di Roma 9 (Bologna, 1941).
  'Le chiese longbarde dopo la conversione al cattolicesimo ed i loro rapporti con il papato', *Settimane* 7 (Spoleto, 1960), 62–94.
  'I vescovi del "*regnum langobardorum*" al tempo dei Carolingi', *Italia Sacra* 5 (1964), 1–26.
  'Carlomagno e Benevento', in H. Beumann (ed.), *Karl der Grosse: Persönlichkeit und Geschichte*, I (Düsseldorf, 1965), pp. 625–31.
  'Ordinamenti militari e strutture sociali dei longobardi in Italia', *Settimane* 15 (Spoleto, 1968), 429–608.
  Scritti scelti di storia medievale di O. Bertolini, ed. O. Banta, 2 vols. (Livorno, 1968).
  Roma e Longobardi (Rome, 1972).
Besta, E. *Fonti del diritto italiano dalla caduta dell'impero sino ai tempi nostri* (Padua, 1938).
  Storia del diritto italiano: diritto pubblico, 2 vols. (Milan, 1949–50).
  'Le fonti del editto di Rotari', *Atti I CISAM* (Spoleto, 1952), 51–69.
Bieler, L. 'Some remarks on the aenigmata laureshamensia', *Romanobarbarica* 2 (1977), 11–15.
Bierbrauer, V. 'Aspetti archeologici di Goti, Alamanni e Longobardi', in P. Caratelli (ed.), *Magistra Barbaritas* (Milan, 1984), pp. 445–508.
Billanovich, G. 'Dall'antica Ravenna alle biblioteche umanistiche', *Aevum* 30 (1956), 316–62.
Billanovich, G. and M. Ferrari 'La trasmissione dei testi nell'Italia nord-occidentale. I. Monza, Pavia, Milano, Bobbio. II. Milano, Nonantola, Brescia', *Settimane* 22 (Spoleto, 1975), 303–55.

Bibliography

Bischoff, B. 'The study of foreign languages in the Middle Ages', *Speculum* 36 (1961), 209–24.

'Scriptoria e manoscritti mediatori di civiltà dal VI secolo alla riforma di Carlo Magno', *Settimane* 11 (Spoleto, 1963), 479–504.

'Wendepunkte in der Geschichte der lateinischen Exegese in Frühmittelalter', *Sacris Erudiri* 6 (1954), 189–279, repr. in his *Mittelalterliche Studien*, I (Stuttgart, 1966), pp. 205–73.

Mittelalterliche Studien: Ausgewählte Aufsätze zur Schriftkunde und Literaturgeschichte, 3 vols. (Stuttgart, 1967–81).

Sammelhandschrift Diez. B. Sant. 66. Grammatici Latini et Catalogus librorum, Codices selecti phototypice impressi 42 (Graz, 1973).

'Centri, scrittori e manoscritti mediatori da civiltà dal VI sec. all'età di Carlomagno', in G. Cavallo (ed.), *Libri e lettori nel medioevo* (Rome and Bari, 1977), pp. 29–72.

Die südostdeutschen Schreibschulen und Bibliotheken in der Karolingerzeit, I, *Die bayrischen Diözesen* (Wiesbaden, 1960).

'Manoscritti nonantoli dispersi dell'epoca carolingia', *La Bibliofilia* 85 (1983), 99–124.

'Italienische Handschriften des neunten bis elften Jahrhunderts in frühmittelalterlichen Bibliotheken ausserhalb Italiens', in C. Questa and R. Rafaelli (eds.), *Il libro e il testo. Atti del convegno internazionale, Urbino 20–23 Settembre 1982* (Urbino, 1984), pp. 169–94.

Latin Palaeography: Antiquity and the Middle Ages, trans. D. Ó Cróinín and D. Ganz (Cambridge, 1993).

Manuscripts and Libraries in the Age of Charlemagne, ed. and trans. M. Gorman (Cambridge, 1994).

Blake, H.M., T.W. Potter and D.B. Whitehouse (eds.). *Papers in Italian Archaeology*, I, BAR 541 (Oxford, 1978).

Blasel, C. 'Die Übertritt der Langobarden zum Christentum', *Archiv für Katholisches Kirchenrecht* 83 (1903), 585–634.

Bloch, H. 'Monte Cassino's teachers in the high Middle Ages', *Settimane* 19 (Spoleto, 1972), 562–603.

Monte Cassino in the Middle Ages, 3 vols. (Rome, 1986).

Blok, D.P. *Ortsnamen, Typologie des Sources du Moyen Age Occidental* 54 (Turnhout, 1988).

Bluhme, F. *Die Gens Langobardorum* (Bonn, 1874).

Bognetti, G.P. *Storia di Brescia* (Rome, 1963).

L'età longobarda, 4 vols. (Milan, 1966–70).

'Longobardi e romani', *L'età*, I, pp. 83–142.

'Le origini della consacrazione del vescovo di Pavia da parte del pontefice romano e la fine dell'arianesimo presso i Longobardi', *L'età*, I, pp. 143–218.

'Il gastaldato longobardo e i giudicati di Adaloaldo, Arioaldo e Pertarido nella lite tra Parma e Piacenza', *L'età*, I, pp. 219–74.

'Il problema monetario dell'economia longobarda e il "panis" e la scutella del cambio', *L'età*, I, pp. 381–415.

'S. Maria foris portas di Castelseprio e la storia religiosa dei Longobardi', *L'età*, II, pp. 12–674.

'L'influsso delle istituzioni militari romane sulle istituzioni longobarde del secolo VI e la natura della "fara" ', *L'età*, III, pp. 1–46.
'I ministri romani dei re longobardi e un'opinione di Alessandro Manzoni', *L'età*, III, pp. 47–66.
'Processo logico e integrazioni delle fonti della storiografia di Paolo Diacono', *L'età*, III, pp. 157–84.
'Storia, archeologia e diritto nel problema dei longobardi', *L'età*, III, pp. 197–266.
'I "loca sanctorum" e la storia della Chiesa nel regno dei Longobardi', *L'età*, III, pp. 303–46.
'Tradizione longobarda e politica bizantina nelle origini del ducato di Spoleto', *L'età*, III, pp. 439–76.
'Il ducato longobardo di Spoleto', *L'età*, III, pp. 485–506.
'I rapporti etico-politici fra oriente e occidente dal secolo V al secolo VIII', *L'età*, IV, pp. 1–56.
'L'Editto di Rotari come espediente politico di una monarchia barbarica', *L'età*, IV, pp. 114–35.
'Carrateri del secolo VII in Occidente', *L'età*, IV, pp. 137–88.
'Un momento storico di Vicenza longobarda e la crisi dello scisma aquileiese', *L'età*, IV, pp. 189–208.
'Problemi di metodo e oggetti di studio nella storia delle città italiane dell'alto medioevo', *L'età*, IV, pp. 221–50.
'La rinascita cattolica dell'Occidente di fronte al arianesimo e allo scisma', *L'età*, IV, pp. 273–94.
'Continuità delle sedi episcopali e l'azione di Roma nel regno longobardo', *L'età*, IV, pp. 301–38.
'Teodorico di Verona e Verona longobarda capitale del regno', *L'età*, IV, pp. 339–79.
'I capitoli 144 e 145 di Rotari e il rapporto tra Como e i magistri commacini', *L'età*, IV, pp. 431–54.
'Il rapporto tra L'Oriente e la Lombardia da Giustiniano a Carlo Magno', *L'età*, IV, pp. 525–38.
'La navigazione padana e il sopravvivere della civiltà antica', *L'età*, IV, pp. 539–56.
'Frammenti di uno studio sulla composizione dell'Editto di Rotari', *L'età*, IV, pp. 585–609.
'Appunti per una storia dei Longobardi in Italia', *L'età*, IV, pp. 611–68.
'L'*exceptor civitatis* ed il problema della continuità', *L'età*, IV, pp. 669–708.
'Navi e navigazione nel diritto pubblico mediterraneo dell'alto medioevo', *L'età*, IV, pp. 709–34.
Böna, I. *The Dawn of the Dark Ages: The Gepids and the Lombards in the Carpathian Basin* (Budapest, 1976).
'I Longobardi in Pannonia', in G.C. Menis (ed.), *I Longobardi* (Milan, 1990), pp. 14–19.
Bonacini, P. 'Regno ed episcopato a Modena nei secoli VII e VIII. Il periodo longobardo', *Studi Medievali* 33 (1992), 73–108.
Bondardo, M. *Il dialetto veronese* (Verona, 1972).
Bonelli, G. *Codice paleografico lombardo* (Milan, 1908).

Bonfante, G. *Latini e Germani in Italia* (Brescia, 1965).
 'Quando si è incominciato a parlare italiano? Criteri fonologici', in *Festschrift für W. von Wartburg* (Basel, 1969), pp. 21–46.
 'La lingua parlata nell'età imperiale', *Aufstieg und Niedergang der Römischen Welt* 29:1 (1983), 413–52.
Bostock, J. *A Handbook on Old High German Literature*, 2nd edn (Oxford, 1976).
Bowman, A.K. 'Literacy in the Roman empire: mass and mode', in J. Humphreys (ed.), *Literacy in the Roman World* (Ann Arbor, MI, 1991), pp. 119–31.
 'The Roman imperial army: letters and literacy in the frontier', in A.K. Bowman and G. Woolf (eds.), *Literacy and Power in the Ancient World* (Cambridge, 1994), pp. 109–25.
Bowman, A.K. and G. Woolf (eds.). *Literacy and Power in the Ancient World* (Cambridge, 1994).
Boyle, L.E. *Medieval Latin Palaeography, Bibliographical Introduction* (Toronto, 1984).
Bracciotti, A. 'La saga di Gambara e dei suoi figli nella *Origo gentis langobardorum*', *Romanobarbarica* 12 (1992–93), 81–6.
 'Il ruolo del Peredeo nell'assassinio di Alboino', *Romanobarbarica* 13 (1994–95), 99–123.
 Origo gentis langobardorum: introduzione, testo critico, commento, Biblioteca di Cultura Romanobarbarica 2 (Rome, 1998).
Braesecke, G. *Die deutschen Worte der germanisch Gesetze*, Beitrage zur Geschichte der deutschen Sprache und Literatur 59 (Halle, 1935).
Bresslau, H. *Handbuch der Urkundenlehre für Deutschland und Italien*, 2 vols. (Leipzig and Berlin, 1889–1931).
Brogiolo, G.P. 'La città tra tardo-antichità e medioevo', in R. Bussi and A. Molinari (eds.), *Archeologia urbana in Lombardia* (Modena, 1985), pp. 46–57.
 'Edilizia residenziale in Lombardia', in *Atti del 4 seminario sul tardoantico e l'altomedievo in Italia centrosettentrionale* (Mantua, 1994), pp. 103–14.
Brogiolo, G.P. and S. Gelichi. 'La ceramica grezza medievale nella pianura padana', in D. Manacorda *et al.*, *La ceramica medievale nel Mediterraneo occidentale* (Florence, 1986), pp. 293–316.
Brown, G. 'The Carolingian Renaissance', in R. McKitterick (ed.), *Carolingian Culture* (Cambridge, 1994), pp. 1–51.
Brown, P.R.L. *The World of Late Antiquity, A.D. 150–750* (London, 1971).
 The Cult of the Saints: Its Rise and Function in Latin Christianity (Chicago, 1981).
 Power and Persuasion in Late Antiquity: Towards a Christian Empire (Madison, 1992).
Brown, T.S. 'The Church of Ravenna and the imperial administration in the seventh century', *English Historical Review* 94 (1979), 1–28.
 Gentlemen and Officers: Imperial Administration and Aristocratic Power in Byzantine Italy, A.D. 554–800 (Rome, 1984).
 'The transformation of the Roman Mediterranean', in G. Holmes (ed.), *The Oxford Illustrated History of Medieval Europe* (Oxford, 1988), pp. 1–62.
 'Ethnic independence and cultural deference: the attitude of the Lombard principalities', *Byzantinoslavica: Revue International des Etudes Byzantines* 54:1 (1993), 5–12.

Bibliography

'Everyday life in Ravenna under Theoderic: an example of his "tolerance" and "prosperity"?', *Atti XIII CISAM* (Spoleto, 1993), 77–100.
'Gibbon, Hodgkin and the invaders of Italy', in R. McKitterick (ed.), *Edward Gibbon and Empire* (Cambridge, 1997), pp. 137–61.
Browning, R. *Medieval and Modern Greek* (London, 1969).
Brozzi, M., C. Calderini and M. Rotili. *L'Italia dei Longobardi* (Milan, 1980).
Bruckner, W. *Die Sprache der Langobarden* (Strasburg, 1895).
Brühl, C.R. *Fodrum, Gistum, Servitium Regis* (Cologne, 1968).
   Studien zu den langobardischen Königsurkunden, Bibliothek des deutschen historischen Instituts in Rom 33 (Tübingen, 1970).
'Chronologie und Urkunden der Herzöge von Spoleto im 8. Jahrhundert', *Quellen und Forschungen aus Italienischen Archiven und Bibliotheken* 51 (1972), 1–92.
'Langobardische Königsurkunden als Geschichtsquelle', in *Studi storici in onore di O. Bertolini* (Pisa, 1972) pp. 47–72.
'Zentral- und Finanzverwaltung im Franken- und im Langobardenreich', *Settimane* 20 (Spoleto, 1973), 64–91.
'Überlegungen zur Diplomatik der spoletinischen Herzogsurkunden', *Atti IX CISAM* (Spoleto, 1983), 124–63.
Bruhölzl, F. 'Der Bildungsauftrag der Hofschule', in B. Bischoff (ed.), *Karl der Grosse: Lebenswerk und Nachleben*, II, *Das Geistige Leben* (Düsseldorf, 1965), pp. 28–41.
   Geschichte der lateinischen Literatur des Mittlelalters, 2 vols. (Munich, 1975).
Brunner, H. *Zur Rechtsgeschichte der römischen und germanischen Urkunde*, I (Berlin, 1880).
   Forschungen zur Geschichte des deutschen und franzoesischen Rechts (Berlin, 1894).
   Deutsche Rechtsgeschichte, 3rd edn with C.F. von Schweim (Berlin, 1961).
Brusin, G. 'Epigrafi aquileisei in funzione di pietre miliari', *Atti dell'Istituto Veneto di Scienze, Lettere e Arti* 1.14 (1955–56), 281–90.
Buchner, R. *Die Rechtsquellen* (Weimar, 1953).
'Die römischen und die germanischen Wesenzüge in der neuen politischen Ordnung des Abendlandes', *Settimane* 5 (Spoleto, 1958), 247–78.
Bullough, D. 'The Counties of the "*regnum Italiae*" in the Carolingian period (774–888): a topographical study', *Papers of the British School at Rome* 23 (1955), 48–168.
   'Leo, *qui apud Hlotharium magni loci habebitur*', *Le Moyen Age* 67 (1961), 221–45.
   '"Baiuli" in the Carolingian "regnum Langobardorum" and the career of Abbot Waldo (+813)', *English Historical Review* 305 (1962), 625–37.
   'Le scuole cattedrali e la cultura dell'Italia settentrionale prima dei communi', *Italia Sacra* 5 (1964), 111–45.
   'An unnoticed medieval Italian *Staf(f)ile* "post, esp. boundary-post", and the significance of the place-names *Staffalo, Staffora*, etc.', *Zeitschrift für Romanische Philologie* 80 (1964), 465–77.
   'The Ostrogothic and Lombard Kingdoms', in D. Talbot Rice (ed.), *The Dark Ages* (London, 1965) pp. 167–74.
   'Urban change in early medieval Italy: the example of Pavia', *Papers of the British School at Rome* 34 (1966), 82–131.
   '*Europae Pater*: Charlemagne and his achievement in the light of recent scholarship', *English Historical Review* 85 (1970), 59–105.

'The writing office of the Dukes of Spoleto in the eighth century', in D. Bullough and R.L. Story (eds.), *The Study of Medieval Records: Essays in Honour of Kathleen Major* (Oxford, 1971), pp. 1–21.

'*Aula renovata*: the Carolingian court before the Aachen palace', *Proceedings of the British Academy* 71 (1985), 267–301, reprinted in D. Bullough, *Carolingian Renewal* (Manchester, 1991), pp. 123–60.

'Ethnic history and the Carolingians: an alternative reading of Paul the Deacon's *Historia Langobardorum*', in C. Holdsworth and T.P. Wiseman (eds.), *The Inheritance of Historiography 350–900*, Exeter Studies in History 12 (Exeter, 1990), pp. 85–105.

Carolingian Renewal: Sources and Heritage (Manchester, 1991).

'Reminiscence and reality: text, translation and testimony of an Alcuin letter', *Journal of Medieval Latin* 5 (1995), 174–201.

Burnham, J. *A Classical Technology Edited from Codex Lucensis 490* (Boston, 1920).

Cagiano de Azevedo, M. 'Memorie della vittoria sul Gargano e il culto di S. Michele a Milano', in C. Carletti and G. Otranto (eds.), *Il Santuario di S. Michele sul Gargano dal VI al IX secolo* (Bari, 1980), pp. 503–14.

Calasso, F. *Medio evo del diritto*, Le Fonti 1 (Milan, 1954).

Calderini, C. 'Il palazzo di Liutprando a Corteolona', *Contributi dell'Istituto di Archeologia* 5 (1975), 174–225.

Calisse, C. *Storia del diritto italiano*, I, *Le fonti* (Florence, 1930). Eng. edition *A History of Italian Law*, trans. L.B. Register, Continental Legal History Series 8 (Boston, 1928).

Cameron, A. *Procopius and the Sixth Century* (London, 1985).

'Texts as weapons: polemic in the Byzantine dark ages', in A. Bowman and G. Woolf (eds.), *Literacy and Power in the Ancient World* (Cambridge, 1994), pp. 198–215.

Cameron, A. and J. Herrin (eds.). *Constantinople in the Early Eighth Century: The Parastaseis Syntomoi Chronikai* (Leiden, 1984).

Cammarosano, P. and S. Gasparri (eds.). *Langobardia* (Udine, 1990).

Campana, A. 'Tutela dei beni epigrafici', *Epigrafica* 30 (1968), 5–8.

Cantino Wataghin, G. 'L'abbazia di Novalesa alla luce delle indagini archeologiche: verifiche e problemi', in *Dal Piemonte all'Europa: esperienze monastiche nella società medievale. XXXIV Congresso storico subalpino, Torino 1985* (Turin, 1988), pp. 569–85.

'Ricerche archeologiche all'abbazia di Novalesa (1978–81)', in *La Novalesa: ricerche, fonti documentarie, restauri* (Susa, 1988), pp. 329–57.

'Monasteri di età longobarda: spunti per una ricerca', *Corso di Cultura dell'Arte Ravennate e Bizantina* 36 (1989), 73–100.

'Monasterium in locum qui vocatur Sexto. L'archeologia per la storia dell'abbazia di S. Maria di Sesto', in G.C. Menis and A. Tilatti (eds.), *L'abbazia di S. Maria di Sesto fra archeologia e storia* (Pordenone, 1999), pp. 3–51.

Caratelli, G.P. (ed.). *Magistra Barbaritas: I Barbari in Italia* (Milan, 1984).

Caretta, A. 'Note sulle epigrafi longobarde di Laus Pompeia del Cremasco', *Archivio Storico Lombardo* 9:3 (1963), 174–95.

Carletti, C. 'Iscrizioni murali', in C. Carletti and G. Otranto (eds.), *Il Santuario di S. Michele sul Gargano dal VI al IX secolo* (Bari, 1980), pp. 7–180.

Bibliography

Carletti, C. and G. Otranto (eds.). *Il Santuario di San Michele sul Gargano dal VI al IX secolo: contributo alla storia della Langobardia meridionale*, Vetera Christianorum, Scavi e Ricerche 2, Atti del Convegno tenuto a Monte Sant'Angelo il 9–10 dicembre 1978 (Bari, 1980).

Carlton, C. *Studies in Romance Lexicology, Based on a Collection of Latin Documents from Ravenna (A.D. 445–700)*, University of North Carolina Studies in the Romance Languages and Literature 54 (Chapel Hill, 1965).

A Linguistic Analysis of a Collection of Late Latin Documents Composed in Ravenna between A.D. 445–700: A Quantitative Approach, Janua Linguarum Studia Memoriae Nicolai van Wijk Dedicata, Series Pratica 58 (The Hague and Paris, 1973).

Carruthers, M. *The Book of Memory: The Study of Memory in Medieval Culture* (Cambridge, 1990).

Casartelli Novelli, S. 'Confini e bottega provinciale delle Marittime nel divenire della scultura longobarda dai primi del VIII secolo all'anno 774', *Storia dell'Arte* 32 (1978), 11–22.

'L'immagine della croce nella scultura longobarda e nell'*entrelacs* carolingio della diocesi di Torino', in A.A. Schmid (ed.), *Riforma religiosa e arti nell'epoca carolingia. Atti del XXIV Congresso internazionale di storia dell'arte* (Bologna, 1983), pp. 109–15.

'Committenza e produzione scultorea "bassa"', *Settimane* 39:2 (Spoleto, 1992), 531–67.

Cassata, L. 'Sul metro (e sul testo) dell'Indovinello veronese', *Annali della Scuola Normale Superiore di Pisa*, cl. di lett. e fil., s.III, v.VIII fasc. (1978), 1229–36.

Castritius, H. 'Das romische Namensystem: von der Dreinamigkeit zur Einnamgkeit', in D. Geunich *et al.* (eds.), *Nomen et gens* (Berlin, 1997), pp. 30–40.

Cattaneo, E. 'Missionari orientali a Milano nell'età longobarda', *Archivio Storico Lombardo* (1963), 216–45.

Cau, E. 'Scrittura e cultura a Novara (secoli VIII–X)', *Ricerche Medievali* 6:9 (1971–74), 1–87.

Cavallo, G. 'La trasmissione dei tesi nell'area benevento-cassinese', *Settimane* 22 (Spoleto, 1975), 356–414.

'Aspetti della produzione dei libraria nell'Italia meridionale longobarda', in G. Cavallo (ed.), *Libri e lettori nel medioevo* (Rome and Bari, 1977), pp. 99–130.

'Scrittura, alfabetismo e produzione libraria nel tardo antico', in *La cultura in Italia fra tardo antico e alto medioevo*, II (Rome, 1981), pp. 523–38.

'Alfabetismo e circolazione del libro', in M. Vegetti (ed.), *Oralità, scrittura, spettacolo* (Turin, 1983), pp. 166–86.

'Le iscrizioni di Ravenna dei secoli VI–VIII. Tracce per uno studio grafico-culturale', *Corso di Cultura sull'Arte Ravennate e Bizantine* 31 (1984), 109–36.

'Libri e continuità della cultura antica in età barbarica', in G.P. Caratelli (ed.), *Magistra Barbaritas* (Milan, 1984), pp. 603–61.

'Dallo scriptorium senza biblioteca alla biblioteca senza scriptorium', in G. Cavallo (ed.), *Dall'eremo al cenobio* (Milan, 1987), pp. 331–424.

'Forme e ideologia della committenza libraria tra Oriente e Occidente', *Settimane* 39 (Spoleto, 1992), 617–45.

'Libri e cultura nelle due Italie longobarde', in C. Bertelli and G.P. Brogiolo (eds.), *Il futuro dei Longobardi: l'Italia e la costruzione dell'Europa di Carlo Magno. Saggi* (Milan, 2000), pp. 85–104.

Cavallo, G. (ed.). *Libri e lettori nel medioevo: guida storica e critica* (Rome and Bari, 1977).

Cavallo, G., C. Leonardi and E. Menestò (eds.), *Lo spazio letterario del medioevo. Medioevo Latino*, I.1, *La produzione del testo* (Rome, 1993).

Lo spazio letterario del medioevo. Il medioevo latino, I.2, *La circolazione del testo* (Rome, 1994).

Cavanna, A. 'Nuovi problemi intorno alle fonti dell'editto di Rothari', *Studia et Documenta Historiae et Iuris* 34 (1968), 269–361.

Cecchelli, C. 'L'arianesimo e le chiese ariane d'Italie', *Settimane* 7 (Spoleto, 1960), 743–74.

Cencetti, G. 'Scriptoria e scritture nel monachesimo benedettini', *Seltimane* 4 (Spoleto, 1957), 187–219; repr. in Cavallo (ed.), *Libri e lettori nel medioevo* (Rome and Bari, 1977), pp. 73–98.

Cesa, M. 'Etnografia e geografia nella visione storica di Procopius di Cesarea', *Studi Classici et Orientali* 32 (1982), 189–215.

Chadwick, H. *Boethius: The Consolations of Music, Logic, Theology and Philosophy* (Oxford, 1981).

Chazelle, C.M. 'Pictures, books and the illiterate: Pope Gregory I's letters to Serenus of Marseilles', *Word and Image* 6 (1990), 138 63.

Chiu, K. 'The introduction of spectacles into China', *Harvard Journal of Asiatic Studies* 1 (1936), 5–34.

Christ, K. *The Handbook of Medieval Library History*, rev. A. Kern, trans. T.M. Otto (Meteuchen, NJ and London, 1984).

Christie, N. 'The archaeology of Byzantine Italy: a synthesis of recent research', *Journal of Mediterranean Archaeology* 2:2 (1989), 249–93.

'Invasion or invitation? The Longobard occupation of northern Italy, A.D. 568–569', *Romanobarbarica* 11 (1991), 79–108.

'Longobard Weaponry and Warfare, A.D. 1–800', *Journal of Roman Military Equipment Studies* 2 (1991), 1–26.

'The survival of Roman settlement along the Middle Danube: Pannonia from the fourth to the tenth century A.D.', *Oxford Journal of Archaeology* 11:3 (1992), 317–39.

The Lombards (Oxford, 1995).

'Barren fields? Landscapes and settlements in Roman and post-Roman Italy', in G. Shipley and J. Salmon (eds.), *Human Landscapes in Classical Antiquity: Environment and Culture* (London, 1996), pp. 254–83.

Christou, K.P. *Byzanz und die Langobarden von der Ansiedlung in Pannonien bis zur endgultigen Anerkennung (500–680)* (Athens, 1991).

Cilento, N. *Italia Meridionale Longobarda*, 2nd edn (Milan and Naples, 1971).

Cipolla, C. *Literacy and Development in the West* (Harmondsworth, 1969).

Cipolla, C. (ed.). *Codici bobbiesi della Biblioteca Nazionale dell'Università di Torino* (Milan, 1936–39).

Monumenta novaliciensia vetustiora: raccolta degli atti e delle chronache riguardanti l'abbazia della Novalesa, Fonti per la Storia d'Italia 31–2 (Rome, 1898–1901).

Bibliography

Clanchy, M. *From Memory to Written Record: England 1066–1307*, 2nd edn (Oxford, 1993).
Clarke, H.B. and M. Brennan (eds.). *Columbanus and Merovingian Monasticism*, British Archaeological Reports, Int. Ser. 113 (Oxford, 1981).
Classen, P. 'Kaiserreskript und Königsurkunde: diplomatische Studien zum römisch-germanischen Kontinuitätsproblem', *Archiv für Diplomatik* 1 (1955), 1–87, and 2 (1956), 1–115.
  'Fortleben und Wandel spätrömischen Urkundenwesens im frühen Mittelalter', in P. Classen (ed.), *Recht und Schrift im Mittelalter*, Vorträge und Forschungen 23 (Sigmaringen, 1977), pp. 13–54.
  Kaiserreskript und Königsurkunde: Diplomatische Studien zum Problem der Kontinuität zwischen Altertum und Mittelalter, Byzantine Texts and Studies 15 (Thessalonika, 1977).
Collins, R. 'Theudebert I, *Rex Magnus Francorum*', in P. Wormald, D. Bullough and R. Collins (eds.), *Ideal and Reality in Frankish and Anglo–Saxon Society: Studies Presented to J.M. Wallace–Hadrill* (Oxford, 1983), pp. 7–33.
  'Visigothic law and regional custom in disputes in early medieval Spain', in W. Davies and P. Fouracre (eds.), *The Settlement of Disputes in Early Medieval Europe* (Cambridge, 1986), pp. 85–104.
  'Literacy and the laity in early medieval Spain', in R. McKitterick (ed.), *The Uses of Literacy in Early Medieval Europe* (Cambridge, 1990), pp. 109–33.
Colman, R.V. 'The abduction of women in barbarian law', *Florilegium* 5 (1983), 62–75.
Conti, P.M. 'L'uso dei titoli onorari ed aulici nel regno longobardo', in *Studi storici in onore di Ottorino Bertolini*, I (Pisa, 1972), pp. 105–76.
Conti, R. *Il tesoro: guida alla conoscenza del Tesoro del Duomo di Monza* (Monza, 1993).
Cornell, T. 'The tyranny of evidence: a discussion of the possible uses of literacy in Etruria and Latium in the Archaic age', in J. Humphreys (ed.), *Literacy in the Roman World* (Ann Arbor, 1991), pp. 7–34.
Cortese, E. 'Per la storia del mundio in Italia', *Rivista Italiana per le Scienze Giuridiche* 8 (1955–56), 323–474.
  'Il processo longobardo tra romanità e germanismo', *Settimane* 42 (Spoleto, 1994), 621–47.
Costamagna, G. and M. Amelotti. *Alle origini del notariato Italiano*, Studi Storici sul Notariato Italiano 2 (Rome, 1974).
Costambeys, M. 'The transmission of tradition: Gregorian influence and innovation in eighth-century Italian monasticism', in Y. Hen and M. Innes (eds.), *The Uses of the Past in the Early Middle Ages* (Cambridge, 2000), pp. 78–101.
Courtois, C. et al. (eds.). *Tablettes Albertini: actes privés de l'époque vandale* (Paris, 1952).
Cracco Ruggini, L. *Economia e società nell'Italia annonaria* (Milan, 1961).
  'Vicende rurali dell'Italia antica dall'età tetrarchia ai Longobardi', *Rivista Storica Italiana* 76 (1974), 261–84.
Cressy, D. *Literacy and Social Order: Reading and Writing in Tudor and Stuart England* (Cambridge, 1980).
Croke, B. 'A.D. 474: the manufacture of a turning point', *Chiron* 13 (1983), 81–119.
Crombie, A. *Augustine to Galileo*, 2 vols., 3rd edn in 1 vol. (London, 1979).

Bibliography

Curtius, E.R. *European Literature in the Latin Middle Ages*, trans. W.R. Trask (New York, 1953).

Cuscito, G. 'Venanzio Fortunato e le chiese Istriane', *Atti e memorie della Società Istriana di Archeologia e storia patria* 78 (Trieste, 1978), 9–25.

'La politica religiosa della corte Longobarda di fronte allo scisma dei Tre Capitoli', *Atti VI CISAM* (Spoleto, 1980), 375–82.

D'Arco Silvio Avalle, G. *Bassa latinità: il latino tra l'età tardo-antica e l'alto medioevo con particulare riguardo all'origine delle lingue romanze. Consonantismo* (Turin, 1969).

Darmstäder, P. *Das Reichsgut in der Lombardei und Piemont, 568–1250* (Strasburg, 1896).

Davies, W. and P. Fouracre (eds.). *The Settlement of Disputes in Early Medieval Europe* (Cambridge, 1986).

Deichmann, F. *Ravenna: Haupstadt des spätantiken Abendlandes*, 3 vols. (Wiesbaden, 1969–76).

Dekkers, E. *Clavis patrum latinorum* (Steenbrugis, 1961; 2nd edn 1995).

Del Giudice, P. 'Le tracce di diritto romano nelle leggi longobarde', in *Studi di storia e diritto* (Milan, 1889), pp. 262–409.

Delogu, P. 'I Longobardi e la scrittura', *in Studi storici in onore di Ottorino Bertolini*, I (Pisa, 1972), pp. 313–24.

Mito di una città meridionale: Salerno, secoli VII–IX (Naples, 1977).

'Il regno longobardo', in G. Galasso (ed.), *Storia d'Italia*, I (Turin, 1980).

'Longobardi e Romani: altre congetture', in P. Cammarosano and P. Gasparri (eds.), *Langobardia* (Udine, 1990), pp. 111–64.

'Patroni, donatori, committenti nell'Italia meridionale longobarda', *Settimane* 39 (Spoleto, 1992), 303–34.

'Lombard and Carolingian Italy', in R. McKitterick (ed.), *NCMH*, II (Cambridge, 1995), pp. 290–319.

Derrida, J. *Of Grammatology*, trans. G.C. Spivak (Baltimore, 1976).

Diaz y Diaz, M.C. 'Un document privé de l'Espagne wisigothique sur ardoise', *Studi Medievali* 3rd ser., 1 (1960), 52–71.

Diehl, C. *Etudes sur l'administration byzantine dans l'exarchat de Ravenne (568–751)* (Paris, 1888).

Diesner, H.J. 'Bemerkungen zur schriftlichen Kultur der Langobarden in Italien', *Philologus* 119 (1975), 264–6.

Di Majo, A., C. Federici and M. Palma. 'La pergamena dei codici altomedievali italiani', *Scriptorium* 39 (1985), 3–12.

Diurni, G. *Le situazioni possessorie nel medioevo: età longobardo-franca* (Milan, 1988).

Di Virgilio, R. 'I buoi "dipari" dell'Indovinello veronese', *Giornale Italiano di Filologia* 15/36:1 (1984), 39–50.

Dold, A. 'Zwei Doppelblätter in Unziale des 7. Jahrhundert mit Text aus den Dialogs Gregor der Grosse', *Zentralblatt für Bibliothekswesen* 55 (1938), 253–8.

'Zum Longobardengesetz', *Deutsches Archiv für Geschichte des Mittelalters* 32 (1941), 1–27.

Zur ältesten Handschrift des Edictus Rothari (Stuttgart, 1955).

DuCange, C.D. *Glossarium mediae et infimae latinitatis*, 10 vols. (London and Niort, 1884–87).

Bibliography

Duchesne, L. 'Les évêchés italiens pendant l'invasion lombarde par Mgr Duchesne', in G. Barni (ed.), *La Conquête de l'Italie par les Lombards*, Le Mémorial des siècles. Les Evénements du sixième siècle (Paris, 1975), pp. 387–418.

Dumville, David N. 'Kingship, genealogies, and regnal lists', in P. Sawyer and I. Wood (eds.), *Early Medieval Kingship* (Leeds, 1977) pp. 72–104.

Dunn, M. 'Mastering Benedict: monastic rules and their authors in the early medieval West', *EHR* 105 (1990), 567–94.

Durando, E. *Il tabellionato o notariato nelle leggi romane, nelle leggi medievali italiane e posteriori* (Turin, 1897).

Durliat, J. 'Le salaire de la paix sociale dans les royaumes barbares', in H. Wolfram and A. Schwarcz (eds.), *Anerkennung und Integration* (Vienna, 1988), pp. 21–72.

De la Ville antique à la ville byzantine: le problème des subsistances (Rome, 1990).

Les Finances publiques de Dioclétien aux Carolingiens (284–889) (Sigmaringen, 1990).

Eigler, U. 'Die *vita walfredi*. Ein spätes Zeugnis "langobardischer" Literatur', in K. Schmidt (ed.), *Vita Walfredi und Kloster Monteverdi* (Tübingen, 1991), pp. 64–74.

Elze, R. 'Die Agilulfkrone des Schatzes von Monza', in H. Beumann (ed.), *Historische Forschungen für W. Schlesinger* (Cologne and Vienna, 1974), pp. 167–84.

Engels, L.J. *Observations sur le vocabulaire de Paul Diacre*, Latinitatis Christianorum Primaeva 16 (Nijmegen, 1961).

Everett, N. 'Barbarian ethnicity and Italian history in Alessandro Manzoni's *Adelchi*', *Convivio: Journal of Ideas in Italian Studies* 6:2 (2000), 112–27.

'The hagiography of Lombard Italy', *Hagiographica* 7 (2000), 49–126.

'Scribes and charters in Lombard Italy', *Studi Medievali* 3rd ser., 41:1 (2000), 39–83.

'The *Liber de apparitione S. Michaelis de Gargano* and the hagiography of dispossession', *Analecta Bollandiana* 120 (2002), 364–91.

Everett, N. and Michel Gorman. 'The *Interrogationes de littera et de vetere testamento*: an eighth-century school text from northeastern Italy (Verona?)', in M. Gorman (ed.), *Lo studio della Bibbia nell'alto medioevo* (forthcoming).

Falkenhausen, V. von. 'I Longobardi meridionali', in *Il mezzogiorno dai Bizantini a Frederico II*, Storia d'Italia III (Turin, 1980), pp. 251–370.

Fanning, S.C. 'Lombard Arianism reconsidered', *Speculum* 56:2 (1981), 241–58.

Fasoli, G. *I Langobardi in Italia* (Bologna, 1965).

Fauber, L. *Narses: Hammer of the Goths* (New York, 1990).

Favreau, R. 'Les Commanditaires dans les inscriptions du haut moyen âge occidental', *Settimane* 39:12 (Spoleto, 1992), 681–722.

Feist, S. *Etymologisches Wörterbuch der gotischen Sprache*, 2nd edn (Halle, 1923).

Ferrari, M. 'Le scoperte a Bobbio nel 1493: vicende di codici e fortuna di testi', *Italia Medievale e Umanistica* 13 (1970), 144–51.

'In Papia conveniant ad Dungalum', *Italia Medioevale e Umanistica* 15 (1972), 1–52.

'Spigilature bobbiesi', *Italia Medioevale e Umanistica* 16 (1973), 9–30.

'Centri di trasmissione: Monza, Pavia, Milano, Bobbio', *Settimane* 22 (Spoleto, 1975), 303–20.

'Libri e testi prima del Mille', in G. Cracco, *Storia della Chiesa di Ivrea: dalle origini al XV secolo* (Rome, 1998), pp. 511–17.

Bibliography

Ferrari, M. and A. Belloni. *La biblioteca capitolare di Monza*, Medioevo e Umanesimo 21 (Milan, 1974).
Fischer-Drew, K. (trans.). *The Lombard Laws*, Sources of Medieval History (Philadelphia, 1973).
Fischetti, G. *Mercurio Mithra Michael: magia mito e misteri nella grotta dell'Arcangelo* (Monte Sant'Angelo, 1973).
Flint, V. *The Rise of Magic in Early Medieval Europe* (Oxford, 1991).
Fonseca, C.D. 'Longobardia minore e Longobardi nell'Italia meridionale', in P. Caratelli (ed.) *Magistra Barbaritas* (Milan, 1984), pp. 127–84.
Fouracre, P. '"*Placita*" and the settlement of disputes in later Merovingian Francia', in W. Davies and P. Fouracre (eds.), *The Settlement of Disputes in Early Medieval Europe* (Cambridge, 1986), pp. 23–44.
Fouracre, P. and G.A. Geberding. *Late Merovingian France: History and Hagiography 640–720* (Manchester, 1996).
Franklin, J.L. Jr. 'Literacy and the parietal inscriptions of Pompei', in J. Humphreys (ed.), *Literacy in the Roman World* (Ann Arbor, MI, 1991), pp. 77–98.
Francovich, R. and G. Noyé (eds.). *La storia dell'altomedioevo italiano alla luce dell'archeologia* (Florence, 1994).
Frankovich, G. De. 'Il problema della scultura cosiddetta "longobarda"', *Atti I CISAM* (Spoleto, 1952), 255–76.
Frau, G. 'Contributo alla conoscenza dell'elemento longobardo nella toponomastica friuliana', *Atti del convegno di studi longobardi* (Udine, 1970), 165–93.
Frezza, P. *L'influsso del diritto Romano Giustinaiano nelle formule e nella prassi in Italia*, Ius Romanum Medii Aevi 1, 2, c ee (Milan, 1974).
Friedrichsen, G.W. *The Gothic Version of the Gospels: A Study of Its Style and Textual History* (Oxford, 1926),
 The Gothic Version of the Epistles (Oxford, 1936).
Friend, W.H.C. 'The missions of the early church 180–700 A.D.', *Miscellanea Historiae Christianae* 3 (1970), 3–23.
Fritz Volbach, W. 'Die langobardische Kunst und ihre byzantinischen Einflüsse', in *La civiltà dei Longobardi in Europa*, Problemi attuali di scienza e storia 189, Accademia Nazionale dei Lincei (Rome, 1974), pp. 144–56.
Fröschl, J.M. 'Imperitia litterarum. Zur Frage der Beachlichkeit des Analphabetismus im römischen Recht', *Zeitschrift der Savigny-Stiftung für Rechtsgeschichte. Romanistiche Abteilung* 104 (1987), 84–155.
Fuchs, S. *Die langobardischen Goldblattkreuze aus der Zone südwärts der Alpen* (Berlin, 1938).
Fumagalli, V. *Coloni e signori nell'Italia settentrionale: secoli VI–XI* (Bologna, 1978).
Gabotto, F. *Storia dell'Italia occidentale nel medio evo, 395–1313*, Biblioteca della Società Storica Subalpina 61–62 (Turin, 1911).
Gailbraith, V.H. 'The Literacy of Medieval English Kings', *Proceedings of the British Academy* 21 (1935), 205–243.
Galante, M. 'Il notaio e il documento notarile a Salerno in epoca longobarda', in *Per una storia del notariato meridionale*, Studi Storici sul Notariato Italiano 6 (Rome, 1982), pp. 71–94.
Gamillscheg, E. *Romania Germanica: Sprach und Siedlungsgeschichte der Germanen auf dem Boden des alten Römerreichs*, 2 vols. (Berlin, 1934–36).

Bibliography

Ganshof, F.L. 'The use of the written word in Charlemagne's administration', in F.L. Ganshof, *The Carolingians and the Frankish Monarchy: Studies in Carolingian History*, trans. J. Sondheimer (Ithaca, NY, 1971), pp. 125–42.

Ganz, D. 'The preconditions for Caroline minuscule', *Viator* 18 (1987), 23–43.

'The Luxeuil Prophets and Merovingian missionary Strategies', *Yale University Library Gazette* 66 (1991), supplement (= R. Babcock (ed.), *Beinecke Studies in Early Manuscripts* (New Haven, 1991), pp. 105–16.)

'Books and book production', in R. McKitterick (ed.), *NCMH*, II, (Cambridge, 1995), pp. 786–808.

Ganz, D. (ed.). *The Role of the Book in Medieval Culture*, 2 vols., Bibliologia, Elementa ad Librorum Studia Pertinentia 3–4 (Brepols, 1986).

Ganz, D. and W. Goffart. 'Charters earlier than 800 from French collections', *Speculum* 65 (1990), 906–32.

Gardiner, K.H.J. 'Paul the Deacon and Secundus of Trent', in B. Croke and A. Emmet (eds.), *History and Historians in Late Antiquity* (Sydney, 1983), pp. 147–53.

Gasparri, S. *I duchi longobardi* (Rome, 1978).

'La questione degli Arimanni', *Bullettino dell'Istituto Storico Italiano per il Medioevo* 87 (1978), 121–53.

'Grandi proprietari e sovrani nell'Italia longobarda del VIII secolo', *Atti VI CISAM* (Spoleto, 1980), pp. 429–42.

La cultura tradizionale dei Longobardi: struttura tribale e resistenze pagane (Spoleto, 1983).

'Strutture militari e legami di dipendenza in età longobarda e carolingia', *Rivista Storica Italiana* 98 (1986), 664–726.

'Pavia longobarda', in *Storia di Pavia*, II, *L'alto medioevo* (Milan, 1987), pp. 19–68.

'Il regno e la legge. Longobardi, Romani e Franchi nello sviluppo dell'ordinamento pubblico (secoli VI–X)', *La Cultura* 28 (1990), 243–66.

'Il regno longobardo in Italia. Struttura e funzionamento di uno stato altomedievale', in P. Cammarosano and S. Gasparri (eds.), *Langobardia*, (Udine, 1990) pp. 237–305.

Prima delle nazioni: populi, etnie e regni fra Antichità e Medioevo (Milan, 1997).

Gaudenzi, A. 'Il monastero di Nonantola, il ducato di Persiceta, e la chiesa di Bologna', *Bullettino dell'Istituto Storico Italiano* 22 (1901), 77–214.

Gaur, A. *A History of Writing*, rev. edn (London, 1992).

Geary, P. 'Ethnic identity as a situational construct in the early middle ages', *Mitteilungen der Anthropologischen Gesellschaft in Wien* 113 (1983), 15–26.

'Extrajudicial means of conflict resolution', *Settimane* 42 (Spoleto, 1994), 569–602.

George, J. *Venantius Fortunatus: A Latin Poet in Merovingian Gaul* (Oxford, 1992).

Geunich, D., W. Haubrichs and J. Jarnut (eds.). *Nomen et gens: zur historischen Aussagekraft frühmittelalterlicher Personennamen. Ergänzungsbände zum Reallexicon der germanischen Altertumskunde* (Berlin, 1997).

Giardina, A. (ed.). *Società romana e impero tardoantico*, III, *Le merci, gli insediamenti* (Rome and Bari, 1986).

Gibbon, E. *The Decline and Fall of the Roman Empire*, ed. J.B.Bury, 7 vols. (London, 1896–1909).

Gibson, M. (ed.) *Boethius: His Life, Thought and Influence* (Oxford, 1981).

Bibliography

Giulotta, G. *Gli antichi cataloghi e i codici della Abbazia di Nonantola*, Studi e Testi 181 (Vatican City, 1955).
Godman, P. *Poetry of the Carolingian Renaissance* (London, 1985).
Goffart, W. *Barbarians and Romans: The Techniques of Accommodation* (Princeton, 1980).
'Old and new in Merovingian taxation', *Past and Present* 96 (1982), 3–21.
'Paul the Deacon's "*Gesta episcoporum mettensium*" and the early design of Charlemagne's succession', *Traditio* 42 (1986), 59–93.
The Narrators of Barbarian History A.D. 550–800: Jordanes, Gregory of Tours, Bede and Paul the Deacon (Toronto, 1988).
'Two notes on Germanic antiquity today', *Traditio* 50 (1995), 9–30.
Golinelli, P. 'Il cristianesimo nella "Venetia" altomedievale. Diffusione, istituzionalizzazione e forme di religiosità dalle origini al secolo X', in A. Castagnetti and G.M. Varanni (eds.), *Il Veneto nel medioevo: dalla Venetia alla Marca Veronese* (Verona, 1989), I, pp. 237–331.
Città e culto dei santi nel medioevo italiano, 2nd edn (Bologna, 1991).
Goody, J. (ed.). *Literacy in Traditional Societies* (Cambridge, 1968).
The Domestication of the Savage Mind (Cambridge, 1977).
The Logic of Writing and the Organisation of Society (Cambridge, 1986).
Goody, J. and Ian Watt, 'The consequences of literacy', in J. Goody (ed.), *Literacy in Traditional Societies* (Cambridge, 1968), pp. 27–68.
Gordon, A.E. *Illustrated Introduction to Ancient Roman Epigraphy* (Berkeley and London, 1983).
Gorman, M. 'The earliest manuscript tradition of St Augustine's *Confessions*', *Journal of Theological Studies* 34 (1983), 114–45.
'Wigbod and biblical studies under Charlemagne', *RB* 107 (1997), 40–76.
'The myth of Hiberno-Latin exegesis', *RB* 110 (2000), 42–85.
'Peter of Pisa and the *Quaestiunculae* copied for Charlemagne in Brussels II 2572, with a note on the Codex Diezianus from Verona', *RB* 110 (2000), 238–60.
Gough, K. 'The implications of literacy in traditional China', in J. Goody (ed.), *Literacy in Traditional Societies* (Cambridge, 1968), pp. 69–83.
Grabar, A. 'Essai sur l'art des Lombards en Italie', *La civiltà dei Longobardi in Europa*, Problemi attuali di scienza e storia, Accademia Nazionale dei Lincei (Rome, 1974), pp. 25–44.
Graff, H.J. *The Literacy Myth: Literacy and Social Structure in the Nineteenth Century City* (New York, 1979).
The Legacies of Literacy: Continuities and Contradictions in Western Culture and Society (Bloomington, 1987).
Graff, H.J. (ed.). *Literacy and Social Development in the West: A Reader* (Cambridge, 1981).
Grandgent, C.H. *From Latin to Italian: An Historical Outline of the Phonology and Morphology of the Italian Language* (Cambridge, MA, 1927).
Graus, F. Review of Wenskus' *Stammesbildung, Historica* 7 (1963), 185–91.
Volk, Herrscher und Heiliger im Reich der Merowinger (Prague, 1965).
Gray, N. 'The palaeography of Latin inscriptions in the eighth and ninth centuries in Italy', *Papers of the British School at Rome* 16 (1948), 38–170.
'The Filocalian Letter', *Papers of the British School at Rome* 24 (1956), 1–23.
The History of Lettering: Creative Experiment and Letter Identity (Oxford, 1986).

Bibliography

Grazi, V. 'Le parole lombarde di origine longobarda', *I Longobardi e la Lombardia: Saggi* (Milan, 1978), pp. 45–53.
Green, D.H. 'Orality and reading: the state of research in medieval studies', *Speculum* 65 (1990), 267–81.
Greenhalgh, M. *The Survival of Roman Antiquities in the Middle Ages* (London, 1989).
Grierson, P. 'The silver coinage of the Lombards', *Archivio Storico Lombardo* 6 (1956), 130–47.
'Symbolism in early medieval charters and coins', *Settimane* 23 (Spoleto, 1976), 603–30.
Grimm, J. and W. Grimm. *Deutsche Sagen*; Eng. trans. Donald Ward, *The German Legends of the Brothers Grimm*, 2 vols. (Philadelphia, 1981).
Grundmann, H. '*Litteratus–illiteratus*: der Wandal einer Bildungsnorm vom Altertum zum Mittelalter', *Archiv für Kulturgeschichte* 40 (1958), 1–66.
Gryson, R. *Le Recueil arien de Vérone*, Instrumenta Patristica (The Hague, 1992).
Gschwantler, O. 'Die Heldensage von Alboin und Rosamund', in H. Birkhan (ed.), *Festschrift für Otto Höfler zum 75. Geburtstag*, Philologia Germanica 3 (Vienna and Stuttgart, 1976), pp. 214–47.
'Formen langobardischer mündlicher Überlieferung', *Jahrbücher für Internationale Germanistik* 11 (1979), 58–85.
Gualazzini, U. 'La scuola pavese con particolare riguardo all'insegnamento del diritto', *Atti IV CISAM* (Spoleto, 1969), 35–73.
Guerra D'Antoni, F. 'A new perspective of the Veronese riddle', *Romance Philology* 36 (1982), 185–200.
Guerra-Medici, M.T. *I diritti delle donne nelle società altomedievale*, Ius Nostrum serie 2a:4 (Naples, 1986).
Guillou, A. *Studies in Byzantine Italy* (London, 1970).
'L'école dans l'Italie byzantine', *Settimane* 19 (Spoleto, 1978), 291–311.
Gulli, L. 'A proposito della più antica tradizione novalicense', *Archivio Storico Italiano* 117 (1959), 306–18.
Haberl, J. and C. Hawkes. 'The last of Roman Noricum: St. Severin on the Danube', in C. and S. Hawkes (eds.), *Greeks, Celts and Romans* (London, 1973), pp. 96–156.
Hachman, R. *Die Goten und Skandinavien*, Quellen und Forschungen zu Sprach- und Kulturgeschichte der germanischen Völker 34 (Berlin, 1970).
Haldon, J.F. *Byzantium in the Seventh Century: The Transformation of a Culture* (Cambridge, 1992).
Hallenbeck, J.T. *Pavia and Rome: The Lombard Monarchy and the Papacy in the Eighth Century*, American Philosophical Society, Transactions 72:4 (1982).
Harris, W. 'Literacy and epigraphy, I', *Zeitschrift für Papyrologie und Epigraphik* 52 (1983), 87–111.
Ancient Literacy (Cambridge, MA and London, 1989).
'*Instrumentum domesticum* and Roman literacy', in *Acta Colloqui Epigraphici Latini* (Sept. 1991), Commentationes Humanarum Litterarum 104 (Rome, 1995), pp. 19–27.
Harrison, D. 'Dark Age migrations and subjective ethnicity: the example of the Lombards', *Scandia* 57:1 (1991), 19–36.
The Early State and the Towns: Forms of Integration in Lombard Italy, AD 568–774, Lund Studies in International History 29 (Lund, 1993).

Bibliography

Hartmann, L.M. *Geschichte Italiens im Mittelalter*, 4 vols. (Gotha, 1900).
  Zur Wirtschaftgeschichte Italiens im frühen Mittelalter (Gotha, 1904).
  'Italy under the Lombards', in *The Cambridge Medieval History*, II (Cambridge, 1911), pp. 194–221.
Hauk, K. 'Lebensnormen und Kulturmythen in germanischen Stammes- und Herrschergeneaologien', *Saeculum* 6 (1955), 182–223.
Hauptfeld, G. 'Zur langobardischen Eroberung Italiens. Das Heer und die Bischöfe', *Mitteilungen des Instituts für Österreichische Geschichtsforschung* 91 (Vienna, Cologne and Graz, 1983), 40–53.
Havelock, E.A. *Preface to Plato* (Cambridge, 1963)
  Prologue to Greek Literacy (Cincinatti, 1971).
  Origins of Western Literacy (Toronto, 1976).
  The Literate Revolution in Ancient Greece and Its Cultural Consequences (Princeton, 1982).
Heather, P. 'Cassiodorus and the rise of the Amals: genealogy and the Goths under Hun domination', *Journal of Roman Studies* 79 (1989), 103–28.
  'The historical culture of Ostrogothic Italy', *Atti XIII CISAM* (Spoleto, 1993), 317–53.
  'Literacy and power in the migration period', in A. Bowman and G. Woolf (eds.), *Literacy and Power in the Ancient World* (Cambridge, 1994), pp. 177–97.
  'The Huns and the end of the Roman empire in Western Europe', *EHR* 110 (1995), 4–41.
  'Theoderic, king of the Goths', *EME* 4:2 (1995), 145–74.
  The Goths (Oxford, 1996).
  'Signs of ethnic identity: disappearing and reappearing tribes', in W. Pohl and H. Reimitz (eds.), *Strategies of Distinction: The Construction of Ethnic Communities, 300–800* (Leiden, Boston and Cologne, 1998), pp. 95–112.
Heather, P. and J.F. Matthews. *The Goths in the Fourth Century* (Liverpool, 1991).
Hen, Y. *Culture and Religion in Merovingian Gaul A.D. 481–751* (Leiden, 1995).
Hen, Y. and M. Innes (eds.), *The Uses of the Past in the Early Middle Ages* (Cambridge, 2000).
Hendy, M.F. *Studies in the Byzantine Monetary Economy, c. 300–1450* (Cambridge, 1985).
Herman, J. 'La situation linguistique en Italie au VI siècle', *Revue de Linguistique Romane* 52 (1988), 55–67.
  'Sur un exemple de la langue parlée à Rome au VIe siècle', in G. Calbioli and S. Guartiero (eds.), *Latin vulgaire–Latin tardif II* (Tübingen, 1990), pp. 145–57.
  'Spoken and written Latin in the last centuries of the Roman empire. A contribution to linguistic history of the western provinces', in R. Wright (ed.), *Latin and the Romance Languages in the Early Middle Ages* (London, 1991), pp. 29–43.
  Le Latin vulgaire (Paris, 1967); trans. R. Wright, *Vulgar Latin* (University Park, PA, 2000).
Herrin, J. *The Formation of Christendom* (Princeton, 1987).
Herzig, E. 'Die langobardische Fragmente in der Abtei S. Pietro in Ferentillo', *Römische Quartalschrift für Christlichen Altertumskunde und für Kirchengeschichte* 20 (1906), 49–81.

Bibliography

Hessen, O. von 'Considerazioni sull'anello a sigillo di Rodchis proveniente dalla tomba n.2 del cimeterio Longobardo di Trezzo sull'Adda', *Quaderni Ticinensi* 7 (1978), 267–73.
    'Anelli a sigillo longobardi con ritratti regali', *Quaderni Ticinensi* 11 (1982), 305–14.
Hillgarth, J.H. 'Popular religion in Visigothic Spain', in E. James (ed.), *Visigothic Spain: New Approaches* (Oxford, 1980), pp. 3–60.
Hodges, R. *Dark Age Economics* (1982).
    'The riddle of St. Peter's Republic', in *La storia economica di Roma nell'alto medioevo alla luce dei recenti scavi archeologici*, Biblioteca di Archeologia Medievale (Florence, 1993), pp. 353–67.
    'In the shadow of Pirenne: San Vincenzo al Volturno and the revival of Mediterranean commerce', in R. Francovich and G. Noye (eds.), *La storia dell'alto medioevo italiano (VI–X secolo) alla luce dell'archeologia* (Florence, 1994), pp. 109–27.
Hodges, R. (ed.). *San Vincenzo al Volturno 1: The 1980–86 Excavations*, Archaeological Monographs of the British School at Rome 7. (London, 1993).
Hodges, R. and J. Mitchell (eds.). *San Vincenzo al Volturno: The Archeology, Art and Territory of an Early Medieval Monastery*, British Archaeological Reports Int. Ser. 252 (Oxford, 1985).
Hodges, R. and D. Whitehouse. *Mohammed, Charlemagne and the Origins of Europe: Archaeology and the Pirenne Thesis* (Ithaca, NY, 1983).
Hodgkin, T. *Italy and Her Invaders*, 8 vols. (London, 1892–99).
    'Sulla relazione ethnologica fra i Longobardi e gli Angli', in *XI Centenario di Paulo Diacono: Atti e memorie del Congresso storico* (Cividale, 1900), pp. 150–63.
Horsfall, N. 'Statistics or states of mind', in J. Humphreys (ed.), *Literacy in the Roman World*, pp. 59–76.
Hout, M. van der. 'Gothic palimpsests of Bobbio', *Scriptorium* 6 (1952), 87–98.
Humphreys, J.H. (ed.). *Literacy in the Roman World*, Journal of Roman Archaeology Suppl. Ser. 3 (Ann Arbor, 1991).
Hyde, J.K. *Literacy and Its Uses: Studies on Late Medieval Italy*, ed. D. Waley (Manchester and New York, 1993).
    'Medieval descriptions of cities', *Bulletin of the John Rylands Library* 48 (1965–66), 308–40. Reprinted in J.K. Hyde, *Literacy and Its Uses* (Manchester and New York, 1993), pp. 1–32.
Innes, M. 'Memory, orality and literacy in an early medieval society', *Past and Present* 158 (1998), 3–36.
Innes, M. and R. McKitterick. 'The writing of history', in R. McKitterick (ed.), *Carolingian Culture* (Cambridge, 1994), pp. 193–220.
Irvine, M. *The Making of a Textual Culture: 'Grammatica' and Literary Theory, 350–1100* (Cambridge, 1994).
    State and Society in the Early Middle Ages: The Middle Rhine Valley 400–1000 (Cambridge, 2000).
Jacobi, R. *Die Quellen der Langobardengeschichte des Paulus Diaconus* (Halle, 1877).
James, E. *The Franks* (Oxford, 1988).
Jarnut, J. *Prosographische und sozialgeschichtliche Studien zum Langobardenreich in Italien (568–774)*, Bonner historische Forschungen 38 (Bonn, 1972).
    Bergamo 568–1098: Verfassung-, Sozial- und Wirtschaftsgeschichte einer langobardischen Stadt im Mittelalter (Wiesbaden, 1979)

Geschichte der Langobarden (Stuttgart, 1982).
'Zur Frügeschichte der Langobarden', *Studi Medievali* 3rd ser., 24:1 (1983), 1–16.
'Die langobardische Ethnogenese', in H. Wolfram and W. Pohl (eds.), *Typen der Ethnogenese unter besondere Berücksichtigung der Bayern*, I (Vienna, 1990), pp. 97–102.
'I Longobardi nell'epoca precedente all'occupazione dell'Italia', in P. Cammarosano and S. Gasparri (eds.), *Langobardia* (Udine, 1990), pp. 3–34.
'Nobilis non vilis, cuius et nomen et genus scitur – a quotation from Isidore of Seville', in D. Geunich, W. Haubrichs and J. Jarnut (eds.), *Nomen et gens* (Berlin, 1997), pp. 116–26.

Jenal, G. *Italia ascetica atque monastica: des Asketen- und Monchtum in Italien von den Anfangen bis zur Zeit der Langobarden (ca. 150/250–604)*, 2 vols., Monographien zur Geschichte des Mittelalters 39 (Stuttgart, 1995).

Johnson, J. *Compositiones variae, from Codex 490, Biblioteca Capitolare, Lucca, Italy*, Illinois Studies in Language and Literature 23, no. 3 (Urbana, 1939).

Johnson, M. 'Toward a history of Theoderic's building program', *Dumbarton Oaks Papers* 42 (1988), 73–96.

Jones, A.H.M. *Later Roman Empire: A Social, Ecomomic and Administrative Survey*, 2 vols. (Oxford, 1973).

Kaster, R.A. 'Notes on primary and secondary schools in late antiquity', *Transactions of the American Philological Association* 113 (1983), 323–46.
Guardians of the Language: The Grammarians and Society in Late Antiquity (Berkeley, 1988).

Kaufmann, M.W. 'Spare ribs: the conception of women in the middle ages and the Renaissance', *Soundings* 56:2 (1973), 135–61.

Kelly, C. 'Later Roman bureaucracy: going through the files', in A. Bowman and G. Woolf (eds.), *Literacy and Power in the Ancient World* (Cambridge, 1994), pp. 161–76.

Kelly, S. 'Anglo-Saxon lay society and the written word', in R. McKitterick (ed.), *The Uses of Literacy in Early Medieval Europe* (Cambridge, 1990), pp. 36–62.

Keppie, L. *Understanding Roman Inscriptions* (London, 1991).

Kessler, H.L. '*Facies bibliothecae revelata*: Carolingian art as spiritual seeing', *Settimane* 41.2 (Spoleto, 1993), 533–94.

Keynes, S. 'Royal government and the written word in late Anglo-Saxon England', in R. McKitterick (ed.), *The Uses of Literacy in Early Medieval Europe* (Cambridge, 1990), pp. 226–57.

Kindersley, D. and L. Lopes Cardozo. *Letters Slate Cut: Workshop Philosophy and Practice* (Cambridge, 1990) (sequel to 1981 edn).

Kiszely, I. *The Anthropology of the Lombards*, British Archaeological Reports, Int. Ser. 61, 2 vols. (Oxford, 1979).
'On the true face of the Lombards', *La cultura in Italia fra tardo antico e alto medioevo*, 2 vols. (Rome, 1981), pp. 54–83.

Kloos, R.M. 'Methoden und Möglichkeiten der lateinischen Epigraphik des Mittelalters', in *Actes du VIIe Congrès international d'épigraphie grecque et latine* (Bucharest and Paris, 1979), pp. 91–103.

Bibliography

'Zum Stil der langobardischen Steininschriften des achten Jahrhunderts', *Atti X CISAM* (Spoleto, 1980), 169–82.
'Die frühmittelalterliche lateinische Epigraphik', in *La cultura in Italia fra tardo antico e alto medioevo*, II (Rome, 1981), pp. 103–32.
Klos, H. 'Neue Fragmente des Hilarius-Papyruskodex', *Mitteilungen des Instituts für Oesterreichische Geschichtsforshung* 63 (1955), 47–52.
Kurze W. 'Zur Kopiertätikeit Gregors von Catino', *Quellen und Forschungen aus Italienischen Archiven und Bibliotheken* 53 (1973), 409–65.
'La lamina di Agilulfo: usurpazione o diritto?', *Atti VI CISAM* (Spoleto, 1980), 224–61.
La Rocca, C. 'Trasformazioni della città altomedievale in "Langobardia"', *Studi Storici* 4 (1989), 993–1011.
Pacifico di Verona: il passato carolingio nella costruzione della memoria urbana (Rome, 1995).
'Using the Roman past. Abandoned towns and local power in eleventh century Piemonte', *EME* 5:1 (1996), 45–69.
'A man for all seasons: Pacificus of Verona and the creation of a local Carolingian past', in Y. Hen and M. Innes (eds.), *The Uses of the Past in the Early Middle Ages* (Cambridge, 2000), pp. 250–77.
Laistner, M.L.W. *Thought and Letters in Western Europe, A.D. 500 to 900* (London, 1957).
Lane Fox, R. 'Literacy and power in early Christianity', in A.K. Bowman and G. Woolf (eds.), *Literacy and Power in the Ancient World* (Cambridge, 1994), pp. 126–48.
Lanzoni, F. *Le diocesi d'Italia dalle origini al principio del secolo VII*, Studi e Testi 35 (Faenza, 1927).
Law, V. *The Insular Latin Grammarians* (Woodbridge, 1982).
'Late Latin grammars in the early Middle Ages: a typological history', *Historiographia Linguistica* 13 (1986), 365–80.
'The sources of the *Ars Donati quam Paulus Diaconus exposuit*', *Filologia Mediolatina* 1 (1994), 71–80.
'The study of grammar', in R. McKitterick (ed.), *Carolingian Culture* (Cambridge, 1994), pp. 88–110.
Grammar and Grammarians in the Early Middle Ages (London and New York, 1997).
Lazzarini, V. *Scuola calligrafica veronese del s. IX* (Venice, 1904).
Lear, S. 'Public law of the Visigothic code', *Speculum* 26 (1951), 1–23.
Leccisotti, T.D. 'Le conseguenze dell'invasione longobarda per l'antico monachesimo italico', *Atti I CISAM* (Spoleto, 1952), 369–76.
'Aspetti e problemi del monachesimo in Italia', *Settimane* 4 (Spoleto, 1956), 319–37.
Leccisotti, T.D. (ed.). *Abbazia di Monte Cassino: i regesti dell'archivio* (Rome, 1964).
Leclercq, J. *Love of Learning and Desire for God: A Study of Monastic Culture*, trans. C. Misrahi (New York, 1960).
Lee, A.D. *Information and Frontiers: Roman Foreign Relations in Late Antiquity* (Cambridge, 1993).
Legnyel, A. and G.T.B. Radan (eds.). *The Archaeology of Roman Pannonia* (Budapest, 1980).

Bibliography

Lehmann, P. *Mittelalterlich Büchertitel*, 2 vols. (Munich, 1949–53).
Leicht, P.S. *Studi sulla proprietà fondaria nel medioevo* (Padua, 1907).
  Formulari notarili nell'Italia settentrionale, excerpt of Mélanges Fitting, II (Montpellier, 1908).
  'Ultime vicende della *mancipatio* in Italia', *Atti del II Congresso nazionale di studi romani* 3 (Rome, 1931), 13–19.
Lencek, R.L. *Jan Baudouin de Courtenay on the Dialects Spoken in Venetian Slovenia and Rezija*, Documentation Series 2, Society for Slovene Studies Newsletter (New York, 1977).
Leoni, A. 'Vitalità della tradizione longobarda nell'Italia meridionale', *Medioevo Romanzo* 6:1 (1979), 3–21.
  'I glossari longobardi–latini', *Atti VI CISAM* (Spoleto, 1980), 267–76.
Levy, E. 'Reflections of the first "Reception" of Roman law in Germanic states', *American Historical Review* 48 (1942), 20–9.
  'The vulgarisation of Roman law in the early middle ages', *Medievalia et Humanistica* 1 (1943), 14–40.
  West Roman Vulgar Law: The Law of Property (Philadelphia, 1951).
Lévi-Strauss, C. *Tristes-Tropiques*, trans. J. and D. Weightman (New York, 1974).
Leyser, C. 'St Benedict and Gregory the Great: another dialogue', in S. Pricoco, F. Rizzo Nervo and T. Sardello (eds.), *Sicilia e Italia suburbicaria tra IV e VIII secolo* (Catania, 1991), pp. 21–43.
Liva, A. *Notariato e documento notarile a Milano, dall'altomedioevale alla fine del settecento*, Studi Storici sul Notariato Italiano 4 (Rome, 1979).
Llewellyn, P.A.B. 'The Roman church in the seventh century: the legacy of Gregory I', *Journal of Ecclesiastical History* 25 (1974), 363–80.
Lloyd, A. and O. Springer (eds.), *Etymologisches Wörterbuch des Althochdeutschen*, I (Göttingen, 1988), A. Lloyd and R. Lühr, II (Göttingen, 1998).
Löfstedt, E. *Studien über die Sprache der langobardischen Gesetze*, Acta Universitatis Upsaliensis, Studia Latina 1 (Stockholm, 1961).
Lomartire, S. 'L'iscrizione della lastra n.12', in *S. Abbondio, lo spazio e il tempo* (Como, 1984), pp. 235–9.
Lopez, R.S. 'Byzantine law in the seventh century and its reception by the Germans and the Arabs', *Byzantion* 16 (1942–43), 445–61.
L'Orange, H.P. and H. Torp. *Il tempietto longobardo di Cividale*, Acta ad archaeologiam et artium historiam pertinentia VII:3 (Rome, 1977).
Lowe, E.A. *The Beneventan Script: A History of the South Italian Minuscule* (Oxford, 1914); 2nd edition, with V. Brown, 2 vols. (Rome, 1981).
  Scriptura Beneventana, 2 vols. (Oxford, 1929).
  '*Codices rescripti*: a list of the oldest Latin palimpsests with stray observations on their origin', *Mélanges Eugène Tisserant*, V, Studi e Testi 235 (Rome, 1934), pp. 67–81.
  Handwriting: Our Medieval Legacy (Rome, 1969).
  Palaeographical Papers, 1907–1965, ed. L. Bieler, 2 vols. (Oxford, 1972).
Lowe, E.A. (ed.). *Codices latini antiquiores*, 12 vols. and *Supplement*. (Oxford, 1934–71).
Lot, F. 'A quelle époque a-t-on cessé de parler Latin', *Archivium Latinitatis Medii Aevi VI Bullentin DuCange* (1931), 97–159.

Bibliography

The End of the Ancient World and the Beginnings of the Middle Ages, trans. P. and M. Leon (London, 1931).

Lülfing, H. 'Libro e classi sociali nei secoli XIV e XV', in G. Cavallo (ed.), *Libri e lettori nel medioevo* (Rome and Bari, 1977), pp. 167–230.

Lusuardi Siena, S. '*Pium super amnem iter*: riflessioni sull'epigrafe di Aldo da S. Giovanni in Conca a Milano', *Arte Medievale* 2nd ser., 4:1 (1990), 1–12.

Maccabruni, C. *Pavia: la tradizione dell'antico nella città medievale* (Pavia, 1990).

McClure, J. 'Bede's Old Testament Kings', in P. Wormald, D. Bullough and R. Collins (eds.), *Ideal and Reality in Frankish and Anglo-Saxon Society: Studies Presented to J.M. Wallace-Hadrill* (Oxford, 1983), pp. 76–98.

McCormick, M. *Triumphal Rulership in Late Antiquity, Byzantium and the Early Middle Ages* (Cambridge, 1986).

McKenna, S. *Paganism and Pagan Survivals in Spain up to the Fall of the Visigothic Kingdom* (Washington, DC, 1938).

McKitterick, R. *The Frankish Kingdoms under the Carolingians 751–987* (Essex, 1983).

'Knowledge of canon law in the Frankish kingdoms before 789: the manuscript evidence', *Journal of Theological Studies* 36 (1985), 96–117.

The Carolingians and the Written Word (Cambridge, 1989).

'Carolingian book production: some problems', *The Library*, ser. 6, 12 (1990), 1–33.

McKitterick, R. 'Text and image in the Carolingian world', in R. McKitterick (ed.), *The Uses of Literacy in Early Medieval Europe* (Cambridge, 1990), pp. 297–318.

'Frauen und Schriftlichkeit im Frühmittelalter', in H.W. Goetz (ed.), *Weibliche Lebensgestaltung im frühen Mittelalter* (Cologne and Vienna, 1991), pp. 65–118.

'Latin and Romance: an historian's perspective', in R. Wright (ed.), *Latin and the Romance Languages in the Early Middle Ages* (London, 1991), pp. 130–45.

'Nuns' scriptoria in England and Francia in the eighth century', *Francia* 19:1 (1992), 1–35.

'Royal patronage of culture in the Frankish kingdoms under the Carolingians: motives and consequences', *Settimane* 39 (Spoleto, 1992), 93–131.

Books, Scribes and Learning in the Frankish Kingdoms: Sixth to Ninth Centuries (Aldershot, 1994).

'The audience for Carolingian historiography', in G. Scheibelreiter and A. Scharer (eds.), *Historiographie im Frühmittelalter* (Vienna, 1994), pp. 96–114.

'Eighth century foundations', in R. McKitterick (ed.), *NCMH*, II (Cambridge, 1995), pp. 681–94.

'Constructing the past in the early Middle Ages: the case of the Royal Frankish Annals', *Transactions of the Royal Historical Society* Coth ser., 7 (1997), 101–29.

McKitterick, R. (ed.). *The Uses of Literacy in Early Medieval Europe* (Cambridge, 1990).

Carolingian Culture: Emulation amd Innovation (Cambridge, 1994).

The New Cambridge Medieval History, II, *c. 700–900* (Cambridge, 1995).

McKitterick, R. and M. Innes. 'The writing of history', in R. McKitterick (ed.), *Carolingian Culture* (Cambridge, 1994), pp. 193–221.

McKitterick, R. and L. Lopes Cardozo. *Lasting Letters* (Cambridge, 1992).

Maitland, F.W. and F. Pollock. *History of English Law*, 2nd edn (Cambridge, 1968).

Manacorda, G. *Storia della scuola in Italia*, 2 vols. (Milan, 1913).

Mango, C. 'Antique statuary and the Byzantine beholder', *Dumbarton Oaks Papers* 17 (1963), 53–75.
Manselli, R. 'Gregorio Magno e due riti pagani dei Longobardi', in *Studi storici in onore di O. Bertolini*, 2 vols. (Pisa, 1972), I, pp. 435–41.
Mariotti, S. 'L'Indovinello veronese', in *Letterature comparate, problemi, metodi: studi in onore di Ettore Paratore* (Bologna, 1981), pp. 987–96.
Markey, T.L. 'Germanic in the Mediterranean: Lombards, Vandals, and Visigoths', in F.M. Clover and R.S. Humphreys (eds.), *Tradition and Innovation in Late Antiquity* (Madison, 1989), pp. 51–72.
Markus, R.A. *The End of Ancient Christianity* (Cambridge, 1990).
'From Caesarius of Arles to Boniface: Christianity and paganism in Gaul', in J. Fontaine and J.N. Hillgarth (eds.), *The Seventh Century: Changes and Continuity* (London, 1992), pp. 154–72.
Gregory the Great and His World (Cambridge, 1997).
Marrou, H.I. *Histoire de l'éducation dans l'antiquité* (Paris, 1948), trans. G. Lamb, *A History of Education in Antiquity* (Madison, 1982).
'L'école dans l'antiquité tardive', *Settimane* 19 (Spoleto 1972), 127–43.
Massa, E. 'Gregorio Magno e l'arte del linguaggio. Alcune osservazioni', in *Gregorio Magni e il suo tempo* (Rome, 1991), II, pp. 59–104.
Mastrelli, C.A. 'L'elemento germanico nella toponomastica toscana', *Atti V CISAM* (Spoleto, 1973), 664–670.
'Vicende linguistiche del secolo VIII', *Settimane* 20 (Spoleto, 1973), 244–79.
'La terminologia longobarda dei manufatti', *La Civiltà dei Longobardi in Europa, Accademia Nazionale dei Lincei: Problemi attuali di scienza e di cultura* (Roma, 1974), pp. 257–269.
'La toponomastica lombarda di origine longobarda', in *I Longobardi e la Lombardia: Saggi* (Milan, 1978), pp. 35–49.
'Le iscrizioni runiche', in C. Carletti and G. Otranto (eds.), *il Santuario di S. Michele sul Gargano del VI al IX secolo* (Bari, 1980), pp. 319–336.
Mastrelli Anzilotti, G. 'Toponomi di origine longobarda nel Trentino-Alto Adige', in G.C. Menis (ed.), *Italia longobarda* (Venice, 1991), pp. 227–34.
Mathisen, R.W. 'Epistolography, literary circles and family ties in late Roman Gaul', *Transactions of the American Philological Association* 111 (1981), 95–109.
'The theme of literary decline in Late Roman Gaul', *Classical Philology* 83 (1988), 45–53.
Matthews, J.F. *Western Aristocracies and the Imperial Court A.D. 364–425* (Oxford, 1975; reprinted 1990).
'Anicius Manlius Severinus Boethius', in M. Gibson (ed.), *Boethius: His Life, Thought and Influence* (Oxford, 1981), pp. 15–43.
Meltzer, E.S. 'Remarks on ancient Egyptian writing with emphasis on its mnemonic aspects', in P. Kolers *et al.* (ed.), *Processing of Visible Language*, II (New York and London, 1980), pp. 22–45.
Melucco Vaccaro, A. *I Longobardi in Italia*, 2nd edn (Milan, 1988).
Menghin, W., T. Springer and E. Warmer (eds.). *Germanen Hunnen und Awaren: Schätze der Völkerwanderungszeit. Die Archäologie des 5. und 6. Jahrhunderts an der mittleren Donau und der östlich-merowingische Reihengräberkreis* (Nuremberg, 1987).
Mengozzi, G. *Ricerche sull'attività della scuola di Pavia nell'altomedievo* (Pavia, 1924).

Bibliography

Menis, G.C. (ed.) *I Longobardi* (Milan, 1990).
  Italia longobarda (Venice, 1991).
Mentz, I. and J. Jarnut. 'Storia e archeologia: prospettive', in P. Cammarosano and S. Gasparri (ed.) *Langobardia* (Udine, 1990), pp. 107–10.
Meslin, M. *Les Ariens d'Occident 335–430*, Patristica Sorbonensia 8 (Paris, 1967).
Meyer, C. *Sprache und Sprachdenkmäler der Langobarden* (Padderborn, 1877).
Migliorini, B. *Storia della lingua italiana* (Florence, 1960).
Milroy, J. and M. 'Linguistic change, social network, and speaker innovation', *Journal of Linguistics* 21 (1985), 339–84.
Mitchell, J. 'Literacy displayed: the use of inscriptions at the monastery of San Vincenzo al Volturno in the early ninth century', in R. McKitterick (ed.), *The Uses of Literacy in Early Medieval Europe* (Cambridge, 1990), pp. 186–225.
  'The display of script and the uses of painting in Longobard Italy', *Settimane* 41.2 (Spoleto, 1994), 887–951.
Mócsy, A. *Pannonia and Upper Moesia* (London and Boston, 1974).
Mohrmann, C. *Etudes sur le Latin des Chrétiens*, Storia e Letteratura 65 (Rome, 1958).
Moisl, H. 'Anglo-Saxon royal genealogies and Germanic oral tradition', *Journal of Medieval History* 7 (1981), 215–48.
  'Kingship and orally transmitted *Stammestradition* among the Lombards and the Franks', in H. Wolfram and A. Schwarcz (eds.), *Die Bayern und ihre Nachbarn* I (Vienna, 1985), pp. 111–19.
Momigliano, A. 'Cassiodorus and the Italian culture of his time', *Proceedings of the British Academy* 41 (1955), 207–45.
Mommsen, T. 'Die Quellen der Langobardengeschichte des Paulus Diaconus' [1880], in *Gesammelte Schriften* 6 (Berlin, 1910) pp. 485–539.
Mommsen, T. 'Petrarch's conception of the Dark Ages', *Speculum* 17 (1942), 226–42.
Moorhead, J. 'Boethius and Romans in Ostrogothic service', *Historia* 27 (1978), 604–12.
  '*Libertas* and *nomen romanum* in Ostrogothic Italy', *Latomus* 46 (1987), 161–8.
  Theoderic in Italy (Oxford, 1992).
  Justinian (London, 1994).
Mor, C.G. 'La manumissione in ecclesia', *Rivista di Storia del Diritto Italiano* 1 (1928), 1–25.
  'S. Colombano e la politica ecclesiastica di Agilulfo', *Bollettino Storico Piacentino* 38 (1933), 49–63.
  'Lo stato longobardo del VII secolo', *Settimane* 5 (Spoleto, 1958), 271–307.
  'La successione al trono nel diritto pubblico', in *Scritti di storia giuridica altomedievale* (Pisa, 1977), pp. 437–64.
Mordek, H. *Bibliotheca capitularium regum francorum manuscripta. Überlieferung und Traditionszusammenhang der fränkischen Herrschererlasse*, MGH Hilfsmittel XV (Munich, 1995).
Morison, S. *First Principles of Typography* (Cambridge, 1951).
  Politics and Script: Aspects of Authority and Freedom in the Development of Graeco-Latin Script from the Sixth Century B.C. to the Twentieth Century A.D. (Oxford, 1972).
Moschetti, G. *Primordi esegetici sulla legislazione longobarda nel secolo IX a Verona secondo il Codice Vat. lat. 5359* (Spoleto, 1954).

Bibliography

Mostert, M. 'Celtic, Anglo-Saxon or Insular? Some considerations on Irish manuscript production and their implications for Insular Latin culture, c. 500–800 A.D.', in D. Edel (ed.), *Cultural Identity and Cultural Integration: Ireland and Europe in the Early Middle Ages* (London, 1995), pp. 92–115.

Mostert, M. (ed.). *Communication in the Middle Ages* (Leiden, Cologne and Boston, 1999).

Moyse, G. 'Monachisme et réglementation monastique en Gaule avant Benoît d'Aniane', in *Sous la Règle de St Benoît: structures monastiques et sociétés en France du moyen âge à l'époque moderne* (Geneva and Paris, 1982), pp. 3–19.

Muhlbergher, S. 'Heroic kings and unruly generals: the Copenhagen continuation of Prosper reconsidered', *Florilegium* 6 (1984), 50–70.

'War, warlords and Christian historians from the fifth to the seventh century', in A.C. Murray (ed.), *After Rome's Fall* (Toronto, Buffalo and London, 1988), pp. 83–98.

Muller, H.F. 'The passive voice in vulgar Latin', *The Romanic Review* 12 (1921), 318–34.

'When did Latin cease to be a spoken *language* in France', *The Romanic Review* 14 (1923), 317–24.

Müller, K.E. *Geschichte der antiken Ethnographie und ethnologischen Theoriebildung*, 2 vols. (Wiesbaden, 1982).

Müller, R. 'Die spätromische Festung Valcum am Plattensee', in W. Menghin, T. Springer and E. Warmer (eds.), *Germanen Hunnen und Awaren: Schätze der Völkerwanderungszeit. Die Archäologie des 5. und 6. Jahrhunderts an der mittleren Donau und der östlich-merowingische Reihengräberkreis* (Nuremberg, 1987), pp. 270–4.

Mullet, M. 'Writing in early medieval Byzantium', in R. McKitterick (ed.), *The Uses of Literacy in Early Medieval Europe* (Cambridge, 1990), pp. 156–85.

Murray, A.C. *Germanic Kinship Structure: Studies in Law and Society in Antiquity and the Early Middle Ages* (Toronto, 1983).

Murray, A.C. (ed.). *After Rome's Fall: Narrators and Sources of Early Medieval History. Essays presented to Walter Goffart* (Toronto, Buffalo and London, 1998).

Musca, G. *L'emirato di Bari 847–871* (Bari, 1964).

Mütherich, F. and A. Peroni (eds.). *Seminario internazionale sulla decorazione pittorica del San Salvatore di Brescia* (Pavia, 1983).

Natale, A.R. 'Note paleografiche sulle carte private della Svizzera italiana nell'alto medioevo. II. La corsiva di Orso *scriptor* in Campione nel 756', *Bollettino Storico della Svizzera Italiana* ser. 4, 25 (1950), 135–43.

'Influenze merovingiche e studi calligrafici nello scriptorium di Bobbio', in *Miscellanea G. Galbiati*, II, Fontes Ambrosiani 26 (Milan, 1951), pp. 1–23.

Neff, K. *Die Gedichte des Paulus Diaconus: Kritiche und Erklärende Ausgabe*, Quellen und Untersuchungen zur lateinischen Philologie des Mittelalters 3.IV (Munich, 1908).

Nehlsen, H. 'Zur Aktualität und Effectivität germanischer Rechtsaufzeichnungen', in P. Classen (ed.), *Recht und Schrift im Mittelalter* (Sigmaringen, 1977), pp. 449–502.

Nellen, D. *Viri litterati: gebildetes Beamtentum und spätromischen Reich im Westen* (Bochum, 1977).

Bibliography

Nelson, J. 'Literacy in Carolingian government', in R. McKitterick (ed.), *The Uses of Literacy in Early Modern Europe* (Cambridge, 1990), pp. 258–96.
'Women and the word in the earlier middle ages', in W. Sheils and D. Wood (eds.), *Women in the Church* (Oxford, 1990), pp. 53–87.
'Gender and genre in women historians of the early middle ages', in *L'Historiographie médiévale en Europe* (Paris, 1991), pp. 149–163.
'Making a difference in eighth-century politics: the daughters of Desiderius', in A.C. Murray (ed.), *After Rome's Fall* (Toronto, Buffalo and London, 1998), pp. 171–90.
Niermeyer, J.F. *Mediae latinitatis lexicon minus* (Leiden, 1976).
Noble, T.F.X. *The Republic of St. Peter: The Birth of the Papal State, 680–825* (Philadelphia, 1984).
'Literacy and the papal government in late antiquity and the early middle ages', in R. McKitterick (ed.), *The Uses of Literacy in Early Modern Europe* (Cambridge, 1990), pp. 82–108.
'Theoderic and the papacy', *Atti XIII CISAM* (Spoleto, 1993), pp. 395–425.
Norberg, D. *Introduction à l'étude de la versification médiévale*, Acta Universitatis Stockholmiensis 5, Studia Latina Stockholmiensia (Stockholm, 1958).
'Le développement du latin en italie de S. Grégoire le Grand à Paul Diacre', *Settimane* 5 (Spoleto, 1958), 485–539.
Ohly, V.F. 'Halbbiblische und ausserbiblische typologie', *Settimane* 23 (Spoleto, 1976), 429–72.
Oliver, G.H. *History of the Invention and Discovery of Spectacles* (London, 1913).
Olivieri, D. *Toponomastica lombarda* (Milan, 1961).
Ong, W.J. *Interfaces of the Word* (Ithaca, 1977).
Orality and Literacy: The Technologising of the Word (London and New York, 1982).
Ongaro, O. *Cultura e scuola calligrafica Veronese del s.X* (Venice, 1925).
Otranto, G. 'Il *Liber de apparitione* e il culto di San Michele sul Gargano nella documentazione liturgica altomedievale', *Vetera Christianorum* 18 (1981), 377–401.
'Il *regnum* longobardo e il santuario micaelico del Gargano: note epigrafia e storia', *Vetera Christianorum* 22 (1985), 165–80.
Pagnin, B. 'Formazione della scrittura carolina italiana', *Atti del Congresso internazionale di storia del diritto*, I (Milan, 1951), 245–66
'Scuola e cultura a Pavia nell'alto medioevo', *Atti IV CISAM* (Spoleto, 1969), 153–181.
'Espressioni scrittorie dell'ambiente culturale veronese dal V al VII secolo', *Ricerche Medievali* 13–14 (1978–80), 5–18.
Panazza, G. *Lapidi e sculture paleocristiane e pre-romaniche di Pavia, Arte del Primo Millennio, Atti 2nd convegno per lo studio dell'arte dell'alto medioevo, tenuto presso l'Università di Pavia nel Settembre 1950* (Turin, 1953).
Pantoni, A. 'Documenti epigrafici sulla presenza di settentrionali a Monte Cassino', *Benedictina* 12 (1958), 205–38.
Paradisi, B. 'Il prologo e l'epilogo dell'Editto di Rotari', *Studia et Documenta Historiae et Iuris* 34 (1968), 1–31.
Parkes, M. 'The literacy of the laity', in D. Daiches and A.K. Thorlby (eds.), *Literature and Western Civilisation: The Medieval World* (London, 1973), pp. 555–77.

Bibliography

'The contribution of insular scribes in the seventh and eighth centuries to the grammar of legibility', reprinted in M., Parkes, *Scribes, Scripts and Readers: Studies in the Communication, Presentation, and Dissemination of Medieval Texts* (London, 1991), pp. 1–18.

Pause and Effect: An Introduction to the History of Punctuation in the West (Aldershot, 1993).

Paschini, P. *Storia del Friuli* (Udine, 1953).

Pattison, R. *On Literacy: The Politics of the Word from Homer to the Age of Rock* (Oxford, 1982).

Pederson, H. *The Discovery of Language*, trans. J.W. Spargo (Indiana, 1962).

Peduto, P. 'Un accesso alla storia di Salerno: stratigrafie e materiali dell'area palaziale longobarda', *Rassegna Storica Salernitana* 2:10 (1988), 2–28.

'Insediamenti longobardi del ducato di Benevento (sec. VI–VIII)', in P. Cammarosano and S. Gasparri (eds.), *Langobardia* (Udine, 1990), pp. 307–73.

Peduto, P. and M. Romito. 'Chiesa di San Pietro a Corte', *Passeggiate Salernitane* 3 (1988), 20–6.

Pellegrini, G.B. 'Terminologia agraria medievale in Italia', *Settimane* 13 (Spoleto, 1966), 647–60.

Peroni, A. 'Pavia *capitale longobarda*. Testimonianze archeologiche e manufatti artistici', in *I Longobardi e la Lombardia: Saggi* (Milan, 1978), pp. 73–81.

Pertusi, A. 'Bisanzio e l'irradiazione della sua civiltà in Occidente nell'alto medioevo', *Settimane* 11 (Spoleto, 1964), 119–31.

Petracco Sicardi, G. 'Latino e romanzo di mano barbarica', *Romanobarbarica* 2 (1977), 183–208.

Petrucci, A. *Notarii: documenti per la storia del notariato italiano* (Milan, 1958).

'Aspetti del culto e del pellegrinaggio di S. Michele Arcangelo sul Monte Gargano', *Atti del IV Convegno di studi sul tema 'Pellegrinaggio e culto dei Santi in Europa fino alla fine della I Crociata'* (Todi, 1963), 154–95.

'Origine e diffusione del culto di S. Michele nell'Italia medievale', *Millénaire monastique du Mont Saint-Michel*, II, *Culte de Saint Michel et pèlerinages au Mont* (Paris, 1971), pp. 49–72.

'Libro, scrittura e scuola', *Settimane* 19 (Spoleto, 1972), 313–38.

'Aspetti simbolici delle testimonianze scritte', *Settimane* 23 (Spoleto, 1976), 813–44.

'La concezione cristiana del libro fra VI e VII secolo', in G. Cavallo (ed.), *Libri e lettori nel medioevo* (Rome and Bari, 1977), pp. 3–26.

La scrittura: ideologia e rappresentazione (Turin, 1980), trans. L. Lapin, *Public Lettering: Script, Power, and Culture* (Chicago and London, 1993).

'Epigrafia e paleografia. Inchiesta sui rapporti fra due discipline', *Scrittura e Civiltà* 5 (1981), 265–312.

'David Cressy: sull'alfabetismo in Inghilterra', *Quaderni Storici* 51/a. Dec. (1982), 1129–33.

'Modello notarile e testualità', in *Il notariato nella civiltà Toscana*, Studi Storici sul Notariato Italiano 8 (Rome, 1985), pp. 123–47.

'Alfabetismo ed educazione grafica degli scribi altomedievali', in P. Ganz (ed.), *The Role of the Book in Medieval Culture* (Brepols, 1986), pp. 109–32.

'Storia della scrittura e storia della società', *Annuario de Estudios Medievales* 21 (1991), 309–22.

Bibliography

'Scrittura e figura nella memoria funeraria', *Settimane* 41 (Spoleto, 1994), 277–97.

Writers and Readers in Medieval Italy: Studies in the History of Written Culture, trans. C.M. Radding (New Haven and London, 1995).

Petrucci, A. and C. Romeo. *Scriptores in urbibus: alfabetismo e cultura scritta nell'Italia altomedievale* (Bologna, 1992).

Petrucci, A. and P. Supino-Martini. 'Materiali ed ipotesi per una storia della cultura scritta nella Roma del IX sec.', *Scrittura e Civiltà* 2 (1978), 45–101.

Picard, J.C. 'De Milan sous Liutprand à Verone sous Pépin Ier d'Italie', in *Hagiographie, cultures et sociétés IVe–XIIe siècles* (Paris, 1981), pp. 455–67.

Le Souvenir des évêques: sépultures, listes épiscopales et culte des évêques en Italie du nord des origines au Xe siècle, Bibliothèque des Ecoles Français d'Athènes et de Rome 268 (Rome, 1988).

Pietrangeli, C. 'I sarcofagi romani dell'abazzia longobarda di Ferentillo', *Atti I CISAM* (Spoleto, 1952), 451–6.

Pinkster, H. 'Evidence for SVO in Latin?', in R. Wright (ed.), *Latin and the Romance Languages in the Early Middle Ages* (London, 1991), pp. 69–82.

Pirenne, H. 'L'instruction des marchands au moyen âge', *Annales d'Histoire Economique et Sociale* 1 (1929), 20–53.

'De l'état de l'instruction des laiques a l'époque mérovingienne' *RB* 46 (1934), 165–77.

Pitmada, L. 'S. Onofrio (Catanzaro) – rinvenimento di cippo miliare', *Notizie degli scavi di Antichità* 6, *Atti dell Accademia dei Lincei*, ser. 8 (1952–53), 343–4.

Pizzani, U. 'S. Gregorio Magno, Cassiodoro, e le arti liberali', *Gregorio Magno e il suo tempo* (Rome, 1991), II, pp. 121–36.

Pohl, W. *Die Awaren: ein Steppenvolk in Mitteleuropa 567–822* (Munich, 1988).

'L'armée romaine et les Lombards: stratégies militaires et politiques, in F. Vallet and M. Kazanski (eds.), *L'Armée romaine et les barbares du IIIe au VIIe siècle* (Rouen, 1993), pp. 291–6.

'Paulus Diaconus und die Historia Langobardorum: text und tradition', in G. Scheibelreiter and A. Sharer (eds.), *Historiographie im frühen Mittelalter* (Vienna, 1994), pp. 375–405.

'Tradition, Ethnogenese und literarische Gestaltung: eine Zwischenbilanz', in K. Brunner and B. Merta (eds.), *Ethnogenese und Überlieferung: Angewandte Methoden der Frühmittelalterforschung*, Veröffentlichungen des Institut für österreichische Geschichtsforschung 31 (Vienna, 1994), pp. 9–26.

'The Empire and the Lombards: treaties and negotiations in the sixth century', in W. Pohl (ed.), *Kingdoms of the Empire: The Integration of Barbarians in Late Antiquity* (Leiden, New York and Cologne, 1997), pp. 75–133.

'Telling the difference. Signs of ethnic identity', in W. Pohl and H. Reimitz (eds), *Strategies of Distinction: The Construction of Ethnic Communities, 300–800* (Leiden, Boston and Cologne, 1998), pp. 17–69.

'Memory, identity and power in Lombard Italy', in Y. Hen and M. Innes (eds.), *The Uses of the Past in the Early Middle Ages* (Cambridge, 2000), pp. 9–28.

Werkstätte der Erinnerung: Monte Cassino und die Gestaltung der langobardischer Vergangenheit (Munich, 2001).

Pohl, W. (ed.) *Kingdoms of the Empire: The Integration of Barbarians in Late Antiquity* (Leiden, New York and Cologne, 1997).

Bibliography

Politzer, R.L. *A Study of the Language of Eighth-Century Lombardic Documents: A Statistical Analysis of the Codice paleografico lombardo* (New York, 1949).
'The interpretation of correctness in Late Latin texts', *Language* 37 (1961), 209–14.
Politzer, R.L. and F.N. Politzer. *Romance Trends in 7th and 8th Century Latin Documents* (Chapel Hill, 1953).
Polonio, V. *Il monastero di S. Colombano di Bobbio dalla fondazione all'epoca carolingia* (Genoa, 1962).
Pratesi, A. 'Note per un contributo alla soluzione del dilemma paleografico: "semicorsiva o precarolina"?', *Annali della Facoltà di Lettere e Filosofia dell'Università di Bari* 3 (1957), 3–13.
Princi Braccini, G. 'Un suggerimento da due glosse di Papia: cadarfida = "retaggio dei detti"?', *Romanobarbarica* 10 (1988–89), 309–66.
'Termini germanici per il diritto e la giustizia: sulle tracce dei significati autentici attraverso etimologie vecchie e nuove', *Settimane* 42 (Spoleto, 1994), 1053–1205.
Rabinowitz, J.J. 'Jewish and Lombard Law', *Jewish Social Studies* 12 (1950), 299–328.
Raby, E.F.J. *A History of Christian Latin Poetry* (Oxford, 1934).
A History of Secular Latin Poetry (Oxford, 1936).
Radding, C.H. *The Origins of Medieval Jurisprudence: Pavia and Bologna 850–1150* (New Haven and London, 1988).
Randsborg, K. *The First Millennium AD in Europe and the Mediterranean: An Archaeological Essay* (Cambridge, 1991).
Rapelli, G. 'L'onomastica personale e familiare nella Lessina Cimbra', in G. Volpato (ed.), *Civiltà Cimbra* (Verona, 1983), pp. 49–55.
'Per una storia dei Cimbri Tredicicomunignani', in G. Volpato (ed.), *Civiltà Cimbra* (Verona, 1983), pp. 75–83.
Testi Cimbri: gli scritti dei Cimbri dei Tredici Comuni Veronesi (Verona, 1983).
Rea, B. 'The context and meaning of popular literacy: some evidence from nineteenth-century rural England', *Past and Present* 131 (1991), 81–129.
Redlich, O. 'Die Privaturkunden des Mittelalters', in G. von Below and F. Meinecke (eds.), *Handbuch der mittelalterlichen und neueren Geschichte* (Berlin, 1911), pp. 1–54.
Reed, R. *Ancient Skins, Parchments and Leathers* (London and New York, 1972).
Restelli, G. *Goti Tedeschi Longobardi: rapporti di cultura e di lingua* (Brescia, 1984).
Reynolds, L.D. (ed.). *Texts and Transmission: A Survey of the Latin Classics* (Oxford, 1983).
Reynolds, L.D. and N.G. Wilson. *Scribes and Scholars: A Guide to the Transmission of Greek and Latin Literature*, 3rd edn (Oxford, 1991).
Riccardi, A. *Le vicende, l'area, e gli avanzi, del Regium Palatium e della cappella e monastero di S. Anastasio dei Re Longobardi, Carolingi e Re d'Italia nella corte regia ed imperiale di Corte Olona, provincia di Pavia* (Milan, 1889).
Richards, J. *The Popes and the Papacy in the Early Middle Ages 476–752* (London and Boston, 1979).
Riché, P. *Education and Culture in the Barbarian West: From the Sixth through Eighth Centuries*, trans. J. Contreni (Columbia, SC, 1976).
'Apprendre à lire et à écrire dans le haut moyen-âge', *Bulletin de la Société Nationale des Antiquaires de France* (1978–79), 193–203.
Ecoles et enseignement dans le haut moyen-âge (Paris, 1979).

Bibliography

Richter, M. 'A socio-linguistic approach to the Latin middle ages', *Studies in Church History* 11 (1975), 69–82. Repr. in *Studies in Medieval Language and Culture* (Dublin, 1995).
'*Urbanitas–rusticitas*: linguistic aspects of a medieval dichotomy', *Studies in Church History* 16 (1979), 149–57. Repr. in *Studies in Medieval Language and Culture* (Dublin, 1995).
'A quelle époque a-t-on cessé de parler Latin? A propos d'une question mal posée', *Annales ESC* 38 (1983), 439–48.
The Formation of the Medieval West: Studies in the Oral Culture of the Barbarians (New York, 1994).
The Oral Tradition in the Early Medieval West, Typologie des Sources du Moyen Age Occidental 71 (Turnhout, 1994).
Righetti Tosti-Croce, M. 'La scultura', in G.C. Menis (ed.), *I Longobardi* (Milan, 1990), pp. 311–12.
Rivers, T.J. 'Legal status of free women in the *Lex Alamannorum*', *Zeitschrift der Savigny-Stiftung für Rechtsgeschichte, Germanische Abteilung* 91 (1974), 175–9.
Roberts, C.H. and T.C. Skeat. *The Birth of the Codex*, 2nd edn (Oxford, 1983).
Robson, C.A. 'L'Appendix Probi et la philologie latine', *Moyen Age* 69 (1963), 37–54.
Roffia, E. *La necropoli longobarda di Trezzo sull'Adda*, Ricerche di Archeologia Altomedievale e Medievale 12–13 (Florence, 1986).
Rohr, C. 'La tradizione culturale tardo-romana nel regno degli ostrogoti – il panegirico di Teoderico a Ennodio', *Romanobarbarica* 16 (1999), 261–84.
Romanini, A.M. 'Problemi di scultura e plastica altomedievali', *Settimane* 12 (Spoleto, 1971), 426–67.
'Il concetto di classico e l'arte medievale', *Romanobarbarica* 1 (1976), 218–23.
'Committenza regia e pluralismo culturale nella "Longobardia major"', *Settimane* 39 (Spoleto, 1992), 57–92.
Romm, J.S. *The Edges of the Earth in Ancient Thought* (Princeton, 1992).
Roncoroni, A. 'L'epitafio di S. Agrippino nella chiesa di S. Eufemia ad Isola. Tradizione classica e storia religiosa nell'Italia longobarda', *Rivista Archeologica dell'Antica Provincia e Diocesi di Como* 162 (1980), 99–149.
Rosen, E. 'The invention of eyeglasses', *Journal of the History of Medicine* 11 (1956), 125–47.
Rosenfeld, H. 'Buch, Schrift, und lateinische Sprachkenntnis bei den Germanen vor der christlichen Mission', *Rheinisches Museum für Philologie* 95 (1952), 203–14.
Rossetti, G. 'I ceti proprietari e professionali: stato sociale, funzioni e prestigio a Milano nei secoli VIII–IX: l'età longobarda', *Atti X CISAM* (Spoleto, 1986), 165–207.
Russo Mailler, C. *Il senso medievale della morte nei carmini epitaffici dell'Italia meridionale fra VI e XI secolo* (Naples, 1981).
Russyscaert, J. *Les Manuscrits de l'abbaye de Nonantola: table de concordance annotée et index des manuscrits*, Studi e Testi 182 (Vatican City, 1955).
Sabatini, F. 'Dalla *scripta latina rustica* alle *scriptae* Romanze', *Studi Medievali* 3rd ser., 9:1 (1961), 321–58.
Riflessi linguistici della dominazione longobarda nell'Italia mediana e meridionale, Atti dell'Accademia Toscana di Scienza e Lettere, 'La Columbaria', 23 (Florence, 1963).

Bibliography

'Sull'origine dei plurali italiani: il tipo in -i', *Studi Linguistici Italiani* 5 (1965), 5–39.
'Lingua parlata, scripta, e conscienza linguistica nelle origini romanze', *Atti del XIV Congresso internazionale di linguistica e filologia romanza* (Naples, 1978), 445–54.
Saenger, P. 'The separation of words and the order of words: the genesis of medieval reading', *Scrittura e Civiltà* 14 (1990), 49–74.
'The separation of words in Italy', *Scrittura e Civiltà* 17 (1993), 5–42.
Space between Words: The Origins of Silent Reading (Stanford, 1997).
Salvioli, G. *L'istruzione in Italia prima del mille* (Florence, 1912).
Storia del diritto italiano (Turin, 1930).
Santifaller, L. *Liber Diurnus: Studien und Forschungen von Leo Santifaller*, ed. H. Zimmermann, Päpste und Papsttum 10 (Stuttgart, 1976).
Saracco Previdi, E. 'Lo *sculdahis* nel territorio longobardo di Rieti (sec. VIII e IX). Dall'amministrazione longobarda a quella franca', *Studi Medievali* 3:2 (1973), 219–75.
Sasel, J. 'Il viaggio di Venanzio Fortunato e la sua attività in ordine alla politica bizantina', *Antichità Altoadriatiche* 19 (1981), 359–75.
Scardigli, P. *Die Goten: Sprache und Kultur* (Munich, 1973).
'Appunti longobardi', in P. Chiarini, C.A. Mastrelli, P. Scardigli and L. Zagari (eds.), *Filologia e critica: studi in onore di V. Santoli* (Rome, 1976), pp. 91–131.
'All'origine dei longobardismi in italiano', in H. Kolb and H. Lauffer (eds.), *Sprachliche Interferenz: Festschrift für Werner Betz zum 65. Geburtstag* (Tübingen, 1977), pp. 335–54.
'Dalla culturale orale all cultura scritta', in G.C. Menis (ed.), *I Longobardi* (Milan, 1990), pp. 152–63.
Scheibelreiter, G. and A. Sharer (eds.). *Historiographie im frühen Mittelalter*, Veröffentlichungen des Institut für österreichische Geschichtsforschung 32 (Vienna, 1994).
Schiaffini, A. 'Problemi del passagio del latino all'italiano (evoluzione, disgregazione, riconstruzione)', in *Studi in onore di Angelo Monteverdi*, 2 vols. (Modena, 1959), II, pp. 691–715.
'I problemi dell'Indovinello veronese', in Schiaffini, *I mille anni della lingua italiana* (Milan, 1961), pp. 71–96.
Schiaparelli, L. *Raccolta di documenti latini*, I, *Documenti romani* (Como, 1923).
Il Codice 490 della biblioteca capitolare di Lucca e la scuola scrittoria Lucchese (secoli VIII–IX), Studi e Testi 36 (Rome, 1924).
'Note paleografiche. Sulla data e provenienza del. cod. LXXXIX della Biblioteca capitolare di Verona (l'Orazionale mozarabico)', *Archivio Storico Italiano* ser. 7, 1 (1924), 106–17.
'Note paleografiche. Intorno all'origine della scrittura curiale romana', *Archivio Storico Italiano* ser. 7, 6 (1926), 165–82.
Influenze straniere nella scrittura italiana dei secoli VIII e IX, Studi e Testi 47 (Rome, 1927).
'Tachigrafia sillabica nelle carte Italiane', *Bullettino dell'Istituto Storico Italiano* 33 (1928), 10–35.
Codice diplomatico langobardo, Fonti per la Storia d'Italia 64–65 (Rome, 1929–32).
'Note paleografiche sulle carte longobarde'.

Bibliography

I. 'I notai nell'età longobarda', *Archivio Storico Italiano* ser. 7 (1932), 3–34.
II. 'Tracce di antichi formulari nelle carte longobarde', *Archivio Storico Italiano* ser. 7, 19 (1933), 3–34.
III. 'La formula *post traditam (chartam)*', *Archivio Storico Italiano* ser. 7, 19 (1933), 34–51.
IV. La formula *post traditam (chartam)* e la *traditio chartae ad proprium* del chartularium langobardicum', *Archivio Storico Italiano* ser. 7, 19 (1933), 52–66.
V. 'La formula *sub stipulatione et sponsione interposita*', *Archivio Storico Italiano* ser. 7, 21 (1934), 1–21.
VI. 'Dictare, ex dictato, ex dicto, dictator', *Archivio Storico Italiano* ser. 7, 21 (1934), 21–37.
VII. 'Note dorsali. *Dicta.*', *Archivio Storico Italiano* ser. 7, 21 (1934), 38–55.
Note paleografiche e diplomatiche, ed. G. Cencetti (Rome, 1967).
Schmidt, K. (ed.). *Vita Walfredi und Kloster Monteverdi: toskanisches Mönchtum zwischen langobardischer und fränkischer Herrschaft* (Tübingen, 1991).
Schmiedt, G. 'Città scomparse e città di nuova formazione in Italia in relazione al sistema di communicazione', *Settimane* 21 (Spoleto, 1974), 503–607.
Schneider, F. *Die Reichsverwaltung in Toskana von der Gründgung des Langobardenreiches bis zum Ausgang der Staufer* (Rome, 1914).
Schneller, C. *Die romanischen Volksmundarten in Südtirol, nach ihren Zusammenhange mit den romanischen und germanischen Sprachen, etymologisch und grammatikalisch Dargestellt* (Gera, 1870).
Schott, C. 'Der Stand der Leges Forschung', *Frühmittelalterliche Studien* 13 (1979), 29–55.
Schumann, R. 'Le fondazioni ecclesiastiche e il disegno urbano di Piacenza tra il tardo romano (350) e la Signoria (1313)', *Bollettino Storico Piacentino* 71 (1976), 159–71.
Schupfer, F. *Delle istituzioni politiche longobardiche* (Florence, 1963).
Schwarzmaier, H. *Lucca und das Reich bis zum Ende des 11. Jahrhunderts: Studien zur Sozialstruktur einer Herzogstadt in der Toscana* (Tübingen, 1972).
Scribner, S. and S.M. Cole. *The Psychology of Literacy* (Cambridge, MA, 1981).
Seaward, M.R.D. and C. Giacobini. 'Lichen-induced biodeterioration of Italian monuments, frescoes and other archaeological materials', *Studia Geobotanica* 8 (1988), 3–11.
Segagni Malacart, A. 'La scultura in pietra dal VI al IX secolo', in *Storia di Pavia*, II (Pavia, 1987), pp. 373–407.
Sestan, E. 'La storiografia dell'Italia longobarda: Paolo Diacono', *Settimane* 17 (Spoleto, 1970), 357–86.
Sheppard, C. 'Subtleties of Lombard marble sculpture of the seventh and eighth centuries', *Gazette des Beaux Arts* 63 (1964), 193–206.
Silvagni, A. 'The *Sylloge* of Cambridge', *Rivista di Archeologia Cristiana* 20 (1943), 74–95.
Simonetti, M. *Studi sull'arianesimo*, Verba Seniorum 5 (Rome, 1965).
Sinatti d'Amico, F. *Le prove giudiziarie nel diritto longobardo: legislazione e prassi da Rotari ad Astolfo*, Fondazione Guglielmo Castelli 40 (Milan, 1968).
'L'applicazione dell'Edictum in Tuscia', *Atti V CISAM* (Spoleto, 1973), 745–81.

Bibliography

Skinner, P. 'Women, wills and wealth in medieval southern Italy', *EME* 2 (1993), 133–52.
'Women, literacy and invisibility in southern Italy 900–1200', in L. Smith and J. Taylor (eds.), *Women, the Book and the Worldly*, II (Cambridge, 1995), pp. 1–11.
'Disputes and disparity: women in court in medieval southern Italy', *Reading Medieval Studies* 22 (1996), 85–104.
Women in Medieval Italian Society 500–1200 (Harlow, 2001).
Solmi, A. 'La formula della *mancipatio* nei documenti piacentini del secolo VIII', *Archivio Storico Italiano* 71:2 (1913), 225–70.
Sot, M. *Gesta episcoporum*, Typologie des Sources du Moyen Age Occidental 57 (Turnhout, 1980).
Spagnolo, A. *I manoscritti della Biblioteca Capitolare di Verona: catalogo descrittivo*, ed. Silvia Marchio (Verona, 1996).
Spinelli, G. 'San Silvestro di Nonantola', in G. Spinelli (ed.), *Monasteri Benedettini in Emilia Romagna* (Milan, 1980), pp. 33–51.
'Origine e primi sviluppi della fondazione monastica sestense (762–967)', in G. C. Menis and A. Tilatti (eds.), *L'abbazia di S. Maria di Sesto fra archeologia e storia* (Pordenone, 1999), pp. 97–121.
Splett, J. *Althochdeutsches Wörterbuch*, 3 vols. (Berlin and New York, 1993).
Squatriti, P. 'Personal appearance and physionomics in early medieval Italy', *Journal of Medieval History* 14 (1988), 191–202.
Water and Culture in Early Medieval Italy (Cambridge, 1998).
Stevens, E.W. Jr. *Literacy, Law, and the Social Order* (Dekalb, 1988).
Stock, B. *The Implications of Literacy: Written Language and Models of Interpretation in the Eleventh and Twelfth Centuries* (Princeton, 1983).
Stone, L. 'Literacy and education in England', *Past and Present* 42 (1969), 69–139.
Supino Martini, P. 'La produzione libraria negli "scriptoria" delle abbazie di Farfa e di S. Eutizio', *Atti IX CISAM* (Spoleto, 1970), 581–607.
'Carolina romana e minuscola romanesca. Appunti per una storia della scrittura latina in Roma tra IX e XI secolo', *Scrittura e Civiltà* 2 (1978), 45–101.
'*Manuum mearum labores*. Nota sulle *chartae rescriptae*', *Scrittura e Civiltà* 3 (1984), 83–103.
Roma e l'area grafica romanesca (sec. X–XIII) (Alessandria, 1987).
'Le sottoscrizioni testimoniali al documento italiano del secolo VIII: le carte di Lucca', *Bullettino dell'Istituto Storico Italiano* 98 (1992), 87–108.
Susini, G. *Il lapicida romano: introduzione all'epigrafia latina* (Bologna, 1966), trans. A.M. Dabrowski and intro. E. Badian, *The Roman Stonecutter: An Introduction to Latin Epigraphy* (Oxford, 1973).
Epigrafia Romana (Rome, 1982).
Svennung, J. *Compositiones lucenses: Studien zum Inhalt, zur Textkritik und Sprache*, Uppsala Universitäts Årsskrift 1941:4 (Uppsala and Leipzig, 1941).
Tabacco, G. *I liberi del re nell'Italia carolingia e postcarolingia* (Spoleto, 1966).
'Dai possessori dell'età carolingia agli esercitali dell'età longobarda', *Studi Medievali*, ser. 3, 10 (1969), 221–68.
'La connessione fra potere e possesso nel regno franco e nel regno longobardo', *Settimane* 20 (Spoleto, 1973), 133–68.

Bibliography

'L'ambiguità delle istituzioni nell'Europa costruita dai Franchi', *Rivista Storica Italiana* 87 (1975), 392–425.

Egemonie sociali e strutture del potere nel medioevo italiano (Turin, 1979), trans. R. Brown Jensen, *The Struggle for Power in Medieval Italy: Structures of Political Rule* (Cambridge, 1989).

'La città italiana fra germanismo e latinità nella medievistica ottocentesca', in R. Elze and P. Schiera (eds.), *Il medioevo nell'ottocento in Italia e Germania* (Bologna, 1988), pp. 23–42.

Tagliaferri, A. *I Longobardi nella civiltà e nell'economia italiana nel primo medioevo* (Milan, 1969).

Tamassia, G. *Le fonti dell'editto di Rotari* (Pisa, 1889).

Tangl, G. 'Die Passvorschrift des Königs Ratchis und ihre Bezeihung zu dem Verhältnis zwischen Franken und Langobarden vom 6.–8. Jahrhundert', *Quellen und Forschungen aus Italianischen Archiven und Bibliotheken* 38 (1958), 1–66.

Themelly, A. 'Note sulla decorazione di alcuni manoscritti bobbiensi VII e VIII secoli', *Romanobarbarica* 12 (1993), 101–22.

Thibault, F. 'L'impôt direct et la propriété foncière dans la royaume des Lombards', *Nouvelle Revue Historique de Droit Français et Etranger* 28 (1904), 53–79.

Thomas, E. 'Die Romanität Pannoniens im 5. und 6. Jahrhundert', in W. Menghin, T. Springer and E. Warner (eds.), *Germanen Hunnen und Awaren* (Nuremberg, 1987), pp. 284–94.

Thompson, E.A. 'Christianity and the northern Barbarians', in A. Momigliano (ed.), *The Conflict between Paganism and Christianity in the Fourth Century* (Oxford, 1963), pp. 56–78.

Thompson, J.W. *The Literacy of the Laity in the Middle Ages* (New Berkeley, 1939; New York, 1960).

Tjäder, J.O. 'Der Codex Argentius in Uppsala und der Buchmeister Viliaric in Ravenna', *Studia Gotica* (Stockholm, 1972), 144–64.

'Considerazioni e proposte sulla scrittura latina nell'età romana', *Palaeographica, diplomatica et archivistica: studi in onore di G. Batelli*, Storia et Letteratura, Raccolta di Studi e Testi 139 (Rome, 1979), I, pp. 31–62.

'Some ancient letter-forms in the later Roman cursive and early medieval script of the *notarii*', *Scrittura e Civiltà* 6 (1982), 5–21.

Tosi, M. 'L'Edictus Rothari nei manoscritti bobiensi', *Archivium Bobiense* 4 (1982), 11–72.

Toubert, P. *Les Structures du Latium médiéval* (Rome, 1973).

Turrini, G. *Indice dei codici capitolari di Verona redatto 1625 dal canonico Agostino Rezzani: testo critico rapportato al Catalogo di Antonio Spagnolo* (Verona, 1965).

Millennium scriptorii veronensis dal IV al XV (Verona, 1967).

Ussani, V. 'Indice provvisorio degli spogli italiani per il dizionario latino dell'altomedioevo', *Bulletin DuCange* 6 (1931), 1–96.

Uytfanghe, M. van. 'Les expressions du type *quod vulgo vocant* dans des texts latins antérieurs au Concile de Tours et aux Serments de Strasbourg: témoinages lexicologiques et sociolinguistiques de la langue rustique romaine?', *Zeitschrift für Romanische Philologie* 105 (1989), 28–49.

Valentini, R. and G. Zuchetti. *Codice topografico della città di Roma*, II (Rome, 1942).

Bibliography

Van der Rhee, F. *Die germanische Wörter in die langobardische Gesetzen* (Rotterdam, 1970).
'Die germanischen Wörter in der *Historia Langobardorum* des Paulus Diaconus, *Romanobarbarica* 5 (1980), 271–96.
Vavaro, A. 'Latin and Romance: fragmentation or restructuring', in R. Wright (ed.), *Latin and the Romance Languages in the Early Middle Ages*, pp. 44–51.
Veit, U. 'Ethnic concepts in German pre-history: a case study on the relationship between cultural identity and archaeological objectivity', in S. Shennan (ed.), *Archaeological Approaches to Cultural Identity* (London, 1989), pp. 35–56.
Venturini, T. *Ricerche paleografiche intorno all'arcidiacono Pacifico di Verona* (Verona, 1929).
Versteegh, K. 'Latinitas, Hellenismos, Arabiyya', *Historiographia Linguistica* 12 (1986), 425–48.
Vigo, P. 'Ricerche su notai e notabili longobardi del Sacro Palazzo di Pavia', *Ricerche Medievali* 4 (1969–70), 94–143.
Vinogradoff, P. *Roman Law in Medieval Europe*, 2nd edn (London, 1929).
Viscardi, A. *Le origini. Storia letteraria d'Italia*, I, 3rd edn (Milan, 1939).
Vismara, G. 'Cristianesimo e legislazioni germaniche: leggi longobarde, alamanne e bavare', *Settimane* 14 (Spoleto, 1967), 397–470.
Edictum Theodorici, Ius Romanum Medii Aevi I, 2 b aa (Milan, 1967).
Volpini, R. 'Placiti del "Regnum Italiae"', in P. Zerbi (ed.), *Contributi dell'Istituto di storia medioevale*, III, pp. 245–520.
Wallace-Hadrill, J.M. *The Barbarian West 400–1000* (London, 1979).
Ward-Perkins, B. *From Classical Antiquity to the Middle Ages: Urban Public Building in Northern and Central Italy A.D. 300–850* (Oxford, 1984).
'Continuitists, catastrophists and the towns of post-Roman northern Italy', *Papers of the British School at Rome* 65 (1997), 156–76.
Wartburg, W. von. *Die Ausgliederung der romanischen Sprachräume* (Berne, 1950).
Wattenbach, W. *Das Schriftwesen im Mittelalter*, 3rd edn (Leipzig, 1896).
Wemple, S. *Women in Frankish Society: Marriage and the Cloister 500–900* (Philadelphia, 1981).
Wenskus, R. *Stammesbildung und Verfassung: das Werden der frühmittelalterlichen Gentes* (Cologne and Graz, 1961).
Wickham, C.J. 'Settlement problems in early medieval Italy: Lucca Territory', *Archeologia Medievale* 5 (1978), 495–503.
Early Medieval Italy: Central Power and Local Society, 400–1000 (London and Basingstoke, 1981).
'The other transition: from the ancient world to feudalism', *Past and Present* 113 (1984), 3–36. Reprinted in C.J. Wickham, *Land and Power* (London and Rome, 1994), pp. 7–42.
'The *terra* of San Vincenzo al Volturno in the eighth to twelfth centuries: the historical framework', in R. Hodges and J. Mitchell (eds.), *San Vincenzo al Volturno* (Oxford, 1985), pp. 227–58.
'Land disputes and their social framework in Lombard–Carolingian Italy, 700–900', in W. Davies and P. Fouracre (eds.), *The Settlement of Disputes in Early Medieval Europe* (Cambridge, 1986), pp. 105–24. Reprinted in C.J. Wickham, *Land and Power* (London and Rome, 1994), pp. 229–56.

Bibliography

'Marx, Sherlock Holmes, and late Roman commerce', *Journal of Roman Studies* 78 (1988), 183–193. Reprinted in C.J. Wickham, *Land and Power* (London and Rome, 1994), pp. 77–98.

The Mountains and the City: The Tuscan Apennines in the Early Middle Ages (Oxford, 1988).

'European forests in the early middle ages', *Settimane* 37 (Spoleto, 1989) 479–548. Reprinted in C.J. Wickham, *Land and Power* (London and Rome, 1994), pp. 155–200.

'Italy and the early middle ages', in K. Randsborg (ed.), *The Birth of Europe* (Rome, 1989), pp. 140–51. Reprinted in C.J. Wickham, *Land and Power* (London and Rome, 1994), pp. 99–120.

'La chute de Rome n'aura pas lieu', *Le Moyen Age* 99:1 (1993), 107–26.

Land and Power: Studies in Italian and European Social History, 400–1200 (London and Rome, 1994).

'Rural society in Carolingian Europe', in R. McKitterick (ed.), *NCMH*, II, *c. 700–900* (Cambridge, 1995), pp. 510–37.

'Aristocratic power in eighth-century Lombard Italy', in A.C. Murray (ed.), *After Rome's Fall* (Toronto, Buffalo and London, 1998), pp. 153–70.

Wild, J.P. 'Loanwords and Roman expansion in north-west Europe', *World Archaeology* 8 (1976), 57–64.

Wilkinson, J. *Jerusalem Pilgrims before the Crusades* (Warminster, 1977).

Wolfram, H. *Intitulatio I. Lateinische Königs- und Fürstentitel bis zum Ende des 8. Jahrhunderts*, Mitteilungen des Instituts für österreichische Geschichtsforschung 21 (Innsbruck, 1967).

'Methodischen Fragen zur Kritik am "sakralen" Königtum germanischer Stämme', in H. Birkhan and O. Gschwantler (eds.), *Festschrift für Otto Höfler* (Vienna, 1968), pp. 473–90.

Die Geschichte der Goten: von den Anfängen bis zur Mittel des sechsten Jahrhunderts. Entwurf einer historischen Ethnographie (Munich, 1979), trans. T.J Dunlap, *History of the Goths* (Berkeley, 1988).

'*Origo et religio*: ethnic traditions and literature in early medieval texts', *EME* 3:1 (1994), 19–38.

Wolfram, H. and W. Pohl (eds.). *Typen der Ethnogenese unter besonderer Berücksichtigung der Bayern*, I (Vienna, 1990).

Wolfram, H. and A. Schwarcz (eds.). *Die Bayern und ihre Nachbarn*, I (Vienna, 1985). *Anerkennung und Integration: zu den wirtschaftlichen Grundlagen der Völkerwanderungszeit (400–600)* (Vienna, 1988).

Wood, I. 'Disputes in late fifth- and sixth-century Gaul: some problems', in W. Davies and P. Fouracre (eds.), *The Settlement of Disputes in Early Medieval Europe* (Cambridge, 1986), pp. 7–22.

'Administration, law and culture in Merovingian Gaul', in R. McKitterick (ed.), *The Uses of Literacy in Early Medieval Europe* (Cambridge, 1990), pp. 63–81.

Woolf, G. 'Power and the spread of writing in the West', in A. Bowman and G. Woolf (eds.), *Literacy and Power in the Ancient World* (Cambridge, 1994), pp. 84–98.

Wormald, P. 'The decline of the Western Empire and the survival of its aristocracy' (Review of J. Matthews, *Western Aristocracies*), *JRS* 66 (1976), 217–26.

Bibliography

'The uses of literacy in Anglo-Saxon England and its neighbours', *Transactions of the Royal Historical Society* 5th ser., 27 (1977), 95–114.

'*Lex scripta* and *verbum regis*: legislation and Germanic kingship, from Euric to Cnut', in P. Sawyer and I. Wood (eds.), *Early Medieval Kingship* (Leeds, 1979) pp. 105–38.

'Bede and the conversion of England: the charter evidence', Jarrow Lecture 1984.

'Charters, law, and the settlement of disputes in Anglo-Saxon England', in W. Davies and P. Fouracre (eds.), *The Settlement of Disputes of Early Medieval Europe* (Cambridge, 1986), pp. 149–68.

The Making of English Law: King Alfred to the Twelfth Century, I, *Legislation and Its Limits* (Oxford, 1999).

Wright, R. *Late Latin and Early Romance in Spain and Carolingian France* (Liverpool, 1982).

Review of Banniard, *Viva voce*, *Journal of Medieval Latin* 3 (1993), 78–94.

Early Ibero-Romance (Newark, 1994).

'Latino e Romanzo: Bonifazio e il Papa Gregorio II', in J. Herman and L. Mondin (eds.), *La preistoria dell'Italiano* (Tübingen, 2000), pp. 219–29.

'Even Priscian nods', *Acts of the Sixth International Conference on Late and Vulgar Latin* (Helsinki, forthcoming).

Wright, R. (ed.). *Latin and the Romance Languages in the Early Middle Ages* (London, 1991).

Zanini, E. 'Ricontando la terra sigillata africana', *Archeologia Medievale* 23 (1996), 677–88.

Le Italie bizantine: territorio, insediamenti ed economia nella provincia bizantina d'Italia (VI–VIII secolo) (Bari, 1998).

Zeiller, J. 'Les églises ariennes de Rome à l'époque de la domination gotique', *Mélanges d'Archéologie et d'Histoire de l'Ecole Française de Rome* 24 (1904), 17–33.

'Etude sur l'arianisme en Italie à l'époque ostrogothique et à l'époque lombarde', *Mélanges d'Archéologie et d'Histoire* 25 (1905), 121–53.

Les Origines chrétiennes dans les provinces danubiennes de l'empire romain (Paris, 1918).

Zelzer, K. 'Zur Stellung der Textus receptus und des interpolitierten Textes in der Textgeschichte der *Regula S. Benedicti*', *RB* 88 (1978), 205–46.

'Von Benedikt zu Hildemar: zur Textgestalt and Textgeschichte der Regula Benedicti auf ihrem Weg zur Alleingeltung', *Frühmittelalterliche Studien* 23 (1989), 112–30.

Zielinski, H. *Studien zu den spoletinischen 'Privaturkunden' des 8. Jahrhunderts und ihre Überlieferung im Regestum Farfense*, Bibliotek des deutschen Historischen Instituts in Rom 39 (Tübingen, 1972).

'Gregor von Catino und das Regestum Farfense', *Quellen und Forschungen aus Italienischen Archiven und Bibliotheken* 55/56 (1976), 361–404.

Zuliani, F. 'L'abbazia di Nonantola', in F. Zuliani and C. Segre Montel (eds.), *La pittura nell'Abbazia di Nonantola: un refettorio affrescato di età romanica* (Nonantola, 1991), pp. 5–28.

INDEX OF MANUSCRIPTS

CLA numbers, where possible, are given in brackets after the shelf mark.

BAMBERG
Staatsbibliothek
Patr. 61 (VIII.1029)   305

BERLIN
Staatsbibliothek
Diez. B.66 (VIII.1044)   302, 303, 304
Frag. 48 (VIII.1046)   313
lat. fol. 381 no.1 + Hildersheim 658 (VIII.1050)   305
Phillipps 1831   314

BERNE
Burgerbibliothek
363   304

BRESCIA
Biblioteca Civica Queriniana
A.III.14   181, 182
B.II.6   302

CAVA DEI TIRRENI
Archivio della Badia
4   93, 102, 193

CIVIDALE
Museo archeologico
S.N. + Prague, Bib. Metr CIM 1 + Venice, S. Marco (III.285)   290

ERFURT
Wissenschaftliche Bibliothek
Ampl. 2.74 (VIII.1190)   286

FLORENCE
Biblioteca Medicea Laurenziana
Digest, S.N. (III.295)   312

GOTHA
Forshcungsbibliothek
I.84   93, 96

IVREA
Biblioteca Capitolare
1 (III.300)   281
34   93
94 (III.301)   305

KARLSRUHE
Badische Landesbibliothek
Aug. LVII (VIII.1077)   314
Aug. CXXXIX   291
Aug. CLXXXI (VIII.1086)   315
Aug. CC (VIII.1093)   313
Aug. CCXXII (VIII.1096)   313
Aug. CCLI (VIII.1110)   315
Aug. CCLXI (VIII.1111)   313

LONDON
British Library
Add. 5463 (II.162)   293
Add. 43460 (II.180–1)   296
Chester Beatty 5 (II.161)   296
Cotton Nero A.II (II.186)   315

LUCCA
Biblioteca Capitolare Feliniana
490 (III.303)   159

MADRID
Biblioteca Nacional
413   93, 102

MILAN
Biblioteca Ambrosiana
B.31 sup. (III.308)   314
C.5 inf. (III.311)   280
C.98 inf. (III.322)   290
C.105 inf. (III.323b)   281
C.301 inf. (III.326)   84
D.268 inf. (III.334)   312
E.147 sup. (I.26b+c)   281

Index of manuscripts

MILAN (cont.)
F.84 sup. (III.341)   282
H.78 sup. + Turin, G.V.15 (III.347)   284
I.1 sup (III.348)   313
I.61 sup. (III.350)   312
L.91 sup. (III.353)   314
O.212 sup. (III.361)   284
S.45 sup. (III.365)   279
Cimelio 1 (III.304)   311

Archivio civico storico
Trivulziano 688 (III.366)   283

MODENA
Archivio Capitolare
O.I.2   93, 95, 96
O.I.11 (III.368)   305
O.I.12 (III.369)   313
O.I.17 (III.370)   314

MOMBELLO DI IMBERSAGO
Archivio del Principe
S.N. (III.371)   311

MONTE CASSINO
Archivio della Badia
353   93
523 (III.380)   282

MUNICH
Bayerische Staatsbibliothek
Clm 6302   291
Clm 13581   317
Clm 14510   317

NAPLES
Biblioteca Nazionale
lat. 1 (Vindobon. 17) (III.388–90)   149
lat. 2 (Vindobon. 16) (III.391–6)   284
IV.A.8 (III.403)   314

NOVARA
Biblioteca Nazionale
2 (III.406)   283

OXFORD
Bodleian Library
100+101+102 (II.255)   286

PARIS
Bibliothèque Mazarine
660   296

Bibliothèque Nationale
Baluze 270   315
lat. 4613   93
lat. 4616   93
lat. 5730 (V.562)   314
lat. 6161   93

lat. 7530 (V.569)   304
lat. 7900a   305
lat. 9427 (V.579)   282
lat. 10318 (V.593)   302
lat. 10616 + 10457 (V.601)   291
lat. 11326 (V.609)   286
lat. 13025   304

PERUGIA
Bibliotheca capitolare
2 (IV.408)   313

PRINCETON, NEW JERSEY
W.H. Scheide Collection
Daniel Fragment (XI.1665)   315

ROME
Biblioteca Nazionale Centrale
1006 (IV.428)   295
1378   295
Sessor.13 (IV.418)   296
Sessor. 39 (IV.419)   296
Sessor. 55 (IV.420a–b)   296
Sessor. 58 (IV.422)   296
Sessor. 77 (IV.423)   296
Sessor. 94 (IV.425)   296
Sessor. 128 (IV.426)   296
Sessor. 590 (IV.427)   295

ST GALL
Stiftsbibliothek
108 (VII.905)   313
207 (VII.920)   313
227 (VII.930)   315
730 (VII.949)   93, 168
908 (VII.953–65)   302
1399 a.3 (VII.997)   315

ST PAUL IN CARINTHIA
Stiftsbibliothek
7.1 (X.1457)   286

ST PETERSBURG
Saltykov-Shchedrin State Public Library
F. XIV.1   244
F. V.1.7 (XI.1603)   315

TURIN
Archivio di Stato
1B.II.27 (IV.438)   279

Biblioteca Nazionale
[A.II.2] (IV.444)   281
F.IV.1 fasc. 5+6 (IV.452)   84
F.IV.1 fasc. 9 (IV.454)   280
G.V.15 (IV.465)see Milan, Amb.
o.212 sup.
G.V.26 (IV.463)   310

Index of manuscripts

VERCELLI
Biblioteca Capitolare Eusebiana
  XXXIX   283
  CXXI   93
  CLVIII (IV.668b)   283
  CLXXXIII (IV.469)   283
  CLXXXIII, fols. 107–111
    (IV.470)   283
  CLXXXVIII (IV.471)   93, 168, 283
  CCII   314

VATICAN CITY
Biblioteca Apostolica Vaticana
  lat. 3314   298
  lat. 4929   301
  lat. 5001   93, 102
  lat. 5359   93
  lat. 5750 (I.26b+c)   286
  lat. 5757 (I.34)   280
  lat. 5758 (I.36)   279
  lat. 5763 (I.39)   281, 314
  lat. 5951   296, 305
  Barb. lat. 679 (I.65)   297
  Pal. lat. 833   243, 247
  Pal. lat. 165   298
  Pal. lat. 187 (I.80 a–b, 81)   305
  Pal. lat. 1547   302
  Reg. lat. 1040 (I.112)   282
  Reg. lat. 1997 (I.113)   313
  Urb. lat. 983   93
  Urb. lat. 293 (I.116)   305

VERONA
Biblioteca Capitolare
  I (1) (IV.472)   286
  II (2) (IV.477)   289
  IV (3) (IV.488)   312
  XIII (11) (IV.484)   288
  XXXVII (35) (IV.493)   289
  XXXVIII (36)(IV.494)   289
  XL (38) (IV.498)   282
  LI (49) (IV.504)   289
  LV (53) (IV.507)   281
  LIX (59) (IV.509)   286
  LX (58) (IV.510)   286
  LXI (59) (IV.511)   286
  LXII (60) (IV.512)   281
  LXXXV (80) (IV.514)   288
  LXXXIX (84) (IV.515)   130
  CLXIII (150) (IV.516)   304

VIENNA
Österreichische Nationalbibliothek
  954 (X.1492)   315

WOLFENBÜTTEL
Herzog-August-Bibliothek
  Weiss. 64 (+ Vat. lat. 5763) (IX.1386, I.39)
    314

GENERAL INDEX

Aachen, 301
abbreviations, *see* script
Adaloald, king, 74, 201
Adelperga, 182
administration, 52–3, 70–7, 170–86, 199–205, 319–20
Africa, 40, 51, 68, 71, 208
African Red Slip, pottery, 15
agents, royal, 91, 159, 192–6, 352; *see also* Gunteram; officials
Agilulf, king, 65, 74, 76, 99, 201, 253, 321
Agnellus of Ravenna, 72
Aistulf, king, 79, 115, 182, 188, 231, 294, 296–7
  legislation of, 178–80
Alahis, *vir magnificus*, 232
Alan, of Farfa, 292–3
Alboin, king, 65–8, 77, 113
Alcuin, 133, 283, 292, 317
aldius/aldia, 116, 178
Aldo, of Milan, 251, 264, 266
allegory, 39, 291
Amalasuintha, queen, 30
Ambrose, St, 283, 285, 312
  Ambrosian rite, 302
Ambrosius Autpert, 293
amund, see *mundium*
anagrip, 118
Ancona, 283
Anglo-Saxons, 243, 268, 297, 307
Anselm, of Nonantola, 294–5, 296, 297
  vita of, 296
Ansoald, notary, 169
Anthologia latina, 302, 313
anthropology, 1, 164, 167, 197, 222
antiquarian, 238–40, 293
Appendix probi, 149
Aquileia, 60, 67, 80, 242, 285, 290
Arator, 43–4
archaeology, 55, 106, 169
archives, 197–202, 224–9; *see also* documents, preservation of
arengae, 224–7

Arezzo, *see* Siena–Arezzo dispute
arga, 111, 114
Arianism, 31, 58–61, 320–21
Arichis I, duke, 97, 241, 250
arimanni, 107, 116, 191
Arioald, king, 60
Aripert II, king, 196, 288, 321
aristocrats
  Roman, 15–18, 74, 239, 319
  Lombard, 111, 128–9, 185, 296–8
army, *see* military
Ars numeri, text (Lucca 490), 159, 323
arschild, see *harischild*
astalin, 122
Atala, abbot, 279
Athalaric, king, 23, 29, 111
Attepert, scribe, 293–4
Audoald, *dux liguriae*, 72, 258–60
Audoald, *vir clarissimus*, 223
Audoin, king, 113
Augustine, St, 22, 28
  works of, 283, 285
Ausonius, 22
Austrasia, 73
Authari, king, 59–60, 65, 74
Avars, 67, 303

Bangor antiphony, 280
Banniard, M., 133
barba, 116
Barbatus, bishop, 63
baro, 116
Baronias, *custos*, 245
baths, 245, 249
Bavarians, 17, 113, 124, 164
Benedict, St, 41, 45–9, 148
  Rule of, 46–9, 148, 212, 299–300
Bergamo, 89, 169, 204, 207, 268
Bible, *see* scriptures, holy
biblical commentaries, 291
biblical literacy, 50, 319
Bieda (*Blera*), 83

374

General index

bilingualism, 100–1, 133, 322
bishops, 34, 61, 63, 121–2, 194, 244, 268;
　see also clergy
bluttare, 119–20
Bobbio, 61, 298, 305, 312, 321, 326;
　see also Atala; Columbanus; Jonas
　catalogue of, 280
Boethius, 4, 26
Boniface, 149, 309
books, 27–8, 286–7, 299–300; see also
　manuscripts
　lay ownership of, 300, 326
boundary markers, 173
Brescia, 105, 181, 268, 298, 302
breve, 192
Brunhild, queen, 45
Bulgars, 114
bureaucracy, 33–5, 99, 135, 193
Byzantium, Byzantine empire, 35, 72, 74, 129,
　164–6, 202, 208, 321
　Byzantine Italy, 14–35, 62, 64, 166, 230, 280,
　322

Caesarius of Arles, 41
Campania, 89, 130, 301
camphio, see duel
Campione, 178, 185, 215
Candidus, see Wizo
Capannori, 224, 226
Carmen de synodo ticinensi, 245–7, 286
Carolingians, 78–9, 149, 187, 192, 197, 200,
　235, 284, 291, 320, 326
　renaissance, 2, 134, 301, 318, 327
Casa Anelli, 237, 254
case, see declensions
Cassiodorus, 4, 24–5; see also Vivarium
　De orthographia, 38, 149–50
　Institutiones, 24, 38, 305
　Variae, 24
Castel Trosino, 272
Castelseprio, 184
Catholicism, 54, 57, 320
cautio, 175
cawerfida, 116–17, 195
chanceries, chancery script, 186–7, 231–3, 314
Charlemagne, 78–9, 112, 234, 297, 301
Charles Martel, 260
charters
　dispositivity of, 211
　dorsal notes on, 211, 232
　private, 141, 197–8, 297, 324
　probative value of, 172, 197, 210
　royal, 67, 78, 120, 124, 170–80, 198, 253,
　288, 321
　size of, 214, 307

Chelles, 299
Chieti, 313
Christianity, and literacy, 57, 83, 171, 213, 272,
　319–21
　names, 108
Chrysologus, Peter, 38–9, 49
church, and state, 82, 170, 321
Cicero, 317, 319
cities, 9, 15, 72, 84, 134, 190–1, 226–7, 239,
　320–6
Cividale, 257, 290, 297
classical literature, see Latin; literature;
　manuscripts
classical norms, orthography, grammar, 46, 52,
　131–5, 226, 263, 306–11, 323
Cleph, king, 65, 68, 74
clergy, 109, 144, 206, 247, 271, 278, 284, 317,
　319
　clerical literacy, 9, 15–31, 144–50, 161, 171,
　287–90
　clericus, 200, 204, 210
　education/training, 82
　Lombard, 43, 223–4; see also Lucca
climate change, 17
Codex Amiatinus, 298
Codex Diezanus, 302–4
Codex Ingilrammi, 312
Codex Nazarianus, 302
Codex Salmasianus, 302
Columba, twice widowed, 246
Columbanus, S., 61, 81, 279, 281, 321
Commachio, see *magistri commacini*
Como, 27, 82, 184, 264
Compositiones, text (Lucca 490), 155–6, 323
Constantinople, 16, 30, 58, 65, 208, 241, 285
contracts, 173, 175
Corbie, 304
Corteolona, 248, 260
countryside, 9, 15, 29, 134, 227, 294, 299,
　326
courts
　ecclesiastical, 190
　Lombard, 72, 115, 121, 155, 172–6, 213,
　223, 324
　royal 78–80, 122, 180, 185, 220, 271–2,
　321–2; *curtes regiae/regis*, 72, 78
Cresconius, 297, 312
Crypta Balbi, 170
Cumianus, of Bobbio, 251–4
Cunincperga, 181, 251, 256
Cunincpert, king, 178, 196, 256–7, 260, 263,
　285, 298, 321
curia, 76, 135, 206, 208
Curtius, E., 131
Cyprian, 32

General index

Damian, bishop of Pavia, 244, 285, 290, 321
Dante, 137
dating
    of charters, 168–9
    of inscriptions, 255, 260
    of legislation, 169
    of manuscripts, 278–9, 326
declamationes, 21
declensions, case usage, 138–9, 227, 323
Decretum de libris recipiendis, 287
Desiderius, king, 120, 184, 187, 250, 294
Deusdona, priest, 224–7
dialects, 134–7, 322
diglossia, 133
diplomacy, 69–70
documents
    preservation of, 40, 197, 226–34, 319, 351; see also archives; *gesta municipalia*; *scrineum*
    redaction of, 211–14
donations, 49, 126–7, 141, 148, 223
Drotculf, 71
duel (*camphio*), 123
dukes, see Lombards

Eberhard, of Friuli, 95–6
Edict, see Rothari
education, 8–9, 20, 167, 215, 219–21, 318; see also *enarratio*; schools
Egypt, 156, 241
Eigenklöster, 299
Emilia-Romagna, 83, 166
enarratio, 21
Ennodius, 4, 23–6, 245, 319
epigraphy
    development of, 263–4, 325
    funerary, 181
    see also inscriptions
Ermedruda, 183
Eusebius, St, of Vercelli, 290
exceptores, 205–8

faderfio, 116
faida, 116, 165
Fanano, 296
fara, 67, 106
Farfa, 187, 199, 204, 292, 293, 298
Faroald II, duke, 298
fegangi, 118
feld, 113
ferquidus, 120–1
fideiussor, see oathhelper
fides publica, 200, 207
Fleury, 304

forgery, 169, 172, 204
formulae, legal, 140, 152–3, 193–4, 225–9; see also *mancipatio*; *post traditam*
formularies, 148, 209, 221
fornaccar, 124
Fortunatus, Venantius, 45, 275
Franks, 2, 18, 66, 69, 110, 112, 146; see also Carolingians; Gaul; Merovingians
    Franco-papal alliance, 322
Fratellus, scribe, 226
Frea, goddess, 88–9, 91, 321
Fredegar, 74, 92
Friuli, 69–70, 105, 112, 294, 297
fulboran, 116
fulcfree, 116–17

gaida et gisel, 127, 128, 177
gairethinx, 116, 127, 163, 165
Gargano, 236, 265–74
gasindii, 179, 193
gastalds, *gastaldi*, 153, 188–90, 204, 231, 320
Gaudentius, scribe, 144–5, 200, 206, 300
Gaul, 22, 209, 318; see also Merovingians
Gelasius, pseudo-, see *Decretum de libris*
Gepids, 61, 67, 103
Gerbert, of Aurillac, 326
Germanic, 318, 320
    ethnicity, 4, 14
    language, 110; see also dialects; Gothic language
        Langobardic language, 100–4, 322
        in Lombard law, 110; see also loan-words; onomastics; place-names;
        Old High German, 88, 100, 103, 322
gesta municipalia, 224–41; see also archives
Gibbon, E., 4, 21
gold, 156
    writing in, 158, 196, 288, 321
goldsmiths, 9, 284
Gospels, swearing upon, 122, 171, 192, 212
Gothic language, 30–2, 57, 60, 100–2, 311
Gothic wars, 14, 18, 76, 207, 277
government, Lombard, 59, 120, 185–6, 194–6; see also administration; state
Grado, 67, 79
graffiti, 145, 259; see also Gargano; Olevano sul Tusciano; Trani
grammar, 14, 20, 73, 148–9, 204, 225, 279, 315–22; see also classical norms; declensions; prepositions; pronouns; syntax; verbs
grammarians, 21–31, 149–62, 196, 263, 291, 308
Grasulf, of Friuli, 69, 166, 250, 320
Gray, N., 254

376

General index

Greek language, 12, 20, 26, 57, 111, 115, 150, 156, 248, 286–7, 303, 317
Gregorio di Catino, 204
Gregory I, pope, 8, 40, 59, 70, 71, 76, 83–4, 134, 247, 283, 319
  Dialogues, 45–51, 62–5
  homilies, 313
  letters of, 50, 62–4, 151, 247, 283
  Moralia, 313
  Pastoral Care, 50, 281–2
Gregory of Tours, 41, 59, 61, 110, 247, 263
Grimoald, king, 89, 94, 267, 269
  legislation of, 168
Gunfred, of Monteverdi, 299
Gunteram, royal agent, 150–2, 189, 201

habeo, 46
Hadrian, pope, 296, 321
hagiography, 11, 94, 290, 299, 318
harischild, 118–19, 140
Harris, M., 237
Hilary of Poitiers, 285, 288
Historia langobardorum codicis gothani (HLCGoth.), 93, 170
history writing, narrative, 86, 170, 181–2, 283, 291
holy men, 298, 319
hospitalitas, 73–4, 183
Hospitius, of Nissa, 110
Huns, 40, 57, 92

iconoclasm, 247
Indovinello veronese, 130, 137
ink, 49, 155, 211, 284, 308
inscriptions, 72, 103, 116, 131, 235, 324
  audience for, 237
  clericalisation of, 258–60
  display of, 236–40, 324
  educational purpose of, 240–7, 324
  figural design/decoration of, 240, 251, 325
  funerary, 238, 325
  and images, 247–8
  Liutprandian, 248–50
  location of, 238
  Lombard style, 236, 254, 325
  Pavese style, 238
insular script/scribal traditions, 280
interpretex, 110–11
interregnum, 65, 73, 76, 87
Ireland/Irish, 301, 307
Isernia, 188
Isidore, of Seville, 87, 92, 283–308
Istria, Istrian churches, 70, 80
Italian language, 113, 149, 159; *see also* proto-Italian, proto-Romance

Italians, primitive, 317
Ivrea, 244, 281

Jerome, 22, 36, 93, 149, 182, 285, 309
Jews, Judaism, 65, 116, 166, 292, 321
John, nephew of Thomas, 246
John Lydus, 33–4
Jonas, of Bobbio, 279
Jordanes, *Getica*, 89–90
judges (*iudex*), 138, 150, 167, 176, 204, 288, 300, 320
Justinian, 14, 18, 55, 58, 166, 202, 232
  Codex, 14, 213, 223, 283
  Novels, 34, 165, 208, 220
  Pragmatic Sanction, 14

land, land-ownership, 75–6, 176–7, 203, 210, 297, 299, 320
language, *see* Germanic language; Greek; Italian; Latin; linguistic development; proto-Italian
Latin, 9, 15, 73, 84, 134, 226–7, 239, 322–6
  glosses, 101, 115
  spoken, 110–11, 131–3, 261–2, 323
  vulgar, 111, 132, 153, 180, 323
  see also formulae; grammar; literature
launichild, 116, 165, 176
law, 49, 92–8, 115, 164
  criminal, 195, 324
  and custom, 76, 118, 244, 318–21; *see also cawerfida*
  family law, 115, 165, 171, 324
  legal culture, 48–9, 115–18, 166–71, 198, 210, 324
  Lombard, 92–8, 201–3, 300, 322
    reactive quality of, 202
  personal, personality of, 95, 173
  property law, 49, 115–19, 167, 198, 203, 324
  Roman, 116, 164–5, 202–3, 323
  'vulgar', 167, 174, 203, 209
layout, of text (*mise en page*), 308
leases, 172, 226
legibility, 306–7, 326
  'grammar' of, 307
Leonine Sacramentary, 287–8
letters, use of, 191–2, 317, 324
Levy, E., 167, 222
Liber diurnus, 83
Liber pontificalis, 19, 66, 149, 155, 190, 283, 321
liberal arts, 14, 245, 319
Liberius, patrician, 32
libraries, 49, 279–80
  catalogues of, 280, 294, 295
librarii, 317
lid in laib, 126–7

377

General index

Liguria, 16–17, 67, 258
linguistic development, 37, 149
  towards Romance, 38, 145, 239, 355;
    see also proto-Romance
literacy
  as capillary, 318
  definitions of, 6, 195, 197–9, 261–71, 306, 318
  'democratisation' of, 327
  illiteracy, 196, 318–19
  legal, 195–6, 234, 318
  levels of, 237, 271
  public display of, 236, 292
  quantitative reckoning of, 9, 237, 318
    and script types, 331; see also legibility, minuscule
    and cursive, 327
literature, 15, 21, 114, 276, 277–8
  classical literary tradition, 277, 326
    preservation of, 300–5
    rare works, see Codex Diezanus
  religious, 277–305, 358; see also patristic
littera notabilior, 307–8
litterae, 19–24, 319
liturgy, 83, 130–1, 285
Liutprand, king, 59, 78, 102, 117, 130, 189–90, 236, 245, 298, 321, 325
  legislation of, 140, 154, 171, 173, 182, 201, 220, 251
  see also inscriptions
livellarium, 177, 231
loan-words, 112–13, 354; see also Germanic language
Lombards
  custom, 62–3, 165–7
  dukes, 72, 74, 109, 110, 147, 170, 193, 232, 254, 258, 320
  ethnic identity, 54–6, 101–2, 165, 321–2
  invited to Italy, 66, 98, 320
  language, see Germanic language
  monarchy, 69, 182, 269; see also court, royal
  numbers of, 67–8
lost texts, 61, 83, 186, 231, 243–4, 292–3, 318
Lowe, E.A., 282
Lucca, 119–21, 147, 179, 185, 220, 221, 224–9, 283, 306
  church of, 121, 145, 200, 211, 224–9, 324
  clergy of, 121, 144, 146–7, 227, 300, 306
  preservation of documents at, 120–2, 211, 224
  school of, 224–8
  see also Capannori; Fratellus; Gaudentius; manuscripts; Osprand; Prandulus; Sicherad

Lucio, *aldius*, 178
luminaria, 232
Luni, 64
Lupus, of Ferrières, 95–6
Luxeuil, 281
  script, 281
Lyons, 282

McKitterick, R., 3, 6, 235
magister, 146, 219, 233, 253, 274
Magnerata, of Campione, 184
mancipatio formulae, 155, 174, 221
manumission, 167, 177–80, 212
  charters of, 172–7
  rituals, 127, 177–8
manuscripts, 168, 237, 277
  attribution of, 277–8, 325
  decoration in, 313
  exemplars of, 156, 326
  marginal additions to, 130, 281, 286–92
  palimpsest, 277, 287
  preservation of, 298, 326
  subscriptions and colophons in, 28, 142, 295, 308
  survival of, 2, 277, 284, 325
  tradition, 46, 92–3, 113, 168–9, 321
  see also books; dating
maraphis, 112, 193
marble, 253, 275
Markus, R., 52
Master, *Rule* of the, 46–7, 301
Maurace, *vir clarissimus*, 154, 200, 207
Maurezius, royal cellarer (*canevaggio regis*), 130, 142, 300
Maximus, of Turin, 290, 313
medicine, medical texts, 14
Memoratio de mercebus magistrorum commacinorum, 122, 253
Merovingians, 37, 79, 197, 225, 229, 234, 237;
  see also Franks, Gaul
  script/scribal traditions, 306, 325; see also Luxeuil
metfio, meta, 116, 185
Metz, 303, 313
Michael, St, archangel, cult of, 267, 273; see also Gargano
Milan, 23, 25, 60–1, 187, 211, 232, 243–4, 285, 325
milestones, 241–2, 325
military, army, 77–9, 102–3, 152, 166, 194
  terms, 122–3
minuscule, see script
missus royal, 153, 184, 189, 201, 231; see also Gunteram
Modena, 254

General index

monasteries, 11, 64, 99, 188–9, 258, 282, 292–300
  numbers of, 298; *see also* Benedict; Master
money, coins, 172, 235
monimen, 179
Monothelite hetesy, 285
Monte Amiata, 292, 297
Monte Cassino, 11, 137, 268–9, 292, 294
Monte Pulciano, 153
Monteverdi, 299–300
Monza, 85, 264, 283
morgingab/morgengab, 116, 185
morphology, 37, 142, 161, 323
morth, 119
Mozarabic Orational, 144, 320; *see also* MS 147
mundium, 78, 116, 165, 178, 226
  mundoald, 116, 179
  amund, 127
  see also women
music, 261

names, personal, 108–9, 132, 268–71, 322
Naples, 28, 279, 301
Narni, 65, 83
Narses, 19, 65, 66, 103, 123
Neustria, 73
Nissa, 110
Nonantola, 292, 294–7
Norberg, D., 134, 262
notary, *notarius*, 85, 121, 141, 143, 199–200, 271, 324
  civitatis, 206
  ecclesiae, 206–7
  royal (*regis*), 183, 189, 201
notitia, 192
  brevis, 185
  de actoribus regis, 171, 192
  traditionis, 184
Novalesa, 292, 293
Novara, 232, 255, 283

oathhelpers, oathtakers, 121, 172
oaths, 167, 171, 176, 212
Odovacer, 27, 33, 60, 208
officials, Lombard, 193, 320
Olevano sul Tusciano, graffiti at, 265
onomastics, 101, 108
Opilio, 32
oral communication, 3, 5, 57, 122, 141, 154, 179, 186
oral traditions, 88, 126–7, 163, 283
Origo gentis langobardorum, 54, 170, 320
orthography, 32–8, 112–15, 146–8, 331; *see also* classical norms

logographic, 143–4, 306
Osprand, scribe, 206, 227
Ostrogoths, 4–5, 19, 23, 30, 61, 68, 104–5, 167, 210, 277, 319

Pacificus, of Verona, 287
paganism, 58, 61–5, 241, 243, 320–1
palace, royal, 79, 85, 153, 201, 248–54, 301
Pannonia, 54–5, 103, 210, 242
pans, *in pans*, 116, 127
papacy, popes, 42, 60, 109, 148–9, 171, 190, 207, 268, 285, 323
  papal hatred of Lombards, 322
papyrus, 197, 241, 328; *see also* Ravenna books, 311
parchment, 155–7, 163, 211, 284, 311, 317
parish, rural, 299
Parkes, M., 307
passports, 192
patristics, texts, 84, 114, 181, 277, 283
patronage, 292
Paul the Deacon, 11, 16–17, 44, 61, 65, 110–14, 127, 166, 181–2, 223, 241, 254, 288–90, 321–2, 325, 327
  and epigraphy, 45, 130, 241, 246, 249, 267, 275, 325
  Historia langobardorum, 44, 88, 112, 244–5, 255
  Historia romana, 45, 90, 182, 241
  and Lombard language, 110–11, 322
  poetry of, 47, 88, 304
Paulinus of Aquileia, 292, 327
Pavia, 45, 64–5, 120, 153, 167, 168, 205, 230, 237, 243, 283–5, 325
  Synod of, 79, 186, 265, 310; *see also Carmen de synodo*
peasants, 77
Pentapolis, 321
Perctarit, king, 90, 201, 256, 260, 298, 321
Peredeo, bishop, 120
Persiceta, 294
Perugia, 70, 83, 283, 302
Peter of Pisa, 292, 303, 327
Piacenza, 78, 79, 112, 154, 174, 179, 206, 207, 221–4, 243, 324
  dispute with Parma, 194
Pignolo, 288
pigs, 80, 182; *see also sonorpair*
Pippin, king, 303
Pippin III, *maiordomus*, 325
Pisa, 109, 130, 144, 231, 299, 300
Pistoia, 230
place-names, 101, 105–8, 322
placitum, 69, 119, 130, 137, 176, 178, 197, 202
plague, 16

379

General index

plough, words for, 124
Po, River, 19, 78, 190, 223, 248
poetry, verse, 25, 290; *see also* Paul the Deacon; rhythmic metres
polemic against rhetoric, 15, 36, 319
Pomerius Julianus, 40–2
popes, *see* Gregory; Hadrian; papacy
post traditam [*cartam*], 212
praeceptum, 180–7, 231
Prandulus, scribe, 200
prepositions, 138–9, 227, 309, 323
Pretonax, 268, 300
Priscian, 150
privatisation, 198
probationes pennae, 187
Procopius, 18, 30–1, 55, 58
pronouns, 140
pronunciation, 108, 133–43, 315, 323
property, and documentation, 39; *see also* land
proprietorial culture, 209
Prosper, chronicle, continuation of (*Prosperi continuatio haveniensis*), 235
proto-Romance, 111, 130–3, 323
Psalms, 47, 50, 264, 285, 288
  psalters, 286
Pseudo-Clemens, 289
public authority, 183, 219–21, 356; *see also* state
public/private distinction, 10, 200, 233–4
publicus, 204
punctuation, 261, 307
  per cola et commata, 307–8
  see also legibility

Quintilian, 20, 26, 241, 319

Ragintruda, queen, 181
Ratchis, king, 70, 86, 121, 123, 187, 192, 231, 297
Ravenna, 14, 38, 60, 72, 208, 214, 275, 287, 301, 321
  church of, 208
  scribes at (*forenses, tabelliones*), 17, 135–6
Ravennate papyri, 135–6, 207–9, 244, 323
recipes, technical/medical, 155–9, 309, 356; *see also Compositiones*; medicine
Reggio, 296
Rhaetia, 124
rhetoric, Latin, 14–15, 69, 251–6, 290, 302, 319
rhythmic metres/verse, 237, 244–7, 325
Riché, P., 237, 244
Rieti, 187
Rodchis, 170
rogator, 211, 217

Roman
  epigraphic heritage, 236, 239–42, 324
  survival of, 236, 275, 318
  see also aristocracy, law
Rome, 14–22, 23, 79, 83, 148–9, 192, 243, 296, 301, 321–3
  St Peter's, 83, 190
Romoald I, II, dukes, 269, 270
Rosamund, queen, 89
Rothari, king, 59, 87, 101, 114, 163, 201, 300, 321
  Edict of, 77, 92, 114–29, 163–71, 321
  language of, 138–40

sala, 107–22
Salerno, 241, 250
San Salvatore, Brescia, 181, 298
San Salvatore, Monte Amiata, *see* Monte Amiata
San Vincenzo al Volturno, 188, 236, 292, 298
Sanctulus, 51
Saracens, 260, 267, 293
Sardinia, 130
Saxons, 67, 118, 158, 181; *see also* Anglo-Saxons
scaffardus, 112
Scandinavia, 55–6, 165
Schiaparelli, L., 187, 198, 212, 283, 318
schools, 11, 39, 135–48, 167, 208, 215, 287, 292
  clerical, 283
  see also education, clergy
scilpor, 112, 193
scriba/scrivane, 201–2
scribes, 152, 188, 218–25, 311–16; *see also* Fratellus; Gaudentius; Lucca; Maurace; notary; Prandulus; Ravenna; Sicherad; *tabelliones*
  titles of, 201–2
scrineum, 232
script
  abbreviations, 143–4, 209, 310, 312, 327
  aerated script, 309
  Beneventan, 295, 316
  capitals, 219, 251, 269
  diversity of, 280–1, 325–6
  elementary scripts, 215–19, 272
  hierarchy of, 308
  ligatures, 161, 257, 270, 302, 309
  scriptura continua, 309, 311
  superscript, 215, 257
script types, 8, 11, 144, 155, 213, 269–72, 279–83
  cursive, 11, 130, 135, 187, 209, 213–15, 273, 281–3, 323, 326
  development of, 213, 311

380

General index

half-uncial, 214, 279, 286
minuscule, 11, 214, 302, 306–15, 326
   Caroline, 214, 315
   cursive minuscule, 289, 306
   development of, 306, 326
   of Nonantola, 295
   pre-Caroline Italian, 278, 295, 326
   uncial, 144, 155, 214, 272–3, 283, 286
scriptorium, 61, 243, 279
scriptures, holy, Vulgate, 36, 50, 122, 132, 146, 170–1, 246–7, 285, 323
   apocryphal, 287
   Vetus latina, 47, 88, 304
sculca, 123
sculdahis, 112–8, 190–1, 193–4; *see also* officials, Lombard
seal rings, 169–70
Secundus, of Trent, 73, 81, 83–4
senate/senators, Roman, 30, 32
Senatur, of Pavia, 182
Seneca, 301–2
Sergius, archbishop of Ravenna, 296
sermo humilis, 15, 41, 134, 239, 320–6
sermons, 51, 290
   De die iudicii, 289
Sesto, 297
shorthand, *see* charters, dorsal notes on; tachigraphy; Tironian notes
Sicherad, scribe, 146
Sicily, 33, 89, 209, 242
Sidonius Apollinaris, 22, 28
Siena, 143, 150, 189, 194, 232
Siena–Arezzo dispute, 150–3, 189–90, 194, 201, 285
slate texts, Visigothic, 77, 210, 219
slaves, slavery (*servus, serva*), 74–5, 178, 242, 247
Slavs, Slavic, 70, 112, 114
snaida, 124, 173
Solomon, 171, 249–50
sonorpair, 124–5, 137
Spain, 68, 77, 130, 156, 280; *see also* Visigoths, slate texts
   Spanish script/scribal traditions, 280, 306
Spoleto, 60, 68, 186, 199, 205, 243, 244, 274, 298
St Denis, 304
state
   late Roman, 14–19
   Lombard, 35, 72–4, 129, 151, 164–6, 200–7, 321
   see also government; public authority
stipulatio, 48, 120; *see also* surety; *wadium*
stolesazo, 101

stupla, 123
subscriptions, 182
   autograph, 182, 197, 215
   see also manuscripts; witnesses; writing
Sulpicius Severus, 279
sunder (sundrius, sundriale), 107, 122
surety, 196; *see also stipulatio*; *wadium*
syllogae, 236–7, 243–8, 325
   Centulensis, 244
   Laureshamensis, 243–4
Symmachus, 26, 29
syngraphus, 193
syntax, 138, 149–52, 193, 325; *see also* word order

tabellarii, 317
tabelliones, 202, 208
Tablettes Albertini, 208, 210
tachigraphy, syllabic, 211
Tacitus, 54, 68
Taido, *gasindius regis*, 179
Tanipert, priest, 224
tax (tolls, tithes), 75, 209, 287, 320
tempore barbarico, 222, 288
Terni, 83, 190
Theodahad, king, 18, 31
Theoderic, king, 25, 30, 60; *see also* Ostrogoths
Theodosian Code, 183, 202, 213
Theodota, 181, 251, 254–6
Theodota school (epigraphy), 236, 254
Theudelinda, queen, 63, 65, 81, 84, 181, 253, 321
thinx, thingatio, thingare, 120, 257; *see also gairethinx*
Thomas, deacon in Pavia, 245–6
Three Chapters dispute/schism, 45, 67, 70, 83, 181, 285–6, 320
threus, 116
Tironian notes, 286
tituli loquentes, 240, 256
titulus, meaning of, 249
Tjäder, J.O., 135, 207
Toto, of Campione, 178, 183, 185
Tours, 323; *see also* Gregory of Tours
Trani, graffiti of, 272
Treviso, 66, 229
trewas, 116
Trezzo d'Adda, 169–70
Tuscany, 68, 78, 190, 227, 231, 284

Udine, 297
Ulfilas, 279, 311
Umbria, 302
Ursicinus, lector, 279–80
usufruct clauses, 225

General index

Valdinievole helmet/visor, 169
Vandals, 68; *see also* Africa
Varsi, S. Pietro, 154, 179, 207, 223
Veneto, 17, 67, 166
verbs, forms, tenses, 138, 227, 291
    deponents, 138, 146
    passive, 138, 142
Vercelllli, 109, 168, 243, 283
Verona, 67, 84, 102, 130, 217, 229, 278, 279–83, 326
Versus in laudem Mediolanensis civitatis, 262, 285, 290
Via Flaminia, 243
Vienna, 279, 293
Vigilantius, scribe, 295, 296
vir clarissimus, 219, 285, 357; *see also* Audoald; Maurace
Visigoths, 77, 210, 219; *see also* Spain
Vivarium, 311

wadium, *see stipulatio*; surety
Walfred, 299
    Vita of, 299
waregang, 116
wergeld, 115–16, 173, 175

Wickham, C., 10, 176, 197
Widsith, poem, 113
wifa, wifare, 118
wills, 179, 210
Winili, 88, 321
wiridibora, 116–17
Witigis, king, 31
witnesses, 189–91, 220–1, 357; *see also* subscriptions
Wizo (Candidus), 317
Woden, 88–9, 92, 321
women, 117, 120, 159–60, 174, 181–6, 215, 222–3, 271, 299
    literacy of, 9, 30, 181–2, 299
    and religious life, 181–2, 255–7
word order, 150–1; *see also* grammar; syntax
word-separation, 261, 308–9
Wormald, P., 128
Wright, R., 133
'writer', 202
writing, 6, 37–8, 62, 149–53, 171, 173, 202–15, 269–71, 283–316
writing tablets, 317

Zachary, pope, 300

Cambridge Studies in Medieval Life and Thought
Fourth series

Titles in series

1 The Beaumont Twins: The Roots and Branches of Power in the Twelfth Century
D.B. CROUCH

2 The Thought of Gregory the Great*
G.R. EVANS

3 The Government of England Under Henry I*
JUDITH A. GREEN

4 Charity and Community in Medieval Cambridge*
MIRI RUBIN

5 Autonomy and Community: The Royal Manor of Havering, 1200–1500*
MARJORIE KENISTON MCINTOSH

6 The Political Thought of Baldus de Ubaldis*
JOSEPH CANNING

7 Land and Power in Late Medieval Ferrara: The Rule of the Este, 1350–1450*
TREVOR DEAN

8 William of Tyre: Historian of the Latin East*
PETER W. EDBURY AND JOHN GORDON ROWE

9 The Royal Saints of Anglo-Saxon England: A Study of West Saxon and East Anglian Cults
SUSAN J. RIDYARD

10 John of Wales: A Study of the Works and Ideas of a Thirteenth-Century Friar*
JENNY SWANSON

11 Richard III: A Study of Service*
ROSEMARY HORROX

12 A Marginal Economy? East Anglian Breckland in the Later Middle Ages
MARK BAILEY

13 Clement VI: The Pontificate and Ideas of an Avignon Pope*
DIANA WOOD

14 Hagiography and the Cult of Saints: The Diocese of Orléans, 800–1200
THOMAS HEAD

15 Kings and Lords in Conquest England*
ROBIN FLEMING

16 Council and Hierarchy: The Political Thought of William Durant the Younger*
CONSTANTIN FASOLT

17 Warfare in the Latin East, 1192–1291*
CHRISTOPHER MARSHALL

18 Province and Empire: Brittany and the Carolingians
JULIA M.H. SMITH

19 A Gentry Community: Leicestershire in the Fifteenth Century, c. 1422–c. 1485*
ERIC ACHESON

20 Baptism and Change in the Early Middle Ages, c. 200–1150*
PETER CRAMER

21 Itinerant Kingship and Royal Monasteries in Early Medieval Germany, c. 936–1075*
JOHN W. BERNHARDT

22 Caesarius of Arles: The Making of a Christian Community in Late Antique Gaul*
WILLIAM E. KLINGSHIRN

23 Bishop and Chapter in Twelfth-Century England: A Study of the *Mensa Episcopalis**
EVERETT U. CROSBY

24 Trade and Traders in Muslim Spain: The Commercial Realignment of the Iberian Peninsula, 900–1500*
OLIVIA REMIE CONSTABLE

25 Lithuania Ascending: A Pagan Empire within East-Central Europe, 1295–1345
S.C. ROWELL

26 Barcelona and Its Rulers, 1100–1291*
STEPHEN P. BENSCH

27 Conquest, Anarchy and Lordship: Yorkshire, 1066–1154*
PAUL DALTON

28 Preaching the Crusades: Mendicant Friars and the Cross in the Thirteenth Century*
CHRISTOPH T. MAIER

29 Family Power in Southern Italy: The Duchy of Gaeta and Its Neighbours, 850–1139*
PATRICIA SKINNER

30 The Papacy, Scotland and Northern England, 1342–1378*
A.D.M. BARRELL

31 Peter des Roches: An Alien in English Politics, 1205–1238*
NICHOLAS VINCENT

32 Runaway Religious in Medieval England, c. 1240–1540*
F. DONALD LOGAN

33 People and Identity in Ostrogothic Italy, 489–554*
PATRICK AMORY

34 The Aristocracy in Twelfth-Century León and Castile*
SIMON BARTON

35 Economy and Nature in the Fourteenth Century: Money, Market Exchange and the Emergence of Scientific Thought*
JOEL KAYE

36 Clement V*
SOPHIA MENACHE

37 England's Jewish Solution, 1262–1290: Experiment and Expulsion*
ROBIN R. MUNDILL

38 Medieval Merchants: York, Beverley and Hull in the Later Middle Ages*
JENNY KERMODE

39 Family, Commerce and Religion in London and Cologne: A Comparative Social History of Anglo-German Emigrants, c. 1000–c. 1300
JOSEPH P. HUFFMAN

40 The Monastic Order in Yorkshire, 1069–1215
JANET BURTON

41 Parisian Scholars in the Early Fourteenth Century: A Social Portrait
WILLIAM J. COURTENAY

42 Colonisation and Conquest in Medieval Ireland: The English in Louth, 1170–1330
BRENDAN SMITH

43 The Early Humiliati
FRANCES ANDREWS

44 The Household Knights of King John
S.D. CHURCH

45 The English in Rome, 1362–1420: Portrait of an Expatriate Community
MARGARET HARVEY

46 Restoration and Reform: Recovery from Civil War in England, 1153–1165
GRAEME J. WHITE

47 State and Society in the Early Middle Ages: The Middle Rhine Valley, 400–1000
MATTHEW INNES

48 Brittany and the Angevins: Province and Empire, 1157–1203
JUDITH EVERARD

49 The Making of Gratian's *Decretum*
ANDERS WINROTH

50 At the Gate of Christendom: Jews, Muslims and 'Pagans' in Medieval Hungary, c. 1000–c. 1300
NORA BEREND

51 Making Agreements in Medieval Catalonia: Power, Order, and the Written Word, 1000–1200
ADAM J. KOSTO

52 The Making of the Slavs: History and Archaeology of the Lower Danube Region, c. 500–700
FLORIN CURTA

53 Literacy in Lombard Italy, c. 568–774
NICHOLAS EVERETT

*Also published as a paperback

OHIO UNIVERSITY LIBRARY

Please return this book as soon as you have finished with it. In order to avoid a fine it must be returned by the latest date stamped below. All books are subject to recall after two weeks or immediately if needed for reserve.

CF